READINGS IN HUMAN DEVELOPMENT:

CONCEPTS, MEASURES AND POLICIES FOR A DEVELOPMENT PARADIGM

Edited by

Sakiko Fukuda-Parr
A. K. Shiva Kumar

D1528969

Human Development Report Office
United Nations Development Programme
New York

OXFORD
UNIVERSITY PRESS

OXFORD
UNIVERSITY PRESS

YMCA Library Building, Jai Singh Road, New Delhi 110001

Oxford University Press is a department of the University of Oxford. It furthers the
University's objective of excellence in research, scholarship, and education
by publishing worldwide in

Oxford   New York

Auckland   Bangkok   Buenos Aires   Cape Town   Chennai
Dar es Salaam   Delhi   Hong Kong   Istanbul   Karachi   Kolkata
Kuala Lumpur   Madrid   Melbourne   Mexico City   Mumbai   Nairobi
São Paulo   Shanghai   Taipei   Tokyo   Toronto

Oxford is a registered trade mark of Oxford University Press
in the UK and in certain other countries

Published in India
By Oxford University Press, New Delhi

ISBN 019 5670523

Printed at Sai Printopack, New Delhi 110020
Published by Manzar Khan, Oxford University Press
YMCA Library Building, Jai Singh Road, New Delhi 110 001

CONTENTS

Book Title: Y20 V

PREFACE

Human development has become a popular phrase today. The term is used extensively by the media, by politicians, by non-governmental organizations and by governments all over the world. Human development as a concept and its measurement are also much discussed by academics in colleges and universities. Since the publication of the first *Human Development Report* in 1990, human development as both a philosophy and an approach has become the cornerstone for the United Nations Development Programme.

The idea of human development has great intuitive appeal. Articulating development as a widening of choices, an expansion of freedoms and a fulfillment of human rights gives it a distinct edge over the more narrow perception of development as economic expansion alone. By bringing into sharp focus issues of deprivation and inequality, human development puts people – and among them, the most deprived – at the centre of development interventions. Embedded in the concept is a firm commitment to democracy, human rights, participation and a deep respect for the environment.

Just as importantly, human development has also altered the way we assess progress. It is not always a matter of monitoring fiscal deficits, inflation rates and balance of payments. These are important, but ultimately the measurements that

matter are at the human level. Progress can be judged only if we see marked improvements in the lives of people – in their health, in their levels of education and in their sense of security. Ultimately, development is about improving the quality of people's lives and advancing human dignity.

Behind the public popularity of human development lies a wealth of intellectual contributions by very eminent scholars. The late Pakistani economist Mahbub ul Haq was the principal architect and advocate of the concept. But backing him were many development thinkers and practitioners. Nobel Prize winning economist Amartya Sen was and continues to be among the leading contributors. Many in the Human Development Report Office have also contributed to giving the concept a practical appeal and policy relevance. Every annual *Human Development Report* has added to extensions and policy applications of the concept. This book pulls together a set of original contributions that have helped shape the contents of the *Human Development Reports*.

I am sure the readings in this book will further stimulate thinking and debate about human development.

Mark Malloch Brown
Administrator, UNDP

Book-title:

FOREWORD

By Amartya Sen

010

Dante lamented in *The Divine Comedy*, "Born to ascend on the wings,/Why do ye fall at such a little wind?" Why indeed? The contrast between what great things human beings can achieve and what limited lives most women and men end up living is truly remarkable. Dante's question, from the early 14th century, remains very alive even today. The potentialities of human beings far exceed what we actually manage to do, and that general contrast characterizes the human predicament in contemporary as well as classical understanding.

This tension is indeed a plausible starting point for the "human development approach". The concept of human development draws on the magnificence of human potentiality amidst the widespread experience of narrowly circumscribed lives. Lack of schooling, meagre health care, inadequate economic opportunities, violation of political liberties, denial of civil rights, and other hostile "winds" can totally frustrate human beings despite their potential to "ascend on the wings".

Human development is, of course, concerned with more worldly aspects of the good life than those that engaged Dante's thoughts in his journey through Inferno, Purgatorio and Paradiso (though the linkages that Dante explored were themselves worldly enough in their own way). However, the twin recognition that human beings can (1) *fare far better*, and (2) *do much more* to bring this about may sensibly be seen as the two central theses of the human development approach.

The perspective of human development incorporates the need to remove the hindrances that people face through the efforts and initiatives of people themselves. The claim is not only that human lives can go very much better and be much richer in terms of well-being and freedom, but also that human agency can deliberately bring about a radical change through improving societal organization and commitment. These are indeed the two central ideas that give cogency to the focus on human development. That focus relates, on one side, to a clearer comprehension of how – and in what ways – human lives can go much better, and on the other, to a fuller understanding of how this betterment can be brought about through a strengthening of human agency. I shall call them, respectively, "the evaluative aspect" and "the agency aspect" of human development.[1] This collection of essays is concerned with both.

HISTORY: SHORT AND LONG

The *Human Development Reports* started being published by the United Nations Development Programme a dozen years ago, from 1990. It is good that UNDP is producing this collection of readings after a period of considerable achievement, including the firm establishment of the human development perspective as an influential approach in the global scene.

The initiation of the approach and the beginning of the annual series of *Human Development Reports* occurred under the remarkable leadership of Mahbub ul Haq, the great Pakistani economist. Even though Mahbub's primary focus was on the evaluative aspect of the human development approach (he questioned, in particular, the commonly used measures of economic success, such as the gross domestic product, on which so much of the development literature had tended to concentrate), he also had deep interest in the agency aspect.[2] Even as he was hammering home the need to judge progress differently, Mahbub was also scrutinizing the ways and means of enhancing – through commitment and determination – the "life chances" that people enjoy in the miserable world in which we live.

I have been privileged to have Mahbub as one of my closest friends from our undergraduate days in Cambridge, right up to his tragic death in 1998. This collection of essays, skilfully edited by Sakiko Fukuda-Parr and A. K. Shiva Kumar, not only reflects the fruits of Mahbub's intellectual leadership, but also serves as a tribute to what that visionary thinker initiated and achieved. I feel very privileged to have the opportunity of expressing my own admiration – and affection – for my extraordinary friend.

One of the subjects that relate closely to Mahbub's concerns is the odd contrast between (1) the broad and humane concerns that led to the birth of economics as a discipline, and (2) the narrow and mechanical nature of the standard measures of progress on which the evaluation of economic success so often depends in contemporary investigations. When Mahbub founded the *Human Development Reports*, under the supportive umbrella of the United Nations Development Programme, he was, to a great extent, returning to the classic motivation that underlay the founding of economics as a discipline.

Indeed, a belief in the central importance of enriching the lives and freedoms of ordinary human beings has been a foundational concern in the social sciences for a very long time. This applies not only to Adam Smith, but also – much earlier – to the pioneering exploration of political economy in the 17th century by Sir William Petty. Petty's classic monograph *Political Arithmetic*, written around 1676 and published posthumously in 1691, was clearly motivated by an interest in the lives of human beings in a way that is not all that removed from the contemporary interest in human development. At the technical level, William Petty did, in fact, pioneer the measurement of the gross national product, the GNP, using both "the income method" and "the expenditure method" of estimating national income. This was a very significant contribution to applied economics, and yet at the same time, Petty was quite clear that the interest in incomes and expenditures lies not in themselves but in their serving as important means

to more profound ends. Among those ends, Petty emphasized such broad concerns as "the Common Safety" and "each Man's particular Happiness".[3] The origin of economics as a subject lies in the interest in the lives of human beings, not just in the production of commodities. Indeed, with a little bit of historical scrutiny, we can see that the interest in human development goes back to much earlier times than the 17th century, for example, to Aristotle's *Nicomachean Ethics* and *Politics* and to Kautilya's *Arthashastra* (that Sanskrit title can be translated as "the discipline of material well-being" or simply as "economics"), both written in the fourth century BC.

The evaluative aspect of the human development approach reclaims the motivational heritage of the discipline of economics. It takes us back to Smith and Petty and Aristotle, and demands that we look for information and analysis that would place human beings again at the centre of our analysis. The tables and the indices – including the human development index – involved a reassertion of the motives that led to the development of the discipline of economics and the related social sciences.

DISCONTENT AND CONSOLIDATION

By the time Mahbub ul Haq became the pioneering leader of the human development approach, there were several movements of discontent that were seeking an approach broader than what standard economic measurement provided. There were development theorists arguing for the recognition of "basic needs". There were advocates of various indicators of "physical quality of life". There were writers focusing on disparities in "living conditions". There were international interventionists – even within the UN family – wanting to focus specifically on "the state of the world's children". There were relief organizations concerned with hunger, morbidity and mortality, rather than only with income poverty. There were humanists voicing the need for social justice in the distribution of opportunities that people have. And there were also some obdurate theory spinners wondering whether the foundations of economic and social evaluation could not be radically shifted from commodities to capabilities – from what people own or have to what they can actually be or do.

It is to the credit of Mahbub's integrating vision that he saw the possibility of harnessing these different discontents into the development of a capacious alternative outlook that would be at once practical and broad, and could accommodate – if only roughly – these different concerns. If the idea of human development had a rapid acceptance, this was made possible by Mahbub ul Haq's skill in coordinating similar but not identical discontents and in weaving them together into a constructive and readily usable format.

Not surprisingly, the same charges were brought against Mahbub's move that had been used earlier to keep economic appraisal narrow and straight. There were plenty of grumbles that the diverse concerns on which Mahbub concentrated did not automatically yield one "operational metric". Of course, it didn't; it could not – and indeed *should not* – have. The domain of social valuation cannot be taken over by some kind of a value-neutral engineering. It is important that evaluative challenges are addressed by clarifying how valuations are used and how can they can be assessed and disputed (rather than just being pushed into "operation"). The system of weights that may be sensibly used is ultimately a matter for social choice, not to be overlooked in a mechanical search for some technical formula that would be free from valuational arguments.

Central to this exercise is enlightened public discussion. The human development approach tries to enhance this exercise by gathering together a wide variety of possibly relevant knowledge (in the form of tables and charts as well as descriptive narratives) and by discussing their potential role in the informational basis of evaluative judgements. Trying to broaden the intellectual support for well-informed public discussion is one of the main glories of the human development enterprise, and in this Mahbub absolutely revelled.

Mahbub's impatience with theory, which (I have to confess) I sometimes found quite exasperating, actually ended up helping him in his chosen purpose of constructing a broad vehicle – a "mahayana" – that accommodated a great many different theoretical approaches, without their differences being necessarily resolved. While he invoked theories and conceptual analyses often enough, his primary goal was to seek a practical accord rather than a conceptual agreement. As a quintessential anti-theorist, Mahbub sought what Cass Sunstein, the legal theorist, has called "an imperfectly theorized agreement". This was not only a helpful move to bolster his wide-ranging exploration of different kinds of information, it also made it possible for the human development approach to be jointly supported, in a broad way, by a diversity of heterodox approaches. Mahbub built on specific points of concordance, without waiting for a general conceptual congruence.

There is one other point I should emphasize here. Mahbub wanted to keep the door always open for revision. The informational coverage could be changed and the system of weights altered if that would follow from open and informed public discussion. Basically, he told the world: "Here we have a broad framework; if you want something else to be included here, which may deserve a table in the *Human Development Report* (and with some luck, may even be considered for inclusion in one of the aggregate indicators we use), tell us *what*, and explain *why* it must figure in this accounting. We *will* listen." The world of evaluation, he announced, was not imprisoned in any given formula, and is quite open to pragmatic reasoning, invoking different kinds of argument within a broad and permissive framework of discussable social evaluation. Human development, as Mahbub saw it, demands a willingness to entertain interminable intellectual engagement.

BEYOND THE HUMAN DEVELOPMENT INDEX

The breadth of the human development approach contrasts with the slender specificity of the human development index - the HDI - which the *Human Development Reports* have made into something of a flagship. The HDI serves the very specific purpose for which it was devised, but it would be a great mistake - alas one that is often made – to identify the capacious human development approach with the use of this useful but intellectually limited index. Since I was privileged to devise the HDI in collaboration with Mahbub, I hope I shall not be taken to be "anti-HDI" in general, but it is important to understand the severe limitations of the HDI, seen from within the human development perspective.

Based on three components, viz. indicators of basic education, longevity, and income per head, it is not exclusively focused on economic opulence, as the GNP is. It serves the purpose of broadening attention from GNP, and other narrowly income-based indicators, to something that responds also to two of the fundamental ingredients of the freedom of living, viz. life expectancy and basic education. I did not, I must admit, initially see much merit in looking for an aggregate indicator, rather than insisting on attention being paid to the rich variety of information that a *Human Development Report* presents. I had expressed to Mahbub considerable scepticism about trying to catch in one simple number a complex reality about human development and deprivation. In contrast with the coarse index of the HDI, the rest of the *Human Development Reports* contain a wealth of information (in extensive collections of tables) on a variety of social, economic and political features that influence the well-being and freedom of human beings. Why give prominence, it was natural to ask, to a crude summary index that could not begin to capture much of the rich information that makes the *Human Development Reports* so engaging and important?

In fact, the crudeness had not escaped Mahbub at all. He did not resist the argument that the HDI could not but be a very limited indicator of development. But after some initial hesitation, Mahbub persuaded himself that the dominance of GNP could not be broken by any set of tables. People will look at the tables respectfully, but when it came to using an overall measure of development, they would still go back to the unadorned GNP, because it is so convenient to have an aggregate index. As I listened to Mahbub, I could not help hearing an echo of T. S. Eliot's poem, "Burnt Norton": "Human kind/Cannot bear very much reality."[4] Mahbub hoped that not only would the HDI be something of an improvement on – or at least a helpful supplement to – the GNP, but also that it would serve to broaden public interest in the other variables that are plentifully analysed in the *Human Development Reports*. In this Mahbub was absolutely right. The success of the HDI, as a rival to GNP, has been quite remarkable, serving as a more humane measure of development than a purely income-based (or a commodity-based) measure like the GNP could possibly be.

Mahbub's basic approach must not be identified simply with the use of the HDI, which he chose mainly as an instrument of public communication. We have to see the human development index as a deliberately constructed crude measure, offered as a rival to the GNP (an overused and oversold index that Mahbub wanted to supplant). He did succeed in getting the ear of the world through the high publicity associated with the transparent simplicity of the HDI as an index. But it is extremely important not to read more into the HDI than is there.

Let me briefly mention some obvious limitations of the HDI seen from the general human development perspective. First, the well-being and freedom that we enjoy have much internal diversity, and they are influenced by a great variety of factors – political, economic, social, legal, epidemiological, and others. These factors are distinct, but they also interrelate with each other.[5] The HDI is based on a heroic selection and puts the focus on some of these features, while totally neglecting others. The problem cannot be rectified by including more factors into this one numerical index, since the inclusion of more variables reduces the importance of each of the other – already included – variables. The loss of informational sensitivity involved in moving from a complex reality to just one number (formally, from an n-tuple or a vector to a scalar) cannot but be great. Depending on the purpose at hand, the particular informational focus of any index, like the HDI, may well be contingently justified, but it cannot do justice to the variety of purposes that can be served by the human development approach.

Second, when the ingredients of a judgement are diverse, any aggregate index with *constant* weights over its diverse constituent elements would tend to oversimplify the evaluative exercise. As is well known in indexing theory, in reducing a vector (reflecting a set of numbers) into a scalar, we tend by and large to get an incomplete ranking (a partial ordering). Furthermore, the ranking that we get will depend on the question that the index is meant to address, and there are important dichotomies here.

For example, in assessing commodity vectors (or bundles of goods and services), we can examine their "welfare-giving" value, or their value as indicators of what the economy can produce – their "production possibility" value.[6] More generally, there is a dichotomy between (1) what an economy or a society has the ability to produce and achieve, and (2) what level of well-being (or freedom) it is actually achieving for the people in that society. The evaluation of each may not give us more than an incomplete ranking, but they will not, except in very special cases, be the same ranking. These may look like technical issues, and in a sense they are, but no "practical" theory of measurement can be immune to the complexities that are endemic to aggregation. The HDI is no exception; nor are any of the other indicators – GNP or any other. The assumed completeness of the HDI as an indicator cannot but be quite deceptive.

Third, another dichotomy involves the time dimension. We have reason to be interested in the current situation as well as future prospects. Indeed, sometimes we are particularly interested in *changes* over time. For example, if a further spread of AIDS and the unfolding of that pandemic would reduce life expectancy sharply, it will be particularly relevant to examine that and also to see how this would tend to restrain or reduce the future values of HDI, of which life expectancy is a component (unless policy initiatives are taken to reverse the downward movement).

Of course, this is not, in itself, an argument against the HDI as an indicator, since we can distinguish between different questions, in particular, "What is the present situation (such as the present level of well-being)?" and "What are the prospects of the future (such as those of future well-being)?" But since some commentators seem to be keen on getting all the different information through just one real number (some all-inclusive index), it is worth noting that any expectation that today's HDI may adequately reflect *both* the present situation and the future prospects would tend to be disappointed. It is important to see that the valuation of today's HDI (or any other such contemporary indicator) would have to be supplemented by estimating the prospects of future HDI (or other indicators), under alternative assumptions (including distinct policy decisions).[7]

Movements over time – both upwards (with the progress of education or health care, or economic growth) as well as downwards (with new epidemics or environmental destruction) – are part of human development analysis, and to investigate them adequately (including bringing out different possible time patterns), different questions have to be properly distinguished. In this context, downward possibilities need particular attention, especially given the spread of the AIDS pandemic, and the damage done to the natural environment.[8] The Hicksian distinction between the use of a real-income index to reflect, respectively, (1) production possibility, and (2) experienced well-being, also needs to be more fully recognized in the literature than it seems to be, given the evident temptation of making one overall index perform many different tasks. Policies to prevent or reverse downward movements can be greatly helped by the investigation of different time patterns of distinct variables under different scenarios.

CONCLUDING REMARKS

This collection of essays will give the reader a good introduction to the human development approach that got its first formulation only a little over a dozen years ago, but which has already achieved considerable success. It is important to be clear as to what its contributions are, how it relates to earlier works (often going back many centuries), and what its future relevance may be (including the possibility of addressing fresh issues and responding to new problems). I have tried to comment briefly on these subjects, but they are further pursued in the assortment of essays included in this useful collection. I end with a few concluding remarks.

First, it is important to distinguish between (1) the popular use of HDI as an index, and (2) the human development approach in general. The fact that there are many variables of relevance to human development that are not included in the HDI has to be fully acknowledged, and adequate room for those variables has to be secured within the informational framework of human development.[9] Further, the fact that the "complete ordering" form of the HDI is a serious oversimplification also needs firm recognition. We also have to distinguish between different questions that are sometimes merged together. Even though they may all be relevant to the human development perspective, they are not necessarily relevant for the same reason, nor best aggregated into one overall index.

Second, Mahbub's heterodoxy not only took the form of being sceptical of the standardly used indicators of development, but also encouraged an openness to new initiatives and departures that the perspective allows. Mahbub himself experimented with some departures, not each of which was a success, but it is important to be open to variations and departures, and not to stifle further broadening on any *a priori* ground. For example, recently the *Human Development Reports* have taken on such big issues as the relationship between human rights and human development, and the demands of deepening democracy in the fragmented world in which we live.[10] From each of these extensions, gains are made in enriching the human development approach. One very much hopes that the human development work will remain open to new departures.

Third, as and when we face new problems, the focus of attention has to adjust to the demands of the new reality. For example, in the early days of human development reporting a decade ago, some countries (the Republic of Korea was a good example) were doing astonishingly well by combining the use of opportunities of expansion in the global market economy with development-oriented social interventions, particularly focused on the expansion of human resources, for example, through education and skill formation. The *Human Development Report* duly recorded their success. But it emerged later (for example, during the Asian economic crisis of 1997) that some of these economies also had basic problems that had not been adequately addressed, such as the lack of democratic institutions and the absence of transparency in business transactions. No less importantly, there was also the extreme vulnerability in a downturn of those whose economic viability depended entirely on a buoyant market – without any social safety net, in case of unemployment or loss of economic opportunities. While people were united on the way up, they were often very divided as they fell. The importance of this phenomenon, and that of "human security" in general, requires a reorientation of factual concentration and its proper reflection in development accounting. This has implications for future work using the human development perspective.

The spread of epidemics, including the AIDS pandemic, has also raised extremely important new questions, which have to be addressed. These concerns, along with many other challenges (such as making use of new information on environmental deterioration), will undoubtedly call for appropriate scrutiny of the applications of the human development discipline. Mahbub ul Haq would have been happy to see that the school of work that he initiated is not resting on its laurels, nor remaining frozen in predetermined paths, but is continuing to use the open-minded approach to which he attached such importance.

If this collection of essays is an account of past achievement, it is also an energizing call to future engagement. We have reason to celebrate both.

ENDNOTES

1. I have tried to discuss the distinctions involved as well as their interconnections in "Well-being, Agency and Freedom: The Dewey Lectures 1984," *Journal of Philosophy*, 82, 1985.

2. The force of his personal commitment and his strong belief in the power of human agency are both well reflected in Mahbub ul Haq, *The Poverty Curtain* (New York: Columbia University Press, 1976).

3. The origins of the idea of "standard of living", including Petty's contribution (among those of other pioneers), are investigated in my 1985 Tanner Lectures in Cambridge, and published in Amartya Sen et al, *The Standard of Living,* ed. Geoffrey Hawthorn, with comments by John Muellbauer, Ravi Kanbur, Keith Hart and Bernard Williams (Cambridge: Cambridge University Press, 1987).

4. On one occasion when I told Mahbub that the one-number index I was then devising at his request could not but be quite "vulgar" because of the inescapable oversimplification that he was demanding, Mahbub replied: "We need a measure of the same level of vulgarity as the GNP, but one that is not as blind to social aspects of human life as the GNP is."

5. I have tried to discuss the conceptual distinctions as well as the interconnections involved in *Development as Freedom* (New York: Knopf, and Oxford: Oxford University Press, 1999). See also Sakiko Fukuda-Parr, "Rescuing the Human Development Concept from the HDI: Reflections on a New Agenda," in *this* collection.

6. To bring out the dichotomy between the two perspectives of welfare and production possibility was one of the major contributions of John Hicks's classic paper, "The Valuation of Social Income," *Economica,* 7 (1940). The discipline of partial orderings in the two cases can take very distinct forms, on which see my "Welfare Basis of Real Income Comparisons," *Journal of Economic Literature,* 17 (1979), reprinted in my *Resources, Values and Development* (Cambridge, Mass.: Harvard University Press, 1984). A good example of measuring national income from the perspective of production possibility can be found in James Mirrlees, "The Evaluation of National Income and an Imperfect Economy," *Pakistan Development Review,* 9 (1969). That production-possibility perspective may be particularly worth pursuing now because of the identifiable loss of natural capital through the deterioration of the physical environment. That will, in turn, affect the possibility of well-being as well, but the diverse questions and connections can be appropriately distinguished.

7. Partha Dasgupta has argued that it is a defect of the HDI that of its three components, only one, viz. adult literacy, "reflects something about future possibilities" (*Human Well-being and the Natural Environment,* Oxford: Oxford University Press, 2001, p. 82). This, combined with Dasgupta's observation that "adult literacy is only one type of capital asset", takes him to his conclusion that the HDI is "not derivable from a coherent view of human well-being" (p. 83). But, surely, the current HDI aims to reflect current well-being and current opportunities (literacy is included because it influences today's well-being, not just future prospects). It is, thus, hardly a cogent criticism to point out that the current HDI does not tell us about future well-being *as well*. To look at future prospects (including future well-being), it would be necessary to estimate the likely values of *future* HDI (based on estimates of the future value of its components, such as life expectancy), taking note of the relevant causal connections, rather than trying to get all this from the one scalar number of *today's* HDI.

8. On the analysis of the latter from the human development perspective, see Sudhir Anand and Amartya Sen, "Human Development and Economic Sustainability," *World Development,* 28 (December 2000).

9. Many of the relevant variables are already covered in the wide-ranging tables in the annual *Human Development Reports,* but there may be need to broaden the coverage further, particularly as neglected aspects of individual well-being and social choice are considered.

10. See *Human Development Report 2000* (New York: Oxford University Press, 2000), and *Human Development Report 2002* (New York: Oxford University Press, 2002).

ACKNOWLEDGEMENTS

For many of us who have had the privilege of working with Mahbub ul Haq, human development has been an "intellectual journey". The vision that drove his work was matched by his never-ending curiosity about new ideas and approaches to grappling with the challenges of poverty, injustice and oppression. He was always in search of innovative concepts, measurement tools and policy initiatives. It is in this spirit of an "intellectual journey" that the *Human Development Reports* have evolved since 1990 to the present day.

This book of readings documents and celebrates that evolution. We owe the book to all those who contributed to the journey, who are more numerous than those whose writings comprise this volume. Simply too many to be mentioned here individually, they include close intellectual associates of Mahbub, who helped him launch the idea of human development and its report; the members of the Human Development Report Office of the United Nations Development Programme, each of whom invested passionately in every word and number in the annual reports; and the many professionals working on national human development strategies and reports at the national, sub-national and regional levels. Their reports now number over 400 and have contributed some of the most interesting innovations over the years. Finally, we owe gratitude to the UNDP Administrators and senior managers who have defended the report in the face of political threats, and have developed and operationalized human development in key policy areas.

In constructing this volume, we thank Professor Amartya Sen for graciously agreeing to contribute a Foreword. We are privileged not only to have his thoughts on the origins and the future of the human development approach, but to have benefited from his decisive contributions over the years. The concept of human development rests on his articulation of the philosophical foundations, and the ongoing dialogue with Amartya for more than a decade has been critical in shaping the "intellectual journey" to this day – we hope it will continue in the future. We would also like to thank UNDP Administrator Mark Malloch Brown for his supportive preface. He has challenged the human development movement with new visions of the role that we can play in shaping world opinion and moving policy debates. His leadership of UNDP is taking the *Human Development Reports* to play an enhanced role in influencing global policy positions.

Special thanks are also due to Gerry Quinn for the design of the book; to Gretchen Sidhu for editorial support; to Sarah Burd-Sharps, Anne Louise Winslov and Oscar Bernal of the Human Development Report Office; and to Kavita Iyengar of Oxford University Press in New Delhi for managing the publication process. All have been extremely patient.

Sakiko Fukuda-Parr and A. K. Shiva Kumar

CONTRIBUTORS

Sudhir Anand
University of Oxford

Håkan Björkman
United Nations Development Programme

Lord Meghnad Desai
London School of Economics and Political
    Science

Nancy Folbre
University of Massachussetts at Amherst

Sakiko Fukuda-Parr
United Nations Development Programme

Late Mahbub ul Haq
Mahbub ul Haq Human Development Centre

Selim Jahan
United Nations Development Programme

Sir Richard Jolly
Institute of Development Studies, University
    of Sussex

Inge Kaul
United Nations Development Programme

Terry McKinley
United Nations Development Programme

Omar Noman
United Nations Development Programme

Alejandro Ramírez
Organisation for Economic Co-operation
    and Development

Gustav Ranis
Yale University

Kate Raworth
Oxfam, U.K.

Amartya Sen
Trinity College, Cambridge

Gita Sen
Indian Institute of Management

A. K. Shiva Kumar
United Nations Children's Fund

David Stewart
United Nations Development Programme

Frances Stewart
University of Oxford

Paul Streeten
University of Boston

Common Abbreviations

CCA	Common Country Assessment	IDA	International Development Association
CIS	Commonwealth of Independent States	ILO	International Labour Organization
DAC	Development Assistance Committee	IMF	International Monetary Fund
EU	European Union	LSE	London School of Economics
GDI	Gender-related development index	NGO	Non-governmental organization
GDP	Gross domestic product	ODA	Official development assistance
GEM	Gender empowerment measure	OECD	Organisation for Economic Co-operation and Development
GESI	Gender-equity-sensitive indicator	PFI	Political freedom index
GNP	Gross national product	PPP	Purchasing power parity
HDI	Human development index	PQLI	Physical quality of life index
HDII	Human development improvement index	R&D	Research and development
HDR	*Human Development Report*	SNA	System of National Accounts
HIV/AIDS	Human immunodeficiency virus/ acquired immunodeficiency syndrome	TAI	Technology achievement index
		UNDP	United Nations Development Programme
HPI-1	Human poverty index (developing countries)	UNESCO	United Nations Educational, Scientific and Cultural Organization
HPI-2	Human poverty index (industrial countries)	UNICEF	United Nations Children's Fund
		UNRISD	United Nations Research Institute for Social Development
IBRD	International Bank for Reconstruction and Development	WHO	World Health Organization

INTRODUCTION

Sakiko Fukuda-Parr and A. K. Shiva Kumar

The term "human development" has come to be accepted in the development economics literature as an expansion of human capabilities, a widening of choices, an enhancement of freedoms and a fulfillment of human rights. Rising incomes and expanding outputs, in the human development framework, are seen as the *means* and not the *ends* of development. Indeed, defining people's well-being as the end of development and treating economic growth as a means have been central messages of the annual *Human Development Reports* published since 1990.

There are several implications in adopting this development approach and framework. First, the policy significance of income expansion, in any society, is clarified. Higher incomes do help many people realize valuable ends and fulfill many aspirations. Income expansion matters, especially to the poor: it enables them to gain access to many goods and services, and, potentially, to an improved quality of life. But higher incomes alone may not always guarantee that which people cherish and value. For example, levels of environmental pollution, safety, crime and domestic violence, or the quality of education and health care, may not be associated with levels of income in any predictable manner. Therefore, the focus of policy cannot be based merely on the generation of more and more income. How additional income is used, and the degree to which it improves the quality of people's lives, must be given equal weight.

Second, and as a corollary, growth in per capita incomes cannot be the dominant criterion for judging how societies are faring. An expansion of income is important but only as a means to valuable ends. The human development approach, therefore, generates a new set of evaluative questions to assess the impact of development policies.

Are people truly enjoying an expansion in their capabilities – the capability to lead a healthy and creative life, to be well nourished, to be secure, to be well informed and educated? Has there been a significant improvement in the quality of people's lives? Do they have more of what they cherish? How free are they? How equal? Ultimately, progress has to be judged by an expansion of freedoms, or as Nobel laureate Amartya Sen puts it: "Freedom to do what you want to do and to be what you want to be."

Third, focusing on human lives as the goal of development results in the articulation of very different policy concerns that are rooted in the advancement of people's well-being. Thus, in the human development framework, discussions on globalization go beyond examining the impact on trade, capital flows and economic growth, to consider the changing opportunities and new insecurities in people's lives. Similarly, a discussion on technology is not confined to its impacts on the economy, or for that matter, to productivity increases, employment creation and trends in the stock market. In the human development framework, technology becomes a mechanism for promoting human development, rather than a reward of higher incomes. The focus, accordingly, is on public policies that make new technologies work for human development – on shifting investment priorities to end human poverty. Likewise, a people-centred approach stresses human security, not military security – that is, security of people, not of territory. In other words, the exercise of policy formulation overall becomes one of ensuring not merely growth as such, but growth that promotes human development.

Fourth, human development is motivated by a concern for freedom, well-being and the dignity of individuals in society, issues that are not conventionally regarded as central to policy formulation. Human development is concerned with the full range of capabilities, including social freedoms that cannot be exercised without political and civil guarantees. Indeed, the human development approach emphasizes political and social freedoms through enhanced participation and inclusive democracy as fundamental to the realization and sustainability of social and economic goals.

Concerns about people in development have been important in other development debates and approaches. The concept of satisfying basic needs as the goal of development was a significant influence in policy debates of the 1970s. Similarly, the concept of human resource development – i.e., investing in the education and health of people as a means of accelerating growth – has been well established in the economics literature and is accepted as a critical element of development policy. But the human development approach, as developed and articulated in the *Human Development Reports*, goes further. People are not regarded as passive beneficiaries of services provided to meet basic needs. Nor does the expansion of people's knowledge and health take place for the sole purpose of promoting the economy. Instead, people are seen as active agents of change.

In creating the *Human Development Report* in 1990, the late Pakistani economist Mahbub ul Haq had an explicit purpose. He wanted to bring people back into the centre of the agenda for national and global development policy at a time when goals of macroeconomic balances and economic growth dominated the agenda, and when structural adjustment sought to "balance economies at the expense of unbalancing human lives". Over the last decade, the annual Reports have sought to develop concepts, measurement tools and policy analyses in a variety of areas. In the process, a human development approach or paradigm has been articulated that has influenced development debates and policies.

Today, human development is no longer confined to the *Human Development Report*. Related concepts and new measurement tools are being elaborated throughout the world – more than 135 countries have prepared similar reports. The reports are used extensively by non-governmental organizations for advocacy, by governments for reviewing policies, by donor agencies for examining priorities, and by academia, media and citizens groups to draw attention to research, news and campaigns for improving human well-being. Research publications as well as policy workshops and seminars organized in different parts of the world regularly discuss conceptual refinements, supplementary measures and the policy implications of adopting a human development approach.

ABOUT THIS BOOK

The following chapters comprise a set of essential readings for those who want to better appreciate the substance and intellectual positions advocated by human development. As the editors of the book, we have attempted to pull together some of the main contributions that have shaped particular concepts, measurement tools and policy perspectives. The book will enable readers to trace the conceptual origins and evolution of the human development approach; to better understand the issues related to its measurement; and to get a flavour of some innovative policy applications. The readings are by no means comprehensive. Nor are they confined to those authors who have made a contribution to the evolution of the notion of human development. In fact, hundreds of scholars, interns, researchers, activists and development practitioners all over the world have helped to shape the human development paradigm, and this widespread participation is one significant reason for the public popularity of the Reports.

We have divided the book into three sections: conceptual foundations, measurement and some policy explorations.

Section 1: Conceptual foundations

Mahbub ul Haq joined the United Nations Development Programme in 1989. He steered the publication and launch of the first five *Human Development Reports* and was largely responsible for much of their public popularity and appeal. Haq was an unusual economist. During a period with the World Bank in the 1970s, he constantly challenged the conventional wisdom of economic growth and the power of markets as the sole means of ending human deprivations. Having persuaded UNDP to sponsor the *Human Development Reports*, Haq called upon his many friends and associates who had been similarly disillusioned with the prevailing economic analysis. To begin, he recruited Amartya Sen, a good friend since their undergraduate days at Cambridge University. Haq was particularly inspired by Sen's articulation of development as an expansion of human capabilities and human freedoms.

Chapter 1.1 of this volume is Sen's paper "Development As Capability Expansion". Written in 1989, a year before the publication of the first *Human Development Report*, it contains many of the intellectual insights and fundamental ideas that have come to shape human development thinking. Sen argues that human beings should be viewed as ends in themselves; distinguishes between commodities and capabilities; and points to the policy implications of expanding capabilities to end human deprivations. These considerations constitute the essential underpinnings of the human development paradigm.

From the beginning, the atmosphere in the Human Development Report Office in New York has been exhilarating. Intense intellectual exchanges and debates between eminent thinkers, development practitioners and social activists on the one hand, and the young and committed professionals in the Human Development Report Team on the other, have led to the crafting and articulation of many compelling ideas. This dynamism is evident in chapter 1.2, Haq's "The Human Development Paradigm", which, in his characteristic style, summarizes the essence of human development and the main messages of the first five *Human Development Reports*.

The wider acceptance and use of the term "human development" has led to widespread confusion as well. Most people tend to mistake human development for social development and to associate it solely with investments in health, education and nutrition, while others mistakenly equate human development with human resource devel-

opment. Many fail to see the essential and vital distinction between human capital formation and an expansion of human capability. In chapter 1.3, "Human Capital and Human Capability", Amartya Sen offers a much-needed clarification: "The former concentrates on the agency of human beings, whereas the latter focuses on the ability of human beings to lead lives they have reason to value most." Sen argues that despite the usefulness of the concept of human capital as a productive resource, it is important to see human beings in a broader perspective than that of human capital.

A major concern of human development has been with poverty – in both developed and developing countries. The persistence of human deprivations in rich societies is as worrisome as it is in less affluent nations of the world: Why do so many in developed countries not have access to basic health care? Why are people denied adequate shelter, even in rich countries, when there is so much wealth? Clearly, poverty cannot be reduced to merely a lack of income, just as development cannot be equated solely to income expansion. Discussions in the Human Development Report Office led to the formulation of the concept of human poverty as a universal concern that extends far beyond a shortfall of income. *Human Development Report 1997*, excerpted in chapter 1.4, argues that from a human development perspective, poverty means "the denial of choices and opportunities for a tolerable life". Poverty manifests itself in human deprivations crying out to be addressed: ill health, ignorance, malnutrition, exclusion from decision-making processes, lack of freedoms, and loss of dignity and self-esteem. In advanced societies, human poverty is different, arising through such forms as social exclusion, homelessness, insecurity, inadequacy of skills and unemployment.

Human rights and political freedoms are two other important concerns of human development. They have not been part of mainstream debates within the realms of economic and social processes. Even in the initial years of the *Human Development Reports*, human freedoms and respect for human rights were regarded as essential aspects of human development. These dimensions remained relatively neglected, however, until the publication of *Human Development Report 2000*, which explores more formally the many interconnections between human rights and human development. *Human Development Report 2000* recognizes that the movements for human rights and for human development have distinct traditions and strategies. United in a broader alliance, each can bring new energy and strength to the other. In chapter 1.5, which originally appeared in *Human Development Report 2000*, Amartya Sen presents a conceptual framework for examining these links.

As the concept of human development has evolved over the years, many hard choices have had to be made. Voting in favour of some positions meant rejecting others, and given the tradition of participation, debate and discussion in the Human Development Report Office, selection or rejection was never an easy task. Inge Kaul, the first Director of the office, from 1990 to 1994, was deeply involved, along with Haq, in many of the decisions that had to be taken. In chapter 1.6, she reveals the political complexities hidden behind many of the seemingly simple choices: the politics of language, of aid, of international cooperation, of North-South biases, of national sovereignty. With the advantage of hindsight, Kaul lists the right decisions that were made.

Paul Streeten has played a major role in shaping the human development paradigm as we recognize it today. Streeten, another old friend of Haq's, was delighted to accept the invitation to join the Human Development Report Team. The two had worked together at the World Bank on basic needs, a conceptual forerunner of human development. During the early years of the Reports, Streeten was closely involved, contributing rare insights and bringing in inspiring interns and young scholars. As the ageless chronicler of economic and world events in "Shifting Fashions in Development Dialogue", which appears as chapter 1.7, Streeten traces the evolution in development thinking from a preoccupation with growth and employment to the adoption of a more comprehensive human development framework.

Sir Richard Jolly, well known for his work on "redistribution with growth" and "structural adjustment with a human face", took over from Mahbub ul Haq as the Special Adviser to the UNDP Administrator on the *Human Development Reports* in 1996. In chapter 1.8, Jolly sets out the differences between the human development approach and the neo-liberal approach, which has shaped the dominant policy known as the Washington Consensus. He highlights many points of common concern and policy emphasis, but also draws attention to major differences in operational terms. Human development and neo-liberalism share some common roots, most notably in the liberal economic tradition that emphasizes the fundamental importance of individual freedoms and choices. Nevertheless, the inter-disciplinary, pragmatic and pluralistic approach advocated by the human development paradigm proves to be more practical than the neo-liberal approach, which focuses on income growth, neglects non-economic issues and assigns a relatively low importance to equality of opportunities.

At the end of the first section, in chapter 1.9, Sakiko Fukuda-Parr, the Director of the Human Development Report Office since 1995, asks why the concept of human development is so frequently misinterpreted to mean social development or human resource development or, simply, the satisfaction of basic needs. She argues for greater attention to the capability of participating in the life of the community and the important decisions that affect a person's life. Fukuda-Parr's article reviews the way in which notions of participation developed with some ambiguity in earlier *Human Development Reports*, and proposes future Reports integrate participation as a capability with the same level of importance as education and health. The chapter raises key questions about the scope of human development as an open-ended concept in which those capabilities that are important for public policy evolve over time and can be different from one social context to another. It is up to the community to decide which are the important choices. The world of 2002, Fukuda-Parr points out, poses new and evolving challenges for human development, which the *Human Development Reports* need to address.

Section 2: Measurement

The computation of the human development index, and ranking of countries on that basis, has been a regular feature of the *Human Development Reports* since 1990, attracting more public attention – and public criticism – than any other part of the Reports. The origins of the HDI can be traced back to the contributions of Meghnad Desai and Amartya Sen, who in the late 1980s wrote about assessing social progress in the context of economic reforms in Latin America. Haq took the lead from here, and helped develop the HDI. Everyone agrees the index is neither perfect nor comprehensive, and Haq himself said the HDI "is of the same level of vulgarity as the GNP". Nonetheless, he felt a strong need for a new measure that would draw attention more meaningfully to issues of central concern to people, "a measure that is not blind to social aspects of human lives, as the GNP is".

Human Development Report 1990 states: "Human deprivation and development have many facets, so any index of human progress should incorporate a range of indicators to capture this complexity. But having too many indicators in the index would blur its focus and make it difficult to interpret and use. Hence the need for compromise to balance the virtues of broad scope with those of retaining sensitivity to critical aspects of deprivation." The Report adds: "People do not isolate the different aspects of their lives. Instead, they have an overall sense of well-being. Thus, there is merit in trying to construct a composite index of human development."

In contrast to the GNP – the only other widely used indicator of a country's overall development – the HDI reflects the average achievements of a country along three dimensions of human development: longevity, educational attainment and command over resources needed for a decent living. Does the HDI capture all aspects of human development comprehensively? It does not. As *Human Development Report 1990* states: "... the human development index captures a few of people's choices and leaves out many that people may value highly – economic, social and political freedoms, and protection against violence, insecurity and discrimination, to name a few."

Not many could have predicted the popularity and public appeal of the HDI, despite its limitations. Sen writes: "I did not, I must admit, initially see much merit in the HDI itself, which, as it happens, I was privileged to help (Haq) devise . . . Why give prominence, it was natural to ask, to a crude summary index that could not begin to capture much of the rich information that makes the *Human Development Reports* so engaging and important?"

Mahbub ul Haq, however, foresaw the enormous political mileage to be gained from the launch of the HDI – and his instincts proved right. In chapter 2.1, "The Birth of the Human Development Index", Haq describes the momentum in the search for a new composite index of socioeconomic progress, and explains the method for constructing the HDI; the rationale for the choice of components and indicators; some of the refinements over time; and the uses to which the HDI can be put. Over the years, Sudhir Anand and Amartya Sen have lent considerable statistical rigour to the index, some aspects of which are discussed in chapter 2.2 on the HDI's methodology and measurement. In chapter 2.3, Selim Jahan addresses some of the deficiencies of the HDI and tracks the changes that have been made over time. Subsequently, in chapter 2.4, Kate Raworth and David Stewart enumerate the many criticisms and charges leveled against the HDI, from the quality of data used to exclusion of certain constituents to choice of indicators. Questions have also been raised about the methodology, and the basis for weighting the components. The Human Development Report Office has responded to some of these criticisms; others have been ignored.

Advocates in several countries have made innovative use of the HDI to attract the attention of policy makers to vital human development concerns. The disaggregation of the HDI has been particularly effective for advocacy and policy analysis. Constructing sub-national HDIs has helped draw attention to low levels as well as glaring inequalities in human development – between rural and urban areas, across states and provinces, and among different ethnic communities. A few attempts have also been made to assess short-term progress in human development. Sakiko Fukuda-Parr, Kate Raworth and A. K. Shiva Kumar, in chapter 2.5, demonstrate the potential for disaggregation and offer a framework for assessing short-term improvements in human development.

A key debate has been the importance of political rights and freedoms, which have been central to discussions on human development. The dimensions of human development captured in the HDI reflect social and economic achievements, however, and do not directly address political freedom. But while political empowerment and economic freedoms are seen as two sides of the same coin, it is certainly possible to have one without the other. China, for instance, fares well on the HDI as a medium human development country, even though its record on human rights and political freedoms remains poor. As Paul Streeten says, "Life expectancy and literacy could be quite high in a well-managed prison. Basic physical needs are well met in a zoo." The human development approach advocates the simultaneous fulfillment of social and economic rights alongside civil and political rights, especially if human development is to be sustainable.

In this spirit, *Human Development Report 1992* argues that political freedom is an essential element of human development: "Many people argue that even if freedom should be debated, it should not be measured. The concept, they point out, is so large and complex that any system of measurement will diminish it. Freedom is too valuable to be reduced to a number. It should, they say, be discussed qualitatively, not quantitatively. Certainly, no measure of freedom can do it full justice." Having said this, however, *Human Development Report 1992* goes on to construct a new political freedom index. The Report defends keeping the PFI and the HDI separate instead of combining them into one. First, the HDI and PFI operate on very different scales. The HDI is likely to be quite stable over time, because economic and social achievements move relatively slowly. Since achievements will not, in the short term, be greatly affected by political change, insulating the HDI from the political shocks of the PFI would offer a truer picture. Second, the HDI depends partly on a country's economic opportunities, while the PFI does not. Countries don't have to censor the press or torture prisoners just because they are poor, but a poor country that makes substantial progress in political freedoms could not hope to see this reflected in an improved ranking in a combined index like the HDI.

The PFI constructed by *Human Development Report 1992* has five components: personal security, rule of law, freedom of expression, political participation and equality of opportunity. Data were collected on 102 countries. Fully aware of the arbitrariness that creeps into any rating of political freedoms, instead of ranking countries, the Report presents the PFI aggregates for high, medium and low HDI countries; for high-, medium- and low-income countries; and for industrial countries and the developing world. The PFI was, however, dropped the next year for diplomatic rather than academic reasons – the political heat generated by the somewhat arbitrary index proved too much to take. Nonetheless, efforts are still being made to construct indices that measure political freedoms. In chapter 2.6, Meghnad Desai discusses many of the conceptual and methodological issues relating to the measurement of political freedoms.

The family of human development indices has grown over the years. In 1995, two new indices were introduced: the gender-related development index and the gender empowerment measure. The GDI uses the same variables as the HDI and adjusts the average achievement of each country in life expectancy, educational attainment and income in accordance with the disparities in achievements between women and men. Sudhir Anand and Amartya Sen, in chapter 2.7 on measuring gender inequality, present the statistical details of the construction of gender-sensitive indices that form the basis of the GDI.

Once again, Anand and Sen discuss the concept of human poverty and human development in

Chapter 2.8. In 1997 and 1998, two more indices were introduced: the human poverty index-1 for developing countries and the human poverty index-2 for industrial countries. As discussed earlier, human poverty in the human development framework is multidimensional. Human poverty also manifests itself differently in different situations. Conditions of human poverty in developing countries tend to be very different from those found in industrialized countries. The HPI-1 concentrates on deprivation in three essential dimensions of human life already reflected in the HDI: longevity, knowledge and a decent standard of living. The first deprivation concerns survival, or vulnerability to death at a relatively early age. The second relates to knowledge in terms of being excluded from the world of reading and communication. The third describes a decent living standard in terms of overall economic provisioning. Indicators identified for each of these dimensions of human deprivation are combined to form a composite HPI-1. The HPI-2 for industrialized countries concentrates on deprivations in four dimensions of human life quite similar to those reflected in the HDI: longevity, knowledge, a decent standard of living and social exclusion. As in the HPI-1, the first deprivation relates to survival – vulnerability to death at a relatively early age; the second to knowledge as in being excluded from reading and communication; and the third to a decent living standard in terms of overall economic provisioning. The fourth concerns non-participation or exclusion. Once again, appropriate indicators identified for each of these dimensions of human deprivation are combined to form a composite HPI-2. Chapter 2.9 presents the various measures of human development introduced in the *Human Development Reports* and shows the computation of the different human development indices.

The launch of the HDI has revived the trend for generating more and more indices. Some claim to modify the HDI, others to offer radically different alternatives. Yet others seek to complement the HDI or to compensate for the many dimensions that are not included. Innovation, refinements and extensions of the HDI must be encour-

aged. There is enormous scope for developing the index, particularly at the country level where many better indicators may be available to capture achievements along the HDI's three basic dimensions. There is a tendency, however, to overdo the quest for new indices. In striving for statistical sophistication, many lose sight of the larger picture, and, worse still, forget the underlying philosophy and motivation behind the construction of such indices. Others, in their desire to show higher national achievements, tend to disregard the indicators used in the global HDI. This practice can be dangerous, misleading and even unwarranted in many cases. Additionally, manipulations of this kind tend to destroy the credibility of the index.

Section 3: Some policy explorations

Viewing human development as an expansion of people's capabilities, an enlargement of choices and the assurance of human rights has several policy implications. To begin with, this approach offers a people-centred analytical framework for designing and assessing public policy interventions. Outcomes are to be judged not in terms of how much production has increased or incomes have grown, but rather in terms of improvements in the quality and security of people's lives.

Gains in human development have been recorded in every region of the world. In developing countries today compared with 1970: a newborn can expect to live 10 years longer; the infant mortality rate has dropped by more than two-thirds; adult literacy is down by nearly half; and combined net primary and secondary enrolment has increased by nearly 50 percent, according to *Human Development Report 2000*. Yet, as the Report also points out: some 1.2 billion people are living below the poverty line on less than US $1 a day; about 1 billion adults are illiterate; more than 2.4 billion people are without basic sanitation; about 100 million are homeless; and approximately 100 million children live or work on the street.

Such lopsided patterns of development – where opulence coexists with public squalor – can be found in every country, rich and poor. They reflect policy failures and, more typically, policy inaction. In many cases, a badly skewed pattern of public investments is the underlying factor, and analysing patterns of public expenditures is a useful starting point for understanding inequalities and discrepancies in human development. For instance, governments frequently spend much more on higher education than on ensuring universal basic education, or more on building a new hospital in a city than on reviving primary health care centers in villages. Cities tend to have an abundance of electricity when many thousands of villages may not even have one light bulb. Residents of cities may be beneficiaries of low-cost housing even if it means the poor in rural areas remain without proper shelter.

How should policy analysts begin to examine patterns of public spending from a human development perspective? Gustav Ranis and Frances Stewart, two prominent contributors to the human development paradigm, propose a framework for expenditure analysis in chapter 3.1, which first appeared in *Human Development Report 1991*. They argue that countries should monitor four ratios to develop a sound basis for analysing public spending on human development: the public expenditure ratio, the social allocation ratio, the social priority ratio and the human expenditure ratio. The human expenditure ratio is the product of the first three ratios. A powerful operational tool, it allows policy-makers who want to restructure their budgets to see clearly the available options.

Concerns of widespread inequality have been central to the *Human Development Reports*. Most alarming has been the persistent inequalities between women and men. What makes gender inequalities particularly disturbing is that discrimination against girls and women tends to be largely invisible and often appears legitimate, having the sanction of society. Chapter 3.2, "Valuing Women's Work", was first published in *Human Development Report 1995*. It has to be read against the simple but far-reaching message of the main Report: Human development, if not engendered, is endangered. *Human Development Report 1995* argues that achieving gender equality is not a technocratic goal. It is a political process requiring struggle and radical shifts in mindsets. The

Report points out that despite significant expansion in women's capabilities all over the world, nowhere do women enjoy the same opportunities and freedoms as men. This is particularly so in the economic and political spheres, where the doors have hardly begun to open for women. A major index of neglect is that a large part of the economic contribution by women is grossly undervalued or not valued at all: *Human Development Report 1995* estimated this to be of the order of US $11 trillion. The failure to value women's work is more than just a matter of accounting or even a question of justice. It concerns the status of women in society. Research initiated by *Human Development Report 1995* has extended to many countries that are making efforts to assess the extent of women's economic contributions. In some places, this has led to a re-examination of the definition of women's work, especially in the activities of field investigators, such as census takers.

In the human development framework, economic growth is an essential means for people, and especially the poor, to realize many of the freedoms they value. Two features of modern development are of particular concern, however. The first is that growth has been failing over much of the past 15 years in about 100 countries with almost a third of the world's population. The second feature is that the links between growth and human development are weak in many more countries that continue to experience lopsided development. Some countries have had good growth but little human development. Others have experienced good human development with little or no growth. A careful investigation into the connections between growth and human development became the focus of *Human Development Report 1995*. Chapter 3.3, originally the overview of this Report, argues that the connections between growth and human development are neither obvious nor automatic. Particularly useful is the identification of the five types of policy failure that occur when the links are broken. In a style characteristic of the *Human Development Reports*, these failures are identified as:

- jobless growth, where the overall economy grows but does not expand the opportunities for employment;
- ruthless growth, where the fruits of economic growth mostly benefit the rich, leaving millions of people struggling in ever-deepening poverty;
- voiceless growth, where growth in the economy has not been accompanied by an extension of democracy or empowerment;
- rootless growth, which causes people's cultural identity to wither; and,
- futureless growth, where the present generation squanders resources needed by future generations.

Human Development Report 1995 argues that the world needs more growth, not less. But getting mesmerized by merely the quantity of growth is a problem. Policy-makers must also pay attention to the structure and quality of growth so that it is directed to supporting human development, eliminating human poverty, protecting the environment and ensuring sustainability.

Another significant policy contribution of the *Human Development Reports* has been the enrichment of discussions on poverty. Policy-makers have traditionally been preoccupied primarily with addressing income poverty alone. Much of the discussion has centred on forms of income transfers that can reduce the proportion of the those living below the poverty line. Such a narrow perception of poverty – as shortfalls in income – serves only a limited purpose. In the human development framework, life is multidimensional and so is poverty. Income poverty is seen as an outcome, and the poverty of opportunities is the underlying cause of income poverty and human deprivations. Therefore, the focus of attention ought to be the poverty of opportunities, not merely the poverty of incomes. And the emphasis is not on economic opportunities alone, but on an equitable expansion of political, social, legal and cultural opportunities as well.

What can be done to address the persistence of human poverty? *Human Development Report*

1997 takes on this question. Apart from a discussion of economic policies and economic interventions that help alleviate human poverty, *Human Development Report 1997* argues that politics, not just economics, determines what we do, or don't do, to address human poverty. What is often lacking is not resources or economic solutions but the political momentum to tackle poverty head on. Political reforms need to go hand in hand with economic reforms if the world is to succeed in eliminating the worst forms of human poverty. Chapter 3.4, which first appeared in *Human Development Report 1997*, examines essential political strategies for eliminating poverty. Drawing on examples of social movements and peoples' struggles around the world, it examines three essential elements of any political strategy: political empowerment of poor people, partnerships for change and the crucial role of an enabling state. A central argument is that ending human poverty requires a democratic space in which people can articulate demands, act collectively and fight for a more equitable distribution of power.

The *Human Development Reports* emphasize the increasing interconnectedness and consequent interdependency between people across the globe. Nowhere is this more apparent than in worldwide consumption patterns and the impact this has had on the environment. *Human Development Report 1998* examines various dimensions and consequences of these unequal consumption patterns, as they exist today. A particularly regrettable outcome has been environmental damage, which has hit the poorest the hardest. The Report argues that even though the poor bear the brunt of environmental damage, the irony is that they are seldom the principal creators of it. Chapter 3.5, which comes from *Human Development Report 1998*, highlights this point and related aspects, presenting some powerful arguments and evidence to support the unequal human impacts of environmental damage on people. Arguing for greater clarity in policy formulation, the chapter seeks to demolish five myths that surround discussions on the poverty-environment nexus:

- subsidies on resources are always for the benefit of poor people;
- poor people are unable or unwilling to contribute to costs;
- developing countries should simply imitate what industrial countries have done in dealing with the environment;
- developing countries should restrain their consumption, industrialization and development, because they will contribute to further environmental damage; and,
- the scope for cheap, effective and politically acceptable anti-pollution policies is very limited in developing countries.

Focusing on people and people's lives draws attention to care, a central feature of any society. Care is an invisible element that is often influenced by policy decisions, but the adverse impacts of economic policies on care are rarely considered. And, typically, it is women who bear a disproportionate burden of the consequences. *Human Development Report 1999* addresses the issue of globalization and human development. An excerpt from the Report, Chapter 3.6, "The Invisible Heart – Care and the Global Economy", argues that much of the focus on the impact of globalization has been confined to incomes, employment, education and other opportunities. In the process, studies have failed to pay adequate attention to the consequences for care and caring labour – the task of providing for dependents, for children, the sick and the elderly. The real challenge is to ensure that globalization does not squeeze out care. A clear policy path is needed that will support incentives and rewards for caring work, both paid and unpaid, to increase its supply and quality. Economic solutions are not enough. Providing caring labour requires adjustments in roles and responsibilities among women and men, and within the state, the family or community, and the employer.

Ultimately, the human development paradigm argues more broadly for pluralistic solutions that are backed by concerted public action. Enriching people's lives cannot be left to the markets. Market expansion may be necessary, but by itself may be inadequate to assure an improvement in the quality of people's lives. Similarly, state action is critical but not sufficient for accelerating human development – people's lives are too valuable to be left to markets and the state. Effective people's participation and inclusion in the processes of decision-making are needed for any intervention to be sustainable. Public action calls for new partnerships and institutional mechanisms that are particularly responsive to the demands of the most disadvantaged in society.

The last chapter in the third section, chapter 3.7, deals with the issue of *inclusive* democracy, which is considered critical in the human development framework for the fulfillment of all human rights. To secure human rights for all requires inclusive democracy, not just majoritarian democracy. The emphasis is not simply on democracy but on the nature of democracy. Elections alone are not sufficient. Democracy must protect the rights of minorities by giving them legitimacy, space and voice. Democracy must also provide separation of powers to ensure that the judiciary is independent, that it protects people from injustices and prevents abuse of power. Again, as the article points out, democratic societies must ensure public accountability, which requires an open civil society, and an independent and free media that is vigilant. Policy-making in a democratic society must also become transparent, and subject to public scrutiny. In the human development approach, ensuring the proper establishment of inclusive democracy is as much a part of the public policy agenda as eradicating human poverty.

CONCLUDING REMARKS

The 1990s witnessed marked changes in development thinking and in the policy environment. First, there were major shifts in the role of the state. Until 1990, policy formulation in most developing countries took place in a planned environment with the state at the centre. Since the collapse of the former Soviet Union and its satellites in Eastern Europe, the old model of state planning has almost become extinct. Today, thinking is far more influenced by the extraordinary role of community action, private initiative and human agency. Instead of a benevolent state planning the future of its people, policy initiatives seek to empower people to decide and act for themselves. Public action has come to mean more than just action by the state. Today, it stands for everything that civil society – people, NGOs, research institutions and other agencies – does collectively. Second, development debates are increasingly moving to integrate political issues into the economic and social spheres. The discourse on human rights has in fact led the way by arguing that development promotes respect for human rights, and that promoting respect for and guarantees of human rights are critical development objectives.

The *Human Development Reports* have played a crucial role in shaping some of the new development ideas. Looking ahead, the thinking about poverty and human development will come to be influenced more and more by the agency of human beings – women in particular. Issues of justice, equality and rights will deepen the discourse on human rights and human development.

SECTION 1:
CONCEPTUAL FOUNDATIONS

1.1
DEVELOPMENT
AS CAPABILITY EXPANSION*

Amartya Sen

INTRODUCTION

In his *Grundlegung zur Metaphysik de Sitten*, Immanuel Kant argues for the necessity of seeing human beings as ends in themselves, rather than as means to other ends: "So act as to treat humanity, whether in thine own person or in that of any other, in every case as an end withal, never as means only".[1] This principle has importance in many contexts – even in analysing poverty, progress and planning. Human beings are the agents, beneficiaries and adjudicators of progress, but they also happen to be – directly or indirectly – the primary means of all production. This dual role of human beings provides a rich ground for confusion of ends and means in planning and policy-making. Indeed, it can – and frequently does – take the form of focusing on production and prosperity as the essence of progress, treating people as the means through which that productive progress is brought about (rather than seeing the lives of people as the ultimate concern and treating production and prosperity merely as means to those lives).

Indeed, the widely prevalent concentration on the expansion of real income and on economic growth as the characteristics of successful development can be precisely an aspect of the mistake against which Kant had warned. This problem is particularly pivotal in the assessment and planning of economic development. The problem does not, of course, lie in the fact that the pursuit of economic prosperity is typically taken to be a major goal of planning and policy-making. This need not be, in itself, unreasonable. The problem relates to the level at which this aim should be taken as a goal. Is it just an intermediate goal, the importance of which is contingent on what it ultimately contributes to human lives? Or is it the object of the entire exercise? It is in the acceptance – usually implicitly – of the latter view that the ends-means confusion becomes significant – indeed blatant.

The problem might have been of no great practical interest if the achievement of economic prosperity were tightly linked – in something like a one-to-one correspondence – with that of enriching the lives of the people. If that were the case, then the pursuit of economic prosperity as an end in itself, while wrong in principle, might have been, in effect, indistinguishable from pursuing it only as a means to the end of enriching human lives. But that tight relation does not obtain. Countries with high GNP per capita can nevertheless have astonishingly low achievements in the quality of life, with the bulk of the population being subject to premature mortality, escapable morbidity, overwhelming illiteracy and so on.

Just to illustrate an aspect of the problem, the GNP per capita of six countries is given in table 1.1.1, along with each country's respective level of life expectancy at birth.

A country can be very rich in conventional economic terms (i.e., in terms of the value of com-

TABLE 1.1.1
Economic prosperity and life expectancy, 1985

Country	GNP per capita	Life expectancy at birth
China	310	69
Sri Lanka	380	70
Brazil	1,640	65
South Africa	2,010	55
Mexico	2,080	67
Oman	6,730	54

Source: World Development Report 1987 (New York, Oxford University Press, 1988). Table 1.

modities produced per capita) and still be very poor in the achieved quality of human life. South Africa, with five or six times the GNP per capita of Sri Lanka or China, has a much lower longevity rate, and the same applies in different ways to Brazil, Mexico, Oman, and indeed to many other countries not included in this table.

There are, therefore, really two distinct issues here. First, economic prosperity is no more than one of the means to enriching the lives of people. It is a foundational confusion to give it the status of an end. Secondly, even as a means, merely enhancing average economic opulence can be quite inefficient in the pursuit of the really valuable ends. In making sure that development planning and general policy-making do not suffer from costly confusions of ends and means, we have to face the issue of identification of ends, in terms of which the effectiveness of the means can be systematically assessed. This paper is concerned with discussing the nature and implications of that general task.

THE CAPABILITY APPROACH: CONCEPTUAL ROOTS

The particular line of reasoning that will be pursued here is based on evaluating social change in terms of the richness of human life resulting from it. But the quality of human life is itself a matter of great complexity. The approach that will be used here, which is sometimes called the "capability approach", sees human life as a set of "doings and beings" – we may call them "functionings" – and it relates the evaluation of the quality of life to the assessment of the capability to function. It is an approach that I have tried to explore in some detail, both conceptually and in terms of its empirical implications.[2] The roots of the approach go back at least to Adam Smith and Karl Marx, and indeed to Aristotle.

In investigating the problem of "political distribution", Aristotle made extensive use of his analysis of "the good of human beings", and this he linked with his examination of "the functions of man" and his exploration of "life in the sense of activity".[3] The Aristotelian theory is, of course, highly ambitious and involves elements that go well beyond this particular issue (e.g., it takes a specific view of human nature and relates a notion of objective goodness to it). But the argument for seeing the quality of life in terms of valued activities and the capability to achieve these activities has much broader relevance and application.

Among the classical political economists, both Adam Smith and Karl Marx explicitly discussed the importance of functionings and the capability to function as determinants of well-being.[4] Marx's approach to the question was closely related to the Aristotelian analysis (and indeed was apparently directly influenced by it).[5] Indeed, an important part of Marx's programme of reformulation of the foundations of political economy is clearly related to seeing the success of human life in terms of fulfilling the needed human activities. Marx put it thus: "It will be seen how in place of the wealth and poverty of political economy come the rich human being and rich human need. The rich human being is simultaneously the human being in need of a totality of human life-activities – the man in whom his own realization exists as an inner necessity, as need."[6]

COMMODITIES, FUNCTIONINGS AND CAPABILITY

If life is seen as a set of "doings and beings" that are valuable, the exercise of assessing the quality of life takes the form of evaluating these functionings and the capability to function. This valuational exercise cannot be done by focusing simply on communities or incomes that help those doings and beings, as in commodity-based accounting of the quality of life (involving a confusion of means and ends). "The life of money-making", as Aristotle put it, "is one undertaken under compulsion, and wealth is evidently not the good we are seeking; for it is merely useful and for the sake of something else."[7] The task is that of evaluating the importance of the various functionings in human life, going beyond what Marx called, in a different but related context, "commodity fetishism".[8] The functionings themselves have to be examined, and the capability of the person to achieve them has to be appropriately valued.

In the view that is being pursued here, the constituent elements of life are seen as a combination of various different functionings (a "functioning n-tuple"). This amounts to seeing a person in, as it were, an "active" rather than a "passive" form (but neither the various states of being nor even the "doings" need necessarily be "athletic" ones). The included items may vary from such elementary functionings as escaping morbidity and mortality, being adequately nourished, undertaking usual movements etc., to many complex functionings such as achieving self-respect, taking part in the life of the community and appearing in public without shame (the last a functioning that was illuminatingly discussed by Adam Smith[9] as an achievement that is valued in all societies, but the precise commodity requirement of which, he pointed out, varies from society to society). The claim is that the functionings are constitutive of a person's being, and an evaluation of a person's well-being has to take the form of an assessment of these constituent elements.

The primitive notion in the approach is that of functionings – seen as constitutive elements of living. A functioning is an achievement of a person: what he or she manages to do or to be, and any such functioning reflects, as it were, a part of the state of that person. The capability of a person is a derived notion. It reflects the various combinations of functionings (doings and beings) he or she can achieve.[10] It takes a certain view of living as a combination of various "doings and beings". Capability reflects a person's freedom to choose between different ways of living. The underlying motivation – the focusing on freedom – is well captured by Marx's claim that what we need is "replacing the domination of circumstances and chance over individuals by the domination of individuals over chance and circumstances".[11]

UTILITARIAN CALCULUS VERSUS OBJECTIVE DEPRIVATION

The capability approach can be contrasted not merely with commodity-based systems of evalua-

tion, but also with the utility based assessment. The utilitarian notion of value, which is invoked explicitly or by implication in much of welfare economics, sees value, ultimately, only in individual utility, which is defined in terms of some mental condition, such as pleasure, happiness, desire-fulfilment. This subjectivist perspective has been extensively used, but it can be very misleading, since it may fail to reflect a person's real deprivation.

A thoroughly deprived person, leading a very reduced life, might not appear to be badly off in terms of the mental metric of utility, if the hardship is accepted with no-grumbling resignation. In situations of long-standing deprivation, the victims do not go on weeping all the time, and very often make great efforts to take pleasure in small mercies and to cut down personal desires to modest – "realistic" – proportions. The person's deprivation, then, may not at all show up in the metrics of pleasure, desire-fulfilment etc., even though he or she may be quite unable to be adequately nourished, decently clothed, minimally educated and so on.[12]

This issue, apart from its foundational relevance, may have some immediate bearing on practical public policy. Smugness about continued deprivation and vulnerability is often made to look justified on grounds of lack of strong public demand and forcefully expressed desire for removing these impediments.[13]

AMBIGUITIES, PRECISION AND RELEVANCE

There are many ambiguities in the conceptual framework of the capability approach. Indeed, the nature of human life and the content of human freedom are themselves far from unproblematic concepts. It is not my purpose to brush these difficult questions under the carpet. In so far as there are genuine ambiguities in the underlying objects of value, these will be reflected in corresponding ambiguities in the characterization of capability. The need for this relates to a methodological point, which I have tried to defend elsewhere, that if an underlying idea has an essential ambiguity, a precise formulation of that idea must try to capture that ambiguity rather than attempt to lose it.[14] Even when precisely capturing an ambiguity proves to be a difficult exercise, that is not an argument for forgetting the complex nature of the concept and seeking a spuriously narrow exactness. In social investigation and measurement, it is undoubtedly more important to be vaguely right than to be precisely wrong.[15]

It should be noted also that there is always an element of real choice in the description of functionings, since the format of "doings" and "beings" permits additional "achievements" to be defined and included. Frequently, the same doings and beings can be seen from different perspectives, with varying emphases. Also, some functionings may be easy to describe, but of no great interest in the relevant context (e.g., using a particular washing powder in doing the washing).[16] There is no escape from the problem of evaluation in selecting a class of functionings as important and others as not so. The evaluative exercise cannot be fully addressed without explicitly facing questions concerning what are the valuable achievements and freedoms, and which are not. The chosen focus has to be related to the underlying social concerns and values, in terms of which some definable functionings and capabilities may be important and others quite trivial and negligible. The need for selection and discrimination is neither an embarrassment nor a unique difficulty for the conceptualization of functioning and capability.[17]

In the context of some types of welfare analysis, for example, in dealing with extreme poverty in developing economies, we may be able to go a long distance in terms of a relatively small number of centrally important functionings and the corresponding capabilities, such as the ability to be well-nourished and well-sheltered, the capability of escaping avoidable morbidity and premature mortality and so forth.[18] In other contexts, including more general problems of assessing economic and social development, the list may have to be much longer and much more diverse.[19] The task of specification must relate to the underlying motivation of the exercise as well as dealing with the social values involved.

QUALITY OF LIFE, BASIC NEEDS AND CAPABILITY

There is an extensive literature in development economics concerned with valuing the quality of life, the fulfilment of basic needs and related matters.[20] That literature has been quite influential in recent years in drawing attention to neglected aspects of economic and social development. It is, however, fair to say that these writings have been typically comprehensively ignored in the theory of welfare economics, which has tended to treat these contributions as essentially *ad hoc* suggestions. This treatment is partly the result of the concern of welfare theory that proposals should not just appeal to intuitions but also be structured and founded. It also reflects the intellectual standing that such traditional approaches as utilitarian evaluation enjoy in welfare theory, and which serves as a barrier to accepting departures even when they seem attractive. The inability of utility-based evaluations to cope with persistent deprivations was discussed earlier, but in the welfare-economic literature the hold of this tradition has been hard to dislodge.

The charge of "*ad hoc*-ness" against the development literature relates to the different modes of arguing that are used in welfare theory and in development theory. As far as the normative structure is concerned, the latter tends to be rather immediate, appealing to strong intuitions that seem obvious enough. Welfare theory, on the other hand, tends to take a more circuitous route, with great elaboration and defense of the foundations of the approach in question. To bridge the gap, we have to compare and contrast the foundational features underlying the concern with quality of life, needs etc. with the informational foundations of the more traditional approaches used in welfare economics and moral philosophy such as utilitarianism. It is precisely in this context that the advantages of the capability approach become perspicuous. The view of human life seen as a combination of various functionings and capabilities, and the analysis of human freedom as a central feature of living, provide a differently grounded foundation route to the evaluative exercise. This informational foundation contrasts with the evaluative bases incorporated in the more traditional foundations used in welfare economics.[21]

The "basic needs" literature has, in fact, tended to suffer a little from uncertainties about how basic needs should be specified. The original formulations often took the form of defining basic needs in terms of needs for certain minimal amounts of essential commodities such as food, clothing and shelter. If this type of formulation is used, then the literature remains imprisoned in the mould of commodity centered evaluation, and can in fact be accused of adopting a form of "commodity fetishism". The objects of value can scarcely be the holdings of commodities. Judged even as means, the usefulness of the commodity-perspective is severely compromised by the variability of the conversion of commodities into capabilities. For example, the requirement of food and of nutrients for the capability of being well nourished may greatly vary from person to person, depending on metabolic rates, body size, gender, pregnancy, age, climatic conditions, parasitic ailments and so on.[22] The evaluation of commodity holdings or of incomes (with which to purchase commodities) can be at best a proxy for the things that really matter, but unfortunately it does not seem to be a particularly good proxy in most cases.[23]

RAWLS, PRIMARY GOODS AND FREEDOMS

The concern with commodities and means of achievement, with which the motivation of the capability approach is being contrasted, happens to be, in fact, influential in the literature of modern moral philosophy as well. For example, in John Rawls' outstanding book on justice (arguably the most important contribution to moral philosophy in recent decades), the concentration is on the holdings of "primary goods" of different people in making interpersonal comparisons. His theory of justice, particularly the "difference principle", is dependent on this procedure for interpersonal comparisons. This procedure has the feature of being partly commodity-based, since the list of primary goods includes "income and wealth", in addition to "the basic liberties", "powers and prerogatives of offices and positions of responsibility", "social bases of self-respect" and so on.[24]

Indeed, the entire list of "primary goods" of Rawls is concerned with means rather than ends; they deal with things that help to achieve what we want to achieve, rather than either with achievement as such or even with the freedom to achieve. Being nourished is not part of the list, but having the income to buy food certainly is. Similarly, the social bases of self-respect belong to the list in a way self-respect as such does not.

Rawls is much concerned that the fact that different people have different ends must not be lost in the evaluative process, and people should have the freedom to pursue their respective ends. This concern is indeed important, and the capability approach is also much involved with valuing freedom as such. In fact, it can be argued that the capability approach gives a better account of the freedoms actually enjoyed by different people than can be obtained from looking merely at the holdings of primary goods. Primary goods are means to freedoms, whereas capabilities are expressions of freedoms themselves.

The motivations underlying the Rawlsian theory and the capability approach are similar, but the accountings are different. The problem with the Rawlsian accounting lies in the fact that, even for the same ends, people's ability to convert primary goods into achievements differs, so that an interpersonal comparison based on the holdings of primary goods cannot, in general, also reflect the ranking of their respective real freedoms to pursue any given – or variable – ends. The variability in the conversion rates between persons for given ends is a problem that is embedded in the wider problem of variability of primary goods needed for different persons pursuing their respective ends.[25] Hence, a similar criticism applies to Rawlsian accounting procedure as applies to parts of the basic-needs literature for their concentration on means (such as commodities) as opposed to achievements or the freedom to achieve.

FREEDOM, CAPABILITY AND DATA LIMITATIONS

The capability set represents a person's freedom to achieve various functioning combinations. If freedom is intrinsically important, then the alternative combinations available for choice are all relevant for judging a person's advantage, even though he or she will eventually choose only an alternative. In this view, the choice itself is a valuable feature of a person's life.

On the other hand, if freedom is seen as being only instrumentally important, then the interest in the capability set lies only in the fact that it offers the person opportunities to achieve various valuable states. Only the achieved states are in themselves valuable, not the opportunities, which are valued only as means to the end of reaching valuable states.

The contrast between the intrinsic and the instrumental views of freedom is quite a deep one, and I have discussed the importance of the distinction elsewhere.[26] Both views can be accommodated within one capability approach. With the instrumental view, the capability one is valued only for the sake of the best alternative available for choice (or the actual alternative chosen). This way of evaluating a capability set by the value of one distinguished element in it can be called "elementary evaluation".[27] If, on the other hand, freedom is intrinsically valued, then elementary evaluation will be inadequate, since the opportunity to choose other alternatives is of significance of its own. To bring out the distinction, it may be noted that if all other than the chosen alternative were to become unavailable, then there would be a real loss in the case of the intrinsic view, but not in the instrumental, since the alternative chosen is still available.

In terms of practical application, the intrinsic view is much harder to reflect than the instrumental view, since our direct observations relate to what was chosen and achieved. The estimation what could have been chosen is, by its very nature, more problematic (involving, in particular, assumptions about the constraints actually faced by the person). The limits of practical calculations are set by data restrictions, and this can be particularly hard on the representation of capability sets in full, as opposed to judging the capability sets by the observed functioning achievements.

There is no real loss involved in using the capability approach in this reduced form if the instrumental view of freedom is taken, but there is loss if the intrinsic view is accepted. For the latter, a presentation of the capability set as such is important.

In fact, neither the instrumental view nor the intrinsic view is likely to be fully adequate. Certainly, freedom is a means to achievement, whether or not it is also intrinsically important, so that the instrumental view must be *inter alia* present in any use of the capability approach. Also, even if we find in general the instrumental view to be fairly adequate, there would clearly be cases in which it is extremely limited. For example, the person who fasts, that is, starves out of choice, can hardly be seen as being similarly deprived as a person who has no option but to starve because of penury. Even though their observed functionings may be the same, at least in the crude representation of functionings, their predicaments are not the same.

In practice, even if in general the capability approach is used in the reduced form of concentrating on the chosen functioning combination, some systematic supplementation would be needed to take care of cases in which the freedom enjoyed is of clear and immediate interest. There may be no great difficulty in doing this supplementation in many cases, once the problem is posed clearly enough and the data search is made purposive and precise. Sometimes it would be useful to redefine the functionings in what is called a "refined" way, to take note of some of the obviously relevant alternatives that were available, but not chosen. Indeed, fasting is an example of a "refined" functioning, and contrasts with the unrefined functioning of "starving", which does not specify whether or not this was by choice.[28] The important issue does not concern the existence or not of some actual word (such as fasting) that reflects the refined functioning (that is largely a matter of linguistic convention), but assessing whether or not such refining would be central to the exercise in question, and if central, deciding how this might be done.

As a matter of fact, the informational base of functionings is still a much finer basis of evaluation of the quality of life and economic progress than various alternatives more commonly recommended, such as individual utilities or commodity holdings. The commodity fetishism of the former and the subjectivist metric of the latter make them deeply problematic. Thus, the concentration on achieved functionings has merits over the feasible rivals (even though it may not be based on as much information as would be needed to attract intrinsic importance to freedom). And in terms of data availability, keeping track of functionings (including vital ones such as being well-nourished and avoiding escapable morbidity or premature mortality) is typically no harder – often much easier – than getting data on commodity use (especially divisions within the family), not to mention utilities.

The capability approach can, thus, be used at various levels of sophistication, and how far we can go would depend much on the practical consideration of what data we can get and what we cannot. In so far as freedom is seen to be intrinsically important, the observation of the chosen functioning bundle cannot be in itself an adequate guide for the evaluative exercise, even though the freedom to choose a better bundle rather than a worse one can be seen to be, in some accounting, an advantage even from the perspective of freedom.[29]

The point can be illustrated with a particular example. An expansion of longevity is seen, by common agreement, as an enhancement of the quality of life (though, strictly speaking, I suppose one can think of it as an enhancement of the quantity of life). This is so partly because living longer is an achievement that is valued. It is also partly so because other achievements, such as avoiding morbidity, tend to go with longevity (and thus longevity serves also as a proxy for some achievements that too are intrinsically valued). But greater longevity can also be seen as an enhancement of the freedom to live long. We often take this for granted on the solid ground that given the option, people value living longer, and thus the observed

achievement of living longer reflects a greater freedom than was enjoyed.

The interpretative question arises at this precise point. Why is it evidence of greater freedom as such that a person ends up living longer rather than shorter? Why can it not be just a preferred achievement, but involving no difference in terms of freedom? One answer is to say that one always does have the option of killing oneself, and thus an expansion of longevity expands one's options. But there is a further issue here. Consider a case in which, for some reason (either legal or psychological or whatever), one cannot really kill oneself (despite the presence in the world of poisons, knives, tall buildings and other useful objects). Would we then say that the person does not have more freedom by virtue of being free to live longer though not shorter? It can be argued that if the person values, prefers and wishes to choose living longer, then the change in question is in fact an expansion of the person's freedom, since the valuation of freedom cannot be dissociated from the assessment of the actual options in terms of the person's evaluative judgements.[30]

The idea of freedom takes us beyond achievements, but that does not entail that the assessment of freedom must be independent of that of achievements. The freedom to live the kind of life one would take to live has importance that the freedom to live the kind of life one would hate to have does not. Thus, the temptation to see more freedom in greater longevity is justifiable from several points of view, including noting the option of ending one's life and being sensitive to the evaluative structure of achievements, which directly affect the metric of freedom. The bottom line of all this is to recognize that the use of the capability approach even in the reduced form of concentrating on the achieved functionings (longevity, absence of morbidity, avoidance of undernourishment etc.) may give more role to the value of freedom than might have been initially apparent.

INEQUALITY, CLASS AND GENDER

The choice of an approach to the evaluation of well-being and advantage has bearings on many exercises. These include the assessment of efficiency as well as inequality. Efficiency, as it is normally defined, is concerned with noting overall improvements, and in standard economic theory, this takes the form of checking whether someone's position has improved without anyone's position having gone down. A situation is efficient if and only if there is no alternative feasible situation in which someone's position is better and no one's worse. Obviously, the content of this criterion depends crucially on the way individual advantage is defined. If it is defined in terms of utility, then this criterion of efficiency immediately becomes that of "Pareto optimality" (or "Pareto efficiency", as it is sometimes – more accurately – called). On the other hand, efficiency can be defined also in terms of other metrics, including that of the quality of life based on the evaluation of functionings and capabilities.

Similarly, the assessment of inequality too depends on the chosen indicator of individual advantage. The usual inequality measures that can be found in empirical economic literatures tend to concentrate on inequalities of incomes or wealth.[31] These are valuable contributions. On the other hand, in so far as income and wealth do not give adequate account of quality of life, there is a case for basing the evaluation of inequality on information more closely related to living standards.

Indeed, the two informational bases are not alternatives. Inequality of wealth may tell us things about the generation and persistence of inequalities of other types, even when our ultimate concern may be with inequality of living standard and quality of life. Particularly in the context of the continuation and stubbornness of social divisions, information on inter-class inequalities in wealth and property ownership is especially crucial. But this recognition does not reduce the importance of bringing in indicators of quality of life to assess the actual inter-class inequalities of well-being and freedom.

One field in which inequalities are particularly hard to assess is that of gender difference. There is a great deal of general evidence to indicate that women often have a much worse deal than men do, and that girls are often much more deprived than boys. These differences may be reflected in many subtle as well as crude ways, and in various forms they can be observed in different parts of the world – among both rich and poor countries. However, it is not easy to determine what is the best indicator of advantage in terms of which these gender inequalities are to be examined. There is, to be sure, no need to look for one specific metric only, and the need for plurality of indicators is as strong here as in any other field. But there is still an issue of the choice of approach to well-being and advantage in the assessment of inequalities between women and men.

The approach of utility-based evaluation is particularly limiting in this context, since the unequal deals that obtain, particularly within the family, are often made "acceptable" by certain social notions of "normal" arrangements, and this may affect the perceptions of women as well as men of the comparative levels of well-being they respectively enjoy. For example, in the context of some developing countries such as India, the point has been made that rural women may have no clear perception of being deprived of things that men have, and may not be in fact any more unhappy than men are. This may or may not be the case, but even if it were so, it can be argued that the mental metric of utility may be particularly inappropriate for judging inequality in this context. The presence of objective deprivation in the form of greater undernourishment, more frequent morbidity, lower literacy etc. cannot be rendered irrelevant just by the quiet and ungrumbling acceptance of women of their deprived conditions.[32]

In rejecting utility-based evaluations, it may be tempting to go in the direction of actual commodities (enjoyed by women and men, respectively) to check inequalities between them. There is here the problem, already discussed earlier in this paper, that commodity-based evaluations are inadequate because commodities are merely means to well-being and freedom and do not reflect the nature of the lives that the people involved can lead. But, in addition, there is the further problem that it is hard – sometimes impossible – to get confirmation on how the commodities belonging to the family are divided between men and women, and between boys and girls.

For example, studies on the division of food within the family tend to be deeply problematic since the observation needed to see who is eating how much is hard to carry out with any degree of reliability. On the other hand, it is possible to compare signs of undernourishment of boys and girls, to check their respective morbidity rates etc., and these functioning differences are both easier to observe and of greater intrinsic relevance.[33]

There are indeed inequalities between men and women in terms of functionings, and in the context of developing countries the contrast may be sharp even in basic matters of life and death, health, illness, education and illiteracy. For example, despite the fact when men and women are treated reasonably equally in terms of food and health care (as they tend to be in the richer countries, even though gender biases may remain in other – less elementary – fields), women seem to have a greater ability to survive than men, in the bulk of the developing economies, men outnumber women by large margins. While the ratio of females to males in Europe and North America tends to be about 1.06 or so, that ratio is below 0.95 for the Middle East (including countries in Western Asia and North Africa), South Asia (including India, Pakistan and Bangladesh) and China.[34] This crude figure of the ratio of survived females to survived males already tells a story that has much informational value in judging inter-gender inequalities. Sometimes there are sharp contrasts even within a country (e.g., the ratio of females to males varies within India all the way from 1.03 in Kerala to 0.87 or 0.88 in Haryana and Punjab). From the point of view of studying both the actual situations and the causal influences operating in the generation of inter-gender inequalities, these regional contrasts may be particularly important.

Being able to survive is of course only one capability (though undoubtedly a very basic one), and other comparisons can be made with information on health, morbidity etc. The ability to read and write is also another important capability, and here it can be seen that the ratio of female to male literacy rates is often shockingly low in different parts of the world. The combined effects of low literacy rates in general (a deprivation of a basic capability across genders) and gender inequalities in literacy rates (unequal deprivation of this basic capability for women) tend to be quite disastrous denials for women. It appears that even leaving out many countries for which no reliable data exist, in a great many countries in the world, the female literacy rate is still below 50 per cent. In fact, it is below even 30 per cent for as many as 26 countries, below 20 per cent for 16 and below 10 per cent in at least five.[35]

In general, the perspective of functionings and capabilities provides a plausible approach to examining inter-gender inequalities. It does not suffer from the type of subjectivism that makes utility-based accounting particularly obtuse in dealing with entrenched inequalities. Nor does it suffer from the overconcentration on means that commodity-based accounting undoubtedly does, and in fact it has better informational sources in studying inequalities within the family than is provided by guesswork on commodity distribution (e.g., who is eating how much?). The case of inter-gender inequalities is, of course, only one illustration of the advantages that the capability approach has. But it happens to be an illustration that is particularly important on its own as well, given the pervasive and stubborn nature of inequalities between women and men in different parts of the world.

CONCLUSION

The assessment of achievement and advantage of members of the society is a central part of development analysis. In this paper, I have tried to discuss how the capability approach may be used to substantiate the evaluative concerns of human development. The focus on human achievement and freedom, and on the need for reflective – rather than mechanical – evaluation, is an adaptation of an old tradition that can be fruitfully used in providing a conceptual basis for analysing the tasks of human development in the contemporary world. The foundational importance of human capabilities provides a firm basis for evaluating living standards and the quality of life, and also points to a general format in terms of which problems of efficiency and equality can both be discussed.

The concentration on distinct capabilities entails, by its very nature, a pluralist approach. Indeed, it points to the necessity of seeing development as a combination of distinct processes, rather than as the expansion of some apparently homogeneous magnitude such as real income or utility. The things that people value doing or being can be quite diverse, and the valuable capabilities vary from such elementary freedoms as being free from hunger and undernourishment to such complex abilities as achieving self-respect and social participation. The challenge of human development demands attention being paid to a variety of sectoral concerns and a combination of social and economic processes.

In the collection of papers of which this one is a part, there are a number of specific studies dealing with such matters as education, health and nutrition, as well as the process of agricultural expansion and industrial development. The problems of resource mobilization and participatory development are also addressed. Some of the subjects thus covered deal with variables that are direct determinants of human capability (e.g., education and health), while others relate to instrumental influences that operate through economic or social process (e.g., the promotion of agricultural and industrial productivity). The uniting feature is the motivating concern with human development and its constitutive characteristics.

In the distinction between functionings and capabilities, emphasis was placed on the importance of having the freedom to choose one kind of life rather than another. This is an emphasis that distinguishes the capability approach from any accounting of only realized achievements. However, the ability to exercise freedom may, to a considerable extent, be directly dependent on the education we have received, and thus the development of the educational sector may have a foundational connection with the capability-based approach.

In fact, educational expansion has a variety of roles that have to be carefully distinguished. First, more education can help productivity. Secondly, wide sharing of educational advancement can contribute to a better distribution of the aggregate national income among different people. Thirdly, being better educated can help in the conversion of incomes and resources into various functioning and ways of living. Last (and by no means the least), education also helps in the intelligent choice between different types of lives that a person can lead. All these distinct influences can have important bearings on the development of valuable capabilities and thus on the process of human development.

There are also other interconnections between the different areas covered in the collection; for example, good health is an achievement in itself and also contributes both to higher productivity and to an enhanced ability to convert incomes and resources into good living. In focusing on human capabilities as the yardstick in terms of which successes and failures of human development are to be judged, attention is particularly invited to addressing these social interconnections. Given clarity regarding the ends (avoiding, in particular, the pitfall of treating human beings as means), the social and economic instrumentalities involved in the ends-means relations can be extensively explored.

One of the most important tasks of an evaluative system is to do justice to our deeply held human values. The challenge of "human development in the 1980s and beyond" cannot be fully grasped without consciously facing this issue and paying deliberate attention to the enhancement of those freedoms and capabilities that matter most in the lives that we can lead. To broaden the limited lives into which the majority of human beings are willy-nilly imprisoned by force of circumstances is the major challenge of human development in the contemporary world. Informed and intelligent evaluation both of the lives we are forced to lead and of the lives we would be able to choose to lead through bringing about social changes is the first step in confronting that challenge. It is a task that we must face.

ENDNOTES

* Editors' note: This chapter has been reproduced from *Journal of Development Planning*, 1989, no.19, pp. 41–58.

1. *Grundlegung* (1785), sect. II: English translation, *Fundamental Principles of the Metaphysics of Morals*, in *Kant's Critique of Practical Reason and Other Works on the Theory of Ethics*, 6th edition, T.K. Abbot, ed (London, Longmans, 1909), p. 47.

2. Amartya Sen, "Equality of what?", in *Tanner Lectures on Human Values*, S. M. McMurring, ed., vol. I (Cambridge, Cambridge University Press, 1980, reprinted in *Choice, Welfare and Measurement* (Oxford, Blackwell: and Cambridge, Massachusetts, MIT Press, 1982)): *Resources, Values and Development* (Oxford, Blackwell; and Cambridge, Massachusetts, Harvard University Press, 1984); *Commodities and Capabilities* (Amsterdam, North-Holland, 1985); "Well-being, agency and freedom, the Dewey lectures 1984", *Journal of Philosophy*, 82 (April 1985); and "Capability and well-being", WIDER conference paper, 1988.

3. Aristotle, *The Nicomachean Ethics*, book I, sect. 7; in the translation by David Ross, *World's Classics* (Oxford, Oxford University Press, 1980), pp. 12–14. Note that Aristotle's term "eudaimonia", which is often misleadingly translated simply as "happiness", stands for fulfilment of life in a way that goes well beyond the utilitarian perspective. Though pleasure may well result from fulfilment, that is seen as a consequence rather than the cause of valuing that fulfilment. For an examination of the Aristotelian approach and its relation to recent works on functionings and capabilities, see Martha Nussbaum, "Nature, function and capability: Aristotle on political distribution", *Oxford Studies in Ancient Greek Philosophy*, supplementary volume 1998.

4. See Adam Smith, *An Inquiry into the Nature and Causes of the Wealth of Nations* (1776), vol. I, book V, sect. II; republished, R. H. Campbell and A. S. Skinner, eds. (Oxford, Clarendon Press, 1976), pp. 869–872; and Karl Marx, *Economic and Philosophic Manuscripts of 1844* (1844); English translation (Moscow Progressive Publishers, 1977).

5. See G. E. M. de Sainte Croix, *The Class Struggle in the Ancient Greek World* (London, Duckworth, 1981); and Martha Nussbaum, "Nature, function and capability...".

6. Karl Marx, *Economic and Philosophic Manuscripts of 1844...*

7. Aristotle, *op. cit.*, book I, sect. 5; in the translation by David Ross, p. 7.

8. Karl Marx, *Capital*, vol. I, English translation by S. Moore and E. Aveling (London, Sonnenschein, 1887), chap. 1, sect. 4, pp. 41–55; see also Karl Marx, *Economic and Philosophic Manuscripts of 1844...*

9. See Adam Smith, *op. cit.*, vol. II, book V, chap. II (section entitled "Taxes upon Consumable Commodities"); republished..., pp. 469–471.

10. There are several technical problems in the representation of functioning n-tuples and of capability as a set of alternative functioning n-tuples, any one n-tuple of which a person can choose. In this paper, I shall not be particularly concerned with these formal matters, for which see *Commodities and Capabilities...*, especially chaps. 2, 4 and 7.

11. Karl Marx and Friederich Engels, *The German Ideology* (1846). The quoted passage is taken from the translation by David McLellan, *Karl Marx: Selected Writings* (Oxford, Oxford University Press, 1977), p. 190.

12. See Amartya Sen, "Well-being, agency and freedom ..."; and *Commodities and Capabilities ....*

13. It is sometimes presumed that to depart from a person's own actual desires or pleasures as the measuring rod of assessment would be to introduce paternalism into the evaluative exercise. This view overlooks the important fact that having pleasure and desiring are not themselves valuational activities, even though the latter (desire) can often result from valuing something, and the former (pleasure) can often result from getting what one values. A person's utility must not be confused with his or her own valuations, and thus tying the evaluative exercise to the person's own utility is quite different from judging a person's success in terms of the person's own valuation. The important distinction to note in this context is that a person may not have the courage to desire a big social change, weighted down by the circumstances in which he or she lives, and yet given the opportunity to evaluate the situation, which is essentially an analytical exercise in this context, the person may well value a change. One advantage of valuing as opposed to feeling is that proper evaluation has to be a reflective exercise – open to critical examination – in a way that feelings need not be (the requirement of critical examination does not apply in the same way to feelings as it does to reflective evaluations). These and related issues are discussed in "Well-being, agency and freedom ...".

14. In many contexts, the formal representations will take the form of partial orderings, or of overdetermined rankings, or of "fuzzy" relations. This is, of course, not a special problem with the capability approach, and applies generally to conceptual frameworks in social theory; see Amartya Sen, *Collective Choice and Social Welfare* (San Francisco, Holden-Day, 1970; republished, Amsterdam, North-Holland, 1979); and *On Ethics and Economics* (Oxford, Blackwell, 1987); see also "Social choice theory", in *Handbook of Mathematical Economics*, K. J. Arrow and M. Intriligator, eds. (Amsterdam, North-Holland, 1985). The formal problems can be dealt with at different levels of precision (i.e. with varying extent of precise representation of ambiguities). The important general point to note here is that it may be, for substantive social theories, both terribly limiting and altogether unnecessary to shun ambiguities.

15. See Amartya Sen, *Choice, Welfare and Measurement ...*, essays 17–20.

16. Bernard Williams raises this issue in his comments on the Tanner Lectures on the standard of living; see *The Standard of Living*, Tanner Lectures of Amartya Sen, with discussions by John Muelbauer, Ravi Kanbur, Keith Hart and Bernard Williams, edited by Geoffrey Hawthorn (Cambridge, Cambridge University Press, 1987), pp. 98–101 and 108–109.

17. I have tried to discuss some of the general methodological issues involved in description in "Description as choice", *Oxford Economic Press*, 32 (1980); reprinted in *Choice, Welfare and Measurement ....*

18. See Amartya Sen, *Resources, Values and Development ...*, chaps. 15, 19 and 20; and "The concept of development", in *Handbook of Development Economics*, H. Chenery and T. N. Srinivasan, eds. (Amsterdam, North-Holland.

19. The range of functionings and capabilities that may be of interest for the assessment of a person's well-being or agency can be very wide indeed; see Amartya Sen, "Well-being, agency and freedom . . .".

20. See, among other contributions, Michael Lipton, *Assessing Economic Performance* (London, Staples Press, 1968); Paul Streeten, *The Frontiers of Development Studies* (London, Macmillan, 1972); Irma Adelman and Cynthia Tuft Morris, *Economic Growth and Social Equity in Developing Countries* (Stanford, Stanford University Press, 1973); Amartya Sen, "On the development of basic income indicators to supplement GNP measures", *Economic Bulletin for Asia and the Far East* (United Nations publication, Sales No. E.74.II.F.4); H. Chenery and others, *Redistribution with Growth* (London, Oxford University Press, 1974); Irma Adelman, "Development economics: a reassessment of goals", *American Economic Review*, Papers and Proceedings, 66 (1976); James P. Grant, *Disparity Reduction Rates in Social Indicators* (Washington, D.C., Overseas Development Council, 1978); Keith Griffin and Azizur Rahman Khan, "Poverty in the third world: ugly facts and fancy models", *World Development*, 6 (1978); Paul Streeten and S. J. Burki, "Basic needs: some issues", *World Development*, 6 (1978); Morris D. Morris, *Measuring the Conditions of the World's Poor: The Physical Quality of Life Index* (Oxford, Pergamon, 1979); Paul Streeten, *Development Perspectives* (London, Macmillan, 1981); Paul Streeten and others, *First Things First: Meeting Basic Needs in Developing Countries* (New York, Oxford University Press, 1981); S. R. Osmani, *Economic Inequality and Group Welfare* (Oxford, Claredon Press, 1982); and Frances Stewart, *Planning to Meet Basic Needs* (London, Macmillan, 1985).

21. This general question of foundations and informational bases is discussed in Amartya Sen, "Informational analysis of moral principles", in *Rational Action*, Ross Harrison, ed. (Cambridge, Cambridge University Press, 1979): and "Well-being, agency and freedom . . . ". In the latter analysis, some distinctions are drawn (especially between agency and well-being and between achievement and freedom) that may be worth pursuing in a more elaborate treatment of this matter, but I shall resist the temptation to go into these issues here.

22. On this general question and on the relation between commodities, characteristics and functionings, see Amartya Sen, *Commodities and Capabilities . . .* , chap. 2.

23. On this question, see Amartya Sen, *Resources, Values and Development . . .* , essays 19 and 20; and Paul Streeten, "Basic needs: some unsettled questions", *World Development*, 12 (1984).

24. John Rawls, *A Theory of Justice* (Oxford, Clarendon Press: and Cambridge, Massachusetts, Harvard University Press, 1971), pp. 60–65

25. See Amartya Sen, "Equality of what?" . . . , and *Resources, Values and Development . . . .*

26. See Amartya Sen, "Freedom of choice: concept and content", Alfred Marshall lecture at the European Economic Association, *European Economic Review*, 1988.

27. See Amartya Sen, *Commodities and Capabilities . . .* , pp. 60–67.

28. See Amartya Sen, "Well-being, agency and freedom . . ." and "Freedom of choice: concept and content . . . ".

29. On the question of the relation between achieved states and the extent of freedom and liberty, see Amartya Sen, "Liberty and social choice", *Journal of Philosophy*, 80 (1983).

30. Indeed, not to take note of the person's own evaluations of states of affairs in providing a measure of freedom can yield a very peculiar view of freedom, which would be seriously at odds with the tradition of seeing freedom as important. On this, see Amartya Sen, "Liberty as control: an appraisal", *Midwest Studies in Philosophy*, 7 (1982); and "Liberty and social choice . . .".

31. See, for example, A. B. Atkinson, *Unequal Shares: Wealth in Britain* (London, Penguin, 1972); and *The Economics of Inequality* (Oxford, Clarendon Press, 1975).

32. I have discussed this question in *Commodities and Capabilities . . .* , appendix B, and also in *Resources, Values and Development . . .* , essays 15 and 16. The importance of perception biases in the continuation of inter-gender inequalities is discussed in "Gender and cooperative conflicts", WIDER working paper, in *Persistent Inequalities*, Irene Tinker, ed.

33. For an attempt to make such functioning-based comparisons between men and women, see Jocelyn Kynch and Amartya Sen, "Indian women: well-being and survival", *Cambridge Journal of Economics*, 7 (1983).

34. See Jocelyn Kynch, "How many women are enough: sex ratios and the right to life", *Third World Affairs 1985* (London, Third World Foundation for Social and Economic Studies, 1985). The ratios of life expectancy seem to have turned in favour of women *vis-à-vis* men, according to reported statistics in most countries (see United Nations Children's Fund, *The State of the World's Children 1988* (New York, Oxford University Press, 1988), table 7), but the undoing of past biases against women in the sex composition of the population tends to be a slow process over the years.

35. United Nations Children's Fund, *The State of the World's Children 1988 . . .* , table 4.

REFERENCES

Adelman, Irma. 1976. "Development Economics: A Reassessment of Goals." *American Economic Review*, Papers and Proceedings 66.

Adelman, Irma and Cynthia Tuft Morris. 1973. *Economic Growth and Social Equity in Developing Countries*. Stanford: Stanford University Press.

Aristotle. 1980. *The Nicomachean Ethics*, book I, sect. 7. In the translation by David Ross, *World's Classics*. Oxford: Oxford University Press, pp. 12–14.

Arrow, K. J. and M. Intriligator (eds.). 1985. "Social Choice Theory." In *Handbook of Mathematical Economics*. Amsterdam: North-Holland.

Atkinson, A. B. 1972. *Unequal Shares: Wealth in Britain.* London: Penguin.

——. 1975. *The Economics of Inequality.* Oxford: Clarendon Press.

Chenery, H. and others. 1974. *Redistribution with Growth.* London: Oxford University Press.

Chenery, H. and T. N. Srinivasan (eds.). 1988–1989. "The Concept of Development." In *Handbook of Development Economics.* Amsterdam: North-Holland.

Grant, James P. 1978. *Disparity Reduction Rates in Social Indicators.* Washington, D.C.: Overseas Development Council.

Griffin, Keith and Azizur Rahman Khan. 1978. "Poverty in the Third World: Ugly Facts and Fancy Models." *World Development* 6.

Hawthorn, Geoffrey (ed.). 1987. *The Standard of Living.* Tanner Lectures of Amartya Sen, with discussions by John Muelbauer, Ravi Kanbur, Keith Hart and Bernard Williams. Cambridge: Cambridge University Press, pp. 98–101 and 108–9.

Kant, Immanuel. 1785. *Grundlegung.* Sect. II: English translation, *Fundamental Principles of the Metaphysics of Morals,* in *Kant's Critique of Practical Reason and Other Works on the Theory of Ethics,* 6th edition, T.K. Abbot (ed.). London: Longmans, 1909, p. 47.

Kynch, Jocelyn. 1985. "How Many Women Are Enough: Sex Ratios and the Right to Life." *Third World Affairs 1985.* London: Third World Foundation for Social and Economic Studies.

Kynch, Jocelyn and Amartya Sen. 1983. "Indian Women: Well-being and Survival." *Cambridge Journal of Economics* 7.

Lipton, Michael. 1968. *Assessing Economic Performance.* London: Staples Press.

Marx, Karl. 1844. *Economic and Philosophic Manuscripts of 1844.* English translation. Moscow Progressive Publishers, 1977.

Marx, Karl and Friederich Engels. 1846. *The German Ideology.* In the translation by David McLellan, *Karl Marx: Selected Writings.* Oxford: Oxford University Press, 1977, p. 190.

Morris, Morris D. 1979. *Measuring the Conditions of the World's Poor: The Physical Quality of Life Index.* Oxford: Pergamon.

Nussbaum, Martha. 1998. "Nature, Function and Capability: Aristotle on Political Distribution." *Oxford Studies in Ancient Greek Philosophy,* supplementary volume.

Osmani, S. R. 1982. *Economic Inequality and Group Welfare.* Oxford: Claredon Press.

Rawls, John. 1971. *A Theory of Justice.* Oxford, Clarendon Press; Cambridge, Mass.: Harvard University Press, pp. 60–65.

Sainte Croix, G. E. M. de. 1981. *The Class Struggle in the Ancient Greek World.* London: Duckworth.

Sen, Amartya. 1970. *Collective Choice and Social Welfare.* San Francisco, Holden-Day, republished, Amsterdam: North-Holland, 1979.

——. 1979. "Informational Analysis of Moral Principles." In Ross Harrison (ed.), *Rational Action.* Cambridge: Cambridge University Press.

——. 1980. "Equality of What?" In S. M. McMurring (ed.), *Tanner Lectures on Human Values,* vol. I, Cambridge, Cambridge University Press. Reprinted in *Choice, Welfare and Measurement.* Oxford, Blackwell: and Cambridge, Mass.: MIT Press, 1982.

——. 1982. "Liberty as Control: An Appraisal." *Midwest Studies in Philosophy* 7.

——. 1983. "Liberty and Social Choice." *Journal of Philosophy* 80.

——. 1984. *Resources, Values and Development.* Oxford, Blackwell; and Cambridge, Mass.: Harvard University Press.

——. 1985. *Commodities and Capabilities.* Amsterdam: North-Holland.

——. 1985. "Well-being, Agency and Freedom: The Dewey Lectures 1984." *Journal of Philosophy* 82, April.

——. 1987. *On Ethics and Economics.* Oxford: Blackwell.

——. 1988. "Capability and Well-being." WIDER conference paper.

——. 1988. "Freedom of Choice: Concept and Content." Alfred Marshall lecture at the European Economic Association, *European Economic Review.*

——. 1990. "Gender and Cooperative Conflicts." In Irene Tinker (ed.), *Persistent Inequalities.* Oxford University Press: New York.

——. "On the Development of Basic Income Indicators to Supplement GNP Measures." *Economic Bulletin for Asia and the Far East* (United Nations publication, Sales No. E.74.II.F.4).

Smith, Adam. 1776. *An Inquiry into the Nature and Causes of the Wealth of Nations.* Vol. I, book V, sect. II. Republished, R. H. Campbell and A. S. Skinner (eds.). Oxford: Clarendon Press, 1976, pp. 869–72.

Stewart, Frances. 1985. *Planning to Meet Basic Needs.* London: Macmillan.

Streeten, Paul. 1972. *The Frontiers of Development Studies.* London: Macmillan.

——. 1981. *Development Perspectives.* London: Macmillan.

——. 1984. "Basic Needs: Some Unsettled Questions." *World Development* 12.

Streeten, Paul and S. J. Burki. 1978. "Basic Needs: Some Issues." *World Development* 6.

Streeten, Paul and others. 1981. *First Things First: Meeting Basic Needs in Developing Countries.* New York: Oxford University Press.

UNICEF (United Nations Children's Fund). 1988. *The State of the World's Children 1988.* New York: Oxford University Press.

1.2
THE HUMAN
DEVELOPMENT PARADIGM*

Mahbub ul Haq

"That's very important," the King said, turning to the jury. They were just beginning to write this down on their slates, when the White Rabbit interrupted: "Unimportant, your Majesty means, of course," he said in a very respectful tone, but frowning and making faces at him as he spoke.

"Unimportant, of course, I meant," the King hastily said, and went on to himself in an undertone, "important – unimportant – unimportant – important –" as if he were trying which word sounded best.

– Alice in Wonderland

The rediscovery of human development is not a new invention. It is a tribute to the early leaders of political and economic thought. The idea that social arrangements must be judged by the extent to which they promote "human good" dates at least to Aristotle (384–322 B.C.). He argued that "wealth is evidently not the good we are seeking, for it is merely useful and for the sake of something else". He distinguished a good political arrangement from a bad one by its successes and failures in enabling people to lead "flourishing lives".

Immanuel Kant (1724–1804) continued the tradition of treating human beings as the real end of all activities when he observed: "So act as to treat humanity, whether in their own person or in that of any other, in every case as an end withal, never as means only." And when Adam Smith (1723–1790), that apostle of free enterprise and private initiative, showed his concern that economic development should enable a person to mix freely with others without being "ashamed to appear in publick", he was expressing a concept of poverty that went beyond counting calories – a concept that integrated the poor into the mainstream of the community. A similar strain was reflected in the writings of the other founders of modern economic thought, including Robert Malthus, Karl Marx and John Stuart Mill.

After the belated rediscovery of human development, it is necessary to give this paradigm some firmer conceptual, quantitative and policy moorings – here and in the next six chapters.

The basic purpose of development is to enlarge people's choices. In principle, these choices can be infinite and can change over time. People often value achievements that do not show up at all, or not immediately, in income or growth figures: greater access to knowledge, better nutrition and health services, more secure livelihoods, security against crime and physical violence, satisfying leisure hours, political and cultural freedoms and a sense of participation in community activities. The objective of development is to create an enabling environment for people to enjoy long, healthy and creative lives.

INCOME AND HUMAN CHOICES

The defining difference between the economic growth and the human development schools is that the first focuses exclusively on the expansion of only one choice – income – while the second embraces the enlargement of all human choices – whether economic, social, cultural or political. It might well be argued that the expansion of income can enlarge all other choices as well. But that is not necessarily so, for a variety of reasons.

To begin with, income may be unevenly distributed within a society. People who have no access to income, or enjoy only limited access, will see their choices fairly constrained. It has often been observed that in many societies, economic growth does not trickle down.

But there is an even more fundamental reason why income expansion may fail to enlarge human options. It has to do with the national priorities chosen by the society or its rulers – guns or butter, an elitist model of development or an egalitarian one, political authoritarianism or political democracy, a command economy or participatory development.

No one will deny that such choices make a critical difference. Yet we often forget that the use of income by a society is just as important as the generation of income itself, or that income expansion leads to much less human satisfaction in a virtual political prison or cultural void than in a more liberal political and economic environment. There is no automatic link between income and human lives – a theme explored at length in the subsequent chapters. Yet there has long been an apparent presumption in economic thought that such an automatic link exists.

It should also be recognized that accumulating wealth may not be necessary for the fulfilment of several kinds of human choices. In fact, individuals and societies make many choices that require no wealth at all. A society does not have to be rich to afford democracy. A family does not have to be wealthy to respect the rights of each member. A nation does not have to be affluent to treat women and men equally. Valuable social and cultural traditions can be – and are – maintained at all levels of income.

Many human choices extend far beyond economic well-being. Knowledge, health, a clean physical environment, political freedom and simple pleasures of life are not exclusively, or largely, dependent on income. National wealth can expand people's choices in these areas. But it might not. The use that people make of their wealth, not the wealth itself, is decisive. And unless societies recognize that their real wealth is their people, an excessive obsession with creating material wealth can obscure the goal of enriching human lives.

The human development paradigm performs an important service in questioning the presumed automatic link between expanding income and ex-

panding human choices. Such a link depends on the quality and distribution of economic growth, not only on the quantity of such growth. A link between growth and human lives has to be created consciously through deliberate public policy – such as public spending on social services and fiscal policy to redistribute income and assets. This link may not exist in the automatic workings of the marketplace, which can further marginalize the poor.

But we must be careful. Rejecting an automatic link between income expansion and flourishing human lives is not rejecting growth itself. Economic growth is essential in poor societies for reducing or eliminating poverty. But the quality of this growth is just as important as its quantity. Conscious public policy is needed to translate economic growth into people's lives.

How can that be done? It may require a major restructuring of economic and political power, and the human development paradigm is quite revolutionary in that respect. It questions the existing structure of power. Greater links between economic growth and human choices may require far-reaching land reform, progressive tax systems, new credit systems to bank on the poor people, a major expansion of basic social services to reach all of the deprived population, the removal of barriers to the entry of people in economic and political spheres and the equalization of their access to opportunities, and the establishment of temporary social safety nets for those who may be bypassed by the markets or public policy actions. Such policy packages are fairly fundamental and will vary from one country to another. But some features are common to all of them.

First, people are moved to centre stage. Development is analysed and understood in terms of people. Each activity is analysed to see how much people participate in it or benefit from it. The touchstone of the success of development policies becomes the betterment of people's lives, not just the expansion of production processes.

Second, human development is assumed to have two sides. One is the formation of human capabilities - such as improved health, knowledge and skills. The other is the use people make of their acquired capabilities - for employment, productive activities, political affairs or leisure. A society needs to build up human capabilities as well as ensure equitable access to human opportunities. Considerable human frustration results if the scales of human development do not finely balance the two sides.

Third, a careful distinction is maintained between ends and means. People are regarded as the ends. But means are not forgotten. The expansion of GNP becomes an essential means for expanding many human options. But the character and distribution of economic growth are measured against the yardstick of enriching the lives of people. Production processes are not treated in an abstract vacuum. They acquire a human context.

Fourth, the human development paradigm embraces all of society – not just the economy. The political, cultural and social factors are given as much attention as the economic factors. In fact, study of the link between the economic and the non-economic environment is one of the most fascinating and rewarding aspects of this new analysis.

Fifth, it is recognized that people are both the means and the ends of development. But people are not regarded as mere instruments for producing commodities – through an augmentation of "human capital". It is always remembered that human beings are the ultimate end of development – not convenient fodder for the materialistic machine.

A HOLISTIC CONCEPT

Nor should human welfare concepts or social safety nets or investment in education and health be equated with the human development paradigm, which includes these aspects, but only as parts of the whole. The human development paradigm covers all aspects of development – whether economic growth or international trade, budget deficits or fiscal policy, saving or investment or technology, basic social services or safety nets for the poor. No aspect of the development model falls outside its scope, but the vantage point is the widening of people's choices and the enrichment of their lives. All aspects of life – economic, political or cultural – are viewed from that perspective.

Economic growth, as such, becomes only a subset of the human development paradigm.

On some aspects of the human development paradigm, there is fairly broad agreement:

- Development must put people at the centre of its concerns.
- The purpose of development is to enlarge all human choices, not just income.
- The human development paradigm is concerned both with building up human capabilities (through investment in people) and with using those human capabilities fully (through an enabling framework for growth and employment).
- Human development has four essential pillars: equality, sustainability, productivity and empowerment. It regards economic growth as essential but emphasizes the need to pay attention to its quality and distribution, analyses at length its link with human lives and questions its long-term sustainability.
- The human development paradigm defines the ends of development and analyses sensible options for achieving them.

Despite the broad agreement on many of these features, there are several controversies about the human development concept – often stemming from some misunderstanding about the concept itself. Fairly widespread is the mistaken view that human development is anti-growth and that it encompasses only social development.

The human development paradigm consistently takes the view that growth is not the end of economic development – but that the absence of growth often is. Economic growth is essential for human development, but to fully exploit the opportunities for improved well-being that growth offers, it needs to be properly managed. Some countries have been extremely successful in managing their economic growth to improve the human condition, others less so. So, there is no automatic link between economic growth and human progress. And one of the most pertinent policy issues concerns the exact process through which growth translates, or fails to translate, into human development under different development conditions.

There are four ways to create the desirable links between economic growth and human development.

First, emphasis on investment in the education, health and skills of the people can enable them to participate in the growth process as well as to share its benefits, principally through remunerative employment. This is the growth model adopted by China, Hong Kong, Japan, Malaysia, the Republic of Korea, Singapore, Thailand and many other newly industrializing countries.

Second, more equitable distribution of income and assets is critical for creating a close link between economic growth and human development. Wherever the distribution of income and assets is very uneven (as in Brazil, Nigeria and Pakistan), high GNP growth rates have failed to translate into people's lives. The link between distribution of assets and the nature of growth can be:

- Growth-led, with favourable initial conditions in asset distribution and mass education, including the participation of people in economic activities (China, the Republic of Korea)
- Unfavourable initial conditions but high growth with corrective public policy action, including people's participation (Chile, Malaysia).
- Low growth with public policy action to provide basic social services, but normally unsustainable over the long term (Jamaica, Sri Lanka).

Third, some countries have managed to make significant improvements in human development even in the absence of good growth or good distribution. They have achieved this result through well-structured social expenditures by the government. Cuba, Jamaica, Sri Lanka and Zimbabwe, among others, achieved fairly impressive results through the generous state provision of social services. So did many countries in Eastern Europe and the Commonwealth of Independent States (CIS). But such experiments generally are not sustainable unless the economic base expands enough to support the social base.

Fourth, the empowerment of people – particularly women – is a sure way to link growth and human development. In fact, empowerment should accompany all aspects of life. If people can exercise their choices in the political, social and economic spheres, there is a good prospect that growth will be strong, democratic, participatory and durable.

Another misconception – closely related to the alleged anti-growth bias of human development models – is that human development strategies have only social content, no hard economic analysis. The impression has grown that human development strategies are concerned mainly with social development expenditures (particularly in education and health). Some analysts have gone further and confused human development with development only of human resources – that is, social development expenditure aimed at strengthening human capabilities. Others have insisted that human development strategies are concerned only with human welfare aspects – or, even more narrowly, only with basic human needs – and that they have little to say about economic growth, production and consumption, saving and investment, trade and technology, or any other aspect of a macroeconomic framework.

These analysts do scant justice to the basic concept of human development as a holistic development paradigm embracing both ends and means, both productivity and equity, both economic and social development, both material goods and human welfare. At best, their critiques are based on a misunderstanding of the human development paradigm. At worst, they are the products of feeble minds.

The real point of departure of human development strategies is to approach every issue in the traditional growth models from the vantage point of people. Do they participate in economic growth as well as benefit from it? Do they have full access to the opportunities of expanded trade? Are their choices enlarged or narrowed by new technologies? Is economic expansion leading to job-led growth or jobless growth? Are budgets being balanced without unbalancing the lives of future generations? Are "free" markets open to all people? Are we increasing the options only of the present generation or also of the future generations?

None of the economic issues is ignored, but they all are related to the ultimate objective of development: people. And people are analysed not merely as the beneficiaries of economic growth but as the real agents of every change in society whether economic, political, social or cultural. To establish the supremacy of people in the process of development – as the classical writers always did – is not to denigrate economic growth but to rediscover its real purpose.

It is fair to say that the human development paradigm is the most holistic development model that exists today. It embraces every development issue, including economic growth, social investment, people's empowerment, provision of basic needs and social safety nets, political and cultural freedoms and all other aspects of people's lives. It is neither narrowly technocratic nor overly philosophical. It is a practical reflection of life itself.

Most of the recent elaboration of the human development paradigm has been carried out by the annual *Human Development Report,* which since 1990 has been commissioned by the United Nations Development Programme and prepared by an independent team of eminent economists and distinguished social scientists.

THE ADVENT OF THE HUMAN DEVELOPMENT REPORT

In economic science, nothing is ever new, and nothing permanent. Ideas emerge, flourish, wither and die, to be born again a few decades later. Such is the case for ideas about human development. The founders of economic thought never forgot that the real objective of development was to benefit people – creating wealth was only a means. That is why, in classical economic literature, the preoccupation is with all of society, not just with the economy. Fascination with industrial chimneys and technology did not replace early economists' concern with real people.

After the Second World War, however, an obsession grew with economic growth models and national income accounts. What was important was what could be measured and priced. People as the agents of change and beneficiaries of development were often forgotten. Learned treatises appeared on how to increase production, but little was written on how to enhance human lives. The delinking of ends and means began, with economic science often obsessed with means.

The late 1980s were ripe for a counter-offensive. It was becoming obvious in several countries that human lives were shrivelling even as economic production was expanding. Some societies were achieving fairly satisfactory levels of human welfare even at fairly modest incomes. But no one could miss the signs of considerable human distress in the richest societies – rising crime rates, growing pollution, spreading HIV/AIDS, a weakening social fabric. A high income, by itself, was no defence against human deprivation. Nor did high rates of economic growth automatically translate into improved lives. New questions were being raised about the character, distribution and quality of economic growth.

Other events hastened such questioning. The human costs of structural adjustment programmes in the 1980s, undertaken in many developing countries under the aegis of the International Monetary Fund and the World Bank, had been extremely harsh. That prompted questions about the human face of adjustment and about whether alternative policy options were available to balance financial budgets while protecting the interests of the weakest and most vulnerable sections of society. Fast-spreading pollution started reminding policy-makers about the external diseconomies of conventional economic growth models. At the same time, the strong forces of democracy started sweeping across many lands – from the communist countries to the developing world – raising new aspirations for people-centred development models.

In this favourable climate, I presented the idea of preparing an annual human development report to the Administrator of the United Nations Development Programme, William Draper III, in the spring of 1989. He readily accepted the basic idea as well as its essential corollary – that such a report should be independent of any formal clearance through the United Nations. We both recognized that only a candid, uninhibited development policy dialogue would serve the interests of the global community.

The first *Human Development Report,* published by Oxford University Press, emerged in May of 1990. Since then, reports have been produced annually. While each report has monitored the progress of humanity – particularly through the country rankings in a new human development index – each also takes up a new policy issue and explores it in depth. This article recapitulates the main messages of the first five reports, and then analyses their policy impact and the healthy controversies they have generated in many fields.

1990: CONCEPT AND MEASUREMENT

Concern with human development seems to be moving to centre stage in the 1990s. For too long, the recurrent question was, how much is a nation producing? Increasingly, the question now being asked is, how are its people faring? The main reason for this shift is the growing recognition that the real objective of development is to enlarge people's options. Income is only one of those options – and an extremely important one – but it is not the sum-total of human life. Health, education, physical environment and freedom – to name a few other human choices – may be just as important as income.

Human Development Report 1990, launched in London on 24 May 1990, addressed some of these concerns and explored the relationship between economic growth and human development. It challenged some of the conventional wisdom, exploded some of the old myths and reached some important policy conclusions that would have significant implications for development strategies for the next decade.

First, it is wrong to suggest that the development process has failed in most developing countries in the past three decades. Judged by real indicators of human development, it has succeeded spectacularly. Average life expectancy has in-

creased by 16 years, adult literacy by 40% and per capita nutritional levels by more than 20%, and child mortality rates have been halved. In fact, developing countries have achieved in the past 30 years the kind of real human progress that industrial countries took nearly a century to accomplish. While the income gap between North and South is still very large – with the average income of the South 6% of that in the North – the human gaps have been closing fast. Average life expectancy in the South is 80% of the northern average, adult literacy 66% and nutrition 85%.

True, the record of the developing world is uneven, with disparities between regions and countries and even within countries. And true, there is still a large unfinished agenda of human development – with one-fourth of the people in developing countries still deprived of basic human necessities, minimum incomes and decent social services. But the overall policy conclusion is that the development process does work, that international development cooperation has made a difference, that the remaining agenda of human development is manageable in the 1990s if development priorities are properly chosen. This certainly is a message of hope, though not of complacency.

Second, it is wrong to suggest that economic growth is unnecessary for human development. No sustained improvement in human well-being is possible without growth. But it is also wrong to suggest that high economic growth rates will automatically translate into higher levels of human development. They may or they may not. It all depends on the policy choices that countries make. And the real world offers too many uncomfortable examples of a wide divergence between income and human development levels. Adult literacy in Saudi Arabia is lower than that in Sri Lanka despite a per capita income that is 16 times higher. Infant mortality in Jamaica is one-fourth that in Brazil, despite Jamaica's per capita income being half that of Brazil. Life expectancy is 76 years in Costa Rica, with a per capita income of $1,870, but only 69 years in Oman, with a per capita income of $6,140.

Why such wide divergences between income and human development? The explanation lies in how equitably – or inequitably – income, physical assets, financial credit, social services and job opportunities are distributed. If income and human development are to be linked more closely, countries must adopt policies that distribute these economic assets and opportunities more equitably.

Third, it is conceptually and practically wrong to regard poverty alleviation as a goal distinct from human development. Most poverty can be explained by inadequate access to income, assets, credit, social services and job opportunities. The only long-term remedy is to invest in poor people, particularly in their education and training, and to bring them back into the mainstream of development. Poverty should not be regarded as a residual of economic growth, treated separately without modifying the growth strategies. Such an approach is inconsistent with human development strategies – which are focused on investment in all the people and on their full participation in human well-being.

Fourth, it is wrong to suggest that developing countries lack enough resources to address their human development goals. In reality, considerable potential exists for restructuring present priorities in their national budgets and in foreign assistance allocations. Many poor countries spend two to three times more on their military than on the education and health of their people. Overall, Third World military spending increased by $10 billion to $15 billion a year during the 1980s, showing the scope for diversion of resources if new concepts of security evolve in the 1990s. There also is considerable scope for saving by reducing inefficient spending on parastatals, subsidies to the richer sections of society and inappropriate priorities in the development budgets.

In bilateral foreign assistance, the share for education and health has declined from 17% to 10% over the past decade, suggesting room for improving aid allocation. Considerable scope also exists for restructuring internal and external debt. So, the potential for restructuring existing priorities is enormous. The scope for reallocating budgetary expenditure opens to serious question the human and social costs of structural adjustment programmes. Most budgets can be balanced without unbalancing the lives of future generations. And that is why aid donors must re-examine policy conditionality: they must insist that human investment will be the last item to be touched in a budget, and only when all other options have been explored and exhausted.

Fifth, it is wrong to pretend that markets alone can deliver balanced patterns of economic growth and human development. Instead, there must be a judicious mix of market efficiency and social compassion. The present situation in many developing countries is topsy-turvy. Governments are intervening inefficiently in productive processes in agriculture and industry, where they hardly belong, but spending inadequately (3–4% of GNP) on social services, which should be their primary responsibility. This situation needs to be reversed. Also necessary is to ensure that social safety nets are not seriously eroded in periods of rapid growth or social transformation. Otherwise, serious political upheavals may disrupt the development process.

The challenge now is to ensure that human development is at the forefront of growth strategies in the decade ahead. The suggested agenda for the 1990s:

- Persuading the developing countries to prepare their own human development goals for the 1990s and to integrate these goals in their overall growth models and investment budgets.
- Assisting developing countries in collecting better data on human development indicators and in undertaking more professional analysis of the link between their economic growth and human development.
- Analysing the impact of specific projects and programmes on people, not only on production.
- Incorporating human development concerns in aid allocations and policy conditionality.

The 1990s offer an exciting challenge to move from new ideas to concrete action and to treat human beings, once again, as both the means and the end of development.

1991: FINANCING HUMAN DEVELOPMENT

Human Development Report 1991, launched in Washington, D.C., on 23 May 1991, reached the conclusion that restructuring existing budgets can provide enough resources to finance basic social services for all the people. It is the lack of political courage to make tough decisions, rather than the paucity of financial resources, that is responsible for the current state of human neglect. There are far too many examples of wasted resources and wasted opportunities: rising military expenditures, inefficient public enterprises, numerous prestige projects, growing capital flight and extensive corruption. If priorities are recast, most budgets can accommodate more spending for human development. As much as $50 billion a year can be found in developing countries for urgent human concerns, just by changing government spending patterns.

More funds for human development can be found by taking four actions:

- *Halting capital flight* – Capital flight from the Philippines was equal to 80% of its outstanding debt between 1962 and 1986.
- *Combating corruption* – In Pakistan, public officials' illegitimate private gain from their positions is unofficially estimated at 4% of GNP.
- *Reforming public enterprises* – The losses public enterprises suffer in Cameroon, for example, exceed the country's total oil revenue.
- *Restructuring debt payments* – Debt repayments take a large share of government budgets. Jordan devotes 39% of its budget to external debt service and 18% to social services. Internal debt now exceeds external debt for many countries – including India, Malaysia, Pakistan, the Philippines and Singapore.

Four ratios could serve as the principal guide to public spending policy: the public expenditure ratio (the percentage of national income that goes into public expenditure earmarked for social ser-

vices); the social allocation ratio (the percentage of public expenditure earmarked for social services); the social priority ratio (the percentage of social expenditure devoted to human priority concerns); and the human expenditure ratio (the percentage of national income devoted to human priority concerns, obtained by multiplying the first three ratios).

These ratios tell volumes about a country's priorities. Argentina spent 41% of its GNP through its government budget in 1988, yet its human expenditure ratio was only 2.3%. So Argentina realized that it could reduce public spending, release more resources for private investment and economic growth, and yet substantially increase spending on human priority concerns – a course it is currently embarked on.

The report came to these conclusions:

- The human expenditure ratio may need to be at least 5% of GNP if a country wishes to do well on human development.
- An efficient way to achieve this result is to keep the public expenditure ratio moderate (around 25%), to allocate much of this expenditure to the social sectors (more than 40%) and to focus on the social priority areas (giving them more than 50%).
- Government spending need not be high if GNP growth is high and rather equitable – or if private and non-governmental organizations (NGOs) are extremely active in the social sectors.
- High government spending with low social priorities is the worst case. If more than 25–35% of national income is channelled through the government budget, and yet less than 2% of GNP goes to human priority concerns (as in Brazil, Sierra Leone and Thailand in 1988), this is the worst of all possible worlds. The public sector is huge, yet the majority of the people do not gain.
- Most countries could use existing resources more efficiently by adopting more decentralized, participatory approaches to development, by making prudent economies and reducing unit costs, by charging many users

for the benefits they receive, and by encouraging private initiative in the financing and delivery of social services.

Many developing countries spend more than 25% of their GNP through their government budgets. But their expenditure on human priority goals – basic education, primary health care, rural water supply, family planning, food subsidies, social security – is generally less than one-tenth of their total public spending. And only a twelfth of total aid is earmarked for human priority goals, showing the potential for releasing more resources for human development by restructuring priorities in aid budgets. If only one-third of today's aid were committed to human priority areas, the aid allocation to these areas would increase fourfold.

The plea for greater efficiency should not be confused with indifference to economic growth or to the mobilization of additional resources. In fact, additional resources are needed, because all the essential human goals for the 1990s cannot be financed without more money. But the best argument for mobilizing more resources is to spend existing resources well. Because today's distribution of resources usually suits those in power and their influential supporters, a workable political strategy is needed to restructure resource allocation priorities. The elements of such a strategy: empowering weaker groups, channelling credit to the poor, building coalitions based on common interests, compensating powerful groups and coordinating external pressures.

1992: INTERNATIONAL DIMENSIONS OF HUMAN DEVELOPMENT

The central thesis of *Human Development Report 1992,* launched in Stockholm on 23 April 1992, is that the search for equitable access to market opportunities must extend beyond national borders to the global system. Otherwise, economic disparities between the richest and the poorest people, having doubled over the past three decades, are likely to explode. The income of the richest billion people is 150 times that of the poorest billion, a dangerously large gap. To put this in perspective, the income disparity between the richest 20% and the poorest 20% of people within nations is far smaller – the income of the richest fifth is five times higher in Sweden, six times higher in Germany, nine times higher in the United States and 32 times higher (the highest) in Brazil. What would be considered politically and socially unacceptable within nations is being quietly tolerated at the global level.

No end appears to be in sight for these widening gaps – since the gaps are not only in current levels of income but also in future market opportunities and in human development. The bottom 20% of the world's population receives only 1.4% of global GNP – and has a share of only 1% in global trade, 0.2% in global commercial lending and 1.3% in global investment. Because of the barriers to the movement of goods and people and because poor nations pay four times higher real interest rates than do the rich, global markets deny as much as $500 billion of market opportunities to poor nations and poor people every year – which is ten times the foreign assistance that poor nations receive. Precision in these numbers is not important. What is important is that the cost of denied market opportunities far exceeds foreign assistance. It is certainly better for the poor to earn their living than to receive indefinite and uncertain international charity. But unless their access to market opportunities is increased, there is little chance for poor people or poor nations to break out of their poverty trap.

The situation looks even more difficult after adding the widening disparities in higher education, technology and information systems to the picture. The tertiary enrolment rate in the South is only a fifth that in the North, research and development expenditure only 4% and scientific and technical personnel only a ninth. These widening human gaps have a telling impact in a world where technological progress accounts for one-third to one-half of the increases in national output. The combination of technological disparities and limited market opportunities can be devastating.

What can be done? The primary responsibility lies with the developing countries, for global reforms can never substitute for national reforms.

The developing countries must improve their economic management, liberate their private initiative and invest in the education of their people and in the technological progress of their societies. The basis for such a further advance has already been laid by the rapid strides in basic education and primary health care in most developing countries. Japan, the Republic of Korea, Singapore and, more recently, China, Malaysia and Thailand have followed this human investment path to development. They made spectacular increases in their share of global markets. East and South-East Asia doubled their share of world trade between 1970 and 1990, as did China. But Sub-Saharan Africa, with minimal investments in human development, had its share in world trade plummet to a fourth of the 1970 level.

A fatal contradiction afflicts the global economic system. As national markets open up – from New Delhi to Rio, from Moscow to Warsaw – can global markets close down further? That is precisely what is happening. The OECD nations have become more protectionist in the past decade, just when additional export surpluses are likely to emerge from the liberalizing markets of developing countries and the former socialist bloc. For example, if India follows the path of the Republic of Korea, it will have at least $60 billion of additional exports to offer the world markets each year.

It does not take a genius to figure out that the ongoing, rapid structural adjustment in the South and in the former socialist bloc has a logical corollary – a structural change in the North. Yet this simple truth is being largely ignored – sometimes even bitterly contested. Buffeted by recession and unemployment, many northern economies are unprepared to invest in changing their production and job structures, not recognizing that their lack of adjustment will greatly frustrate the liberal market experiments they are so actively encouraging all over the world.

Many of the poorest nations, particularly in Africa, cannot even begin to fully make use of market opportunities without additional financial help. Market efficiency must be balanced by social equity. Even in the market economies of the United States and the United Kingdom, about 15% of GNP is recycled in medicare, food stamps, unemployment benefits and social security payments. In the Nordic countries, the social safety nets consume roughly a third of GNP. But what about the developing world, where 1.2 billion people barely survive below an absolute poverty line of about $400? The rich nations can spare only 0.3% of GNP for official development assistance, the closest approximation to an international social safety net. This, with about 100 million people below the official poverty line of around $5,000 in income a year.

Even more relevant than the inadequacy and unpredictability of such a social safety net is whether it catches the most deserving people. Twice as much aid per capita goes to high military spenders in the developing world than to more moderate military spenders. Only a quarter of official development assistance is earmarked for the ten countries containing three-fourths of the world's absolute poor. India, Pakistan and Bangladesh have nearly one-half of the world's poor but get only one-tenth of total aid. Less than 7% of global aid is spent on human priority concerns of basic education, primary health care, family planning, safe drinking water and nutritional programmes. Even mighty international institutions like the World Bank and the IMF now take more money from the developing world than they put in, adding to the reverse transfer of around $50 billion a year to the commercial banks.

Much of today's pattern of development cooperation was shaped by the anxieties of the cold war, and the link with global poverty or human development is far from clear. A new framework of development cooperation is needed, one focused more directly on people.

Who can persuade the rich nations that it is in their interest to open their markets, to design a people-centred framework for development cooperation and to prepare their economic systems for a structural change? International institutions of global governance – supposedly with an international reach – are often confined to influence only in poor nations. The IMF's structural adjustment programmes are enforced only in the developing world – which accounts for less than 10% of global liquidity. And as little as 7% of global trade conforms to the GATT rules – since textiles, agriculture, tropical products, services, intellectual property and trade-related investment flows are all outside the GATT's purview and awaiting the ratification of the Uruguay Round of Multilateral Trade Negotiations. The global institutions, so charitably described as the international economic system, are hardly global. To make these institutions truly global in their reach, in their policy frameworks and in their management structures, an Economic Security Council within the United Nations is proposed as a manageable forum for global economic policy coordination.

For the global institutions to become truly global will take time. What about now? What pressures are there for both North and South to move toward equitable access to global markets, to people-centred development cooperation and to structural changes in their economies? For the North, pressure could derive from a combination of hope and fear – a mixture of self-interest and leadership. The high cost of protectionism must be explained to the people. Consumers in the United States pay $70 billion a year more in higher prices for protected goods. There is one hopeful sign: global military spending has been declining since 1987. Still missing, however, is a clear link between reduced military spending and greater attention to the neglected national and global human agendas. A part of the peace dividend could be invested in worker training and in technological development to prepare the northern societies for the future.

Fear may prove to be an even greater motivating force than hope. Fear of international migration of people – as people begin to travel towards opportunities when opportunities fail to travel towards them. Or fear of the migration of poverty – since poverty respects no international frontiers. Or fear of global pollution and the growing threats to common survival. It may not be possible to make the world environmentally safe for anyone unless it is made safe for everyone. The global environment is closely linked to global poverty.

For the South, the sterile dialogue of the 1970s must give way to a more enlightened dialogue on new patterns of development cooperation in a changing world – mutual interests, not unilateral concessions; two-sided responsibility, not one-sided accusations; more equitable access to global opportunities, not massive transfers of financial resources; more open markets, not more managed markets. Yes, there should be pressure for developing countries to reduce their military expenditures. But there should be a similar pressure at the global level to replace military assistance by economic assistance, phase out military bases, restrain arms shipments and eliminate export subsidies for defence industries. And yes, more attention should go to reducing corruption in developing countries. But there should be as much accountability for the multinational corporations that bribe officials and for the banks that park the illegal gains of corruption – accountability tracked by a new NGO, perhaps an Honesty International.

1993: PEOPLE'S PARTICIPATION

Across the globe, people are uniting in a common struggle: to participate freely in the events and processes that shape their lives. From Russia to Poland, from the Republic of Korea to Brazil, from the turbulent slums of Los Angeles to the restless ghettos of Johannesburg, the forces of people's participation are gathering momentum. These forces, constrained neither by time nor by tradition, respect no geographical boundaries or ideological frontiers. They are the messengers of a new age – an age of people's participation – and the central theme of *Human Development Report 1993*, launched in New Delhi on 25 May 1993.

Despite the impatient urge for people's participation, too many barriers still block the way. Our world is still a world of difference.

- It is a world where more than a billion people still languish in absolute poverty – surviving at the bare margins of existence, below any common concept of human dignity.
- It is a world that calmly tolerates a huge global income disparity, with the top one billion

people receiving 150 times more income than the bottom one billion, even as disparities only a tenth as large within nations are leading to convulsions in many countries.

- It is a world where women still earn only half as much as men and despite casting about half the votes, secure less than 10% of the representation in parliaments.
- It is a world where many ethnic minorities still live like a separate nation within their countries, creating tremendous potential for ethnic explosions. Despite commendable efforts at national integration in the United States, the country's whites rank number 1 in the world in the human development index – ahead of all nations – while its blacks rank only number 31, behind Trinidad and Tobago.

Few people have the opportunity to participate fully in the economic and political lives of their nations. And the dangerous potential for human strife that often emerges from the irresistible urge for people's participation clashing with inflexible systems must be recognized.

Needed today is a fundamental change in the management of economic and political systems – from markets to governance to institutions of civil society.

Today's markets are marvels of technology, and open markets are often the best guarantee for unleashing human creativity. But not enough people benefit from the opportunities that markets normally create. Insufficient human investment may mean that many people enter the market at a considerable disadvantage. With literacy rates below 50% in South Asia and Sub-Saharan Africa, about a billion people lack even the basic education and skills to take advantage of market opportunities. The very poverty of many people makes them uncreditworthy – and the same goes for nations. Paradoxically, where the need for credit is the greatest, the market creditworthiness may be the lowest. In Kenya, less than 5% of institutional credit goes to the informal sector. And the bottom 20% of the world's population receives only 0.2% of global commercial credit. People enter the markets with unequal endowments and naturally leave the markets with unequal rewards. It should come as no surprise that the playing fields of life are uneven.

Policy actions must be taken to ensure that people participate fully in the operations of markets and share equitably in their benefits. Markets must be made people-friendly. This is where the state comes in – not to replace markets but to enable more people to share market opportunities. The state has a major role in levelling the playing field by improving the access of all people to human resource investments, productive assets, credit facilities, information flows and physical infrastructure. The state also has to serve as a referee – correcting the price signals and the incentive system, disallowing the exploitation of future generations for present gains (as in the case of the environment) and protecting the legitimate interests of producers, consumers, workers and vulnerable groups in society. In addition, the state must extend a social safety net to the victims of the market-place for temporary periods – to enable them to get back into the market to take advantage of its full opportunities.

The presumption of a conflict between the state and the market is thus false – and dangerous. People must be empowered to guide both the state and the market – to serve the interests of the people.

That is all the more necessary in a period in which markets fail to create enough jobs and not all people are participating in productive market opportunities, even in industrial nations. Witness the new and disturbing phenomenon: jobless growth. Output is increasing, but jobs are lagging way behind. In Germany, the output index increased from 100 in 1960 to 268 in 1987, but the employment index fell from 100 to 91. In developing countries, the increase in employment has been proceeding at about half the rate of increase in output in the past three decades. The great strides in human productivity – thanks to automation and new technological innovations – are to be cheered. But not enough people are participating in this productivity growth. Rising unemployment not only denies income opportunities – it strips away human dignity. And merely expanding unemployment benefits is not the solution to this disturbing phenomenon of jobless growth.

Developing countries are experiencing double-digit unemployment rates. They need to create one billion new jobs in the 1990s to stay abreast of increases in the labour force and to absorb the reservoir of unemployed workers. They need to learn from the experience of Japan and the industrializing tigers of East Asia, and to experiment with new employment strategies. These strategies should stress massive investment in education, skills and training. They should also stress the restructuring of the credit system to make it accessible to the majority of the people and the establishment of more open, people-friendly markets. And they should stress government support to small-scale enterprises and the informal sector, greater fiscal incentives for labour-intensive technologies, and employment safety nets in areas and periods of severe unemployment. It would be folly for the state to displace markets in the name of fancy employment generation schemes. But it would also be a folly to fail to take the policy actions necessary to open market opportunities to increasing numbers of people – particularly investing vigorously in education, skills and infrastructure and opening the credit system to more people.

The industrial nations face even more fundamental dilemmas. Reduced working hours, innovative proposals for work-sharing and redefined concepts of work are all on the policy agenda. These nations may have to consider whether it is better for most people to work five days a week – to support some people on unemployment benefits – or for all people to work, say, four days a week. People's participation in these decisions may create new norms of work and employment.

At the same time, new patterns of national and global governance are needed to accommodate the rising aspirations of the people. The nation-state is already under pressure. It is too small for the big things, and too big for the small. Only meaningful decentralization can take decision-making closer to the people. But new patterns of global governance must be designed for an increasingly interdependent world.

Most developing countries are overcentralized. On average, less than 10% of their budgetary spending is delegated to local levels, compared with more than 25% in industrial nations. Even foreign aid has a centralizing influence. Most decision-making is kept in the hands of a small, central elite. These patterns of governance are inappropriate in societies that have considerable ethnic and cultural diversity and where people increasingly resist dictates from above. What may save these societies from internal explosions is a sweeping decentralization of decision-making powers and faster movement towards economic and political democracy. Unless this is done before people begin to agitate for their rights, the change may come too late and prove too disruptive.

Democracy is rarely so obliging as to stop at national borders. The gathering forces of participation are likely to affect all institutions of global governance. They may lead to more democratic decision-making in the World Bank and the IMF and to a strengthened socioeconomic role for the UN system. The new demands are for the security of people, not just for the security of nation-states. And the new conflicts are increasingly between people, rather than between nations – as in Somalia, Bosnia, Cambodia, Angola and Sri Lanka. Soldiers in uniform – even when in blue berets – are only a poor short-term response to these emerging crises. Needed instead are new participatory socioeconomic processes. To play a greater role in this area, the UN system needs a new socioeconomic mandate, vastly increased financial resources, and a manageable decision-making forum – maybe an Economic Security Council – to meet the new demands of preventive diplomacy and human security.

Although the forces of people's participation demand new structures for markets and the state, they can find their ultimate fulfilment only in the institutions of a civil society that enable people to take control of their own lives. Rule of law, freedom of expression, non-governmental organizations and other community associations are an integral part of such a civil society. NGOs in particular have become very important in recent years, especially in their advocacy of such emerging policy concerns as the environment, women's development, ethnic protection and human rights. Often, people are ahead of their governments – and by organizing themselves, they can bend their governments to the popular will, particularly in a democratic framework in which politicians are sensitive to every shift in public opinion.

There has been an explosion in the number of NGOs in the past decade, with more than 50,000 major NGOs reaching more than 250 million people and channelling more than $5 billion of aid funds a year to the developing countries. But the role of NGOs must be put in its proper perspective. Although they create the necessary pressure for new policy directions and often supplement government action, they can never replace it. The scale and impact of even the most successful of NGOs are surprisingly limited. For instance, the Grameen Bank in Bangladesh – one of the internationally renowned NGOs providing credit to the poor – accounts for only 0.1% of total national credit. The major achievements of NGOs lie in generating new policy pressure for change, in organizing the weak and the vulnerable, and in designing innovative ways of reaching the people in a cost-effective manner.

In sum: people's participation is a powerful and overarching concept. It must inspire a search for a people-centred world order built on five new pillars:

- New concepts of human security that stress the security of people, not only of nations.
- New strategies of sustainable human development that weave development around people, not people around development.
- New partnerships between the state and the market, to combine market efficiency with social compassion.
- New patterns of national and global governance, to accommodate the rising tide of democracy and the steady decline of the nation-state.
- New forms of international cooperation, to focus assistance directly on the needs of the people rather than only on the preferences of governments.

The rising tide of people's participation must be channelled into the foundation for a new human society – where people finally take charge of their own destiny.

1994: HUMAN SECURITY

Human Development Report 1994, launched in Copenhagen on 1 June 1994, underscored the new imperatives of human security in the post-cold war era. Security is now increasingly interpreted as the security of people in their daily lives – in their homes, in their jobs, in their streets, in their communities and in their environment.

Many perceptions have to change. Human security must be regarded as universal, global and indivisible. Just imagine for a moment that every drug that quietly kills, every disease that silently travels, every form of pollution that roams the globe and every act of senseless terrorism all carried a national label of origin, much as traded goods do. That would bring sudden realization that human security concerns today are more global than even global trade.

A second perception must change: it must be recognized that poverty cannot be stopped at national borders. Poor people may be stopped. But not the tragic consequences of their poverty: drugs, AIDS, pollution and terrorism. When people travel, they bring much dynamism and creativity with them. But when only their poverty travels, it brings nothing but human misery.

One more perception must change: it must be seen that it is easier, more humane, and less costly to deal with the new issues of human security upstream rather than downstream. Did it make sense in the past decade to incur the staggering cost of $240 billion for HIV/AIDS treatment when investing even a small fraction of that amount in primary health care and family planning education might have prevented such a fast spread of this deadly disease? Is it a great tribute to international diplomacy to spend $2 billion in a single year on soldiers in Somalia to deliver humanitarian assistance when investing the same amount much earlier in increased domestic food production and social development might have averted the final human tragedy – not just for one year, but for a long time to come? Is it a reflection of human ingenuity to spend hundreds of billions of dollars on administrative control of drug trafficking and on the rehabilitation of drug addicts but not even a small part of that amount for drug education of consumers or alternative livelihoods for producers?

It is time to fashion a new concept of human security that is reflected not in better weapons for countries but in better lives for people. Countries that have ignored the security of their people could not protect even the security of their nations. In 1980, Iraq, Somalia and Nicaragua had the highest ratios of military to social spending. By the 1990s, these countries were beginning to disintegrate. By contrast, Costa Rica invested one-third of its national income in the education, health and nutrition of its people and nothing in the army that it had abolished in 1948. Any wonder that Costa Rica survived as the only prospering democracy in the inflamed Central America of the past few decades?

The emerging concept of human security will lead to many fundamental changes in thinking.

First, new models of human development will treat GNP growth as a means, not as an end; enhance human life, not marginalize it; replenish natural resources, not run them down; and encourage grass-roots participation of people in the events and processes that shape their lives. The real issue is not just the level of economic growth, but its character and distribution. Those who postulate a fundamental conflict between economic growth and human development do no service to the poor nations. To address poverty, economic growth is not an option, it is an imperative. But what type of growth? Who participates in it? And who derives the benefits? These are the real issues.

For a long time, it was quietly assumed that high levels of economic growth would automatically translate into high levels of human development. But that does not necessarily happen, so there is no automatic link between economic growth and human lives. The practical experience of many nations demonstrates this reality. Sri Lanka and Guinea show exactly the same GNP per capita: $500. But they display stark contrasts

in the quality of life in their societies. Life expectancy is 71 years in Sri Lanka, only 44 years in Guinea. Adult literacy is 89% in Sri Lanka, only 27% in Guinea. Infant mortality is 24 per thousand in Sri Lanka and 135 in Guinea. It is not just the level of income that matters. It is how society spends that income. Also important are the many choices that human beings make – particularly in social, cultural and political areas – that may be largely independent of their income. The quality of growth is more important than quantity.

The emerging concept of sustainable human development is based on equal access to development opportunities, for present and for future generations. The heart of this concept is equity – in access to opportunities, not necessarily in results. What people do with their opportunities is their concern. But they should not be denied an equal opportunity to develop and to use their human capabilities. We must acknowledge the universalism of life claims for every individual.

The concept of sustainable human development focuses attention not only on the future generations but also on the present ones. It would be immoral to sustain the present levels of poverty. Development patterns that perpetuate today's inequities are neither sustainable nor worth sustaining. Indeed, an unjust world is inherently unsustainable. A major restructuring of the world's income and consumption patterns – especially a fundamental change in the current life styles of the rich nations – may be a necessary precondition for any viable strategy of sustainable human development.

Second, a new framework of development cooperation must be based on global compacts among nations, not on charity. Foreign assistance must emerge from the shadows of the cold war. Even today, foreign aid is more often linked to strategic alliances from the past than to any specific human development, from slowing population growth to improving the physical environment. Only one-third of official development assistance is earmarked for the ten countries containing two-thirds of the world's absolute poor. Twice as much ODA per capita goes to the richest 40% in the developing world as to the poorest

40%. Less than 7% of bilateral ODA goes to the human priority concerns of primary health care, basic education, safe drinking water, nutrition programmes and family planning services. So, enormous scope still exists to get much more policy mileage and much better allocations from existing aid funds.

At the same time, the concept of development cooperation must be broadened to include all development flows – including trade, investment, technology and labour. It is simply unacceptable that while aid transfers so few resources to the developing world, several times more is taken away through trade protection, immigration barriers and an increasing debt burden. In such a situation, it is critical for poor nations to bargain for more equitable access to global market opportunities.

The 1994 report outlined a new design for development cooperation in the coming decades:

• Aid is regarded as an essential investment by the rich nations in their own human security.
• Developing countries are compensated for trade and immigration barriers imposed by the rich nations.
• Polluting nations are made to pay for their overuse of the global commons.
• The potential peace dividend of nearly $500 billion between 1995 and 2000 is earmarked primarily for the priority human development agenda.
• Global compacts are negotiated in specific areas – population, environment, drug control – between rich and poor nations based on two-way cooperation, not on one-way conditionality or coercion.

Third, the new imperatives of global human security demand an entirely new system of global governance – particularly a greatly strengthened role of the United Nations in development. The nature of conflicts has changed dramatically. Of the 82 conflicts in the early 1990s causing more than a thousand deaths, 79 were within – not between – nations. Many developing countries are already heading towards social disintegration, and behind every failed state, there lies a long trail of failed development or unacceptably high socio-economic disparities. These countries require preventive development, not more weapons of war. The United Nations should be enabled to play a more significant role in social and human development of these poor nations. Only by designing an early warning system and by undertaking upstream preventive development can the United Nations help these nations avert a national collapse. It can no longer fight the battles of tomorrow with the weapons of yesterday.

In this context, the 1994 report offered at least six concrete proposals for consideration by the global community:

• A world social charter, to arrive at a new social contract among all nations and all people.
• A 3% annual reduction in global military spending, with 20% of the savings by rich nations and 10% of those by poor nations earmarked for global human security.
• A 20:20 compact for human development – to provide basic education, primary health care, safe drinking water and essential family planning services to all people over the next decade, by earmarking 20% of existing developing country budgets and 20% of existing aid allocations to these basic human priority concerns.
• A global human security fund – financed from such global taxes as the "Tobin tax" on speculative movements of international funds, an international tax on the consumption of non-renewable energy, global environmental permits and a tax on arms trade.
• A new framework of development cooperation, in which developing and industrial countries would graduate from their present aid relationship to a more mature development partnership – by including trade, technology, investment and labour flows in a broader design to be negotiated among nations.
• An Economic Security Council in the United Nations, as the highest decision-making forum to consider basic issues of human security

such as global poverty, unemployment, food security, drug trafficking, global pollution, international migration and a new framework of sustainable human development.

These proposals demand much from the international community – but they are feasible. What is more, they are urgently needed if we are to design a new architecture of peace through development in the 21st century.

A final observation. The world has seen more hopeful changes in the past decade than ever before – from the collapse of communism to the fall of the Berlin Wall, from the end of apartheid in South Africa to a dim outline of peace in occupied Palestine. This is the time to build a new edifice of human security throughout the world.

Since its birth in San Francisco 50 years ago, the United Nations has committed itself to the first pillar of global security – to freedom from fear, to territorial security, to peace between nations. Can a "second birth" of the United Nations be engineered at the time of its 50th anniversary, giving rise to a United Nations committed to the second pillar of human security – to freedom from want, to socioeconomic development, to peace within nations? That is the supreme challenge. And the 1994 report is a modest attempt to respond to that challenge.

IMPACT OF THE HUMAN DEVELOPMENT REPORT

The impact of the *Human Development Report* on the global policy dialogue has exceeded expectations. More than 100,000 copies of the report now circulate in 13 languages. The report has been prescribed as a text in most leading universities – a tribute to its professional quality. In its first five years, it became one of the most influential reports – not only for governments, donors and international institutions but even more so for the grass-roots movements, media and institutions of civil society. Many commentators describe it as one of the most eagerly awaited reports of the year.

This response is rather unusual for a report from the UN system. What has made the *Human Development Report* an invaluable addition to the global policy dialogue is its intellectual independence and its professional integrity – its courage more than its analysis. It has not hesitated to present unpleasant facts in a fairly blunt fashion. It has chosen to identify specific country experiences – both successes and failures – rather than to bury them in vague generalizations. It has quantified social progress – and even attempted for a brief period to rank countries by political freedom. It has ventured into many areas where international dialogue had remained somewhat muted – from the high human costs of military spending to the new imperatives of human security, from lack of a clear link between ODA allocations and global policy objectives to the corruption and waste in many societies.

Controversies have accompanied the report from its inception. This was inevitable. Most governments and their representatives abroad do not like to be criticized in international reports. What irks them even more is when NGOs and the media take up the issues in the report and generate pressure for change on their own governments. The tendency for many governments has been to go after the messengers rather than to listen to the message. It is a tribute to the *Human Development Report* that it has withstood such onslaughts year after year.

What is the real impact of the *Human Development Report?* First, the report has greatly influenced the global search for new development paradigms. It is now broadly accepted that economic growth does not automatically translate into a better quality of life. For that to happen, policies must be initiated to ensure a more equitable distribution of growth as well as to change the very pattern of growth in response to people's aspirations. It is also recognized that development opportunities must be created not only for the present generations but for the future generations, by making growth models responsive to the need to regenerate natural capital. No debate is complete today without reference to people-centred, environmentally sound development strategies –

irrespective of the precise label given to such strategies. What is more, one can detect some accommodating gestures coming out of the citadels of economic growth – the World Bank and the IMF – though how far this conversion to human development is real rather than rhetorical has yet to be seen.

Second, the *Human Development Report* has helped launch many new policy proposals. For instance, the report has focused on the human costs of military spending, especially in poor nations, and made concrete proposals for reaping a peace dividend by investing in people rather than in arms. The report has also documented the great potential for restructuring existing budgets, the basis of the 20:20 global compact. The report has suggested several innovations in global governance – including the setting up of an Economic Security Council within the United Nations to deal with global socioeconomic issues and an international NGO, Honesty International, to monitor corruption. *Human Development Report 1994* was the first attempt to identify a concrete agenda for the World Summit on Social Development.

Third, the real impact of the report can be seen in the human development strategies that many developing countries have begun to formulate. Several countries have taken major steps on

the road to formulating and implementing their own long-term human development plans: for example, Bangladesh, Bhutan, Bolivia, Botswana, Cameroon, Colombia, Egypt, Ghana, Malawi, Nepal, Pakistan, the Philippines, Tunisia and Turkey. Many others are beginning to take concrete action to move towards human development programmes. UNDP technical assistance has supported these exercises, but real leadership has emerged within the developing countries – and the new strategies are fully owned by the implementing nations themselves.

Fourth, one of the most influential devices – though also one of the most controversial – has been the human development index and the ranking of countries by this index. The index – particularly in its disaggregated form – holds a mirror up to all societies so that policy-makers can see how the people in their societies live and breathe, and where the key tension points are for urgent attention.

ENDNOTE

* Editors' note: This chapter has been reproduced from extracts from Mahbub ul Haq, 1995, *Reflections on Human Development*, chapters 2 and 3, Oxford University Press.

1.3
HUMAN CAPITAL
AND HUMAN CAPABILITY*

Amartya Sen[1]

I would like to comment on the connection as well as contrast between two distinct but related areas of investigation in understanding the processes of economic and social development: the accumulation of "human capital" and the expansion of "human capability". The former concentrates on the agency of human beings – through skill and knowledge as well as effort – in augmenting production possibilities. The latter focuses on the ability of human beings to lead lives they have reason to value and to enhance the substantive choices they have. The two perspectives cannot but be related since both are concerned with the role of human beings, and in particular with the actual abilities that they achieve and acquire.

Given her personal characteristics, social background, economic circumstances, etc., a person has the ability to do (or be) certain things that she has reason to value. The reason for valuation can be *direct* (the functioning involved may directly enrich her life, such as being well nourished or being healthy), or *indirect* (the functioning involved may contribute to further production, or command a price in the market). The human capital perspective can – in principle – be defined very broadly to cover both types of valuation, but it is typically defined – by convention – primarily in terms of indirect value: human qualities that can be employed as "capital" in production in the way physical capital is. In this sense, the narrower view of the human capital approach fits into the more inclusive perspective of human capability, which can cover both direct and indirect consequences of human abilities.

Consider an example. If education makes a person more efficient in commodity production, then this is clearly an enhancement of human capital. This can add to the value of production in the economy and also to the income of the person who has been educated. But even with the same level of income, a person may benefit from education, in reading, communicating, arguing, in being able to choose in a more informed way, in being taken more seriously by others, and so on. The benefits of education thus exceed its role as human capital in commodity production. The broader human-capability perspective would record – and value – these additional roles. The two perspectives are, thus, closely related but distinct.

The significant transformation that has occurred in recent years in giving greater recognition to the role of "human capital" is helpful for understanding the relevance of the capability perspective. If a person can become more productive in making commodities through better education, better health, and so on, it is not unnatural to expect that she can also directly achieve more – and have the freedom to achieve more – in leading her life. Both perspectives put humanity at the center of attention.

Altogether, this involves, to a great extent, a return to an integrated approach to economic and social development championed particularly by Adam Smith (both in *The Wealth of Nations* and in *The Theory of Moral Sentiments*). In analysing the determination of production possibilities, Smith emphasized the role of education as well as division of labour, learning by doing, and skill formation. The development of human capability in leading a worthwhile life as well as in being more productive is quite central to Smith's analysis of "the wealth of nations".

Indeed, Adam Smith's belief in the power of education and learning was peculiarly strong. Regarding the debate that continues today on the respective roles of "nature" and "nurture", Smith was an uncompromising "nurturist", and this fitted in with his massive confidence in the improvability of human capabilities:

The difference of natural talents in different men is, in reality, much less than we are aware of; and the very different genius which appears to distinguish men of different professions, when grown up to maturity, is not upon many occasions so much the cause, as the effect of division of labour. The difference between the most dissimilar characters, between a philosopher and a common street porter, for example, seems to arise not so much from nature, as from habit, custom, and education. When they come into the word, and for the first six or eight years of their existence, they were, perhaps, very much alike, and neither their parents nor play-fellows could perceive any remarkable difference.[2]

It is not my purpose here to examine whether Smith's emphatically "nurturist" views are right, but it is useful to see how closely he links the productive abilities to the ability to lead different types of lives. That connection is quite central in seeing human capital in the broader context of the human-capability perspective.

There is, however, also a crucial difference between the two approaches – a difference that relates to some extent to the distinction between means and ends. The acknowledgement of the role of human qualities in promoting and sustaining economic growth – momentous as it is – tells us nothing about *why* economic growth is sought in the first place. If, instead, the focus is, ultimately, on the expansion of human freedom to live the kind of lives that people have reason to value, then the role of economic growth in expanding these opportunities has to be integrated into that more foundational understanding of the process of development as the expansion of human capability to lead freer and more worthwhile lives.[3]

The distinction has a significant practical bearing on public policy. While economic prosperity helps people to lead freer and more fulfilling lives, so do more education, health care, medical attention, and other factors that causally influence the effective freedoms that people actually enjoy. These "social developments" must directly count as "developmental", since they help us to lead longer, freer, and more fruitful lives, *in addition* to the role they have in promoting productivity or economic growth or individual incomes. (To a considerable extent the *Human Development Reports* of the United Nations Development Programme have been motivated by the need to take a broader view of this kind.) The use of the concept of "human capital", which concentrates only on one part of the picture (an important part, related to broadening the account of "resources"), is certainly an enriching move, but it needs supplementation. This is because human beings are not merely means of production (even though they excel in that capacity), but also the end of the exercise.

Indeed, in arguing with David Hume, Adam Smith had the occasion to emphasize that to see human beings in terms of their usefulness only is to slight the nature of humanity:

. . . it seems impossible that the approbation of virtue should be of the same kind with that by which we approve of a convenient or a well-contrived building, or that we should have no other reason for praising a man than that for which we commend a chest of drawers.[4]

Despite the usefulness of the concept of human capital as a productive resource, it is important to see human beings in a broader perspective than that of human capital (breaking the analogy with "a chest of drawers"). We must go *beyond* the notion of human capital, after acknowledging its relevance and reach. The broadening that is needed is additional and cumulative, rather than being an alternative to the "human capital" perspective.

Finally, it is important to take note also of the instrumental role of capability expansion in bringing about *social* change (going well beyond *economic* change). Capability serves as the means not only to economic production (to which the perspective of "human capital" usually points), but also to social development. For example, as various empirical studies have brought out, expansion of female education may reduce gender inequality in intrafamily distribution and also help to cut down fertility rates. Expansion of basic education may also improve the quality of public debates. These instrumental achievements may be ultimately quite important even though the instrumental role involved is not that of a factor of production in the making of conventionally defined commodities.

In looking for a fuller understanding of the role of human capabilities, we have to take note of:

- their direct relevance to the well-being and freedom of people;
- their indirect role through influencing economic production; and
- their indirect role through influencing social change.

The relevance of the capability perspective incorporates each of these contributions, and the different contributions relate closely to each other.

ENDNOTES

* Editors' note: This chapter is reproduced from an article in *World Development*, 1997, 25 (12), pp. 1959–61.

1. The analysis presented here has been more fully explored in my lectures as Presidential Fellow at the World Bank on "Social Justice and Public Policy" in the fall of 1996.

2. Smith 1776 (Smith 1976, pp. 28–29).

3. I have tried to discuss this issue in Sen 1983 and Sen 1985.

4. Smith 1790 (Smith 1975, p. 188).

REFERENCES

Sen, A. 1983. "Development: Which Way Now?" *Economic Journal* 93.

———. 1985. *Commodities and Capabilities.* Amsterdam: North-Holland.

Smith, A. 1975. *The Theory of Moral Sentiments* (1790). D. D. Raphael and A. L. Macfie (eds.), vol. 4, p. 24. Oxford: Clarendon Press.

———. 1976. *An Inquiry into the Nature and Causes of the Wealth of Nations* (1776). R. H. Campbell and A. S. Skinner (eds.), vol. 1, p. 2. Oxford: Clarendon Press.

1.4

THE CONCEPT
OF HUMAN POVERTY*

United Nations Development Programme

It is in the deprivation of the lives that people can lead that poverty manifests itself. Poverty can involve not only the lack of the necessities of material well-being, but the denial of opportunities for living a tolerable life. Life can be prematurely shortened. It can be made difficult, painful or hazardous. It can be deprived of knowledge and communication. And it can be robbed of dignity, confidence and self-respect – as well as the respect of others. All are aspects of poverty that limit and blight the lives of many millions in the world today.

DEFINING POVERTY IN THE HUMAN DEVELOPMENT PERSPECTIVE

Since its launch in 1990, the *Human Development Report* has defined human development as the process of enlarging people's choices. The most critical ones are to lead a long and healthy life, to be educated and to enjoy a decent standard of living. Additional choices include political freedom, other guaranteed human rights and various ingredients of self-respect – including what Adam Smith called the ability to mix with others without being "ashamed to appear in public". These are among the essential choices, the absence of which can block many other opportunities. Human development is thus a process of widening people's choices as well as raising the level of well-being achieved.

If human development is about enlarging choices, poverty means that opportunities and choices most basic to human development are denied – to lead a long, healthy, creative life and to enjoy a decent standard of living, freedom, dignity, self-respect and the respect of others.

The contrast between human development and human poverty reflects two different ways of evaluating development. One way, the "conglomerative perspective", focuses on the advances made by all groups in each community, from the rich to the poor. This contrasts with an alternative viewpoint, the "deprivational perspective", in which development is judged by the way the poor and the deprived fare in each community. Lack of progress in reducing the disadvantages of the deprived cannot be "washed away" by large advances – no matter how large – made by the better-off people.

Interest in the process of development concerns both perspectives. At a very basic level, the lives and successes of everyone should count, and it would be a mistake to make our understanding of the process of development completely insensitive to the gains and losses of those who happen to fare better than others. It would go against the right of each citizen to be counted, and also clash with the comprehensive concerns of universalist ethics. Yet a part – a big part – of the general interest in the progress of a nation concentrates specifically on the state of the disadvantaged.

Poverty has many dimensions

Concerns with identifying people affected by poverty and the desire to measure it have at times obscured the fact that poverty is too complex to be reduced to a single dimension of human life. It has become common for countries to establish an income-based or consumption-based poverty line. Although income focuses on an important dimension of poverty, it gives only a partial picture of the many ways human lives can be blighted. Someone can enjoy good health and live quite long but be illiterate and thus cut off from learning, from communication and from interactions with others. Another person may be literate and quite well educated but prone to premature death because of epidemiological characteristics or physical disposition. Yet a third may be excluded from participating in the important decision-making processes affecting her life. The deprivation of none of them can be fully captured by the level of their income.

Also, people perceive deprivation in different ways – and each person and community defines the deprivation and disadvantages that affect their lives. Poverty of lives and opportunities – or human poverty – is multidimensional in character and diverse rather than uniform in content.

How does human poverty relate to other approaches?

Over the years the concept of poverty has been defined in different ways (box 1.4.1).

Poverty in the human development approach draws on each of these perspectives, but draws particularly on the capability perspective. In the capability concept the poverty of a life lies not merely in the impoverished state in which the person actually lives, but also in the lack of real opportunity – due to social constraints as well as personal circumstances – to lead valuable and valued lives.

In the capability concept the focus is on the functionings that a person can or cannot achieve, given the opportunities she has. Functionings refer to the various valuable things a person can do or be, such as living long, being healthy, being well nourished, mixing well with others in the community and so on.

The capability approach concentrates on functioning information, supplemented by considering, where possible, the options a person had but did not choose to use. For example, a rich and healthy person who becomes ill nourished through fasting can be distinguished from a person who is forced into malnutrition through a lack of means or as a result of suffering from a parasitic disease. In practice such discrimination is difficult when dealing with aggregate statistics (as opposed to detailed micro studies of individuals), and the practical uses of the capability concept in poverty analysis have been mainly with simple functioning data. The *Human Development Report* too presents information that is essentially about living conditions and functionings.

In choosing particular aspects of living for special investigation in a poverty study, there is need for public discussion. There is an inescapable

---

BOX 1.4.1

Three perspectives on poverty

- *Income perspective.* A person is poor if, and only if, her income level is below the defined poverty line. Many countries have adopted income poverty lines to monitor progress in reducing poverty incidence. Often the cut-off poverty line is defined in terms of having enough income for a specified amount of food.

- *Basic needs perspective.* Poverty is deprivation of material requirements for minimally acceptable fulfilment of human needs, including food. This concept of deprivation goes well beyond the lack of private income: it includes the need for basic health and education and essential services that have to be provided by the community to prevent people from fall-

ing into poverty. It also recognizes the need for employment and participation.

- *Capability perspective.* Poverty represents the absence of some basic capabilities to function – a person lacking the opportunity to achieve some minimally acceptable levels of these functionings. The functionings relevant to this analysis can vary from such physical ones as being well nourished, being adequately clothed and sheltered, and avoiding preventable morbidity, to more complex social achievements such as partaking in the life of the community. The capability approach reconciles the notions of absolute and relative poverty since relative deprivation in incomes and commodities can lead to an absolute deprivation in minimum capabilities.

element of judgement in any such selection. In constructing any index of poverty (such as the human poverty index, HPI-1, presented in *Human Development Report 1997*), the selections and the weights have to be explicitly stated and clarified so that public scrutiny can occur. It is very important that the standards to be used are not determined on a top-down basis, but are open to – if possible, emerge from – a participatory, democratic process. One of the purposes of the *Human Development Report* has been precisely to facilitate such a process, and this applies to poverty analysis as well.

The "sustainable livelihood approach" to the study of poverty has particularly emphasized the need for local participation. In this approach each community can define criteria of well-being and the key elements of deprivation as they appear in the local context. This process brings out the concerns and worries of vulnerable people that are persistently neglected in national statistics and in many studies of poverty (box 1.4.2).

In the 1970s the concept of *social exclusion* came into the literature to analyse the condition of those who are not necessarily income-poor – though many are that too – but who are kept out of the mainstream of society even if not income-poor.

The inadequacy of traditional definitions of poverty, based on incomes and consumption, was widely acknowledged to explain these new concerns.

MEASUREMENT OF POVERTY AND THE HUMAN POVERTY INDEX

Can the concept of human poverty be targeted and monitored? Can an overall measure of poverty be developed that can inform as well as be used for policy? Can an internationally comparable measure be defined?

Human Development Report 1997 introduces a human poverty index (HPI-1 for developing countries) in an attempt to bring together in a composite index the different features of deprivation in the quality of life to arrive at an aggregate judgement on the extent of poverty in a community. *Human Development Report 1996* attempted this through a particular version of the "capability poverty measure". The HPI pursues the same approach, focusing on a broader and more representative set of variables, in a consistent relationship to the human development index (HDI).

Like many other concepts, human poverty is larger than any particular measure, including the

---

BOX 1.4.2

Criteria of ill-being

The following criteria drawn from various participatory studies were used by local people in Asia and Sub-Saharan Africa for defining poverty and ill being:

- Being disabled (for example: blind, crippled, mentally impaired, chronically sick)
- Lacking land, livestock, farm equipment, a grinding mill
- Being unable to decently bury their dead
- Being unable to send their children to school
- Having more mouths to feed, fewer hands to help
- Lacking able-bodied family members who can feed their families in a crisis

- Having bad housing
- Suffering the effects of destructive behaviours (for example, alcoholism)
- Being "poor in people", lacking social support
- Having to put children in employment
- Being single parents
- Having to accept demeaning or low-status work
- Having food security for only a few months each year
- Being dependent on common property resources

Source: Chambers 1997.

HPI. As a concept, human poverty includes many aspects that cannot be measured – or are not being measured. It is difficult to reflect them in a composite measure of human poverty. Critical dimensions of human poverty excluded from the HPI for these reasons are lack of political freedom, inability to participate in decision-making, lack of personal security, inability to participate in the life of a community and threats to sustainability and intergenerational equity.

The human development index and the human poverty index

While human development focuses on progress in a community as a whole, human poverty focuses on the situation and progress of the most deprived people in the community.

The distinction between the two is analogous to the distinction between GNP and the income-based poverty index. In the income-based perspective, poverty incidence is needed to monitor progress in eliminating poverty. In the same way, the HPI is needed to judge the extent of human poverty in a country and to monitor its progress.

The growth rate of GNP per person gives an account of progress seen in the conglomerative perspective – everyone's income counts in the GNP total. In contrast, the reduction of an income-based poverty index – such as the decline in the proportion of people below the poverty-line income – uses the deprivational perspective, concentrating only on the incomes of the poor. In this income-based perspective, it would make little sense to argue that since GNP is already based on income information, any income-based poverty measure must be a substitute for GNP. Nor would it be sensible to suggest that the availability of GNP as an indicator makes it redundant to seek a measure of income poverty. GNP and the income poverty measures use the income information in different perspectives – with GNP taking a conglomerative view and the income poverty measures focusing specifically on people poor in income.

Perspective	Income	Human life
Conglomerative	GNP per capita	HDI
Deprivational	Headcount index	HPI

The relationship between the HDI and the HPI has to be seen in a similar way. Both have to use the rich categories of information associated with human development – characteristics of human lives and quality of living that go far beyond what income information can provide. But while the HDI uses these characteristics in the conglomerative perspective, the HPI must use them in the deprivational perspective. The availability of GNP measures does not obviate the need for an income-based poverty indicator, nor does the HDI measure eliminate the need for an HPI.

Poverty depends on the context

The nature of the main deprivations varies with the social and economic conditions of the community in question. The choice of indicators in the HPI cannot but be sensitive to the social context of a country. For example, an index that concentrates on illiteracy and premature mortality may be able to discriminate between Pakistan and Sri Lanka more easily than it can between, say, France and Germany.

Issues of poverty in the developing countries involve hunger, illiteracy, epidemics and the lack of health services or safe water – which may not be so central in the more developed countries, where hunger is rare, literacy is close to universal, most epidemics are well controlled, health services are typically widespread and safe water is easy to tap. Not surprisingly, studies of poverty in the more affluent countries concentrate on such variables as social exclusion. These can be forceful deprivations and very hard to eliminate in all countries. But they take on relatively greater prominence in the affluent ones. There is no real possibility of constructing an index of human poverty that would be equally relevant in the different types of countries.

Given the pervasiveness of poverty in poor countries, the HPI-1 developed is aimed at that context and the variables chosen reflect that (box 1.4.3). The nature of poverty in rich countries deserves a specialized study – and a more specialized index – focusing on those deprivations particularly relevant for those countries.

The three indicators of HPI-1

The HPI-1 for developing countries concentrates on the deprivation in three essential elements of human life already reflected in the HDI – longevity, knowledge and a decent living standard.

The first deprivation relates to survival – the vulnerability to death at a relatively early age – and is represented in the HPI-1 by the percentage of people expected to die before age 40.

The second dimension relates to knowledge – being excluded from the world of reading and communication – and is measured by the percentage of adults who are illiterate.

The third aspect relates to a decent standard of living, in particular, overall economic provisioning. This is represented by a composite of three variables – the percentage of people with access to health services and to safe water, and the percentage of malnourished children under five.

A few observations must be made about this last variable and about why income does not figure in the HPI-1. The logic underlying the construction of the economic provisioning variable is that

---

BOX 1.4.3

The HPI – useful for policy-makers?

The human poverty index can be used in at least three ways.

1. *As a tool for advocacy.* If poverty is to be eradicated, public opinion and support need to be mobilized to the cause. The HPI can help summarize the extent of poverty along several dimensions, the distance to go, the progress made. Income poverty also needs to be measured – but income alone is too narrow a measure.

2. *As a planning tool for identifying areas of concentrated poverty within a country.* The HDI has been used in many countries to rank districts or counties as a guide to identifying those most severely disadvantaged in terms of human development. Several countries, such as the Philippines, have used such analyses as a planning tool. The HPI can be used in a similar way to identify those most seriously affected by human poverty. Though ranking by any one index alone would be possible – say by illiteracy rate, lack of access to health services or the percentage in income poverty – the HPI makes possible a ranking in relation to a combination of basic deprivations, not one alone.

3. *As a research tool.* The HDI has been used especially when a researcher wants a composite measure of development. For such uses, other indicators have sometimes been added to the HDI. The HPI could be similarly used and enriched – especially if other measures of

poverty and human deprivation were added, such as unemployment.

Although greeted with controversy when first launched in 1990, the HDI has found an increasing following as a simple measure of human development. The HDI provides an alternative to GNP for assessing a country's standing in basic human development or its progress in human development over time. It does not displace economic measures but can serve as a simple composite complement to other measures like GNP.

The HPI can similarly serve as a useful complement to income measures of poverty. It will serve as a strong reminder that eradicating poverty will always require more than increasing the incomes of the poorest.

Further work is merited to explore how the HPI and the HDI could be enriched and made more robust in situations where a wider range of data on different aspects of poverty and human development are available.

What the HPI does not show: The HPI provides a measure of the incidence of human poverty in a country (or among some other group), say 25%. This means that judged by the HPI, an "average" of some 25% of the country's population is affected by the various forms of human poverty or deficiency included in the measure. But unlike with a headcount measure, it is not possible to associate the incidence of human poverty with a specific group of people or number of people.

---

the GNP included in the HDI is actually an amalgam of private and public facilities, since public services are paid out of aggregate national income.

Private income could not be an adequate indicator of an individual's economic facilities, which also include crucial public services (such as health care arrangements and a safe water supply). But why is private income not chosen to supplement the information on public facilities?

One of the problems in assessing the prevalence of income poverty is that the use of the same poverty line in different countries can be very misleading because of the variation in "necessary" commodities. Depending on the prevailing patterns of consumption – clothing, accommodation and such tools of communication and interaction as radios and telephones – many provisions are taken to be essential for social participation in one community without being treated as such in another. As a result, the minimum income needed to escape social estrangement can be quite different between communities.

Given the social pressure, these felt "needs" may compete – for relatively poor people in rich countries – even with the provision of resources for food, nutrition and health care. This can explain the prevalence of some hunger and malnutrition, especially among children, even in the United States, where incomes are high but inequalities generate a heavy burden of "necessity" in the direction of socially obligated consumption, often to the detriment of health and nutritional spending. So, the assessment of poverty on the basis of a low minimum cut-off income used for poor countries fails to show any poverty in generally affluent societies, even when the relatively poor in those societies may lack social participation and may even suffer from hunger and malnutrition.

An alternative is to use different poverty lines in different countries. But it is not easy to decide what the appropriate variations would be and how the respective poverty lines could be estimated. The official national lines cannot serve this purpose, since they reflect other influences, especially political ones, and cannot be used for international comparisons. The general need for a variable cut-off line of poverty is easier to appreciate than it is to find adequate values for variable poverty lines in different communities.

A more practical possibility is to be less ambitious and focus on material deprivation in hunger and malnutrition, not on income. A very high proportion of personal income goes to food and nourishment, especially for poor people in poor countries.

For this we can use information on food intake, which relates to personal incomes. Alternatively, there are estimates of malnutrition, but these are influenced by a number of variables, such as metabolic rate, climatic conditions, activity patterns and epidemiology. Since our concern is with the lives that people can lead, there is a case for going straight to the prevalence of malnutrition, and this is what is done in the HPI-1, concentrating specifically on the malnutrition of children, which is relatively easier to measure and for which usable data are more uniformly available.

For public provisions, access to health services and to safe water were chosen. Combining these two access variables with the prevalence of malnutrition gives a fairly broad picture of economic provisioning – private and public – to supplement the information on survival and literacy.

These are the basic informational ingredients of the HPI-1. It must be emphasized that there is some inescapable arbitrariness in any such choice. The choice was made on the basis of balancing considerations of relevance on the one hand, and the availability and quality of data on the other. There are inevitable compromises made, and it would be idle to pretend that even the variables that have been included have high-quality data for every country. There has been an attempt, in these selections, to strike a balance between the demands of relevance and the need for tolerably usable data, and these choices would certainly remain open to criticism and public scrutiny.

Weighting and aggregation[1]

The process of aggregation can be sensitive to the overlaps in the three dimensions of the HPI-1. For example, consider a case in which in each of the three categories of deprivation, 30% of people fail to meet the minimum requirement. This can be so because the same 30% fail in all three fields. But it can also be that a different 30% fail in each category. Or we may have some combination of the two extremes. In the first extreme case only 30% are affected by poverty, but they are deprived on all three fronts. In contrast, in the second extreme case as many as 90% of the population are deprived altogether, but each group has inadequacy in merely one field. Even though information on overlaps (or covariance) is not easy to obtain (since data regarding the different variables come from different sources), these distinctions can be important in describing poverty. They can also be crucial for causal analysis, since deprivation of one kind often feeds others.

However, when it comes to constructing an index, it is not easy to decide whether 30% of people with inadequacies of all three types represents larger social poverty than 90% of people having one deficiency each. It is a matter of the importance to be given to depth vis-à-vis breadth. For the purpose of the HPI, the two cases have been treated as equivalent, so that in some sense depth and breadth have been equally considered.

There is a further issue to be addressed in deriving an aggregate index, namely that of substitutability between the three components of the HPI-1. This is done through an explicit procedure of using an additional weight (α). When α is taken to be 1, perfect substitutability is presumed, and the aggregate is obtained by simply averaging the three deprivations. The opposite case of no substitutability corresponds to α being taken to be infinity. In that case the largest of the percentage shortfalls rules the roost. For example, if 30% fail in field one, 50% in field two and 45% in field three, then the overall extent of poverty, in this case, is simply 50%.

Perfect substitutability is too extreme an assumption, and goes against the sensible requirement that as the deprivation in some field becomes relatively more acute, the weight placed on removing deprivation in that field should increase. Nor is the other extreme, zero substitutability, very easy to support, since it implies that any increase in deprivation in any category other than the one with the highest rate of deprivation must leave the aggregate poverty measure completely unchanged. Both extremes are avoided by choosing an intermediate value of α.

MEASURING HUMAN POVERTY IN INDUSTRIAL COUNTRIES

Poverty and deprivation are not only a problem of the developing countries.

- On the basis of an income poverty line of 50% of the median personal disposable income, more than 100 million people are income-poor in OECD countries.
- At least 37 million people are without jobs in OECD countries, often deprived of adequate income and left with a sense of social exclusion from not participating in the life of their communities.
- Unemployment among youth (age 15–24) has reached staggering heights, with 32% of young women and 22% of young men in France unemployed, 39% and 30% in Italy, and 49% and 36% in Spain.
- About 8% of the children in OECD countries – including half or more of children of single parents in Australia, Canada, the United Kingdom and the United States – live below the income poverty line of 50% of median disposable personal income.
- Nearly 200 million people are not expected to survive to age 60.
- More than 100 million are homeless, a shockingly high number amid the affluence.

To capture the multiple dimensions of poverty in a composite measure, an HPI-2 for industrial countries is introduced, focusing on deprivation in the same three dimensions of human life as the HPI-1, but replacing the measures with ones that better reflect social and economic conditions in these countries. And it adds a fourth dimension – social exclusion – for which the HPI-1 does not include a quantitative measure because no reliable data could be found. For industrial countries appropriate data are available.

The nature of deprivation in human life varies with the social and economic conditions of a community or country. Studies of poverty in the developing countries – with low levels of resources and human development – focus on hunger, epidemics, illiteracy and lack of health services and safe water. These issues are less dominant in industrial countries, where hunger is not as pervasive, primary schooling is nearly universal, most epidemics are well controlled, health services are typically widespread and safe water is easily available. Not surprisingly, typical studies of poverty in the more affluent countries concentrate on social exclusion, a complex and persistent deprivation difficult to eliminate in all countries, industrial and developing alike.

Although the dimensions used in the HPI-1, for developing countries, are equally relevant to industrial countries, the indicators used are not. A second index is needed, using indicators that reflect the way poverty is manifested in industrial countries.

The HPI-2 comprises:

- Deprivation in survival, measured by the percentage of the population likely to die before age 60.
- Deprivation in knowledge, measured by the percentage of the population functionally illiterate – lacking an ability to read and write adequate for the most basic demands of modern society, such as reading instructions on a medicine bottle or reading stories to children.
- Deprivation in economic provisioning, measured by the proportion of people whose disposable personal income is less than 50% of the median, leaving them unable to achieve the standard of living necessary to avoid hardship and to participate in the life of the community.
- Social exclusion, measured by one of its most critical aspects – the percentage of long-term unemployed (those out of work 12 months or more) in the total labour force.

The HPI-2 uses the same measures as the HPI-1 for survival and knowledge, applying a higher cut-off point. For economic provisioning and exclusion, new measures are used. These require explanation.

Social exclusion takes many forms, varies considerably from one community to another and is difficult to measure. But long-term unemployment, which is consistently monitored in most industrial countries, is a suitable proxy for exclusion. It reflects exclusion from the world of work and the social interaction associated with employment, which is an important part of social exclusion in most communities.

For economic provisioning the HPI-1 uses a combination of malnourishment and lack of access to water and health services, while the HPI-2 uses a headcount measure of income poverty. These divergent approaches were followed for three reasons.

First, the HPI-1 incorporates economic provisioning from both public and private income. Public provisioning is an important source of consumption for poor households, and key deprivations in this area are captured in lack of access to such services as health care and water. Deprivation in private provisioning focuses on food consumption, since by far the largest proportion of personal incomes of the poorest households in the poorest countries goes to food – more than 50%, sometimes more than 80%. For the HPI-2 these would not have been the most suitable measures because in industrial countries food is not the principal component of private income and because most people already have access to such basic public services as water.

Second, deprivation in income is a more appropriate measure for industrial countries because it reflects deprivation in the material means that people require. But the use of a single international poverty line can be misleading – because of variations in what are defined as "essential" commodities. Differences in the prevailing patterns of consumption – of clothing, housing and such means of communication as radios, televisions and telephones – mean that many goods considered essential for social participation in one community might not be seen as essential in another. Thus the minimum income needed to avoid social exclusion can be quite different across countries. For this reason 50% of the country's median personal disposable income was used as the poverty line, reflecting what is appropriate for each country. Moreover, this measure of income poverty is now the standard used in the European Union for making international comparisons.

Third, data availability and quality are an important concern. Income poverty data are available for only 48 developing countries and rely on many estimates. Data on malnourishment and access to public services have broader coverage. In industrial countries comparable data on income poverty are available.

CONCLUDING REMARKS

Just as life is multidimensional, so is human poverty. The merit of the HPI lies in the fact that it incorporates, for the first time, non-income dimensions of poverty. However, no measure can adequately capture all aspects of human deprivation and poverty. Clearly, the concept of human poverty shall remain much larger than the measures that the *Human Development Reports* have proposed.

ENDNOTES

* Editors' note: This chapter has been adapted from the 1997 and 1998 *Human Development Reports*.

1. For additional discussion on the statistical features of the HPI, see chapter 2.6 by Anand and Sen in this book. Also, for the methodology for the construction of HPI-1 and HPI-2, see chapter 2.9 or, for the latest modifications, the technical appendix in the most recent *Human Development Report*.

REFERENCES

Anand, Sudhir and Amartya K. Sen. 1997. "Concepts of Human Development and Poverty: A Multidimensional Perspective." Background paper for *Human Development Report 1997*. UNDP, New York.

Bratton, Michael and Nicolas van de Walle. 1997. *Democratic Experiments in Africa: Regime Transitions in Comparative Perspective*. New York: Cambridge University Press.

Bread for the World Institute. 1996. *Hunger 1996: Countries in Crisis*. Silver Spring, Md.

———. 1998. *Hunger 1998: Hunger in a Global Economy*. Silver Spring, Md.

Chambers, Robert. 1997. *Whose Reality Counts? Putting the First Last*. London: Intermediate Technology Publications.

De Haan, Arjan and Simon Maxwell (eds.). 1998. "Poverty and Social Exclusion in North and South." *IDS Bulletin* (Sussex) 29(1).

The Economist. 1998. "AIDS in Kenya: Serial Killer at Large." 7 February: 97–176.

Egypt, Institute of National Planning. 1996. *Egypt Human Development Report 1996*. Cairo.

Euromonitor. 1997. *World Consumer Markets 1997/98*. CD-ROM. London.

Forbes Magazine. 1997. "The Global Power Elite." 28 July: 49–50.

IILS. 1996. "Social Exclusion and Anti-Poverty Strategies." International Labour Organization, Geneva.

Jaura, Ramesh. 1997. "South Still Arming Heavily for 1998." Inter Press Service, New York.

Lipton, Michael. 1996. "Defining and Measuring Poverty: Conceptual Issues." Background paper for *Human Development Report 1997*. UNDP, New York.

Mongkolsmai, Dow and Somchai Suksirserekul. 1997. "Linkages between Globalization, the Resultant Consumption Patterns and the Impact on Human Development: Country Study on Kenya." Country Study for *Human Development Report 1998*. UNDP, New York.

OECD, Human Resource Development Canada and Statistics Canada. 1997. *Literacy Skills for the Knowledge Society: Further Results from the International Adult Literacy Survey*. Paris and Ottawa.

Ranis, Gustav and Frances Stewart. 1998. "A Pro-Human Development Adjustment Framework for the Countries of East and South-East Asia." UNDP, Regional Bureau for Asia and the Pacific, New York.

Rodgers, Gerry, Charles Gore and Jose B. Figueiredo (eds.). 1995. *Social Exclusion: Rhetoric, Reality, Responses*. Geneva: International Labour Office.

Stanecki, Karen A. and Peter O. Way. 1997. "The Demographic Impacts of HIV/AIDS: Perspectives from the World Population Profile, 1996." US Bureau of Census, Washington D.C.

Tujinman, Albert. 1998. "Adult Literacy in OECD Countries." Background note for *Human Development Report 1998*. UNDP, New York.

UN (United Nations). 1994b. Economic and Social Council, Commission on Human Rights, Fiftieth Session. New York. E/CN.4/1995/42.

——. 1997a, "The World Conferences: Developing Priorities for the 21st Century." UN Briefing Papers. Department of Public Information. New York.

——. 1997b, *World Drug Report.* International Drug Control Programme. New York: Oxford University Press.

UNAIDS and WHO (Joint United Nations Programme on HIV/AIDS). 1997. *Report on the Global HIV/AIDS Epidemic.* Geneva (December).

UNDP (United Nations Development Programme). 1995. *Human Development Report 1995.* New York: Oxford University Press.

——. 1996a. *Human Development Report 1996.* New York: Oxford University Press.

——. 1996b. *Human Development Report Nigeria 1996.* Lagos.

——. 1997a. *Latvia Human Development Report 1997.* Riga.

——. 1997b. *Namibia Human Development Report 1997.* Windhoek.

——. 1997c. *Philippine Human Development Report 1997.* Jakarta.

——. 1997d. *Rapport sur le Développement Humain au Benin.* Cotonou.

——. 1997e. *Zambia Human Development Report 1997.* Lusaka.

——. 1998. *Desarrollo Humano en Bolivia 1998.* La Paz.

UNDP (United Nations Development Programme) and the Government of El Salvador. 1997. *Informe sobre Indices de Desarrollo Humano en El Salvador.* San Salvador.

UNDP (United Nations Development Programme) and the Government of Niger. 1997. *Premier Rapport National sur le Développement Humain.* Niamey.

UNDP (United Nations Development Programme) and Instituto de Pesquisa Econômica Aplicada. 1996. *Relatório Sobre o Desenvolvimento Humano no Brazil 1996.* Brasilia.

UNDP (United Nations Development Programme), UNFPA (United Nations Population Fund) and UNICEF (United Nations Children's Fund). 1994. *The 20/20 Initiative.* UNDP, New York.

UNICEF (United Nations Children's Fund). 1996. *The State of the World's Children 1996.* New York: Oxford University Press.

——. 1997. *The State of the World's Children 1997.* New York: Oxford University Press.

——. 1998a. "Information: Impact of Armed Conflict on Children." Data available at http://www.unicef.org. January.

——. 1998b. *The State of the World's Children 1998.* New York: Oxford University Press.

US Bureau of the Census. 1998. *World Population Profile: 1998.* Washington, D.C.

Worldwide Research, Advisory and Business Intelligence Services. 1997. Data available at http://www.find. svp.com. December.

1.5

HUMAN RIGHTS
AND HUMAN DEVELOPMENT*

The basic idea of human development – that enriching the lives and freedoms of ordinary people is fundamental – has much in common with the concerns expressed by declarations of human rights. The promotion of human development and the fulfilment of human rights share, in many ways, a common motivation, and reflect a fundamental commitment to promoting the freedom, well-being and dignity of individuals in all societies. These underlying concerns have been championed in different ways for a long time (the French Declaration of the Rights of Man and of the Citizen came in 1789), but the recent literatures on human development and on human rights have given new shape to old aspirations and objectives.

Extensive use of these two distinct modes of normative thinking, respectively invoking human development and human rights, encourages the question of whether the two concepts can be viewed together in a more integrated way, gaining something through being combined in a more comprehensive vision. To answer this question, it is important not only to have a clear understanding of what the two concepts – human development and human rights – mean, but also to examine their commonalities and their differences. Indeed, it is necessary to undertake two basic diagnostic inquiries:

- How compatible are the normative concerns in the analyses of human development and human rights? Are they *harmonious enough* – to be able to complement rather than undermine each other?
- Are the two approaches sufficiently distinct so that each can add something substantial to the other? Are they *diverse enough* – to enrich each other?

The answers to both of these foundational questions are definitely in the affirmative. Human development and human rights are close enough in motivation and concern to be compatible and congruous, and they are different enough in strategy and design to supplement each other fruitfully. A more integrated approach can thus bring significant rewards, and facilitate in practical ways the shared attempts to advance the dignity, well-being and freedom of individuals in general.

COMMON MOTIVATION
AND BASIC COMPATIBILITY

The idea of human development focuses directly on the progress of human lives and well-being. Since well-being includes living with substantial freedoms, human development is also integrally connected with enhancing certain capabilities – the range of things a person can do and be in leading a life. We value the freedom of being able to live as we would like and even the opportunity to choose our own fate.

Capabilities and freedoms

Capabilities can vary in form and content, though they are also often closely interrelated. They include, of course, the basic freedoms of being able to meet bodily requirements, such as the ability to avoid starvation and undernourishment, or to escape preventable morbidity or premature mortality. They also include the enabling opportunities given by schooling, for example, or by the liberty and the economic means to move freely and to choose one's abode. There are also important "social" freedoms, such as the capability to participate in the life of the community, to join in public discussion, to participate in political decision-making and even the elementary ability "to appear in public without shame" (a freedom whose importance was well discussed by Adam Smith in *The Wealth of Nations*).

The human development approach is concerned, ultimately, with all the capabilities that people have reason to value. The human development index (HDI) incorporates the most elementary capabilities, such as living a long and healthy life, being knowledgeable and enjoying a decent standard of living, and the various indices, tables and more elaborate discussions in the body of the *Human Development Reports* provide information on many other valuable capabilities. Indeed, longevity is itself an important means to other capabilities, since one does not have the freedom to do much unless one is alive.

What about human rights? The idea of an individual right must involve, directly or indirectly, a claim that one person has over others – individuals, groups, societies or states. The claims can take different forms, as has been analysed by legal theorists, from John Austin and Jeremy Bentham to H.L.A. Hart and Stig Kanger. Some rights take the form of immunity from interference by others; libertarians have tended to take a particular interest in such rights. Others take the form of a claim on the attention and assistance of others to be able to do certain things; champions of social security have tended to emphasize such rights.

But diverse as these rights are, they share the characteristic of entailing some entitlements to help from others in defence of one's substantive freedoms. The claim to help may involve a demand for positive support and facilitation, or take only the negative form of assurance that there will be no hindrance from others. But all of these claims are aimed at securing the freedoms of the persons involved – to do this or be that – in one way or another. In this way, human rights are also ultimately grounded in the importance of freedoms for human lives.

Social, political and economic concerns

Given this founding connection between human development and human rights – particularly the involvement of each in guaranteeing the basic free-

doms that people have reason to value – the ideas of human development and those of human rights are linked in a compatible and complementary way. If human development focuses on the enhancement of the capabilities and freedoms that the members of a community enjoy, human rights represent the claims that individuals have on the conduct of individual and collective agents and on the design of social arrangements to facilitate or secure these capabilities and freedoms.

Despite the compatibility of the two approaches, their strategic form and focus are rather different. It is sometimes presumed that these approaches differ because they are concerned with different kinds of freedoms. The human rights literature has often focused primarily or exclusively on political liberties, civil rights and democratic freedoms. But these rights have not figured in some of the aggregate human development indicators, such as the HDI, for example, which concentrates on longevity, literacy and other socioeconomic concerns. The domain of interest of the human development approach goes much beyond what is measured by the HDI, however. Political and civil rights and democratic freedoms also have their place in the human development perspective, though they are much harder to quantify, having resisted attempts in earlier *Human Development Reports* to measure them with composite indicators.

An adequate conception of human development cannot ignore the importance of political liberties and democratic freedoms. Indeed, democratic freedom and civil rights can be extremely important for enhancing the capabilities of people who are poor. They can do this directly, since poor people have strong reason to resist being abused and exploited by their employers and politicians. And they can do this indirectly, since those who hold power have political incentives to respond to acute deprivations when the deprived can make use of their political freedom to protest, criticize and oppose. The fuller human development approach does not ignore these concerns that figure so prominently in the human rights literature.

Similarly, the human rights literature is concerned not only with political and civil liberties, but also with the rights to education, to adequate health care and to other freedoms that have received systematic investigation in *Human Development Reports*. Indeed, recent documents, such as the Declaration on the Right to Development and the Vienna Declaration and Programme of Action, emphasize that economic, social and cultural rights are no less weighty than civil and political rights. The contrast between the two concepts of human rights and human development does not, therefore, lie in any basic difference in their subject matter.

WHAT HUMAN RIGHTS ADD TO HUMAN DEVELOPMENT

Since there are substantive differences between these two approaches that share common motivations and aims, it is important to investigate whether they are sufficiently distinct to complement and enrich each other. Even more important, what do practitioners of each approach stand to gain from the analyses of the other? How can the aims of each be better promoted by an integration of these approaches?

To have a particular right is to have a claim on other people or institutions that they should help or collaborate in ensuring access to some freedom. This insistence on a claim on others takes us beyond the idea of human development. Of course, in the human development perspective, social progress of the valued kind is taken to be a very good thing, and this should encourage anyone who can help to do something to preserve and promote it. But the normative connection between laudable goals and reasons for action does not yield specific duties on the part of other individuals, collectivities or social institutions to bring about human development – or to guarantee the achievement of any specified level of human development, or of its components.

This is where the human rights approach may offer an additional and very useful perspective for the analysis of human development. It links the human development approach to the idea that others have duties to facilitate and enhance human development. What precise form the link between rights and duties should take is, of course, a different – and, in some ways, later – question (to be addressed shortly).

The first step is to appreciate that assessments of human development, if combined with the human rights perspective, can indicate the duties of others in the society to enhance human development in one way or another. And with the invoking of duties comes a host of related concerns, such as accountability, culpability and responsibility. For example, to assert a human right to free elementary education is to claim much more than that it would be a good thing for everyone to have an elementary education – or even that everyone *should* have an education. In asserting this right we are claiming that all are *entitled* to a free elementary education, and that, if some persons avoidably lack access to it, there must be some culpability somewhere in the social system.

This focus on locating accountability for failures within a social system can be a powerful tool in seeking remedy. It certainly broadens the outlook beyond the minimal claims of human development, and the analysis of human development can profit from it. The effect of a broader outlook is to focus on the actions, strategies and efforts that different duty bearers undertake to contribute to the fulfilment of specified human rights and to the advancement of the corresponding human development. It also leads to an analysis of the responsibilities of different actors and institutions when rights go unfulfilled.

Consider further the example of the right to a free elementary education. If a girl is not schooled because her parents refuse to send her to school, then the responsibility for the failure – and the corresponding blame – can be placed on the parents. But if she cannot be sent to school because the government forbids her going there (as, regrettably, some governments have excluded girls), then the blame can come down not on the parents but on the government. The failure may be more complex when the girl cannot go to school for one, or some combination, of the following reasons:

- The parents cannot afford the school fees and other expenses.

- The school facilities are inadequate. For example, the school may be unable to guarantee that teachers will be regularly present, so that the parents think that it would be unsafe for the young girl to go there.
- The parents can afford the school expenses but at the cost of sacrificing something else that is also important (such as continuing the medical treatment of one of their other children).

The attribution or sharing of blame can be quite important here, and it is important to recognize how the effects of different inadequacies in a social system tend to aggravate one another. The willingness of parents to make sacrifices for their children's schooling will often be diminished when they have reason to doubt that this schooling will significantly benefit their children. The sacrifice of human development is much the same in all these cases, but the analysis of rights, duties and responsibilities must be quite different. In this respect, concern with duties enhances the ways of judging the nature and demands of progress. Since the process of human development often involves great struggle, the empowerment involved in the language of claims can be of great practical importance.

There are other substantial ways in which ideas of human rights contribute tools to the analysis of social progress offered by the human development approach. Development thinking has traditionally focused on the outcomes of various kinds of social arrangements. And although human development thinking has always insisted on the importance of the process of development, many of the tools developed by the human development approach measure the outcomes of social arrangements in a way that is not sensitive to *how* these outcomes were brought about. Human rights thinking offers tools that amplify the concern with the process of development in two ways:

- Individual rights express the limits on the losses that individuals can permissibly be allowed to bear, even in the promotion of noble social goals. Rights protect individuals and minorities from policies that benefit the community as a whole but place huge burdens on them.
- Rights thinking incorporates a distinction between how institutions and officials treat citizens and how they affect them. Human rights monitoring has traditionally focused on the conduct of public officials and the institutional structure within a society. This focus may be unduly narrow, but it reflects something important. Even if arbitrarily harsh police procedures such as torture and execution without trial minimize the number of violent deaths within a society overall by creating fear and disincentives to crime, they are not celebrated as promoting the human rights to life, liberty and security of the person. Human rights thinking gives special weight to threats from certain official sources, capturing the idea that there is something particularly wrong about harm to people carried out by those responsible for ensuring justice.

Finally, human rights analysis can enrich our assessments of social progress by helping us to become more attuned to features of a society that might not be adequately emphasized in pure human development accounting. Human rights are fulfilled when individuals enjoy certain goods and freedoms and when there are measures in place to secure these goods and freedoms. Human rights analysis thus involves assessments of the extent to which institutions and social norms are in place that provide security to the human development achievements within a society.

Gains in human development are not always attended by gains in human rights fulfilment, and subsequently a pure human development accounting may fail to pick up on the vulnerability of individuals and groups within a society. The East Asian financial crisis vividly illustrates how societies that have fared extremely well in terms of composite human development indicators were overly dependent on a buoyant market. The instability of the market combined with inadequate social security provisions exposed the insecurity of East Asia's human development gains.

Human rights assessment involves a reorientation of factual concentration which can broaden and enrich human development accounting. Assessments of human rights fulfilment would, for example, focus not only on what progress has been made so far, but also on the extent to which the gains are socially protected against potential threats. The profound concern of the human rights literature with the duties of others in helping each human being live a better and less unfree life is thus quite relevant in considering both the ways and the means of promoting human development.

WHAT HUMAN DEVELOPMENT ADDS TO HUMAN RIGHTS

Just as human rights contribute something important to human development, so human development helps to augment the reach of the human rights approach. First, there is a tradition of articulation and definiteness in the analysis of human development which can add something to the literature of human rights. Human development analysis has been undertaken at various levels, qualitative and quantitative, and has made use of both inclusive table and exclusive composite indicators. These different types of investigation, used discriminatingly, can help to give concreteness to human rights analysis. This can be significant, but there are also other advantages – more than clarificatory and presentational – that human development can bring to human rights.

Second, promoting the fulfilment of a right often requires an assessment of how different policy choices will affect the prospects for fulfilling the right. Assessing the human rights impact of various policies will involve both an analysis of the probable human achievement outcomes of the policy and a balancing of claims to different types of achievements – not all of which may be at once attainable. Such an exercise in the evaluation of achievement can sensibly be characterized as an exercise much like human development analysis. For example, the government of a non-affluent country may find it impossible to guarantee the fulfilment of all the identified human rights – including social and economic rights. The alternative scenarios of accomplishment and failure to safeguard the different human rights can be seen as alternative human development achievements, related particularly to each set of policy decisions and the related patterns of rights fulfilment and non-fulfilment.

Human rights advocates have often asserted the indivisibility and importance of all human rights. This claim makes sense if it is understood as denying that there is a hierarchy of different kinds of rights (economic, civil, cultural, political and social). But it cannot be denied that scarcity of resources and institutional constraints often require us to prioritize concern for securing different rights for the purposes of policy choice. Human development analysis helps us to see these choices in explicit and direct terms.

Third, while human rights are ultimately matters of individual entitlement, their fulfilment depends on appropriate social conditions. The goal of human development is to create an enabling environment in which people's capabilities can be enhanced and their range of choices expanded. By attending to this process of human development, human rights analysis can get a fuller assessment of what is feasible given the resource and institutional constraints that prevail within a society, and a clearer understanding of the ways and means of making a more attractive set of policy choices feasible. While the human rights literature has been concerned with the analysis of duties, the human development literature has constantly emphasized the importance of institutional complementarity and resource constraints and the need for public action to address them.

Focusing on causally important institutional and operational variables, the human development literature brings to discussion and analysis of human rights some additional understanding of policies that will best promote human rights in a world that is inescapably pluralist in terms of causal influences and interactive impacts.

Fourth, the idea of human development involves change, and in this sense it has an inescapable dynamism that the specification of a given set of human rights may lack. Human development includes an abiding concern with progress, with things moving on from where they were earlier. The insistence on a dynamic view can be particularly useful in considering human rights over time. When a country is very poor, it may not be capable of achieving the fulfilment of every right that is judged important. But this is not an argument for giving priority to economic rights over civil and political rights. Economic entitlements complement rather than outweigh the importance of civil and political rights. But regardless of which kind of right is at issue, varying extents of crucial freedoms may be incorporated in different formulations of each right. Within the right to health, for example, the freedom to receive standard or primary medical care must be taken to be more basic than the freedom to receive costly surgical procedures. A poor country must insist on providing the former, but may have to wait until it is much richer to guarantee the second.

In this way, there may be a progression (indeed, "development") in the human rights that receive priority, even though all such rights ultimately have value and importance. By adding the perspective of change and progress in conceptual and practical reasoning about human rights, human development can help to deepen the understanding and broaden the usefulness of the human rights approach. Indeed, the dynamic view inherent in human development analysis has already been partially integrated into human rights thinking, most obviously in the appreciation that some rights must be progressively realized. Human development analysis can give more structure and concreteness to this idea.

THE NATURE OF DUTIES ASSOCIATED WITH HUMAN RIGHTS

What form should the nature of duties associated with human rights take? To whom do they apply? With what degree of compulsion? In many writings on rights – geared rather rigidly to legal rights – it is assumed that rights make no sense unless they are combined with exact duties imposed – without fail – on specified persons or agents who would make sure that these rights are fulfilled. A person's right to something must, then, be inflexibly coupled with another person's (or another agent's) duty to provide the first person with that something. This corresponds to what the great 18th-century philosopher Immanuel Kant called "perfect duty", strictly linking rights perfectly to prespecified exact duties of particular agents (in form, perfect duties in an ethical system are rather close to legal duties). In contrast, imperfect duties – also a concept explored by Kant – are general and non-compulsive duties of those who can help. This is a far less rigid system (as Amartya Sen explained in 1999 in "Consequential Evaluation and Practical Reason"), since imperfect duties leave open both *how* the duty can be discharged, and how forceful the duty is. Nevertheless, the neglect of the demands of an imperfect duty also involves a serious moral – or political – failure.

Those who insist on the rigid linkage of rights and duties, in the form of perfect duties, tend typically to be rather impatient with invoking the rhetoric of "rights" without exactly specifying particular agents whose precisely defined (and inescapable) duty it is to ensure the fulfilment of those rights. Not surprisingly, they are often very critical of the use of the concept of "human rights" without exact specification of responsible agents and their precise duties to bring about the fulfilment of these rights. Demands for human rights may then appear, in this line of reasoning, as largely "loose talk".

They are not loose talk. Indeed, if this view were to be fully accepted, the human development literature would need to be kept analytically delinked from the approach of human rights – even if the rhetorical and agitprop merits of the language of human rights may be readily conceded when it comes to exposition or to "consciousness raising". But to divorce the rhetoric from the substance of an approach goes entirely against the tradition of the human development literature, which has been committed, right from the beginning, to standing on articulated concepts and exacting argumentation, rather than concentrating on moving language and stirring phrases not matched by explicit defence.

Legal rights and human rights

The issue of the relationship between rights and duties must be seized at a critical level. It has already been argued that rights and duties must be linked in some form, but why the insistence on exactly matching rights with prespecified duties that apply rigidly to particular agents? It can be argued that the insistence on a rights-duties tie-up in this rigid form is simply a hangover from the empire of law, making all invoking of rights – even in ethics and politics – ultimately parasitic on the concepts and ideas that apply specifically to legal rights.

This rather severe view tallies with Jeremy Bentham's argument that a "declaration of rights would be but a lop-sided job without a declaration of duties". It tallies also with Bentham's rejection of the ethical claims of "natural rights" as "nonsense" and the concept of "natural and imprescriptible rights" as "nonsense on stilts" (presumably, artificially elevated nonsense). It refers to this sense of illegitimacy in taking the idea of rights beyond what Bentham, along with many others, thought to be the proper use of an essentially legal concept.

This way of seeing rights – essentially in legal or quasi-legal terms – does, however, militate against the basic idea that people have some claims on others and on the design of social arrangements regardless of what laws happen to be enforced. Indeed, it is a commitment to common fellowship and solidarity, quite well expressed in Article 1 of the Universal Declaration of Human Rights, that inspires the idea that all persons have duties both to refrain from harming others and to help them. The Universal Declaration demands protection from unjust laws and practices on the ground that no matter what the laws may be, individuals have certain rights by virtue of their humanity, not on the basis of their citizenship or contingent facts about the legal reality of the country of which they are citizens. Human rights are moral claims on the behaviour of individual and collective agents, and on the design of social arrangement. Human rights are fulfilled when the persons involved enjoy secure access to the freedom or resource (adequate health protection, freedom of speech) covered by the right. In many contexts, establishing legal rights may be the best means of furthering the fulfilment of human rights. Nevertheless, legal rights should not be confused with human rights – nor should it be supposed that legal rights are sufficient for the fulfilment of human rights.

This is indeed the approach to rights invoked by such general political theorists as Tom Paine, in his *Rights of Man,* Mary Wollstonecraft, in *A Vindication of the Rights of Woman* (both published in 1792), and also by earlier writers in the social contract tradition such as John Locke and Jean-Jacques Rousseau. All of them asserted that all human beings are endowed with rights prior to the formation of social institutions that constrain both the design of institutions and the conduct of other individuals. The insistence that the discourse of rights cannot go beyond the limits of legal demands does less than justice to the sense of solidarity and fairness in social living, commitments that are not parasitic on the exact laws that may have been enacted in a society.

Human rights and imperfect duties

There is, however, a different kind of rationale for insisting on the rigid rights-duties linkage in the form of perfect duties. It can be asked how we can be sure that rights are, in fact, realizable unless they are matched by corresponding duties that ensure their fulfilment. This argument is invoked to suggest that to be effective, any real right must be matched by a specific duty of a particular agent, who will see to the actual fulfilment of that right.

It is certainly plausible to presume that the performance of perfect duties would help a great deal towards the fulfilment of rights. But why cannot there be *unfulfilled* rights? There is no contradiction involved in saying (indeed lamenting): "These individuals have these rights, but alas the rights were not fulfilled." The question of the fulfilment of rights must be distinguished (as Amartya Sen has argued) from the issue of their existence. We need not jump from regretting the *non-fulfilment* of rights all the way to the denial of the existence – or the cogency – of the rights themselves. Often, rights are unfulfilled precisely because of the failure of duty bearers to perform their duties.

In normative discussions human rights are often championed as entitlements, powers or immunities that benefit all who have them. But even when universal and unblemished fulfilment of human rights for all may be very hard to achieve, the articulation of these rights can help to mobilize support from a great many people in their defence. Even though no particular person or agency may be charged with bringing about the fulfilment of the rights involved, the articulation of imperfect duties may be both an assertion of normative importance and a call for responsible action to be undertaken by others. For example, we can argue that women have a human right to be free from discrimination on the basis of gender independent of whether this right is protected by laws and social arrangements. Gender discrimination is not merely a crime practised by individuals who are violating their perfect duties to particular women. Gender discrimination is an injustice entrenched in the social norms and institutions of all societies. This injustice is expressed both in laws and in other social norms and informal practices of discrimination against women.

Women's human rights give them a claim that male-only suffrage and many other practices be ended through social, legal and institutional reforms. The duties correlated with this right cannot easily be allocated to particular duty bearers because the task of reforming these unjust practices falls on the group as a whole. Yet individuals surely have imperfect duties correlative to this right, and speaking of this right clearly expresses something of great normative importance.

Even if it were to be the case that a particular government does not, right now, have the resources (or the possibility of raising the resources) needed to bring about the fulfilment of specified rights for all, it is essential to encourage the government to work towards making their fulfilment feasible. Credit can still be given for the extent to which these alleged rights are fulfilled. This can help to focus attention on these human rights – and to promote their fulfilment. It can also enrich the understanding of processes that lead to successes and failures in human development. The combination of the two perspectives gives us something that neither can provide alone.

The Ongoing Global Struggle for Human Rights

Struggles and historical events	Conferences, documents and declarations	Institutions
Through the 17th century		
Many religious texts emphasize the importance of equality, dignity and responsibility to help others	Codes of conduct – Menes, Asoka, Hammurabi, Draco, Cyrus, Moses, Solon and Manu	1809 Ombudsman institution established in Sweden
Over 3,000 years ago Hindu Vedas, Agamas and Upanishads; Judaic text the Torah	1215 Magna Carta signed, acknowledging that even a sovereign is not above the law	1815 Committee on the International Slave Trade Issue, at the Congress of Vienna
2,500 years ago Buddhist Tripitaka and Anguttara-Nikaya and Confucianist Analects, Deanne of the Mean and Great Learning	1625 Dutch jurist Hugo Grotius credited with birth of international law	1839 Antislavery Society in Britain, followed in 1860s by Confederação Abolicionista in Brazil
2,000 years ago Christian New Testament, and 600 years later, Islamic Qur'an	1690 John Locke develops idea of natural rights in *Second Treatise of Government*	1863 International Committee of the Red Cross
		1864 International Working Men's Association
18th–19th centuries		1898 League of Human Rights, an NGO, in response to the Dreyfus Affair
1789 The French Revolution and the Declaration of the Rights of Man and of the Citizen	**1792** Mary Wollstonecraft's *A Vindication of the Rights of Woman*	
1815 Slave revolts in Latin America and in France	**1860s** In Iran Mirza Fath Ali Akhundzade and in China Tan Sitong argue for gender equality	**1902** International Alliance for Suffrage and Equal Citizenship
1830s Movements for social and economic rights – Ramakrishna in India, religious movements in the West	**1860s** Rosa Guerra's periodical *La Camelia* champions equality for women throughout Latin America	**1905** Trade unions form international federations
1840 In Ireland the Chartist Movement demands universal suffrage and rights for workers and poor people	**1860s** In Japan Toshiko Kishida publishes an essay, *I Tell You, My Fellow Sisters*	**1910** International Ladies' Garment Workers' Union
1847 Liberian Revolution	**1860–80** More than 50 bilateral treaties on abolition of the slave trade, in all regions	**1919** League of Nations and Court of International justice
1861 Liberation from serfdom in Russia		
The 20th century 1900–29		
1900–15 Colonized peoples rise up against imperialism in Asia and Africa	**1900** First Pan-African Congress in London	
1905 Workers movements in Europe, India and the US; in Moscow 300,000 workers demonstrate	**1906** International convention prohibiting night work for women in industrial employment	
1910 Peasants mobilize for land rights in Mexico	**1907** Central American Peace Conference provides for aliens' right to appeal to courts where they reside	
1914–18 First World War	**1916** Self-determination addressed in Lenin's *Imperialism, the Highest Stage of Capitalism*	

The 20th century—*Continued*

1914 onward Independence movements and riots in Europe, Africa and Asia

1915 Massacres of Armenians by the Turks

1917 Russian Revolution

1919 Widespread protests against the exclusion of racial equality from the Covenant of the League of Nations

1920s Campaigns for women's rights to contraceptive information by Ellen Key, Margaret Sanger, Shizue Ishimoto

1920s General strikes and armed conflict between workers and owners in industrialized world

1918 Self-determination addressed in Wilson's "Fourteen Points"

1919 Versailles Treaty stresses right to self-determination and minority rights

1919 Pan-African Congress demands right to self-determination in colonial possessions

1923 Fifth Conference of the American Republics, in Santiago, Chile, addresses women's rights

1924 Geneva Declaration of the Rights of the Child

1924 US Congress approves Snyder Act, granting all Native Americans full citizenship

1926 Geneva Conference adopts Slavery Convention

1919 International Labour Organization (ILO), to advocate human rights embodied in labour law

1919 Women's International League for Peace and Freedom

1919 NGOs devoted to women's rights start addressing children's rights; Save the Children (UK)

1922 Fourteen national human rights leagues establish International Federation of Human Rights Leagues

1920s National Congress of British West Africa in Accra, to promote self-determination

1925 Representatives of eight developing countries found Coloured International to end racial discrimination

1928 Inter-American Commission on Women, to ensure recognition of women's civil and political rights

1930–49

1930 In India Gandhi leads hundreds on long march to Dandi to protest salt tax

1939–45 Hitler's Nazi regime kills 6 million Jews and forces into concentration camps and murders Gypsies, Communists, labour unionists, Poles, Ukrainians, Kurds, Armenians, disabled people, Jehovah's Witnesses and homosexuals

1942 Rene Cassin of France urges creation of an international court to punish war crimes

1942 US government interns some 120,000 Japanese-Americans during Second World War

1942–45 Antifascist struggles in many European countries

1949 Chinese Revolution

1930 ILO Convention Concerning Forced or Compulsory Labour

1933 International Convention for the Suppression of the Traffic in Women of Full Age

1941 US President Roosevelt identifies four essential freedoms – of speech and religion, from want and fear

1945 UN Charter, emphasizing human rights

1948 Universal Declaration of Human Rights

1948 ILO Convention on the Freedom of Association and Protection of the Right to Organize

1949 ILO Convention on the Right to Organize and Collective Bargaining

1933 Refugee Organization

1935–36 International Penal and Penitentiary Commission, to promote basic rights of prisoners

1945 Nuremberg and Tokyo trials

1945 United Nations

1946 UN Commission on Human Rights

1948 Organization of American States

1949 Council of Europe

Continued

The Ongoing Global Struggle for Human Rights—*Continued*

Struggles and historical events	Conferences, documents and declarations	Institutions
1950–59		
1950s National liberation wars and revolts in Asia; some African countries gain independence	**1950** European Convention on Human Rights	**1950** ILO fact-finding commission deals with violations of trade union rights
1955 Political and civil rights movement in US; Martin Luther King Jr. leads the Montgomery bus boycott (381 days)	**1951** ILO Equal Retribution Convention	**1951** ILO Committee on Freedom of Association
	1957 ILO Convention Concerning Abolition of Forced Labour	**1954** European Commission of Human Rights
	1958 ILO Convention Concerning Discrimination in Employment and Occupation	**1959** European Court of Human Rights
1960–69		
1960s In Africa 17 countries secure right to self-determination, as do countries elsewhere	**1965** UN International Convention on the Elimination of All Forms of Racial Discrimination	**1960** Inter-American Commission on Human Rights holds its first session
1962 National Farm Workers (United Farm Workers of America) organizes to protect migrant workers in US	**1966** UN International Covenant on Civil and Political Rights	**1961** Amnesty International
1960s–70s Feminist movements demand equality	**1966** UN International Covenant on Economic, Social and Cultural Rights	**1963** Organization of African Unity
	1968 First World Conference on Human Rights, in Tehran	**1967** Pontifical Commission for International Justice and Peace
1970–79		
1970s Human rights issues attract broad attention – apartheid in South Africa, treatment of Palestinians in occupied territories, torture of political opponents in Chile, "dirty war" in Argentina, genocide in Cambodia	**1973** UN International Convention on Suppression and Punishment of the Crime of Apartheid	**1970** First commissions on peace and justice in Paraguay and Brazil
1970s People protest against Arab-Israeli conflict, Viet Nam war and Nigeria-Biafra civil war	**1973** ILO Minimum Age Convention	**1978** Helsinki Watch (Human Rights Watch)
1976 Amnesty International wins Nobel Peace Prize	**1974** World Food Conference in Rome	**1979** Inter-American Court of Human Rights
	1979 UN Convention on the Elimination of All Forms of Discrimination Against Women (CEDAW)	
1980–89		
1980s Latin American dictatorships end – in Argentina, Bolivia, Paraguay, Uruguay	**1981** African Charter on Human and Peoples' Rights	**1983** Arab Organization for Human Rights
1988 In the Philippines peaceful People's Power Movement overthrows Marcos dictatorship	**1984** UN Convention Against Torture and Other Cruel, Inhuman or Degrading Treatment or Punishment	**1985** UN Committee on Economic, Social and Cultural Rights
1989 Tiananmen Square	**1986** UN Declaration on the Right to Development	**1988** African Commission on Human and Peoples' Rights
1989 Fall of the Berlin Wall	**1989** UN Convention on the Rights of the Child	

The 20th century—*Continued*
1990–2000

1990s Democracy spreads across Africa; Nelson Mandela released from prison and elected president of South Africa

1990s Ethnic cleansing in former Yugoslavia, and genocide and massive human rights violations in Rwanda

1998 Spain initiates extradition proceedings against General Pinochet of Chile

1999 Doctors without Borders wins Nobel Peace Prize

2000 Court in Senegal charges former Chadian dictator Hissene Habre with "torture and barbarity"

1990–96 Global UN conferences and summits on the issues of children, education, environment and development, human rights, population, women, social development and human settlements

1998 Rome statute for establishing International Criminal Court

1999 CEDAW Optional Protocol for Individual Complaints

1999 ILO Worst Forms of Child Labour Convention

1992 First Organization for Security and Cooperation in Europe (OSCE) High Commissioner for National Minorities

1993 First UN High Commissioner for Human Rights, appointed at the Vienna Conference

1993–94 International criminal tribunals for former Yugoslavia and Rwanda

1995 South African Truth and Reconciliation Commission

1995–99 Ten countries launch national plans of action for the protection and promotion of human rights

Source: Lauren 1998; Ishay 1997; UN 1997a, 1997b; An-Na'im 2000; Olcott 2000; Mendez 2000; Silovic 2000; Pinheiro and Baluarte 2000; Vizard 2000; Akash 2000.

ENDNOTES

* Editors' note: Reproduced here is chapter 1 from *Human Development Report 2000.*

REFERENCES

Aksah, M.M. 2000. "Rights-Based Approach to Development and Right to Land." Background paper for *Human Development Report 2000*. UNDP, New York.

An-Na'im, Abdullahi A. 2000. "Human Rights in the Arab World – A Regional Perspective." Country/regional study for *Human Development Report 2000*. UNDP, New York.

Bentham, Jeremy. 1996. *Works*. Oxford: Clarendon Press.

Dworkin, Ronald. 1978. *Taking Rights Seriously*. Cambridge, Mass.: Harvard University Press.

Hart, H.L.A. 1961. *The Concept of Law*. Oxford: Clarendon Press.

Ishay, Micheline R. (ed.). 1997. *The Human Rights Reader. Major Political Writings, Essays, Speeches, and Documents – From the Bible to the Present*. New York: Routledge.

Kanger, Stig. 1985. "On Realization of Human Rights." *Acta Philosophica Fennica* 38.

Kant, Immanuel. 1956. *Critique of Practical Reason*. Translated by L. W. Beck. New York: Bobbs-Merrill.

Lauren, Gordon Paul. 1998. *The Evolution of International Human Rights: Visions Seen*. Philadelphia: University of Pennsylvania Press.

Mendez, Juan E. 2000. "Human Rights in Latin America and the Caribbean – A Regional Perspective." Country/regional study for *Human Development Report 2000*. UNDP, New York.

Nussbaum, Martha and Amartya Sen (eds.). 1991. *The Quality of Life*. Oxford: Oxford University Press.

Olcott, Martha Brill. 2000. "Regional Study on Human Development and Human Rights – Central Asia." Country/regional study for *Human Development Report 2000*. UNDP, New York.

O'Neill, Onora. 1996. *Towards Justice and Virtue*. Cambridge: Cambridge University Press.

Pinheiro, Paulo Sergio and David Carlos Baluarte. 2000. "Study on National Strategies – Human Rights Commissions, Ombudsmen, Specialized Agencies and National Action Plans." Background paper for *Human Development Report 2000*. UNDP, New York.

Pogge, Thomas. 1992. "O'Neill on Rights and Duties." *Grazer Philosophische Studien* 43: 223–47.

Sen, Amartya. 1985. *Commodities and Capabilities*. Amsterdam: North Holland.

——. 1999a. "Consequential Evaluation and Practical Reason." Trinity College, Department of Economics, Cambridge.

——. 1999b. *Development as Freedom*. New York: Alfred Knopf.

——. 1999c. "Human Rights and Economic Achievements." In Joanne Bauer and Daniel Bell (eds.) *The East Asian Challenge for Human Rights*. Cambridge: Cambridge University Press.

Sen, Amartya and Sudhir Anand. 2000. "Human Rights and Human Development." Background paper for *Human Development Report 2000*. UNDP, New York.

Sengupta, Arjun. 1999. "Study on the Current State of Progress in the Implementation of the Right to Development Pursuant to Commission Resolution 1988/72 and General Assembly Resolution 53/155." United Nations document E/CN.4/1999/WG.18/2. New York.

Shue, Henry. 1980. *Basic Rights: Subsistence, Affluence, and U.S. Foreign Policy*. Princeton, N.J.: Princeton University Press.

Silovic, Darko. 2000. "Regional Study on Human Development and Human Rights in Central and Eastern Europe." Country/regional study for *Human Development Report 2000*. UNDP, New York.

UN (United Nations). 1997a. *Human Rights. A Compilation of International Instruments*. Vol. 1, *Universal Instruments*. New York.

——. 1997b. *Human Rights. A Compilation of International Instruments*. Vol. 2, *Regional Instruments*. New York.

Vizard, Polly. 2000. "The Evolution of the Idea of Human Rights in Western and Non-Western Thought." Background paper for *Human Development Report 2000*. UNDP, New York.

1.6
ECONOMIC GROWTH AND
HUMAN DEVELOPMENT

Gustav Ranis, Frances Stewart, and Alejandro Ramirez*

1. INTRODUCTION

Human development has recently been advanced as the ultimate objective of human activity in place of economic growth.[1] Its intellectual antecedents may be traced to the earlier basic needs approach of the ILO and the World Bank, as well as Sen's concept of capabilities.[2] Human development has been defined as enlarging people's choices in a way which enables them to lead longer, healthier and fuller lives.[3] The definition of HD as "enlarging people's choices" is very broad. For the purpose of exploring the links between HD and EG theoretically, and especially empirically, we need to narrow it down. We shall consider the HD of a country as consisting of the health and education of its people, recognizing that this is very much a reductionist interpretation. Clearly, there exists a strong connection between economic growth (EG) and human development (HD). On the one hand, EG provides the resources to permit sustained improvements in HD. On the other, improvements in the quality of the labor force are an important contributor to EG. Yet, while this two-way relationship between HD and EG may now be widely accepted, the specific factors linking them have not been systematically explored. Nor has the question of priorities in the phasing of policy. The purpose of this paper is to sharpen understanding of the two-way links between HD and EG at both theoretical and empirical levels. This in turn permits us to analyze priorities in the phasing of policy and to examine the usual assumption that EG must precede progress on HD.[4]

Section 2 identifies the major links between EG and HD. Section 3 presents some empirical crosscountry evidence on these links. Section 4 develops a typology of country cases, some representing the mutual enhancement of HD and EG and some demonstrating asymmetric performance. The final section investigates the movement of countries from one category to another and reflects on the implications for policy.

2. THE TWO CHAINS

We view HD as the central objective of human activity and economic growth as potentially a very important instrument for advancing it. At the same time, achievements in HD themselves can make a critical contribution to economic growth. There are thus two distinct causal chains to be examined: one runs from EG to HD, as the resources from national income are allocated to activities contributing to HD; the other runs from HD to EG, indicating how, in addition to being an end in itself, HD helps increase national income. The two chains are pictured in Figure 1.6.1.

(a) Chain A: from EG to HD

GNP contributes to HD mainly through household and government activity; civil society, e.g., through community organizations and other nongovernmental organizations (NGOs), also plays a role. The same level of GNP can lead to very different performance on HD according to the allocation of GNP among and within these institutions and variations in their behavior.

Households' propensity to spend their after-tax income on items which contribute most directly to the promotion of HD in poor countries, e.g., food, potable water, education and health, varies, depending on such factors as the level and distribution of income across households as well as on who controls the allocation of expenditure within households. In general, poor households

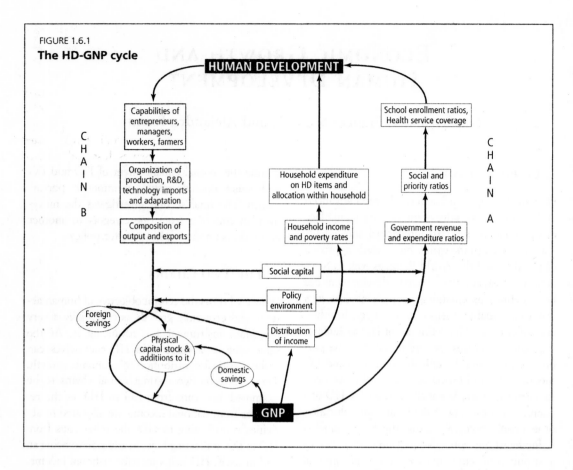

FIGURE 1.6.1

The HD-GNP cycle

HUMAN DEVELOPMENT

CHAIN B

CHAIN A

Capabilities of entrepreneurs, managers, workers, farmers

School enrollment ratios, Health service coverage

Organization of production, R&D, technology imports and adaptation

Household expenditure on HD items and allocation within household

Social and priority ratios

Composition of output and exports

Household income and poverty rates

Government revenue and expenditure ratios

Social capital

Policy environment

Foreign savings

Distribution of income

Physical capital stock & additiions to it

Domestic savings

GNP

spend a higher proportion of their incomes on HD items than those with higher incomes, and similar results flow from greater female control over household income.

When levels of poverty in a country are high, either because per capita income is low or badly distributed, the expenditure of many households on HD is bound to be low. While evidence [5] indicates that, in general, poverty is reduced with economic growth, the extent of the reduction varies greatly with the distribution of income and its change over time.[6] The way in which growth translates into income distribution and poverty reduction depends on the nature of the growth process – in particular, the extent to which it is based on the generation of employment and on increasing rural incomes, e.g., if the output mix is labor intensive and rural incomes rise rapidly in-

come distribution is more likely to improve and poverty reduction to occur than if growth is urban biased and capital intensive.[7]

Expenditure on HD-related items is strongly affected by the rate of poverty reduction. Not surprisingly, if poor households receive extra income, they increase their food expenditure and calorie consumption significantly.[8] Empirical evidence – for example, for Bolivia, Brazil, Chile, Côte d'Ivoire, Ghana, India, Indonesia, Pakistan, Philippines, Malaysia, Nicaragua and Peru – also indicates the positive effects of family income change on child schooling.[9] For example, a cross-country study of the determinants of secondary education found that more egalitarian countries had higher secondary enrollment rates.[10] One estimate suggests that if the distribution of income in Brazil were as equal as Malaysia's, school enrollments among poor children would be 40% higher.[11] While the evidence on the relations between income and health is less extensive, studies in Brazil, Chile, Côte d'Ivoire and Nicaragua suggest that household income also has a significant effect on the demand for health,[12] some showing a much higher relative response for low than for high-income households.[13]

Where women control cash income, it appears that expenditure patterns are geared relatively more toward HD inputs, such as food and education. For example, among Gambian households, the larger the proportion of food under women's control the larger household calorie consumption.[14] Similarly, in the Philippines it has been shown that consumption of calories and proteins increases with the share of income accruing directly to women.[15] In the Côte d'Ivoire, an increase in women's share of cash income was associated with significantly higher spending on food and reduced spending on alcohol and cigarettes.[16]

Turning to the government, the allocation of resources to improving HD is a function of total public sector expenditure, of how much of this flows to the HD sectors, and of the way in which it is allocated within these sectors. This can be expressed in the form of three ratios:[17] the public expenditure ratio, defined as the proportion of GNP spent by the various levels of government; the HD-allocation ratio, defined as the proportion of total government expenditure going to the HD-sectors; and, finally, the HD priority ratio, defined as the proportion of total HD-sector expenditure going to "priority areas." Within the HD-sectors, some expenditures are clearly much more productive in terms of achieving advances in HD than others; for example, basic education, especially at an early stage of development, is generally recognized to have a larger impact on HD than tertiary education. But the precise definition of what constitutes a "priority area" will inevitably vary according to a country's stage of development, rendering this third ratio more arbitrary and difficult to measure than the other two. There are very large variations across countries in each of these ratios, which means that the same level of GNP

may be associated with very different levels of government spending on HD priorities.[18]

The underlying determinants of these three ratios are complex, but include the following: (i) the tax capacity of the system; (ii) the strength of the demand for military expenditure and for other non-HD priorities of the government; (iii) the varying interplay between bureaucratic forces, vested interests and popular pressures. It should be noted that all three ratios are affected by the extent of decentralization of government: country evidence suggests that real decentralization, i.e. devolution, tends to increase the total revenue available; it often raises the HD-allocation ratio; and it almost always improves the HD-priority ratios.[19]

The significance of public expenditure choices for improving HD is illustrated by a comparison between Kenya and Malawi. In the 1980s, a similar proportion of national income went to public expenditure (27% in Kenya; 30% in Malawi) but Kenya had a significantly higher social allocation ratio (47% compared to 35%) and social priority ratio (34% compared to 14%) so that the proportion of GDP going directly to HD-improving priorities in Kenya was over three times that of Malawi (5.1% compared to 1.5%).[20]

The importance of economic growth for raising resources to promote HD is illustrated by a comparison between Botswana and Sudan. In 1970 public expenditure on health and education per person was similar in the two countries ($96 in 1987 prices in Sudan, and $65 in Botswana). During 1970–92 per capita expenditure increased more than seven times in Botswana, while remaining practically unchanged in Sudan. Hence, by 1992, Sudanese expenditure was less than a quarter of that in Botswana ($114 versus $466). This was not due to differences in the public expenditure ratio, which was higher in Sudan during the 1970s and equal to Botswana's during the 1980s, but to the much faster income growth in Botswana. With a similar share of Botswana's GNP going to health and education, real expenditure rose much faster there.

Finally, NGO or other civil society activity, on which information is more scattered, is typically heavily oriented toward HD objectives (e.g., generating incomes for the poor and on schools, nutrition and health projects). Resources are derived from private donations and government, in each case including both foreign and domestic sources. There are considerable variations in the extent, vitality and effectiveness of NGO activities across countries, depending on their history, culture, tax laws and actual or perceived government deficiencies in providing services. In most contexts, NGOs play a supplemental or even marginal role, but in a few areas – e.g., BRAC and the Grameen Bank in Bangladesh, the Harambee Schools in Kenya and the "Comedores Populares" in Peru – they appear to represent a major source of HD-enhancement.[21]

Expenditures on HD inputs are clearly not objectives in themselves, but rather constitute instruments for achieving advances in various dimensions of basic well-being. A further important link in Chain A, therefore, is the effectiveness of these expenditures in raising HD levels, i.e. what type of provision is most productive at what level of development, and how different combinations effect a change in HD. We shall call this link in the chain the "HD improvement function" (HDIF); it resembles a production function in that it relates the inputs into HD, such as public expenditure on health services or water, to the HD objective of achieving better health. An illustration of the type of relationship represented in the HDIF is whether and how far the provision of safe water is complementary to or substitutes for education in contributing to improvements in health. Another is what combination of family planning expenditure, improved nutrition and immunisation levels most effectively yield improvements in infant mortality. The relationships embodied in the HDIF are complex, depending on individual and community behavior and local knowledge about relevant technologies. Moreover, the relevant arguments of the HDIF are bound to differ at different stages of development.

Some aspects of the HDIF have been greatly illuminated by detailed empirical work.[22] An example of the potential usefulness of an improved understanding of this production function is the abundant evidence that education, especially female, tends to improve infant survival and nutrition.[23] Another study, for Brazil, showed that an increase in the nonlabor income of women increased the probability of child survival by 20 times that of a comparable increase in the nonlabor income of men.[24] Research in Ghana has shown that in rural areas the provision of basic health services, including adequate drugs, increases child health and survival significantly, while the evidence is less clear on urban services.[25]

Conditions liable to bring about an improvement in the efficiency of the HDIF include better information about available technologies and the appropriate combinations of inputs; the generation of new and more effective technologies; and the enhancement of the motivation to make use of available options, e.g., to send children to schools and clinics. Such motivation appears to be influenced by education levels, the power structure within the family, incentives and the magnitude of the opportunity costs.

It should be clear from this discussion of the various links in the ED-HD chain that, in general, we would expect important causal connections to exist between the economy and HD achievements, but these connections are *not automatic*: the strength of the links in Chain A varies according to a large range of factors, including the structure of the economy, the distribution of assets, and the policy choices made. The richness of the so-called social capital[26] of a society presumably also affects these choices and the strength of links at each stage; when people act together to promote their well-being, when public morality is high, when the community monitors malfeasance, and when it participates extensively in public life, *ceteris paribus*, we can expect all the links in Chain A to be stronger.

In summary, we would hypothesize from this review of the links in Chain A that the connection between GNP to HD is likely to be stronger:

A.i – the lower the proportion of the population below the poverty line; for a given level of GNP per capita, this means the more equally income is distributed;

A.ii – the more income households allocate to HD at a given income level; this may be related both to the level of female education and to female control over income within the household.

A.iii – the higher the proportion of GNP devoted to priority social expenditure by the government;

A.iv – the more effective the contribution of social capital, including community organizations and other NGOs;

A.v – the more efficient the HDIF.

We shall test some of these hypotheses; others we do not test, either because of conceptual problems or data constraints, notably A.iv. and A.v.

(b) Chain B: from HD to EG

Turning our attention to the second chain, from HD to EG, ample evidence suggests that as people become healthier, better nourished and educated they contribute more to economic growth, although some important dimensions of HD, such as making the lives of the terminally ill tolerable, do not directly lead to enhanced productivity.[27] Higher levels of HD, in addition to being an end in themselves, affect the economy through enhancing people's capabilities and consequently their creativity and productivity. Clearly, the health and education of a population are among the main determinants of the composition and growth of output and exports, and constitute an important ingredient in a system's capacity to borrow foreign technology effectively.

Specifically, (i) health, primary and secondary education and nutrition raise the productivity of workers, rural and urban; (ii) secondary education, including vocational, facilitates the acquisition of skills and managerial capacity; (iii) tertiary education supports the development of basic science, the appropriate selection of technology imports and the domestic adaptation and development of technologies; (iv) secondary and tertiary

education also represent critical elements in the development of key institutions, of government, the law, the financial system, among others, all essential for economic growth.

Empirical evidence at both micro and macro levels lends support to the importance of these relationships.

At a *micro*-level, numerous studies indicate that increases in earnings are associated with additional years of *education*, with the rate of return varying with the level of education.[28] While social rates of return (which deduct the publicly financed costs of education but make no other adjustments to the private returns) are below the private, they are still typically greater than returns to most physical investment.[29] These rate of return estimates are sometimes interpreted as indicating the magnitude of the impact of education on productivity; but this view has also been challenged by the argument that education performs a signalling function, distinguishing among people of different innate ability, rather than itself raising productivity. But, investigations in rural Pakistan, and in urban Kenya and Tanzania, differentiating between additional earnings due to cognitive achievement and those due simply to schooling, showed that cognitive achievement accounted for a high proportion of the extra earnings.[30]

In agriculture, evidence suggests positive effects of education on productivity among farmers using modern technologies, but less impact, as might be expected, among those using traditional methods.[31] In Thailand, farmers with four or more years of schooling were three times more likely to adopt fertilizer and other modern inputs than less educated farmers.[32] Similarly, in Nepal, the completion of at least seven years of schooling increased productivity in wheat by over a quarter, and in rice by 13%.[33]

Education is also an important contributor to technological capability and technical change in industry. Statistical analysis of the clothing and engineering industries in Sri Lanka, to cite just one example, showed that the skill and education levels of workers and entrepreneurs were positively related to the rate of technical change of the firm.[34] Education alone, of course, cannot transform an economy. The quantity and quality of investment, domestic and foreign, together with the overall policy environment, form other important determinants of economic performance. Yet the level of human development has a bearing on these factors too. The quality of policy-making and of investment decisions is likely to be influenced by the education of both policymakers and managers; moreover, the volume of both domestic and foreign investment will probably be larger when a system's human capital supply is more plentiful.

Improved *health and nutrition* have been shown to have direct effects on labor productivity, especially among poorer individuals.[35] A range of labor productivity gains has been observed associated with calorie increases in poor countries,[36] including studies of farmers in Sierra Leone, sugar cane workers in Guatemala, and road construction workers in Kenya.[37] In these cases productivity enhancement appears to follow fairly immediately as current intakes of calories or micro-nutrients are increased. In other cases the effects are medium-run (as reflected in weight) or long-run (as reflected in height), based on evidence from Bangladesh, Brazil, India, Sri Lanka, and the Philippines.[38] A longitudinal study of a sample of children in Chile concluded that providing nutritional supplements to children to prevent malnutrition would generate benefits six to eight times the cost of the intervention in terms of additional productivity.[39] A similar study of Cali, Colombia found that a health and nutrition program increased the lifetime earnings of individuals to from 2.5 to 8.9 times those of an illiterate worker.[40]

It is difficult to capture the effects of ill-health (other than malnutrition) as there are few accurate estimates of the incidence of illness. But studies in both Ghana and Côte d'Ivoire show the negative impact of morbidity, with men who reported that their activities had been curtailed by illness having lower hourly wage rates, reduced hours of work and a smaller probability of being in the labor force.[41] In some contexts the evidence even indicates larger productivity effects arising from health and nutrition than from formal schooling, although the impact of education has been much more emphasized in the development literature.

From a *macro*-perspective, the "new growth theories" aim to endogenize technical progress by incorporating some of these same effects, emphasizing education as well as learning and research and development (R&D). According to Lucas (1988), for example, the higher the level of education of the workforce the higher the overall productivity of capital because the more educated are more likely to innovate, and thus affect everyone's productivity. In other models a similar externality is generated as the increased education of individuals raises not only their own productivity but also that of others with whom they interact, so that total productivity increases as the average level of education rises.[42] A complementary view is that technical progress depends on the level of R&D in an economy. By investing labor and capital in R&D a firm is able to improve not only its own profitability but also the productivity of the firms which consume its output. Again, education plays a key role, both in contributing to R&D and via interactive learning.[43] A number of empirical studies have shown the positive effect of education on economic growth at a macro level, with its size varying according to the measure of education and the particular macro growth model adopted.[44]

The impact of education on the nature and growth of exports, which, in turn, affect the aggregate growth rate, is another way in which human development influences macro performance. The education and skills of a developing country's labor force influence the nature of its factor endowment and consequently the composition of its trade. It has been argued that even "unskilled" workers in a modern factory normally need the literacy, numeracy and discipline which are acquired in primary and lower secondary school.[45] Theoretical models incorporating skills and learning as important determinants of comparative advantage have led to modifications of the simple two factor Heckscher-Ohlin model, helping to explain the Leontief Paradox and the dramatic success in the manufactured export growth of some developing countries, notably those of East Asia.[46] Investigations have shown a significant positive correlation between the growth of manufactured exports and the growth of GDP, although serious identification problems remain.[47]

There is also a positive feedback from improved education to greater income equality which, in turn, is likely to favor higher rates of growth. As education becomes more broadly based, low-income people are better able to seek out economic opportunities. For example, a study of the relation between schooling, income inequality and poverty in 18 countries of Latin America in the 1980s found that one-quarter of the variation in workers' incomes was accounted for by variations in schooling attainment; it concludes that "clearly education is the variable with the strongest impact on income equality."[48] Another study suggested that a 1% increase in the labor force with at least secondary education would increase the share of income of the bottom 40 and 60% by between 6 and 15% respectively.[49] An investigation of the determinants of income distribution in 36 countries found secondary enrollment rates to be significant.[50]

Finally, education may affect per capita income growth via its impact on the denominator, i.e. population growth. For example, a study of 14 African countries for the mid-1980s showed a negative correlation between female schooling and fertility in almost all countries, with primary education having a negative impact in about half the countries and no significant effects in the other half, while secondary education invariably reduced fertility.[51] The three success countries in terms of reduced fertility, Kenya, Botswana and Zimbabwe, had the highest levels of female schooling as well as the lowest child mortality rates.[52]

As in Chain A, the strength of the various links in Chain B varies considerably and there is no *automatic* connection between an improved level of HD and increases in per capita GNP. It is not enough to create a larger pool of educated people; there must also be opportunities for them to be productively employed or it might simply increase the number of educated unemployed. Rele-

vant to the demand-side are the savings and investment rates, technology choice and the overall policy setting.

Although high rates of saving and investment by themselves, as shown by past East European experience, do not guarantee high levels of sustained growth, normally a positive relationship between investment and growth prevails, with its strength depending on such factors as the policy environment, the quantity and quality of human resources, the availability of technology choices and the flexibility of the institutional framework. As pointed out earlier, both domestic investment and direct foreign investment are influenced by a country's HD level – particularly the education and skill levels of the workforce.[53] But differences in economic growth across societies are again not only due to the level of inputs but also by how effectively they are used and for what purpose. One important influence is the incentives set by economic policy. Another derives from people's motives and behavior patterns.

Income distribution again appears to be important in Chain B, as it was in Chain A. Recent empirical evidence suggests that the distribution of assets and income has an effect on economic growth, with a more equal distribution favoring higher rates of growth.[54] Among the explanations put forward for this, one is derived from the relationships in Chain A, i.e., that a more equal distribution of income implies better nutrition and a stronger demand for education and hence raises labor productivity. Others derive from political economy considerations and relate to Chain B, e.g., that an unequal distribution of income may be associated with greater political and economic instability, more likely to interrupt economic progress.[55]

In summary, the connection between HD and GNP, represented by Chain B, is likely to be stronger:

B.i – the higher the investment rate;
B.ii – the more equal the distribution of income;
B.iii – the more appropriate the economic policy setting.

Because of difficulties in defining and measuring hypothesis B.iii we shall confine our tests to B.i and B.ii.

3. EMPIRICAL FINDINGS

The discussion above led us to a set of hypotheses about the links between HD and EG for both causal chains – from EG to HD (Chain A) and from HD to EG (Chain B), some of which we test with crosscountry regressions for 1960–92. Our sample consists of 35 to 76 developing countries, according to the availability of data for particular variables. We generally use lags of the original variables as instruments to reduce the simultaneity bias that would have resulted from applying ordinary least squares (OLS). Lagged values are reasonable candidates as instruments since the correlation between the residuals in the two periods analyzed is not substantial.

(a) Chain A

For Chain A the variable chosen as a proxy for achievement in human development was life expectancy shortfall reduction, 1970–92, from a maximum of 85 years.[56]

The explanatory variables selected were:

– lagged GDP per capita growth rate (for 1960–70) as a measure of overall EG;
– social expenditure (defined as public expenditure on education and health) as a percentage of GDP for the whole period (1970–92), as well as lagged (1970–80). The hypothesis advanced earlier was that HD improvement would depend in part on the proportion of GDP devoted to social expenditure; priority social expenditure data were viewed as somewhat too arbitrary for deployment here;
– several measures of income distribution, i.e. income share of the bottom 20% or 40%, 1960–92, and the ratio of income share of the top to the bottom quintile, 1960–92;
– female primary school gross enrollment rate in 1965; this is a proxy for the change in the stock of educated females. The latter is

likely to be associated with greater female control over household expenditure, thus tending to improve the HDIF;
– regional dummies, with East Asia allocated a zero value.

Table 1.6.1 summarizes the results for Chain A. GDP per capita growth proved significant and quite strong in all of the equations, with higher growth of per capita income leading to better HD performance. According to equation (1), a one percentage point increase in the average growth rate of GDP per capita is estimated to reduce life expectancy shortfall by more than three percentage points over the period. The social expenditure ratio also proved significantly positive in all but one case. For every percentage point increase in the average share of GDP invested in health and education, when lagged, the life expectancy shortfall decreases by about 1.75 percentage points (equations (1) and (3)).

An interesting finding is the mechanism through which the social expenditure ratio seems to affect human development. As regressions (4), (5) and (6) indicate, the female primary enrollment rate for 1965 has a significant but small impact on the rate of improvement of life expectancy. We attribute this to the impact on household behavior of female income, knowledge and control within the household. Moreover, it should be noted that when this variable is added, social expenditure becomes less significant, which suggests that much of the impact of social expenditure appears to occur through its effect on female education. According to equations (4), (5) and (6), a 1% increase in the female primary gross enrollment rate is estimated to reduce the life expectancy shortfall by 0.1%.

The income distribution variables run counter to our expectations, i.e. a more equal distribution does not seem to advance human development.

Both the African and Latin American dummies are negative and significant throughout, as we might have expected, given that the comparator is highly successful East Asia. In each case the coefficient is quite small. The regional dummies include a number of region-specific features, including the level of per capita income.

TABLE 1.6.1
Chain A – ordinary least squares regressions dependent variable: life expectancy shortfall reduction 1970–92

Variable	1	2	3	4	5	6	7	8	9
GDP/n Growth rate 1960–70	3.25*	1.66*	3.19*	1.27**	2.65*	2.70*	2.10*	2.14**	2.31*
	(4.09)[a]	(3.61)	(4.06)	(2.56)	(3.17)	(3.17)	(2.82)	(2.52)	(2.95)
Social Expenditures as a % of GDP 1970–92	–	1.03*	–	–	–	–	–	–	–
		(2.84)							
Social Expenditures as a % of GDP	1.73**	–	1.75**	–	1.36	1.51***	1.28***	1.54***	1.36***
	(2.37)		(2.56)		(1.64)	(1.74)	(1.91)	(1.76)	(1.91)
Income share of bottom 40% 1960–92	-0.004	–	–	-0.004	–	-0.002	–	–	–
	(-0.93)			(-1.29)		(-0.45)			
Income share of bottom 20% 1960–92	–	–	–	–	–	–	–	-1.66***	-1.88**
								(-1.76)	(-2.26)
Ratio of income share top to bottom 20% 1960–92	–	–	0.002	–	0.002	–	0.005*	–	–
			(1.19)		(1.01)		(3.02)		
Female primary gross enrollment rate 1965	–	–	–	0.12**	0.10***	0.10***	–	0.05	–
				(2.59)	(1.94)	(1.85)		(0.71)	
Latin America dummy	–	–	–	–	–	–	-0.08**	-0.08***	-0.07***
							(-2.35)	(-1.98)	(-2.02)
Africa dummy	–	–	–	–	–	–	-0.16*	-0.12**	-0.13*
							(-4.34)	(-2.49)	(-3.63)
South Asia dummy	–	–	–	–	–	–	0.003	0.003	0.02
							(0.06)	(0.50)	(0.39)
Middle East dummy	–	–	–	–	–	–	-0.09	-0.07	-0.09
							(-1.01)	(-0.67)	(-0.97)
Intercept	0.15	0.28*	0.06	0.23*	0.02	1.07	0.16*	0.25**	0.30*
	(1.51)	(6.09)	(1.17)	(3.36)	(0.51)	(0.68)	(2.92)	(2.08)	(3.59)
# of observations	41	76	41	54	38	38	41	38	41
Adj. R-squared	0.38	0.27	0.38	0.26	0.41	0.40	0.59	0.51	0.55

[a] T-Statistics are given in parentheses.
*Significant at 1%.
**Significant at 5%.
***Significant at 10%.

(b) Chain B

For Chain B, the dependent variable chosen was GDP per capita growth, 1970–92.

The explanatory variables selected were:

- log GDP per capita in 1960, to test for convergence of income levels as countries approach high income levels;
- initial levels of HD, using three different measures, log life expectancy in 1962, adult literacy 1970–72, and a combined index of life expectancy and literacy for 1970 (HDI*);[57]
- changes in HD over time for two of the measures of HD, the change in the log of life expectancy, 1962–82; and HDI* shortfall reduction 1960–80;[58]
- gross domestic investment as a % of GDP for the period as a whole (1960–92);
- income distribution, lagged, (1960–70), using three alternative measures, the ratio of the income share of the top to bottom quintiles, the income share of the bottom 40% of the population, and the income share of the bottom 20%;
- regional dummies, as in Chain A.

The results are summarized in Table 1.6.2. Our measures of the initial level of human development invariably proved significant, although with low coefficients; i.e. the initial level of life expectancy in equations (10)–(12), as well as (18)–(22) were all highly significant. Adult literacy 1970–72 was significant in equations (13), (16) and (17); and the HDI* for 1970 was significant in equations (14) and (15), all with low coefficients. The change in life expectancy, 1962–82, was positive and significant in all cases but one (see equations (18)–(22)). The change in HDI* shortfall reduction, 1960–80, was significant in equation (23), but the initial level of HDI* was not significant.

The domestic investment rate was always significant except when the regional dummies were included (equations (15) and (22)). The lagged income distribution variables virtually all gave results with the expected sign (i.e. a more equal income distribution is associated with higher economic growth), and were almost always significant – if with very low coefficients – except when the regional dummies were included. Moreover, income distribution is apparently more strongly related to GDP growth when changes as well as levels of human development, however measured, are included. The ratio of income shares of the top to bottom quintiles, 1960–70, showed significance in equations (11), (13) and (21); the share of the bottom 40% was significant in equations (14), (17), (19), (20) and (23), but the lagged income distribution variable was not significant in equations (12), (15) and (22), although the signs were in the "right" direction. Regional dummies for Latin America were significantly negative in both instances when deployed and, in one case, also for Africa. In all equations, except when the regional dummies were introduced (equation (15)), the initial level of GDP per capita was significant, with a negative sign, indicating weak convergence, i.e. with a low coefficient.

In summary, the two chains, taken as a whole, showed a significantly positive effect of economic growth on HD and a significantly positive effect of HD on economic growth. With respect to specific links in each of the chains, our findings broadly confirmed the tested hypotheses, except for income distribution in Chain A. For Chain A, the higher social expenditure, the higher adult literacy, and the higher the female education enrollment for a given level of GNP per capita, the larger the improvement in HD. The most surprising finding, counter to our expectations, was that a more equal distribution of income did not improve HD performance; indeed, in some equations the opposite result obtained. One explanation of this may well be that we restricted the definition of HD in our Chain A regressions to life expectancy shortfall reduction which is mainly affected by public expenditures on health and education, particularly female, and less by household expenditures. For Chain B, the relationship between HD and economic growth was stronger the higher the investment rate and the more equally distributed the income. The regional dummies were generally negative for both Africa and Latin

TABLE 1.6.2
Chain B – ordinary least squares regressions dependent variable: average real GDP/n growth 1970–92

Variable	10	11	12	13	14	15	16	17
Log GDP/n 1960	-0.01*	–	-0.01*	-0.01**	-0.01**	-0.009	-0.01**	-0.01**
	(-3.01)[a]		(-3.04)	(-2.87)	(-1.87)	(-1.42)	(-2.38)	(-2.55)
Adult literacy rate 1970–72	–	–	–	0.03**	–	–	0.03**	0.03**
				(2.45)			(2.19)	(2.21)
Log life expectancy 1967	0.06*	0.03**	0.09*	–	–	–	–	–
	(3.79)	(2.09)	(3.90)					
Gross domestic investment as a % of GDP 1960–92	0.12*	0.14**	0.12**	0.12***	0.13**	0.06	0.12**	0.12**
	(3.83)	(2.72)	(2.37)	(1.99)	(2.26)	(1.06)	(2.07)	(2.09)
Income share of bottom 40% 1960–70	–	–	0.001	–	0.001***	–	–	0.001**
			(1.52)		(1.70)			(2.20)
Income share of bottom 20% 1960–70	–	–	–	–	–	–	0.40**	–
							(2.18)	
Ratio of income share of top to bottom quintile 1960–70	–	-0.0007**	–	-0.0007**	–	-2.21	–	–
		(-2.17)		(-2.06)		(-0.05)		
HDI* 1970	–	–	–	–	0.06**	0.07**	–	–
					(2.38)	(2.58)		
Latin America dummy	–	–	–	–	–	-0.02**	–	–
						(-2.57)		
Africa dummy	–	–	–	–	–	-0.01***	–	–
						(-1.90)		
South Asia dummy	–	–	–	–	–	-0.003	–	–
						(-0.31)		
Middle East dummy	–	–	–	–	–	0.01	–	–
						(0.57)		
Intercept	-0.17*	-0.14**	-0.28*	0.12**	0.03	0.04	0.07	0.07
	(-3.71)	(-2.30)	(-3.93)	(2.74)	(0.64)	(1.08)	(1.46)	(1.54)
# of observations	73	38	36	24	35	35	24	24
Adj. R-squared	0.34	0.29	0.45	0.37	0.30	0.41	0.38	0.38

continued on next page

TABLE 1.6.2 – continued
Chain B – ordinary least squares regressions dependent variable: average real GDP/n growth 1970–92

Variable	18	19	20	21	22	23
Log life expectancy 1962	0.06*	0.07*	0.05*	0.05**	0.08	–
	(5.48)	(3.98)	(3.04)	(2.65)	(2.88)	
Change in the log of life expectancy 1962–82	0.13*	0.17**	0.14*	0.12	0.14***	–
	(3.81)	(2.48)	(2.01)	(1.65)	(1.78)	
Gross domestic investment as a % of GDP (1970–92 average)	–	–	0.12**	0.13**	0.06	0.13**
			(2.44)	(2.39)	(1.17)	(2.42)
Income share of bottom 40% 1960–70	–	0.002*	0.002*	–	–	0.002*
		(2.83)	(3.16)			(2.96)
Ratio of income share of top to bottom quintile 1960–70	–	–	–	–0.0008**	–0.0002	–
				(–2.49)	(–0.62)	
HDI* 1960	–	–	–	–	–	–0.0007
						(–0.03)
HDI* shortfall reduction 1960–80	–	–	–	–	–	0.09**
						(2.08)
Latin America dummy	–	–	–	–	–0.02**	–
					(–2.71)	
Africa dummy	–	–	–	–	–0.005	–
					(–0.57)	
South Asia dummy	–	–	–	–	0.003	–
					(0.29)	
Middle East dummy	–	–	–	–	0.004	–
					(0.34)	
Intercept	0.27*	–0.33*	–0.29*	–0.23	–0.33*	–0.03*
	(–5.37)	(–3.96)	(–3.56)	(–2.81)	(–2.81)	(–3.84)
# of observations	79	39	38	38	38	37
Adj. R-squared	0.27	0.30	0.38	0.32	0.44	0.33

a T-Statistics are given in parentheses.
*Significant at 1%.
**Significant at 5%.
***Significant at 10%.

America in both chains but with small coefficients. Since, on average, Africa experienced a decline in GDP per capita over the period, this indicates that the fall in per capita incomes was not proportionately translated into a slowdown or reversal in HD improvements.[59]

4. Virtuous and Vicious Cycles and Lop-Sided Development

The existence of two chains linking HD and economic growth is thus strongly supported by both our framework, drawing on micro and macro studies in the literature, and our empirical results. This means that an economy may be on a mutually reinforcing upward spiral, with high levels of HD leading to high growth and high growth in turn further promoting HD. Conversely, weak HD may result in low growth and consequently poor progress toward HD improvement. The strength of the links in the two chains influences the extent of mutual reinforcement between HD and EG, in either direction.

Country performance can therefore be usefully classified into four categories, *virtuous*, *vicious* and two types of *lop-sidedness*, i.e. lopsided with strong HD/weak growth (called HD-lopsided); and lopsided with weak HD/strong growth (EG-lopsided). In the virtuous cycle case, good HD enhances growth, which in turn promotes HD, and so on. In the vicious cycle case, poor performance on HD tends to lead to poor growth performance which in turn depresses HD achievements, and so on. The stronger the linkages in the two chains described above the more pronounced the cycle of economic growth and HD, either in a positive or dampening direction. Where linkages are weak, cases of lop-sided development may occur. On the one hand, good economic growth may not bring about good HD, if, for example, there are such weak linkages as a low social expenditure ratio; on the other hand, good HD performance may not generate good EG if there is a dearth of complementary resources because of low investment rates. Such cases of lop-sided development are unlikely to persist. Either the weak partner in the cycle eventually acts as a brake on the other partner, leading to a vicious cycle case, or, if the linkages are strengthened, possibly by policy change, a virtuous cycle case results.

One way of classifying countries into the four categories is to compare their performance on HD and EG with the average performance of all developing countries. Figure 1.6.2 presents this classification for 1960–92 for all developing countries for which data were available. The vertical and horizontal grid lines represent the average performance for the period, with countries weighted by their populations in 1992. Most developing countries appear as either virtuous (NE quadrant), or vicious (SW quadrant); a significant number showed an HD-lopsided pattern, and very few an EG-lopsided one. A strong regional pattern emerges, with East Asia heavily represented in the virtuous cycle case (seven out of the eight cases are East or South East Asian, the eighth being Botswana). Of the 37 countries in the vicious cycle quadrant, 21 are from sub-Saharan Africa, nine from Latin America. Latin America is also strongly represented in the HD-lopsided quadrant, i.e. 10 of the 13 are from that region. In the EG-lopsided category there are just four countries – Egypt, Pakistan, Mauritius and Lesotho.

The important issue for policy purposes is how a country may move towards inclusion in the virtuous cycle category. Much can be learned about this by looking at the ways in which countries moved across categories over time. Taking the movements of countries over the three decades 1960–70, 1970–80 and 1980–92 (see Table 1.6.3 and Figure 1.6.3), we find the following:

– Over half the countries in the vicious-cycle category in 1960–70, i.e. 18 out of 35, remained in that category throughout. Most of these countries were in sub-Saharan Africa, which started with very low levels of HD, handicapping their growth potential; their low growth rates and, subsequently, the debt crisis prevented them from generating the resources necessary for improvements in HD.
– Six countries moved from vicious cycle to EG-lopsided between the 1960s and the 1970s, but four of them fell back to the vi-

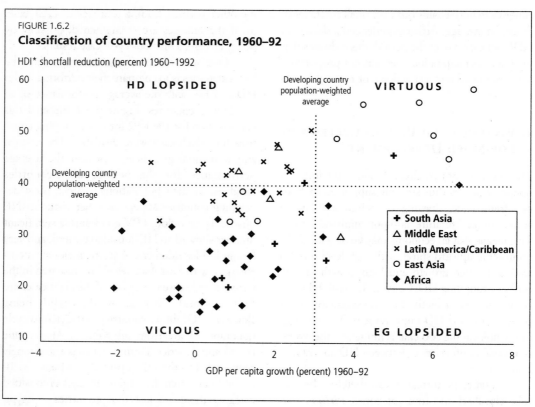

FIGURE 1.6.2

Classification of country performance, 1960–92

HDI* shortfall reduction (percent) 1960–1992

Legend:
- **+** South Asia
- **△** Middle East
- **×** Latin America/Caribbean
- **○** East Asia
- **◆** Africa

X-axis: GDP per capita growth (percent) 1960–92

Quadrant labels: HD LOPSIDED, VIRTUOUS, VICIOUS, EG LOPSIDED

Developing country population-weighted average

cious cycle category in the 1980s. Three moved from vicious to HD-lopsided, including Honduras, Algeria and Madagascar, and only Madagascar returned to the vicious cycle category. Kenya, which moved from vicious to virtuous in the 1970s, also subsequently fell back to vicious. Only two countries managed to move from the vicious to virtuous category on a sustained basis – i.e. Sri Lanka and Botswana.

– Of the eight countries which were EG-lopsided in 1960–70, none stayed in that category throughout, but all moved into the vicious category. One – Pakistan – reverted to EG-lopsided in the 1980s. Brazil and Egypt enjoyed relatively fast growth during the 1960s and 1970s (over 3% in the 1960s and about 6% in the 1970s) but did not utilize this opportunity to improve the levels of HD substantially. In the case of Brazil the highly unequal income distribution (with a Gini of 0.634, one of the worst in the world) was one

reason why growth did not translate into HD improvements. In both Pakistan and Egypt, public expenditure on health and education was low, partly due to heavy expenditure on the military, while Pakistan's HD performance suffered especially from discrimination against females.

– Of the 13 HD-lopsided countries in the 1960s, only Costa Rica stayed in that category throughout: four moved into a virtuous cycle – Chile, China, Colombia and Indonesia (Colombia later falling back to HD-lopsided). In these cases, early progress in human development meant that they were able to take advantage of policy reforms for generating growth. Egalitarian income distribution also assisted the movement toward a virtuous cycle. Four moved initially from HD-lopsided into the vicious category (Venezuela, Myanmar, Peru, and El Salvador[60] – the latter two moving back into HD-lopsidedness in the 1980s).[61] Three – Dominican

TABLE 1.6.3

Virtuous, vicious and lop-sided performance 1960–92

	1960–70	1970–80	1980–92
Africa			
Benin	Vicious	Vicious	Vicious
Botswana	Vicious	Virtuous	Virtuous
Burkina Faso	Vicious	Vicious	Vicious
Burundi	Vicious	Vicious	Vicious
Cameroon	Vicious	EG lop-sided	Vicious
Central African Republic	Vicious	Vicious	Vicious
Chad	Vicious	Vicious	Vicious
Congo	Vicious	EG lop-sided	Vicious
Côte d'Ivoire	EG lop-sided	Vicious	Vicious
Gabon	EG lop-sided	Vicious	Vicious
Ghana	Vicious	Vicious	Vicious
Kenya	Vicious	Virtuous	Vicious
Lesotho	Virtuous	EG lop-sided	Vicious
Madagascar	Vicious	HD lop-sided	Vicious
Malawi	Vicious	EG lop-sided	Vicious
Mali	Vicious	Vicious	Vicious
Mauritius	HD lop-sided	EG lop-sided	EG lop-sided
Niger	Vicious	Vicious	Vicious
Nigeria	Vicious	Vicious	Vicious
Rwanda	Vicious	Vicious	Vicious
Senegal	Vicious	Vicious	Vicious
Sierra Leone	EG lop-sided	Vicious	Vicious
South Africa	Virtuous	Vicious	Vicious
Sudan	Vicious	Vicious	Vicious
Tanzania	Vicious	Vicious	Vicious
Zaire	Vicious	Vicious	Vicious
Zimbabwe	Vicious	Vicious	Vicious
Latin America & Caribbean			
Argentina	Vicious	Vicious	HD lop-sided
Barbados	Virtuous	HD lop-sided	HD lop-sided
Bolivia	Vicious	Vicious	HD lop-sided
Brazil	EG lop-sided	EG lop-sided	Vicious
Chile	HD lop-sided	HD lop-sided	Virtuous
Colombia	HD lop-sided	Virtuous	HD lop-sided
Costa Rica	HD lop-sided	HD lop-sided	HD lop-sided
Dominican Republic	HD lop-sided	EG lop-sided	Vicious
El Salvador	HD lop-sided	Vicious	HD lop-sided
Guatemala	HD lop-sided	EG lop-sided	Vicious
Haiti	Vicious	Vicious	Vicious
Honduras	Vicious	HD lop-sided	HD lop-sided
Jamaica	Virtuous	Vicious	Vicious
Mexico	Virtuous	Virtuous	HD lop-sided
Nicaragua	Virtuous	Vicious	HD lop-sided
Panama	Virtuous	Virtuous	HD lop-sided

continued on next page

TABLE 1.6.3 – *continued*
Virtuous, vicious and lop-sided performance 1960–92

	1960–70	1970–80	1980–92
Latin America & Caribbean			
Paraguay	Vicious	EG lop-sided	Vicious
Peru	HD lop-sided	Vicious	HD lop-sided
Togo	EG lop-sided	Vicious	Vicious
Trinidad & Tobago	Vicious	EG lop-sided	HD lop-sided
Uruguay	Vicious	Vicious	HD lop-sided
Venezuala	HD lop-sided	HD lop-sided	Vicious
South Asia			
India	Vicious	Vicious	EG lop-sided
Nepal	Vicious	Vicious	Vicious
Pakistan	EG lop-sided	Vicious	EG lop-sided
Sri Lanka	Vicious	Virtuous	Virtuous
Bangladesh	Vicious	Vicious	Vicious
East Asia			
China	HD lop-sided	Virtuous	Virtuous
Hong Kong	Virtuous	Virtuous	Virtuous
Indonesia	HD lop-sided	Virtuous	Virtuous
Korea Republic	Virtuous	Virtuous	Virtuous
Malaysia	Virtuous	Virtuous	Virtuous
Myanmar	HD lop-sided	Vicious	Vicious
Philippines	HD lop-sided	EG lop-sided	Vicious
Singapore	Virtuous	Virtuous	Virtuous
Thailand	Virtuous	Virtuous	Virtuous
Middle East			
Algeria	Vicious	HD lop-sided	HD lop-sided
Egypt	EG lop-sided	EG lop-sided	Vicious
Morocco	Vicious	EG lop-sided	HD lop-sided
Turkey	Virtuous	HD lop-sided	HD lop-sided

Republic, Guatemala and the Philippines – initially moved to EG-lopsided and subsequently fell back into the vicious category. Among the reasons for the failure to move into high economic growth were the debt situation, poor economic policies and internal disturbances. Consequently, they were unable to maintain the rate of progress in HD because of slow economic growth.

– Thirteen countries were in the virtuous cycle category in the 1960s; five retained this position throughout; and five fell back to the HD-lopsided and three to the vicious category.[62] Mostly, the countries that fell back were subject to the depressing effects of the 1980s debt crisis on economic growth.

It is important to note that lopsidedness was a temporary condition in all cases except Costa Rica.[63] Our most significant finding is that, while HD-lopsidedness permitted movement towards a virtuous cycle (occurring in about a third of the cases), *in the case of EG-lopsidedness, all the cases reverted to a vicious cycle.* Very few coun-

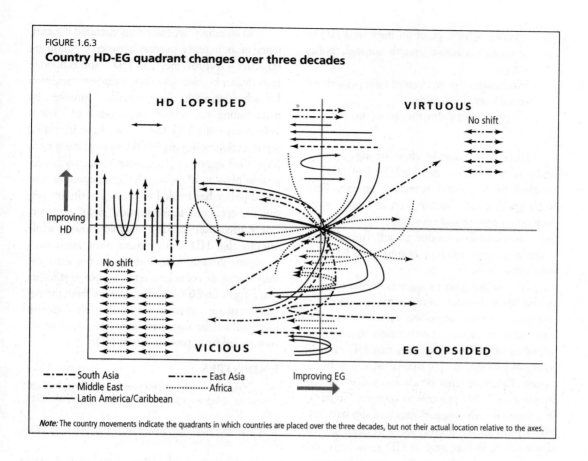

FIGURE 1.6.3

Country HD-EG quadrant changes over three decades

HD LOPSIDED

VIRTUOUS

No shift

Improving
HD

No shift

VICIOUS

EG LOPSIDED

—·—·— South Asia   —··—··— East Asia   Improving EG
— — — Middle East   ············ Africa
———— Latin America/Caribbean

Note: The country movements indicate the quadrants in which countries are placed over the three decades, but not their actual location relative to the axes.

tries managed to go directly from vicious to virtuous; but some succeeded in moving to HD-lopsided, from where it was possible to move into the virtuous category. Our analysis suggests that it is not possible to move to virtuous via EG-lopsidedness, as this proved a dead end.

Hence the process we need to examine more closely is that leading to a movement from vicious to HD-lopsided, from HD-lopsided to virtuous, or the very unusual case, undoubtedly difficult, of taking the direct route from vicious to virtuous.

Our earlier review of the links in the two chains suggests that to move from vicious to HD-lopsided one needs to strengthen the links in Chain A, which may be achieved by adopting some of the following policies:

– those leading to a shift in resource allocation toward education and health services,

especially those serving the majority of the people, as apparently occurred in Argentina with enhanced decentralization.

– those generating a more equitable income distribution (for example, through land and tax reform or a move toward a more employment-intensive pattern of output). Algeria is an example, with land reform in the 1960s and some large-scale employment programs in the 1970s.[64]

– those providing extensive opportunities for the unemployed, for example Bolivia's Social Fund in the 1980s, which received substantial support from donors.

Movement from the HD-lopsided to the virtuous category requires strengthening the links in Chain B by, for example:

- taking advantage of an improved HD to promote economic growth through policy reform;
- increasing the investment rate, possibly assisted from the outside;
- improving the distribution of income.

Chile is an example where strong economic reforms, combined with a high level of HD, accounted for improved economic growth. Relatively good income distribution in China, along with policy reform and very high investment rates, led to accelerated economic growth. In Indonesia, a similar process was heavily supported by external capital flows.

We do not wish to argue here that any particular set of policies would achieve a particular movement across categories; rather we want to emphasize an important conclusion about the sequencing of policy change, i.e. that HD must be strengthened *before* a virtuous cycle can be attained. Policy reforms which focus only on economic growth are unlikely to succeed. Countries in a virtuous cycle category may well slip back into HD-lopsidedness, if, for some reason, growth slows down, but as long as HD stays high such cases have a good chance of resuming their virtuous cycle pattern.

Whenever either or both chains appear to be weak, leading to lop-sided or vicious cycles, it is important to identify where the weak links are and what the appropriate policies might be to strengthen such links. These policies must, moreover, be viewed in an evolutionary context. Even countries initially successful in both HD and EG will need to change their policies as development proceeds in order to sustain their success. In an early phase, for example, priority should be given to primary education and some comprehensive health interventions, both from the perspective of improving HD and that of increasing economic growth. At a later stage, the roles of science and technology institutions and higher education become more important for strengthening Chain B, while, along Chain A, hospitals assume a greater role than before.

In summary, we have demonstrated the existence of an iterative process between the ultimate objective – improvements in HD – and economic growth as a necessary but not sufficient condition for achieving such improvements. Moreover, by investigating the relative importance of various links connecting HD and EG we have identified the direction policy might take to strengthen such links. One important conclusion concerns the desirable phasing of policy change. Economic and social policy has tended to focus priority on getting the economic fundamentals "right" as a necessary precondition for economic growth, while arguing that HD improvement must await such economic growth. Our findings do not deny the importance of economic reforms, but emphasize that a focus on HD must be included from the beginning of any reform program. Economic growth itself will not be sustained unless preceded or accompanied by improvements in HD.

ENDNOTES

*We are grateful for very helpful comments on an earlier draft from three anonymous referees. Final revision accepted: 19 July 1999.

Reprinted from *World Development*, Vol. 28, No. 2, pp. 197–219, 2000, with permission from Elsevier.

1. See especially the UNDP's *Human Development Reports*, starting in 1990.

2. See, e.g., Sen (1984); Streeten, Burki, ul Haq, Hicks and Stewart (1981); Fei, Ranis and Stewart (1985).

3. The first UNDP *Human Development Report* stated that: "The basic objective of development is to create an enabling environment for people to enjoy long, healthy and creative lives" (UNDP, 1990, p. 9), and defined human development as "a process of enlarging people's choices" (p. 10).

4. One notable exception is Adelman and Morris (1973) who argued that educational investment should be given sequencing priority.

5. E.g. Fields (1989); Deininger and Squire (1996).

6. Bruno, Ravallion and Squire (1995), for example, in a study of 20 developing countries, show that a 10% increase in average income per capita, 1984–93, was associated with a 20% fall in the proportion of people living on less than $1 a day. See also Ravallion and Datt (1991).

7. Lipton (1977); Ranis (1979); Stewart (1977); Lipton and Ravallion (1995).

8. Strauss and Thomas (1995). Of 38 studies in different countries one-third indicate that at least one-half of additional income is spent in this way. See also Bouis and Haddad (1992).

9. E.g., Alderman, Behrman, Khan, Ross and Sabot (1995, 1996a); Behrman and Wolfe (1987a,b); Birdsall (1985); Deolalikar (1993); King and Lillard (1987).

10. Williamson (1993).

11. Birdsall, Ross and Sabot (1995).

12. Blau (1986); Harbert and Scandizzo (1982); Thomas, Strauss and Hanriques (1990, 1991); Thomas, Lavy and Strauss (1992).

13. Gertler, Locay and Sanderson (1987).

14. von Braun (1988).

15. Garcia (1990).

16. Hoddinott and Haddad (1991).

17. See UNDP (1991).

18. See UNDP (1991) Chapter 3, and UNDP (1996) Chapter 3.

19. Decentralization of publicly provided services recently has been introduced in a wide range of countries. Tentative conclusions about their effectiveness are mixed, with apparent relative success in promoting efficiency and contributing to HD in Indonesia, Malaysia, Chile and Karnataka in India, but less so in Argentina, Bangladesh and Brazil. Mostly, local governments have been severely constrained in their ability to raise taxes as well as in the freedom of allocative decision-making, and full democratic devolution has been rare. See Behrman (1995b); Prud'homme (1995); Klugman (1995); Ranis and Stewart (1994); Tanzi (1995).

20. UNDP (1996, p. 71). These calculations adopt a narrow definition of social priority expenditure, including pre-primary and first-level education plus primary health care only.

21. Riddell, Robinson deConinck, Muir and White (1995).

22. See, e.g., the review by Strauss and Thomas (1995).

23. See e.g., Rosenzweig and Schultz (1982); Wolfe and Behrman (1987); Barrera (1990).

24. Thomas (1990).

25. Lavy, Strauss, Thomas, deVreyer (1995).

26. A term used broadly to describe civil society networks – see Coleman (1988); North (1990) and Helliwell and Putnam (1995) for the development of the concept and some empirical evidence. Tendler and Freedheim (1994) provide evidence.

27. This clearly does not detract from the intrinsic value of improving the lives of the unemployable, who may account for a significant proportion of the population.

28. See surveys in Behrman (1990a,b,c, 1995a); Behrman and Deolalikar (1988), King and Hill (1993); King and Bellew (1988); Psacharopolous (1994); Schultz (1988, 1993a,b); Strauss and Thomas (1995).

29. Following the work of Psacharopolous, the conclusion that the returns to education are highest for primary education has become part of the accepted wisdom; but in fact this is by no means always the case – see, e.g., Schultz (1993a,b). However, since secondary education necessarily requires prior attendance at primary school, the usual measures of returns to primary education which do not allow for this may understate the total returns.

30. Boissiere, Knight and Sabot (1985); Alderman, Behrman, Khan, Ross and Sabot (1996b).

31. Schultz (1975); Welch (1970); Rosenzweig (1995); Foster and Rosenzweig (1994); Behrman, Rosenzweig and Vashishtha (1995).

32. Birdsall (1993).

33. Jamison and Moock (1984). A similar level of education was estimated to increase farm productivity by 10% or more, according to studies in India and Pakistan (Azher, 1991; Butt, 1984; Duraisamy, 1992). Studies in Malaysia, Ghana and Peru show that, on average, an extra year of schooling of a farmer is associated with an annual increase in output of 2–5% (Birdsall, 1993). Examination of the early stages of India's Green Revolution indicates that the benefits from schooling arose more from conferring on farmers the capacity for learning from their own experience or from those of others, rather than from providing them with an initial information advantage (Foster & Rosenzweig, 1995).

34. Deraniyagala (1995).

35. See Behrman and Deolalikar (1987) and surveys in Behrman (1993, 1996).

36. See Cornia and Stewart (1995).

37. Strauss (1986); Immink and Viteri (1981); Wolgemuth, Latham, Hall and Crompton (1982).

38. Behrman and Deolalikar (1989); Behrman and Lavy (1995); Deolalikar (1988); Foster and Rosenzweig (1993); Haddad and Bouis (1991); Pitt, Rosenzweig and Hassan (1990); Sahn and Alderman (1988); Strauss and Thomas (1996).

39. Selowsky and Taylor (1973).

40. Selowsky (1981).

41. Schultz and Tansel (1993).

42. Perotti (1993).

43. See Romer (1990); Grossman and Helpman (1991); Gemmell (1995).

44. E.g., Barro (1991); Barro and Lee (1993, 1994).

45. Wood (1994); Owens and Wood (1995).

46. See Kenen (1965); Keesing (1966); Pack and Westphal (1986); Leamer (1993).

47. E.g. Michaely (1977); Krueger (1978); Ram (1985); Rana (1988); Edwards (1993).

48. Psacharopolous, Morley, Fiszbein, Lee and Wood (1992, p. 48).

49. Bourguignon and Morrisson (1990).

50. Bourguignon (1995).

51. See Birdsall, Ross and Sabot (1995); Jayaraman (1995); Strauss and Thomas (1995); Thomas, Strauss and Henriques (1991); Behrman and Wolfe (1987a).

52. Ainsworth, Beegle and Nyamete (1995).

53. OECD/DAC (1995); World Bank (1995a).

54. Alesina and Rodrik (1994); Alesina and Perotti (1994); Persson and Tabellini (1994); Birdsall et al. (1995).

55. Alesina and Rodrik (1994).

56. As incorporated in the Human Development Index – see UNDP (1995). We also tried regressions with changes in adult literacy rates and a combined, equally weighted, measure of the two. The results were similar but the number of observations more limited.

57. HDI* is a modified version of the Human Development Index of UNDP, including only the nonincome components, i.e. educational attainment as measured by a combination of adult literacy (2/3 weight), mean years of schooling (1/3 weight), and longevity as measured by life expectancy at birth.

58. When changes over time were introduced, the dates of the initial level of HD were also changed, so that log life expectancy was for 1962 and HDI* for 1960.

59. One explanation is that there were important specific interventions (notably immunization) that affected HD positively throughout the world in the 1970s and 1980s. In a sense these weakened the links in Chain A by rendering HD improvements more independent of incomes. In Africa, this would translate into a reduced negative impact on HD of falling incomes.

60. Iraq made the same move between the 1960s and 1970s, but data are not available for the later period, when conflict is likely to have damaged both HD and growth.

61. The Philippines moved from HD-lopsided to EG-lopsided and then returned to HD-lopsided in the 1980s.

62. Lesotho moved from virtuous to vicious by way of EG-lopsided.

63. One of the explanations of why Costa Rica was able to sustain HD achievements despite low economic growth resides in its early, strong and sustained commitment to HD, exemplified by abolition of its army in 1948 and its heavy investment (at 10% of GDP) on health and education during 1970–92.

64. El-Ghonemy (1990).

REFERENCES

Adelman, I., & Morris, C. T. (1973). *Economic growth and social equity in developing countries*. Stanford, CA: Stanford University Press.

Ainsworth, M., Beegle, K., & Nyamete, A. (1995). *The impact of female schooling on fertility and contraceptive use: a study of fourteen sub-Saharan African countries*. SMS Working Papers, 110, World Bank, Washington, DC.

Alderman, H., Behrman, J., Khan, S., Ross, D., & Sabot, R. (1996b). The returns to endogenous human capital in Pakistan's rural wage market. *Oxford Bulletin of Economics and Statistics*.

Alderman, H., Behrman, J., Khan, S., Ross, D., & Sabot, R. (1996a). The income gap in cognitive skills in rural Pakistan. *Economic Development and Cultural Change, 44*.

Alderman, H., Behrman, J. R., Ross, D., & Sabot, R. (1995). Decomposing the gender gap in cognitive skills in a poor rural economy. *Journal of Human Resources, 31*.

Alesina, A., & Perotti, R. (1994). The political economy of growth: a critical survey of the recent literature. *The World Bank Economic Review, 8*.

Alesina, A., & Rodrik, D. (1994). Distributive politics and economic growth. *Quarterly Journal of Economics, 109*.

Azher, R. A. (1991). Education and technical efficiency during the green revolution in Pakistan. *Economic Development and Cultural Change, 39*.

Barro, R. J., & Lee, J. -W. (1993). International comparison of educational attainment. *Journal of Monetary Economics, 32*.

Barro, R. J., & Lee, J. -W. (1994). Losers and winners in economic growth. In *Proceedings of the World Bank annual conference on development economics, 1993*. Washington, DC: IBRD.

Barro, R. (1991). Economic growth in a cross-section of countries. *Quarterly Journal of Economics, 106*.

Barrera, A. (1990). The role of maternal schooling and its interaction with public health programs in child health production. *Journal of Development Economics, 32 (1)*, 69–91.

Behrman, J. R. (1990b). *The action of human resources and poverty on one another: what we have yet to learn*. LSMS Working Paper 74. Washington, DC: World Bank.

Behrman, J. R. (1990c). *Women's schooling and non-market productivity: a survey and a reappraisal*. Mimeo, University of Pennsylvania, Philadelphia.

Behrman, J. R. (1993a). The economic rationale for investing in nutrition in developing countries. *World Development, 21*.

Behrman, J. R. (1995a). *The impact of distributive policies, governmental expenditure patterns and decentralization on human resources*. Philadelphia: Mimeo, University of Pennsylvania.

Behrman, J. R. (1995b). Intra-household allocation of resources: is there a gender bias? *In Sex differentials in infant and child mortality*. Population Division, United Nations, New York.

Behrman, J. R. (1996). Impact of health and nutrition on education. *World Bank Research Observer, 11*.

Behrman, J. R., & Deolalikar, A. B. (1987). Will developing country nutrition improve with income? a case study for rural south India. *Journal of Political Economy, 95.*

Behrman, J. R., & Deolalikar, A. B. (1988). Health and nutrition. In H. B. Chenery & T. N. Srinivasan. *Handbook of development economics,* vol. 1. Amsterdam: North Holland.

Behrman, J. R., & Deolalikar, A. B. (1989). Wages and labor supply in rural India: the role of health, nutrition and seasonality. In D.E. Sahn, *Causes and implications of seasonal variability in household food security.* Baltimore, MD: The Johns Hopkins University Press.

Behrman, J. R., & Lavy, V. (1995). *Production functions, input allocations and unobservables: the case of child health and schooling success.* Mimeo, University of Pennsylvania, Philadelphia.

Behrman, J. R., & Wolfe, B. L. (1987a). How does mother's schooling affect the family's health nutrition medical care usage and household? *Journal of Econometrics, 36.*

Behrman, J. R., & Wolfe, B. L. (1987b). Investments in schooling in two generations in pre-revolutionary Nicaragua: the roles of family background and school supply. *Journal of Development Economics, 27.*

Behrman, J. R. (1990a). *Human resource led development: review of issues and development.* ARTEP/ILO, New Delhi.

Behrman, J. R., Rosenzweig, M. R., & Vashishtha, P. (1995). Location-specific technical change, human capital and local economic development: The Indian Green Revolution experience. In H. Siebert, *Locational competition in the world economy.* Kiel: Kiel Institute of World Economics.

Birdsall, N. (1985). Public inputs and child schooling in Brazil. *Journal of Development Economics, 18.*

Birdsall, N. (1993). *Social development is economic development.* World Bank policy research working papers, WPS, 1123, World Bank, Washington, DC.

Birdsall, N., Ross, D., & Sabot, R. (1995). Inequality and growth reconsidered: lessons from East Asia. *World Bank Economic Review, 9.*

Blau, D. (1986). Fertility child nutrition and child mortality in Nicaragua: an economic analysis of interrelationships. *Journal of Developing Areas, 20.*

Boissiere, M., Knight, J. B., & Sabot, R. H. (1985). Earnings schooling ability and cognitive skills. *American Economic Review, 75.*

Bouis, H. E., & Haddad, L. J. (1992). Are estimates of calorie-income elasticities too high? A recalibration of the plausible range. *Journal of Development Economics, 39.*

Bourguignon, F. (1995). *Equity and economic growth: Permanent questions and changing answers?* Background paper prepared for the 1996 Human Development Report, UNDP, New York.

Bourguignon, F., & Morrisson, C. (1990). Income distribution development and foreign trade: a crosssectional analysis. *European Economic Review, 34.*

Bruno, M., Ravallion, M., & Squire, L. (1995). *Equity and growth in developing countries: old and new perspectives on the policy issues.* Paper presented at International Monetary Fund Conference on Income Distribution and Sustainable Growth, Washington, DC, June 1–2.

Butt, M. S. (1984). Education and farm productivity in Pakistan. *Pakistan Journal of Applied Economics, 3.*

Coleman, J. (1988). Social capital in the creation of human capital. *American Journal of Sociology, 94* (suppl. S95–S120).

Cornia, G.A., & Stewart, F. (1995). Two errors of targeting. In F. Stewart, *Adjustment and poverty: options and choices.* London: Routledge.

Deininger, K., & Squire, L. (1996). A new data set measuring income inequality. *World Bank Economic Review, 10.*

Deolalikar, A. B. (1988). Nutrition and labor productivity in agriculture: Estimates for rural south India. *Review of Economics and Statistics, 70.*

Deolalikar, A. B. (1993). Gender differences in the returns to schooling and school enrollment rates in Indonesia. *Journal of Human Resources, 28.*

Deraniyagala, S. (1995). *Technical change and efficiency in Sri Lanka's manufacturing industry.* Ph.D. dissertation, University of Oxford, UK.

Duraisamy, P. (1992). Effects of education and extension contacts on agricultural production. *Indian Journal of Agricultural Economics, 47.*

Edwards, S. (1993). Openness trade liberalization and growth in developing countries. *Journal of Economic Literature, 31.*

El-Ghonemy, M. (1990). *The political economy of rural poverty: the case for land reform.* New York: Routledge.

Fei, J. C. H., Ranis, G., & Stewart, F. (1985). *Towards viable balanced growth strategies: A locational perspective.* Paper prepared for UNIDO.

Fields, G. S. (1989). Changes in poverty and inequality in developing countries. *World Bank Research Observer, 4.*

Foster, A. D., & Rosenzweig, M. R. (1993). Information, learning, and wage rates in low-income rural areas. *Journal of Human Resources, 28.*

Foster, A. D., & Rosenzweig, M. R. (1994). *Technical change and human resources and investments: Consequences of the Green Revolution.* Mimeo, Philadelphia: University of Pennsylvania.

Foster, A. D., & Rosenzweig, M. R. (1995). Learning by doing and learning from others: Human capital and technical change in agriculture. *Journal of Political Economy, 103.*

Garcia, M. (1990). *Resource allocation and household welfare: A study of personal sources of income on food consumption, nutrition and health in the Philippines.* Ph.D. dissertation, Institute of Social Studies, The Hague.

Gemmell, N. (1995). *Evaluating the impacts of human capital stocks and accumulation on economic growth: Some new evidence.* Center for Research in Economic Development and International Trade, UK: University of Nottingham.

Gertler, P., Locay, L., & Sanderson, W. (1987). Are user fees regressive? The welfare implications of health care financing proposals in Peru. *Journal of Econometrics, 36.*

Grossman, G. M., & Helpman, E. (1991). *Innovation and growth in the global economy.* Cambridge, MA: MIT Press.

Haddad, L., & Bouis, H. (1991). The impact of nutritional status on agricultural productivity: Wage evidence from the Philippines. *Oxford Bulletin of Economics and Statistics, 53.*

Harbert, L., & Scandizzo, P. L. (1982). *Food distribution and nutrition intervention: the case of Chile.* Staff Working Paper 512. Washington, DC: World Bank.

Helliwell, J. F., & Putnam, R. (1995). Economic growth and social capital in Italy. *Eastern Economic Journal, 21.*

Hoddinott, J., & Haddad, L. (1991). *Household expenditures, child anthropometric status and the intra-household division of income: evidence from the Côte d'Ivoire.* Research Program in Development Studies, Discussion Paper 155, Woodrow Wilson School.

Immink, M., & Viterri, F. (1981). Energy intake and productivity of Guatemalan sugarcane cutters: An empirical test of the efficiency wage hypothesis. *Journal of Development Economics, 9.*

Jamison, D., & Moock, P. (1984). Farmer education and farm efficiency in Nepal: The role of schooling, extension services and cognitive skills. *World Development, 12.*

Jayaraman, R. (1995). On the meta-production front: An evidence-gathering exercise. Processed for UNDP, New York.

Keesing, D. B. (1966). Labor skills and comparative advantage. *American Economic Review, 56.*

Kenen, P. B. (1965). Nature capital and trade. *Journal of Political Economy, 73.*

King, E. M., & Bellew, R. (1988). *Education policy and schooling levels in Peru.* Mimeo the World Bank, Washington DC.

King, E. M., & Hill, M. A. (1993). *Women's education in developing countries: barriers, benefits, and policies.* The Johns Hopkins University Press, published for the World Bank, Baltimore.

King, E. M., & Lillard, L. A. (1987). Education policy and schooling attainment in Malaysia and the Philippines. *Economics of Education Review, 6.*

Klugman, J. (1995). Decentralization: A survey of the literature from a human development perspective. *Human Development Report Office Occasional Papers No. 12.*

Krueger, A. (1978). *Foreign trade regimes and economic development: liberalization attempts and consequences.* Cambridge, MA: Ballinger.

Lavy, V., Strauss, J., Thomas, D., & deVreyer, P. (1995). *The impact of the quality of health care on children's nutrition and survival in Ghana.* LSMS Working Papers, 106. Washington, DC: World Bank.

Learner, E. (1993). Factor-supply differences as a source of comparative advantage. *American Economic Review, 83.*

Lipton, M., & Ravallion, M. (1995). Poverty and policy. In J. R. Behrman & T. N. Srinivasan. *Handbook of development economics*, Vol. 3. Amsterdam: North Holland.

Lipton, M. (1977). *Why poor people stay poor: urban bias in world development.* London: Temple Smith.

Lucas, R. E. (1988). On the mechanics of economic development. *Journal of Monetary Economics, 22.*

Michaely, M. (1977). Exports and growth: an empirical investigation. *Journal of Developing Economies, 4.*

North, D. (1990). Institutions and their consequences for economic performance. In K. Cook & M. Levi, *The limits of rationality* (pp. 383–401). Chicago: University of Chicago Press.

OECD/DAC (1995). *Development Cooperation: Efforts and Policies of the Members of the Development Assistance Committee,* OECD, Paris.

Owens, T., & Wood, A. (1995). *Export-oriented industrialization through primary processing?* IDS Working Paper 19, Institute of Development Studies. University of Sussex, Brighton.

Pack, H., & Westphal, L. (1986). Industrial strategy and technological change: theory versus reality. *Journal of Development Economics, 22.*

Perotti, R. (1993). Political equilibrium income distribution and growth. *Review of Economic Studies, 60.*

Persson, T., & Tabellini, G. (1994). Is inequality harmful for growth?. *American Economic Review, 84.*

Pitt, M. M., Rosenzweig, M. R., & Hassan, M. N. (1990). Productivity health and inequality in the intrahousehold distribution of food in low-income countries. *American Economic Review, 80.*

Prud'homme, R. (1995). The dangers of decentralization. *The World Bank Research Observer, 10.*

Psacharopolous, G., Morley, S., Fiszbein, A., Lee, H., & Wood, B. (1992). *Poverty and income distribution in Latin America: the story of the 1980s.* Washington, DC: World Bank.

Psacharopolous, G. (1994). Returns to investment in education: a global update. *World Development, 22* (9), 1325–1343.

Ram, R. (1985). Exports and economic growth: some additional evidence. *Economic Development and Cultural Change, 33,* 415–425.

Rana, P. (1988). Exports policy changes and economic growth in developing countries after the 1973 oil shock. *Journal of Developing Economies, 8,* 261–264.

Ranis, G. (1979). Appropriate technology in the dual economy: reflections on Philippine and Taiwanese experience. In A. Robinson, *Appropriate technologies for Third World development.* New York: Macmillan.

Ranis, G., & Stewart, F. (1994). Decentralization in Indonesia. *Bulletin of Indonesian Economic Studies, 30.*

Ravallion, M., & Datt, G. (1991). *Growth and redistribution components of changes in poverty measure: A decomposition with applications to Brazil and India in the 1980s.* LSMS Working Papers #83. Washington, DC: World Bank.

Riddell, R., Robinson, M., deConinck, J., Muir, A., & White, S. (1995). *Nongovernmental organizations and rural poverty alleviation.* New York: Oxford University Press.

Romer, P. M. (1990). Endogenous technological change. *Journal of Political Economy, 98.*

Rosenzweig, M. R., & Schultz, T. P. (1982). Child mortality and fertility in Colombia: individual and community effects. *Health Policy and Education, 2,* 305–318.

Rosenzweig, M. R. (1995). Why are there returns in schooling? *American Economic Review, 85* (2).

Sahn, D. E., & Alderman, H. (1988). The effect of human capital on wages, and the determinants of labor supply in a developing country. *Journal of Development Economics, 29* (2).

Schultz, T. P. (1988). Education investments and returns. In H. Chenery & T.N. Srinivasan, *Handbook of Development Economics.* Amsterdam: North Holland.

Schultz, T. P. (1993a). Returns to women's education. In E. M. King & M. A. Hill, *Women's education in developing countries: barriers, benefits, and policies.* The Johns Hopkins University Press, published for the World Bank, Baltimore, MD.

Schultz, T. P. (1993b). Investments in the schooling and health of women and men: quantities and returns. *Journal of Human Resources, 28.*

Schultz, T. P., & Tansel, A. (1993). Measurement of returns to adult health. LSMS 95, World Bank, Washington, DC.

Schultz, T. W. (1975). The value of the ability to deal with disequilibria. *Journal of Economic Literature, 13.*

Selowsky, M. (1981). Nutrition health and education: The economic significance of complementarities at an early age. *Journal of Development Economics, 9.*

Selowsky, M., & Taylor, L. (1973). The economics of malnourished children: an example of disinvestments in human capital. *Economic Development and Cultural Change, 22*.

Sen, A. K. (1984). Rights and capabilities. In A. Sen, *Resources, values, and development*. Cambridge, MA: Harvard University Press.

Stewart, F. (1977). *Technology and underdevelopment*. London: Macmillan.

Strauss, J. (1986). Does better nutrition raise farm productivity?. *Journal of Political Economy, 94*.

Strauss, J., & Thomas, D. (1995). Human resources: Empirical modeling of household and family decisions. In J. R. Behrman & T. N. Srinivasan. *Handbook of development economics,* Vol. 3. Amsterdam: North Holland.

Strauss, J., & Thomas, D. (1996). Health, wealth and wages of men and women in urban Brazil. *Journal of Econometrics*.

Streeten, P., Burki, S. J., ul Haq, M., Hicks, N., & Stewart, F. (1981). *First things first: meeting basic needs in the developing countries*. New York: Oxford University Press.

Tanzi, V. (1995). *Fiscal federalism and decentralization: A review of some efficiency and macroeconomic aspects*. Mimeo, International Monetary Fund, Washington, DC.

Tendler, J., & Freedheim, S. (1994). Trust in a rent-seeking world: health and government transformed in northeast Brazil. *World Development, 22* (12), 1771–1791.

Thomas, D., Strauss, J., & Henriques, M. H. (1990). Child survival height-for-age and household characteristics in Brazil. *Journal of Development Economics, 33*.

Thomas, D., Strauss, J., & Henriques, M. H. (1991). How does mother's education affect child height. *Journal of Human Resources, 26*.

Thomas, D. (1990). Intrahousehold resource allocation: An inferential approach. *Journal of Human Resources, 25*, 4.

Thomas, D., Lavy, V., & Strauss, J. (1992). *Public policy and anthropometric outcomes in the Côte d'Ivoire*. LSMS Working Paper 89. Washington, DC: World Bank.

UNDP (various). *Human Development Report*. New York: Oxford University Press.

von Braun, J. (1988). Effects of technological change in agriculture on food consumption and nutrition: rice in a West African setting. *Economic Development and Cultural Change, 37*.

Welch, F. (1970). Education in production. *Journal of Political Economy, 78*.

Williamson, J. (1993). Human capital deepening, income inequality and demographic events along the Asia-Pacific Rim. In N. Ogawa et al. *Human resources in development along the Asia-Pacific rim*. Singapore: Oxford University Press.

Wolfe, B. L., & Behrman, J. R. (1987). Determinants of women's health status and health-care utilization in a developing country: a latent variable approach. *Review of Economics and Statistics, 56*.

Wolgemuth, J. C., Latham, M. C., Hall, A., & Crompton, D. (1982). Worker productivity and nutritional status of Kenyan road construction laborers. *American Journal* of *Clinical Nutrition, 36*.

Wood, A. (1994). North-South trade, employment and inequality: Changing fortunes in a skill-driven world. *IDS Development Studies Series*. Oxford: Oxford University Press.

World Bank (1995a). *Global economic prospects and the developing world*. Washington, DC: World Bank.

1.7

CHOICES THAT SHAPED
THE HUMAN DEVELOPMENT REPORTS

Inge Kaul

When we started work on the *Human Development Report*, the concept of human development, as we know it today, did not yet exist. In fact, it was not at all certain that the Reports would ever carry the *Human Development Report* label. And even after we had opted for the term "human development", it took us several years of intensive debates before the essential features of the concept found consensus within the Report team and made their way into the publication.

In the following paper, I review the ten basic conceptual choices we made – "we" being the Report team under the guidance of Mahbub ul Haq, together with our core consultants, notably Meghnad Desai, Gustav Ranis, Amartya Sen, Frances Stewart and Paul Streeten. Re-examining these choices from the vantage point of hindsight, I feel we mostly selected the right options, in the sense that the alternatives would by now have been at odds with global development realities, and the *Human Development Report* might not have remained as relevant and alive as it has. This may have been just luck on our part. But it also reveals Mahbub's approach to development and policy analysis. His advice was to keep our feet firmly rooted in the ground but to set our eyes on the stars; to link bold and radical ideas for change to incipient real-life changes. The Report did not dream up opportunities for reform – it helped to name them.

Choice 1: Human condition or human development?

Mahbub's original intention was to write a report about the human condition. The first background studies that we initiated in the spring of 1989 were very much focused on assessing the impact of the past decades of development on people's well-being. The studies explored how well economic growth, in different countries and under different policy regimes, had succeeded or failed in being translated into enhanced human capabilities, such as an expansion of life expectancy, better health or improved levels of education.

Yet what occurred to us when reading these studies was that while they presented a tremendous wealth of empirical facts and figures, people were invisible. The studies discussed human development in such categories as expenditures on basic education, changes in the rates of infant mortality or trends in (un)employment. But the voices of people speaking on how they saw and experienced development could not be heard; nor was there much debate about what people could do to better their own lives and contribute to global development if critical obstacles were removed.

We realized that simply assessing the impact of growth and other development dimensions on the human condition would make our analyses view people as passive beings to whom development was being handed out, if not handed down. This was not consistent with our interest in producing a report that would examine development from people's viewpoints and that would help work out how people could participate pro-actively in shaping and improving the conditions in which they live.

Thus, the challenge was to choose a term that would allow us to cover three important dimensions: whether and to what extent people have a say in matters that concern their lives; whether they have fair opportunities to contribute to development; and whether and to what extent they have a chance to obtain a fair share of the fruits of development. This meant searching for a term that described a process of human-centred development. It was on this basis that "human development" was selected.

Choice 2: Reducing poverty or improving well-being?

There was never any question that the first and most urgent task of any human development strategy had to be poverty reduction. Yet many debates centred on the issue of whether the *Human Development Report* and its main tools, such as the human development index (HDI), should focus exclusively on poverty or include the wider issue of human development up to *and beyond* the poverty line. Figure 1.6.1 illustrates this choice.

Two reasons in particular persuaded us to opt for the wider lens.

First, as many *Human Development Report* analyses have shown, poverty is often more a matter of lack of political will than an unavoidable reality. Hence, it constitutes a social debt. Reducing poverty will bring people to the point "zero" of development, which in all earnest will only start after that. From the viewpoint of the poor, it would

have been disappointingly modest if we had limited our ambitions merely to enabling them to cross the poverty line. Certainly, the enjoyment of basic human capabilities is critical. But human development beyond the poverty line does not happen automatically. It, too, needs to be carefully analysed, devised and promoted, even struggled for. Consider the many human development challenges that even rich countries face, ranging from problems of old-age security to environmental sustainability to control of communicable diseases.

Second, a report and strategies aimed exclusively or primarily at poverty reduction would have probably failed to mobilize requisite political support. By defining human development in a broader way as a process of widening human choices and improving well-being for all, we were able to attract the attention of politically more powerful and influential groups than the poor themselves. In fact, the wider notion of human development was particularly well received among people in the more advanced developing countries and in richer countries.

People in Latin America, for example, were attracted to the concept because of their negative experiences during the "lost development decade" of the 1980s. Indeed, they were strongly opposed to the original design of the HDI, which capped income and considered only basic education. For people in industrial countries, "human development" often provided an organizing concept for naming and synthesizing their experiences with decades of rapid economic growth accompanied by growing environmental challenges and a fraying social fabric. Many wholeheartedly agreed that, as the *Human Development Report* said, "Income is not the sum total of human life."

It was the choice we made for focusing on the improved well-being of all that led us to present the country rankings in terms of the HDI for all countries, in one table, beginning with the very first *Human Development Report*.

Choice 3: Closing gaps or widening human choices?

In some respects, this choice posed similar issues to the previous one. Like poverty reduction, "clos-

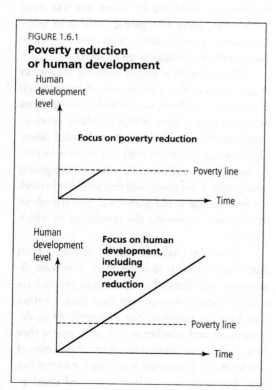

FIGURE 1.6.1

Poverty reduction or human development

Human development level

Focus on poverty reduction

----- Poverty line

→ Time

Human development level

Focus on human development, including poverty reduction

----- Poverty line

→ Time

ing a gap" suggests a norm, a desirable goal. "Widening people's choices", like the notion of the improved well-being of all, is a more open-ended concept. It entails the possibility of people choosing their own and sometimes even an alternative path of development.

I will never forget the admonition we received from a decisive Dutch feminist on this issue. The "gap tables", which appeared in the *Human Development Report* from 1990 to 1995, included one that expressed women's human development achievements in terms of those of men. No doubt, the data in this table were sometimes breathtaking in the enormous disparities they revealed. Nevertheless, the Dutch feminist contended that the goal of women is not to become like men, as our gap table seemed to suggest. Other similar tables measured the gaps in human development between rural and urban areas or between industrial and developing countries.

Interlocutors from developing countries also had doubts about the messages implied by the tables. In particular, they pointed to the situation of older persons in developing countries and the breakdown of family and local community ties, querying whether economic growth really warranted such costs. Many readers clearly welcomed and preferred our moving away from measuring gaps and the implicit suggestion that development should mean "more" of everything. They appreciated the Report's growing emphasis on participatory development – people having a say in matters that determine their lives, including choosing their own and distinctive path of development – because mounting evidence showed that a fairer process of decision-making and policy-making is an important, though not necessarily sufficient, precondition of a more just development outcome.

Choice 4: National human development or global human development?

Most of the human development comparisons presented in the early *Human Development Reports* compare the average human development levels achieved in one country to those of other countries. It was Amartya Sen, in particular, who underscored the importance of measuring (in)equity not only within countries or between countries but also globally – dispensing with national borders and looking at people just as people, not as citizens or residents of particular nations.

Of course, cross-border measurements of human development pose many conceptual and methodological challenges. Nevertheless, we followed Amartya's advice, and in *Human Development Report 1992* as well as in subsequent Reports we presented analyses that looked at the poor and the rich, irrespective of where they lived. These analyses echoed what many civil society organizations, among them human rights advocates, feminists and environmentalists, had long recognized – many of people's concerns cut across, and are oblivious to, national borders. They relate to universal life claims, shared objectives and common goals. To study them in a compartmentalized way, nation-state by nation-state, would be incorrect, since human-drawn borders may obstruct the realization of common claims and rights.

It was a daring step in the early 1990s to conduct development analyses "without borders". Today, with globalization more deeply entrenched, this approach seems quite obvious and normal.

Choice 5: National human development or disaggregated human development?

A related and similarly daring decision in the early 1990s was the disaggregation of the HDI according to sub-national groups, such as provinces, regions and states; rural and urban; male and female. We realized that a disaggregated HDI entailed a risk similar to the gap tables mentioned earlier. It could send the wrong signal – that the desired state of human development should be set at the level of the cities, the men or the rich. We took pains to avoid this message and to stress that the intention of the disaggregated HDI is to show which population groups enjoy the better human capabilities and hence the chance to shape future development according to their interests and concerns. It also reveals which groups have lost out in the past and risk being left behind in the future.

At the beginning of the 1990s, discussing national development trends in global reports was not yet a familiar phenomenon. The mindset of many policy-makers and diplomats was still that of the Cold War era, when governments had insisted on full policy-making sovereignty behind national borders, even if their policies were in violation of universal human rights, or ran counter to international commitments and treaties. Yet we felt that "putting people first" – making people's well-being the end of development, and political and economic actions and mechanisms the means towards this end – would require the Report to examine not only national averages and disparities between countries, but also inequities within countries.

Choice 6: Growth first or at least concurrently, versus no country is too poor to afford human development?

The *Human Development Report* initially came out in favour of the notion that no country is too poor to afford human development. It really does not cost much to end discrimination against women. Nor does it require a high income to stop torturing people or to guarantee freedom of speech and association. Even basic education and health care would often be within the reach of poor countries if they did not spend so much money on debt repayments, on the military, or on prestige and luxury projects.

If the goal is to go beyond poverty reduction, however, then economic growth and income expansion become important. We later modified our initial choice, as outlined in Choice 7 below. This repositioning of the human development concept was not unique; Choice 8 presents another example. We were quite proud of these modifications. Most of them resulted from extensive debates with various interlocutors and focus groups. They urged the change, and we thought that we should "walk our talk". If we suggested that people ought to have a say in matters that affect their lives, they should certainly have a say in defining the concept of human development, which is intended to enhance their visibility in development theory and practice. Let us now see why we opted for giving more weight to economic growth, income and wealth.

Choice 7: Human development for all or equitable human development?

Over several years, the *Human Development Reports* identified a trend towards growing inequity in global income. The figures are well known: between 1960 and the early 1990s, the ratio between the income of the world's richest quintile and that of its poorest quintile increased from 30:1 to 65:1 and later on to about 80:1. In drawing attention to these figures, our intention was not, in the first place, to be methodologically and statistically precisely right. We realized that the ratios used raise many issues and require refinements and corrections. Our main purpose was to highlight the question of whether the international community would be satisfied if human development, meaning betterment for all, is accompanied by rising inequities and inequalities, or whether the goal ought to be more equitable human development (figure 1.6.2).

If current human development did show a trend towards increasing inequity, the question

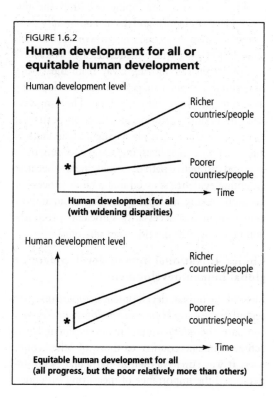

FIGURE 1.6.2
Human development for all or equitable human development

would be how to halt or even reverse that trend. Was there a mechanism of path dependency at work, which would cause present inequity to generate even wider inequity in the future? Did we have to consider leapfrogging options? What would these strategies require, in terms of accelerated social development as well as infrastructure and other types of economic development?

While each subsequent *Human Development Report* has made some added concessions to economic growth, a clear difference has remained between the Report's approach and that of other major reports, such as the World Bank's *World Development Reports*. We have tried to emphasize and explain that not just any type of economic growth would do; human development concerns have to be woven into the growth strategies selected. We have stressed that the type of economic growth that ignores people and relies on "re-distribution, if needed, later" may be less efficient in the long run than one that takes equity into account from the outset.[1] Just think of the high transaction costs involved in the recent demonstrations of civil society organizations at the international trade debates in Seattle in 1999 or at the global finance discussions in Prague in 2000. Or consider how long it took for national policymakers in developing countries and civil society organizations to find an international audience for their analyses of the shortcomings of the original Washington Consensus reform policies. As *Human Development Report 1991* stated, early structural adjustment programmes often attempted to balance budgets by unbalancing people's lives. The result was stifled human development, and hence stifled opportunities for entrepreneurship, growth and development.

So, while giving added importance to economic growth, the *Human Development Reports* always insisted that the pattern of growth matters: it ought to be growth that gives people a voice, involves them and benefits all. It is for the same reason that the *Human Development Reports* in recent years have strongly emphasized issues of global governance, including those related to knowledge management, and that UNDP has initiated a second strand of policy inquiry, viz. studies on global public goods.[2]

Choice 8: Pure human development or human development freed, greened and engendered?

Although telling us more about development than the GNP per capita measure, the HDI still reflects only a limited number of variables related to life expectancy, education and income. (For a more detailed discussion on the HDI, see section 2 of this volume.) Hence, it should not be a surprise that we have received many suggestions for the inclusion of further variables in the index from a large number of readers and interlocutors.

During the first five to six years of the Report's life, we resisted that temptation. (In later years, that choice was reversed somewhat with good reason.) Our motivation for keeping the original HDI more or less intact – at least in terms of the basic variables – was that it measured the key human capabilities that people the world over need in order to help themselves. It reflected universal human concerns.

Nevertheless, we realized that other issues matter enormously to human development – whether or not a society recognizes gender equity; whether or not it engages in racial discrimination; whether or not it degrades its environment; and whether or not it curtails political freedom.

In 1993, we factored gender into the HDI for the first time, and the ranking of many countries changed quite significantly: those with high degrees of gender equity moved up the HDI ranking ladder, while those with gender discrimination slipped down.

We tried to green the HDI in the early 1990s, but abandoned the effort because there were still many blank spots in the environmental data. Today, the greening of the index would be much more achievable, considering the wealth of data generated by the follow-up to the 1992 United Nations Conference on Environment and Development and its five-year review in 1997.

In 1991, we also attempted to construct a political freedom index (PFI). The reasoning was that human development, which implies the widening of human choices, could not occur under conditions of political repression. Human development and political freedom had to go hand in hand. Our intention was that one day, should the PFI find academic and political acceptance, we would be able to express the link between political freedom and human development by multiplying the value of the PFI by that of the HDI. The discussion in *Human Development Report 1991* on political freedom and the measures we presented there met with considerable criticism, however, notably from countries that at the time still had a long way to go towards democracy and political, social and economic pluralism. Therefore, in 1992, we made a modified attempt at introducing the issue. This time, we avoided individual country rankings and presented "collapsed" PFIs, in other words, measures for regions that hid individual country situations. Nevertheless, the topic was still too far ahead of its time. Reforms in terms of democracy, enhanced governance, accountability and transparency had just started and were still controversial in some countries. We realized, as many critics had argued, that assessing countries in terms of their current political freedom conditions could result in downgrading their first and very difficult and sensitive reform efforts. Another obstacle to the PFI was a series of conceptual and methodological problems. Political freedom was not so deep or well researched at that time, and our analyses had relied too strongly on Western, industrial-country-based studies and no doubt reflected some sociocultural biases.

Concerned that with so few PFI supporters among our worldwide readership we might lose our audience, we abandoned the PFI in 1993. But we were convinced that progress in human development would make the issue of political freedoms resurface one day, raised by people themselves, from the bottom up. So we concentrated on furthering a better understanding of human development. And in this we seem to have been proven right: the issue of fair and just participation in policy-making, nationally and internationally, is emerging as one of the key issues of the next decade. Fundamental questions are being raised about interactions between the state, civil society and business. A vibrant discussion is also taking place about the decision-making structures and distribution of voting power in intergovernmental organizations, a number of which were created at a time when many developing countries had not yet achieved their political independence.

Clearly, there is a need today for new measures of political freedom and political participation.

Choice 9: Global reports or national strategies?

Initially, the Report team was lean, and resources were limited and hard to obtain. In a bureaucratic context, innovation tends to meet with considerable opposition, and our initiative was no exception in this respect. We were faced with a tough choice: should we invest all available resources in the production of an annual Report or should we be bold, spread ourselves somewhat thinly and complement the global Report with national reports and country strategies for human development?

Mahbub's verdict was unambiguous: both are needed. He based his judgement on his experience as a minister of finance and planning in Pakistan. He often told us that no national minister would act on global analyses, however fascinating they were. Moreover, how much detail could we provide in the Report's usual 70 pages? Not enough.

We started the first round of five country reports and strategies in 1991/92. Today, more than 135 countries have prepared national human development reports, some written by civil society organizations, some by academics and some by government entities. Throughout the world, people and their leaders have an interest in finding out more precisely how people fare in development – in their country, state, province and district. This level of curiosity demonstrates how much more normal and human it is to be concerned about a good life than about the rather abstract indicators most other development studies contain. The *Human Development Report* and its national complements responded to an unmet information demand – a demand that revealed itself so clearly because of the choice to "go national", to add country, context and colour to the global analyses.

Choice 10: Academic correctness or effective communication?

Many excellent academic analyses never get heard. They may be written in a style that is not broadly accessible, or presented in a lengthy way that requires more time and attention than busy policy-makers can devote to any particular issue. Or the key findings may be accompanied by so many qualifications that by the end the reader may not know, for example, whether a specific trend is moving up or down.

Publishing a global Report on a worldwide basis, with the UN and UNDP name attached to it – even remotely – is a major responsibility. It demands correct and reliable analyses and policy recommendations that are credible and well thought through in terms of possible consequences, intended and unintended.

We have always aimed for the highest quality and reliability. But we have also wanted to be heard. This has often required us to be somewhat sharp in our statements, which in turn has sometimes meant skipping qualifications lest we confuse our audiences. Initially, it was a hard choice to make, especially since many of us came from an academic tradition. Yet we soon realized that communication was an art to be learned. Much to our relief, some of our most pointed statements have proven to be some of the most effective. We have found that a message needs a certain amount of "penetration force". If one presents all pros and cons, people tend to hear primarily the more familiar side of the story, not the new and really important dimension.

While the *Human Development Reports'* more focused outgoing messages may have been somewhat unbalanced, the end results have been positive. In striving to highlight our key points, we had to expand our vocabulary, to make it less dry and more accessible and striking. For example, instead of talking about "deteriorating terms of trade", we chose to say, "Poor farmers are compelled to sell their crops at dusk at cut-throat prices." Or, our critique of aid conditionality was couched in phrases such as, "Policy ownership is a plant that wilts under foreign pressure." And instead of acknowledging matter-of-fact current migration trends, we would say, "Poverty travels without a passport across borders." By now this type of language has become a hallmark of the Report.

CONCLUSION

The ten conceptual choices reviewed by this paper have played a significant role in defining the notion of human development as we know it today. Yet there was one critical point that the Human Development Report Team never debated. We all agreed with, and enthusiastically followed, one of Mahbub's basic principles of research and analysis. He taught us never to focus on figuring out why a good idea may not be achieved. While it is often important to know that, Mahbub urged us to think of change and to say, "Why not? Let's figure out how to make it work!"

I hope that besides enhancing our understanding of human development, the *Human Development Reports* have contributed to encouraging this spirit among our readers, and have evoked the determination to make change feasible and never to lose sight of the politics of change. Human development must place a priority on poverty reduction, but it must also offer something to the non-poor. It ought to be about widening human choices and improving well-being *for all*.

ENDNOTES

1. In fact, it was only in the 2000/2001 *World Development Report* that the World Bank team began in any systematic way to base its analyses on a participatory development concept. See: The World Bank. 2000. *The World Development Report 2000/2001*. New York: Oxford University Press.

2. See, for example: Kaul, Inge, Isabelle Grunberg and Marc A. Stern (eds.). 1999. *Global Public Goods: International Cooperation in the 21st Century*. New York: Oxford University Press. See also Faust, Michael, Inge Kaul, Katell Le Goulven, Grace Ryu and Mirjam Schnupf. 2001. *Global Public Goods: Taking the Concept Forward*. ODS Discussion Paper 17. UNDP, New York.

1.8
SHIFTING FASHIONS IN DEVELOPMENT DIALOGUE*

Paul Streeten

It used to be said that there are three forms of discourse: monologue, dialogue, and Balogh. My old tutor, mentor and friend, Thomas Balogh, who indeed practised a unique form of conversation, once wrote a book about fads and fashions in monetary economics. Had he been asked to write on the subject that I have chosen to attempt, he would probably have begun by saying that the models produced by the fads of development economics are elegant and shapely, but lack the vital organs. I would not have agreed.

It is true that sometimes the change in the fashions of thinking about development appears like a comedy of errors, a lurching from one fad to another, a wild goose chase. Economic growth, employment creation, jobs and justice, redistribution with growth, basic needs, bottom-up development, participatory development, sustainable development, market-friendly development, development as liberation, as liberalization, as freedom, human development; thus goes the carousel of the slogans. My own view is that there has been an evolution in our thinking about development, though there have also been periods of regress. Both internal logic and new evidence have led to the revision of our views. Previous and partly discarded approaches have taught us much that is still valuable, and our current approach will surely be subject to criticisms and be replaced by new insights. A brief survey of the progress of our thinking may be helpful. Our thinking about development and the place of people in it has, as I said, undergone an evolution, an uneven progress. Both internal logic and new evidence have led to the continual revision of our views. Previous and partly discarded approaches have taught us much that is still valuable, and our current approach will surely be subject to criticisms and be overtaken.

Thinking about the purpose of our social arrangements goes back at least to Aristotle. The full development of human beings as the end of all our activities was a recurring theme in the writings of most philosophers from the ancient Greeks to David Hume, Immanuel Kant, and John Stuart Mill, and of such political economists as Adam Smith, Karl Marx, Alfred Marshall, John Maynard Keynes and Mahbub ul Haq.

The discussion was resumed in the 1950s, when economic growth was emphasized as the key to poverty eradication. Even at this early stage, sensible economists and development planners were quite clear that economic growth is not an end in itself, but a performance test of development. In 1955 the Nobel Prize winning West Indian economist Arthur Lewis defined the purpose of development as widening "the range of human choice", exactly as the *Human Development Reports* since 1990 have done. The only difference is that Lewis had faith in the efficacy of economic growth for promoting this objective.

Three justifications were given for the emphasis on growth as the principal performance test. One justification assumed that through market forces – such as the rising demand for labour, rising productivity, rising wages, lower prices of the goods bought by the people – economic growth would spread its benefits widely and speedily, and that these benefits are best achieved through growth. Even in the early days some sceptics said that growth is not necessarily so benign. They maintained that in certain conditions (such as increasing returns, restrictions to entry, monopoly power, unequal initial distribution of income and assets), growth gives to those who already have; it tends to concentrate income and wealth in the hands of the few.

This is where the second assumption came in. It was that governments are concerned with the fate of the poor. Therefore progressive taxation, social services and other government interventions would spread the benefits downwards. The reduction of poverty would not be automatic (as on the first assumption), but governments would take action to correct situations in which market forces by themselves concentrated benefits in the hands of the few.

The third assumption was more hard-headed than the previous two. It said that the fate of the poor should not be a concern at the early stages of development. It was thought necessary first to build up the capital, infrastructure and productive capacity of an economy, so that it can improve the lot of the poor later. For a time – and it could be quite a long period – the poor would have to tighten their belts and the rich would receive most of the benefits. But if the rewards of the rich are used to provide incentives to innovate, to save and to accumulate capital, which could eventually be used to benefit the poor, the early hungry years would turn out to have been justified. Classical, neoclassical, and palaeo-Marxist economists all agreed on this. Some radical liberal philosophers such as John Rawls[1] would sanction such a strategy. Inequalities, in their view, are justified if they are a necessary condition for improving the lot of the poor.

Another powerful influence was the so-called Kuznets curve.[2] Named after Nobel laureate Simon Kuznets, it relates average income levels to an index of equality and suggests that the early stages of growth are accompanied by growing inequality. Only at an income per head of about $1,000 (in 1979 dollars) is further growth associated with reduced inequality. One measure of inequality is the share of the bottom 40 per cent of the population in total national income.

This association has been suggested by tracing the course of the same country over time (time series), and of different countries, with different incomes per head, at the same time (cross section). In the early stages of development, as income per head increases, inequality tends to grow. This may mean that absolute poverty for some groups also increases. But eventually the turning point, the bottom of the U-curve, is reached, after which growing income is accompanied by greater equality and, of course, reduced poverty. The golden age is ushered in.

None of the assumptions underlying these three justifications turned out to be universally true. Except for a very few countries – with special initial conditions, such as a radical land reform, and special policies, such as heavy emphasis on mass education and health measures – there was no automatic tendency for increasing incomes to be spread widely. Nor did governments often take corrective action to reduce poverty. Governments were themselves often formed by people who had close psychological, social, economic and political links with the beneficiaries of the process of concentrated growth, even though their motives were often mixed. And it certainly was not true that a period of enduring mass poverty was needed to accumulate savings and investment and to raise productivity. It was found that small farmers saved at least as high a proportion of their incomes as big landowners; that they were more productive, in terms of yield per acre; that entrepreneurial talent was widespread and not confined to large firms; and that some forms of consumption by the poor made them more productive. Prolonged mass poverty was therefore not needed to accumulate capital and to stimulate entrepreneurship.

To judge by the growth of the gross national product, the development process since World War II has been a spectacular, unprecedented and unexpected success. But at the same time there was increasing diversity of growth between different developing countries, and increasing dualism within many of them. Despite high rates of growth of industrial production and continued general economic growth, not enough employment was created for the rapidly growing labour force. Nor were the benefits of growth always widely spread, and the lower income groups often did not benefit.

In a much-quoted, classical article, Arthur Lewis had predicted that poor and low-productivity subsistence farmers and landless labourers would move from the countryside to the high-income, urban, modern industries.[3] This move would increase inequality in the early stages (so long as rural inequalities were not substantially greater than urban inequalities), but when more than a critical number of rural poor had been absorbed in modern industry, the golden age would be ushered in, when growth would be married to greater equality. In this way one explanation for the statistical association of the Kuznets curve was provided. It became evident, however, that the Lewis model, which strongly dominated not only academic thought but also political action, did not always work in reality. It did not apply for four reasons. First, the rural-urban differentials were much higher than had been assumed, owing to trade union action on urban wages, minimum wage legislation, differentials inherited from colonial days, and other causes. This produced an excess of migrants to the towns. Second, the rate of growth of the population and with it that of the labour force was much larger than expected: between 2 and 3 per cent per year. Third, the technology transferred from the industrial countries to the urban industrial sector of the developing countries was labour-saving, and although it raised labour productivity it did not create many jobs. Fourth, in many developing countries a productivity-raising revolution in agriculture was a precondition for substantial and widespread progress in industry, and this revolution had not occurred.

It was not surprising, then, that attention turned away from GNP and its growth. Some even wanted to "dethrone GNP" in the 1960s, not for the currently fashionable reason of environmental protection, but because it neglected employment and income distribution, jobs and justice. Since 1969 the International Labour Organization had attempted under the World Employment Programme to promote jobs in the developing countries. It had organized employment missions to several countries – Colombia, Kenya, the Philippines, Iran, Sri Lanka, the Dominican Republic, the Sudan and Egypt – to explore ways of creating more productive and remunerative employment. While this was an extremely useful learning exercise, it soon became evident that unemployment was not really the main problem. "Employment" and "unemployment" make sense only in an in-

dustrialized society where there are employment exchanges, organized and informed labour markets, and social security benefits for the unemployed, who are trained workers, willing and able to work, but temporarily without a job. Much of this does not apply to the poorest developing countries, in which livelihoods are more important than wage employment.

Another Nobel laureate, Gunnar Myrdal, tried to replace the concept of "employment" by the concept of "labour utilization". It has numerous dimensions when applied to self-employed subsistence farmers, landless labourers, artisans, traders, educated young people, saffron-clad monks, beggars, caste-conscious Brahmins, or women, in societies without organized labour markets. "Employment" as interpreted in industrial countries was found not to be the appropriate concept. To afford to be unemployed, a worker has to be fairly well off. To survive, an unemployed person must have an income from another source. The root problem, it was found, is frequently poverty, or low-productivity employment, not unemployment. Many of the moderately poor are not unemployed but work very hard and long hours in unremunerative, unproductive forms of activity. True, among the poorest of the poor, unemployment can be a common form of suffering, but even then its roots are quite different from those of unemployment in industrial countries.

The discovery that the problem is often unremunerative work of low productivity drew attention to the informal sector: the street traders, garbage collectors and casual workers, as well as many in small-scale production such as blacksmiths, carpenters, sandal makers, builders and lamp makers. These people often work extremely hard and long hours, are self-employed or employed by their family, and are sometimes very poor. Attention was also directed to the women who, in some cultures, perform hard tasks without being counted as members of the labour force because their production is not sold for cash. The problem was then redefined as that of the "working poor".

Labour utilization covers more dimensions than the demand for labour (the lack of which gives rise to Keynesian unemployment) and the need for cooperating factors of production such as machinery and raw materials (the lack of which gives rise to Marxian "non-employment"). There is a good deal of evidence that not only labour but also capital is grossly underutilized in many developing countries. This suggests other causes for underutilization than surplus labour in relation to scarce capital. More specifically, the causes of low labour utilization can be classified under four headings: consumption and levels of living (including education and health), attitudes, institutions and policies.

Nutrition, health and education are elements of the level of living that are important for fuller labour utilization. They have been neglected because in advanced societies they count as consumption and this has no effect on human productivity. The only exceptions that have been admitted in the literature until recently are some forms of education. In poor countries, however, better nutrition, health, education and training can be very productive forms of investment in human capital. This is one thread that goes into the later fabric of human development.

The second dimension, attitudes, makes a difference in the kinds of jobs people will accept. In Sri Lanka, for example, a large part of unemployment is the result of the high aspirations of the educated, who are no longer prepared to accept "dirty" manual jobs. Caste attitudes in India also present obstacles to fuller labour utilization. In Africa those with primary education wish to leave the land and become clerks in government offices. In many societies manual work or rural work is held in contempt.

The third dimension is the absence or weakness of such institutions as labour exchanges, credit facilities, marketing organizations, centres of information and a system of land ownership or tenancy that provides incentives and ability to till the soil. As a result, labour is underutilized.

Finally, wrong policies for fuller labour utilization are often adopted: labour in the organized sector is overpriced, capital is underpriced, food bought from the small growers is underpriced, the exchange rate is overvalued, making labour-intensive exports difficult, etc.

For reasons such as these the concepts of unemployment and underemployment as understood in the North were found to be not applicable, and an approach to poverty that assumes levels of living, skills, attitudes and institutions fully adapted to full labour utilization has turned out to be largely a dead end. Unemployment can coexist with considerable labour shortages and capital underutilization.

Inappropriate attitudes and institutions can also frustrate some approaches to meeting basic needs. Focusing on the needs of men, women and children draws attention to the appropriate institutions (such as land reform, public services, and credit facilities) to which households need access, and to the attitudes (such as those towards women's welfare) that need changing to secure better distribution within the household.

The employment concept was questioned for other reasons too. The creation of more employment opportunities, far from reducing unemployment, increases it. Those who come from the countryside to the towns in search of jobs balance the expectation of high earnings against the probability of getting a job.[4] As job opportunities increase, they attract more people. The influx of migrants in turn contributes to the high rate of urban drift and the growth of shantytowns. The employed urban workers, though poor by Western standards, are among the better-off when measured against the distribution of income in their own countries.

These difficulties turned the development debate to the question of income distribution. One of the landmarks was the book published in 1974 for the Development Research Center of the World Bank and the Sussex Institute of Development Studies, entitled *Redistribution with Growth*.[5] Among many questions about the relations between growth and redistribution were the following: do conventional measures of growth involve a bias against the poor, and how can this be changed? How can strategies of redistribution be combined with strategies of growth? Is it possible to identify groups whose members have common characteristics and to direct strategies towards those groups? What are the principal instruments of policy? The book also raised two sets of questions, of special interest in the present context:

- What can be done to increase the productivity of the small-scale, labour-intensive, informal sector "discovered" by the ILO employment mission to Kenya? How can we remove discrimination against this sector and improve its access to information, credit and markets? The question is: how does redistribution affect efficiency and growth? Does helping the "working poor" mean sacrificing productivity? Is it an efficient way of promoting growth?
- To turn the question the other way around, how does economic growth affect distribution? It was quite clearly seen that in low-income countries economic growth is a necessary condition for eradicating poverty, but it also seemed that economic growth sometimes reinforced and entrenched inequalities in the distribution of incomes, assets and power. Not surprisingly, when growth began with an unequal distribution of assets and power, it was more difficult to redistribute incomes and to eradicate poverty. And the results of redistributing out of incremental income turned out to be pitifully small. According to one simulation exercise, an annual transfer of 2 per cent of GNP over 25 years into public investment to build up the stock of capital available to the poor – thought to be a very "dynamic" policy – would, after 40 years, raise the consumption of the poorest 40 per cent of the population by only 23 per cent; that is to say, their rate of consumption growth would accelerate by 0.5 per cent a year: $1 for a $200 income. The model excludes, however, the human capital aspects of some forms of consumption and the impact on labour utilization, which are stressed by the basic needs approach.

In spite of its title, most of *Redistribution with Growth* is concerned not with relative income shares but with the level and growth of income in low-income groups. Much of the redistribution literature measures inequality by the Gini coefficient, which runs through the whole range of incomes, from the richest to the poorest. It measures somewhat meaningless percentiles instead of socially, regionally, or ethnically significant deprived groups. It does not tell who is in these decile groups, for how long, or for what reasons. Nor does it indicate the scope for mobility or the degree of equality of opportunity. Normally there is no particular interest by those concerned with poverty reduction in redistribution to the middle, which would reduce inequality but leave poverty untouched. Nor is the fate of income deciles as such of much interest, for these are not sociologically, politically, or humanly interesting groups.

An empirical question is how economic growth affects the reduction of inequality and poverty, and how this reduction in turn affects efficiency and economic growth. The answers to these questions will depend on the initial distribution of assets; the policies pursued by the government; the available technologies; the scope for labour-intensive exports, which enlarges the application of labour-intensive technologies; and the rate of population growth. Land reform and access to basic mass education are preconditions for equitable growth, but they are not enough. Continuing policies and vigilance are needed to prevent large inequalities from reestablishing themselves, even if they are eliminated initially. Another important empirical question is how policies to reduce inequalities and meet basic needs affect freedom and human rights.

It is true that we do not have a production function for meeting adequate standards of nutrition, health, education and family planning. It is not known precisely which financial, fiscal, and human resources and policies produce these desirable results. The causes are multiple and interact in a complex and still partly unknown manner. But at least it is fairly clear when the objective has been attained, and the criteria by which it is judged are also clear.

After the disappointment with growth, after the dead end of "employment" as interpreted in industrial countries, and after the limitation and irrelevance of egalitarianism and redistribution, basic human needs were the next logical step in development thinking. The basic needs approach emphasized that income increases are not enough to reduce poverty. Mass education, safe water, family planning, health services and other priorities depend on public action. Some poor people are incapable of earning income. The basic needs approach has also always called for participatory community involvement and self-governing institutions in the design and implementation of projects and programmes. The best shorthand way of describing the basic needs approach is: incomes + public services + participation.

The basic needs approach had at least four advantages over previous approaches to growth, employment, income redistribution and poverty eradication. First, the basic needs concept is a reminder that the objective of development is to provide all human beings with the *opportunity* for a full life. However a "full life" is interpreted, the opportunity for achieving it presupposes meeting basic needs. In the previous decades those concerned with development have sometimes become lost in the technical intricacies of means – growth rates, production, productivity, savings ratios, export ratios, capital-output ratios, tax ratios, and so on – and lost sight of the end. They also emphasized the economic component of development at the expense of non-material components that contribute to human development. They came near to being guilty, to borrow a term from Karl Marx, of "commodity fetishism". Being clear about the end obviously must not imply neglecting the means: on the contrary, it means efforts are directed at choosing the right means for the ultimate ends that are desired. In the past, planners have moved away from one aim of development, which is meeting basic needs, to some conglomeration of commodities and services valued at market prices, irrespective of whether they are air conditioners or bicycles, luxury houses or rural shelters, whether they benefit the rich or the poor, and irrespective of non-economic costs and benefits such as human rights, freedom and participation. The basic needs approach recalled the fundamental concern of development, which is human beings and their needs.

Second, the approach went behind abstractions such as money, income or employment. These aggregates have their place and function;

they are important concepts and, though in need of revision, should not be abandoned; but they are useless if they conceal the specific, concrete objectives that people themselves seek. To consider basic needs is to move from the abstract to the concrete, from the aggregate to the specific, from commodities to people.

The evolution sketched above shows that the concepts have become decreasingly abstract and increasingly disaggregated, concrete, and, above all, centred on people. Starting with GNP and its growth, a highly abstract and unspecified conglomerate of goods and services, irrespective of what, how, for whom, and for what, development thinking then turned to employment, a somewhat more specific goal. The discussion was then narrowed down to particular groups of unemployed: school leavers, recent migrants to the city, landless labourers, small-scale farmers without secure water supply and so forth. But "employment" also was seen to have serious limitations. Ideas were next further narrowed to identify deprived groups of individuals and families – women, children under five, the elderly, youths with specific needs, ethnic groups discriminated against, communities in distant and neglected regions. Economic growth is no longer the ultimate objective of economic development, but an incidental result of aiming at the right composition, distribution and use of production, and a satisfying way of accomplishing it, for the present and future generations.

Third, the basic needs approach appealed to members of national and international aid-giving institutions and was therefore capable of mobilizing resources, unlike vaguer (though important) objectives, such as raising growth rates to 6 per cent, contributing 0.7 per cent of GNP to development assistance, redistributing for greater equality, or narrowing income gaps. People do not share normally lottery prizes or other gains in wealth with their adult brothers and sisters, but they do help when their siblings are ill, or their children need education, or some other basic need has to be met. The same is true in the wider human family. Meeting basic needs has some of the characteristics of a public good. One person's satisfaction from knowing that a hungry child is fed does not detract from other people's satisfaction. The basic needs approach therefore has the power to mobilize support for policies that more abstract notions lack.

Fourth, the basic needs approach has great organizing and integrating power intellectually, as well as politically. It provides a key to the solution of problems that are at first sight separate, but, on inspection, prove to be related. If basic needs are made the starting point, these otherwise recalcitrant problems fall into place and become solvable.[6]

In one sense, this was a homecoming. For when the world embarked on development more than half a century ago, it was primarily with the needs of the poor in mind. Third World leaders wanted economic as well as political independence, but independence was to be used for people's self-fulfilment. The process got sidetracked, but many important discoveries about development were made: the importance of making small-scale farmers and members of the informal urban sector more productive and raising their earning power; the scope for "efficient" redistribution, that is, redistribution that contributes to more equitable economic growth; the numerous dimensions of labour markets; and the importance of creating demand for certain types of products and the labour producing them.

A common minimum formulation of the objectives of development is sustainable growth (of consumption) with equity, or, better, with rapid poverty reduction. Equity means that there should not be unfair or unjustified discrimination. Some poverty reduction may have to be unequal, in the sense that not all the poor can become better off at the same time, so that some groups, or some regions, may have to be favoured, at least for a time. This is particularly important if the selective policy favouring one group eventually helps to eradicate more speedily the poverty of those left behind.

We should distinguish between inequality and inequity. If A, whose situation is in all relevant respects the same as E's, has more than E, that is inequality; if he or she has more *because E has less*, or if E has less *because A has more*, that is inequitable or iniquitous. But even where exploitative and iniquitous inequality is absent, we should still be concerned with the fate of the poor.

Both poverty and some forms of inequality are evils, but poverty is the greater evil.

And inequality can also be a source of hope when those left behind rightly think that they can catch up with those ahead and grasp the opportunities for advance by their own efforts.

Equality can refer to many things: income, resources, utility, achievements, primary goods, opportunities, freedom, human rights, the right to vote, etc. Equality in one dimension means inequality in another. Even those most wedded to free markets who think that more productive work deserves higher rewards believe in equality of opportunity; those who believe in markets believe in equality of freedom to choose. The basic aim is to find a practical conception of equality that can give people a sense that they receive equal consideration from society and so have a stake in it. The kind of equality denounced by Anatole France when he wrote "the law in its majestic equality forbids the rich as well as the poor to sleep under bridges, to beg in the streets, and to steal bread" is not enough. Equality of freedom to choose is generally acknowledged as desirable.

Raising production and productivity of the poor, although important, is not enough. Many productivity gains in the Third World have been passed on to foreign buyers (e.g., in lower prices of export crops) or to large multinational corporations, or to the better-off groups at home. The gains must also be remunerative for the poor, as well as productive.

But basic needs comprises more than economic benefits. We may also wish to add the objective of security and stability: economic, political and legal.

Greatly fluctuating gains and insecure jobs are discounted, even if their average is larger than a more stable, though lower level. So, as a first approximation, the objective became productive, remunerative, sustainable, stable and equitable growth of consumption (or, to remove the ambiguities in "equity", growth with rapid reduction of absolute poverty).

But this does not exhaust the range of objectives. Some of the most important contributions to poverty reduction, reflected in what poor people actually want, do not show up in growth figures, and are not achieved by economic growth. Poverty is multidimensional and cannot be subsumed under one or two or a few indicators of deprivation.

As the basic needs concept entered the North-South dialogue all sorts of misconceptions and misinterpretations grew around it.[7] First, it was said that basic needs are confined to basic commodity bundles and that the choices are limited: educational services, health services, food, shelter. It amounts to a prescription of "count, cost and deliver": count the poor, cost the bundle and deliver it to the "target groups" (people who are not only got at, but, metaphorically, shot at, instead of being regarded as active agents). Second, it was thought that the role allotted to the state was too powerful, both in determining what basic needs are and in providing for their being met, and that this type of paternalism is both inefficient and unworthy. Third, it was held that there was a neglect of opening up opportunities to people: access to jobs, income, assets, credit, power were neglected in favour of so many calories, so many yards of cloth.

Opposition in developing countries also grew, particularly to the use of the concept by donor countries. Some of the objections raised by the developing countries were justified, such as the use of the concept as an excuse to reduce development aid and to put up protectionist barriers, or its use to divert attention from the need to reform the system of international relations; others reflected the vested interests of the rich in the poor countries who resist attempts to reduce their power and wealth. Similarly, the rich countries raised both legitimate and illegitimate objections. The result was that the concept faded away in international conversations, although it has still adherents among many of the drafters of plans in the developing countries, among private voluntary organizations and activists, and among thinkers and those with common sense.

The 1980s were a period of crisis, of setbacks and retreats. The debt problem, and adjustment and stabilization policies were the principal concern. Stabilization was sought through deflationary policies that reduced output and employment. The poor were either forgotten or, instead of seeking ways to reduce their number, ways were sought to prevent an increase.

Many criticisms were voiced against the prescriptions of the International Monetary Fund. Among them was the charge that IMF recommendations attempt to solve structural problems, such as an oil price increase in oil-importing countries, or a permanent deterioration in the terms of trade for some other reason, by monetary restrictions, thereby inflicting unnecessary unemployment, underutilization of capacity and forgone production, as well as being counterproductive by depriving firms of the means to invest in the exploration of new deposits and in related industries, in oil substitutes and in conservation.

Another criticism is that the Fund concentrates on reducing demand instead of increasing supplies, on cutting imports rather than expanding exports. During the 1980s many countries, instead of raising exports and reducing imports, found that both their exports and imports were reduced. It is almost always possible to achieve stabilization and correction of the balance of payments by policies that reduce income, demand and employment sufficiently, without reallocating resources to investment and exports, in other words without fundamental adjustment. The criticism is that the IMF has advocated this kind of "stabilization without adjustment".

At the same time, this period witnessed a world-wide surge to freedom, democratic government and demand for participation. During the 1980s, and while stabilization and adjustment policies were pursued, new concerns were incorporated in the development dialogue: the role of women (and children), the physical environment, population, habitation, human rights, political freedom and governance, empowerment, corruption, the waste of military expenditure and the "peace dividend", and the role of culture among them. The basic needs approach was regarded as too narrowly focused on commodity bundles delivered to people by the government, and it had to carry the ballast of past misinterpretations.

At this time in the 1980s several authors proposed a variety of "new growth theories". These have a bearing on the relation between human development and economic growth. The observation that output has grown faster than population for over 200 years, while different countries have remained on different growth paths, was an important motivation for the construction of these new models. In the older growth theories growth is seen as the result of the accumulation of productive factors and of exogenous technological progress that makes factors more productive. In the new growth theories the emphasis is switched to the way the changes in total factor productivity can be related to several external economies (benefits from investment to others than those who incur the costs) that are present in most economies and to the acquisition of knowledge, education and on-the-job training. In this framework the long-term growth rate is not determined by the exogenous rate of technical progress, but by the behaviour of people responsible for the accumulation of productive factors and knowledge.

There are two implications of this switch. First, growth is not explained by technological progress that comes from outside the economic system but by the "endogenous" behaviour of people. Second, education and knowledge, particularly in the form of research and development (R&D), incorporated in human or physical capital or in books and blueprints, play an important part in increasing total productivity and thus in enhancing growth.

The impact of higher levels of education is twofold. First, a better-educated and trained workforce raises the productivity of the cooperating factors because better educated people are more likely to innovate and to be more efficient in general. Second, better education benefits others who can now earn more, in addition to the educated person.

R&D similarly improves not only the productivity and profitability of the firm that invests in it, but also those of other firms or individuals who buy its products. Moreover, some discoveries are freely accessible to all firms that can benefit from them. In these ways investing in human capital can overcome the diminishing returns of investing in physical capital. It follows from the external benefits of education, R&D and knowledge generally that private agents will tend to underinvest in them and that public interventions such as subsidies are necessary to ensure adequate investment.

A problem with any model that emphasizes a single factor, such as education or R&D, as the driving force of development is that it is easy to point to counter-examples. Although it is true that, looking at many countries, a correlation between economic growth and education can be found, there are also important exceptions. Sri Lanka had high levels of widespread education without spectacular growth, while Brazil enjoyed high growth rates with low levels of education. Reality is more complicated than single factor models suggest.

The 1980s were also the time when Amartya Sen set out to propose an alternative approach to utility and "welfarism", expanding and deepening the basic needs approach. People value commodities, he argued, not in their own right but for their characteristics and for the needs they meet. But going beyond this, he noted that the results of consuming commodities depend also on the characteristics of the consumer (whether he or she is able-bodied or disabled) and the society of which he or she is a member. Sen also emphasized that freedom to choose is important to well-being. The well-being of a fasting monk is different from that of a starving pauper. The standard of living should be judged by a person's "capability" to lead the life that he or she values, from being well fed and healthy to achieving self-respect and participating in the life of the community.

The time had come for a wider approach to improving the human condition that would cover all aspects of human development, for all people, in both high-income and developing countries, both now and in the future. It went far beyond narrowly defined economic development to cover the full flourishing of all human capabilities. It emphasized again the need to put people, their needs, their aspirations, and their choices, at the centre of the development effort. And to assert the unacceptability of any biases or discrimination, whether by class, gender, race, nationality, religion, community or generation. Human development had arrived.

The first *Human Development Report* of the United Nations Development Programme, published in 1990 under the inspiration and leadership of its great architect, Mahbub ul Haq, came after a period of crisis and retrenchment, in which concern for people had given way to concerns for balancing budgets and payments. It met a felt need and was widely welcomed. Human development was defined as a process of enlarging people's choices, not just between different detergents or television channels or car models, but of jobs, education and leisure pursuits. These choices can change over time and can, in principle, be infinite. Yet, infinite choices without limits and constraints can become pointless and mindless. Choices have to be combined with allegiances, rights with duties, options with bonds, liberties with ligatures. It is true that bonds without options are oppressive; but options without bonds are anarchic. Indeed, choices without bonds can be as oppressive as bonds without choices.

Just as at the end of the 19th century the reaction against extreme Manchester liberalism took the form of "collectivism", not nowadays a popular concept, so today we see a reaction against the extreme individualism of the free market approach towards what has come to be called communitarianism. The exact combination of individual and public action, of human agency and social institutions, will vary from time to time and from problem area to problem area. Institutional arrangements will be more important for achieving environmental sustainability, personal agency more important when it comes to the choice of household articles or marriage partners. But some complementarity will always be necessary.

Among the most important choices is the ability of people to lead a long and healthy life, to acquire knowledge, and to have access to the resources needed for a decent standard of living. If these essential choices are available, many other opportunities are opened. These three basic choices are reflected in the human development index. But many additional choices are valued by people. These range from political, social, economic and cultural freedoms to opportunities for being productive and creative, and enjoying self-respect and human rights.

Human development has two sides: (1) the formation of human capabilities, such as improved health, knowledge and skills, and (2) the use people are willing, able and permitted to make of these capabilities: for leisure, productive purposes, or participation in cultural, social and political activities. The rapid expansion of these capabilities – including those associated with education, health, social security, credit, gender equality, land rights, and local democracy – depends crucially on public action that is neglected by many developing countries. On the other hand, by removing itself from excessive regulation and bureaucratic interventions in production and trade, the government can also contribute to expanding social opportunities.

The use of these capabilities can be frustrated if the opportunities for their exercise do not exist or if people are deprived of these opportunities as a result of discrimination, obstacles or inhibitions: if there is no demand for their productive contributions so that people are unemployed, or if there are legal or social or conventional restrictions on their employment, or if they do not have enough leisure, or if political oppression or deprivation of human rights prevents them from full participation in the life of their communities. There can be "jobless" growth, there can be "voiceless" growth, there can be "rootless" growth, and there can be jobless, voiceless and rootless nongrowth. Different countries illustrate each of these cases.

Getting income is one of the options people would like to exercise. It is an important, but not an all-important option. Human development includes the expansion of income and wealth, but it includes many other valued and valuable things as well.

For example, in investigating the priorities of poor people, one discovers that what matters most to them often differs from what outsiders assume. More income is only one of the things desired by poor people. Adequate nutrition, safe water at hand, better medical services, more and better schooling for their children, cheap transport, adequate shelter, continuing employment and secure livelihoods, and productive, remunerative, satisfying jobs do not show up in higher income per head, at least not for some time.

There are other non-material benefits that are often more highly valued by poor people than material improvements. Some of these partake in the characteristics of rights, both positive and negative, others in those of states of mind. Among these are good and safe working conditions, freedom to choose jobs and livelihoods, freedom of movement and speech, self-determination and self-respect, independence, mobility, liberation from oppression, violence and exploitation, less dependence on patrons, security from persecution and arbitrary arrest, not having to move in search of work, a satisfying family life, the assertion of cultural and religious values, access to power or direct empowerment, recognition, status, adequate leisure time and satisfying forms of its use, a sense of purpose in life and work, the opportunity to join and participate actively in the activities of civil society, and a sense of belonging to a community. These are often more highly valued than income, both in their own right and as means to satisfying and productive work. They do not show up in higher income figures. No policy-maker can guarantee the achievement of all, or even the majority, of these aspirations, but policies can create the *opportunities* for their fulfilment.

Economic growth can be quite rapid without an improvement in the quality of life of the majority of the people, and many countries have achieved a high quality of life with only moderate growth rates of income. It has been observed that there is a positive correlation between income per head and the indicators of human development. Some have drawn the erroneous conclusion that it is only income that matters. But, first, this relationship is far from perfect, and interesting questions are raised by the outliers and particularly by countries that have achieved high human development at low levels of income; and, second, this relation depends entirely on the extra income that arises from growth being used for public education and health and for specific attacks on poverty. If these two conditions are absent, the correlation disappears.[8] Much depends also on the initial distribution of assets. If land ownership is fairly equally distributed and mass education is widespread, the benefits of economic growth will be reflected in good human development.

Economic growth is often considered to be an essential component of human development. But growth (in the narrow sense of a continuing increase in the quantity of goods and services produced and consumed over time) is simply the intertemporal dimension of any policy objective, although it has been wrongly monopolized by production and consumption: it should apply to poverty reduction, employment, investment, a more equitable income distribution, environmental protection, leisure, and, of course, also to income. But once you specify for income, consumption and production – the what? to whom? by whom? for what? and when? – growth becomes the incidental result, not the objective, of a sensible economic policy. Growth is too unspecified, abstract, aggregate and unbounded to be a sensible objective of policy. It also implies an infinite horizon, without limits to increases in income. What matters is the composition of the national income; to what uses it is put; its distribution among beneficiaries, now and for future generations; and with how much effort and in what conditions it is produced. If and only if the extra resources resulting from growth go largely to the poor, and if they are spent on public health and education, will a contribution to human development result.

National income is a quite inadequate measure of human development for several reasons. It counts only goods and services that are exchanged for money, leaving out of account the large amount of work done inside the family, mainly by women, and work done voluntarily for children or older people or in communities. Public services are counted at their cost, so that doubling the wages of all public servants appears to double their contribution to welfare or development. National income accounting does not distinguish between goods and regrettable necessities, like military or anti-crime expenditure, products needed to combat "bads". Addictive eating and drinking is counted twice: when the food and the alcohol are consumed, and when large sums are spent on the diet industry and on cures for alcoholism. Much of what is now counted as economic growth is really either combating evils, and fixing blunders and social decay from the past, or borrowing resources form the future, or shifting functions from the community and household to the market.[9]

National income accounting does not add leisure gained by fewer working hours on earlier retirement age, and does not subtract from the extra income generated by the leisure lost if women are forced (or desire) to take on jobs outside the family, or men to take on a second job. Environmental degradation, pollution and resource depletion are not deducted, so that the earth is treated, it has been said, like a business in liquidation. Freedom, human rights and participation are ignored. It would be perfectly possible to attain high incomes per head and the satisfaction of all material needs in a well-managed prison. Most important, the conventional measure does not allow for the distribution of the income, counting all goods and services at their market prices.

Increasing the production of whisky, bought by rich men, counts for much more than increasing the production of milk that would have gone to a starving child. Attempts have been made here and there to correct these faults and omissions, but national income remains a quite inadequate measure of economic welfare or of human development.

Some of these shortcomings can be removed by adjustments in the accounting methods. These concern those components of well-being that can be, in principle, brought into relation with the measuring rod of money. A monetary value can be attached to leisure time. Income distribution can be allowed for by attaching greater weights to the incomes and their growth of the bottom 20 per cent or 30 per cent or 40 per cent of the population. Depletion of non-renewable raw materials can be evaluated and a measure for sustainable income can be designed.

For other components of choice and welfare monetary measurement is much more difficult or may be impossible. The enjoyment we derive from an unspoiled wilderness; the satisfaction from work; political engagement that results from participation; the sense of community, brotherhood and sisterhood that grows out of social activities; the freedom, peace and sense of security that are common in a well-run society – these cannot easily be reduced to dollars and cents. Yet they form the essence of human development.

The contributing tributaries to human development can be grouped under five headings: (1) economic growth, (2) human resource development, (3) human rights and participation, (4) peace and security, and (5) sustainability. The role of culture is discussed under the heading of human rights and participation. Issues of equity and in particular of gender equity run through all five tributaries.

We now live in a "risk society". People are bombarded with assessments of the risks of decisions (from what they eat to whether they should build nuclear power stations). They have lost the old certainties about how their lives will turn out: no more jobs, or marriages, for life.

Human development is the end, the tributaries are the means; but they can also acquire end characteristics themselves. Environmental sustainability, peace, participation, human resources and by some even economic growth are valued in their own right. To the extent that they are ends, they all have to be included in human development. The five tributaries can augment each other, for example, when human resources contribute to higher growth, or respect for human rights advances peace. There are also feedbacks from achievements in human development to further improvements in human development. These may be indirect by improving the five components (economic growth, human resource development, human rights and participation, peace and security, and sustainability), or they may be direct. The latter occur within and between families when knowledge is passed on and when better education of mothers has an impact on their children. Several studies have shown that women's education, control over cash income, and access to power, in addition to being desirable in themselves, improve the health, nutrition and education of children, reduce fertility, reduce infant mortality, reduce health hazards to adults arising from low birth weight, raise productivity, reduce inequality, are beneficial for the environment, and increase the range and effectiveness of public debates.

Gender issues are particularly important for reproductive freedom, for people, especially women, to be able to choose the size of their families. There is now a wealth of evidence to show that given the opportunity to choose smaller families without adverse economic and social consequences, smaller families are indeed chosen. With human development, that is with the expansion of education, especially of girls and women, the reduction of infant mortality rates, and the provision of medical facilities (including the opportunity of birth control), fertility rates have come down sharply. It may seem paradoxical that reduced infant mortality rates should contribute to reduced population growth. But there is overwhelming evidence that parents try to over-insure themselves against the deaths of their children (particularly sons) and that more surviving children reduce the desired family size. Human development is the best way to reduce population growth, and reduced population growth advances human development. Human development, in addition to longer life expectancy, better education and securer lives, makes it possible for people to opt for smaller families.

It is thought that some of these links lend themselves more easily to measurement than others. The human resources of education can be captured under literacy rates and school enrolment rates; of health under life expectancy and infant mortality. It is for this reason that more attention has been paid to these links than to others, such as that between participation and human development, not so readily brought into relation with a measuring rod. Some may have become victims of the fallacy that what cannot be counted does not count or even exist. But it may be questioned whether the quality of education or the attitudes that a good education instills, such as punctuality, discipline, team work, etc., are caught under the conventional statistical social indicators. The same goes for health measures. Economic growth, based on increases in GNP, has, of course, been the archetypical case of counting and has attracted the limelight of attention.

The most eye-catching and headline-making contribution of the *Human Development Reports* has been the human development index. It comprises (1) the logarithm of GDP per head, calculated at the real purchasing power, not at exchange rates, up to the international poverty line;

(in Reports after the 1990 Report this was modified in various ways); (2) literacy rates (and, since the 1991 Report, mean years of schooling); and (3) life expectancy at birth. These disparate items are brought to a common denominator by counting the distance between the best and worst performers and thereby achieving a ranking of countries. Critics have said that not only are the weights of the three components arbitrary, but also what is excluded, and what is included.

Another problem with the HDI is the implicit trade-off between life expectancy and income. For a country with an income per head less than the world average ($5,711 per year at 1993 purchasing power parity, which is about the income per head of Costa Rica), an increase of annual GDP per head of $99 will exactly compensate for one year less of life expectancy, so as to keep the HDI constant.[10] If the people in one poor country have one year less of life expectancy but $100 higher GDP per head than in another country, this country will have a higher HDI. The value attached to longevity rises sharply with income. For a country with twice the average income (about the income per head of Malta), an extra year of life is valued at $7,482 in income per head. At three times the average (about the income in the United Kingdom) it is worth $31,631, about twice the country's income per head. At four times the average (about Switzerland's income) its value reaches $65,038, about three times actual income. The implication is that life is far less valuable in poor countries than in rich ones. The value judgments underlying these trade-offs have been rightly rejected. So "human development" and the human development index are not ultimate insights and other ideas will take their place. We are all free to guess what these will be.

ENDNOTES

* This chapter appears in the *International Journal of Applied Economics and Econometrics* 11 (1), January–March 2003.

1. John Rawls 1971, p. 302.

2. Simon Kuznets 1955, pp. 1–28; and 1963, pp. 1–80.

3. W. A. Lewis 1954, pp. 139–91.

4. John R. Harris and Michael P. Todaro 1970, pp. 126–42.

5. Hollis Chenery and others 1974.

6. Paul Streeten 1975, pp. 1–9.

7. For a discussion of these, see Paul Streeten and others 1981, chapter 8.

8. Sudhir Anand and Martin Ravallion 1997.

9. Clifford Cobb, Ted Halstead and Jonathan Rowe 1995.

10. Martin Ravallion 1997

REFERENCES

Anand, Sudhir and Martin Ravallion. 1993. "Human Development in Poor Countries: On the Role of Private Incomes and Public Services." *The Journal of Economic Perspective* 7 (1): 133–50.

Chenery, Hollis and others. 1974. *Redistribution with Growth*. London: Oxford University Press.

Cobb, Clifford, Ted Halstead and Jonathan Rowe. 1995. *The Genuine Progress Indicator: Summary of Data and Methodology*. San Francisco, Calif.: Redefining Progress.

Harris, John R. and Michael P. Todaro. 1970. "Migration, Unemployment, and Development: A Two-Sector Analysis." *American Economic Review* 60 (1): 126–42.

Kuznets, Simon. 1955. "Economic Growth and Income Inequality." *American Economic Review* 45 (1): 1–28.

——. 1963. "Quantitative Aspects of Economic Growth of Nations, VIII: Distribution of Income by Size." *Economic Development and Cultural Change* 11 (2): 1–80.

Lewis, W. A. 1954. "Economic Development with Unlimited Supplies of Labour." *Manchester School of Economic and Social Studies* 22 (2): 139–91.

Ravallion, Martin. 1997. "Good and Bad Growth: The *Human Development Reports*." World Development 25 (5): 631–38.

Rawls, John. 1971. *A Theory of Justice*. Cambridge, Mass.: Harvard University Press.

Streeten, Paul. 1975. "Industrialisation in a Unified Development Strategy." In Sir Alec Cairncross and Mohinder Puri (eds.), *Employment, Income Distribution and Development Strategy: Essays in Honour of W. H. Singer,* Macmillan, and in *World Development* 3(1): 1–9.

Streeten, Paul and others. 1981. *First Things First: Meeting Basic Human Needs in Developing Countries*. Ch. 8. Oxford: Oxford University Press.

HUMAN DEVELOPMENT AND NEO-LIBERALISM: PARADIGMS COMPARED

Richard Jolly

There is an emerging international consensus on goals for poverty reduction, the importance of sustainable human development and the opportunities of globalization. There are calls for social principles to be introduced in global governance to ensure that the poorest countries and people benefit.

But this consensus hides some important differences: on other goals, on the means to be used, and on the whole approach to development to be followed. While strong reservations have been expressed about the neo-liberal paradigm, it continues to set the framework for economic policy internationally.

Within the UN system, UNDP's series of *Human Development Reports* has set out many of the objectives and mechanisms for a coherent and comprehensive approach, incorporating the goals noted above but going beyond them in several crucial respects. Drawing on the fundamental work of economist Amartya Sen, the human development approach embodies a robust paradigm, which may be contrasted with the neoclassical paradigm of the Washington Consensus. There are places of overlap, but also important points of difference in objectives, assumptions, constraints; in the key policy areas; and in the indicators for assessing results. These are set out in the main section of the chapter that follows.

Different parts of the UN system have always been more sympathetic to ideas of human development than the Bretton Woods institutions, in part because the latter have been more aligned with neoclassical economics and with thinking and interests in the Anglo-Saxon world. The principles of human development share many values and ideas with the Anglo-Saxon tradition as well, but also draw from a wide range of other sources. In particular, an emphasis on human rights and the importance of freedom in development give human development a more fundamental appeal to countries seeking to work within the tradition of inclusive democracy. But to enlarge appeal will require broader thinking in development and a willingness to bring human rights and human choices and capabilities more fully into analysis and policy-making.

The human development paradigm also offers guidelines for policy-making in the industrial countries, providing a more robust frame of analysis and policy-making for parties and countries wanting to pursue a third way between the old political alignments of left and right. By drawing on the international analysis of the *Human Development Reports*, concepts of human security and actions to moderate the extremes of international inequalities in income, power and human well-being could evolve in ways that will be increasingly necessary in the 21st century.

HUMAN DEVELOPMENT –
A SEDUCTIVE APPEAL REQUIRING CLEAR DEFINITIONS IF VAGUE GENERALITIES ARE TO BE AVOIDED

There is still much lack of clarity about the definition, strategies and policies embodied in human development. In part, this is because human development is an approach, not a dogma or a doctrine. Human development has deep foundations, analysed in the work of Amartya Sen and summarized and elaborated in the 12 *Human Development Reports* issued since 1990. Each of these reports has carefully used the term human development to refer to "a process of enlarging human choices and strengthening human capabilities".

Most of the reports have amplified or footnoted the link with Sen's work, as well as connected basic ideas about human development to the concepts of "functionings" and "capabilities" (i.e., what people are able to do or be, such as being healthy, being able to read and write, and being able to participate in the life of the community). Sen has himself carried forward these ideas in a recent book, *Development as Freedom*.[1]

The human development approach has also been applied and elaborated in a large number of different economic and social situations. Some 300 national human development reports have been prepared in over 135 countries during the last decade, analysing aspects of human development in various national contexts.[2] These reports cover all six regions of the developing world; one has also been prepared for the United Kingdom and two are underway for the United States. There are also four regional reports for South Asia, three summary reports for countries in transition, and regional reports for Africa, the Southern African Development Community, Central America and the Pacific Islands.

In spite of this flowering of initiatives, or perhaps because of it, the core definitions and the strategies and policies to implement a human development approach are still used in very different ways. Several reasons may account for this:

- First, the seductive appeal of the very idea of human development, "putting people at the centre", readily encourages many policy-makers and politicians to use the phrase casually in order to pin a positive label on all manner of policies or actions that have a vaguely human focus.
- Second, economists and development strategists long ago discovered the importance of human resources in the development process. This has led to an emphasis on human resource investment, which often gets confused with human development. Confusion has increased through a broad use of terms. For example, the name of the World Bank unit responsible for education and health is the Human Development Unit.

- Third, a decentralized system has been adopted in UNDP, with no attempt to ensure a standardized approach or standardized definitions in the preparation of national human development reports in different parts of the world. Perhaps this is a praiseworthy example of consistency with the very idea of human development, which encourages free choice and decentralization. It has also been the result of limited resources and reluctance to take on the major administrative task that consistent, top-down monitoring and control would require. But the result has been a diversity of approaches and sometimes of definitions.

There is another quite different explanation for some of the confusion. The term "human development" is not new and not restricted to economic development. Paediatricians and child psychologists often use the term to refer to the intellectual and social development of the individual child. Psychologists in general use the term as well. These professional applications have caused the term to spread into more casual usage, where it retains its positive connotation.

The broad use of the human development term underlines the importance of returning to its core definitions and also elaborating their implications for development strategy and policy. This is done in the section that follows. It presents the key elements of human development and compares them to the ruling neoclassical paradigm.

The reason for the comparison with the neoclassical approach needs a further word of explanation. In spite of important modifications over the last decade, the Washington Consensus is still the dominant international economic paradigm. Poverty reduction as a priority has been added to this paradigm, and the paradigm itself has been modified since the rigid forms it took in the early years of structural adjustment policy in the 1980s. But its core elements are still there. The Washington Consensus, or perhaps better, the neo-Washington Consensus still rules.

In contrast, a full-blooded adoption of human development would go much further, both in the pursuit of poverty reduction and as a strategy for a more humanly sensitive and participatory approach to development. The various *Human Development Reports* have already set out much of what this would involve, but usually within the scope of the specifics of policy rather than in more general terms. The purpose of this presentation is to illustrate the latter. Contrasting human development with the neo-liberal approach helps explain the operational differences and also emphasizes the practicality of human development. Although there are important differences at every stage, these are not as complete as many might imagine. This is hardly surprising. Both human development and neo-liberalism share many common roots, most notably in the liberal economic tradition, which emphasizes the fundamental importance of individual choices and the value of well-functioning markets to enable individuals to exercise these choices.

Thus, the presentation that follows emphasizes overlap as well as contrasts in four areas: objectives and strategies, common ground, policy priorities and a comparison of paradigms. The final section of the paper views structural adjustment within the context of the two approaches.

OBJECTIVES AND STRATEGIES

At first sight, there are important similarities in the objectives and major points of strategy between the human development and the neo-liberal paradigms. Both stress freedom of choice for the individual and the enlargement of choices as key elements in development. In this, both draw on a long liberal tradition in philosophy and economics. But underlying these similarities are important differences.

As summarized in Table 1.8.1, the key objective in human development is the enlargement of human voices made possible by the expansion of human opportunities and capabilities. Because people are the central focus of concern, they are the ends towards which all analysis and policy are directed. The guiding principle is equity. In contrast, the objective of the neo-liberal analysis is the maximization of economic welfare. The focus of

concern in analysis and policy is markets and the functioning of markets – and thus on the means rather than the ends of development. The guiding principle is efficiency.

These differences are obvious in the indicators used to measure goals and achievements. In the human development approach, the indices are multidimensional. The human development index (HDI) is a composite index gathering GDP per capita and health and education achievements. The human poverty index (HPI) measures the lack of access to the three central human capabilities, a decent income, health and knowledge. The gender-related development index (GDI) tries to capture the gender bias in the central human capabilities, with women usually scoring much worse than men.

Under the neo-liberal approach, GNP and GNP growth form the central indicators of success, along with inflation and various indicators of economic balance, such as the balance of payments and the surplus or deficit in public expenditure. Neo-liberalism is totally silent about the ends towards which these economic indicators lead. It may address the increase in income, but it does not consider what that income actually brings to people's lives and whether they enjoy better living conditions or not.

TABLE 1.8.1
Objectives and strategies compared

Human development	Neo-liberalism
• Objective: expansion of human opportunities and capabilities	• Objective: maximization of economic welfare
• Focus of concern: people	• Focus of concern: markets
• Guiding principle: equity and justice	• Guiding principle: economic efficiency
• Emphasis: ends	• Emphasis: means
• Trend focus: poverty reduction	• Trend focus: economic growth
• Poverty definition: population in multidimensional deprivation	• Poverty definition: population below minimum income line
• Key indicators: HDI, GDI, GEM and per cent of HPI	• Key indicators: GNP, GNP growth and per cent below income poverty line

COMMON GROUND –
BUT FOR DIFFERENT REASONS

The areas where the human development and neo-liberal paradigms do overlap have often given rise to confusion. But even when there are common points of focus or concern, they often stem from different rationales and choices, as can be seen in Table 1.8.2.

Democratic governance is one example of both similarities and differences. Both human development and neo-liberalism emphasize the need for human rights and for a democratic state as key elements of governance. But neo-liberalism tends to propound a minimal state while human development stresses the importance of a core of state functions. (Even on this, the neo-Washington Consensus appears to have shifted from its strictly minimalist view of the 1980s to a somewhat more expansive outlook in the late 1990s.)

The human development view recognizes many areas where state action is vital: in strengthening the human capabilities of all the population; in ensuring a fair distribution of opportunities through a fair distribution of income; in creating active policies to ensure markets work with equity as well as efficiency, which includes monitoring market outcomes and allowing interventions, where necessary, to offset extreme inequalities of market power; and in encouraging the formation or strengthening of local institutions that provide opportunities for participation and empowerment in a whole range of activities and services, from schools and health services to specialized services needed to ensure opportunities for the disabled and otherwise handicapped. It is not so much that the neo-liberal approach ignores all these, but it generally accords them lower importance than the goal of economic efficiency.

There is also common ground in health and education and on issues of discrimination. Differences are revealed, however, when one considers the priorities. Human development recognizes education and health as human rights, while neo-liberalism considers them investments with high returns. There is of course mutual reinforcement in both of these positions. But by recognizing education and health as human rights, the human development approach accepts the need to ensure these rights even to groups like the severely disabled or those past working age for whom education and basic health will not lead to a high economic return.

TABLE 1.8.2
Common ground – but for different reasons

Human development	Neo-liberalism
Underlying philosophy	
• Freedom of choice – but by developing and strengthening human capabilities and functionings • Emphasizes all human rights • Concern for equity and justice	• Freedom of choice – but by increasing utilities and satisfaction of preferences • Emphasizes mainly political and civil rights
Education, health and nutrition	
• Important in themselves • As a means of empowerment • As human rights	• Important as investments in human capital
Ending discrimination	
• A human right • For fairness	• A human right • For efficiency
Governance	
• Democratic and inclusive • Important state functions • Focus on all human rights	• Democratic • Minimal state • Focus on political and civil rights

Similarly, human development transforms a strong anti-discrimination stance into an active agenda to end discrimination and to support positive measures in favour of minorities and other groups that start with handicaps because of previous discrimination in society. And while both approaches recognize the importance of women's education, human development highlights expanding knowledge and ending discrimination as important means to empower women and to strengthen their role in development. This may not always involve high net costs. Many forms of discrimination against women, present or past, already involve high economic costs that are not acknowledged because of a heavy overlay of traditional beliefs and customs. Ending discrimination in the name of human rights may in fact produce good economic returns, even though the motivation is the principle of equity, not efficiency.

The most fundamental difference between the human development and the neo-liberal approaches is one of underlying philosophy. Human development rests on the foundations of capabilities and functionings, while neo-liberalism is based on the utility approach to well-being. Neo-liberal economic theory views utility as the underlying rationale for individual preferences. Even though the cardinal measurement of utility in "utils" is no longer used or needed, many residuals from this line of reasoning remain. These have been set out by Sen[3] and Sen and Williams[4]:

- Consequentialism judges all choices according to their consequences or their results. Principles are not good in themselves, but only insofar as they yield good consequences.
- Welfarism maintains that comparisons and judgements about the relative worth of different states of affairs lie entirely in their utilities.

The combination of consequentialism and welfarism is that every choice – and every policy – can and should be judged in terms of the utility generated.

This line of reasoning leads to serious deficiencies. Sen and Nussbaum have highlighted two of these. Sen[5] emphasizes how narrow forms of consequentialism such as utilitarianism (where an action is evaluated according to the consequences in the levels of utility) leads to the neglect of rights and freedoms. Sen argues that tough actions have to be evaluated in terms of their consequences and not so much in terms of deontological principles. Consequences need to include space beyond just utility, namely the space for freedoms and rights (what Sen has called "broad consequentialism").

Another problem with utility consequentialism is that everything is assessed in principle by a single evaluative measure, utility. So, if one chooses to work hard during weekends, at the expense of the time spent with one's family, then the working time can be "compared", and even "measured", in terms of an increase in utility. But is it possible for people to "measure" in terms of wage equivalents the poor quality of their family life? While the neo-liberal paradigm claims that people can do this – that everything eventually amounts to a matter of "opportunity costs" – the human development paradigm claims that these types of benefits are intrinsically different and each must be valued for its own sake. Hence, for example, a human development policy trying to promote women's participation in economic activity will try to create the structures for work flexibility and give incentives "in kind" to promote women's participation. A neo-liberal policy, in contrast, would tend to give money incentives, as if an increase in salary could compensate for the time that women could not spend with their families.

The analysis of deficiencies in utility theory can go even further. For instance, the social and mental adaptation and conditioning of individuals can lead them to accept situations of low status and deprivation.[6] The active conditioning of slaves in slave societies is an egregious case. But the less visible conditioning of minorities or other social groups discriminated against in contemporary societies is probably more widespread. Women, for example, can become accustomed to being undereducated, so that this becomes an accepted part of their lives. Consequently, when asked if they want to receive education, women may well reply that they "prefer" remaining uneducated. The distinction between preference, free choice and social conditioning is indeed a difficult one, and by assuming that preference equals someone's free choice, the neo-liberal paradigm reveals its weak theoretical foundations, which nevertheless have large implications for the real world.

PRIORITIES FOR POLICY – POVERTY REDUCTION, NATIONAL POLICY AND INTERNATIONAL PRIORITIES

POVERTY REDUCTION: The consensus on poverty reduction reached internationally over the last five years or so is both important and perhaps unprecedented. In a world of extraordinary wealth, with total incomes exceeding US $30 trillion per year, tackling the human needs and social situations of the 3 billion people with estimated annual incomes of less than $700 per year has become an extremely important human rights issue. For just over $1 trillion – barely 3 per cent of the world's income – it would be possible to double the incomes of the poorest people, who form half of the world's population. The changes and mechanisms for achieving this would of course be vastly complicated, but in terms of the magnitude of the economic costs, the task is much less than many people seem to realize.

Table 1.8.3 sets out the main elements of poverty reduction strategies that have emerged from the human development and the neo-liberal approaches. The World Bank's 1990 *World Development Report* defined the neo-liberal approach as emphasizing economic growth, investment in education and health, and social safety nets – the so-called "two-and-a-half" strategy, since the shortage of resources in the poorer countries meant that social safety nets could never be more than a half leg in the strategy tripod. In the latest *World Development Report*, this strategy has been reinforced by a strong focus on the need for empowering the poor and promoting their active participation in local institutions and activities. This is an important advance for the Bank, though it is not entirely clear how much this can be taken as an operational statement of Bank policy, since the release of this document was preceded by the resignation of two of the Bank's most senior economists, each of whom was closely involved with this particular report.

The human development approach to poverty reduction has embraced a broader range of policy concerns: empowerment of the poor, through strengthening their capabilities; gender equity; access to assets; pro-poor growth; and international action to enhance opportunities for poor people and poor countries. Human development generally gives more emphasis to goals to guide national and international action and to the need for monitoring. But again, to be fair, it is even less clear how much this can be taken as an indication of UNDP policy, let alone of UN system-wide policy. The *Human Development Reports* are always issued with the disclaimer that: "The analysis and recommendations of the Report do not necessarily reflect the views of the United Nations Development Programme, its Executive Board or its Member States. The Report is an independent publication commissioned by UNDP."

TABLE 1.8.3
Priorities compared – poverty reduction and growth

Human development	Neo-liberalism
Key assumption: Growth must be consciously made pro-people and pro-poor	*Key assumption:* Trickle down can be expected
Goal-oriented poverty strategy: • Empower the poor • Aim for gender equity • Ensure poor have access to assets • Accelerate pro-poor growth • International support for national action	*Growth-oriented poverty strategy:* • Ensure adequate economic growth • Expand social sectors • Build in safety nets as affordable • Open economy policies and international aid

NATIONAL POLICY: It is by setting poverty reduction in the frame of human development that the differences most clearly emerge. For this underlines the fact that poverty reduction is not an end in itself, nor an add-on to development as usual, but a step to something better. This something better is human development, an enhancement of human choices and a strengthening of human capabilities. The very basics of this definition reveal potential guidelines for the future, when the economy has grown and the levels of income make possible not only the eradication of mass poverty but also a wider range of choices and an improved quality of life for the whole population.

Again there are similarities. Both the human development and the neo-liberal paradigms highlight choice and the need for using the market to expand opportunities for individuals and households to exercise these. But whereas the neo-liberal paradigm focuses on the *market conditions* to ensure free choice – free markets, getting prices right, prevention of monopoly and following the guidance of rates of return to achieve efficiency – the human development paradigm keeps the emphasis on people and on the *human and social conditions* for achieving free choice.

Thus, further strengthening of human capabilities is kept in sharp relief at all income levels by the human development approach as a necessary condition for broadening choices and opportunities. This does not imply some top-down, all-wise paternalistic guidance from the state, but rather achieving and maintaining the conditions for democratic participation and community action at all levels, whether local, regional, national or international. Local level community action is especially important – for schools, health services, local government, transport, and certainly for conservation and sustainable development. The principle of subsidiarity is a useful guide. Nothing should be decided at a higher level than is necessary to ensure that the interests of all stakeholders are taken into account.

As a further condition for achieving such participation, action is needed to moderate inequality, not only to remove poverty but also to prevent extremes in income, to overcome obstacles to serious participation, and to achieve reasonable levels of service in health and education.

It would be a serious mistake to imagine that a human development approach involves a plan and a succession of technocratic decisions made by applying a few precise human development principles. How much participation, what degrees of inequality, what regulations are required to moderate imbalances of power, how much government support is needed to strengthen which human capabilities – all these and many other issues are ones for which no clear guidelines can be provided. They must be determined by a democratic political process. The human development approach provides just that: an approach, not a timetable and a social work plan. It offers an ordering of issues and priorities to be weighed and considered, not a checklist of decisions to be taken. Above all, human development provides a clear view on the human focus to be maintained and on the true test of achievement – that all people in a community, region, country and ultimately the world are in situations where their rights are achieved and they face an enlargement of choices and opportunities.

INTERNATIONAL PRIORITIES: This brings us to the international conditions for achieving poverty reduction and human development on a glo-

---

TABLE 1.8.4
Priorities compared – national policy

Human development	Neo-liberalism
• Broadening choices and opportunities	• Free markets
• Strengthening human capabilities	• Getting prices right
• Participation	• Prevention of monopoly
• Moderating inequality	• More efficiency
• Education and health as essentials of human development	• Human resource investment
• Restructuring national budgets	• Education and health when rates of return indicate a good investment
	• Reducing national budgets

bal scale. In the last five years, since the World Summit for Social Development in 1995 and the Development Assistance Committee High Level Meeting in 1996, a number of serious commitments have been made nationally and internationally that have already set in motion an unprecedented focus on global action to halve the worst extremes of poverty within the next 15 years. It is a remarkable set of commitments and everything possible needs to be done to maintain them and to encourage their full implementation country by country, in all developed and developing nations. The following analysis is provided within this spirit.

The national policies required to achieve poverty reduction – and, in the long run, poverty eradication objectives – have already been set out. But for many of the poorer and weaker countries, various forms of international action will be required if they are to reduce poverty and set national development on a path that will achieve human development. This is not to deny that some of the larger and more powerful countries have demonstrated the capacity to rapidly reduce poverty and attain considerable measures of human development with only limited international support. But the very size and strength of some of these countries, or other favourable factors, seem often to explain at least part of their success. It would be a

mistake to imagine that all countries today can achieve poverty reduction and human development without a more enabling international environment, including some special support.

From a human development perspective, there are several categories of action required to achieve international support for human development. Many of these are treated differently by the neo-liberal approach, which underscores opening international markets, removing all barriers to trade and capital flows, and offering only the poorest countries some aid for a limited period. By contrast, the human development perspective has a more structuralist view. It emphasizes the *potential* benefits of the open global economy, but also recognizes the need for special action if the poorer and weaker countries are to find opportunities to participate fully and effectively. As elaborated in *Human Development Report 1999,* this objective requires action to ensure a level playing field and support to strengthen the negotiating position of poorer and weaker countries. It also entails more aid and special assistance for the least developed countries.

More controversially, the human development approach would suggest the introduction of human principles into the rules and regulations governing the global market. At the national level in most industrial countries, rules and regulations have been enacted that require trade and transactions to meet certain minimum standards of health and safety. These also mandate paying workers minimum wages, and define labour rights and working conditions. From a human development perspective, similar steps should be implemented in the global economy today. There is a need for social principles linked to human rights on a global scale.

Another area for action is to restore peace and security in countries suffering from war. Most of the initiatives for this must grow out of the countries and communities concerned. But there are many people, women and men, in every war-torn country who are ready and anxious to take such initiatives with appropriate international support and protection. In cases such as these, international action becomes an important if not essen-

TABLE 1.8.5
Priorities compared – international action and support

Human development	Neo-liberalism
• More democratic global governance to level the global playing field	• Remove all barriers to trade and capital flows
• Strengthen bargaining position of weak and poor countries	
• Positive attitude to international migration	• Some aid
• Aid, especially support for the least developed countries	• Military security
• Human security (and reducing military expenditures)	

tial complement to national action. And in the longer run, international action to reduce nationally and regionally the weapons and threats of conflict are important measures for increasing and sustaining global security.

Here the concept of human security, as elaborated in the 1994 and 1999 *Human Development Reports*, has much to contribute. The post-cold-war world is threatened by many causes of conflict and social disruption – crime, drugs, human trafficking, and the trade and proliferation of small arms and other weapons, new and second-hand. National and international security policies need to shift to these intra-country issues and away from the former international preoccupation with inter-country military conflict.

PARADIGMS COMPARED

It is time to draw the threads together. What can we learn about human development and neo-liberalism as paradigms of development? A concluding contrast is set out in Table 1.8.6.

The human development paradigm is multi-disciplinary and pragmatic, emphasizing ends and decentralized approaches. By contrast, the neo-liberal paradigm is economic and dogmatic, emphasizing means and aspiring to general equilibrium.

Weighing the balance of strengths and weaknesses is not easy. The neo-liberal approach has great strengths, including strong theoretical foundations that are sufficient for a wide range of economic and financial issues and have been used to establish empirical conclusions of considerable generality. The power of the human development paradigm is that it focuses on fundamentals and explores subjects often neglected by the neo-liberal paradigm. These include the non-economic factors, the issues beyond the market such as intra-household income distribution and gender inequalities, the human concerns of the aged and the socialization of young children. All these are important in terms of recognizing human values and strengthening human capabilities. However, they do not fit easily or reasonably into the neo-liberal worldview, with its insistence on maximizing returns and ensuring market efficiency.

It is true that the human development strengths are bought at a price. Human development's multidisciplinary paradigm often leads to casual analysis based on weak data. It lacks the tough empiricism of the propositions and testing of the neo-liberal approach. But, as no less than a Nobel laureate in economics has pointedly asked: "Would you rather be roughly right or precisely wrong?"

ADJUSTMENT WITH A HUMAN FACE – AN EXAMPLE IN PRACTICE

In real life, the choices presented by such a dilemma may seem less difficult, at least with hind-

TABLE 1.8.6
Paradigms compared

Human development	Neo-liberalism
• Multidisciplinary	• Economic
• Pragmatic	• Dogmatic
• Emphasizes decentralized approaches	• Aspires to general equilibrium
• Emphasizes ends	• Emphasizes means
Strengths	
• Focus on fundamentals	• Strong economic theory and financial analysis
• Choices, opportunities and capabilities	• Much economic data of good quality and up to date
• Non-market issues like time, intra-household distribution	
Weaknesses	
• Analysis often casual	• Neglect of non-economic issues
• Often weak data	

sight. We may take the example of structural adjustment in the 1980s. Presented with evidence of severe economic imbalances in many countries of sub-Saharan Africa and Latin America, the neo-liberal approach called for urgent economic action and harsh programmes of structural adjustment. In economic terms, the programmes were hardly an unqualified success. Inflation was controlled, and usually the most severe imbalances in the balance of payments were reduced – but most often at the cost of major declines in economic growth and considerable human suffering. Only after five years of intense national and international debate and opposition were some modifications introduced, and then, as is still true today, only to a limited extent.

An alternative approach had also been set forth, sharing many elements of a human development approach, though not as formally based on human development analysis as might today be the case. This alternative, Adjustment with a Human Face, emphasized different objectives, policies and modalities.[7]

The AWHF objectives, like the human development approach, stressed the need to focus on the human situation, making the maintenance of people's health, nutrition and welfare a central concern, rather than the by-product of restoring economic health, as in the orthodox neo-liberal programmes.

The policies also were different from those advocated by neo-liberalism. Though attention was given to restoring economic balances, keeping human concerns at the centre meant that much more attention was given to meso and micro policy and to the human impact of all actions. Meso policy emphasized the need for actions at a level midway between the macro and the micro, such as improving the allocation of public expenditure and assessing the poverty impact of tax, tariff and price controls. Micro policy dealt with increasing production and income in ways that benefited the poor and vulnerable.

Although AWHF required some tough and restrictive actions, they were to be assessed and adjusted from the beginning to ensure the maintenance of minimum standards of nutrition, health

and such basics as school enrolments. Moreover, the goal was not only *to prevent deterioration* in essential human standards, but also *to ensure some positive progress* towards longer-run goals of poverty reduction and human development. This could be achieved through low-cost means, such as bolstering production by small-scale urban and rural producers, and maintaining productive opportunities for informal sector workers.

It was in the modalities of the AWHF compared with the neo-liberal approach that the differences become most clear. The AWHF emphasized three areas of concern if it was to be realized effectively:

- A broader group of government and non-government actors would need to be brought into policy- and decision-making. Thus in government, policy-making could not be left only to economic and financial decision-makers. Other ministries, especially those concerned with nutrition, health and education would need to play a full part in the process. Outside of government, communities would need to be included at local levels and higher, to ensure a human focus and a clear understanding of the options and what was needed to keep human opportunities open.
- Instead of the exclusive focus on economic and financial indicators, human and social indicators would be given equal value. Particular importance would be assigned to human indicators that enable tracking of the human situation and responding to urgent human needs. These include indicators of nutritional status, reasons for health clinic attendance and supplies of essential drugs in primary health care centres. Similar tracking would also be needed in schools – of drop-outs and supplies of books and school materials. Again, the test would not only be to avoid deterioration, but to ensure the maintenance of progress towards the mid-term and longer goals of poverty reduction and human development.
- The urgency of the situation would require a new approach internationally. This could comprise more rapid and flexible support –

financially, in access to markets and in other forms such as peacekeeping troops. To ensure adequate planning and political support, a broader group of international agencies and donors would need to be involved as full partners who could contribute ideas and experience. They would not simply be viewed as extra donors for an already determined programme.

It is possible to dismiss the human development alternative as unrealistic idealism. To do so, however, would be misguided and defeatist. Examples can be found of virtually every element of the human development approach being implemented somewhere in recent years, at reasonable cost and often with considerable success. The human development paradigm is closely aligned with the human rights commitments that most governments have now adopted, including virtually all of the richer countries. Indeed, the relevant human rights agreements include specific commitments by richer countries to do all within their power to assist poorer countries to carry out their own commitments.

Mahbub ul Haq, the founder and creator of the *Human Development Report*, began his final book, *Reflections on Human Development*,[8] with a section entitled "Towards a New Development Paradigm". He ended the book by quoting approvingly from Barbara Ward: "Ideas are the prime movers of history. Revolutions usually begin with ideas."

Mahbub saw human development as a vision for future human advances, not merely as an analytical tool. But he also recognized the intellectual hurdles. He often used to say that the main obstacle to implementation of the human development paradigm was not a lack of resources but a lack of intellectual courage. This is the challenge today.

ENDNOTES

1. Sen 1999.

2. See the National Human Development Report Corporate Policy.

3. Sen 1999, chapter three.

4. Sen and Williams 1982, introduction.

5. Sen 2000.

6. Nussbaum 2000, chapter two.

7. The ideas were set out in several places, but the most comprehensive was Cornia, Jolly and Stewart (eds.) 1987.

8. Haq 1995.

REFERENCES

Cornia, Giovanni Andrea, Richard Jolly and Frances Stewart (eds.). 1987. *Adjustment with a Human Face: Protecting the Vulnerable and Promoting Growth*, vols. 1 and 2. Oxford: Clarendon Press.

Haq, Mahbub ul. 1995. *Reflections on Human Development*. New York: Oxford University Press.

Nussbaum, Martha. 2000. *Women and Human Development: A Study in Human Capabilities*. Cambridge: Cambridge University Press.

Sen, Amartya K. 1999. *Development as Freedom*. New York: Oxford University Press.

——. "Non-consequentialist Evaluation of Freedom." *Journal of Philosophy*, September 2000.

Sen, A. K. and B. Williams. 1982. *Utilitarianism and Beyond*. Cambridge: Cambridge University Press.

1.10

RESCUING THE HUMAN DEVELOPMENT CONCEPT FROM THE HDI: REFLECTIONS ON A NEW AGENDA

Sakiko Fukuda-Parr*

INTRODUCTION: HUMAN DEVELOPMENT MISUNDERSTOOD

In the 1990s, development economics and policy debates acknowledged that development is about more than the growth of material output and should serve broader objectives of human well-being. In particular, it is now widely accepted that expansion of education and health constitute important goals, and the monitoring of poverty has come to explicitly include progress in these areas.[1] The annual *Human Development Reports* have been a major force behind this shift, constituting one of the strongest voices advocating attention to the non-income dimensions of human well-being, and raising dissatisfaction with the notion that human well-being is to be advanced primarily through expanding incomes.

But this new consensus is by no means a recognition of the full concept of human development. Indeed, for myself and several other co-authors of the *Human Development Reports*, the most nagging frustration with the recent evolution of development thinking has been the continued misinterpretation of human development, which is an application of the "capabilities approach" conceived by Amartya Sen and explained in more detail in other chapters of this book. Despite the broad and complex nature of human development, an assumption has arisen that it is essentially about education and health, which adds little to concepts of human capital and basic needs.

There has also been a tendency to imprison human development strategies and ideas within the human development index. Ironically, the success of the HDI has only served to reinforce the narrow interpretation of human development. Two flaws in the initial design of the HDI – the simplification of a complex idea, and the exclusion of references to political freedoms and participation – continue haunt the concept. Despite careful efforts to explain that the notion of human development is much broader than its measure, the HDI's message is that the essential human development objectives are to expand education, literacy, health and survival, and to raise incomes. The power of the HDI as a communications tool has proved difficult to moderate.

This chapter focuses on how human development differs from the human capital, human resource development and basic needs approaches. It also reviews how human development concepts have evolved in the *Human Development Reports* over the last decade, and why the perception continues that human development is about education and health.

Maintaining that human development is broader than education and health because human capabilities extend well beyond these areas and are arguably infinite, the chapter shows how human development differs from other approaches in three important ways:[2]

- definition of ends and means,
- concern with human freedoms and dignity, and
- concern with human agency – the role of people in development.

Finally, the chapter identifies gaps and outlines an agenda for future work on concepts, measures and policies.

HUMAN ENDS AND ECONOMIC MEANS

In the human development framework, development is about people's well-being and the expansion of their capabilities and functionings. Expansion of material output is treated as a means and not an end. The ends-means relationship is reversed in theories of human capital formation or human resource development, in which human beings are treated as a means to economic growth. While the human development approach views investment in education and health as having intrinsic value for human lives, the human resource development approach stresses how education and health enhance productivity, and have important value for promoting economic growth.[3] The basic needs approach focuses on access to social services to meet basic material needs for a decent life. This approach does not elaborate on the reasons why certain needs are important. In the absence of such considerations, the basic needs approach ends up emphasizing the supply of materials rather than what these material goods allow people to do.[4]

In embracing the human development approach, the *Human Development Reports* have highlighted two central messages: defining well-being as the purpose of development and treating economic growth as a means. This ends-means relationship has been developed in new concepts and measures, and in articulating policy priorities.

For example, successive Reports have shown that countries with similar incomes can achieve very different levels of human development. *Human Development Report 1996* explores this relationship further, revealing that there is no automatic link. Growth can be ruthless, rootless, futureless, voiceless and jobless – but when the links are strong, growth and human development are mutually reinforcing.

With ends being defined in terms of human ends, deprivation and inequalities must also be defined in non-income terms. Thus, *Human Development Report 1997* made an important conceptual breakthrough on poverty, defining it as deprivation in lives and choices rather than in material goods and income. The Report introduces a concept of "human poverty" as distinct from "income poverty". While the standard measure of poverty focuses on incomes or food consumption below a threshold, *Human Development Report 1997* debuts a measure focussing on human de-velopment achievements below a threshold level in human survival, literacy, nutrition and access to public income.

Similarly, analysis of deprivations and inequalities in the *Human Development Reports* focuses less on material goods and more on capabilities and choices. For example, *Human Development Report 1995* introduced a measure of human development that takes account of gender inequalities (the gender-related development index, or GDI) and another on the disparities between women and men in participation in decision-making processes (the gender empowerment measure, or GEM).

Human Development Reports have also introduced an approach to measuring inequalities based on capabilities by the use of HDIs, and through disaggregating the HDI by region, gender and ethnic groups. Such assessments have led to lively national debates and policy responses – for example, in Brazil, where regional HDIs display a huge range, the lowest comparable to the lowest in the world and the highest comparable to the highest in the world.[5]

The most obvious policy implication of this ends-means framework is that economic growth alone will not be enough to promote human development. Greater attention needs to be paid to other human development goals. Focussing on human lives as the end of development can frame the analysis of almost any development challenge and drive the agenda of policy concerns that will be addressed. Each annual *Human Development Report* has carefully applied this framework to its chosen theme.

In considering globalization, for instance, *Human Development Report 1999* goes beyond the impact of trade and capital liberalization on economic growth. It focuses instead on the changing opportunities in people's lives and raises concerns over new insecurities that are being created. The conceptual framework of *Human Development Report 2001* sees technology as a tool for promoting human development, not as a reward of higher incomes. This contrasts with growth-oriented studies of the current technology revolution, which deal primarily with impacts on the economy such as productivity increases, employment creation and stock market trends.

Human Development Report 2001 looks at public policies to "make new technologies work for human development" – for example, by shifting priorities for research and development investment to tackle enduring problems such as tropical diseases, low agricultural productivity and lack of access to energy. The Report introduces a new measurement tool, the technology achievement index, which focuses on how basic technologies are spread through a country. India, for instance, which is now a world class centre of innovation, has a relatively low index because large parts of the country are still without access to basic technologies such as electricity and telephones. The TAI also incorporates the human capacity to innovate and adapt.

In addition, the *Human Development Report* has taken new approaches to the consumption/environment debates, which have been dominated by concerns about economic growth and expansion in consumption as sources of environmental stress. *Human Development Report 1998* focuses on the impact on people, especially on the different burdens and needs of the underconsumers, who are not consuming enough even to meet basic needs, and the overconsumers, whose consumption is huge and growing. Not only do the overconsumers create more environmental stress, but the underconsumers are most likely to suffer from the environmental consequences, from air pollution to rising sea levels.

Another human-centred concept that has had considerable impact on public debates is the notion of human security. *Human Development Report 1994* calls upon policy-makers and researchers to focus on the security of people rather than on the security of national borders. The implications of this concept are profound. It challenges notions of foreign policy by proposing that countries protect people against serious harm and violations of human rights even when a state is unwilling or unable to do so. It indicates the need for national economic policies to set up measures against the catastrophic consequences of economic downturns and natural disasters. Human security is a major current of international deliber-ations, which have given rise to the establishment of two world commissions in 2000 and 2001.[6]

HUMAN FREEDOM AND DIGNITY – INCLUDING SOCIAL AND POLITICAL FREEDOMS

Human development is motivated by the search for freedom, well-being and the dignity of individuals in all societies, concerns that are absent from concepts of social development, human capital formation and basic needs. The human development approach also maintains that all capabilities expand human freedoms, and emphasizes attaining the full range of these capabilities, including the social freedoms, which cannot be exercised without a guarantee of political and civil rights.

As *Human Development Report 2000* states, capabilities comprise "the *basic freedoms* of being able to meet bodily requirements, such as the ability to avoid starvation and undernourishment, or to escape preventable morbidity or premature mortality. They also include the enabling opportunities given by schooling . . . or the liberty and economic means to move freely and to choose one's abode. There are also important '*social*' freedoms, such as the capability to participate in the life of the community, to join in public discussion, to participate in political decision-making and even the elementary ability 'to appear in public without shame'."[7] (Emphasis added.)

From the outset, the *Human Development Reports* have underscored political and social freedoms as integral to human development, recognizing them as a policy priority. The authors of the *Human Development Reports* also have acknowledged that the biggest flaw in the HDI has been the lack of an indicator of political freedom. Serious efforts were made to develop a measure starting in 1990, with the human freedom index published in 1992 followed by the political freedom index in 1993. Unfortunately, these measures were technically flawed as well as politically unacceptable. They created bitter controversy and had to be discontinued.[8]

So, in spite of the human development emphasis on the importance of political and social freedoms, these capabilities have never been given as much attention as basic capabilities – improved health, education and incomes. Part of the reason has to do with the complexity of measuring and monitoring such freedoms, a factor that is reflected in the assessment of trends in human development that forms a chapter in each *Human Development Report*. For example, the 1990, 1991 and 1992 *Human Development Reports* make strong assertions about the importance of human freedoms and contain serious attempts to develop composite measures of them. Yet ironically, while the chapters on progress in human development provide detailed analyses of trends in life expectancy, education and basic incomes, they barely contain a mention of trends in political freedom, human rights and participation. Similarly, the balance sheets of human development graphically display progress and deprivation in life expectancy, health, sanitation, food and nutrition, women, children, human security, environment – all essentially economic and social issues with no reference to political freedoms.

Two exceptions to this pattern are the 1995 and 2000 *Human Development Reports*, which explicitly recognize the significance of political freedoms. The 1995 Report on gender emphasizes the importance of equal rights to political freedom and participation. The GEM includes the political empowerment of women as an indicator of women's overall standing. *Human Development Report 2000*, on human rights, also leaves no ambiguity in assessing human progress – in development and rights – by giving equal attention to economic, social, political and civil concerns.

Human Development Report 2000 in particular afforded a major conceptual breakthrough in clarifying the relationship between human rights and human development. The Report identifies seven freedoms as inherent to both. These span the spheres of social, economic, political and civil life, including freedom from discrimination, from fear, of speech, from want, to develop and realize one's human potential, from injustice and violations of the rule of law, and to obtain decent work.

Human Development Report 2000 also addresses policies needed to promote political and civil freedoms. It highlights "inclusive democracy" as a political system that safeguards the rights of all and identifies the exclusion of minorities as a pitfall of majoritarian democracies. It also shows that civil and political freedoms can help people take collective action and demand other rights.

PEOPLE, PARTICIPATION AND CHANGE

Intrinsic to the human development approach is the notion of human agency. People cannot be considered as passive beneficiaries of economic and social progress, but must be regarded as active agents of change. By contrast, the basic needs approach treats human beings as beneficiaries rather than as participants in making progress. While the human resources approach sees human beings as agents of change, the focus is on their productive capacity.

Human development is also concerned with human agency in diverse areas, especially participation in the life of a community, in community decision-making and in collective action to promote change. Freedom and enjoying the respect of others are not only goals but also have instrumental value. Human beings can be agents of change through both individual and collective activities – through education and health that enhance productive potential, through knowledge that betters health, and through the use of civil and political liberties to promote political change. All of the *Human Development Reports* have reflected issues related to individual and collective actions.

In terms of the former, the Reports have consistently stressed the importance of investing in education and health as a cornerstone of human development – the perception that human development is more or less the same as human resource development strategies is therefore not surprising. For instance, *Human Development Report 1991*, on the theme of financing human development, focuses on investing in education and health to ensure equitable access to all. Innovative measures in the Report, such as the human priority measure, call for an analysis of public expenditures. *Human Development Report 1991* also supports the 20:20 initiative, a major policy advocacy effort to raise expenditures on basic human priorities.

In looking at mobilizing human agency through collective action, *Human Development Report 1993*, on participation, broke ground in arguing for the importance of people's role in governance. It proposes two strategies – strengthening institutions of civil society and decentralizing power from capital cities to regions and villages.[9] *Human Development Report 2000* goes further, explicitly addressing civil and political freedoms as a means for empowering people. As in the celebrated analysis of famines by Amartya Sen, which shows that famines are not allowed to persist in democracies, the expansion of civil and political freedoms empowers people to take collective action. The 1995 and 2000 *Human Development Reports* also contend that through history, human rights, including women's rights, have not been won by technocratic planning but by social advocacy movements.

However, the *Human Development Reports* overall have placed more attention on human agency through individual action rather than collective mobilization, resulting in many gaps. For example, in *Human Development Report 1990*, a section on using capabilities discusses employment, migration, popular participation and NGO movements, but does not mention the guarantee of political and civil liberties as a necessary condition for participation. The message behind this section is that "skilled, healthy and well-educated people are in a better position than others to take their lives into their own hands".[10]

While the Reports have acknowledged the importance of collective agency, they have not developed a more elaborate understanding of how collective action can be facilitated, where it can be effective, what can go wrong. *Human Development Report 1993* details only the positive benefits of the rise of civil society, without an assessment of constraints that may still exist, the mixed results of new movements and the pitfalls. *Human Development Report 1995* says little about how women's participation in political life can be enhanced. And *Human Development Report 1996* offers interesting insights into a strategy for collective mobi-

lization but does not give a more comprehensive treatment of the subject. The 1995 and 2000 *Human Development Reports* show that collective action – in the form of social movements – has been the essential motor behind progress in achieving gender equality and protection of human rights. But these Reports also neglect to explore this process.

THE SCOPE OF HUMAN DEVELOPMENT

The foregoing review shows that the *Human Development Reports* have emphasized capabilities related to education and health as well as the human-centered approach to development challenges, while paying much less attention to political freedoms, participation and the importance of collective action. This has fostered a widespread misconception of human development, but it also raises broader questions: What should be the scope of human development? Which capabilities should be included? Human development is certainly wider than education and health; important capabilities extend far beyond these two concerns.

The capabilities approach leaves open the priorities to be assigned to different capabilities.[11] However, public policy is about setting priorities. So one of the most difficult questions to be faced involves selecting which capabilities are important.[12] The range is infinite and the values that individuals assign to each capability vary from one person to another. Many of these are not relevant – such as a brand of washing powder[13] or the colour of a car[14]. Some clearly deserve greater attention for public policy. But even those that are important or relevant can vary with social context – from one community or country to another, and from one point of time to another. Thus, "the task of specification must relate to the underlying motivation of the exercise as well as dealing with the social values involved".[15]

The *Human Development Reports* have applied two criteria in identifying key capabilities. First, they must be capabilities that are universally valued, since the purpose of the Reports is to make a global assessment of progress in achieving human well-being that will be meaningful for nearly

200 countries at vastly different levels of income and social development. Second, these capabilities must be basic to life, in the sense that their lack would foreclose many options.

Four important capabilities for human development have been identified as basic: to be able to survive, to be knowledgeable, to have access to resources necessary for a decent standard of living, and to participate in the life of a community. Of these four, three are included in the HDI; the last is not because it is not measurable. The set has evolved over the years, and there are built-in ambiguities and an open-endedness in how it has been emphasized. While the first two capabilities are consistently in the definition of human development, the other two have been qualified and evolved. Access to resources needed for a decent standard of living is a reflection of "all other capabilities" that are not captured by education and health.[16] Participation has been included in the definition of human development from the first *Human Development Report* published in 1990, but it was referred to under "other important capabilities". This qualification was dropped in 2001. The shift is apparent in the following excerpts:

Human development is a process of enlarging people's choices. In principle, these choices can be infinite and change over time. But at all levels of development, the three essential ones are for people to lead a long and healthy life, to acquire knowledge and to have access to resources needed for a decent standard of living. If these essential choices are not available, many other opportunities remain inaccessible. But human development does not end there. Additional choices, highly valued by many people, range from political, economic and social freedom to opportunities for being creative and productive, and enjoying personal self respect and guaranteed human rights.[17]

Human development ... is about creating an environment in which people can develop their full potential and lead productive, creative lives in accord with their needs and interests. ... Fundamental to enlarging choices is building human capabilities – the range of things people can do or be in life. The most basic capabilities for human development are to lead long and healthy lives, to be knowledgeable, to have access to resources needed for a decent standard of living and to be able to participate in the life of the community. Without these, many choices are simply not available and many opportunities in life remain inaccessible.[18]

Should other capabilities be included? Are there others that are both universal and fundamental? A number might be considered, for example, the capability to be free from physical danger, to be free from violence. This is a concern of people the world over as violence manifests itself in diverse forms, from battery in the home to street crime to wars and conflicts.

HUMAN DEVELOPMENT STRATEGIES – FROM THE ERA OF NATIONAL PLANNING TO THE ERA OF GLOBALIZATION

It is not surprising that the *Human Development Reports* initially emphasized education and health, paid less attention to political and social freedoms, and underscored individual rather than collective agency. As noted in *Human Development Report 1990*, capabilities that are important can change over time and from place to place.

The first *Human Development Report* was published in 1990, at the tail end of the "planning" era of development thinking. The opening chapter of Mahbub ul Haq's *Reflections on Human Development* carries the title, "The Missing People in Development Planning." Advocacy for human development focused on shifts in planning priorities, and on what investments and actions were needed by the state. In that context, what the state could do to expand capabilities in areas of education and health constituted an important part of human development strategy, both for the intrinsic as well as the instrumental values of education and health.

Today, we are in the era of rapid globalization. Economic and political liberalization shape the context of development and have shifted priorities. Capabilities to participate and the collective agency of social action have become more important. Against the economic entrepreneurship driving markets, social entrepreneurship is expected to impel policy debates on issues that matter for people's well-being – for human development. Collective actions by people and actors other than the state, notably civil society groups, now play a larger role in shaping the course of development, and there is an emerging consensus on the importance of civil society in the promotion of development. The political shifts of the 1980s and 1990s have also built greater consensus around the intrinsic value of political freedoms and all human rights.

A future agenda for the *Human Development Reports* should be to give more balanced emphasis to political freedoms and collective agency. Over the next decade, they can contribute more to development debates by providing innovative concepts, measures and policy analyses that focus on the instrumental value of these issues for development.

ENDNOTES

* The author is grateful to Saras Menon and A. K. Shiva Kumar for their useful comments.

1. Kanbur 2001.

2. The contrasts have been explained in each report from the start. For example, see *Human Development Report 1990*, p. 11. Chapter 2 of *Human Development Report 1996*, "Growth as a Means to Human Development," elaborates the evolution of development thought, traces how ideas about human development have emerged, and provides many useful insights into the differences between human development and earlier approaches.

3. The difference between human capital and human capabilities is fundamental. See chapter 2.3.

4. See chapter 2.1.

5. *Brazil National Human Development Report, 1996.*

6. The government of Canada established an international commission in 2000 to propose principles and conditions for humanitarian interventionism. In 2001, the government of Japan set up a World Commission on Human Security to provide public advocacy, conceptual clarification and a programme of action on the multiple dimensions of human security.

7. *Human Development Report 2000*, p. 19.

8. Since then, a number of efforts have been made to collect data on and measures of political freedom – such as the Free-

dom House Index, Gurr's Polity Index and dozens of others. These are interesting measures but are concerned with political institutions. The human freedom index and the political freedom index remain important experiments in measuring human enjoyment of freedom rather than the existence of institutional arrangements. For assessments of this experience, see Haq 1995 and *Human Development Report 2000*, box 5.2.

9. *Human Development Report 1993*. See especially the overview and chapters 4 and 5.

10. *Human Development Report 1990*, p. 26.

11. Several scholars have written on this complex issue. See, for example, Nussbaum 2000.

12. The capabilities approach to development – and human development, its application – leaves open the final definition of valuable ends to social and individual values. According to Sen (1989), "There are many ambiguities in the conceptual framework of the capability approach." These ambiguities are in fact part of the concept.

13. Sen 1989.

14. *Human Development Report 1999*, pp. 16–17.

15. Sen 1989.

16. Anand and Sen 1997.

17. *Human Development Report 1990*, box 1.1.

18. *Human Development Report 2001*, p. 9.

REFERENCES

Anand, Sudhir and Amartya K. Sen. 1997. "Concepts of Human Development and Human Poverty: A Multidimensional Perspective." *Human Development Papers 1997*. United Nations Publications, New York.

Freedom House. 2001. *Freedom in the World*. [http://www.freedomhouse.org/research/freeworld/2001/index.htm]. April 2002.

Haq, Mahbub ul. 1995. *Reflections on Human Development*. New York: Oxford University Press.

ICISS (International Commission on Intervention and State Sovereignty). 2000. "About the Commission." [http://www.iciss-ciise.gc.ca/background-e.asp]. April 2002.

Kanbur, Ravi. 2001. "Economic Policy, Distribution and Poverty: The Nature of Disagreements." *World Development* 29 (6): 1083–94.

The Ministry of Foreign Affairs of Japan. 2001. "Plan for Establishment of the Commission on Human Security." [http://www.mofa.go.jp/policy/human_secu/speech0101.html]. April 2002.

Nussbaum, Martha C. 2000. "Women and Human Development: The Capabilities Approach." Cambridge: Cambridge University Press.

Polity IV. 2002. "Political Regime Characteristics and Transitions, 1800–2000." [http://www.bsos.umd.edu/cidcm/inscr/polity/index.htm]. April 2002.

Sen, Amartya. 1989. "Development as Capability Expansion." *Journal of Development Planning* 19: 41–58.

UNDP (United Nations Development Programme). 1990. *Human Development Report 1990*. New York: Oxford University Press.

———. 1991. *Human Development Report 1991*. New York: Oxford University Press.

———. 1992. *Human Development Report 1992*. New York: Oxford University Press.

———. 1993. *Human Development Report 1993*. New York: Oxford University Press.

———. 1994. *Human Development Report 1994*. New York: Oxford University Press.

———. 1995. *Human Development Report 1995*. New York: Oxford University Press.

———. 1996. *Human Development Report 1996*. New York: Oxford University Press.

———. 1997. *Human Development Report 1997*. New York: Oxford University Press.

———. 1998. *Human Development Report 1998*. New York: Oxford University Press.

———. 1999. *Human Development Report 1999*. New York: Oxford University Press.

———. 2000. *Human Development Report 2000*. New York: Oxford University Press.

———. 2001. *Human Development Report 2001*. New York: Oxford University Press.

UNDP and IPEA (Institute of Applied Economic Research). 1996. *Brazil National Human Development Report*. Brasília.

SECTION 2:
MEASUREMENT

2.1

THE BIRTH OF THE
HUMAN DEVELOPMENT INDEX*

Mahbub ul Haq

After a while [Alice] remembered that she still held the pieces of mushroom in her hands, and she set to work very carefully, nibbling first at one and then at the other, and growing sometimes taller and sometimes shorter, until she had succeeded in bringing herself down to her usual height.

—Alice in Wonderland

Any measure that values a gun several hundred times more than a bottle of milk is bound to raise serious questions about its relevance for human progress. It is no surprise, then, that since the emergence of national income accounts, there has been considerable dissatisfaction with gross national product as a measure of human welfare. GNP reflects market prices in monetary terms. Those prices quietly register the prevailing economic and purchasing power in the system – but they are silent about the distribution, character or quality of economic growth. GNP also leaves out all activities that are not monetized – household work, subsistence agriculture, unpaid services. And what is more serious, GNP is one-dimensional: it fails to capture the cultural, social, political and many other choices that people make.

There has been a long search for a more comprehensive measure of development that could capture all, or many more, of the choices people make – a measure that would serve as a better yardstick of the socioeconomic progress of nations. Several difficulties have marked this search. First, some analysts came out with scores of economic and social indicators but did not aggregate them into a composite index – so policy-makers found such measures hard to digest. Second, several composite measures lacked a sound methodological base and were abandoned after brief trials. Third, not enough investment was made in constructing measures that were alternatives to GNP – nor was the effort sustained long enough to develop, refine and test such socioeconomic indices.

EMERGENCE OF THE HDI

The search for a new composite index of socioeconomic progress began in earnest in preparing the *Human Development Report* under the sponsorship of UNDP in 1989.[1] Several principles guided this search. First, the new human development index (HDI) would measure the basic concept of human development to enlarge people's choices. These choices covered the desire to live long, to acquire knowledge, to have a comfortable standard of living, to be gainfully employed, to breathe clean air, to be free, to live in a community. Obviously, not all these choices could be quantified or measured. The basic idea was to measure at least a few more choices besides income and to reflect them in a methodologically sound composite index.

Second, the new index would include only a limited number of variables to keep it simple and manageable. Initially, life expectancy was chosen as an index of longevity, adult literacy as an index of knowledge, and GNP per capita adjusted for purchasing power parity (PPP) as an index of access to a multiplicity of economic choices. Several other variables were considered and discarded. They showed a significant correlation with the variables already chosen – infant and child mortality, for instance, has almost perfect correlation with life expectancy. Or they inadequately reflected real situations – for example, average calorie supply data failed to show how food was actually distributed among the population so that considerable hunger could coexist with "satisfactory" national averages.

Third, a composite index would be constructed rather than a plethora of separate indices. This posed several problems. Unlike GNP, for which money serves as a "common measuring rod", there is no such common currency for measuring socioeconomic progress. Life expectancy is measured in years, adult literacy in percentages of adults, and real income in PPP-adjusted dollars. How to reduce these indicators to a common denominator? The methodological breakthrough was to measure actual progress in each indicator as relative distance from a desirable goal. The maximum and minimum observed values for each variable were reduced to a scale between 0 and 1: each country was at some point on this scale. The advantage of this methodology: every nation's actual progress was measured in relation to a goal. The disadvantage, of course, was that all values became relative to each other, a disadvantage later removed by agreeing on certain fixed goal posts – an aspect that is discussed later. Another problem in the composite index was that of weighting. Equal weights were decided for the three variables on the simple premise that all these choices were very important and that there was no *a priori* rationale for giving a higher weight to one choice than to another. Besides, experimentation with different weights yielded no significantly different results.

Fourth, the HDI would cover both social and economic choices. A mistake in the past had been to construct separate measures for economic progress (GNP) and for social progress (such as the physical quality of life index, or PQLI). Such a formulation misses the synergy between social and economic progress. Economic growth increases the resources and options available for social progress. And social progress creates a conducive environment for economic growth. Progress of nations and individuals must be measured on both fronts, not separately, in any comprehensive index of development. This reasoning led to the inclusion of real income (PPP dollars) as well as life expectancy and educational attainment in the HDI.

Some critics have regarded it as a weakness of the HDI that income, essentially a means, is aggregated with variables that represent the real ends of development. This is not a valid criticism, as discussed later, because it is based on a misunderstanding of the manner in which income is treated in the index. The merging of economic and social indicators is one of the distinctive features and chief strengths of the HDI.

Fifth, one of the most important decisions was to keep the coverage and methodology of HDI quite flexible – subject to gradual refinements as analytical critiques emerged and better data became available. National income accounts had taken five decades of investment and research, and yet many aspects of these accounts were still being investigated. If a worthwhile socioeconomic index were to emerge, it would also require patient, long-term investigation, research and investment.

Sixth, even though an index can be only as good as the data fed into it, a lack of reliable and up-to-date data series was not allowed to inhibit the emergence of the HDI. Instead, HDI country rankings would be used as a pressure point to persuade policy-makers to invest adequate amounts in producing relevant data and to encourage international institutions to prepare comparable statistical data systems. The HDI calculations still suffer from some inadequate and unreliable data, but the production of the index has already put considerable pressure on the global community to improve the quality of underlying social and human statistics.

METHOD FOR CONSTRUCTING THE HDI[2]

The HDI has three key components: longevity, knowledge and income.[3] Longevity is measured by life expectancy at birth as the sole unadjusted indicator. Knowledge is measured by two education variables: adult literacy and mean years of schooling, with a weight of two-thirds to literacy and one-third to mean years of schooling. Initially, only adult literacy was in the index. Mean years of schooling were added later because, unlike developing countries, few industrial countries maintain separate figures for adult literacy, and there was a need to differentiate the performance of countries already close to 100% literacy.

The third variable, income, has proved more troublesome. Some critics even contend that it does not belong in the index because the HDI is concerned with ends, not means, and income is a means. Moreover, the HDI is a stock figure, while income is a flow figure. But this perception is based on a misunderstanding, for income in the HDI is merely a proxy for a bundle of goods and services needed for the best use of human capabilities. It is thus important to understand the treatment of income in the HDI.

The HDI is based on a cut-off point defined by a level of income regarded as adequate for a reasonable standard of living and for a reasonable fulfilment of human capabilities. Initially, this cut-off point was derived from the poverty-level income of the industrial countries, as reflected in the Luxembourg Income Study, with values updated and translated into purchasing power parity dollars. Later, it was taken as the current global average real GDP per capita in PPP dollars. In both cases, the threshold income is around $5,000. The difference in methodology is analytical rather than statistical and is based on certain pragmatic considerations of political acceptability.

The HDI treats income up to the cut-off point as having full value. But beyond the cut-off point, income has a sharply diminishing return – for which a specific formulation is used. The premise is that people do not need an infinite amount of income for a decent life. Wherever the upper line is drawn will always remain somewhat controversial – as will the rate of discount applied to income beyond the cut-off point.

The HDI method thus emphasizes sufficiency rather than satiety. It does not treat income as a means but reinterprets it in terms of the ends it serves. That is why, for example, the high income of the industrial countries is de-emphasized in the HDI and an overwhelming weight is given to the social progress they have achieved with this income.

With these basic variables – longevity, knowledge and income – the HDI is constructed in three simple steps.

The first step is to define a country's measure of deprivation for each of the three basic variables. Minimum and maximum values are defined for the actual observed values of each of the three variables in all countries. The deprivation measure then places the country in the 0–1 range, where 0 is the minimum observed value and 1 the maximum. So, if the minimum observed life expectancy is 40 years and the maximum 80 years, and a country's life expectancy is 50 years, its index value for life expectancy is 0.25. Similarly for the other variables.

The second step is to compile an average indicator by taking a simple average of the three indicators. As mentioned earlier, it is difficult to argue for giving different weights to the different choices that people make. The third step is to measure the HDI as one minus the average deprivation index. The value of the HDI shows where a country is placed relative to other countries.

For the first few years, this relative nature of the index created several problems of comparison. The minimum value of each dimension – longevity, knowledge and income – was set at the level of the poorest-performing country and the maximum at that of the best-performing country. But maximums and minimums changed each year – following the performance of the countries at the ends of the scale. A country could thus improve its performance and yet see its HDI fall because the countries at the top or bottom had done even better. The shifting goal posts also meant that the progress of each nation could not be measured by the rate of change in the absolute value of its HDI over time.

Recently, the HDI methodology was changed to solve this problem. Rather than constantly shifting goal posts, fixed goal posts have been adopted. Now, the maximum and minimum values are not actually observed values in the best- and worst-performing countries, but the most extreme values observed over the previous three decades or expected over the next three decades. These fixed goal posts permit meaningful comparisons of countries' performance over 60 years.

THE HDI VERSUS GNP

The HDI does not replace GNP, but it adds considerably to an understanding of the real position of a society in several respects:[4]

- Besides income, the HDI measures education and health and is thus multidimensional, rather than one-dimensional.
- It focuses the attention of the policy-makers on the ultimate objectives of development, not just the means.
- It is more meaningful as a national average than GNP because there are much greater extremes in income distribution than in the distribution of life expectancy and literacy.
- It shows that the human development gaps between nations are more manageable than the ever-widening disparities in income. The average income of the South may be only 6% of the North's – but its life expectancy is 80%, its nutrition level 85% and its adult literacy rate 66% of the North's.
- The HDI can be disaggregated by gender, ethnic group or geographical region and in many other ways – to present relevant policy inputs as well as to forecast impending trouble. Indeed, one of the HDI's greatest strengths is that it can be disaggregated in ways that hold a mirror up to society.

Some argue that the income of a society reflects all its other achievements, so a separate index for those achievements is unnecessary. This is patently false. There is no automatic translation of the income of a society into the lives of its people. Several telling examples:

- Saudi Arabia has a per capita income 16 times that of Sri Lanka but a much lower literacy rate.
- The infant mortality rate in Brazil is four times higher than that in Jamaica even though Brazil enjoys twice the per capita income.

- Oman has three times the per capita income of Costa Rica but about one-third its literacy rate and seven fewer years of life expectancy, and it lacks most political and economic freedoms.
- The life expectancy of black males in Harlem, in New York City, is lower than that in Bangladesh or Sudan.

These examples can be multiplied. The point is that GNP, by itself, reveals little about how the people in a society live and breathe. Ideally, a high income brings within reach many social services and improvements in human life. But whether this happens depends on many other factors: What is the composition of this income? What is being produced and consumed? How is the income distributed?

It is the actual distribution and use of the income that is decisive, not just its level – an obvious fact that is often forgotten. For this reason, if for no other, the HDI is a useful supplement to GNP in understanding and analysing a society. Compare the HDI and GNP rankings of countries. Of 173 countries included in these rankings, there is no difference in the ranks for four countries and less than a five-rank difference for 29 countries. But for most other countries, the differences are substantial.

The HDI and GNP ranks of more than a third (60) of the countries differ by more than 20 places (table 2.1.1). There are differences of more than 40 ranks for 10 countries and more than 30 ranks for 26 countries. These comparisons of HDI and GNP ranks raise serious doubts about the notion that there is a perfect trickle-down of income growth to all members of society or that the quality of human lives in each country is correlated with its per capita income.

These comparisons also bring out different development strategies. Some countries give a high priority to the provision of basic social services to all their people as a matter of deliberate public policy: notable examples are China, Colombia, Costa Rica, Cuba, Jamaica and Sri Lanka. The results are fairly high indicators of education and health at fairly modest incomes. For other countries, income distribution has been very uneven, and government policy has not focused on provision of social services. Their HDI ranks are significantly below their per capita GNP ranks, as for Papua New Guinea, Gabon and several other countries in Sub-Saharan Africa.

Several Arab nations also show an HDI rank less favourable than their GNP per capita rank: Oman, United Arab Emirates, Iraq, Libya, Algeria, Qatar, Saudi Arabia, Bahrain, Kuwait and Lebanon. Many of them acquired their new wealth only after the rise in the price of oil in the mid-1970s. It is taking them some time to translate this financial wealth into the well-being of their people. But the process has accelerated considerably in the past two decades. The Gulf states have made much faster progress than the average developing country in the past 20 years. Saudi Arabia increased its HDI from 0.386 in 1970 to 0.688 in 1990 – among the largest increases in HDI during

Table 2.1.1

GNP and HDI rankings of selected countries *(GNP per capita rank minus HDI rank)*

More favourable HDI rank		Less favourable HDI rank	
More favourable by more than 40 ranks		*Less favourable by more than 40 ranks*	
China	+49	Gabon	−72
Guyana	+44	Oman	−54
Colombia	+41	United Arab Emirates	−52
		Guinea	−44
		Seychelles	−44
		Namibia	−43
		Iraq	−41
More favourable by more than 30 ranks		*Less favourable by more than 30 ranks*	
Sri Lanka	+38	Djibouti	−38
Costa Rica	+36	Libyan Arab Jamahiriya	−38
Lithuania	+35	Algeria	−37
Viet Nam	+34	Suriname	−37
Nicaragua	+33	Qatar	−36
Madagascar	+31	Saudi Arabia	−36
Poland	+30	Angola	−35
		South Africa	−33
		Mauritania	−31
More favourable by more than 20 ranks		*Less favourable by more than 20 ranks*	
Czechoslovakia	+29	Botswana	−29
Bulgaria	+28	Senegal	−29
Chile	+28	Vanuatu	−26
Ecuador	+28	Bahrain	−25
Thailand	+28	Central African Rep.	−25
Lao People's Dem. Rep.	+24	Congo	−23
Hungary	+23	Kuwait	−23
Panama	+23	Saint Kitts and Nevis	−23
Ukraine	+23	Gambia	−22
Jamaica	+22	Iran, Islamic Rep. of	−22
Tanzania	+22	Singapore	−22
Azerbaijan	+21	Niger	−21
Cuba	+21	Papua New Guinea	−21
Kenya	+21	Swaziland	−21
Syrian Arab Rep.	+21	Lebanon	−20
Armenia	+20	Saint Lucia	−20
Uruguay	+20		
Zaire	+20		

Source: Human Development Report 1994.

that period. Thus, while there is a link between income and human development, the nature of that link depends on the development priorities that countries choose.

Several countries have similar levels of per capita GNP but vastly different social progress (table 2.1.2). Malaysia and Iraq have the same per capita GNP (around $2,500). But life expectancy in Malaysia is five years longer, adult literacy about 17 percentage points higher and infant mortality less than one-fourth that in Iraq. In such cases, GNP per capita is totally misleading as an indicator of human development.

But an HDI rank higher than a GNP per capita rank is not always a cause for celebration. East European countries and the former Soviet Union enjoyed such a status for a long time. But because their social progress was not supported by economic growth, the long-term sustainability of their human development levels became dubious.

To summarize, to examine the link between economic and social progress, we must see how income is distributed and used in a society and how far it has been translated into the lives of people. If a country's HDI rank is more favourable than its GNP per capita rank, this should reassure policymakers that their social priorities are headed in the right direction, and that the country is building up an adequate base of human capital for accelerated growth. It should also remind them that social

progress cannot be sustained for long without an adequate economic base – so they should also correct the imbalance on the economic growth side.

But if the HDI rank is far less favourable than the GNP per capita rank, this should signal to policy-makers that the benefits of national income are not being distributed to the people. It should prompt them to examine whether the problem lies in maldistribution of income or assets, or in wrong development priorities, or in lack of public policy attention to social services. Comparison with other countries with similar incomes should reassure them that it is possible to generate greater human welfare at that level of income. So, there should be no tension between the HDI and GNP measures. Both can inform public policy.

What the HDI reveals

The HDI captures far more reality than GNP does. It can also be disaggregated by income class, gender, geographical region, ethnic group or other classifications to bring out a graphic profile of society – and this is one of its chief virtues.

It captures many aspects of the human condition:

NATIONAL PRIORITIES. Even a quick glance at HDI rankings shows which countries are combining economic progress with social development

Table 2.1.2
Similar incomes, different HDIs, 1991/92

Country	GNP per capita (US$)	HDI value	HDI rank	Life expectancy (years)	Adult literacy rate (%)	Infant mortality (per 1,000 live births)
GNP per capita around $500						
Sri Lanka	500	0.665	90	71.2	89	24
Guinea	500	0.191	173	43.9	27	135
GNP per capita around $1,000 to $1,100						
El Salvador	1,090	0.543	112	65.2	75	46
Congo	1,040	0.461	123	51.7	59	83
GNP per capita around $2,500 to $2,600						
Malaysia	2,520	0.794	57	70.4	80	14
Iraq	2,550	0.614	100	65.7	63	59

Source: Human Development Report 1994, p. 15.

and which lag behind. Such rankings are particularly effective in putting pressure on policy-makers to improve their performance. The HDI measure also reveals the area – whether education, health or income – in which their country's performance lags behind other comparable countries. The publication of HDI rankings each year has generated an enormous amount of attention, controversy and follow-up.

POTENTIAL GROWTH. The HDI can reveal the future potential for economic growth in a country. If a country has built up considerable human capital, it can accelerate its GNP growth by choosing the right macroeconomic policies – as is true for many formerly socialist countries now in transition to a market economy. But if human capital is largely missing, it would take a country considerable time to create the human infrastructure needed for sustainable growth – which is true for much of Sub-Saharan Africa today. Moreover, if there has been a significant investment in education and health, there is a reasonable prospect that people will be able to gain access to market opportunities so that economic growth will be more equitable.

DISPARITIES BETWEEN PEOPLE. The HDI can be disaggregated to bring out disparities between various sections of society. The *Human Development Report* has disaggregated the HDI by income class, gender, ethnic group and geographical region. These exercises have led to some important conclusions.

For instance, gender-adjusted HDI comparisons have revealed the shocking reality that no country treats women as well as men. And when countries see their HDI ranking decline or improve significantly as a result of adjustment for gender disparities, it evokes controversy and helps galvanize policy action (table 2.1.3).

The policy impact is even greater for disaggregations by ethnic group. *Human Development Report 1993* brought out the HDI disparity among whites, blacks and Hispanics in the United States. It pointed out that, if considered as separate nations, whites would outrank all other countries, blacks would rank number 31 (after Trinidad and Tobago), and Hispanics would rank number 35 (next to Estonia). So, ethnic disparities persist in the United States despite many legal battles, considerable mobility of labour and fast-opening market opportunities. Naturally, the comparison led to much excited debate.

EARLY WARNING SYSTEM. Ideally, it should be possible to disaggregate the HDI measure so that a society can see all its strengths, blemishes and tension points. Such an exercise depends on the availability of relevant data, which countries sometimes are reluctant to collect. Many countries have already started preparing detailed HDI estimates in a fairly disaggregated form – among them, Bangladesh, Bolivia, Egypt, India, the Philippines, South Africa and Turkey. This is politically courageous and timely, since one of the key uses of the HDI can be to provide an early warning about impending trouble.

Widening disparities in the HDI among regions or ethnic groups suggests a possibility of open

Table 2.1.3
Gender-disparity-adjusted HDI

Country	HDI rank	Gender-disparity adjusted HDI rank	Difference between HDI rank and gender-disparity-adjusted HDI rank
Improved rank			
Finland	16	3	+13
Denmark	15	4	+11
New Zealand	18	8	+10
Czechoslovakia	25	15	+10
Iceland	14	6	+8
Fallen rank			
Japan	3	19	–16
Switzerland	2	17	–15
Canada	1	9	–8
Hong Kong	22	30	–8

Note: Only 43 countries are included in the exercise to calculate gender-disparity-adjusted HDI because of limited availability of data. HDI ranks are therefore recalculated for this exercise, taking as the total universe 43 countries rather than the 173 countries included in the total exercise. The differences in ranks in the last column are extremely significant in the context of this limited universe.
Source: Human Development Report 1994.

conflict or violence. For instance, *Human Development Report 1993* documented disparities between components of the HDI for Mexico's Chiapas region and the Mexican national average – a year before Chiapas erupted in open revolt. The 1994 report documents even wider disparities in Brazil, China, Egypt and Nigeria (table 2.1.4). Such gaps should be treated as a timely warning, not a source of national embarrassment. In fact, an obligatory part of preparing national development plans should be to draw up a disaggregated profile of society over time to see which sections of society are gaining or losing in the development race and where the future tension points are likely to be.

CHANGE OVER TIME. With the adoption of fixed goal posts, it has become possible to make meaningful comparisons of countries by their HDI values over time (table 2.1.5). The main conclusions:

- In 1960, the majority of the world's people, 73%, were in the low human development category, but in 1992, only 35% were in that category. So, nearly two-thirds had shifted to the medium or high human development category.

- Developing countries more than doubled their average HDI between 1960 and 1992, while industrial countries, starting from a much higher level, increased theirs by only 15%. This rapidly closed the HDI gaps between North and South – from nearly 70% in 1960 to around 40% in 1992.

- The fastest progress in accelerating human development between 1960 and 1992 was in East Asia and the Arab States.

- Many countries with modest incomes – such as Botswana, China, Costa Rica, Malaysia and the Republic of Korea – increased their education and health investments rapidly during 1960–92, which enabled them to accelerate their economic growth as well.

- Among the industrial countries, Japan made the most extraordinary progress, jumping from an HDI rank of 23 in 1960 to 3 in 1992.

CURRENT CRITICISMS AND POSSIBLE REFINEMENTS

The HDI is still evolving. It must continue to respond to constructive criticism so that a more useful measure emerges. In that spirit, it is worthwhile

Table 2.1.4
Disaggregated HDIs

Reflecting regional disparities

Country	Region with highest HDI value		Region with lowest HDI value		Index[a]
Mexico	Nuevo Leon	0.868	Chiapas	0.619	140
Brazil	Southern region	0.839	Northeast region	0.544	154
China	Shanghai (Beijing)	0.860	Tibet	0.400	215
Egypt	Cairo	0.738	Rural Upper Egypt	0.444	362
Nigeria	Bendel	0.666	Borno	0.156	427

Reflecting ethnic disparities

Country	Ethnic group with highest HDI value		Ethnic group with lowest HDI value		Percentage difference[b]
United States	Whites	0.990	Blacks	0.890	11
South Africa	Whites	0.878	Blacks	0.462	90
Malaysia (1970)	Chinese	0.580	Malays	0.400	45
Malaysia (1991)	Chinese	0.900	Malays	0.730	23

[a] Index of highest regional HDI value with lowest regional HDI value = 100.
[b] Percentage difference calculated by taking lowest HDI value as the denominator.
Source: Human Development Report 1993 and Human Development Report 1994.

to summarize some of the key suggestions made in recent years and to explore how the index can be further refined.

MORE VARIABLES. Several critics have pointed out that the variables included in the HDI are very limited. Several additional indices of socioeconomic progress have been advanced with varying intensity – food security, housing, environment. These deserve serious consideration and should be added when adequate and reliable data become available. Some critics believe that a human development index that does not include political freedoms is incomplete. This criticism is justified. But some suggestions are more difficult to pursue – such as including cultural and spiritual values, since any attempt at quantification will raise more issues than it settles.

More variables will not necessarily improve the HDI. They may confuse the picture and blur the main trends. It is best to recognize that the HDI will remain a partial reflection of reality. And there is some virtue in keeping the index sharp and simple, studying other legitimate concerns alongside the HDI rather than trying to integrate everything into the HDI.

NO COMPOSITE INDEX. Several critics have suggested that it is better to produce a series of separate indicators to document different aspects of social progress rather than a composite index – which raises serious issues about the weights chosen or the methods used for compiling the index. This is academic puritanism taken too far, for the same criticism can apply to all composite indices – particularly GNP. Moreover, practical considera-

Table 2.1.5
Changes in HDI over time

	1960	1992	Change 1960–92 (%)
Distribution of people (%)			
High human development group	16	23	+44
Medium human development group	11	42	+282
Low human development group	73	35	−47
HDI value by country group			
Developing countries	0.260	0.541	+108
Industrial countries	0.799	0.918	+15
World	0.392	0.605	+54
HDI value by region			
East Asia	0.255	0.653	+156
Arab States	0.277	0.631	+128
South Asia	0.202	0.376	+86
Sub-Saharan Africa	0.200	0.357	+78
Latin America and the Caribbean	0.467	0.757	+62
Notable Performers (HDI value)			
Botswana	0.207	0.670	+224
China	0.248	0.644	+160
Korea, Rep. of	0.398	0.859	+159
Malaysia	0.330	0.794	+141
Costa Rica	0.550	0.848	+54
Japan	0.686	0.929	+54

Source: Human Development Report 1994.

tions dictate the evolution of a composite index: busy policy-makers cannot absorb a host of separate social indicators pointing in all directions. For any useful policy index, some compromises must be made. But such compromises must not sacrifice the professional integrity of the broad picture that the composite index intends to convey.

It helps to keep reminding ourselves that human development is a much richer concept than the HDI can ever hope to capture. The HDI is not intended to replace the other detailed socioeconomic indicators essential for understanding the real situation in any country. It should be regarded as a useful measure for some policy purposes, supplemented by other, more detailed socioeconomic indicators.

DIFFERENT HDIs FOR DIFFERENT COUNTRY GROUPS. The HDI measures only the most elementary human achievements: life expectancy at birth, basic education and literacy, and income up to only a low cut-off point (normally around $5,000). So, some have argued that, although the HDI may capture the priorities of the poorest nations of Sub-Saharan Africa and South Asia, it does not do full justice to regions where human development priorities have already moved beyond these basic levels, such as East Asia and Latin America. The criticism is even more valid for industrial countries: they already have high levels of adult literacy, and their incomes have little impact on their HDI values because of the sharply diminishing returns assumed for income beyond the cut-off point. The ranking of industrial countries then corresponds more to the differences in their life expectancy than to any other variable – and fails to capture the full range of their socioeconomic progress.

The argument is valid, but it raises a dilemma. Comparisons across all countries require a simple index for which data are available for most countries. Yet there is a need to differentiate among groups of countries at different stages of development. The *Human Development Report* has resolved this dilemma by keeping the HDI estimates focused on the three basic variables – but supplementing them by detailed human development indicator tables, particularly for industrial countries,

which bring out the full profile of their socioeconomic progress. Another way of dealing with this issue, proposed by Anand and Sen, is to supplement the HDI with three separate indices for low, medium and high human development categories that better reflect their stage of human progress.[5] Supplementary tables on these lines can be compiled to illustrate the additional light they throw on the human development achievements in different groups of countries.

INADEQUATE AND UNRELIABLE DATA. Some critics have pointed out that the underlying data for HDI estimates are weak and unreliable.[6] While this concern is valid, it should be used to improve the quality of data rather than to abandon the exercise. To stop the production of the HDI on this reasoning would be to throw out the baby rather than change the bath water. In fact, the preparation of HDI estimates and rankings have persuaded many countries to invest more resources and effort in preparing better statistical series. Several countries have noticed the poor quality of their data only after it has embarrassed them in the country rankings. The only sensible solution, therefore, is to earmark more resources to improve statistics. Meanwhile, HDI values should be treated as indicating a sense of direction rather than precise magnitudes.

ALLOCATION CRITERIA AND AID CONDITIONALITY. There has been considerable nervousness among policy-makers in the developing world that aid donors will adopt the HDI for allocating their funds and base their policy conditionality on it. This concern is difficult to understand since the availability of statistical measures does not by itself dictate whether there will be aid conditionality. The donors first decide on their aid conditionality and then look for relevant statistical measures to judge the performance of the recipient countries. Today, country performance is measured largely by GNP growth and other macroeconomic indicators. Why should it hurt the developing countries if their progress is judged not only on economic criteria but also on human development criteria, where they have made far more rapid progress in the past three decades than in GNP?

Should the HDI be used as the basis for aid allocations? This is a difficult issue. Should aid go to countries with low HDIs – to the needy? Or should it go to countries with the fastest improvement over time – to the speedy? A case can be made for both options. Perhaps the best option is to focus aid on countries that have a low HDI but are making a determined effort to raise it. The point is that the HDI reveals much more about the socioeconomic progress of a country than GNP does, and there is no reason not to use it increasingly in the development policy dialogue.

To conclude, the HDI is neither perfect nor fully developed. It requires continuous analysis and further refinement. And one of the key questions is whether the HDI should incorporate some measure of political freedom.

ENDNOTES

not collection of articles [handwritten annotation]

* Editors' note: This article has been reproduced from Mahbub ul Haq's *Reflections on Human Development*, 1995, chapter 4, Oxford University Press.

1. A small group was assembled under the direction of the author to prepare the new index. Those who made significant contributions at an initial stage included Amartya Sen and Meghnad Desai, later joined by Gustav Ranis, Frances Stewart, Paul Streeten, Inge Kaul and Sudhir Anand. Many more from among the consultants and staff of the Human Development Report Office contributed to this collective exercise.

2. Editor's note: The methodology for the construction of the HDI has undergone revisions since the publication of this article. See chapter 2.9 or, for the latest modifications, the technical appendix in the most recent *Human Development Report*.

3. For a fuller treatment of the HDI methodology, see the technical notes in the 1991, 1992 and 1993 *Human Development Reports*. See also chapter 5 in *Human Development Report 1994*. A detailed analysis is given in Anand and Sen 1994.

4. I am grateful to Paul Streeten for pointing out some of these characteristics of the HDI.

5. See Anand and Sen 1994, pp. 12–14.

6. See, for example, Srinivasan 1994.

REFERENCES

Anand, Sudhir and Amartya Sen. 1994. "Human Development Index: Methodology and Measurement." Human Development Report Office Occasional Paper 12. UNDP, New York.

Srinivasan, T. N. 1994. "Human Development: A Paradigm or Reinvention of the Wheel?" Paper presented at American Economic Association meeting, 3 January, Boston.

UNDP (United Nations Development Programme). 1991. *Human Development Report 1991*. New York: Oxford University Press.

———. 1992. *Human Development Report 1992*. New York: Oxford University Press.

———. 1993. *Human Development Report 1993*. New York: Oxford University Press.

———. 1994. *Human Development Report 1994*. New York: Oxford University Press.

HUMAN DEVELOPMENT INDEX:
METHODOLOGY AND MEASUREMENT*

Sudhir Anand and Amartya Sen**

THE CONCEPT OF HUMAN DEVELOPMENT

As the 1990 *Human Development Report* argued, a basic distinction needs to be made between the *means* and the *ends* of development. Human beings are the real end of all activities, and development must be centered on enhancing their achievements, freedoms, and capabilities. It is the lives they lead that are of intrinsic importance, not the commodities or income that they happen to possess. Income, commodities ("basic" or otherwise), and wealth do of course have instrumental importance but they do not constitute a direct measure of the living standard itself. A person's income level, for example, does not reveal what expectation of life the person has, whether he or she is presently healthy (or suffering from a disease), is disabled and incapable of moving about freely, etc. Even for those features of the living standard where the instrumental significance of private income is likely to be greater, such as adequate nutrition, there is enormous variation in converting income into achieved well-being.[1] People's metabolic rates vary, as do their activity levels and the climatic conditions in which they live. People living in mountainous areas *need* more energy from food and fuel because they *lose* more body energy in the colder ambient temperature. A handicapped person with a physical disability needs more income to achieve the same degree of mobility than a normal person does.[2] The same is true of elderly and infirm people.

To some extent, one can adjust private household incomes for differences in certain very specific and limited needs. For example, a child needs less food to achieve the same level of nutrition as an adult. A large household needs more income than a small household to achieve the same

level of consumption of goods and services, though not quite in proportion to the number of its members because of "economies of scale" in such consumption. A household living in a high-price region needs more income to purchase the same food and other commodities than one living in a low-price area. For these differences in needs, and only these, we can adjust household income to take them into account. We do this through so-called "equivalence scales" which correct household income for the size and age-sex composition of its members.[3] And we use price indices to correct for regional and temporal price differences. But it is simply *not* possible, through income, to account for individual differences in morbidity, mortality or disability – and these features would seem to deserve priority in any assessment of the living standard. There are also other, non-private, economic goods and services which cannot be captured adequately through household incomes. These are the standard public or publicly provided goods – the environment, infrastructure (such as roads), electricity, transport and communication facilities, epidemiological protection, etc. Thus private incomes fail to capture even some very basic instrumental features of the standard of living in developing countries.

Hence the motivation to focus directly on the lives that people lead – what they succeed in being and doing. Do they have the capability to live long? Can they avoid mortality during infancy and childhood? Can they escape preventable morbidity? Do they avoid illiteracy? Are they free from hunger and undernourishment? Do they enjoy personal liberty and freedom?

These are basic features of well-being which derive from looking at people as the center of all development activity. Enhancing their capabilities to function in these elementary ways is what lies at the core of human development. The achievements of people – be it in terms of long life or functional literacy – are valued as *ends* in themselves. This should be contrasted with more mainstream economic approaches which discuss human *resource* development. Here the focus is on human beings as a resource – an input into production activities. The development of human resources is seen in terms of their contribution to income generation – as an investment, like any other, in enhancing the productive potential.

Whereas the human development approach values capabilities related to, say, health, nutrition, and basic education as ends in themselves – and income only as a means to achieve these – human resource development (like "human capital" investment) is based on precisely the opposite valuation. This approach assesses investment in human capital – including health, nutrition, and education – entirely in terms of the extra income or output the investment generates, judging it to be worthwhile if the rate of return exceeds the capital cost. By contrast, proponents of the human development approach would argue for the enhancement of people's ability to read and write, or to be well-nourished and healthy, even if the conventionally measured economic return to investment in literacy, or improved food intake and health care, were zero (though, of course, they are typically quite high anyway).

AGGREGATIVE INDICATORS AND INTRAPOPULATION INEQUALITY

The usual measures of group performance (such as the gross national product, net national income, life expectancy at birth) tend to be aggregative indicators that are based on averaging the individual circumstances. This inevitably involves the loss of some valuable information. A situation in which, say, three people have respectively income levels (1, 9, 11) looks much like one in which the three respectively have (7, 7, 7), even though the two social situations can scarcely be seen as equivalent in terms of our concerns and values. There is, thus, an understandable demand to see whether

distribution-sensitive measures could not be used instead of the usual aggregate indicators based on simple averages.

In understanding this demand, we have to distinguish between two different aspects of the problem that are sometimes lumped together. First, there is some loss of detailed information in using an aggregate number (a "scalar") for a bunch of numbers representing individual circumstances (a "vector"). Secondly, the procedure of simple averaging overlooks the actual distribution pattern of the bunch of numbers and concentrates only on their mean value. In seeking a distribution-sensitive measure, the object is to tackle the second problem. But even a distribution-sensitive scalar measure would continue to involve some loss of information, since there is no way of capturing the entire wealth of knowledge embedded in a *set* of numbers in *one* real number. For example, while a distribution-sensitive measure would respond both to the average value and in some ways to the dispersion around that average value, it would not be able to tell between (i) how much of a change is due to a shift in the average value, and (ii) how much a result of a changed distributional pattern. Indeed, such a measure could remain stationary even when both the average and the distributive pattern changes, if the two effects cancel each other out. There are also many different ways of assessing inequality, and any particular distribution-sensitive measure would have to pick one and thus can be insensitive to the rationale of the other measures of dispersion. The case for a distribution-sensitive measure must not, therefore, be seen simply in terms of having "more" information, but rather in terms of using "more relevant" information, which incorporates distributional concerns along with aggregative ones.

There is a further distinction that is worth making in interpreting the search for distribution sensitivity, and this concerns the distinction between the "efficiency argument" and the "equity argument" for more equality.[4] The former relates to the fact that many of the indicator variables (such as income) are means to other ends. They are not valuable in themselves – only for the ends they serve – and the functional relation relating these means to the real ends may involve "diminishing returns". The traditional utilitarian argument for a more equal distribution of incomes (given the total income to be distributed) has never rested on wanting a more equal distribution of *utilities* themselves, but on the efficiency advantage of distributing incomes more equally in generating more *total* utility, given the diminishing marginal utility of a shared utility function. Indeed, utilitarianism does not value at all the distribution of what it takes to be the real ends (i.e., utilities), and concentrates instead entirely on the distribution-independent total size of the aggregate of utilities generated.

In contrast to that approach, it is possible to incorporate into the evaluation a concern for the equity of the distribution of utilities themselves, or of other variables (quality of life, capabilities, etc.) that are taken to be intrinsically valuable – not just instrumentally so. For example, in Rawls's theory of justice as fairness, the Difference Principle pays a good deal of attention to the distribution of indices of primary goods – the indicator that Rawls uses to judge individual advantage – and concentrates in fact on a formula that gives priority to the advantage of the "worst off" sections of the community.[5] Within the more traditional "welfarist" framework based on utilities, James Meade develops his theory of economic justice by combining a distributive concern about utilities themselves along with taking note of the diminishing marginal utility from income in generating utilities.[6] While utilitarians would readily accept the case for a more equal distribution of incomes based on the latter (efficiency) argument, they are committed to opposing the former (equity) argument in this form. It is possible to debate this issue extensively, but what is most important for conceptual clarity is to understand the differences between the distinct arguments for equality of *means-variables* (such as incomes) and the disparate bearing they have on the assessment of equality of *ends-variables* (such as utilities).

Income distribution and poverty

The human development index (HDI), as used in the first *Human Development Report* (UNDP 1990), had three components, dealing respectively with (1) life expectancy at birth, (2) the proportion of literacy among the adult population, and (3) the logarithm of the gross national product (up to the level of the internationally fixed poverty line). Of the three, both life expectancy and literacy can be seen to be valuable in themselves (even though they may also be useful for pursuing other ends too). Income, however, is quintessentially a means to other ends.[7] The case for a distribution-sensitive measure of incomes can, therefore, be very firmly linked both with the efficiency and equity arguments for equality. A more equal distribution of income would generate more desirable ends (such as utilities, capabilities, and so on), but can also serve to bring about a more equal distribution of these end-variables, given a homogeneous population.

The use of the logarithm of income can serve, to some extent, the purpose of equality preference on either or both grounds, since it is a strictly concave transformation, and the average of the logarithms of incomes tends to increase as the given total income is more equally distributed. However, in the actual use of this formula in the 1990 *Human Development Report*, the logarithmic transformation was applied not to the individual incomes but to the *average* income of the nation, and this immediately obliterates that possibility of equality-preference in assessing the national situation. The unfortunate fact, however, is that the information we have on individual incomes is very limited indeed for most countries (and nearly absent for some), so that any attempt to use such a distributive correction on the basis of detailed individual income data is bound to be unrealistic at the present time. This is not the only respect in which practical feasibility limits the scope for using more adequate criteria of human development, and the compromises reflect what can be sensibly done here and now.

However, in the context of the more advanced countries (such as those in North America or in Europe, or Japan), the distributional information is much better. This is among the arguments for trying to do some *additional* analysis for a particular group of countries, even though the same exercise would not be useful for another group (see the final section of this chapter). In taking note of inequality in the distribution of incomes, it is possible to use various alternative measures of inequality. Perhaps the most widely available information on income distribution is that given by the Gini coefficient. This measure of inequality has many limitations, and it is not particularly easy to use in building up an overall picture of inequality on the basis of inequalities within and between groups.[8]

On the other hand, it does also have some merit in terms of conceptual understandability and axiomatic interpretation.[9] It can even be shown that calculated with appropriate price indices, a view of social welfare based on rank-order weighted individual income levels is well expressed by a Gini-corrected mean national income. That is, when G is the Gini coefficient, and m is the mean national income, the average income corrected by rank-order weights, W, is given by:

$$W = m(1 - G).$$

If the social value of a commodity j going to individual i is seen to depend in a multiplicative way on the price of that commodity j (positively related) and on the income level y_i of person i (negatively related), and if furthermore the latter relation is seen in the simple terms of attaching a weight of n to each dollar of the n-th richest person (that is, a higher weight on a poorer person's dollar given by the rank in the income order), then m(1 − G) does indeed turn out to be quite significant. In particular, if one nation has a higher value of m(1 − G) in terms of its own price structure than another, then it can be seen as having a higher social welfare level than the latter, given the specified interpretations.[10]

This model does, of course, have many limiting assumptions, and its focus on commodities as the only ultimate source of individual well-being or social welfare is clearly a gross oversimplification. But the commodity concentration can indeed be supplemented by other criteria that focus on other aspects of human development. For example, for the more advanced countries, the possibility of using Gini-corrected income measures (reflecting one aspect of human development) can be supplemented by information on life expectancy and related criteria such as maternal mortality and child (under-five) mortality, and also by educational information – not just literacy but also the proportions of secondary and higher-educated population.

Life expectancy and inequality

Is there an exactly similar case for using some distribution corrected measure of life expectancy as there is for income level? The case cannot in fact be exactly similar, since life expectancy clearly has an intrinsic importance in a way that income does not, so that the efficiency argument for equality applies more simply in the case of incomes than with life expectancies. For example, the utilitarian argument for a more equal distribution of incomes on grounds of shared diminishing marginal utility simply does not translate into an argument for a more equal distribution of life expectancies, if life expectancies are seen, unlike incomes, as valuable in themselves.

The line, however, is not really very sharp, since life expectancy can be thought to be *both* valuable in itself and also helpful for pursuing other objectives. There may well be diminishing returns in the pursuit of those other objectives. Thus, the efficiency argument is not entirely irrelevant to the importance of reducing inequalities in the distribution of life expectancies. Furthermore, there is also the "equity argument" for the distribution of longevities. Taking both these into account, there remain good reasons to be concerned not only with the average life expectancy value, but also with its distributive pattern, even though the case is not altogether analogous to that of income distribution.

The distributive issue in the context of life expectancies also differs in another respect from the income distributional question. Life expectancy is, by its very nature, an average figure, representing the expected value of the number of living years of a group member. A person does not have a life expectancy in the same way as he or she has an individual income – as a particular achievement. A person has a life expectancy *as a member of a group,* and this is a statistically expected value. So the concept of individual life expectancy is not viable in the way that individual income is, and the problem of distribution must, of necessity, take an *intergroup* form in the context of life expectancies.

Life expectancies can indeed be separately calculated for a population classified according to class, gender, and other categories, and they can be very useful in understanding the overall social picture. Unfortunately, the quality of life-expectancy data is often not very good, and this has caused some worries in interpreting and using the HDI from past Reports.[11] The scope for using reliable life expectancy figures for different groups within a nation is typically quite limited. However, there are exceptions in those cases in which the demographic information is collected in an already well-classified form.

This applies to the distinction between males and females, and to some extent also to differences between regions in a country (such as states in India or provinces in China). The case for using sex-specific life expectancy is particularly strong for a different reason as well. There is considerable medical evidence to suggest that if males and females receive similar health care, nutritional opportunities, and so on, women tend to have significantly lower death rates at most age groups and end up living much longer than men do. This is so despite the fact that in many parts of the world men outnumber women by a large margin. This is so not just because of the fact that more males are born than females (as they are all over the world). Indeed, despite that higher male ratio at birth, women are much more numerous than men – by about 5 percent or so – in Europe and North America, mainly because of systematically lower age-specific death rates. In those countries in the world – mostly in Asia and North Africa – where males predominate in number, there is evidence of serious neglect of women vis-à-vis men (and particularly of girls vis-à-vis boys).[12] There seems to be little reason to doubt that as the inequalities of attention between males and females reduces and disappears (and as general life expectancy rises), these countries too will have a preponderance of females over males.

The higher potential life expectancy of females vis-à-vis males is anticipated in the demographic projections for the future as well. For example, a projected life expectancy of 87.5 years for females and 82.5 years for males have been averaged to give something like 85 years of average life expectancy for some countries in 2050.[13]

In the context of this difference between life expectancy potentials, the lower actual life expectancy of females in many parts of the world may be thought to be particularly unfortunate. This point may be readily accepted, but a related point that is sometimes ignored concerns the fact that an equal life expectancy of males and females may still indicate a systematic anti-female bias in the distribution of health care, nutrition, and other ingredients of living. If such unequal treatment is thought to be itself objectionable, no matter how equal or unequal the resulting life expectancies are, then there is a good case for not trying to eliminate inequality in life expectancies irrespective of gender. In fact, a distributional correction (for example, like that through the Gini coefficient) applied here – in analogy with the income distribution correction – can, in this context, end up being highly *inegalitarian* in terms of its impact on basic equality of treatments. Since it is, in general, easier to expand the life expectancy of females than of the males when they have the *same* level of life expectancy, it can even be argued that concentrating on enhancing the simple *average* of life expectancy is more fair than the use of a distribution-corrected life expectancy would be (in this specific respect).

In the 1993 *Human Development Report* the overall HDI uses life expectancy in the aggregated form, but at the same time the life expectancies of females and males are also identified and analysed separately in particular applications (see the subsection below "Disaggregation of the HDI by gender").

Literacy and education

The question of distribution correction is not a terribly central one for an index of education that is based simply on whether or not the person *is* literate (as the literacy part of the traditional HDI is). The individual value of achievement can then take only a 0 or 1 form, and the problem of diminishing returns does not directly arise.

On the other hand, it is possible to go into the distributional question when the attention shifts to more variegated indicators of education. Here again, there is some advantage in looking at intergroup differences, rather than purely at the size distribution of educational attainments, given the social interest in intergroup contrasts. The difference between male and female educational achievements is particularly important both because of questions of gender justice and because of the practical importance – confirmed in many empirical studies – of the long-run impact of women's education on the social well-being of both women and men.[14]

REVIEWING THE CONSTRUCTION OF THE HUMAN DEVELOPMENT INDEX

In the *Human Development Reports* of 1990, 1991, and 1992, the HDI has been formulated in terms of a country's deprivation or shortfall in each of three separate dimensions – life expectancy (X_1), education (X_2), and adjusted income (X_3). The shortfall perspective has some merit in drawing attention to the distance a country still has to travel in order to achieve what is regarded as a desirable target or goal. Thus the 1990 Report defined I_{ij} as the deprivation indicator for country j with respect to variable X_i as

$$I_{ij} = \frac{\max_{k}\{X_{ik}\} - X_{ij}}{\max_{k}\{X_{ik}\} - \min_{k}\{X_{ik}\}}$$

By construction each deprivation indicator for country j, I_{ij}, $i = 1,2,3$, lies between 0 and 1. An average deprivation index I_j for country j across the three variables was defined as a simple unweighted average of the I_{ij}:

$$I_j = \frac{1}{3}\sum_{i=1}^{3} I_{ij}.$$

The shortfall in the human development index for country j was then defined to be just this average deprivation. Thus if H_j is the human development index for country j, we have, by definition $1 - H_j = I_j$ or $H_j = 1 - I_j$.

For some purposes, however, it is preferable to express the human development index H_j in terms of the attainments rather than shortfalls of country j. This formulation certainly seems more natural if one wishes to assess changes in HDI over time. The attainment perspective is more relevant in assessing how *well* a country is doing, whereas the shortfall perspective is more relevant in looking at the *difficulty* of the task still remaining.[15] Which perspective we adopt depends on the nature of the exercise.

We now express H_j directly in terms of the attainment levels X_{ij}. From the above,

$$H_j = 1 - \frac{1}{3}\sum_{i=1}^{3} I_{ij}.$$

$$= \frac{1}{3}\sum_{i=1}^{3}(1 - I_{ij})$$

$$= \frac{1}{3}\sum_{i=1}^{3}\left[1 - \frac{\max_{k}\{X_{ik}\} - X_{ij}}{\max_{k}\{X_{ik}\} - \min_{k}\{X_{ik}\}}\right]$$

$$= \frac{1}{3}\sum_{i=1}^{3}\frac{X_{ij} - \min_{k}\{X_{ik}\}}{\max_{k}\{X_{ik}\} - \min_{k}\{X_{ik}\}}$$

$$= \frac{1}{3}\sum_{i=1}^{3} H_{ij},$$

where

$$H_{ij} = \frac{X_{ij} - \min_{k}\{X_{ik}\}}{\max_{k}\{X_{ik}\} - \min_{k}\{X_{ik}\}}$$

is the ith variable's contribution to the human development index for country j.

Some commentators on the *Human Development Report 1990* have been disconcerted by this normalization of each component H_{ij} of the aggregate index H_j. They point out, for example, that an improvement in the achievement of the lowest-achieving country in the sample would decrease the HDI for country j, and this is not the sort of externalities that one wants in an index. But the human development index in the 1990 (and subsequent) Reports was constructed expressly as a measure of *relative performance* across countries at a point in time. No special significance is attached to the absolute value of the index, the entire analysis being conducted in terms of the *ranking* of countries *relative to one another*. Thus although a higher value of

$$\min_k\{X_{ik}\} \text{ or of } \max_k\{X_{ik}\}$$ would indeed decrease

H_{ij} for country j, it would do so for all other countries 1 too, and in proportion to the gap $(H_{ij} - H_{il})$ between countries j and 1. This, of course, has the effect – given the basic information – of leaving the relative ranking of countries unchanged.[16]

As defined, the human development index H_j for country j is invariant to positive affine transformations of the underlying variables X_i, $i = 1,2,3$. Thus if one were to substitute for each $i = 1,2,3$, $Z_i = a_i X_i + b_i$ where $a_i > 0$, the absolute value of each H_{ij}, and therefore also of H_j, would remain the same. In particular, if one changed the units of measurement of X_i by either scale changes ($a_i > 0$) or level changes ($b_i \neq 0$), the indices H_{ij} and H_j would have the same numerical values as before.

Measuring human development over time

While the first two *Human Development Reports* have been careful to avoid intertemporal comparisons of HDI for a given country j, we should enquire whether H_j as defined above can satisfactorily measure progress in human development over time. In taking the time derivative of H_j, which we denote as $\dot{H}_j$, it is clear from the definition that $\dot{H}_j$ will depend on $\dot{X}_{ij}$ for $i = 1,2,3$, i.e. the changes in attainment by country j along each of the three dimensions of human development. But $\dot{H}_j$ will *also* depend on the time derivatives of

$\min_k\{X_{ik}\}$ and $\max_k\{X_{ik}\}$ for $i = 1,2,3$ – in other words, the performance over time of the worst and best performers in the sample of countries for each variable i. Whereas this is *not* a problem for *inter-country* comparisons at a given point in time (as demonstrated in the previous subsection), for the purposes of comparing a given country's performance over time, the "goalposts" for each variable X_i must be held constant. In this way changes in HDI over time for country j will depend only on changes in X_{ij} over time for country j – and not on how the worst- and best-performing countries are also doing.[17]

Granted that the "goalposts" need to be fixed if the HDI is to be comparable over time, we need to ask how the goalposts should be determined. It will not be enough to fix the range of values for each X_i by simply looking at the minimum and maximum levels achieved *retrospectively*, say in the period from 1960 to 1990. We also need to look *prospectively* at the projections for each X_i and ensure that individual country levels will remain inside the range forecast in the future, in other words, over the *entire* period – backward and forward – during which intertemporal comparisons are required to be undertaken.

In the main this affects the range for the longevity variable. Looking back in time to a point when sufficient data were available for intercountry comparisons (e.g. the year 1960), the minimum level of life expectancy at birth achieved was about 35 years. For comparisons in the future going as far as 2050, *national* life expectancy at birth has been projected to reach 85 years for some countries (Torrey 1992). Thus keeping to the basic definition of HDI, we choose as our *fixed* endpoints for X_1 a minimum value of 35 years and a maximum value of 85 years. This range encompasses the lower and upper bound of life expectancy estimates over which *both* cross-country and intertemporal comparisons of HDI are envisaged.

As far as the literacy variable is concerned we choose the natural range of 0 to 100 percent. Although the lower end of the range is at the present time unlikely to be experienced at a national level, there are disaggregations we are proposing for which literacy rates even today fall below 10 percent (e.g. the female adult literacy rate in Burkina Faso or Somalia). Moreover, if intertemporal comparisons were to start back from 1960, we would indeed be approaching the lower end of the 0 to 100 percent range in some cases. Hence, we take 0 to 100 percent as the min-max interval for adult literacy.[18]

The final component of the HDI is the logarithm of per capita GDP in 1987 Kravis dollars truncated at the average official poverty line income in nine developed countries. The logarithmic transform of income is taken in order to reflect diminishing returns to transforming income into human capabilities. The ceiling on income at the poverty line is imposed because of the particular relevance of poverty removal in human development (Desai 1991, p. 355).[19] The upper bound of the min-max range for the income variable is kept constant over time at the logarithm of PPP$4,861 in 1987 prices. The lower bound for the variable again poses a slight difficulty: we choose a value of 0 to reflect negligible human development beyond the minimal levels of life expectancy and literacy achieved in the past in some countries.

Disaggregation of the HDI by population subgroups

We shall often want to examine the state of human development *within* population subgroups in a country. Such subgroups may be defined relative to geographical or administrative region, stratum (i.e. urban-rural residence), ethnicity, or occupation and other characteristics of the household head. Our formulation of the HDI in terms of fixed goalposts allows us to measure human development within such subgroups in a reasonably consistent manner. With the ranges of X_1 (life expectancy), X_2 (literacy), and X_3 (logarithm of per capita GDP up to the poverty line) as above, the HDI for country j can be expressed simply as:

$$H_j = \frac{1}{3}\left[\frac{X_{1j} - 35}{50} + \frac{X_{2j}}{100} + \frac{X_{3j}}{3.687}\right]$$

It is useful in some contexts to be able to express the overall index as a weighted average of its subgroup indices for any partition of the national population into mutually exclusive and exhaustive subgroups (such as regions within a country). The HDI is *not*, however, disaggregable in a strictly subgroup-consistent manner, such that the overall index can be built up from information about the subgroup index values and population (or income) shares only. There are two reasons why such disaggregation proves to be impossible. First, and most importantly, the variable X_3 is *non-linear* in income – it is, specifically, the logarithm of income. The population-weighted average of the logarithm of per capita income for each subgroup is *not* the logarithm of average per capita income for the national population as a whole.[20] Secondly, the average life expectancy at birth and average literacy rate for the national population are not strictly speaking the population-weighted averages of life expectancy and literacy at the subgroup level. In the case of life expectancy, the appropriate weights are the subgroup shares of total *births*, and in the case of literacy, the appropriate weights are the subgroup proportions of *adults* aged 15 and above. These latter sets of weights will not necessarily be the same as the *population* shares of the subgroups.

Disaggregation of the HDI by gender

As discussed in the above subsection "Literacy and education", there is considerable evidence of anti-female bias in some countries in the world. This takes the form of unequal treatment in access to food, health care, education, employment and income-earning opportunities – and is reflected in differential achievements of women relative to men. Gender bias exists both within the household *and* outside the household, for example, in the labour market or in access to public health services. We should like to use the HDI to illuminate the gender disparities that result from such unequal treatment.

Unlike conventional measures of development, such as those based on income or the possession of commodities, the HDI is particularly well-suited to examining gender inequalities. The reason is that the informational requirements of resource-use measures such as income – especially when estimation of their allocation *within* the household is involved – makes them very problematic in shedding light on *inter-individual* differences.[21] By contrast, the consequences of female disadvantage and gender bias, both intra- and extra-household, will be reflected in the achievements of the individuals concerned in terms of their life expectancy, literacy, survival chances, and so on. Data on these achievements are collected not at the household level through household income and expenditure surveys, but at the individual level through demographic surveys and population censuses. There is, thus, a strong practical reason – in addition to concern for what is intrinsically important – in adopting the HDI to examine gender and other inter-individual disparities.

In considering the disaggregation of the HDI by gender, we must take note – as argued in the above subsection "Literacy and education" – of the higher potential life expectancy of females vis-à-vis males. For fixing the separate goalposts of life expectancy for females and males over the period in question (from around 1960 to around 2050), the minimum and maximum average levels of life expectancy are taken to be 37.5 and 87.5 years for women, and 32.5 and 82.5 years for men. Thus the life expectancy range is 50 years for both women and men; this implies that a unit increase in longevity for either sex (over time) will contribute the *same* increment to the overall HDI. This procedure is in keeping with a "distributive concept" in which, as Aristotle argued, "people should do best *in so far as their circumstances admit*".[22]

The range for adult literacy is the same for females and males, as is that for the logarithm of per capita GDP truncated at the poverty line income. While separate adult literacy figures are in general available by gender, sex-specific estimates of income *use* are difficult, if not impossible, to establish with any accuracy even for the advanced industrial countries (for the reasons mentioned earlier). Thus if F and M refer to females and males, respectively, the female and male HDIs for country j are given by

$$H_j(F) = \frac{1}{3}\left[\frac{X_{1j}(F) - 37.5}{50} + \frac{X_{2j}(F)}{100} + \frac{X_{3j}(F)}{3.687}\right]$$

and

$$H_j(M) = \frac{1}{3}\left[\frac{X_{1j}(M) - 32.5}{50} + \frac{X_{2j}(M)}{100} + \frac{X_{3j}(M)}{3.687}\right].$$

As argued above in the subsection "Disaggregation of the HDI by population subgroups", the overall HDI for country j, H_j, will not be equal to the population-weighted average of the two subgroup HDIs for females and males, $H_j(F)$ and $H_j(M)$, respectively.

SUPPLEMENTARY CRITERIA FOR MEASURING HUMAN DEVELOPMENT IN MORE ADVANCED COUNTRIES

The concept of human development that we have discussed hitherto has been concerned only with the enhancement of the very basic capabilities of people. We have assessed these capabilities in terms of the elementary achievements of life expectancy at birth, adult literacy, and a logarithmic transform of income up to the poverty line. It is not surprising, therefore, that the HDI which incorporates just these three variables will not have much cutting power to distinguish between the performance of various advanced industrial countries. Most countries in this group have per capita GDP levels which *exceed* the average poverty line income specified, and thus have a value for this component of HDI (H_{3j}) equal to unity. Moreover, the adult literacy rates for the advanced countries – whether empirically estimated or assumed – are all in the high 90s.[23] Thus the discrimination among countries with the highest levels of HDI (say the top 15 or 20 countries) is largely due to their small life expectancy differences. In one sense, this is how it should be if the HDI is trying to measure only *basic* human development; survival would seem to be a prerequisite for the enjoyment of any *other* capability or functioning.

Yet once we take note of the high and similar levels of achievement of basic capabilities, it becomes relevant to assess performance using more refined capabilities. Indeed one can divide all countries into *three* groups – on the basis of their achieved HDI values – as has been done in the 1990 *Human Development Report*. For countries

TABLE 2.2.1

Three levels of human development

Human development level	Low	Medium	High
Human development indicators	1.1 Life expectancy	1.1 Life expectancy	1.1 Life expectancy
		1.2 Under-5 mortality	1.2 Under-5 mortality
			1.3 Maternal mortality
	2.1 Adult literacy	2.1 Adult literacy	2.1 Adult literacy
		2.2 Secondary school enrollment	2.2 Secondary school enrollment
			2.3 Tertiary enrollment
	3.1 Log per capita GDP (up to international poverty line)	3.1 Log per capita GDP (up to international poverty line)	3.1 Log per capita GDP (up to international poverty line)
		3.2 Incidence of poverty	3.2 Incidence of poverty
			3.3 Gini-corrected mean national income

with a "low" level of human development (say with a recomputed HDI value on HDR 1990 data of 0.610 or less), we simply use the basic HDI to rank and assess their performance. For countries with a "medium" level of human development (say with a recomputed HDI value on HDR 1990 data greater than 0.610 but less than or equal to 0.820), we add one supplementary indicator belonging to each of the three categories of basic variables. In the survival (longevity) category, we add under-five (i.e., infant and child) mortality; in the education category, we add secondary school enrollment; and in the income category, we add the incidence of income poverty (headcount ratio) in the country. For countries with a "high" level of human development (say with a recomputed HDI value on HDR 1990 data greater than 0.820), we add a *further* supplementary indicator to the two already existing for each category in the "medium" human development group. In the survival (longevity) category, we add the maternal mortality rate; in the education category, we add tertiary enrollment; and in the income category, we add the Gini-corrected mean national income (i.e., per capita GDP multiplied by (1G)) – as discussed in the above subsection "Income distribution and poverty".

ENDNOTES

* Editors' note: This article is reproduced from Human Development Report Office Occasional Paper 12, 1994, UNDP, New York. For the methodology for the construction of the HDI, see chapter 2.9, or for the latest modifications, the technical appendix to the most recent *Human Development Report*. Also, for a discussion on the treatment of income, see Sudhir Anand and Amartya Sen, 2000, "The Income Component of the Human Development Index," *Journal of Human Development* 1 (1).

** We are grateful to Meghnad Desai, Mahbub ul Haq, Inge Kaul, Leo Goldstone, Saras Menon, Paul Streeten and Barbara Torrey for helpful discussions and comments.

1. The need for income to achieve any specified living conditions can, in fact, vary greatly with various physiological, social, cultural, and other contingent features. For example, to reach the same level of nutrition as another, one needs a larger command over food if one has a higher metabolic rate (or a larger body frame), or if one is pregnant (or breastfeeding), or if one has a disease that makes absorption more difficult, or if one lives in a colder climate, or if one has to toil a lot, or if food has other uses (such as for entertainment, ceremonies or festivals) (Sen 1987, p. 16).

2. The handicapped, in fact, suffer from a double disadvantage. Not only is it harder for them to convert income into well-being, it is also harder for them to earn income in the first place.

3. See Deaton and Muellbauer (1980, 1986) for an analysis of different approaches to the construction and estimation of household equivalence scales.

4. On this and related matters, see Sen 1993a.

5. See Rawls 1971; also Phelps 1973.

6. See Meade 1976; also Atkinson 1983.

7. Although other end-state measures of well-being, such as those related to nutrition and health, may seem more appropriate than income as the third component of the HDI – especially for low-income countries – there are both conceptual and data difficulties in incorporating them. The standard commonly used measures of food security or availability (e.g. calorie supply) are again means-variables, and do not take account of differences in requirements among individuals or populations (see footnote 1 of the present paper; also see Anand and Harris 1992). There are some measures of *nutritional status*, or end-states, proposed to identify chronic energy deficiency. The most common indicators for children are low birthweight, low weight-for-age, wasting (low weight-for-height), and stunting (low height-for-age) [see UNICEF 1993]. For adults, the most famous measure is the Body Mass Index (BMI) proposed by Quetelet (1836, 1870) [see also Rowett Research Institute 1991]. This is defined simply as the weight in kilograms divided by the square of the height in meters. Although BMI is a relatively robust measure of nutritional status for adults, data on it are not available on anything like an international basis. (Even on a national basis, such fragmentary data as do exist are usually not representative.) Other measures like arm circumference and skinfold thickness are also sometimes used (see Willett 1990, ch. 10) – especially to assess acute undernourishment among starving people in famine situations.

8. The problem is one of lack of decomposability of the Gini coefficient; see Anand 1983.

9. See Sen 1973, 1976; Pyatt 1976, 1987; Anand 1983.

10. On this and related results, see Sen 1976; Hammond 1978; Roberts 1980.

11. See Srinivasan 1992; also Chamie 1992.

12. See Sen 1992b and the literature cited therein.

13. See Torrey 1992.

14. See Schultz 1992; also Caldwell 1986 and Preston 1975.

15. The distinction between assessing what Hicks (1939) referred to as "substitution" (as in welfare indifference curves) and "transformation" (as in production possibilities), respectively, is relevant here.

16. Even more can be said. If we were to apply a monotonic-increasing transformation $\Phi(.)$ to the original X_i, the ranking of countries by H_{ij} would remain the same. In other words,

$$\frac{X_{ij} - \min_{k}\{X_{ik}\}}{\max_{k}\{X_{ik}\} - \min_{k}\{X_{ik}\}} > \frac{X_{i\ell} - \min_{k}\{X_{ik}\}}{\max_{k}\{X_{ik}\} - \min_{k}\{X_{ik}\}}$$

if and only if

$$\frac{\Phi(X_{ij}) - \min_{k}\{\Phi(X_{ik})\}}{\max_{k}\{\Phi(X_{ik})\} - \min_{k}\{\Phi(X_{ik})\}} > \frac{\Phi(X_{i\ell}) - \min_{k}\{\Phi(X_{ik})\}}{\max_{k}\{\Phi(X_{ik})\} - \min_{k}\{\Phi(X_{ik})\}}$$

for all $\Phi(.)$ such that $\Phi'(.) > 0$. In this sense, each component H_{ij} of H_j is an *ordinal* measure.

17. This has to be slightly modified if there is more than one worst- or best-performing country at a point of time. In this case, it is the slope of the lower and upper *envelope* of the time paths of X_{ik} for all countries k with respect to which the relevant derivatives must be defined.

18. A lower bound of 0 for life expectancy is much harder to defend. Using a range of [35, 85] instead of [0, 85] for life expectancy will incidentally have the effect of increasing the weight on longevity relative to literacy in the HDI. However, using a [0, 85] range creates a problem for the male-female disaggregation of the HDI that we propose to undertake (see the subsection "Disaggregation of the HDI by gender").

19. Recent cross-sectional evidence lends support to this view. Anand and Ravallion (1993) show that the significantly positive relationship between life expectancy (or infant or under-five mortality) and average income across countries vanishes once one controls for the incidence of poverty and public health spending. Using reasonably comparable statistics on the distribution of income for 22 developing countries (from research done for the 1990 *World Development Report* on poverty), and measuring average income and the poverty line at purchasing power parity (PPP) exchange rates, they obtained the following results in explaining life expectancy (LE) – suitably transformed to measure the proportionate reduction in shortfall of LE from a maximum of 80 years (UNDP 1990, p. 13–14) – with absolute t-ratios shown in parentheses:

$$-\log(80 - LE) = -6.15 + 0.45 \log(\text{GNP per person}) \quad R^2 =$$
$$(2.07) \quad (4.00) \quad 0.45.$$

On adding the poverty index and public health spending per person to this regression, they obtained:

$$-\log(80 - LE) = -1.08 - 0.28 \log(\text{GNP per person})$$
$$(2.34) \quad (1.34)$$

$$-0.21 \log(\text{Proportion of the population consuming less than} \quad (2.36) \quad \text{PPP \$1 per day in 1985})$$

$$+0.30 \log(\text{Public health spending per person}$$

$$(3.02)$$

$$R^2 = 0.71.$$

With the addition of these two variables, the coefficient on log (GNP per person), in fact, reverses sign though it ceases to be significantly different from zero.

20. The population-weighted average of the logarithms of per capita income is equal to the logarithm of the *geometric* mean of per capita incomes of the subgroups, not their *arithmetic* mean (which is what would be required for subgroup-consistent disaggregation). Nor would it help to define the HDI as the geometric mean of the three variables – because the other two variables are measured in non-log form.

21. See, however, Deaton 1987.

22. See Aristotle, *Politics*, VII.1. See also the paper by Julia Annas in Nussbaum and Sen 1992.

23. Most of the assumed adult literacy rates for this group of countries are as high as 99 percent (UNDP 1990).

REFERENCES

Adelman, Irma. 1975. "Development Economics: A Reassessment of Goals." *American Economic Review*, Papers and Proceedings 65(2), May: 302–9.

Anand, Sudhir. 1983. *Inequality and Poverty in Malaysia: Measurement and Decomposition*. New York: Oxford University Press.

——. 1991. "Poverty and Human Development in Asia and the Pacific." United Nations Development Programme, New York, May: 1–39.

Anand, Sudhir and Christopher J. Harris. 1992. "Issues in the Measurement of Undernutrition." In S. R. Osmani (ed.), *Nutrition and Poverty*. Oxford: Clarendon Press.

Anand, Sudhir and Martin Ravallion. 1993. "Human Development in Poor Countries: On the Role of Private Incomes and Public Services." *Journal of Economic Perspectives* 7(1), Winter: 133–50.

Atkinson, Anthony B. 1983. *Social Justice and Public Policy*. Brighton: Wheatsheaf; and Cambridge, Mass.: MIT Press.

Baster, Nancy. 1985. "Social Indicator Research: Some Issues and Debates." Chapter 2 in Hilhorst and Klatter, 1985.

Caldwell, John C. 1986. "Routes to Low Mortality in Poor Countries." *Population and Development Review* 12(2): 171–220.

Chamie, Joseph. 1992. "Population Databases in Development Analysis." Paper prepared for the Conference on Database of Development Analysis, Yale University, New Haven, Conn., 15–16 May.

Chenery, Hollis B., Montek S. Ahluwalia, Clive L. G. Bell, John H. Duloy, and Richard Jolly. 1974. *Redistribution with Growth*. New York: Oxford University Press.

Chenery, Hollis B. and T. N. Srinivasan (eds.). 1988. *Handbook of Development Economics*, vol. I. Amsterdam: Elsevier Science Publishers BV.

Das, Tarun K. 1992. "UNDP Human Development Index – Some Methodological Issues and Alternative Measures." Ministry of Finance, Government of India, New Delhi. Mimeographed.

Dasgupta, Partha. 1990. "Well-being in Poor Countries." *Economic and Political Weekly*, 4 August: 1713–20.

——. 1993. *An Inquiry into Well-Being and Destitution*. Oxford: Oxford University Press.

Dasgupta, Partha and Martin Weale. 1992. "On Measuring the Quality of Life." *World Development* 20(1): 119–31.

Deaton, Angus S. 1987. "The Allocation of Goods within the Household: Adults, Children and Gender." LSMS Working Paper No. 39, World Bank, Washington, DC.

Deaton, Angus S. and John N. J. Muellbauer. 1980. *Economics and Consumer Behaviour*. Cambridge: Cambridge University Press.

——. 1986. "On Measuring Child Costs: With Applications to Poor Countries." *Journal of Political Economy* 94(4): 720–44.

Desai, Meghnad. 1989. "Potential Lifetime (PLT): A Proposal for an Index of Social Welfare." In F. Bracho (ed.), *Towards a New Way to Measure Development*. Caracas, Venezuela: Office of the South Commission.

——. 1990. "Poverty and Capability: Towards an Empirically Implementable Measure." Development Economics Research Programme Discussion Paper No. 27, September, STICERD, London School of Economics.

——. 1991. "Human Development: Concepts and Measurement." *European Economic Review* 35: 350–57.

Desai, Meghnad and A. R. Shah. 1988. "An Econometric Approach to the Measurement of Poverty." *Oxford Economic Papers* 40, November.

Drewnowski, J. and W. Scott. 1966. "The Level of Living Index." United Nations Research Institute for Social Development, Report No. 4, Geneva, September.

Drèze, Jean P. and Amartya K. Sen. 1989. *Hunger and Public Action*. Oxford: Clarendon Press.

Goldstein, Joshua S. 1985. "Basic Human Needs: The Plateau Curve." *World Development* 13(5): 595–609.

Grant, James P. 1978. *Disparity Reduction Rates in Social Indicators*. Washington, D.C.: Overseas Development Council.

Hammond, Peter J. 1978. "Economic Welfare with Rank-Order Price Weighting." *Review of Economic Studies* 45.

Hicks, John R. 1939. *Value and Capital*. Oxford: Clarendon Press.

Hicks, Norman and Paul Streeten. 1979. "Indicators of Development: The Search for a Basic Needs Yardstick." *World Development* 7: 567–80.

Hilhorst, J.G.M. 1985. "Social Indicators: A General Introduction." Ch. 1 in Hilhorst and Klatter 1985.

Hilhorst, J.G.M. and M. Klatter. 1985. *Social Development in the Third World*. London: Croom Helm.

Hopkins, Michael. 1991. "Human Development Revisited: A New UNDP Report." *World Development* 19 (10), October: 1469–73.

ILO (International Labour Office). 1976. *Employment, Growth and Basic Needs: A One-World Problem*. ILO, Geneva.

Kelley, Allen C. 1991. "The Human Development Index: 'Handle with Care'." *Population and Development Review* 17(2), June: 315–24.

Larson, D. A. and W. T. Wilford. 1979. "The Physical Quality of Life Index: A Useful Social Indicator?" *World Development* 7: 581–84.

Lisk, F. 1979. "Indicators of Basic Needs-Oriented Development Planning." *Labour and Society* 4(3).

Marx, Karl. 1867. *Capital*, Vol. I. English translation. London: Allen and Unwin, 1938.

McGillivray, Mark. 1991. "The Human Development Index: Yet Another Redundant Composite Development Indicator?" *World Development* 19(10), October: 1461–68.

McGillivray, Mark and Howard White. 1992. "Inter-Country Quality of Life Comparison: Does Measurement Error Really Matter?" Deakin University, Geelong, Australia. Mimeographed.

——. 1993. "Measuring Development? The UNDP's Human Development Index." *Journal of International Development*, March.

McGranahan, D. V., C. Richaud-Proust, N. V. Sovani, and M. Subramanian. 1972. *Contents and Measurement of Socio-economic Development*. New York: Praeger.

McGranahan, D. V. and P. Pizarro. 1985. *Measurement and Analysis of Socio-Economic Development*. UNRISD, Geneva.

Meade, James E. 1976. *The Just Economy*. London: Allen and Unwin.

Moon, M. and E. Smolensky (eds.). 1977. *Improving Measures of Economic Well-Being*. New York: Academic Press.

Morris, Morris D. 1979. *Measuring the Condition of the World's Poor: The Physical Quality of Life Index*. New York: Pergamon.

Moss, M. (ed.). 1973. *The Measurement of Economic and Social Performance*. Studies in Income and Wealth, 38. New York: NBER.

Nussbaum, Martha C. and Amartya K. Sen (eds.). 1992. *The Quality of Life*. Oxford: Clarendon Press.

Phelps, Edmund S. 1973. *Economic Justice*. Harmondsworth: Penguin.

Pomfret, R. 1992. *Diverse Paths of Economic Development*. Hemel Hempstead, UK: Harvester/Wheatsheaf.

Preston, Samuel H. 1975. "The Changing Relation between Mortality and Level of Economic Development." *Population Studies* 29(2), July: 231–48.

Pyatt, F. Graham. 1976. "On the Interpretation and Disaggregation of Gini Coefficients." *Economic Journal* 86.

——. 1987. "Measuring Welfare, Poverty and Inequality." *Economic Journal* 97.

——. 1991. "Poverty: A Wasted Decade." *European Economic Review* 35: 358–65.

——. 1992. "There is Nothing Wrong with the HDI, but..." Department of Economics, University of Warwick, United Kingdom, August. Mimeographed.

Quetelet, Lambert Adolphe Jacques. 1836. *Sur l'Homme et le Développement de ses Facultés, ou Essai de Physique Sociale*, 2 volumes. Brussels: Louis Hauman. (Translated into English by Robert Knox as *A Treatise on Man and the Development of His Faculties*, 1842. Edinburgh: Chambers.)

——. 1870. *Anthropométrie ou Mesure des Différentes Facultés de l'Homme*. Brussels, Leipzig, Gand: C. Muquardt.

Rao, V. V. Bhanoji. 1991. "Human Development Report 1990: Review and Assessment." *World Development* 19(10), October: 1451–60.

Rawls, John. 1971. *A Theory of Justice*. Cambridge, Mass.: Harvard University Press.

Rieger, Hans Christoph. 1989. "The Quality of Life in Singapore: A Foreigner's Reflections." In Sandhu and Wheatley 1989.

Roberts, Kevin W. S. 1980. "Price-Independent Welfare Prescriptions." *Journal of Public Economics* 13.

Rowett Research Institute. 1991. "Body Mass Index: An Objective Measure for the Estimation of Chronic Energy Deficiency in Adults." Aberdeen, United Kingdom, July.

Sandhu, K. S. and P. Wheatley. 1989. *The Management of Success: The Moulding of Modern Singapore.* Singapore: Institute of Southeast Asian Studies.

Schultz, T. Paul. 1992. "The Benefits of Educating Women." In E. King and M. A. Hill (eds.), *Women's Education in Developing Countries.* Baltimore, Md.: Johns Hopkins University Press.

Sen, Amartya K. 1973. *On Economic Inequality.* Oxford: Clarendon Press; and New York: Norton.

——. 1976. "Real National Income." *Review of Economic Studies* 43.

——. 1981. "Public Action and the Quality of Life in Developing Countries." *Oxford Bulletin of Economics and Statistics* 43(4): 287–319.

——. 1984. "The Living Standard." *Oxford Economic Papers* 36, Supplement: 74–90.

——. 1985. *Commodities and Capabilities.* Amsterdam: North-Holland.

——. 1987. *The Standard of Living,* The Tanner Lectures. Cambridge: Cambridge University Press.

——. 1988. "The Concept of Development." Chapter 1 in Chenery and Srinivasan 1988.

——. 1992a. *Inequality Reexamined.* Oxford: Clarendon Press; and Cambridge, Mass.: Harvard University Press.

——. 1992b. "Missing Women." *British Medical Journal* 34: 7 March.

——. 1993a. "Life Expectancy and Inequality: Some Conceptual Issues." In a festschrift for K. N. Raj published by Oxford University Press.

——. 1993b. "The Economics of Life and Death." *Scientific American* 268(5): May, 40–47.

Smith, Adam S. 1776. *An Inquiry into the Nature and Causes of the Wealth of Nations.* Republished London: Home University, 1910.

Smith, Peter. 1992. "Measuring Human Development." Department of Economics, University of Southampton, United Kingdom, August. Mimeographed.

Srinivasan, T. N. 1992. "Data Base for Development Analysis: An Overview." Paper prepared for the Conference on Database of Development Analysis, Yale University, New Haven, Conn., 15–16 May.

Srinivasan, T. N. and Pranab K. Bardhan. (eds.) 1974. *Poverty and Income Distribution in India.* Calcutta: Statistical Publishing Society.

——. 1988. *Rural Poverty in South Asia.* New York: Columbia University Press.

Stewart, Frances J. 1985. *Planning to Meet Basic Needs.* London: Macmillan.

Streeten, Paul P. 1984. "Basic Needs: Some Unsettled Questions." *World Development* 12 (9): 973–1780.

Streeten, Paul P., S. Javed Burki, Mahbub ul Haq, Norman Hicks, and Frances J. Stewart. 1981. *First Things First: Meeting Basic Human Needs in the Developing Countries.* New York: Oxford University Press.

Torrey, Barbara. 1992. Personal communication to Amartya Sen, Population Reference Bureau, Inc., Washington, D.C.

Trabold-Nübler, Harald. 1991. "The Human Development Index – A New Development Indicator?" *Intereconomics,* September/October: 236–43.

——. 1992. "Making the Human Development Index Comparable Over Time." German Institute for Economic Research (DIW), Berlin, July. Mimeographed.

UNDP (United Nations Development Programme). 1990. *Human Development Report 1990.* New York: Oxford University Press.

——. 1991. *Human Development Report 1991.* New York: Oxford University Press.

——. 1992. *Human Development Report 1992.* New York: Oxford University Press.

UNICEF (United Nations Children's Fund). 1993. *The State of the World's Children 1993.* Oxford: Oxford University Press.

Willett, Walter. 1990. *Nutritional Epidemiology.* Monographs in Epidemiology and Biostatistics, vol. 15. New York: Oxford University Press.

World Bank. 1990. *World Development Report 1990: Poverty.* New York: Oxford University Press.

——. 1993. *World Development Report 1993: Investing in Health.* New York: Oxford University Press.

2.3

EVOLUTION OF THE HUMAN DEVELOPMENT INDEX

Selim Jahan

INTRODUCTION

Historically, development has been mainly perceived in terms of economic performance. We have long been preoccupied with material production and have sought an acceptable way of measuring it – most often by turning to per capita income. Why has this measurement dominated the scene? First, it is an attractive single indicator for assessing economic performance. Second, it is useful for dividing the world into groups – rich and poor, developed and developing – that constitute an international framework for allocating official development assistance. Finally, reliable and solid data on national income accounts are widely available to calculate per capita income at a point in time and also over time.

But over the years, perspectives on development and its rationale and measures have changed. A fundamental shift occurred in 1990, with the introduction of the concept of human development and the publication of the first *Human Development Report*. Today, development extends far beyond economic performance. It focuses on people and their well-being, with the rationale that improving people's lives is the ultimate objective. Economic growth cannot be an end in itself; rather, its benefits must be translated into people's daily realities.

Out of this conceptual shift has grown a search for new measures of human well-being. Various human development indices and indicators have evolved, with the human development index becoming the crown jewel of them all. The HDI was not the outcome of a whim or an arbitrary decision, but rather the reaction to real needs and intellectual and policy demands. It was also proactive, setting the directions of the new approach.

The objective of the following chapter is to trace the evolution of the HDI, looking not only at historical and chronological developments, but also discussing the HDI's impacts on policy-making, advocacy and future research. The chapter will also attempt to identify future challenges.

THE HUMAN DEVELOPMENT PARADIGM AND THE NEED FOR NEW MEASURES

A particular vision was the driving force behind the human development paradigm and its measurements. This vision is articulated in the question posed by the Irish dramatist George Bernard Shaw in his 1921 play *Back to Methuselah*, viz:

*Some people see things as they are
And say 'why'?
We dream things that never were
And ask 'why not'?*

The "why not" question has constantly fuelled the search for new paradigms and new measures: Why not have a development paradigm that puts people at the centre of development? Why not have a measure that may be as vulgar as GNP per capita, but not as blind towards human lives?

Attempts to answer these questions led to the concept of human development presented in the first *Human Development Report*, and a new understanding that:

- Development is about enlarging people's choices by enhancing their functioning and capabilities.
- Development is *of* the people, *for* the people and *by* the people – "*of* the people" referring to human capital formation and human

resources development through nutrition, health and education; "*for* the people" stressing the need for the benefits of economic growth to be translated into people's lives; and "*by* the people" meaning that people must be able to influence a process that affects their lives.

- Development must be shaped to fit people, as opposed to people being shaped to fit development.

This new perspective simultaneously fostered a reconsideration of the ways development is measured and monitored. Since economic performance by itself was no longer the objective of development, per capita income could not be an adequate measure. As Robert Kennedy has pointed out:

Too much and too long, we seem to have surrendered community excellence and community values in the mere accumulation of material things. Our gross national product is the largest in the world, but that GNP – if we should judge our nation by that – counts air pollution and cigarette advertising, and ambulances to clear the highways of carnage. It counts special locks for our doors and the jails for those who break them. It counts the destruction of our redwoods and the loss of natural wonder in chaotic sprawl. It counts napalm and the cost of a nuclear warhead, and the armoured cars for police who fight riots on our streets. . . . Yet the gross national product does not allow for the health of our children, the quality of their education, or the joy of their play. It does not include the beauty of our poetry or the strength of our marriages, the intelligence of our public debate or the integrity of our public officials. It measures neither our wit nor our courage; neither our wisdom nor our learning; neither our compassion nor our devotion to country; it measures everything, in short, except that which makes life worthwhile.[1]

No better rationale could be provided for new measures to monitor the new perception of development as human development. The search for such measures, and their evolution over time, was concentrated in five areas:

- Identification of a single summary measure of human development. As Mahbub ul Haq put it, "Just one number which is of the same level of vulgarity as the GNP, but a measure that is not as blind to the social aspects of human lives as the GNP is."[2]
- Construction of other composite indices that go beyond measures of average achievements to assess aspects of gender inequality and other deprivations in human development.
- Disaggregation of composite indices in terms of regions, states or provinces, gender, races, ethnic groups or the rural/urban divide. These can serve as mirrors to assess trouble spots in societies.
- Identification and the innovative presentation of indicators that go beyond but also supplement composite indices and highlight various aspects of human development.
- The search for new, improved, robust and reliable data to reflect meaningful and consistent human development indicators.

THE HUMAN DEVELOPMENT INDEX: A SINGLE SUMMARY MEASURE

Extensive research and reflection in the first area led to the creation of the HDI, which emerged from the tension between two approaches: Should we aspire to a measure that is statistically pure, scientifically perfect, and absolutely, logically correct? Or should we seek one that is not so pure, not so perfect, but effective both for advocacy and policy-making? In the end, the HDI struck a balance between the two. It is a measure that is quite rigorous, but also capable of attracting attention.

Once that debate was settled, devising criteria for the measure was easier. Those in the forefront were:

- Simplicity – simple is powerful and has a more predictive potential

- Universality – with a focus on basic capabilities that can be applied to both developed and developing countries
- Sufficiently engaging to attract the broadest cross section of development actors, including policy-makers, academics and activists
- Pluralism and not mono-centricity
- A focused synthesis reflecting the breadth of information provided by all the human development indicators, data and statistics

The final criterion needs further elaboration. The HDI measures average achievement in basic human capabilities. It is constructed from three components – longevity, educational attainment and a decent standard of living. This contrasts with the exclusive focus of the GNP on economic opulence, and it broadens empirical attention in assessing the process of development.

In his memorial lecture on the sad demise of Mahbub ul Haq in 1998, Nobel laureate Professor Amartya Sen, one of the architects of the HDI, said: "I did not, I must admit, initially see much merit in the HDI itself, which, as it happens, I was privileged to help him devise. I had expressed to Mahbub considerable scepticism about trying to focus on a crude index of this kind, attempting to catch in one simple number the complex reality of human development and human deprivation. Why give prominence, it was natural to ask, to a crude summary index that could not begin to capture much of the rich information that makes the *Human Development Reports* so engaging and important."[3]

But the conviction was that GNP dominance could not be broken by a set of tables. People would view them respectfully, but when it came to using a summary measure of development, they would go back to the unadorned GNP, which is crude but convenient. A viable alternative that could challenge GNP would have to be a summary measure like the HDI. In fact, the HDI can be seen, in the words of Professor Sen, "as a deliberately-constructed crude measure, offered as a rival to the GNP, an overused and oversold index that Mahbub wanted to supplant".[4]

This is precisely what the HDI is supposed to do. Since its inception, however, competition over country rankings has led some people to attribute to the HDI things that it does not stand for. It does not represent "happiness" or the "best place on earth to live", nor is it a comprehensive measure embracing all aspects of human development. Since it draws only on three basic dimensions of human development, it has a limited scope. Viewing a larger picture of human development requires supplementing the HDI with other useful, important and rich indicators, a number of which appear in each year's *Human Development Report*. In a sense, human development accounting is like a house and the HDI is like the door to the house. If we pass through the door, we can appreciate all that the house has to offer.

The analytical framework of the HDI can be discussed with respect to its focus, its variables and its formula. The *focus* of the HDI is to measure average achievements in human development in a society by combining three basic indicators. Does the HDI concentration on these aspects of human life mean that other issues are unimportant? The answer is no. It just means that these basic capabilities are essential for human well-being. When significant levels of human development are achieved as measured by the HDI, then doors open for other opportunities – human rights, participation, non-discrimination, security – which are also essential for human development.

The *variables* chosen to represent the dimensions of human well-being in the HDI are: life expectancy at birth; educational attainment both in terms of adult literacy rate and the combined gross enrolment ratio at the primary, secondary and tertiary levels; and GDP per capita (PPP$). There are three critical issues with regard to these variables: scaling, weights and treatment of income.

SCALING: In constructing the HDI, the variables are normalized through a process of scaling. A maximum and a minimum value are selected for each variable and the difference between these values defines the scale. The normalized variable is constructed in the following way: First, the difference between the observed value and the minimum value is identified to show the path covered by the society in the selected variable. Second, this difference is shown as a proportion of the difference between the maximum and minimum values – a difference that represents the total path to be covered by every society in the variable in question.

Thus the normalized variable, which is a pure number, shows for a particular variable the path covered by a society as a proportion of the path to be covered. If a society remains at the minimum for a particular variable, the normalized value of the variable will be 0. If it has attained the maximum value, the normalized value of the variable will be 1. In this way the scale is set for each variable between 0 and 1.

Scaling and the normalized value are required for two reasons. First, the variables included in the HDI have different units – life expectancy is in years, adult literacy rate in percentages and the GDP per capita in PPP$. By normalization, one gets rid of units and derives pure numbers. Such a transformation is needed for additive purposes while constructing a composite index. Second, scaling enables comparisons of how countries have fared in each dimension as well as identification of the unfinished paths.

WEIGHTS: The variables are given equal weights not because of simplicity, but because of the philosophical reasoning that all the dimensions included in the HDI are equally important and desirable in their own right for building human capabilities. Furthermore, equal weights make sense because there is no assumption of substitution among the dimensions or the variables representing them. This means, for example, that a question related to the amount of income that can be given up to get an additional year of life is irrelevant in the HDI framework. In the HDI there is, however, an assumption of transformation – education is transformed into knowledge and enhances human capabilities; income is transformed into other dimensions of human development not captured in the HDI.

TREATMENT OF INCOME: Income is a means to human development, not an end in itself, so the HDI considers income as a proxy for all the dimensions not included under a long and healthy

life and knowledge. The issue here is how income is transformed to enhance human attainment in those areas. Even with a little income, a lot can be achieved given the right transformation. This notion and the concern that income should not dictate the value of the HDI have resulted in income being adjusted as it enters the HDI – as income increases, its value is adjusted downwards through mathematical treatment. An extra dollar when the income is $10,000 is not equally important as an input to human development as an extra dollar when the income is $100.

Finally, there is the HDI's *formula*. Once all the variables are normalized with all the necessary adjustments, a simple mean is taken, which is the HDI. The maximum value of the HDI is 1 and the minimum value is 0.

REFINEMENTS IN THE METHODOLOGY OF THE HDI OVER TIME

From its outset, the HDI caught the attention of academics, researchers, policy-makers and development activists. It was praised for its broad perspective on human well-being, yet it was also scrutinized rigorously in terms of its analytical framework, methodology and data. Critiques of the index have appeared in various academic journals.[5] Most of these articles have reviewed the HDI's internal consistency, robustness and predictive power; presented constructive criticism; and suggested refinements to the HDI's methodology. In other arenas, policy-makers have expressed interest in determining whether the index can guide policy in diverse situations, while development activists have been concerned with finding innovative ways to use the index for advocacy.

Responding to such a variety of requirements has meant constant refinements of the index. On behalf of the Human Development Report Office, Professor Sen and Professor Sudhir Anand[6] have effectively responded to this challenge, leading research to develop the HDI's analysis and methodology and to identify more robust data.

When the HDI was introduced, it had five characteristics. First, it was constructed from a deprivation perspective, in a rather roundabout way: the composite of average deprivation was identified by going through deprivations in each variable; the HDI was then represented as one minus the composite average deprivation. Second, in the educational attainment component, there was only one variable – adult literacy rate. Third, income was logged irrespective of levels. Fourth, there was an observed maximum and minimum for each variable. Fifth, the HDI was constructed only for 130 countries.[7]

Over the years, with better understanding of issues, academic reactions, policy responses and demands from development activists, the HDI has undergone a series of methodological refinements. The major refinements are as follows:

- *Direct calculation of the HDI:* This started in 1991 to avoid the roundabout method and to give the index a more positive spin. The tradition continues today.
- *Educational attainment variable*: In the 1991 Report, mean years of schooling was added as a second component to adult literacy to form the variable for educational attainment. A second variable was included to lend a sense of educational attainment by people not covered by adult literacy. Adult literacy was given two-thirds weight and mean years of schooling one-third weight, as adult literacy is more representative of a stock variable for attainment. But the mean years of schooling component was constructed in a fuzzy way, and some of the data did not necessarily reflect reality. As a result, in 1995 it was replaced by combined gross enrolment at the primary, secondary and tertiary levels.
- *Maxima and mimina*: Until 1994, observed maxima and minima were used in normalizing variables. This created a serious problem. First, there was no way of knowing whether the changes in the HDI value of a country were because of its improved performance or because the goalposts had shifted. Second, since the observed maxima and minima alter from year to year, representing changes in the goalposts themselves, any meaningful inter-temporal comparison was not possible. To

deal with these issues, fixed maxima and minima were introduced in 1994. These were no longer observed, but rather based on the trends of the variables and their probable values in the next 25 years.[8] Fixing the maxima and minima for variables made it possible to carry out meaningful trend analysis of the HDI.

- *Treatment of income*: Even though income was logged in the HDI in 1990, for the next eight years income above a cut-off point was adjusted using a highly regressive formulation. Three observations are pertinent to this adjustment. First, the cut-off point was the average world income based on the assumption that every person as a member of the global community should have at least this level of income for building basic capabilities. Second, the adjustment was so drastic that $35,000 (above the $5,000 cut-off point) was reduced to $321. Third, this formulation penalized middle-income countries unduly. In 1999, the formulation of logging income throughout was reintroduced. This approach is less severe and it does not unduly punish middle-income countries since the asymptote starts quite late.[9]

It is necessary to mention here that along with these methodological refinements, there were also attempts to generate more reliable, consistent and robust data. In this area, the Human Development Report Office played a leading role. It voiced the need for better data in different fora, it interacted with various UN agencies and international organizations to demand the production of such data, and it impressed on the national statistical offices the need to generate the data. It should be emphasized at this point that the national human development reports contributed significantly as a depository for innovative and disaggregated data at the country level. Without the improved data that resulted from all of these efforts, the methodological refinements in the HDI could not have been tested.

In order to be credible to users and for the purpose of productive discussion, all methodological changes as well as improvements in data series or sources must be properly documented in a timely fashion. In recent times, the *Human Development Reports* and the Human Development Report Office have been careful to provide such documentation, thus enhancing the transparency of the exercise. This has led to constructive debates that have provided useful guidance for future work.

ACHIEVEMENTS OF THE HDI

When the HDI was first introduced in 1990, its proponents did not have the slightest idea that it would go so far – impacting policy decisions in significant ways, being used as a major advocacy tool, becoming the focus of serious academic inquiries. Over the years, the HDI has achieved much, but there are five particularly distinctive accomplishments that must be highlighted.

First, the HDI has changed the way development is perceived and analysed. Income is no longer seen as the sum total of human life, and per capita income cannot be considered the measure of human well-being. As a result, development today is viewed more broadly than economic growth. This notion of development with a human face has gone way beyond rhetoric to impact policies, resource allocations and institution building.

The macroeconomic polices of various developing countries in Asia, Africa and Latin America have begun explicitly to take various issues of human development into consideration. Policy-makers have moved away from the growth-centric perspective of development to begin concentrating on broader dimensions of human well-being. In many parts of the world, new and emerging development concerns have started to dominate development dialogue. In countries such as Botswana and South Africa, the implications of HIV/AIDS for development have become a serious issue. (In March 2001, the President of Botswana made a decision to provide free access to anti-retroviral drugs for the 17 per cent of the country's population with HIV/AIDS.) The erosion of basic social services in Eastern Europe and the CIS has been dominating the policy dialogues in that region. And the human impact of the East Asian crisis drew the attention of policy-makers in the 1990s.

The focus of development on basic human concerns has also changed the ways resources are allocated. With the publication of Egypt's first *National Human Development Report,* the Upper Egypt region was found to be lagging behind the Cairo region in every area of human development. This led to a formal policy discussion of resource allocation between the governors of 17 provinces in the country, and the entire resource allocation pattern was changed to funnel more funds to Upper Egypt.

The new focus has also raised questions and spurred the identification of reasons for shortfalls in human development. In the Philippines, the 1997 *National Human Development Report* identified as a crucial factor for development the allocation of a threshold amount for basic social services at the local government level. This led to a presidential directive requiring all local governments to devote at least 20 percent of domestic revenue to human development priorities.

In many countries, with the HDI at centre stage, new institutions have evolved to move the agenda for human development forward. In Bolivia, for instance, a new ministry for human development was established. Globally, a discussion is taking place on whether bilateral aid and the core funds of multilateral agencies can be allocated on the basis of the HDI.

A second achievement is that the HDI has motivated desirable and healthy competition among countries to surpass neighbours or competitors in rankings. In Norway, people compare their ranking to Sweden's; in India, the first interest is determining their score next to Pakistan's. Such competition forces policy-makers to examine why their country is lagging behind and induces them to undertake policies to overcome the relevant shortcomings. This implies thorough scrutiny of development strategies, a review of priorities, an assessment of resource allocation patterns, and the adoption of policies that guide each of these aspects toward basic human concerns.

Third, the HDI has served as a powerful instrument of public communication, playing a strong advocacy role and contributing significantly to policy debates and dialogues. NGOs and institutions of civil society in different countries have used it for highlighting their demands and pressing their governments on various issues. The regional disparities revealed by the disaggregated HDI in Brazil's *National Human Development Reports* have prompted civil society institutions to highlight the issue of inequality and demand measures to reduce it. Brazil is now constructing HDIs at the state, district and municipal levels. Such exercises have been carried out in a range of countries, including Bulgaria, India, Poland and Venezuela.

The HDI has also been used as an effective advocacy tool at different international and global events. In 1995, at the Fourth World Conference on Women in Beijing, disaggregated HDI in terms of gender was used by NGOs to highlight the disparities women face in capability-building but more so in relation to opportunities. At the Habitat II Conference in Istanbul in 1996, various civil society organizations used differences in the rural and urban HDIs in many countries to underscore disparities in housing.

Fourth, the HDI has led to various exercises for monitoring and evaluation and also for generation of more systematic and reliable data, both nationally and internationally. In Kuwait, the Ministry of Planning, with the help of the HDI, has started to monitor human development and incorporate it in indicators for strategic planning. At the global level, whether in the area of monitoring Millennium Development Goals or the United Nations System-wide Common Country Assessment (CCA) Framework, the HDI has been used to provide contextual information.

Finally, the HDI has sparked serious academic research and empirical studies that have not only concentrated on a substantive review of the index – its consistency, statistical properties, robustness, predictive power – but also suggested various refinements. Some of the research has concentrated on the issue of including other dimensions of human development in the index. Other studies have reviewed the possibility of using further innovative indicators to represent these dimensions in the HDI. In fact, a number of national and sub-national human development reports, such as the report of the state of Madhya Pradesh in India, have experimented with indicators more relevant to the local context. Additionally, more than a dozen graduate dissertations have been conducted on the HDI and scholars have explored the subject in a variety of academic articles.[10]

While there is much to appreciate in all the HDI has achieved, it is equally important to have a clear idea of what the HDI is *not*. This understanding helps in avoiding misuse of the index, such as forcing it to highlight that which it does not represent. Here it is worth restating that:

- The HDI is *not* a perfect index that fully captures the concept of human development. Any concept is broader than its proposed measurement because no measurement can fully reflect the concept. Thus there is no pretension that the HDI fully and perfectly captures the whole of human development.

- The HDI does *not* take into account every aspect of human development. It focuses on three dimensions of basic capabilities – a long and healthy life, knowledge and a decent standard of living. But the HDI in no way undermines the fact that other aspects of human life, such as participation, political freedom and human security, are equally important. The rationale for concentrating on three basic dimensions is that the achievement of these opens opportunities in other areas.

- The HDI does *not* provide a comprehensive picture of human development in any situation, as it is just a summary measure. Nor can it be a substitute for all the rich information contained in various tables on human development indicators in the *Human Development Reports*. When the HDI is supplemented with this rich information, only then can one get a full assessment of the human development situation in any society.

GOING BEYOND THE HDI

Even though the HDI was widely extolled as a major policy instrument and a useful policy tool within a few years after its introduction, it was recognized first as a measure of average achievements in human development. It can reflect neither the deprivation nor the distributional aspects of development, particularly the issue of inequality.

Over the years, attempts have been made to rectify this situation. First, in 1995, composite indices were constructed to account for gender inequalities. Second, in 1997, a composite index was proposed and constructed for measuring the multidimensionality of poverty. Third, these composite indices were disaggregated in terms of regions, states, provinces, gender, races, ethnic groups and the rural-urban divide.

THE GENDER-RELATED DEVELOPMENT INDEX AND THE GENDER EMPOWERMENT MEASURE:

A gender-related development index (GDI) and a gender empowerment measure (GEM) emerged in 1995. The GDI measures achievements in the same dimensions and variables as the HDI, but takes into account inequality in achievements between women and men.[11] The greater the gender disparity in human development, the lower is a country's GDI compared to its HDI. The GDI is simply the HDI adjusted downwards for gender inequality. The GEM indicates whether women are able to actively participate in economic and political life. It focuses on participation, measuring gender inequality in key areas of economic and political participation and decision-making.

The exercises with the GDI and GEM have established that greater gender equality in terms of building human capabilities or providing opportunities to women does not depend on income level or stage of development. They also reveal that gender equality can be achieved across a range of cultures.

Together, the GDI and the GEM fulfil several useful purposes:

- The GDI, through its construction, incorporates the degree of the concerned society's aversion to gender inequality and in this regard reflects social choices.
- Women's groups, feminist activists and civil society movements have used both the GDI and the GEM extensively as an advocacy tool in global meetings such as the Fourth World Conference on Women in Beijing.
- Policy-makers have found the GDI and GEM extremely relevant for formulating pro-women policies and programmes.

THE HUMAN POVERTY INDEX:

In 1997, a composite measure for multi-dimensional poverty, the human poverty index (HPI), was introduced. The idea was first to look at human development from a perspective of deprivation, and second to assess how the benefits of human development – as measured by the average achievements represented by the HDI – are distributed. People sometimes argue that since the highest possible value of the HDI is 1, then 1 minus the achieved HDI value is a measure of deprivation, which is not correct. The HDI basically measures shortfalls in average achievements, but it cannot reflect the two issues above. Therefore, the HPI was constructed both for developing countries (HPI-1) in 1997 and for industrial countries (HPI-2) in 1998.

The HPI measures deprivations in basic human development in the same dimensions as the HDI, while also including the aspect of participation or social inclusion.[12] For HPI-1, the deprivation in long and healthy life is measured by the percentage of people born today but not expected to survive to age 40; deprivation in knowledge by the adult illiteracy rate; and deprivation in economic provisioning by the percentage of people lacking access to health services and safe water as well as the percentage of children under five who are malnourished. Two observations may be pertinent. First, for economic provisioning in developing countries, public provisioning may be more important than private income. At the same time, more than four-fifths of private income is spent on food. Thus in developing countries, lack of access to health services and safe water and the level of malnutrition capture deprivation in economic provisioning more practically and meaningfully than other indicators. Second, the absence of a suitable indicator and lack of data prevent the HPI-1 from reflecting deprivation in terms of social inclusion in developing countries.

For the HPI-2, the deprivation in long and healthy life is measured by the percentage of people born today but not expected to survive to age 60; deprivation in knowledge by the percentage of functionally illiterate adults; deprivation in economic provisioning by income poverty incidence (as private income is the most important source of economic provisioning in developed countries) and deprivation in social inclusion by long-term unemployment.

The HPIs have served a number of purposes:

- However imperfect, they provide a single measure of the multidimensionality of poverty. They have also established that if income is not the sum total of human lives, lack of it cannot be the sum total of human deprivation either. They have been effective in showing the distribution of the average achievements of human development, as reflected in the HDI.
- They recognize the fact that poverty is not only a southern phenomenon, but very much a northern problem as well.
- HPI-2 enabled us to differentiate the human development situation among countries whose average achievements in human development are extremely close. A high human development ranking does not automatically imply low levels of human deprivation.

DISAGGREGATION OF COMPOSITE INDICES – MIRRORS TO SOCIETIES: Disaggregation of the composite indices has provided the clearest reflection to societies of prevailing realities, highlighting disparities in human achievements or deprivations in terms of regions, states, provinces, gender, races, ethnic groups and the rural-urban divide. Some studies have been carried out by individual researchers; others have been commissioned by the Human Development Report Office.[13] But a majority of these exercises have been spearheaded by the national human development reports.

Three observations on the disaggregated composite indices are pertinent. First, disparities in human development are not exclusive to developing countries. There are serious human development disparities in the developed world as well. Second, in many countries, disaggregation of human development composite indices and indicators has been carried out at the district level, as in Venezuela, and at the municipal level, for instance in Brazil. These have provided new insights for designing local level policies and programmes. Third, in many countries, disaggregation of composite human development indices has had important impacts on policy dialogues and decisions.

THE HDI – LOOKING FORWARD

More than a decade after its introduction, the HDI has established itself as a major measure of development. Its uses for advocacy, its importance for policy guidance and its potential for inducing further research are now well recognized. But to continue to play a constructive and provocative role in all these areas in the future, the HDI has to be subjected to constant scrutiny, refinements and innovation. In the coming years, the following issues have to be addressed:

KEEPING IT SIMPLE: The HDI's universality, advocacy value and policy relevance derive from the fact that it is simple. It should be kept this way, bearing in mind two basic points. First, there are certain aspects of human lives and well-being where qualitative assessments may be more meaningful. Such areas may include human rights, culture, political freedom and so on. Experiences with the human freedom index in 1991 and the political freedom index in 1992 have clearly shown that quantitative assessments based on too much subjective judgement may be misleading and unproductive. Every aspect of human life cannot be and should not be given a number, particularly if that number represents a totally subjective valuation. Second, with respect to quantitative indicators, renewed attempts should be made to explore new possibilities in such areas as the environment, sustainability and governance. However, the idea is not to reflect all these areas in the HDI, because that would overburden the index and destroy its simplicity and predictive power. For example, in earlier years, attempts were made to "green" the HDI. It was soon found that such a measure would not be universal as there is no common set of environmental indicators that could capture the realities of both developed and developing countries.

REFINING THE EDUCATIONAL ATTAINMENT VARIABLE: Over the years, various ways were explored to refine the educational attainment variable. There were serious methodological and data problems with mean years of schooling; combined gross primary, secondary and tertiary enrolment ratios have been viewed by many as not particularly meaningful. There is also the issue of combining a stock variable (adult literacy) and a flow variable (combined enrolment ratio). Suggestions have been made to come up with variables such as years of school expectancy. But to construct data for years of schooling, one would need data on age-specific net enrolment ratios, which does not exist.

SHORT-TERM CHANGES IN HUMAN DEVELOPMENT: The HDI is composed of stock variables and thus cannot capture the short-term changes in human development in a country. It is also not very sensitive to policy changes and as such may frustrate policy-makers. The Human Development Report Office, in collaboration with a number of UNDP Country Offices, is seeking to identify short-term progress indicators of average achievements, deprivation and inequalities that are also more reflective of policy shifts. Proposals for these indicators were presented in the 2000 *Human Development Report*.

MORE INNOVATIVE INDICATORS: The value and relevance of the HDI is enhanced if the rest of human development accounting is strengthened.

Since the 1990 *Human Development Report*, there have been continuous searches for relevant and meaningful indicators on various aspects of human development, experiments to provide them with a policy twist and innovative approaches to present them in user-friendly ways. All of these initiatives were guided by three considerations.

First, human development is broader than the composite indices. As Professor Sen observed, "In contrast with the coarse index of HDI, the rest of the *Human Development Reports* contain, in extensive collections of tables, a wealth of information on a variety of social, economic and political features that influence the nature and quality of human life."[14]

Second, policy twists to basic human development indicators can guide policy-makers. For example, a traditional indicator like military expenditure as a percentage of GDP may be of little use as a policy guide. This is because by only looking at such figures it cannot be determined whether military expenditure at, say, five percent of GDP is worse than if it were at two percent of GDP. It is only by going beyond the percentage to look at the fact that the GDP in the first case is $100, while in the second case it is $10,000, that we can see how in absolute terms more resources are spent on the military in the second situation. Additionally, if military expenditure is shown as a ratio of expenditures on health and education, immediately the misplacement of priorities in terms of resource allocation is made visible and can offer new policy directions.

Third, the users of the human development indicators must find the presentation of data attractive. Otherwise, the purpose of using them for advocacy, policy dialogues and social debates will be lost.

NEW, IMPROVED, ROBUST AND RELIABLE DATA: Whatever innovative indicators and indices are proposed for monitoring human development, one cannot go far if reliable, consistent, robust and timely data are not available. Today, economic data are more readily available, but not social data. More up-to-date data can be found at the country level, but there are gaps in internationally standardized data at the global level. Sometimes, snapshot information for a particular year may be obtained, but not panel data representing a time series over a period of years. In every case, the HDI is always constrained as a secondary user of global data.

Over the years, serious efforts have, however, resulted in three developments. First, more national data have been made available to respective UN agencies and international organizations in a more timely fashion. Second, new searches are being carried out at the national levels for more social, disaggregated and innovative data. National human development reports have played a role in this respect. And third, there is now more emphasis on building statistical capabilities at the country level. The international community is actively supporting this process.

But much more needs to be done if a number of desired refinements are to be made. For example, to have years of school expectancy as an indicator for educational attainment in the HDI requires age-specific net enrolment ratios within the primary school age group. If there were gender disaggregated income data, one could construct a more meaningful GDI and GEM. The absence of any reliable data on the issue of access to health services has forced the estimate of HPI-1 to rely on the other two variables included in economic provisioning. And in general, the lack of data has restricted the estimates of GDI, GEM and HPI-1 to less than 100 countries.

International organizations, working closely with country statistical offices and interacting within themselves, can help close some of these gaps in the future. Together, they can build networks for initiating new surveys and data collection mechanisms, and devise a framework for regularly publishing reliable and standardized data.

CONCLUSIONS

The HDI as a more meaningful measure of development is now established. Its value, importance and relevance are also recognized. This does not mean that its imperfections should be overlooked. The HDI shares the shortcomings of other composite indices, including the GDP. If we can live with the GDP for nearly 50 years, the HDI, which is only 12 years old, deserves a chance.

All the human development composite indices and indicators including the HDI are in the process of evolution. With regard to the HDI, as has been pointed out, refinements have been made over the years both with regard to methodological issues as well as statistical sophistication.

Monitoring human development is important for assessment, policy-making and enhancing the lives of millions. State-of-the-art monitoring is evolving slowly but surely, while research is being conducted both within the Human Development Report Office and in academic and research institutions. We have advanced a long way, but we still have a far distance to go.

ENDNOTES

1. Quoted in Haq 1990.
2. UNDP 1999.
3. Sen 1998.
4. UNDP 1999.
5. Raworth 1998.
6. Anand and Sen 1994 and 1998.
7. UNDP 1990.
8. UNDP 1994.
9. Anand and Sen 1998.
10. Raworth 1998.
11. Anand and Sen 1995.
12. Anand and Sen 1997.
13. Two of the earliest individual research works in this area are Akder 1990 and Shiva Kumar 1991. For studies commissioned by the Human Development Report Office, please see UNDP 1994.
14. UNDP 1999.

REFERENCES

Akder, Halis. 1990. "Turkey: Country Profile – Human Development Indices for All Turkish Provinces." Middle Eastern Technical University, Department of Economics. UNDP, Ankara. Mimeographed.

Anand, Sudhir and Amartya Sen. 1994. "Human Development Index: Methodology and Measurement." Human Development Report Office Occasional Paper 12. UNDP, New York.

——. 1995. "Gender Inequality in Human Development: Theories and Measurements." Human Development Report Office Working Paper 19. UNDP, New York.

——. 1997. "Concepts of Human Development and Poverty: A Multidimensional Perspective." In *Human Development Papers 1997*. UNDP, Human Development Report Office, New York.

——. 1998. "The Income Component of the Human Development Index." UNDP, Human Development Report Office, New York. Mimeographed.

Fukuda-Parr, Sakiko. 1999a. "Human Development Indicators as Benchmarks in Measuring Progress in Economic, Social and Cultural Rights." UNDP, Human Development Report Office, New York. Processed.

——. 1999b. "In Search of Indicators of Culture and Development: Review of Progress and Proposals for Next Steps." Paper prepared for the *World Cultural Report 1999*. New York.

Haq, Mahbub ul. 1990. "Human Development Paradigm." UNDP, Human Development Report Office, New York. Mimeographed.

Jahan, Selim. 1999a. "Gender Equality Indices in the *Human Development Reports:* Concepts, Measurements and Impacts." In Stone, Leroy and others (eds.), *Gender Equality Indicators: Public Concerns and Public Policies*. Statistics Canada, Ottawa, January.

——. 1999b. "Measurement of Human Development: Evolution of Indices and Indicators." Paper presented at the First Global Forum on Human Development. New York, July.

——. 2000. "Measurements of Human Development: Seven Questions." Presentation at the First Human Development Course at Oxford University. September.

——. 2001. "Indicators at Work Around the World: The Human Development Index." Keynote speech at the National Conference on Sustainable Development Indicators, organized by the Round Table on the Environment and the Economy (NRTEE) in Ottawa, Canada, 27 March.

Raworth, Kate. 1998. "Academic Critique of the Human Development Index." UNDP, Human Development Report Office, New York. Mimeographed.

Sen, Amartya. 1998. "Mahbub ul Haq: The Courage and Creativity of His Ideas." Speech at the Memorial Meeting for Mahbub ul Haq at the United Nations. New York, 15 October.

Shiva Kumar, A. K. 1991. "UNDP's Human Development Index: A Computation for Indian States." *Economic and Political Weekly*. Bombay, 12 October.

UNDP (United Nations Development Programme). 1990. *Human Development Report 1990*. New York: Oxford University Press.

——. 1994. *Human Development Report 1994.* New York: Oxford University Press.

——. 1999. *Human Development Report 1999*. New York: Oxford University Press.

2.4

CRITIQUES OF THE
HUMAN DEVELOPMENT INDEX: A REVIEW

C4/3 010

Kate Raworth and David Stewart

"The HDI has opened new perspectives on measuring and analysing human development ... there can be no doubt that the work in this area is still at its beginning. Much more research is needed ... UNDP would welcome any contribution to this topic."

(*Human Development Report 1992*)

This chapter provides a summary of the academic critiques of the human development index that have been put forward since its inception in 1990. Over 40 articles have been written on the HDI, with opinions ranging from broad agreement to pointed criticism. This chapter aims to set out the full range of views covered in these articles, and to provide some of the Human Development Report Office's responses. The first section sets a context for critiques of the HDI, with a brief consideration of the aims of the HDI and the data requirements that any proposed new indicators need to meet. The second and third sections outline the significant changes in the construction of the HDI since 1990, reflecting the incorporation of several major criticisms. The fourth section considers the remaining critiques of the HDI as currently formulated and the fifth section concludes.

INCORPORATING CRITIQUES: THE AIMS AND REQUIREMENTS OF THE HDI

The Human Development Report Team actively seeks ways of improving the HDI and, as this chapter will show, many of the critiques made over the past ten years have significantly contributed to this process. In order for a critique to be incorporated in the HDI, however, it must satisfy two con-

ditions: it must fit in with the concept and purpose of the HDI and, if it involves introducing a new indicator, adequate data must be available to make it feasible.

This is, of course, not to say that critiques that cannot be incorporated into the HDI are not constructive. Not only do critiques build on each other until changes can be incorporated, but many add to the understanding of the theoretical underpinning and purpose of the HDI. In addition, those that are impracticable due to lack of data underline where new or better data are needed.

This section considers the questions of for whom and what the HDI is intended, and the data requirements for indicators that constitute the HDI, and thus provides a context for many of the critiques of the HDI subsequently considered.

Uses and users – who and what is the HDI for?

Since 1990, academic descriptions of possible uses of the HDI have included:

- "Exposing the impacts of policy manipulation" (Kelley 1991).
- "Understanding the underlying sources and potential causes of problems" (Akder 1994).
- "Measuring the human capital component of a nation's competitiveness" (Ivanova and others 1994a).
- "Reorienting the assessment of development levels away from income to more broadly based measures" (McGillivray and White 1993).
- "Acting as a tool for governments to assess their performance one year after another" (Khatib 1994).

- "Measuring the stock of human development at a point in time" (Hopkins 1993).
- Answering questions such as "When has human development occurred? What has caused it?" (Kelley 1991).
- "Being used by governments and companies in determining their activities and operations world-wide, by providing an overall evaluation of the quality of a country's workforce" (Ivanova and others 1994a).
- "Formulating human development objectives in a multi-objective planning programming problem" (Osman 1994).
- "Assessing a nation's capital for aid discussion" (Ivanova 1994).

These academic quotations can be put into the following broad categories:

- challenging GDP as a measure and target of development,
- helping focus planning objectives,
- measuring a nation's stock of human wealth,
- reflecting the impact of policy,
- analysing alternative development strategies, and
- directing aid allocations.

How can any single index be expected to perform so many functions: to be both prescriptive and descriptive, a final output and an input, analytical and also an overview, a tool and a target? With such breadth expected of the HDI, it is unsurprising that so many adjustments and alternatives have been put forward. To prevent the HDI becoming a "Jack of all trades and master of none", an exploration is needed of the uses and users of the HDI, so the focus can be on making the HDI a master where it should be.

In the context of the *Human Development Reports*, the HDI is intended to allow policy-makers to draw a basic picture of their country's level of human development *(Human Development Report 1990,* p. 17). This leads to two fundamental tenets on which the HDI should be based for it to be an effective tool: it is important that the HDI is kept simple for wide comprehension, and

that it is based on fundamental dimensions of human development. Of the six issues identified from the quotations above, the first four are of particular relevance to policy-makers. As such, the interest and usefulness of the HDI to policy-makers would be maximized if the HDI could be:

- an ideological alternative to GDP,
- a measure of the stock of human development,
- a tool for focusing planning objectives (when disaggregated nationally by region/gender/ethnicity), and
- a reflection of the impact of their policies.

As such, the aim of the HDI is to be as useful as possible for these purposes, while remaining as simple as possible and based on the fundamental dimensions of human development. For a critique to be incorporated in the HDI it needs to adhere to these principles. As will be shown in this chapter, there have been many useful critiques in these areas, some of which have been incorporated as improvements in the index.

Data requirements – what it takes to become an HDI indicator

The HDI is currently composed of three dimensions: the capabilities of leading a long and healthy life, being knowledgeable and having a decent standard of living. As will be described in the following sections, various indicators are used to measure these dimensions. Many of the critiques of the HDI call for the inclusion of additional or alternative indicators – either as measures of existing dimensions, or as measures of new dimensions suggested for inclusion in the HDI.

The data requirements for an indicator to be feasible for the HDI are, however, very difficult to meet: data, rather than conceptual issues, are the chief constraint on the HDI better meeting its aims outlined above. For an indicator to be feasible for inclusion in the HDI, the data need to be:

- internationally comparable,
- available for a large proportion of the world's countries,
- of reasonable quality,

- valid – based on identifiable criteria that measure what they are intended to measure, and
- policy relevant – based on criteria that can be influenced, directly or indirectly, by policy action.

Data in the HDI come from international statistical agencies which, in general, assures they are globally comparable and of a reasonable quality. Many international series, however, are not available for all the countries for which the HDI is currently calculated. Whether an indicator is valid or not is less easily determined: there is no simple rule, and a case by case assessment is required.

While there is a large number of international data series, there is a dearth of human development data that are globally available, comparable, valid and of a reasonable quality. This severely impairs the measurement of human development, both through the HDI and more broadly. The rest of this chapter will examine critiques of the HDI in this light.

THE ORIGINAL CONSTRUCTION OF THE 1990 HDI

In 1990, the three dimensions of the HDI (the capabilities of leading a long and healthy life, being knowledgeable and having a decent standard of living) were measured, respectively, by the indicators of life expectancy at birth, literacy of adults over 25 years, and the log of gross domestic product per capita (GDPpc) in purchasing power parity dollars (PPP$). A simple intermediate index was created for each dimension by setting each indicator on a scale of 0–1 using maximum and minimum scaling values as given in the table below. For each country, a simple average of the three in-termediate indices was calculated, giving its HDI value for the year.

CRITIQUES INCORPORATED

Critiques of the 1990 HDI that have since been incorporated into the index are as follows:

Eliminate relative maximum and minimum values

The rationale for using the concept of relative deprivation – and hence the use of levels of extreme countries each year as maximum and minimum values – was criticized for sacrificing the more important benefits to be had from creating a comparable time series which, by definition, cannot have "shifting goalposts". The relativity, it was pointed out, caused undesirable externalities whereby the indices of all countries can change simply due to changes in the extreme countries. In place of relative maximum and minimum values, fixed levels were advocated within which all countries will lie (Kanbur 1990; Kelley 1991; Trabold-Nubler 1991; Pyatt 1992; Pal and Pant 1992; McGillivray and White 1993; Khatib 1994; Ivanova 1994).

Supplement literacy with another indicator

Many countries at the top end of the HDI spectrum do not produce literacy data, and so are assumed to have the same rate. Critics pointed out that this caused bunching at the top, so in order to discriminate further between them, a second education indicator was suggested for all countries (Desai 1990, 1991; Murray 1991; Kelley 1991).

Improve the adjustment of income

Although the concept of diminishing returns to income is accepted for measuring the utility of re-

---

TABLE 2.4.1

Dimensions, indicators and parameters of the 1990 HDI

Dimension	Indicator	Maximum value	Minimum value
Longevity	Life expectancy at birth	Maximum observed value	Minimum observed value
Knowledge	Literacy of adults 25yrs +	100%	Minimum observed value
Living standards	Log GDPpc in PPP$	log y* (see below†)	Minimum observed value

†The maximum value for log GDPpc in PPP$ (log y*) was calculated as the average income poverty line of nine industrial countries.

sources, there have been many critiques of the method used. The initial formulation was to take the logarithm of GDPpc, with a cut-off point of income at the average poverty level of nine industrial countries. However, critics felt that the use of the logarithm had not been justified (Rao 1991), and that the cut-off point was excessively low and disregarded the obvious role that additional income does play in enlarging people's choices (Desai 1990; Murray 1991; McGillivray and White 1993; Ivanova 1994; Ivanova and others 1994b).

These views were incorporated and the log GDPpc was replaced by an adjusted Atkinson's formula for discounting the utility of income. This involved heavily discounting any income above the average world GDPpc (see annex 2.4.1). However, some argued that this threshold was too low, and disregarded the obvious contribution that income over this level makes to human development (Hopkins 1991; Murray 1991; Trabold-Nubler 1993; McGillivray and White 1993). Some claimed income below the threshold level should also be discounted (Trabold-Nubler 1991), although others argued that it does not make sense to talk of diminishing returns to utility for someone whose basic needs are not yet met (Desai 1990). It was also claimed that the adjusted Atkinson's formula was unnecessarily complex and did not bring additional discriminatory power. Indeed, the various treatments of income all had a high correlation with the HDI and so the simple method of log GDPpc was advocated instead (McGillivray and White 1993).

Add dimensions of deprivation

Some called for adding measures of deprivation, using indicators such as under-five mortality rates, maternal mortality rates, poverty incidence, and lack of access to housing, safe water and sanitation (Das 1993; Pant and Pal 1991; Ramirez 1995).

More details on data

More information on the source, year and reliability of each statistic cited was called for (Murray 1991; Boer and Koekkoek 1993). "A particularly dangerous trend is the appearance of collections of cross-country distributional statistics on the developing world, crowned by the World Bank's annual indicators in the *World Development Reports*. While often invaluable, this source is singularly weak on where the numbers come from and how reliable they are. But simply by being listed in tables without qualifications, they implicitly receive the Bank's stamp of approval" (Moll 1992). Though addressed to the World Development Indicators, this critique implicitly applied to the HDI as well.

Use no estimates

Critics of estimated data urged that the HDI only use actual data and not estimates, arguing that the practice of estimation merely hides the urgent need for the collection of quality data: "Who will take seriously efforts to measure mortality or education, if convenient estimates are available each year from prestigious international compendiums?" (Murray 1991).

Resulting changes in the HDI

The above critiques have been taken into account through the following changes:

- Relative maximum and minimum values have been changed to fixed levels.
- Combined gross enrolment ratios (combining the primary, secondary and tertiary enrolment ratios) have been added to literacy for the knowledge dimension to enhance discrimination between the HDI values of the top countries.
- To account for diminishing returns over the full range of income, the HDI has reverted from Atkinson's formula to log GDPpc. The fixed maximum and minimum values used, however, ensure that there is no threshold beyond which achievements are not recognized.
- *Human Development Report 1997* on poverty introduced a human poverty index (HPI-1) for developing countries that focused on deprivations in the same dimensions used in the HDI. This was supplemented in *Human Development Report 1998* by a human poverty index for industrialized countries (HPI-2) which included a fourth dimension of social exclusion.[1]

- Increased attention has been given to the selection of statistical series, with thorough documentation and referencing of the sources used.
- While the HDI continues to use a few limited estimates and assumptions for certain data points in order to include as many countries as possible in the HDI, these estimated figures are not printed in the table – to make clear that data does not exist for these countries.

As a result of these changes the current construction of the HDI is reflected in table 2.4.2:

CURRENT CRITIQUES OF THE HDI

The current critiques of the HDI which have not been incorporated can be divided into the following main categories: conceptual issues, choice of dimensions, choice of indicators, data measurement and error, aggregation issues, redundancy and use of the HDI in analysis.

Conceptual issues

CONCEPTUAL FOUNDATIONS: The theory from which the HDI is derived intends to measure capabilities through their associated functionings, but income, it is argued, is not a functioning (Srinivasan 1993). The rationale for including income, however, is that it acts as the closest feasible proxy for all choices other than those captured by longevity and knowledge indicators, and so is a proxy for the capability to have a decent standard of living and hence provides access to other functionings.

STOCKS AND FLOWS: The HDI is criticized for mixing stock variables (adult literacy and life expectancy) with flow variables (income per capita per annum and gross enrolment ratios). Due to the lags of policy impact on adult literacy and life expectancy, the index is also criticized for partially measuring the outcomes of past efforts and not just the present situation. The combined effect is erratic movements in the rankings on the release of new census data for the stock variables. Critics point out that it also makes unclear what the comparison of GDP and HDI rankings signifies, given that the former is a flow and the later a combination of stocks and flows (Hopkins 1991; Pyatt 1992; Ivanova 1994; Ivanova and others 1994b; Ephrenesis 1994).

One proposed solution to this problem would be to construct a complementary index – the Human Development Improvement Index (HDII) – consisting only of indicators that reflect current flows into improving the HDI stock (Hopkins 1993). This innovation would certainly fit with the HDI's aim of reflecting the impact of policies, and the Human Development Report Office is working on developing measures of improvements in human development in the shorter run: initial work on this appeared in *Human Development Report 2000* (pp. 108–11). A major stumbling block in constructing an HDII is the severe lack of globally available, comparable and quality data that capture short-run changes in the human development situation in a country.

A SINGLE COMPOSITE INDEX? A common critique is that economic and social indicators should not be combined into a single figure but rather analysed in tandem (Kanbur 1990; Pyatt 1992; Ryten 2000). In response, others argue that the HDI is important in that it confronts the most widely used single-figure development indicator, GDPpc, with another single figure, and so creates an alternative and allows comparison (Trabold-

TABLE 2.4.2

Dimensions, indicators and parameters of the HDI in Human Development Report 2000

Dimension	Indicator	Maximum value	Minimum value
Longevity	Life expectancy at birth, in years	85	25
Knowledge	⅔ adult (25yrs +) literacy and	100%	0%
	⅓ combined gross enrolment ratios	100%	0%
Living standards	Log GDPpc in PPP$	$40,000	$100

Nubler 1991; Anand and Sen 1995). The HDI is also supported for being more comprehensible than many other composite indicators (Ivanova and others 1994b). Likewise, the HDI "contributes to an intellectual muscle therapy that helps us avoid analytical cramps" (Streeten 1994).

SILENT ON DISTRIBUTION: The HDI's silence on issues of distribution by gender, region, ethnicity, income and occupation has been widely noted (Akder 1994; Trabold-Nubler 1991; Kelley 1991; Ephrenesis 1994; Osman 1994; Hicks 1997; Ryten 2000; Indrayan and others 1999). The HDI is indeed a summary measure of average human development that is quite distinct from the distribution (by any criteria) of human development – and some argue that it is the latter that should be the focus for those interested in closing gaps (Akder 1994). Making the HDI distribution-sensitive, however, would entail a loss of information because scores would vary both with changes in the average value and with changes in the distribution around that value, making it impossible to distinguish the cause of shifts (Anand and Sen 1993). A further constraint is that distribution-sensitive data are simply not available for a sufficiently large number of countries.

Instead of requiring the HDI alone to reflect multiple distribution concerns, several attempts have been made since the inception of the HDI to create supplementary indices that take distribution into account. Income-distribution adjusted HDIs for countries with adequate data available were shown in the *Human Development Reports* between 1990 and 1994. Gender-disparity adjusted indices were also produced and then superceded by the gender-related development index (GDI) and the gender empowerment measure (GEM) in 1995. Disaggregations have been carried out by a large number of countries at the national level by region, gender, ethnicity, language and income.

Choice of dimensions

A number of critics argue that new dimensions should be added to the index in order to increase its discriminatory power among countries and to make a more complete measure of human development (McGillivray 1991; Ivanova and others 1994a). While the concept of human development is inevitably broader than its measurement, new dimensions could possibly be added to the HDI without significantly compromising its simplicity and transparency. Any additional dimensions would, however, need appropriate indicators to measure them that meet the stringent data criteria described in the first section – namely global availability and comparability, reasonable quality and validity. These conditions are very hard to meet. Suggested additional dimensions include:

A POLITICAL FREEDOM/CIVIL AND POLITICAL RIGHTS DIMENSION: Political freedom/civil and political rights are an integral part of human development and many have objected to their absence from the HDI (Trabold-Nubler 1991; Rao 1991; Hopkins 1991; Desai 1991; Dasgupta and Weale 1992; Boer and Koekkoek 1993; Khatib 1994). Some have suggested that this has not yet been included due to political pressure from some UN members whose ranking would suffer as a result (Hopkins 1991; Trabold-Nubler 1991; Boer and Koekkoek 1993). The real reason behind the lack of a civil/political rights dimension in the HDI, however, is the extreme difficulty of finding adequate measures of any aspect of these. Commonly used measures of civil and political rights are subjective ratings, but these are open to obvious contestation about the knowledge and bias of the rater. Furthermore, such ratings may be expressed as numbers but they do not meet the criteria of reliability and validity, and so cannot be combined with real data (Raworth 2001).

AN ENVIRONMENTAL DIMENSION: Since environmental quality affects the living standards of the present generation and the prospects of the next, it has an obvious bearing on human development. Some argue that not taking it into account creates a false incentive to deplete the natural resource base in order to increase current GDP (Murray 1991; Khatib 1994).

The inclusion of an environmental dimension in the HDI has been explored since 1994, but, as with civil and political rights, there are many problems of capturing environmental status in internationally comparable, valid and reliable data. Indicators relevant to environmental status vary from one country to the next, and there is no clear agreement on what outcomes should be judged as desirable (Desai 1994).

Other suggested dimensions include: nutritional status, autonomy (Murray 1991), culture (Khatib 1994), uncertainty/unpredictability, mobility (Ryten 2000), freedom from crime and violence (Rao 1991; Ryten 2000), self-respect, and the opportunity to be creative and productive (Rao 1991).

Though all of these dimensions are valuable aspects of human development, there are difficulties with including each of them in the HDI. Some, such as nutritional status, overlap with existing dimensions. Others, such as culture, autonomy and mobility, are exhibited in such disparate ways across the world that attempts to measure them by universally applicable indicators would inevitably be highly biased.

One proposal for including more dimensions of human development is to create a ten-dimension measure for countries with high human development and sufficient data, including: environment, food security, job security, housing, personal security, political freedom, transport and communication, safe water and health, education and real income (Hopkins 1993). Such an index could potentially be calculated, though even among similar and industrialized countries, adequate indicators for many of these dimensions would be very hard to find.

Choice of indicators

Given the existing dimensions of the HDI, some critiques focus on the validity, quality and comparability of the indicators used.

ADULT LITERACY: There is no universal definition of literacy and so, due to language differences, the level of knowledge required varies greatly: compare a phonetic language such as Spanish with Chinese, for which several thousand characters must be mastered. Using adult literacy as an indi-

cator has been criticized since a greater amount of linguistic knowledge is required across languages for the same level of literacy (Ivanova and others 1994a, 1994b; Hopkins 1991; Lind 1991). This may be true, but it is the ability to read – literacy – that is the desired outcome to be measured, whatever the linguistic inputs required.

Others argue that the literacy measure does not capture the quality of literacy. Indeed, an Organisation for Economic Co-operation and Development (OECD) survey has found that 20% of Canadians are not functionally literate in that they cannot read and understand a simple set of instructions.[2] Despite this, illiteracy in Canada is implicitly shown in the HDI as 1% (Ivanova and others 1994a, 1994b). Literacy data are not available for most of the industrialized countries so for the purpose of the HDI a rate of 99% is assumed. Nevertheless, the crudity of the literacy test certainly does not make it an ideal indicator: better data on functional literacy are available but only for some OECD countries, and so functional illiteracy is included in the human poverty index for industrialized countries (HPI-2).

Since literacy measures the stock of a nation's education, it is very slow to respond and does not capture the flow of education being achieved (Smith 1995). In order to make it more sensitive to current educational achievements, it has been suggested to narrow the literacy sample group to those aged 15–29 or 15–39 (Murray 1991). Instead of narrowing the age range of literacy, however, the inclusion of the gross enrolment ratio in the HDI is an alternative solution to reflecting the flow of education being achieved.

COMBINED GROSS ENROLMENT: The gross enrolment ratio is critiqued because it includes pupils outside the relevant age groups and repeaters who failed the previous year. Although the former could be positively correlated with human development, the latter certainly cannot. In order to overcome this error of over-counting, the net, rather than gross, combined enrolment ratios has been recommended, if and when data are available (Khatib 1994; Ramirez 1995). Such a change to the HDI is highly desirable, however, the net enrolment ratio is, at present, not available for a sufficient number of countries to be used in constructing the HDI (UNESCO 2000). It has also been argued that while the gross enrolment ratio is used it should not be capped at 100% for the purpose of calculating the HDI, as this ignores large numbers of people enrolled in school who are over age in countries where this ratio is over 100% (Castles 2000). This is an emerging problem: in *Human Development Report 2001* only six countries had their gross enrolment capped. One solution would be to change the goalposts for enrolment, but in order to avoid continual adjustments to the HDI any change to these goalposts should be made at the same time as changes in income and life expectancy, where for some countries the data will also soon exceed the maximum. A preferable solution would be an alternative enrolment indicator – and in meetings with the United Nations Educational, Scientific and Cultural Organisation (UNESCO) there have been discussions towards the development of new education indicators.

LIFE EXPECTANCY OR INFANT MORTALITY?

Age-specific mortality rates are not highly correlated with each other so, it has been argued, it is not obvious which age group to use. This is because life expectancy at birth takes account of infant mortality rates that can change significantly while other age rates remain fairly stable (Murray 1991). Others claim that life expectancy at birth is correlated with income and infant mortality so since income is already included in the HDI, infant mortality should be used instead of life expectancy (Pyatt 1991). Although this may be true for countries with low human development, data on infant mortality are not sufficiently discriminating for highly developed countries: it is therefore preferred to use life expectancy at birth over the full range of countries *(Human Development Report 1993)*. Critiques remain of the quality of data: age-specific mortality rates are said to be unavailable for many countries (Srinivasan 1993), and rural health is said to be often under-reported and therefore under-represented in statistics (Murray 1991; Khatib 1994).

Data measurement and errors

GROSS OR NET DOMESTIC PRODUCT? The gross domestic product is a flow measure and so does not take into account any depletion or accrual of the capital stock of a country – including its natural resource base. This creates an incentive to deplete the stock in order to increase current GDP, so inducing unsustainable economic development. Rather than adding new indicators for an environmental dimension, one suggestion is to replace gross domestic product with net domestic product in order to account for the depletion of the natural resource base. This critique would ideally be incorporated into the HDI, but data for NDP are not yet sufficiently reliable, internationally comparable or widely available (Commission of the European Communities and others 1993).

GDP DISCREPANCIES: Several critics have argued that data on GDP are incomplete and biased due to the varying levels of economic integration and the varying structures of economies, making international data ultimately incomparable (Das 1993; Srinivasan 1993; Ivanova and others 1994b). In countries where remittances are high, for example, it is argued that GNP is a better measure of income (Murray 1991) but still open to the above problems. Furthermore, the conversion to PPP$, though necessary for international price comparability, has been criticized because the PPP conversion rates are only updated periodically and for a number of countries, and so the rest must be extrapolated (Murray 1991; Srinivasan 1993).

EDUCATION DATA QUALITY: Data on adult literacy and life expectancy are not updated annually by statistical agencies and so estimates for intervening years may be far off course, with significant impacts on HDI values and rankings (Castles 1998). This concern with data accuracy is recurring in the use of statistics. It emphasizes the importance of not focusing on year-on-year changes in the HDI and of continuing the call for more resources and attention to be committed to improving data quality.

ARE MORE INDICATORS NEEDED? The HDI has been criticized for being too heavily concentrated on dimensions relevant to low levels of human development, making it limited in its range and application to high human development countries (Kelley 1991). One suggestion to deal with this limitation is to introduce a two- or three-tiered index using more relevant indicators for countries with high and medium human development, in which accurate data are more likely to be available (Anand and Sen 1993). Against this idea is the objection that, by introducing different indicators for different groups of countries, the comparability of the HDI would be lost over the full range of all countries (Ramirez 1995). Others argue that it is only by the addition of a new dimension – not by adding more indicators for the same ones – that greater discriminatory power will be created (McGillivray 1991; McGillivray and White 1993; Ivanova and others 1994b).

COMPARING DISPARATE DATA: There are inherent problems involved in any attempt to compare international data, including differences in: definitions used, sampling techniques, methodology, social and political environments, and the motivations of the researchers. The combined effect has been challenged in its seriously compromised capacity for meaningful comparisons to be made (Akder 1994; Murray 1991; Das 1993; Srinivasan 1993; Khatib 1994). To this end, it has been argued that improvements in the HDI should be concentrated not on the details of its construction, but rather on the issue of improving basic data quality (Hopkins 1991; Pyatt 1992). In response to this apparent problem, robustness tests were carried out that found, while allowing for data margins of error of +/– 15 %, that the rankings of the HDI were not significantly changed, indicating that the data are robust to some measurement error (McGillivray and White 1993).

Aggregation issues

The principle of aggregation has been criticized for reducing the quantity of information available. For example, HDI outcomes depend on the de-

mography and prevailing conditions in a country, as well as on the policies enacted, and so the HDI value and ranking compound these distinct variables (Ryten 2000). This is certainly true; however, the HDI intends to capture a measure of the state of people's lives in a country, and this will depend on both of the mentioned variables and others. The different rates of change of the indicators used in the HDI are also raised as a critique: income per person usually shows greater variations year-on-year than life expectancy, literacy or school enrolments, hence the income component generally drives change in the HDI (Ryten 2000). This is certainly true for year-on-year comparisons, but such annual comparisons are discouraged in the *Human Development Reports* for this reason and because of data fluctuations. Long-term trend tables of HDI values since 1975, given at five-year intervals, show a far more meaningful picture of longer-term evolution in all of the dimensions of the HDI (see for example *Human Development Report 2001*, pp. 145–8).

The weighting of the three dimensions has been criticized as arbitrary, despite claims of it being a "simple average" (Kelley 1991; Das 1993). Behind the aggregation, it has been pointed out, is an implicit social welfare function that should be explicitly stated (Kanbur 1990; Trabold-Nubler 1991). Some find there is relatively too little weight given to the income component, and that the implicit trade-off that is made should be a matter of public choice and hence not be assumed to hold constant across all countries or time (Ravillion 1997). In contrast, another author found that principal components analysis suggests that the equal weighting of the components is "not a serious problem" (Noorbakhsh 1998).

One critic claimed that the summation of the three main dimensions implies perfect substitutability between longevity, knowledge and living standards, which is not conceptually the case (Hopkins 1991). Another demonstrated that a constant marginal return to longer life in the HDI, combined with a sharply falling marginal return to income produces the undesirable implication that the monetary valuation of an extra year of life rises from a remarkably low level in poor countries to a very high level in rich ones (Ravallion 1997). To remove these implications, it has been suggested that the indices be combined in log additive form so that the effect is multiplicative, and there is very limited substitutability (Desai 1991).

Redundancy

INTER-CORRELATION AND REDUNDANCY: Several critics have claimed that there is high positive correlation between the HDI and each of its components (McGillivray 1991; Ivanova 1994; Ivanova and others 1994a, 1994b; Ogwang 1994). There is also high positive correlation between each component of the HDI and an index made of the other two components, and so, it is argued, the inclusion of all three brings little additional insight (McGillivray and White 1993). These critics found that that the HDI is redundant over the full sample of countries, but it is least redundant when used to analyse groups of similar countries, i.e., within the categories of low, medium and high human development (McGillivray and White 1993; Dietz and Gibson 1994). It has also been claimed that the HDI is no better than other indices in discriminating among countries with low and high levels of human development, and it is at its most discriminating for countries of medium human development (Ivanova and others 1994b; Dietz and Gibson 1994).

Not all research has reached these conclusions. After analysing groups of countries ranked in the HDI, Noorbakhsh found that the components of the HDI are not highly correlated with each other or the index, and that there is "little evidence to support the suggestion that (the HDI), as compared with (its) components, is redundant". In addition to this empirical defense, the HDI is still justifiable on conceptual grounds because it values the dimensions as fundamental capabilities of human development and ends in themselves (McGillivray and White 93).

Use of the HDI in analysis

The *Human Development Reports* have been criticized for making analyses that compare HDI ranks with GDPpc ranks. The assertion that countries that have a higher HDI rank than GDPpc rank have been relatively successful at using their economic growth to enhance the lives of their people has been shown to be questionable when other data are brought into consideration (Castles 1998). Likewise, higher HDI ranking may not be a sign of effective spending on health and education at a given level of income, but rather a sign of poor economic policies and performance for a given level of health and education in a country (Castles 1998). These criticisms rightly point out the limited analytical power of such simple comparisons between HDI and GDPpc ranking, which do not take into account other factors that may explain these differences in rank.

CONCLUSION

The idea to measure human, rather than economic, development is not a new one – but it is an important one. Other major reports, such as the *World Development Report,* are also giving more attention to social indicators, and so the Human Development Report Office was warned in 1991 that the HDI must carve out a distinct niche for itself by engaging in greater conceptual analysis if it was not to become a "fad" (Hopkins 1991; Trabold-Nubler 1991; Boer and Koekkoek 1993). Ten years on, 135 countries have produced national human development reports in which many of them have disaggregated the HDI by gender, ethnicity, income and region, and received substantial interest in the results: in this respect, the HDI does not appear to be a fad. Despite academics' calls for greater conceptual analysis, the HDI remains a widely used tool.

The HDI was designed for policy-makers to act as a summary measure of the human development situation in a country. As such, it is important that it remains simple for wide comprehension and is based on fundamental dimensions of human development. The Human Development Report Office has encouraged critiques and research on the HDI to help it fulfil its purpose. There have been a large number of critiques in the past ten years – many of which have been incorporated into the HDI.

Many other critiques of the HDI have not been incorporated. Some, such as including extra dimensions for countries with high human development, do not help move the HDI closer to its fundamental goals. Others, such as net enrolment ratios, cannot be included due to the lack of globally available, comparable and valid data of reasonable quality. The problem points to the continuing need for better quality data.

ANNEX 2.4.1: Atkinson's formula for discounting the utility of income is

$$
\begin{aligned}
W(y) &= y^* & \text{for } 0 < y < y^* \\
&= y^* + 2[(y-y^*)^{1/2}] & \text{for } y^* < y < 2y^* \\
&= y^* + 2(y^{*1/2}) + 3[(y-2y^*)^{1/3}] & \text{for } 2y^* < y < 3y^* \\
&= y^* + 2(y^{*1/2}) + 3(y-2y^*)^{1/3}] + \ldots + n\{[1-(n-1)y^*]\}^{1/n} & \text{for } (n-1)y^* < y < ny^*
\end{aligned}
$$

where $W(y)$ is the well-being derived from income.

ENDNOTES

1. In *Human Development Report 2001*, the indicators included in HPI-1 were: probability at birth of not surviving to age 40, adult illiteracy rate, population without access to safe water, population without access to health services and per cent of underweight children under age five. Those used in HPI-2 were: probability at birth of not surviving to age 60, functional illiteracy, population below income poverty line and long-term unemployment.

2. OECD and Statistics Canada. 2000.

REFERENCES

Akder, Halis. 1994. "A Means to Closing Gaps: Disaggregated Human Development Index." Human Development Report Office Occasional Papers No. 18. UNDP, New York.

Anand, Sudhir and Martin Ravallion. 1993. "Human Development in Poor Countries: On the Role of Private Incomes and Public Services." *Journal of Economic Perspectives*, 7(1).

Anand, Sudhir and Amartya Sen. 1993. *Human Development Index: Methodology and Measurement.* Cambridge, Mass.: Harvard University.

——. 1995. "Gender Inequality in Human Development: Theories and Measurement." Human Development Report Office Occasional Papers No. 19. UNDP, New York.

Banerjee. Paritosh. 1995. "Human Development Index (HDI): A Note On." University of Lucknow, Lucknow, India. Mimeographed.

Boer, Leen and Ad Koekkoek. 1993. "Human Development Report: Fad or Fixture?" *Development Policy Review* 11.

Castles, Ian. 1998. "The Mismeasure of Nations: A Review Essay on the Human Development Report 1998." *Population and Development Review* 24(4), December.

——. 2000. "The Human Development Report 1997." Room document for the United Nations Statistical Commission. March.

Commission of the European Communities, International Monetary Fund, Organisation for Economic Cooperation and Development, United Nations and World Bank. 1993. *System of National Accounts 1993.* Brussels/Luxembourg, New York, Paris, Washington, D.C.

Das, Tarun Kanti. 1993. "UNDP Human Development Index – Some Methodological Issues and Alternative Measures." Mimeographed.

Dasgupta, Partha and Martin Weale. 1992. "On Measuring the Quality of Life." *World Development* 20(1).

Desai, Meghnad. 1990. "Improving the HDI." Mimeographed.

——. 1991. "Human Development: Concepts and Measurement." *European Economic Review* 35.

——. 1992. "Human Development Index: A Survey of Recent Reviews." Mimeographed.

——. 1994. "Greening of the HDI?" Mimeographed.

Dietz, James and Louise Gibson. 1994. "What is Development? – the Human Development Index, a New Measure of Progress." Paper presented at the Association for Institutional Economics meetings, Albuquerque, New Mexico, April.

Ephrenesis, Dag. 1994. "Policy Uses of HDI: Goals and Strategies." SIDA Planeringssekretariatet.

Hamilton, Kirk. 1994. "Greening the Human Development Index." Statistics Canada, Ottawa. Mimeographed.

Hicks, Douglas. 1997. "The Inequality-Adjusted Human Development Index: A Constructive Proposal." *World Development* 25(8): 1283–98.

Hopkins, Michael. 1991. "Human Development Revisited: A New UNDP Report." *World Development* 19(10).

——. 1993. "A Note on Adding Components (Dimensions) to the HDI." UNDP, Human Development Report Office, New York. Mimeographed.

Indrayan, A., M. J. Wysocki, A. Chawla, R. Kumar and N. Singh. 1999. "Three Decade Trend in Human Development Index in India and Its Major States." *Social Indicators Research* 46: 99–120.

Ivanova, Ianita. 1994. "A Quantitative Measure of the Competitive Advantage of Nations." Paper presented at the Atlantic Schools of Business Conference 1994, Nova Scotia.

Ivanova, I, F. J. Arcelus and G. Srinivasan. 1994a. "Information Validity and Axiomatic Characterisation of the Human Development Index." Working Paper 94-010. University of New Brunswick, New Brunswick, Canada.

——. 1994b. "Effects of the Human Development Index's Social and Economic Components on Country Rankings." University of New Brunswick, New Brunswick, Canada. Mimeographed.

Kanbur, Ravi. 1990. "Poverty and Development: the Human Development Report and the World Development Report 1990." Discussion Paper 103. University of Warwick, Coventry, England.

Kelley, Allen C. 1994. "The Human Development Index: Handle with Care." *Population and Development Review,* June 1994.

Khatib, Dr. Hishman. 1994. "The HDI as a Policy and Planning Tool." A paper prepared for the Human Development Report Office. UNDP, New York.

Lind, Niels. 1991. "Some Thoughts on the Human Development Index." University of Waterloo, Institute for Risk Research, Waterloo, Ontario. Mimeographed.

McGillivray, Mark. 1991. "The Human Development Index: Yet Another Redundant Composite Development Indicator?" *World Development* 19(10).

McGillivray, Mark and Howard White. 1993. "Measuring Development? The UNDP's Human Development Index." *Journal of International Development* 5(2).

Moll, Terence. 1992. "Mickey Mouse Numbers and Inequality Research in Developing Countries." *The Journal of Development Studies* 28(4).

Murray, Christopher. 1991. "Development Data Constraints and the Human Development Index." Le Ministere delegue aupres du Premier Ministre charge du Plan au Maroc and The United Nations Research Institute for Social Development. Presented at a meeting of experts on social development indicators. Morocco. Mimeographed.

Noorbakhsh, Farhad. 1998. "The Human Development Index: Some Technical Issues and Alternative Indices." *Journal of International Development* 10: 589–605.

Ogwang, Tomson. 1994. "The Choice of Principle Variables for Computing the Human Development Index." *World Development* 22(12).

OECD (Organisation for Economic Co-operation and Development) and Statistics Canada. 2000. *Literacy in the Information Age: Final Report on the International Adult Literacy Survey*. Paris.

Osman, Osman M. 1994. "The Use of the HDI as a Statistical Tool of Policy Programming." A paper prepared for the Human Development Report Office. UNDP, New York.

Pal, S. P. and D. K. Pant. 1992. *An Alternative Human Development Index*. National Council for Applied Economic Research, India.

Pyatt, Graham. 1991. Personal communication with Inge Kaul.

——. 1992. "There is Nothing Wrong with the HDI but . . ." University of Warwick, England. Mimeographed.

Ramirez, Alejandro. 1995. Comments on the three-tiered human development index. Mimeographed.

Rao, V. V. Bhanoji. 1991. "Human Development Report 1990: Review and Assessment." *World Development* 19(10).

Ravallion, Martin. 1997. "Good and Bad Growth: The Human Development Reports." *World Development* 25(5).

Raworth, Kate. 2001. "Measuring Human Rights." *Journal of Ethics and International Affairs* 15(1).

Ryten, Jacob. 2000. "Should There Be a Human Development Index?" Paper presented at the International Association for Official Statistics meeting, Montreux, 5 September.

Smith, Peter. 1995. "Measuring Human Development." University of Southampton. Mimeographed.

Srinivasan, T. 1993. "Human Development: A New Paradigm or Reinvention of the Wheel?" Paper presented at the American Economic Association meeting, Boston, 3 January. Mimeographed.

Streeten, Paul. 1994. Personal communication with the Human Development Report Office.

Trabold-Nubler, Harald. 1991. "The Human Development Index – A New Development Indicator?" *Intereconomics,* September/October.

UNDP (United Nations Development Programme). 1990. *Human Development Report 1990.* New York: Oxford University Press.

——. 1992. *Human Development Report 1992.* New York: Oxford University Press.

——. 1993. *Human Development Report 1993.* New York: Oxford University Press.

——. 1997. *Human Development Report 1997.* New York: Oxford University Press.

——. 2000. *Human Development Report 2000.* New York: Oxford University Press.

UNESCO (United Nations Educational, Scientific and Cultural Organization). 2000. Personal communication on net enrolment ratios with the Human Development Report Office. Paris.

2.5

USING THE HDI
FOR POLICY ANALYSIS

Sakiko Fukuda-Parr, Kate Raworth and A. K. Shiva Kumar

Since its launch in 1990 in the first *Human Development Report*, the human development index has captured the attention of governments, the media and civil society. People in different countries compare their ranking with those of their neighbours', often asking why achievements in the quality of life made elsewhere have not been made at home.

past decade has seen indicators being increasingly used as tools for policy dialogue, providing monitoring information for advocacy and change. Policy debates have likewise made increasingly sophisticated use of data. This chapter reviews the ways in which the HDI has been employed as a policy tool for evaluating and contrasting human development achievements across countries, between groups within countries and over time. It explores the limitations of the HDI and the challenges facing those attempting to develop new indices. Finally, the chapter reflects on the last decade of policy debates, utilizing the HDI in order to identify the features that have been critical to its usefulness and acceptability.

CHALLENGING COUNTRIES

The HDI's global ranking of countries provides an assessment of a nation's average achievement in human development, comparing it with the progress of other countries. Table 2.5.1, for instance, shows a set of HDI values and incomes.

The data in table 2.5.1 illustrate the lack of determinism between per capita income and HDI achievements. Several implications follow.

First, it is possible to have similar levels of human development (as captured by the HDI) but very different levels of per capita income. Brazil and the Philippines, for instance, have similar HDI values, but the per capita income in Brazil is 85% higher than that of the Philippines.

Second, it is possible to have similar levels of income but very different levels of human development. Jamaica and Guatemala are close in income, but Guatemala's HDI value is 15% lower than Jamaica's.

Third, and derived from these two observations, a higher income does not by itself imply a higher level of human development. Saudi Arabia, South Africa and Brazil, for instance, are richer in terms of per capita income than Costa Rica and yet remain at much lower levels of the HDI.

Fourth, it is not necessary for a country to become rich first before it can assure people a decent level of human development. Sri Lanka, for instance, continues to have a relatively low level of income and still reports a relatively high HDI value.

Fifth, misplaced priorities, and not necessarily a shortage of resources, often prevent coun-

Table 2.5.1
HDI and income levels for select countries

Country	HDI value 1999	GDP per capita (PPP US$) 1999
Brazil	0.750	7,037
Philippines	0.749	3,805
Jamaica	0.738	3,561
Guatemala	0.626	3,674
South Africa	0.702	8,908
Sri Lanka	0.735	3,279
Costa Rica	0.821	8,860
Saudi Arabia	0.754	10,815

Source: Human Development Report 2001.

tries from assuring people universal access to basic health and education. As Costa Rica, Sri Lanka and Jamaica have shown, it is indeed possible to ensure near universal provisioning of health and education even at relatively low levels of income.

Comparisons of this kind have attracted public attention and carry the potential to initiate a more detailed discussion on development strategies and priorities. In several instances, cross-country comparisons have contributed to a re-examination of national development policies and priorities.

FOCUSING ON INTERNAL DISPARITIES

It is often possible to disaggregate the HDI within a country by regions, provinces, ethnic groups, or rural and urban areas. Such disaggregated indices, by drawing attention to both *levels* of human development and the extent of *inequality* within a country, can force public debates and discussions on why differences persist. HDI rankings of regions, states, provinces or counties are a particularly powerful tool in the hands of local politicians and media who can ask for explanations and demand higher allocations to the more backward regions. Several examples of such disaggregation can be found in the national human development reports; a sample is given below.

Disaggregation by regions

In many countries, levels of human development vary according to geographical regions. Table 2.5.2 shows the computed HDI values for five of Brazil's regions.

Table 2.5.2
Disaggregated HDI for Brazil

| Region | HDI value | | |
	1970	1980	1990
North	0.385	0.577	0.582
Northeast	0.245	0.384	0.474
Southeast	0.619	0.734	0.784
South	0.528	0.752	0.799
Mideast	0.427	0.674	0.741

Source: Spindola 1993.

Disparities in levels of human development within Brazil are striking, and HDI achievements have been uneven. In 1990, the South fared the best with an HDI value of 0.799 – almost 68% higher than the HDI value reported by the Northeast. One way of assessing the disparities is to examine which of the regions has made the best progress towards the goal of an HDI of 1.000. Table 2.5.3 below gives the results of such an analysis.

Between 1970 and 1990, the South, which enjoyed an historical advantage, did the best in terms of closing the gap on human development. On the other hand, the North and Northeast recorded the slowest progress – they were the same two regions that reported the lowest HDI values in 1970. Use of such disaggregated HDIs is, of course, only the beginning of a more detailed investigation into factors that have prevented the North and Northeastern regions from achieving high human development more rapidly.

Disaggregation by states and provinces

Disaggregating the national HDI by states or provinces within the country is another useful way of reporting on intranational levels and disparities in human development. The HDI constructed for 15 Indian states in 1991, for example, revealed striking inequalities. Kerala, the state with the highest HDI value at 0.651, ranked above Indonesia and Botswana. In contrast, Uttar Pradesh (with an HDI of 0.292) and Bihar (with an HDI of 0.306) ranked alongside Rwanda and Zaire. Levels of human development in these states, which are two

Table 2.5.3
Progress in human development across regions in Brazil

| Region | HDI value | | % reduction in HDI shortfall |
	1970	1990	
South	0.528	0.799	57.4
Mideast	0.427	0.741	54.8
Southeast	0.619	0.784	43.3
North	0.385	0.582	32.0
Northeast	0.245	0.474	30.3

Source: Computed on the basis of data in Table 2.5.2.

Table 2.5.4
Disaggregated HDI values for China – 1982 and 1990

Province	HDI value	
	1982	1990
Shanghai	0.990	0.985
Beijing	0.824	0.896
Shanxi	0.516	0.556
Hunan	0.451	0.490
Sichuan	0.357	0.454
Ningxia	0.337	0.425
Yunnan	0.180	0.304

Source: Zhizhou 1994.

Table 2.5.5
Disaggregated HDI for Turkey 1990

	HDI Values	
	Urban	Rural
MUaLA	0.91	0.67
NEVPtsEHijR	0.85	0.78
TRABZON	0.86	0.54
ZONGULDAK	0.82	0.47
HATAY	0.80	0.51
SAKARYA	0.80	0.52
KAYSERij	0.79	0.52
CANKIRI	0.77	0.48
ADANA	0.75	0.58
UptsAK	0.74	0.56
GUMUPtsHANE	0.70	0.42
ERZURUM	0.58	0.32
DijYARBAKIR	0.50	0.36
VAN	0.50	0.22

Source: Akder 1992.

of India's most populous, were less than half of those reported in Kerala. Similarly, disaggregation of China's 30 provinces reveals striking differentials. In 1990, the HDI value for Yunnan was less than one-third of the value reported for Shanghai. See table 2.5.4 above.

Rural-urban disparities

Throughout the world, it is common to find higher levels of human development in urban than in rural areas. But just how wide are the disparities? Separate construction of the HDI for rural and urban areas helps highlight the gaps. Table 2.5.5, for example, breaks down the HDI values in some of Turkey's 67 provinces.

The data presented in Table 2.5.5 reveal, for instance, that in Turkey, urban HDIs are higher than rural HDIs and in all the provinces. It is also clear that in some cases the disparities are wide. The most advanced region – urban MUaLA, with an HDI value of 0.91 – ranks higher than South Korea. The other extreme is rural VAN with an HDI value of only 0.22, ranking along with countries such as Togo and Yemen, among the lowest in the world.

Ethnic disaggregation

Some countries have attempted to disaggregate the HDI according to ethnicity. Table 2.5.6 above shows the HDI values for different ethnic groups in Malaysia and Gabon.

Table 2.5.6
HDI by ethnicity

	HDI value
Malaysia	
Chinese	0.954
Indians	0.796
Malays	0.777
All races	0.845
Gabon	
Fang	0.580
Shira-Panu	0.523
Nzabi-Duma	0.483
All races	0.519

Source: Obame 1993; Leng and Aziz 1993.

WHAT DOES – AND DOESN'T – THE HDI REVEAL?

The high profile of the HDI has on occasion led to its misuse or misinterpretation. There are a number of caveats that need to be considered in putting it to use. Many relate, as discussed in other contributions to this book, to data concerns and missing capabilities.

However desirable disaggregated HDIs may be, they can be difficult to compute in practice. Data at the sub-national and local levels are not easy to obtain for many of the indicators. For instance, depending upon the population size of the country, estimates of life expectancy at birth below the national level are sometimes unobtainable. Less problematic are indicators for educational attainment: adult literacy rates are typically obtained from censuses and are available at practically every level of disaggregation. The difficulty, however, is in obtaining annual estimates, especially given that censuses are typically conducted every ten years. Gross enrolment rates are also available as part of every state's educational statistics, but the problem in some situations here lies in vouching for the authenticity of such administratively reported data. In many countries of South Asia, for instance, enrolment figures are exaggerated for a variety of reasons, with actual school attendance far below the levels suggested by the data.

In addition to the HDI's data constraints, the index by no means captures all dimensions of human development. To that extent, it may not always be true that the quality of people's lives is improving whenever the HDI increases. It is quite possible that political repression, crime, pollution and racial discrimination may be on the rise even as HDI values move upward. Similarly, the HDI may not capture effectively the impact of natural disasters such as droughts, cyclones, floods or earthquakes – even when they are severe. The HDI focuses on two capabilities that are basic to all people and without which other capabilities would be foreclosed – being knowledgeable and leading a long and healthy life – as well as a third – having a decent standard of living – as a proxy for many other capabilities. The index does not explicitly cover three important capabilities: political freedoms, personal security and participation in the life of the community. These are basic concerns for people universally, but cannot be quantified reliably or universally, and data are not available. Furthermore, national HDIs show the average achievements of a country without taking into account disparities among groups, or between present and future generations.

MEASURING PROGRESS IN HUMAN DEVELOPMENT

When countries' HDI rankings rise from one year to the next, governments may be tempted to claim credit, pointing to their own recent policies. Likewise, when a ranking falls or stays the same, the media and political opposition may be tempted to blame the current government and its policies. The HDI does not, however, reflect such short-term impacts of policies. Two of its indicators are slow to change: adult literacy and life expectancy. And although combined gross enrolments and average incomes may vary more year to year, when expressed as national averages, they still do not respond much to policies that focus on raising

Table 2.5.7
Fastest and slowest progress in human development, 1975–98
For 101 countries with available data

Country	1975 HDI	1998 HDI	Absolute change 1975–98
Starting from low human development (0–0.499)			
Fastest progress			
Egypt	0.430	0.623	0.193
Nepal	0.291	0.474	0.183
Slowest progress			
Central African Republic	0.332	0.371	0.039
Dem. Rep. of the Congo	0.416	0.430	0.014
Zambia	0.444	0.420	–0.024

Source: Human Development Report 2000.

enrolments among illiterate communities or tackling income poverty among the most deprived. *Human Development Report 1999* produced the first long-term trend data for the HDI, for 1975–97. Even across 22 years, progress is gradual at every level of development.

Neither governments nor the public can wait 20 years to find out whether policies have promoted human development. Indicators are needed that capture the shorter-term impacts of policies and that reflect the priorities and principles of human development. These indicators could:

- Reveal who are the most deprived and how their lives are affected by policies. This calls for disaggregation to identify social groups with the worst outcomes so that their progress can be tracked.
- Reflect disparities between groups – such as by gender, ethnicity, region and urban or rural dwelling – to help identify current or historical discrimination and to show whether policies are reducing or exacerbating the gaps.
- Respond to policy measures so that the findings help in assessing government performance. This calls for using variables that respond in the short term – for instance, the literacy rate among 15 to 19 year olds rather than adult literacy rate – but lack of data is a

common problem. Responsiveness also calls for using data that are updated frequently – at least every five years, for example – but this, too, is still often not possible.

To reflect these demands, three perspectives need to be applied simultaneously:

- average perspective, showing overall progress in the country;
- deprivation perspective, showing progress by the most deprived groups; and
- inequality perspective, showing progress in narrowing inequalities.

The framework shown in table 2.5.8 can be applied in every country using variables most relevant to each nation's most pressing issues. But it requires disaggregated data. More and more such data are being collected at the national level, disaggregated by gender, ethnicity, urban and rural dwelling, district, income level, education level and other relevant characteristics.

Progress in the HDI has typically been assessed through the average perspective, but, as the data show in table 2.5.7, the results are too gradual to be useful for assessing the impacts of specific policy phases. More attention needs to be given to the deprivation and inequality perspec-

Table 2.5.8
Three perspectives for assessing progress

Time frame	Average perspective	Deprivation perspective	Inequality perspective
One period	What is the national average?	Who are the most deprived by: • income quintile • gender • region • rural or urban • ethnic group • education level	What is the disparity between: • bottom and top income quintile • females and males • worst-off and best-off regions • rural and urban • worst-off and best-off ethnic groups • no education and higher education
Over time	Has the national average changed?	How have the most deprived social groups progressed?	How have disparities between social groups changed – have they widened or narrowed?

tives. For all three perspectives, however, the methodology for measuring progress first needs to be addressed.

There are three common ways of measuring progress in the HDI and other human development indicators: (1) absolute change, (2) percentage change and (3) shortfall reduction. The following hypothetical example illustrates the three approaches. Suppose two countries, A and B, record the following trends in adult literacy:

Adult literacy rate:	1980	1995
Country A	60%	70%
Country B	80%	90%

In terms of ranking, Country B does better than Country A in 1980 as well as in 1995. But how should we rank the performance of the two countries in promoting literacy between 1980–95? The outcomes using the three methods yield different results. (See table 2.5.9 below.)

The above example illustrates how rankings change depending upon which method is adopted. Each has its own advantages and drawbacks.

The *absolute change method* is simple to compute, easy to comprehend and biased in favour of low human development countries, which have more scope for improving absolute levels of achievement.

The *percentage change method* is also fairly easy to compute and favours low human development countries (as the base for computing percentage changes is lower than that of high human development countries).

Table 2.5.9
Comparing methods of assessing progress: adult literacy, 1980–95

	Country A	Country B	
Absolute change	10%	10%	
Rank	1	1	Same rank
Percentage change	16.7%	12.5%	
Rank	1	2	A better
Shortfall reduction	25%	50%	
Rank	2	1	B better

The *shortfall reduction method* is more difficult to compute and to communicate. But it has three major advantages:

- It recognizes the difficulty of "reaching the unreached" and gives credit to countries that make special efforts to close the gap as their achievement levels rise.
- It conveys better the idea of "progressive realization of human rights". Even countries with high levels of achievements need to keep up their efforts to move towards universal coverage.
- It is possible that even though a country may be ranked lowest in terms of the level of achievement – and may continue to remain so – its ranking in terms of shortfall reduction can be better. And to that extent, the shortfall reduction method provides the necessary incentive for accelerating human development.

Table 2.5.10 illustrates the point. Even though Venezuela ranked fifth out of the six countries in 1970 and 1995, it ranked first in terms of performance by shortfall reduction over the 25-year period. On the other hand, even though Uruguay held first rank in both 1970 and in 1995, its performance in terms of reducing illiteracy was the worst.

Use of the absolute change method has certain clear advantages over the other two methods. First of all, it is the most transparent of the three methods. It is very simple to compute, requiring little mathematical sophistication. It favours countries with low levels of achievement and provides an incentive for them to do better, in the form of the ranking. At the same time, ranking based on the absolute method also puts pressure on the more developed countries – who typically will appear at the bottom of the rankings list – to end educational deprivation even when it means advancing towards universal literacy by just a few percentage points. In most societies, those who are left out are the most deprived. Appearing at the bottom of the ranking sends a signal to the developed countries to assign top priority to their neglected groups.

Table 2.5.10
Comparing ranks and progress

	Adult literacy rates for selected countries (%)					
	1970	Rank	1995	Rank	% reduction in shortfall	Rank
Uruguay	93	1	97	1	57.1	6
Costa Rica	89	2	96	2	63.6	2
Paraguay	82	3	93	3	61.1	4
Panama	80	4	92	4	60.0	5
Venezuela	77	5	92	5	65.2	1
Mexico	76	6	91	6	62.5	3

Source: Human Development Report 1998.

Assessing progress from the deprivation perspective

Disaggregating data reveals which social groups are worst off. These data can then be used to assess relative rates of progress, especially comparing progress made by the most deprived to that of the average or best group.

In Benin in 1994, for example, there were wide disparities in school enrolments, by gender and by district (figure 2.5.1). National average net enrolment in primary school was 52% – but just 38% for girls compared with 65% for boys. Likewise, there were large differences across districts,

with just 30% of all children in Borgou enrolled in school. From the deprivation perspective, assessing progress must then focus on female enrolments and those in Borgou. By 1997, national average enrolment had risen 7 percentage points to 59%. How much progress was made for the most deprived? Female enrolment across the country rose 8 points to 46%, total enrolment in Borgou rose 9 points to 39%, and female enrolment in Borgou rose 9 points to 31%. The most deprived groups made slightly faster progress than the average, but not enough to reduce the significance of their deprivation compared to other groups.

FIGURE 2.5.1
Making progress: how much for the most deprived?
Once the most deprived groups have been identified, data can reveal whether they benefit from national progress – or are excluded from it.

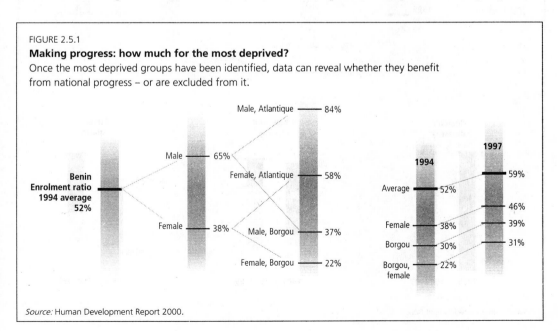

Source: Human Development Report 2000.

Assessing progress from the inequality perspective

Disaggregating and comparing data by different kinds of social groups – by ethnicity compared to region, gender and so on – can reveal the characteristics of inequality within a country and then be used as a means for monitoring reduction of disparities. Data on under-five mortality in Guatemala, for example (see figure 2.5.2), were disaggregated by ethnicity (indigenous/non-indigenous) and location (urban/rural). Both cases revealed inequalities, which data from 1998–99 show are being reduced. It is clear, however, that where urban/rural inequalities fell 17 percentage points, inequalities related to ethnicity declined only 2 points. From the inequality perspective, progress in reducing ethnic inequalities is significantly lagging.

THE STAYING POWER OF THE HDI AND ITS LESSONS

When the HDI was first launched in 1990, it was something of a trial balloon. Convinced by the need for such an index, the authors were nonetheless fully conscious that it could be rejected and further publication stopped in the face of either methodological or political objections. Over the last decade, the HDI has in fact weathered the

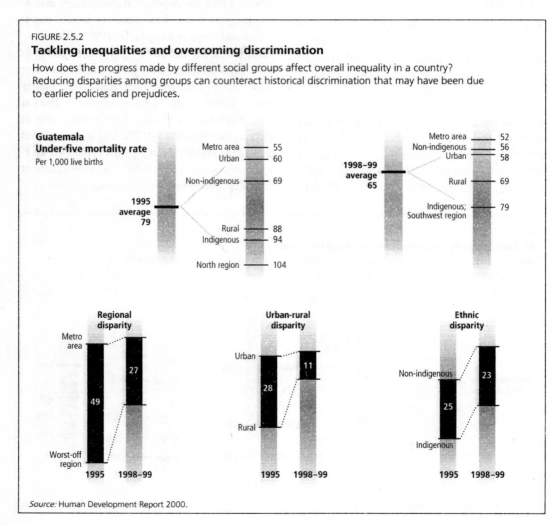

FIGURE 2.5.2

Tackling inequalities and overcoming discrimination

How does the progress made by different social groups affect overall inequality in a country?
Reducing disparities among groups can counteract historical discrimination that may have been due to earlier policies and prejudices.

Guatemala
Under-five mortality rate
Per 1,000 live births

1995 average 79

Metro area — 55
Urban — 60
Non-indigenous — 69
Rural — 88
Indigenous — 94
North region — 104

1998–99 average 65

Metro area — 52
Non-indigenous — 56
Urban — 58
Rural — 69
Indigenous; Southwest region — 79

Regional disparity
Metro area
49 (1995), 27 (1998–99)
Worst-off region
1995   1998–99

Urban-rural disparity
Urban
28 (1995), 11 (1998–99)
Rural
1995   1998–99

Ethnic disparity
Non-indigenous
25 (1995), 23 (1998–99)
Indigenous
1995   1998–99

Source: Human Development Report 2000.

storms of controversy reasonably well, and has become well established and accepted. While controversies remain, there are few voices that would argue for abandoning it. And in fact, of the multiple efforts to develop composite indices of national progress that focus on non-economic dimensions, the HDI is not only one of the most well known and used, but the only one that is published by an intergovernmental organization. It has flourished even under the scrutiny of the world.

In our view, the HDI owes its survival not only to sound methodology, but also to two other factors: policy relevance and acceptability. First, policy-makers have found it useful and wanted to see it continue. Second, they have accepted it even if they have not always liked the results. In fact, those who have theoretical objections to composite indices often grant an exception to the HDI on the grounds that it has had a positive policy impact. (See, for example, Handoussa 2000).

Four aspects of the HDI have been critical to ensuring policy relevance and acceptability:

- conceptual clarity that facilitates the HDI's power as a tool of communication;
- a reasonable level of aggregation;
- use of universal criteria amenable to inter-country comparisons; and
- use of standardized international data that have been legitimized through official processes.

Conceptual clarity

In developing composite indices, the first step is to define what is to be measured in terms that can be understood easily by the average user. The specification of the HDI was derived from a clearly defined concept, not the other way round. This logic may seem obvious, but indices of governance, corruption or environmental sustainability are often developed without the foundation of a clear conceptual framework.

The strength of the HDI as a tool of communication also lies in its clarity for the average reader, who can easily identify with the notion that the three components of the HDI – being knowledgeable, leading a long and healthy life, and having a decent standard of living – represent fundamental goals of human well-being.

Thus, it is easy for policy-makers around the world to quickly and intuitively grasp the idea that the HDI is measuring aspects of well-being not captured in GDP, but that are important goals for any society. Few would dispute that a low score on the HDI is a cause for concern and a high score is a source of pride. In contrast, many other composite indices are "black boxes" with complex conceptual frameworks and methodologies. To compound this effect, there is a lack of transparency in the publication of tables without a full technical explanation of how the index is calculated or what the data sources are.[1]

A reasonable level of aggregation

The power of the HDI, as of any composite index, is in the policy message it conveys. Including too broad a set of issues would make that policy signal unclear. Deciding on the level of aggregation is obviously a matter of judgment.

Many composite indices have fallen into the temptation to aggregate too much, or sometimes too little.[2] The choice made by the *Human Development Reports* was to aggregate at the level of basic capability achievements and to develop complementary indices for other issues, such as gender empowerment and human poverty. Not only would folding such notions into the HDI be methodologically difficult, but the policy impact and analytical usefulness of the index would be compromised by too high a level of aggregation. In contrast to many other indices, which include dozens of dimensions and measurement indicators, the HDI only comprises three dimensions represented by four indicators.

Universally relevant criteria

The HDI is based on dimensions that are clearly comparable across countries, with indicators that are universally relevant. Composite indices that rank countries are necessarily judgmental: they are evaluative measures, not just descriptive ones, in which more is definitely better than less. There is a high degree of consensus across the world on the indicators being used as important development objectives, namely health, education and incomes. Contrast this to more context specific indicators – such as the area of woodland, often used in environmental sustainability measures, or the frequency of elections, often used in governance measures – for which more is not necessarily better.

Legitimized data

Data availability is a problem that affects all measurement challenges in all sectors. In fact, many countries lack information on key social or economic issues, such as employment or even basic education and health, on which specialized data are not available uniformly for all countries. Much of what we would want to monitor quantitatively has not been measured. A good number of issues of concern, such as political freedom, have not been measured at all.[3]

Data used in the HDI are limited to international statistical series that have been published by intergovernmental organizations and originate in official national statistics. Almost all countries have data on literacy, school enrolment, life expectancy and per capita income. There are still data problems: purchasing power parity estimates could be based on more recent and comprehensive surveys; and for measuring knowledge, net enrolment or mean years of schooling would be preferable. As with all statistical series, the cross-country quality does vary. But the HDI is able to use data that have near universal coverage and have also been through a review process – i.e., data that have been produced and published after a legitimization process, including an assessment of their intercountry comparability.

Often, attempts at developing composite indices do not use such legitimized data; many employ estimates to fill gaps in data coverage. Not only does this lead to indices that use unreliable data of poor quality, but also to data that have no credibility or legitimacy. Most indices of governance – such as corruption and political freedom – have particular problems of legitimacy because they depend on indicators of subjective perceptions.

However accurate the data and however sound the methodology, an index cannot be considered legitimate when the underlying data have not themselves been through the legitimization process.

DOING THE DOABLE AND NO MORE

From the conceptual point of view, the HDI is frustratingly limited. It misses many important capabilities, such as political participation and freedom, and important development concerns, such as environmental sustainability and equity. Many of the critiques of the HDI have pointed out such gaps. And while separate measures of gender inequality and poverty have been developed, measures of other important factors in evaluating human development, such as human rights, have not been developed in the *Human Development Reports*.[4]

The Reports have not excessively pushed the limits of the possible in measurement of human development. Our indices have remained within the limits of what can be done while respecting the four principles set out above. The third and fourth principles, of measuring only those achievements for which universal standards can be applied and of using legitimate data, have been particularly rigidly upheld.

As a consequence, the design of the HDI was necessarily simple. It seems deceptively limited: compromises are not made to estimate a large number of data or to include dimensions that are unquantifiable; the concept of human development is clearly larger than the HDI; and the HDI does not reflect many important social achievements. But these concerns are characterized by priorities that are specific to certain locations, or are not easily measurable, or have not yet been measured. The attempt to develop a political freedom index failed for these reasons – not just because there were serious objections from some governments, but also because the index could not be defended as using objective and legitimate measures.

The HDI is therefore pared down to a bare minimum of dimensions and indicators, and as such, it is limited in its meaning. It is important to recognize that the HDI is a "summary measure" of key human development outcomes. Nonetheless, a composite index that combines achievements in knowledge, survival and the standard of living is a major step forward for evaluating development from a human point of view.

CONCLUSION

Creative use of the HDI can effectively draw attention to low levels of human development and, importantly, to areas of inequality. However, it is critical to remember that the HDI has its limitations – including the fact that it is a composite index. For good reasons, Amartya Sen points out that "the selection of an aggregate index is inevitably one of 'tragic choice' ".[5] Any composite index needs to be disaggregated in order to understand trends in the index values. Clearly, it is necessary to develop other sets of indicators – particularly those that are more sensitive in the short run to policy changes, and those that reflect political freedom, personal security and participation.

ENDNOTES

1. The Environmental Sustainability Index (ESI) [http://www.ciesin.org/indicators/ESI] is an example in which the method of calculation and the data sources are not fully published along with the tables.

2. In our view, the ESI is an example of over-aggregation. It not only includes stock or status (environmental systems) but also improvement (reducing environmental stress and human vulnerability) and institutional issues (social and institutional capacity).

3. A notable example is the index of health systems published by the World Health Organization in 2000. This index used data that were not officially published and were often estimated. It also included qualitative indicators.

4. A measure of political freedom was attempted in 1991 and 1992, but then dropped because of inadequacies in the methodology and the absence of a process legitimizing the data.

5. Human Development Report Office internal working paper.

REFERENCES

Akder, A. Halis. 1994. "A Means to Closing Gaps: Disaggregated Human Development Index." Human Development Report Office Occasional Papers No. 18. UNDP, New York.

Handoussa, Heba. 2000. Discussion at the IAOS conference "Statistics, Development and Human Rights,"
session I-PL 6/7: "Human Development: Design of Indicators." Montreux, 7 September.

Leng, Y. K. and Aziz, T. 1993. "Disaggregated Human Development Index (HDI) of Malaysia." An unpublished study for UNDP, cited in Akder 1994. New York.

Obame, J. C. 1993. "Etude sur les Indices Sectoriels du Developpement Humain au Gabon." An unpublished study for UNDP, cited in Akder 1994. New York.

Shiva Kumar, A. K. 2000. "Measuring Progress in Human Development: Tracking Inputs, Assessing Efforts, Evaluating Outcomes." Background paper for Human Development Report 2000. UNDP, New York.

Spindola, A. G. 1993. "The HDI and Other Development Indicators of Brazil." An unpublished study for UNDP, cited in Akder 1994. New York.

UNDP (United Nations Development Programme). 1991. Human Development Report 1991. New York: Oxford University Press.

——. 1998. Human Development Report 1998. New York: Oxford University Press.

——. 2000. Human Development Report 2000. New York: Oxford University Press.

——. 2001. Human Development Report 2001. New York: Oxford University Press.

The World Economic Forum's Global Leaders for Tomorrow Environment Task Force, The Yale Center for Environmental Law and Policy, and the Columbia University Center for International Earth Science Information Network (CIESIN). 2002. Environmental Sustainability Index (ESI). [http://www.ciesin.org/indicators/ESI/]. April 2002.

WHO (World Health Organisation). 2000. The World Health Report 2000 – Healthsystems: Improving Performance. WHO, Geneva.

Zhizhou, C. 1994. "Disaggregation and Analysis of Human Development Indicators in China." An unpublished study for UNDP, cited in Akder 1994. New York.

2.6
MEASURING
POLITICAL FREEDOM*

Meghnad Desai**

INTRODUCTION

The collapse of the Soviet Empire and its satellites has revived some age-old ideas in the social sciences. Perhaps the most famous of these was the notion of the "end of history" in the sense of the Hegelian programme of Universal History. Francis Fukuyama, who first wrote about this in an article in 1989, expanded later into a serious and thought-provoking book in 1992, raises two simple questions: Why capitalism? Why liberal democracy? Why is it that, at the end of the twentieth century, we find ourselves with capitalism as "the only game in town", the only mode of production, when its demise was frequently predicted by friends and foes alike – Schumpeter and Lenin can serve as an example of each of these two categories. Why, despite many distractions and fears about the death of democracy, some as recently as the mid-1970s, are more and more countries adopting multiparty parliamentary democracy as their preferred political system?[1]

Fukuyama's answers are quite subtle, though they can be encapsulated as "science and technology" for the first question and "desire for self-respect and recognition" for the second. It is not my intention to examine Fukuyama's arguments here directly.[2] I wish in this essay to act as a social scientist not as a philosopher or an historian, neither of which can I claim to be. For a social scientist, especially an LSE social scientist who wishes to know the cause of things, the question is: is there any causal link between capitalism and democracy; between freedom and development? It is a question, which has been much explored but not settled.[3] One of the many reasons for this is that the notion of causation needs to be separated from that of correlation, and to do so requires some adequate measurement of the pair of variables under study.

There has been a history of measurement of economic development and of the standard of living. The history of attempts to measure political freedom is a relatively shorter one, being mostly a post-1945 phenomenon, or indeed a 1960s one. It is a subject surrounded in controversy and much has been written on it.[4] My purpose here is not to review these attempts, but to outline a method of measuring political freedom. The measure is of interest because, among its other peculiarities, it uses analogies of concepts from economics. The notions of private and public goods and the notion of a utility tree are used to yield a measure of political freedom.

The paper stops at the measurement problem and does not go on to address the larger question of correlation/causation. The larger question is being addressed in future work. In what follows, I outline the general problem of development/freedom correlation. Then I go into details of the definitions of freedom and the problems encountered in measuring it.

HISTORICAL PERSPECTIVES
ON FREEDOM AND DEVELOPMENT

Development used to be perceived in narrow economic terms of per capita income, ratio of investment to income, the proportion of labour force in the industrial sector, the volume of steel output, etc. This perspective is now being increasingly replaced by the notion that development is about human beings and their lives – human development.

Human development is about enabling people to have wider choice, choice about life style, about social relations, about the kind of civil and political society that they wish to live in. This way of perceiving human development has been vindicated by the events of the last five years, which have witnessed a political upsurge on behalf of peoples of many nations for a society with expanding freedom, even if it were to come at the cost of the loss of economic security.[5]

Development is not a narrow economic process defined merely in terms of the availability of goods and services. It is a process of enrichment which spans social, cultural and political dimensions. It is in this context that freedom becomes a vital ingredient of development. Although freedom is notoriously difficult to define, its absence results in all-too-visible signs of repression, arbitrary threats to the person and a fragile artificial stability of the unfree society. The absence of freedom manifests itself as a threat to the integrity of the self – torture, arbitrary arrest, illegal killings by the state or by private agents; it manifests itself as the absence of the rule of law, the lack of redress against the illegal actions of others. Its absence is seen as a lack of voice in how one's political life is run; it is manifested in denial of equality before the law.

Historically, free societies were contrasted with despotic ones. During the Enlightenment, it became a persistent concern of moral philosophers – Montesquieu, David Hume, Adam Smith, Turgot – to search for the causes of freedom in the type of government: monarchy or oligarchy, despotism or the rule of law, aristocracy or democracy. It seemed to these philosophers that there was a parallel progression in history; as the conditions of life improved, so did the possibility of freedom. The notion that societies pass through stages of development, from the primitive hunting and gathering to sophisticated commerce, gained currency in western thought in the mid-18th century. The stadial theory of history, as articulated by Adam Smith, first married the notions of economic development (the natural progress of opulence, as he called it) and freedom. Commercial societies, then the highest stage, were also the freest. Of course, they could be freer if the governments understood the powerful mechanism of self-interest and *laissez faire,* but this economic freedom had to create a society in which the poor could go about without a sense of shame; in other words development had

to be broad as well as deep; it had to cover the economic as well as the political.

Through much of the 19th century the relation between freedom and development was repeated in rhetoric but denied in practice to the majority of the people of the world. Except in the north west of Europe and in North America, political freedom did not accompany economic development; in many colonies, people felt that unfreedom accompanied underdevelopment. Nationalism became a force and identified imperialism as a denial of freedom as well as of the opportunity for development. Some countries, Germany and Japan most prominently, experienced economic development without political freedom. The historical evidence for Adam Smith's contention seemed to be lacking; while the most developed country of the 19th century, Britain, was the freest, beyond and below that, no match could be made between freedom and development. It was argued that the relationship was perhaps a normative one – freedom would lead to the most rapid development if adopted as a policy by the state, especially if it took the form of *laissez faire* in economic affairs. Freedom, in this way of thinking, was a recipe for development rather than its fruit.

As the former colonies became independent in the 20th century, economic development began to be a concern of national and international policy-makers. It was at this stage that economic historians re-examined the relationship between freedom and economic development. By then development had taken place in most western European countries as well as in North America and the antipodes. Russia had undergone a socialist revolution and had developed a new form of political state. Alexander Gerschenkron, summarizing the experience of late industrializing countries, argued that rapid economic growth required, or was at least facilitated by authoritarian regimes. He cited Germany, Italy, Russia and many other examples in his support.[6]

Through much of the past half century, these two doctrines existed uneasily side by side – that rich societies are free societies and that if a country wanted to get rich quickly it had to sacrifice the freedom of its citizens. Policy-makers condoned the existence of dictatorships or of drastic restrictions on freedoms on the grounds that this was the price to pay for growth. But there were significant variants to this argument. There has been a long-standing distinction between *economic freedoms* and *political freedoms* and between two different meanings for economic freedom – as freedom *from* constraint and freedom *to* have a secure economic living. Thus, authoritarian governments are those which deny political freedom but allow *laissez faire* (negative economic freedom), while totalitarian governments deny negative political and economic freedoms in the avowed pursuit of positive economic freedom in the sense of security.

A similar problem existed about political freedom, which is defined in two different senses, although the second sense has now receded from public debate. At the height of the Cold War, it used to be said that political freedom in the usual sense of liberal democratic freedom had to be contrasted with *real* freedom in people's democracies – that socialist legality was superior to bourgeois legality. The collapse of the many Leninist one-party governments in Eastern Europe and in the Soviet Union has settled this argument so that political freedom is now more clearly defined than economic freedom is.

Thus the relation between freedom and development has been debated in a fluid way, opposite views being argued and contradictory definitions being advanced. No wonder it is a confused, unsettled debate. The evidence in favour of one or another view has changed with the passage of time. What can be unambiguously asserted is:

- In the contemporary world, the economically better off countries, as measured by GDP or HDI, are those with a large measure of political freedom.
- There is no certainty that the mere lack of political freedom (i.e., authoritarian or one-party governments) necessarily delivers either economic growth or economic security; for each China or South Korea or Hong Kong, there is a Zaire, or a Malawi, or a Philippines under Marcos.

- It is no longer possible to argue that poor people value economic benefits more than political freedoms; there seems to be across the world a genuine desire for both economic betterment and political freedom.
- The evidence of history is inconclusive.

Given the dual definition of economic freedom as *laissez faire* and as secure economic entitlements, it is more appropriate to concentrate on political freedom as a co-variable of human development for any test of association. But while human development can be (imperfectly) measured with the human development index, political freedom is difficult to measure. If, however, we are to answer the age-old issue of freedom and development, a matching measure of political freedom is needed to supplement the HDI to further enrich our understanding of the process of human development.

CAN FREEDOM BE MEASURED?

Freedom is difficult to define in any way that commands universal agreement: it is even harder to measure. There are many who may question whether it is desirable to measure freedom even if it were possible. The very act of measuring freedom in their view diminishes it.

There are several responses to these arguments. First, the concept of freedom is much larger than its measure, howsoever sophisticated. This is also true of human development and of more narrow economic notions, such as income or liquidity or competition. It is, thus, important to remember that there is always a distance between the *concept* and the *measure* of freedom. Secondly,

Table 2.6.1
Types of freedom

	Economic	Political
Positive	Social security	Franchise/political participation
Negative	Laissez faire	Rule of law

In Table 2.6.1, in each column an example of a particular type of freedom is given. Thus social security stands for a system of guaranteed income entitlements (safety nets) which guarantee a positive freedom. One could describe it as freedom from want but it is better described as a freedom to enjoy a decent standard of living.

it should be remembered that freedom is a latent variable. There are no directly observable instances of freedom; from much qualitative and some quantitative data, we have to make inferences about freedom indirectly. Most typically, we observe the violations of human rights (as indicators of freedom) more often than positive exercise of freedom. Thus evidence of torture, of denial of free elections are more likely to be helpful in detecting the absence of freedom than any positive signs of its exercise. Thirdly, it has to be said that we accept readily today measures of phenomena previously thought unmeasurable; heat is one instance, which until the efforts of Celsius was thought to be unmeasurable. Sound, light, the genetic structure of DNA are other examples. To measure sound waves is not the same as to measure music, but sound waves and music are related.

Another argument about the measurement of freedom relates not so much to its measurability as such but to the most appropriate way to measure it. The choice is between many separate indicators of freedom, as against a single aggregate index – a vector, as against a scalar measure. In a vector measure, each country has several indicators defined; in some it may be above another country, in others below. The final verdict would depend on how different indicators are weighted. Some authors believe that no final answer is possible; all we can hope for is a *partial ordering*. In a scalar measure, the weighting is explicitly carried out and it is possible to rank countries in a *complete ordering*.

My own preference, pursued here, is to weight components of an overall freedom index explicitly and to present a single index number. This is done in the belief that, whatever its shortcomings, a scalar measure is simpler to understand and to criticize than a vector measure. It is also likely to have more impact on public debate about the value of freedom and its relation to human development.

In measuring human freedom, certain problems arise; some of these are generic to any attempt at measuring a latent variable, be it inflation, or freedom. Others are more specific to the nature of political freedom – the importance of

qualitative information, the relevance of historical context, the importance of avoiding cultural or subjective bias, etc. The generic issues can be classified under four headings: the content; the proximate indicators; the quantitative measures; and the weighting scheme for aggregation.

The content of freedom

A frequently employed distinction in defining freedom is that between positive and negative freedoms, or "freedom from" and "freedom to". Sometimes these categories are (wrongly) identified with political (negative) freedoms and economic (positive) freedoms. But political freedoms can be negative (freedom from arbitrary arrest) as well as positive (the right to vote at elections). The freedom from want is a negative freedom in one sense, but it connotes many freedoms to be able to do various things.

A better way of defining the content of freedom is to re-examine the basis for human development. This was defined in terms of capabilities. Thus human development was to ensure that everyone had certain basic capabilities – to lead a long and healthy life, to be able to engage in and profit by productive work, to communicate freely and have access to information, and to participate in the political and social life of the community.[7] Political freedom has to be seen as providing a capability, especially the last two of the above-mentioned capabilities: to communicate and to participate in the community.

Particular freedoms contribute to making these capabilities secure. In speaking of a free society or a free individual, it is usually implied that an individual in such a society is capable of doing certain things. By analogy with consumption and the standard of living, some particular freedoms are like private consumption goods; they are personal to the individual. They have to be provided to each and every individual to be able to ensure that everyone is capable of certain basic acts. Food is such a consumption good, which ensures that no one is starving. Similarly, to ensure the integrity of the human person, it is necessary to ensure that torture is not prevalent nor is arbitrary arrest or extrajudicial killing. Every individual has to have that guarantee.

Other freedoms are more aggregative, like public goods, which all can enjoy at the same time without excluding the others. Clean air is a public good; freedom from censorship is vital to everyone's freedom. In some cases, as for example the inoculation against contagious disease, deprivation of some may harm others not deprived. The freedom from discrimination on ethnic, racial or gender grounds is one such example. A society practising apartheid is one where not even the favoured race is free.

Thus political freedom can be defined as the condition of individual existence in a collectivity where every individual concerned enjoys certain particular freedoms either personally or collectively. These freedoms make the individual capable of communicating with other individuals and of participating in the daily political life of the community, and this can involve trying to change the government of the day or some laws and regulations without fear. These freedoms have to be legally available as well as actually exercised. Any measurement of freedom has to deal both with these aspects of formal availability and with actual experience. The former is a matter of checking the legal framework, while the latter can be measured only by detailed accounts of life in the community.

Available measures of political freedom

A number of attempts can be cited in which authors have attempted to measure political freedom. It is not my intention to discuss them in detail or to try to contrast my approach with theirs, except by implication. In table 2.6.2, a tabular summary is provided of six existing attempts to measure political freedom. Of these Humana's work is perhaps the best known and his Guide went through three editions.[8] Humana took the Universal Declaration of Human Rights as his basis for constructing 40 questions, but in scoring the performance of countries with regard to these questions he used his own judgement. He gave extra weight to seven questions which had to do with issues of integrity of the self (torture, inhuman imprisonment, etc). He graded his answer as firm YES, mild yes, mild no, and firm NO, depending on the extent to which a freedom was guaranteed.[9]

Three other publications share a methodology. The Freedom House in the USA has, over a number of years, graded countries for their political rights and civil liberties. There are 22 indicators – nine political and 13 civil. Answers are graded from one (most free) to seven (least free). Raymond Gastil, who is the principal researcher at Freedom House, uses his judgement in grading countries. Taylor and Jodice, who publish a two-volume *Handbook of Political Indicators*, rely on the Freedom House for their political and civil measures.[10]

The remaining two efforts have only a partial coverage. Vanhanen has a measure of the degree of democracy of a country based on the number of political parties and the degree of concentration in voting shares. Mitchell and McCormick use the data from Amnesty International to derive a measure of "civil integrity of the person". This is based on two indicators – arbitrary imprisonment, and killing and torture.[11]

The proximate indicators

Since Freedom is generated by many particular freedoms, it is necessary to make the relative contribution of these particular freedoms explicit. A suitable parallel in consumer theory is the notion of a utility tree with separate branches along which particular wants/goods can be evaluated in terms of their contribution to total activity. There is substitutability within a branch but not across branches. Freedom (in the wider sense) can be defined in terms of five clusters, each of which will in turn combine several distinguishable, but interrelated, rights or freedoms. The clusters themselves stand independently as complementary pillars of freedom. These clusters are, therefore, weighted to generate an overall index of political freedom.

The five clusters are:

- Integrity of the self/personal security
- Rule of law
- Political participation
- Freedom of expression
- Equality before the law

Table 2.6.2
Comparison of methodologies

	Categories of rights / data measured	No. of indicators	Weighting	Data	Assessment scheme	No. of countries
Humana	Civil and political; also, right to work, trade unions and protection of children from economic and social exploitation	40 questions. Very free translations of rights	Overtly 7 questions weighted by 3; overlap of questions makes for more	UN, World Bank and 12 other sources	4 grades: unqualified respect; qualified respect; some violations; constant violations. These receive respectively 3, 2, 1 and 0 points.	89
Freedom House	Political rights and civil liberties	Political: 9 Civil: 13 (unclear which examples given)	Judgement of Freedom House as to intensity. High score political = 18; high score civil = 26	Unstated?	7 categories (1 most free). Criteria for these categories not stated but included in earlier Raymond Gastil work. Political & civil separately assessed; 0–2 points per checklist item; also 3 large categories: free, partly free, not free	All
Taylor & Jodice	Political rights (popular participation)	Based on Freedom House	See Freedom House	Freedom House: 1973–79	Mean scores based on Freedom House data and indication of maximum shift	86
Taylor & Jodice	Civil rights (freedom of expression and independent judiciary)	Based on Freedom House	See Freedom House	Freedom House: 1973–79	Mean scores based on Freedom House data and indication of maximum shift	86
Vanhanen	Democracy: –competition –participation	2: smaller party share and voter turnout		Vanhanen. Years 1980, 1984, 1988	Subtraction of largest party % from 100: % of voters from whole population	147
Mitchell & McCormick	Civil: integrity of the person	2: arbitrary imprisonment and killing and torture	None	Amnesty International Report, 1985 (1984 data)	5 points: 0 = never violations; 1 = rarely; 2 = sometimes; 3 = often; 4 = very often	All in Amnesty Report

Each of these clusters can in turn be related to a set of indicators for which qualitative and quantitative data can be gathered. In one sense, the individual indicators are correlates of the individual human rights in the Universal Declaration of Human Rights as well as various other covenants and conventions signed by the countries to whom the index relates. (See table 2.6.3 at the end of this chapter for an exhaustive checklist.) Information on the violations or fulfilment of these rights is gathered regularly by a number of government and non-governmental organizations. Sometimes the information from different sources is in conflict, but mostly the sources supplement each other. The openness of a society typically generates more information about the violations of rights, if for example the press is freer than in more repressive societies. Thus, information has to be contextualized and the history and background to the events being reported upon are also important.

Integrity of the self

This cluster tells us about freedom from torture and arbitrary arrest. Extrajudicial killing and the state's connivance at, or failure to prosecute, non-state violence are also part of this cluster. In a sense this is the most basic of all human freedoms. It is also one on which there is universal agreement. While countries may not agree on the value of multiparty elections or freedom from censorship, no state claims to regard the right to torture innocent citizens as a positive act. This is also the area in which many human rights groups are most actively involved. The information is plentiful though it is difficult to construct quantitative measures. There is no permissible or correct per capita level of torture, though more is worse than less.

Rule of law

This cluster relates to due process, the right to a fair and speedy trial and the independence of the judiciary from executive or legislative interference. As said above, while there was some debate about these freedoms being western or bourgeois during the Cold War, it is now almost universally agreed that, although these freedoms were first mooted in West-

ern Europe, they are of value to all citizens everywhere. These freedoms ensure that an individual exercising his or her right to participate politically, even if attempting to change the government, would be free from the fear that, if legally arrested, he or she would not be victimized by the judicial system, even as a result of the law's delays, much less the complicity of the judiciary with the executive.

Political participation

This cluster relates to the institutions of multiparty free and fair elections in which the citizens have reasonable prospect, in principle at least, of changing the government. It relates to the quality of political democracy in a country. It should take into account not only the quantitative indicators of the number of parties and the frequency of elections, but also the access that the opposition parties have to resources to get their views across to the voters, the actual extent of single party dominance and the overall culture of political tolerance. Continued rule by a single party can, in some instances, be a sign of the lack of democracy – but this is not always so independent of the context. For example, Sweden had an uninterrupted rule by the Social Democratic Party for 40 years, but with the climate of Swedish democracy this was not a sign of lack of freedom. Thus, the context is as important here as the raw information on elections, etc.

Freedom of expression

This cluster relates to the extent of censorship of the press, television, radio and films. Information is plentiful here but, even so, it has to be put in context. State ownership of radio and TV can, in some instances, be oppressive but, in other cultures (for example, the UK and the BBC, at least in pre-Thatcher years), these media may enjoy relative autonomy. Privately owned media may suffer from excessive concentration in a few hands, thus jeopardizing freedom. The openness of a system has to be judged qualitatively.

Equality before the law

This cluster relates to non-discrimination on grounds of race, ethnicity, gender, religion, etc. It defines equality about all the other rights and freedoms in a basic way. Non-discrimination is analogous, as argued above, to non-contagion. (Recall Camus's image of the plague for fascism.) The 20th century has witnessed one of the greatest tragedies in this respect with the Holocaust. But racial discrimination, as under apartheid, is only now on the wane. Gender discrimination is universal and societies are only more or less guilty of practising it. Violence against ethnic minorities and against nations struggling for recognition is, if anything, on the rise. Such actions constitute a basic violation of freedom. Non-discrimination is a *sine qua non* of all the other clusters; a person who is the object of discrimination cannot be said to be fully enjoying any of the other freedoms which the average person in that society may enjoy.

Quantitative measures

Individual indicators within a cluster contribute towards an overall value for a society about the freedom it provides its members. As should be clear from the emphasis on context above, the value attributed to a country for a cluster cannot be arrived at by simply adding up the scores for individual indices. There is an implicit "production function" relating the information available in the appropriate historical context to the final value. The evaluation has to be done so as to avoid subjective bias. For instance, a small group of evaluators can examine the evidence for each cluster/country and, after discussion, assign a commonly agreed value. Often there may have to be recalculations by members of such a group to ensure intercountry consistency. Such evaluations should then be checked against the judgement of additional groups given the same evidence as was made available to the first group. The final evaluation should thus be an inter-subjective qualitative exercise aiming to arrive at a quantitative value, say between 1–100 for each country/cluster.

Weighting the clusters

In adding up the scores for individual clusters various methods are possible. Thus one could take the average of the five scores, or the product of the five scores, or, again, the minimum of all the five scores as the overall score. A simple average is the easiest to understand and the most forgiving; shortfalls in one cluster are compensated by high scores in another. The product measure compounds shortfalls. Two scores of 50 each averages to 50 but the product is 25. The minimum rule is the most punishing one; it pinpoints the weakest spot in a country's human rights performance and judges it as good as its worst performance.

All these are schemes which assign equal weights to the individual clusters. Other schemes exist which may assign unequal weights to the clusters.[12] The clusters are, however, each in itself equally important; they are complementary pillars of political freedom.

The political freedom index is a simple average of the scores of the five clusters. The individual cluster scores are given to enable alternative weighting systems to be applied by others. But the comparison with the HDI again urges the use of a simple averaging for the PFI.

Implementing the methodology

It is an immense task to implement this methodology on a consistent basis for a number of countries. There are enough sources for data – NGOs such as Amnesty International and Human Rights Watch; official bodies such as the US State Department (which is under statutory obligation to report on the human rights situation in all countries with which the USA has diplomatic relations); the Report of the Lawyers Committee for Human Rights which, in its turn, monitors the State Department for bias; the UN Commission on Human Rights, etc.[13]

These sources are ample for allowing an individual or a group of individuals to check for violation of human rights by way of any of the five clusters. A checklist of questions can be drawn up and information sought from the source on particular violations. Thus, for instance, "are there acts of mental or physical torture?" and "is there any incommunicado detention?", are two of the many questions relating to personal security.[14]

Having got the checklist, a group of individuals could examine the evidence and give a score under each question for each cluster. These scores can then be totalled. In scoring, as well as

in totalling, some consensus needs to be established as some of these data are utterly "soft" and
qualitative – and, furthermore, they need to be
contextualized given the culture and history of the
country concerned. To check for bias, ideally another group (or groups) should carry out the same
exercise independently, but with the same checklist and same sources.

Political pitfalls of political freedom

At this stage in any social science research done in
an academic environment, one would present the
results. But research on political freedom is not so
straightforward. Since this research was undertaken with a view to incorporation in *Human
Development Report 1992,* it had a diplomatic
rather than academic environment to cope with.
The methodology proposed here was explained to
the relevant committee of the UN Economic and
Social Council and was approved. But when the
actual score for 101 countries was computed, a
number of countries objected officially in the UN
General Assembly and elsewhere. It was not contended that the results were wrong or contained
errors. The argument was made that UNDP had
no mandate to work on human rights and so could
not publish such an index!

The non-publishability of the full scores is a
barrier that can be partially circumvented, however. In table 2.6.4 at the end of this chapter,
results are presented in which two of the above

clusters – integrity of the self and rule of law, are
merged under the latter. Since "integrity of the
self" asked questions about torture, the separate
score under the cluster was the most objectionable
statistic for many UN member countries. By hiding
it under another cluster (dis) honour is preserved.

Thus table 2.6.4 gives results for four clusters for 101 countries. Under each cluster a score
is given between 0–100 and the overall score is a
simple average of the four cluster scores. As we
can see, the Scandinavian countries score high in
political freedom – they are three out of the top
five. At the bottom, there are nine countries with
scores below 25. These are countries whose human rights record is known to be poor and who
have no political democracy.

CONCLUSION

The results of the political freedom index thus
conform to what one would expect about the
"goodies" and "baddies" of political freedom. The
results should be seen as a preliminary check on
the methodology proposed here. The methodology is designed to ensure inter-subjective consistency, a wide almost universal coverage of the content of political freedom as well as in terms of
countries. It would not be an easy task to repeat
the exercise, but some day, away from the diplomatic wrangling of the UN, I hope to do so when
sufficient funding becomes available.

Table 2.6.3
Related articles in seven major international human rights instruments and six regional instruments (by frequency)*

	UD	ICESCR	ICCPR	ICERD	CEDAW	CAT	CRC	Afr. C.	ECHR & ESC	AmerC & CASC	CSCE
No discrimination of race, colour, sex, language, religion, political or other opinion, national or social origin, property, birth or other status	2	2 (1), 3	2 (1), 3.26	2	2		2	1.18 (3)	14.1	1 – Amer 43-CASC	
Thought, conscience, religion	18		18	5 (d) (vii)			14	8	9	21 Amer	Intro
Opinion and expression	19		19	5 (d) (viii)			13	9	10	13 Amer	Intro
Association	20		22	5 (d) (ix)			15	11	11	16 Amer	Intro
Education	26	13		5 (e) (v)	14 (2) d		28	17 (1)	Prot. 1 Art. 2	47 CASC	
Life, liberty, security	3		Life-6 Lib, sec-9	5 (6)			6.37	4, 6	2.5	4,7 (1)	
Freedom of movement and residence within state	13		12	5 (d) (i)				12 (1)	Prot. 4 Art. 2 (1)	22 (1) Amer	Intro
Right to leave country and return to own country	13		12	5 (d) (ii)				12 (2)	Prot. 4 Art. 2 (2)	22 (2)	Intro
Assembly	20		21	5 (d) (ix)			10	11		15 Amer	Intro
Right to work, and free choice thereof	23	6		5 (e) (i)	11 (1) (a)+ 11 (1) (c)			(15)		4, 8	43 (b)
Just and favourable conditions of work	23	7		5 (e) (i)	11 (1) (f)			15	2, 3	43 (b) CASC	
Trade unions	23	8	-22	5 (e) (ii)			32		5.6	43 (c) CASC	
Adequate living standards	25	11		ICERD (housing only)	14 (b) (living conditions only)		27		4	43 (a) 43 (b) CASC	

*For explanations of abbreviations used here, see table 2.6.5

Table 2.6.3 continues on next page

Table 2.6.3 (continued)
Related articles in seven major international human rights instruments and six regional instruments (by frequency)

	UD	ICESCR	ICCPR	ICERD	CEDAW	CAT	CRC	Afr. C.	ECHR & ESC	AmerC & CASC	CSCE
Care and assistance to motherhood	25	10	24	5 (e) (iv)	(11)		3		7, 19		
No torture, or cruel, inhuman or degrading treatment or punishment	5		7			4.16	37	5		5 (2)	Intro
No *ex post facto* laws	11		15				40 (a)	7 (2)	7	7 (2), 9 Amer	Intro
Privacy	12		17				16		8 (1)	11 Amer	
Right to marriage with free and full consent	16		23	5 (d) (iv)	16 (a) & (b)				12	17	
Right to property	17			5 (d) (v)				14	Prot. 1	21	
Social security	22			5 (e) (iv)	14 (2)(c) + 11 (1)(e)			(18)	12	43 (b), CASC	
Participation in cultural life	27	15		5 (e) (vi)	13 (c)			17 (2)			
No slavery or servitude	4		8				35	5		6 (1)	
Effective remedy for violation of fundamental rights	8		2 (3)					7 (1)(a)	6, 13	25	
No arbitrary arrest, detention or exile	9		9				37		5	7 (3), 7 (6)	
Fair and public hearing	10		14				40 (b)		6	8 (1)	
Presumption of innocence	11		14				40 (b)		6 (2)	8 (2)	
Nationality	15		24	5 (d) (iii)			7			20	
Equal access to public service	21		25		7 (b)			13 (2)		23 Amer	
Periodic elections	21		25		7 (a)				Prot. 4, Art. 3	23 Amer	
Equal pay for equal work	23	7		5 (e) (i)				15			
Just and favourable remuneration	23	7		5 (e) (i)					4	43 (b)	

Highest physical and mental trial	12			24	16 (1)	11	43 (b), CASC
Prompt information or charges and trial before judge if arrested		9.14		37 (d), 49 (b)	7 (1) (d)	5 (4)	7 (5) Amer
Limitations on freedom of thought, conscience, religion		18		14	8		12 (3)
Limitations on right to freedom of opinion and expression		19		13	10	10	13 (2)-(4) Amer
Restrictions on peaceful assembly		21		15		11	15 Amer
Restrictions on free association		22		15	10		16 Amer
Restrictions on freedom of movement		12			12 (1)	Prot. 4, Art. 2	22 (1), 22 (3) Amer
Recognition as a person		16			5	5	3
Equal protection of the law		14.26			3	3	24
Guarantees necessary for defence		14		37 (d), 40 (b)			8 (2), 7(3) Amer
Asylum from persecution			3 (1)		12 (3)	12 (3)	22 (7), 22 (8)
Equal rights as to marriage		23	16 (c)				17
Participation in government		25	11 (1) (e)		13	13	23 Amer
Rest and leisure	7	24				2	
Freedom from compulsory labour		8			(5)	8 (3)	6 (2) Amer
Right of compensation for miscarriage of justice		14	14		5 (5)	5 (5)	10 Amer
Protection against unemployment		23	5 (e) (i)		1	1	

Table 2.6.3 continues on next page

Table 2.6.3 (continued)
Related articles in seven major international human rights instruments and six regional instruments (by frequency)

	UD	ICESCR	ICCPR	ICERD	CEDAW	CAT	CRC	Afr. C.	ECHR & ESC	AmerC & CASC	CSCE
Care and assistance to childhood		10								19	
Duties to the community	29							28.29		32 Amer	
Peoples' right to self-determination		1	1 (1)					20			
Peoples' right to dispose of natural resources		1 (2)	1 (2)					21 (1)			
Free functioning of trade unions		8		5 (e) (iv)						43 (c) Amer	
Strike		8			14 (2) (b)					43 (c) Amer	
Derogation			4						15	27 Amer	
No death sentence under 18 years of age			6 (5)				37 (a),			4 (4) Amer	
Treatment of prisoners with humanity and respect			10				37 (c)			5 (4), 5 (5)	
No imprisonment for failure to fulfil contract		11							Prot 1, Art. 1	7 (7) Amer	
Expulsion of aliens only after legal decision			13					12 (4)		22 (6) Amer	
Traffic in children, women and prostitution					6		34, 35			5 (1) Amer	
Restrictions on right to leave and return to country								12 (2)	Prot. 4, Art. 2	22 (3), 22 (4) Amer	
Prohibition of mass expulsion of aliens								12 (5)	Prot. 4, Art. 2	22 (9)	
Parents choice of education	26	13									
Death sentence only for serious crimes			6							A (2) Amer	
Right to seek pardon or commutation of death sentence			6 (4)							4 (6) Amer	

Table 2.6.3 continues on next page

Right								
Limitation on right to public trial			14				6 (1)	
Right to review of conviction			14					
No trial again after conviction or acquittal			14					8 (4) Amer
Right of minorities to religion and language			27		30			
Right to social services				5 (e) (iv)	40		13, 14	
Right to access to any public place or service				5 (f)		13 (3)		
Right to vocational training and retraining				11 (c)			9, 10, 15	
Right to family benefits				13 (a)			16	
Right to special protection of child separated from parents						20		19 Right of child to special measures of protection
Right of child to protection from economic exploitation						32	7	
Duty to assist family		10				18		
Peoples' right to satisfactory environment favourable to development						24	6	
Independence of courts						26	6	
No expulsion from own country, individually or collectively							Prot. 4, Art. 3	
Protection of moral and material interests	27							22 (5) Amer
Social and international order	28							
Limitations on rights determined by law		4						
No genocide			6 (2)					

Table 2.6.3   (continued)
Related articles in seven major international human rights instruments and six regional instruments (by frequency)

	UD	ICESCR	ICCPR	ICERD	CEDAW	CAT	CRC	Afr. C.	ECHR & ESC	AmerC & CASC	CSCE
No propaganda for war			20								
No segregation or apartheid				3							
No dissemination of racist ideas				4							
No racist organizations or propaganda				4							
Right to inherit				5 (d) (vi)							
Equal rights to acquire, change, retain nationality					9						
Equal rights as to children's nationality					9						
Equal employment opportunities					11 (b)						
Right to promotion, job security and all benefits					11						
Equality of treatment in work					11 (1) (d)						
Right to bank loans, mortgages, etc.					13 (b), 14 (2) (g)						
Right of rural women to participation in development planning					14 (2) (a)						
Right of rural women to organize self-help groups and co-operatives					14 (2) (e)						
Rural women to participate in community activities					14 (2) (f)						

Rural women – other		
No use of statements under torture	14 (2) (g)	16
Right to a home	7	
Right to know and be cared for by parents	7	
Right to preserve identity	8	
Child's right to express self and be heard in proceedings	12	
Right to protection from illicit drug use	(33)	
Child's right to prompt legal assistance	37	
Child's right to privacy during legal proceedings	37	
No punishment of child below minimum age	37	
State's duty to promote and protect morals and traditional values	18	
Rights to special protection of aged and disabled	18	
Equality of peoples	19	
Right of colonized peoples to free themselves	20 (2)	

Table 2.6.3 continues on next page

Table 2.6.3 (continued)
Related articles in seven major international human rights instruments and six regional instruments (by frequency)

	UD	ICESCR	ICCPR	ICERD	CEDAW	CAT	CRC	Afr. C.	ECHR & ESC	AmerC & CASC	CSCE
Right of peoples to assistance in liberation struggles								20 (3)			
Right of dispossessed people to lawful recovery of property and compensation								21 (3)			
Right of peoples to economic, social and cultural development								22 (1)			
States' duty to ensure right to development								22 (2)			
Peoples' right to national and international peace and security								23			
Public judgement and limitations									6		
Limitation on right to privacy									8 (2)		
Restrictions on aliens' political activity									17		
Collective bargaining									6		
Rights of migrant worker									19		
No punishment for political offenses										4 (4) Amer 5 (3)	
Right to respect for physical, mental, moral integrity										5 (1)	
Right of reply										14	

Table 2.6.4
Political freedom index

	Political participation	Rule of law	Freedom of expression	Non-discrimination	PFI
High political freedom					
1. Finland	100	100	100	95	98.8
2. Sweden	100	97	97	100	98.4
3. Switzerland	100	100	100	90	97.5
4. Belgium	100	97	100	93	97.3
5. Norway	100	100	100	85	96.3
6. New Zealand	100	100	100	85	96.3
7. Netherlands	100	97	90	95	95.4
8. Denmark	100	91	100	90	95.3
9. Germany	100	94	100	85	94.8
10. USA	100	93	100	85	94.6
11. Costa Rica	100	94	90	93	94.1
12. Ireland	100	100	90	85	93.8
13. Austria	90	94	100	90	93.5
14. Spain	100	94	90	90	93.5
15. France	100	97	95	80	92.9
16. Canada	100	100	95	75	92.5
17. Portugal	100	88	90	90	92.0
18. Uruguay	100	88	100	80	92.0
19. Trinidad & Tobago	100	94	100	70	91.0
20. United Kingdom	100	81	90	85	88.9
21. Italy	100	88	80	85	88.3
22. Australia	100	88	90	73	87.6
23. Hungary	70	100	100	75	86.3
24. Jamaica	90	70	100	85	86.3
25. Benin	65	93	100	83	85.2
26. Czechoslovakia	70	97	100	73	84.8
27. Greece	100	94	80	65	84.8
28. Argentina	100	64	90	83	84.1
29. Botswana	100	94	90	45	82.3
30. Japan	100	88	80	60	82.0
31. Poland	65	82	100	80	81.8
32. Nicaragua	80	64	90	90	81.0
33. Ecuador	100	70	80	70	80.0
34. Bolivia	85	69	100	65	79.8
35. Venezuela	100	58	90	70	79.5
36. Papua New Guinea	90	70	80	75	78.8
Reasonable political freedom					
37. Colombia	100	55	70	68	73.1
38. Panama	70	64	80	75	72.3
39. Chile	70	76	70	70	71.5
40. Senegal	90	46	70	80	71.5
41. Singapore	55	82	70	75	70.5

Table 2.6.4 continues on next page

Table 2.6.4 (continued)
Political freedom index

	Political participation	Rule of law	Freedom of expression	Non-discrimination	PFI
42. Bulgaria	55	97	60	70	70.4
43. Korea, South	80	64	50	85	69.8
44. Dominican Rep.	65	82	70	60	69.3
45. Honduras	90	46	70	70	69.0
46. Romania	60	82	70	60	68.0
47. Ivory Coast	50	88	50	80	67.0
48. Mexico	70	40	70	85	66.3
49. Malaysia	70	64	60	70	66.0
50. Peru	100	28	70	65	65.8
51. India	90	46	70	55	65.3
52. Zimbabwe	30	82	60	85	64.3
53. Thailand	40	76	70	70	64.0
54. Brazil	70	40	90	53	63.1
55. Paraguay	60	64	70	55	62.3
56. Philippines	80	34	70	65	62.3
57. Pakistan	70	58	70	45	60.8
58. Togo	20	82	60	80	60.5
59. Jordan	35	76	70	60	60.3
60. El Salvador	65	28	80	68	60.1
61. Bangladesh	60	66	60	50	59.0
62. Algeria	35	73	70	53	57.6
63. Nepal	45	64	60	60	57.3
64. Zambia	20	64	70	75	57.3
65. Guatemala	65	28	70	65	57.0
66. Sierra Leone	20	76	70	60	56.5
67. Sri Lanka	90	13	50	70	55.8
68. Tanzania, U. Rep. of	30	82	40	70	55.5
69. Turkey	70	35	50	60	53.8
70. Tunisia	40	70	30	75	53.8
71. Haiti	30	50	60	75	53.8
72. Nigeria	30	46	70	65	52.8
73. Kenya	20	52	70	65	51.8
74. Yemen	20	73	60	50	50.8
Modest political freedom					
75. Uganda	20	27	70	75	47.9
76. Ghana	20	82	30	58	47.4
77. Egypt	40	34	50	65	47.3
78. Mozambique	20	46	60	60	46.5
79. Rwanda	20	46	50	65	45.3
80. Oman	10	93	20	55	44.6
81. Zaire	15	28	60	65	42.0
82. Kuwait	10	50	50	55	41.3
83. Cameroon	15	70	20	60	41.3

Table 2.6.4   (continued)
Political freedom index

	Political participation	Rule of law	Freedom of expression	Non-discrimination	PFI
84. Indonesia	30	40	40	50	40.0
85. Ethiopia	20	30	40	65	38.8
86. Malawi	10	64	10	65	37.3
87. Morocco	20	46	30	45	35.3
88. Cambodia	10	50	10	70	35.0
89. Libyan Arab Jamabiriya	10	53	10	60	33.3
90. Angola	20	19	10	80	32.3
91. Cuba	10	30	10	78	31.9
92. Saudi Arabia	10	60	40	10	30.0
Low political freedom					
93. Myanmar	10	13	10	65	24.6
94. China	10	17	20	50	24.2
95. Syrian Arab Rep.	10	20	10	55	23.8
96. Vietnam	10	25	10	50	23.8
97. Iran	30	13	10	40	23.3
98. Afghanistan	10	34	10	35	22.3
99. Korea, North	10	10	10	55	21.3
100. Sudan	10	23	20	30	20.8
101. Iraq	10	10	10	35	16.3

Table 2.6.5
Symbols and basic information

UD	Universal Declaration of Human Rights
ICESCR	International Covenant on Economic, Social and Cultural Rights Opened December 1966, entry into force 1976
ICCPR	International Covenant on Civil and Political Rights Opened December 1966, entry into force 1976
ICERD	International Convention on the Elimination of All Forms of Racial Discrimination Opened December 1965, entry into force 1969
CEDAW	Convention on the Elimination of All Forms of Discrimination against Women Opened December 1979, entry into force 1981
CAT	Convention against Torture and Other Cruel, Inhuman or Degrading Treatment or Punishment Opened December 1984, entry into force 1987
CRC	Convention on the Rights of the Child Opened January 1990, entry into force September 1990
Afr. C	The African Charter on Human and People's Rights Opened June 1981, entry into force October 1986
ECHR	European Convention on the Protection of Human Rights and Fundamental Freedoms and Protocols Signed November 1950, entry into force September 1953
ESC	European Social Charter Signed October 1961, entry into force February 1965
Amer. C.	American Convention on Human Rights of 22 November 1969, "The Pact of San José, Costa Rica" Signed November 1969, entry into force July 1978
OASC	Organization of American States Charter
CSCE.C.	Charter of Paris of the Conference on Security and Co-operation in Europe Signed November 1990

ENDNOTES

* Editors' note: This chapter is reproduced from Discussion Paper 10, 1994, Centre of the Study of Global Governance, London School of Economics.

** This chapter reports on some work undertaken as a consultant to UNDP for *Human Development Report 1992*. I have used much material that was a result of team effort. I am grateful to Bernard Hausner, Gilhan Dell, Kees Kingma, Saras Menon, Inge Kaul and Mahbub ul Haq, all of the UNDP Human Development Report Office. However, all the opinions and errors in this paper are my own.

1. Fukuyama 1989, 1992.

2. For critical comments, see McCarney 1992, 1993.

3. For references see the 1991 and 1992 *Human Development Reports*; see also Adelman 1980; Adelman and Morris 1967, 1973; Dasgupta 1990, 1993; Scully 1988.

4. See Redfern 1994 for a recent survey.

5. *Human Development Report 1990*.

6. Gerschenkron 1962, 1968.

7. See *Human Development Report 1990*, ch. 1; see also Desai 1990, 1991.

8. See Redfern 1994 for further details.

9. Humana 1986, 1993.

10. R. Gastil 1987, 1990; Taylor and Jodice 1983.

11. Vanhanen 1990; Mitchell and McCormick 1988.

12. As, for example, done by Humana in his index: Humana 1980, 1993; see also Redfern 1994.

13. See "Sources of Data on Political Freedom: Technical Annex 3" in *Human Development Report 1992*, p. 104.

14. See "An illustrative checklist of indicators of political freedom," *Human Development Report 1992*, box 2.2, p. 31.

REFERENCES

Adelman, I. 1980. "Economic Development and Political Change in Developing Countries." *Social Research* 47 (2): 213–34.

Adelman, I. and C. Taft Morris. 1967. *Society, Politics and Economic Development: A Quantitative Approach*. Baltimore: Johns Hopkins University Press.

——. 1973. *Economic Growth and Social Equity in Developing Countries*. Stanford: Stanford University Press.

Dasgupta, P. 1990. "Well-Being and the Extent of Its Realization in Developing Countries." *Economic Journal,* 1990 Supplement: 1–32.

——. 1993. *An Inquiry Into Well-Being and Deprivation*. Oxford: Oxford University Press.

Desai, M. J. 1990. "Poverty and Capability: Towards an Empirically Implementable Measure." Development Economics Research Group discussion paper. London School of Economics.

——. 1991. "Human Development: Concepts and Measurement." *European Economic Review* 35: 350–57.

Fukuyama, F. 1989. "The End of History?" *The National Interest* 16, Summer: 3–16.

——. 1992. *The End of History and the Lost Man*. London: Hamish Hamilton.

Gastil, R. 1987. *Freedom in the World: Political and Civil Liberties 1986–87*. New York: Freedom House.

——. 1990. "The Comparative Survey of Freedom: Experiences and Suggestions." *Studies in Comparative International Development* 25(1): 25–50.

Gerschenkron, A. 1962. *Economic Backwardness in Historical Perspective*. Cambridge, Mass: Harvard University Press.

——. 1968. *Continuity in History and Other Essays*. Cambridge, Mass: Belknap Press.

Humana, C. 1986. *World Human Rights Guide.* Second edition. London: Hodder & Stoughton.

——. 1993. *World Human Rights Guide*. Third edition. New York: Oxford University Press.

McCarney, J. 1992. "Endgame" (on Fukuyama). *Radical Philosophy* 62, Autumn: 35–38.

——. 1993. "Shaping Ends: Reflections on Fukuyama." *New Left Review* 202, November-December: 37–63.

Mitchell, N. and J. McCormick. 1988. "Economic and Political Explanations of Human Rights Violations." *World Politics* 40(4): 476–98.

Redfern, P. 1994. "Measuring Human Rights." Centre for the Study of Global Governance, London School of Economics.

Scully, D. W. 1988. "The Institutional Framework and Economic Development." *Journal of Political Economy* 3: 652–62.

Taylor, C. and D. Jodice. 1983. *World Handbook of Political and Social Indicators, Vol. 2: Political Protest and Government Change*. New Haven: Yale University Press.

UNDP (United Nations Development Programme). 1990. *Human Development Report 1990*. New York: Oxford University Press.

——. 1991. *Human Development Report 1991*. New York: Oxford University Press.

——. 1992. *Human Development Report 1992*. New York: Oxford University Press.

Vanhanen, T. 1990. *The Process of Democratization: A Comparative Study of 147 States, 1980–88*. New York: Crane Russak.

2.7

GENDER INEQUALITY IN HUMAN DEVELOPMENT: THEORIES AND MEASUREMENT[1]

Sudhir Anand and Amartya Sen

MOTIVATION

Over the past five years, a great deal has been achieved by the *Human Development Report* of the UNDP in shifting the focus of attention of the world community from such mechanical indicators of economic progress as GNP and GDP to indicators that come closer to reflecting the well-being and freedoms actually enjoyed by populations. Even though the *Human Development Report* has been influential primarily because of the extensive and detailed statistical analyses of achievements and limitations of living conditions of people in different parts of the contemporary world, the aggregative human development index (HDI) also has played some part in bringing about this reorientation. Despite the obvious limitations of the HDI (arising in part from its attempt to capture a complex reality in a summary form with imperfect data), it has served as something of a rival to the other summary indicator – the aggregative GNP, which hitherto had been almost universally used as the premier index of the economic achievement of nations. The HDI has clearly been able to present some aspects of human development that the GNP tends to miss.

From the beginning, the *Human Development Report* has been concerned with inequalities in the opportunities and predicaments of women and men. Although this perspective has received some attention in past Reports, there is a strong case at this time for concentrating specifically on that issue for a more comprehensive investigation of gender inequality in economic and social arrangements in the contemporary world.

In performing this task, there is need for fresh economic and social analyses as well as careful and probing empirical research. Women and men share many aspects of living together, collaborate with each other in complex and ubiquitous ways, and yet end up – often enough – with very different rewards and deprivations. This note is specifically concerned with developing a framework for "gender-equity-sensitive indicators" of achievements and freedoms. The methodology for this is explored in the sections that follow, ending with specific recommendations to be put into practice.

While this exercise must be a crucial part of the important task that is now being undertaken by the programme of the *Human Development Report*, there are two other aspects of gender deprivation to which this Report must also pay some attention. First, aside from developing "gender-equity-sensitive indicators", the approach must also look at gender inequality *per se*. The investigation of such inequalities must have a close link with the development of equity-sensitive overall indicators, and it would be important to explore how the inequality measures should relate to the approach of using gender-equity-sensitive indicators (GESI).

Secondly, aside from looking at the state of advantages and deprivations that women and men respectively have, there is an important need to look at the contrast between (1) the efforts and sacrifices made by each, and (2) the rewards and benefits respectively enjoyed. This contrast is important for a better understanding of gender injustice in the contemporary world. The exacting nature of women's efforts and contributions, without commensurate rewards, is a particularly important subject to identify and explore.

Thus characterized, the new initiative in the *Human Development Report 1995* has three distinct departures to make, concerning respectively:

(1) the development and use of gender-equity-sensitive indicators;

(2) the formulation and utilization of measures of gender equality and inequality; and

(3) the identification of efforts and contributions made by women that go unrecognized in standard national income and employment statistics.

This paper is primarily concerned with the first two of these three fields, but some analysis of the last problem will also be presented.

GROUP INEQUALITY AND AGGREGATION: THE BASIC STRUCTURE

Aggregate indicators of life expectancy, literacy, and other advantages used in the UNDP's *Human Development Report* have tended to ignore distributional concerns, using a simple arithmetic average of achievement (or shortfall), in each dimension, over the entire population.[2] Such an average overlooks systematic and potentially large differences between distinct groups of people, in particular women and men, but there are disparities also between different classes, racial groups, regional populations, and so on. We focus here on gender differentials in achievement, but the issues discussed would, to a considerable extent, apply to other inequalities as well.

We may begin by examining the inequality between women and men in a dimension where the "potentials" of the two groups are not really different. Literacy is an obvious example. In contrast, in the case of life expectancy, we must take note of the evident biological advantage in survival of females over males (on this, see Waldron 1983, Sen 1992b, Anand 1993, and the references cited there). Given symmetric treatment in nutrition, health care, and other conditions of living (including the duration and intensity of work), women have systematically lower age-specific mortality rates than men, resulting in a life expectancy for women that is significantly higher than that for men – possibly by some five years or more. There is no corresponding difference in the potential for adult literacy (that is, in the percentage of the population aged 15 and above that is literate).

For a given level of mean achievement, *relative* inequality between groups has some obvious simplicity when there are just two groups. For example, if the first element of the pair (X_f, X_m) represents the female literacy rate for a country, and the second element the male literacy rate, the *Human Development Report 1994* (table 5, pp. 138–39) shows three countries with the same mean or overall literacy rate of 80 percent distributed between females and males as follows: China (68, 92), Malaysia (72, 89), and Mauritius (75, 85). Comparing these three countries, it seems clear that gender inequality in literacy is highest in China and lowest in Mauritius. Similarly, at a higher level of mean achievement of 84 percent literacy rate, gender inequality in Indonesia (77, 91) is greater than in the Dominican Republic (83, 86).

The assessment of relative inequality in achievement can be reasonably perspicuous when there are only two groups – as in the case of gender. The larger the gender gap, holding the overall mean constant, the larger is inequality as measured by *any* index belonging to the Lorenz class (see Anand 1983, appendix D); this class includes most commonly used inequality measures such as the Gini coefficient, the two Theil indices, the Atkinson index, and the squared coefficient of variation. A bigger gender gap, with the same overall mean (and the same population proportions of the two groups) is equivalent to a simple *mean-preserving regressive transfer*. (In terms of Lorenz curves, this would correspond to an unambiguously lower curve.) In the special 2-group case, disparity ratios *or* gaps will unambiguously reflect the inequality in achievement between the two groups. Given equality preference and the same overall mean, more relative inequality will indicate a worse social state of affairs, and this evaluative feature must be reflected in the gender-equity-sensitive indicators.

This simple recognition still leaves open the question of what would be appropriate standards of comparison when the overall or mean levels of achievement are *different*. In particular, how might we think about "trading off" more relative equality against a higher absolute achievement? Honduras, for example, has a total literacy rate of

75 percent divided between females and males as (73, 78).[3] Should this social outcome be judged worse or better than the case of China, which has a total literacy rate of 80 percent distributed as (68, 92) between females and males? Honduras has less gender inequality in literacy levels than China, but it also has a lower overall rate of literacy. A comparison between the two countries now calls for some way of assessing the comparative claims of more relative equality against higher absolute achievement. An explicit evaluative exercise on this "trade off" will be required in such situations.

We begin with the approach explored by A. B. Atkinson (1970) for the purposes of measuring relative income inequality, and extend this analysis to fit our task.[4] Let X be the indicator of achievement, and let X_f and X_m refer to the corresponding female and male achievements. If n_f and n_m are the numbers of females and males in the population, respectively, then the overall or mean achievement $\overline{X}$ is given by

$$\overline{X} = (n_f X_f + n_m X_m)/(n_f + n_m)$$

We posit a social valuation function for achievement which is additively separable, symmetric, and of constant elasticity marginal valuation form

$$V(X) = \begin{cases} \dfrac{1}{1-\varepsilon} X^{1-\varepsilon} & \varepsilon \geq 0, \varepsilon \neq 1 \\ \log X & \varepsilon = 1 \end{cases}$$

up to a positive affine transformation. Only values of $\varepsilon \geq 0$ are considered so as to reflect a preference for equality in the social valuation function.

For any pair (X_f, X_m) of female and male achievements, we can construct an "equally distributed equivalent achievement" X_{ede}. This is defined to be the level of achievement which, if attained *equally* by women and men, as (X_{ede}, X_{ede}), would be judged to be *exactly* as valuable socially as the actually observed achievements (X_f, X_m). According to the formula for social valuation, for a given ε, X_{ede} is thus defined through the equation

$$(n_f + n_m)\frac{X_{ede}^{1-\varepsilon}}{1-\varepsilon} = n_f \frac{X_f^{1-\varepsilon}}{1-\varepsilon} + n_m \frac{X_m^{1-\varepsilon}}{1-\varepsilon},$$

which implies that

$$X_{ede} = (n_f X_f^{1-\varepsilon} + n_m X_m^{1-\varepsilon})^{\frac{1}{1-\varepsilon}} / (n_f + n_m)^{\frac{1}{1-\varepsilon}}$$

$$= (p_f X_f^{1-\varepsilon} + p_m X_m^{1-\varepsilon})^{\frac{1}{1-\varepsilon}},$$

where we define the proportions $p_f = n_f/(n_f + n_m)$ and $p_m = n_m/(n_f + n_m)$. Hence X_{ede} is formed from (X_f, X_m) by taking what we shall call a "$(1-\varepsilon)$-average" of X_f and X_m rather than a simple arithmetic average of the female and male achievements.[5] In the case when $\varepsilon = 0$, X_{ede} reduces to $\overline{X}$, the simple arithmetic average; here there is no concern for equality, and the arithmetic mean indicates the social achievement. But when $\varepsilon > 0$, there is a social preference for equality (or an aversion to inequality) which is measured by the magnitude of the parameter ε.

Assuming that female achievement falls short of male achievement, i.e. $(0 \leq) X_f < X_m$, the following results can be demonstrated for "$(1-\varepsilon)$-averaging"[6]:

(1) $X_f \leq X_{ede} \leq X_m$.
(2) The larger is ε, the smaller is X_{ede} (given X_f, $X_m > 0$).
(3) $X_{ede} \leq \overline{X}$ for $\varepsilon \geq 0$ (with equality holding when $\varepsilon = 0$).
(4) $X_{ede} \to X_f$ as $\varepsilon \to \infty$.

Result (4) corresponds to the Rawlsian maximin situation where social achievement is judged purely by the achievement of the worst-off group, which in the case of gender may typically refer to women.[7] If $X_f < X_m$ in every country, and if $\varepsilon \to \infty$ (equity preference tending to infinity), then social achievement across countries will be measured by female achievement alone: in the averaging, the weight given to male achievement in excess of female achievement will tend to zero. In this case, the equally distributed equivalent achievement index X_{ede} reduces to the index for the relatively deprived group (typically women), and countries are ranked according to the absolute achievement of women in those countries.

As mentioned earlier, X_{ede} is a "$(1-\varepsilon)$-average" of X_f and X_m. When $\varepsilon = 0$, $X_{ede} = \overline{X}$, the *arithmetic* average of X_f and X_m. When $\varepsilon = 1$, X_{ede} is the *geometric* average; and when $\varepsilon = 2$, X_{ede} is the *harmonic* mean of X_f and X_m.[8] When $\varepsilon \to \infty$, $X_{ede} \to$ Min $\{X_f, X_m\}$. The equally distributed equivalent achievement can be calculated for each country for different values of ε, the parameter of equity preference. Thus if the preference for equity is small (ε close to 0), China's literacy rates of (68, 92) for females and males, respectively, corresponding to an overall literacy rate of 80 percent, will be judged to be better than Honduras's figures of (73, 78), corresponding to an overall rate of 75 percent. As the equity preference parameter ε is raised, Honduras's achievement will overtake that of China's; in the limit, as ε tends to infinity, Honduras's equally distributed equivalent achievement will be 73 while China's will be 68. For all values of ε above the critical cut-off 5.693, at which the two countries' achievements are the same, Honduras's achievement will be judged to be better than China's.

The equally distributed equivalent achievement X_{ede}, applied to gender differences, yields a measure that is, in fact, a gender-equity-sensitive indicator (GESI). This is, of course, an index of *overall* achievement which takes *note* of inequality, rather than a measure of gender *equality* as such. But it uses – explicitly or by implication – equity-sensitive weights on the achievements of the two groups, rather than the unweighted mean of the two sets of achievements that is more commonly used (including, hitherto, in the *Human Development Report*). It incorporates *implicitly* something like a gender equality index. The index of relative equality E that underlies X_{ede} can be defined simply as

$$E = X_{ede} / \overline{X}.$$

This can vary from 0 to 1 as equality is increased[9]; its properties are examined in appendix A.2.7.3, "Properties of the relative gender-equality index E". Hence, the measure of social achievement $X_{ede} = E.\overline{X}$ is just the relative equality index E

multiplied by the overall or mean achievement measure $\overline{X}$. Relative equality and mean absolute achievement are thus integrated into the gender-equity-sensitive indicators. Applying the correction for equality to *each* of the "human development" indicator (HDI) variables and aggregating them would yield a new gender-equity adjusted measure of "human development" – to be called the gender-related development index (GDI).

EQUITY-SENSITIVE AGGREGATION AND LIFE EXPECTANCY

So far the analysis has been confined to achievements in which the "potentials" of women and men do not differ (for example, each group has the same range of achievable *literacy*, from 0 to 100 percent). The situation is different, however, when it comes to mortality rates and life expectancy (as was mentioned earlier). Given the evidence of biological differences in survival rates favouring women (with comparable care),[10] we are forced to address the question of the appropriate comparable scales of achievement of life expectancy respectively for women and men. And we have to integrate that differential scaling into the general evaluative scheme of gender-equity-sensitive indexes.

Letting (L_f, L_m) denote the life expectancy at birth of females and males, respectively, the *Human Development Report 1994* shows the following comparisons for some advanced countries: Italy (81, 74), Finland (80, 72), France (81, 73), United States (80, 73), Japan (82, 76). For all high-income countries together, the gender gap in life expectancy in 1992 was six years. The higher potential life expectancy of females relative to males is anticipated in demographic projections of the future as well. For the year 2050, for example, life expectancy projections of (87.5, 82.5) years for females and males, respectively, averaging to 85 years, have been made for the developed countries (*Human Development Report 1993*, p. 111).

In considering the disaggregation of the Human Development Index (HDI) by gender, in our paper (Anand and Sen 1993) for the *Human Development Report 1993* we had suggested separate goalposts for maximal life expectancy of 87.5

and 82.5 years for females and males, respectively, that is, a five-year gender gap. The minimum life expectancy levels have been taken to be 37.5 and 32.5 years for women and men, respectively, giving the *same* range of variation (viz. 50 years) for both sexes. When no adjustment is made for gender inequality, this implies that a unit increase in longevity for either sex will contribute the same increment to the overall HDI.

In the corresponding disaggregation of HDI in *Human Development Report 1993*, female and male achievements in life expectancy, X_f and X_m respectively, have been assessed through

$$X_f = (L_f - 37.5)/50$$
$$X_m = (L_m - 32.5)/50.$$

The simple arithmetic average $\overline{X}$ of X_f and X_m, assuming female and male population proportions of ½ each, is then calculated as

$$\overline{X} = \frac{1}{2}X_m + \frac{1}{2}X_f$$

$$= (\overline{L}1 - 35)/50$$

where $\overline{L} = (L_f + L_m)/2$ is the average life expectancy attained in the population.

Equality between persons can be defined in two quite distinct ways, in terms of *attainments*, or in terms of the *shortfalls* from the maximal values that each can respectively attain. For "attainment equality" of achievements, we have to compare the absolute levels of achievement. For "shortfall equality", what must be compared are the shortfalls of actual achievement from the respective *maximal* achievements of each group. Each of the two approaches has some considerable interest of its own.[11] Shortfall equality takes us in the direction of equal use (relative or absolute) of the *respective potentials*. In contrast, attainment equality is concerned with equal absolute levels of achievement (irrespective of what the maximal potentials are).

In those cases in which human diversity is so powerful that it is impossible to equalize the maximal levels that are *potentially* achievable, there is a basic ambiguity in assessing achievement, and in judging equality of achievement (or of the freedom

to achieve). If the maximal achievement of person 1 – under the most favourable circumstances – is, say, x, and that for person 2 is 2x, then equality of *attainment* would invariably leave person 2 below her potential achievement. Partly as a response to such issues, Aristotle had incorporated, in his *Politics*, a parametric consideration of what a person's "circumstances admit" and had seen his "distributive conception" in that light. "For it is appropriate, if people are governed best that they should do best, *in so far as their circumstances admit* – unless something catastrophic happens."[12] It is possible to question this Aristotelian view in terms of the more rough-and-ready rationale of attainment equality, but there is force in the conception of shortfall equality as well, and it is that approach that is being used here for assessing gender equality in the context of life expectancy variations. The gender-equity-sensitive indicators can also be made to take note of the logic behind this approach.

Thus, the approach to adjusting for gender inequality in achievement in the case of life expectancy must first involve a re-scaling to take note of the potentially higher longevity of women. Such adjustments are, in fact, a part of the already used methodology of the *Human Development Report*, since these re-scalings have to be done whether or not we wish to take explicit note of gender inequality. However, instead of taking a simple arithmetic average $\overline{X}$ of the female and male achievements X_f and X_m, we take a "$(1-\varepsilon)$-average" with $\varepsilon > 0$. As before, we form the average X_{ede}, given for $\varepsilon \neq 1$ through

$$X_{ede}^{1-\varepsilon} = \frac{1}{2}X_f^{1-\varepsilon} + \frac{1}{2}X_m^{1-\varepsilon},$$

which reduces to $\overline{X}$ when $\varepsilon = 0$.[13] Thus we define L_{ede} through

$$[(L_{ede} - 35)/50]^{1-\varepsilon} =$$
$$\frac{1}{2}[L_f - 37.5)50]^{1-\varepsilon}$$
$$+\frac{1}{2}[(L_m - 32.5)/50]^{1-\varepsilon}.$$

When $\varepsilon = 0$, $L_{ede} = \overline{L}$. For $\varepsilon > 0$, $L_{ede} < \overline{L}$.

GENDER DIFFERENCES IN EARNING AND REWARDED EMPLOYMENT

The human development index H for a country has been defined to be

$$H = \frac{1}{3}\left[\frac{\overline{L} - 35}{50} + \frac{LIT}{100} + \frac{LPCY}{3.687}\right]$$

where $\overline{L}$ is the average life expectancy attained in the country, LIT is the average percentage literacy rate among adults, and LPCY is the logarithm of per capita GDP (in "purchasing power parity" dollars) truncated at the average official poverty line income in nine developed countries, with 3.687 being the-then value of the logarithm of the poverty level (Anand and Sen 1993).

For the gender-equity-sensitive HDI, we simply replace the arithmetic average attainments in each component by the equally distributed equivalent achievements. Thus the first component ($\overline{L}$ – 35)/50 is replaced by (L_{ede} – 35)/50. The second component LIT/100 is replaced by X_{ede}/100, where X_{ede} is now the (1–ε)-average of the female and male literacy rates. No *corresponding* correction can be made for the third component of HDI, because gender-specific attributions of income per head cannot be readily linked to the aggregate GDP per capita used in these calculations, and inequalities within the household are difficult to characterize and assess (Sen 1992a; Anand and Sen 1993).

It is important to distinguish between two different aspects of incomes, viz. *earning* and *use*. If we wish to concentrate on the *use* aspect, the within-family division of income use between women and men would have to be identified to assess income use by gender. But the empirical and conceptual problems in getting at these divisions within the family are formidable indeed.

In contrast, the earning aspect looks at women and men not as income users, but as people who *earn* incomes. The total gross national product can then be seen in terms of aggregate earnings of all women and all men, making up something like the total national income. An *approximate* idea of the income earnings of women and men can be obtained by looking at their respective employment ratios and their relative wages.

What significance can be attached to such income earning estimates? Indeed, there is some tension in concentrating on the earning aspect when the entire approach of the *Human Development Report* has been based on identifying what people get *out* of the means they can use, rather than on the means they *earn* – possibly to be used by their families. On the other hand, the earning contrasts between men and women do point to an important asymmetry between them in most – nearly all – existing societies. While women very often work as hard as – or harder than – men, much of their work is of the unpaid kind that does not yield remuneration.[14] There is also considerable evidence to indicate that earning explicitly recognized "incomes", and working in sectors that are treated as evidence of being "economically active", can significantly and favourably influence the "deal" that women tend to get in the division of benefits and chores within the family.[15]

There is, thus, a case for doing some gender division even for the "real income" component of HDI, trying to note the differences between the earnings of women and men. It would be hard to get anything like the degree of precision with earnings "allocated" between women and men on the basis of rough calculations that gender-specific measures of literacy or life expectancy can offer. But even some estimates of relative earnings of women and men would give the gender-equity-sensitive indicator (GESI) another component with some bite. If this were to be done, then the total GDP per head can be notionally "split" between women and men in the ratio of the respective *products* of *employment rates* and *wage rates per unit of employment*. It would, however, be necessary then to explain clearly that (1) this procedure looks at income from the "earning" perspective rather than the "use" perspective (even though gender inequalities seem to link the latter to the former), and (2) the evaluations of earnings of women and men are fairly "soft" estimates, to be interpreted with much caution.

EXTENT OF INEQUALITY AVERSION ε

As was discussed earlier, the values of the parameter ε can be taken to range from zero to infinity, reflecting the extent of social preference for equality. In fact, ε as a parameter stands for the elasticity of the marginal social valuation of the respective achievement, and tells us how quickly the marginal value falls as the achievement level rises (that is, how strongly diminishing the marginal social returns are), ε can, in fact, be seen as a reflection of the extent of inequality aversion. When ε is taken to be zero, there is no decline in marginal values, so that the simple arithmetic mean does well enough. At the other extreme, when ε is taken to be infinity, the sensitivity is so great that we end up picking only the lower of the two numbers in a pair, ignoring the achievement of the better-off. It would be interesting to calculate the gender-equity-sensitive (GESI) adaptation of HDI for several parametric values of ε, such as 0, 1, 2, 3, 5, 10, ∞. We call this class of "corrected" HDI the gender-related development index, or GDI for short. Typically we will use the value $\varepsilon = 2$.

The implications of different choices of ε can be gauged by examining the effects on X_{ede}, the equally distributed equivalent achievement. We can compare the relative increase in X_{ede} through a unit increase in female achievement X_f compared to a unit increase in male achievement X_m. From equation (2) in appendix A.2.7.1, we have

$$\frac{\partial X_{ede} / \partial X_f}{\partial X_{ede} / \partial X_m} = \frac{p_f V'(X_f)/V'(X_{ede})}{p_m V'(X_m)/V'(X_{ede})}$$

$$= \frac{V'(X_f)}{V'(X_m)} \text{ assuming } p_f = p_m = 1/2$$

$$= X_f^{-\varepsilon} / X_m^{-\varepsilon} = (X_m / X_f)^{\varepsilon}$$

if the social valuation function $V(X)$ has a constant elasticity of marginal valuation ε.

According to this, if male achievement X_m is *twice* female achievement X_f, i.e. $(X_m/X_f) = 2$, and if $\varepsilon = 1$ (i.e. we have the logarithmic form for $V(X)$), then a unit increase in female achievement will contribute *twice* as much to X_{ede} as a unit increase in male achievement (see table 2.7.1). If (X_m/X_f) remains equal to 2, but $\varepsilon = 2$, then a unit increase in female achievement contributes *four* times as much as a unit increase in male achievement. Holding (X_m/X_f) constant (at any value above 1), as ε is increased there is an *increase* in the relative contribution to X_{ede} from a unit increase in X_f compared to a unit increase in X_m.[16] Table 2.7.1 estimates the relative contribution to X_{ede} of a unit increase in female achievement compared to a unit increase in male achievement for different values of ε and different ratios of male-to-female achievement (X_m/X_f).

For particular values of ε, how different would GDI be from HDI (bearing in mind that HDI is, in fact, a special case of GDI, with $\varepsilon = 0$)? Clearly, the distributional correction would tend to pull down the value of HDI, and we expect GDI to be quite significantly below the corresponding HDI values in a systematic way, for relatively high values of ε.

Table 2.7.1

Relative contributions to X_{ede} of unit increases in X_f and X_m, i.e. $\left[\dfrac{\partial X_{ede} / \partial X_f}{\partial X_{ede} / \partial X_m}\right]$, for alternative values of ε and (X_m/X_f)

(X_m/X_f) ε	0.0	1.0	1.5	2.0	2.5	3.0	5.0	10.0	∞
1.0	1	1	1	1	1	1	1	1	1
1.5	1	1.5	1.8	2.3	2.8	3.4	7.6	57.7	∞
2.0	1	2.0	2.8	4.0	5.7	8.0	32.0	1,024.0	∞
2.5	1	2.5	4.0	6.3	9.9	15.6	97.7	9,536.7	∞
3.0	1	3.0	5.2	9.0	15.6	27.0	243.0	59,049.0	∞
4.0	1	4.0	8.0	16.0	32.0	64.0	1,024.0	1,048,576.0	∞

Note: The relative contributions to X_{ede} in this table are estimated under the assumptions that $p_f = p_m = 1/2$, and that $V(X)$ has a constant elasticity of marginal valuation ε.

This does not, however, imply that the *rankings* would be necessarily much changed. That would depend on the *relative differences* in the extent of gender inequality. While there are often substantial differences between the gender inequality levels of the relevant parameters between high-achieving and low-achieving countries, the patterns of gender inequalities may often be quite close to each other for countries at similar levels of human development. This would tend to make the rankings of GDI rather similar to those of HDI. However, some differences can be expected between low-achieving countries in Asia and low-achievers in Sub-Saharan Africa, since the extent of gender inequality in many fields has tended to be substantially less in the latter countries.[17]

GENDER-EQUALITY MEASURES AND GESI

The appendix A.2.7.3 ("Properties of the relative gender-equality index E") draws attention to the fact that the relative level of gender equality can be well captured by comparing the values of GESI with the uncorrected average measure. That average (gender-blind) measure is based on taking an *arithmetic* average (as with HDI) over the entire population, whereas the formula for GESI permits an entire class of "$(1-\varepsilon)$-averaging" to take note of – and to weigh against – inequalities. In the special case in which ε is taken to be 2, the GESI formula corresponds to the *harmonic* mean. The equally distributed equivalent achievement corresponding to $\varepsilon = 2$, i.e. $X_{ede}(2)$ is then given (for equal proportions of women and men) by the formula

$$X_{ede}(2)^{-1} = \frac{1}{2}X_f^{-1} + \frac{1}{2}X_m^{-1}.$$

Hence,

$$X_{ede}(2) = 2[(1/X_f) + (1/X_m)]^{-1}$$

which is the harmonic mean of X_f and X_m. If we take the ratio of the harmonic mean to the arithmetic mean, we then get a measure of "gender equity" that has obvious interest.

For reasons discussed in the last section, the values of GDI and HDI may not diverge in a way that makes the respective rankings very different. When the values of GDI and HDI are shifted in similar ways – without much of a relative change – the ratios may not tell us very much either. It must, however, be remembered that the GESI formula can be applied to other variables as well, specifically chosen to highlight *differences* in gender disparities. We must, in general, distinguish between (1) the GESI *formula* of $(1-\varepsilon)$-averaging, and (2) the "space" on which it is applied (that is, the variables for which achievements and gender disparities are scrutinized).

It should be noted here that the procedure used for inequality correction in GDI involves the estimation of inequality-corrected achievements in terms of different focus variables, and then putting them together in one aggregate measure of inequality-adjusted performance. In some respects, this procedure is a little deceptive, since the different variables might, in principle, work in somewhat opposite directions, moderating the influence of each other in the inequality between individuals. For example, if person A has a higher achievement in longevity while person B does better in terms of education, it could be thought that these inequalities must, to some extent, counteract each other, so that in terms of a weighted average of achievements, A and B may be less unequal than in terms of each of the two variables. And this opposite-direction case would be different from the one in which one of the individuals, say A, is better off in terms of *both* the variables. In terms of the procedure used here, we cannot discriminate between these two types of cases, since the aggregation is done, first, in terms of specific variables, and then they are put together in an index of overall achievement.

This defect is, however, fairly inescapable at the individual level, given the data availability. There is no obvious way of relating the individual identities in the distribution of one variable with those for the other variable. There is, thus, no serious alternative to the kind of procedure we have used. As a matter of fact, this is not, however, a very serious limitation in the present context. This is partly because the individual deprivations very often go together and reinforce – rather than counteract – each other. For example, the educationally deprived person is often also the one with the lower longevity, as we know from statistical studies of development characteristics.

More importantly, it should be borne in mind that the exercise of gender-equity adjustment is being made here at a high level of aggregation, dealing with the *mean* positions of women and men. At this aggregated level, the inequalities almost always go together, with women being in a more deprived position, on the average, than men. The exceptions come from a handful of countries – such as the Scandinavian ones – where in terms of one variable, viz. life expectancy, women seem to have actually gone significantly ahead of men in terms of the standard correction for expected longevity (with five extra years expected in female longevity). In such cases, the disparity in life expectancy may go in the opposite direction to the disparity in education or income earning. If note were to be taken of this connection, these countries would be placed higher in terms of overall achievement, since the inequality adjustments would have, to some extent, counteracted each other. But since these countries are, in any case, towards or at the top of the international "league tables", the effect of this correction would be only to reinforce that positional lead.

ON SPACES AND FORMULAS

This paper has been primarily concerned with proposing, explaining, and defending a particular approach to constructing gender-equity-sensitive measures of human development. It has not been directly concerned with the choice of variables, even though the argument has been developed in terms of the "classic" components of human development indicators, beginning with *Human Development Report 1990*.

The choices of variables – in particular, life expectancy and literacy – were primarily governed by the ability to discriminate among the relatively less affluent countries. For the high-achieving developed countries, there is relatively little sensitivity in the use of these variables, at least as far as the rankings are concerned. It is for this reason that we had earlier suggested (in Anand and Sen 1993) that different variables may be used in a supplementary way to discriminate between middle- and high-achieving countries, respectively. We stick to the logic behind that position, since the variables needed to discriminate *between* the advanced countries tend to dilute the importance of some of the basic features of human development that the "classic" variables capture, thereby turning a partially blind eye to the relative failures and successes of poorer countries in bringing about achievements in basic fields (such as literacy and life expectancy). However, it is not the purpose of this paper to insist that we must use only the classic HDI variables, or the pyramid structure proposed in Anand and Sen (1993). That is ultimately a question to be determined at the UNDP. But we would like to emphasize that even if we depart from the variables with which this note has been specifically concerned, there will be scope for using the methodology developed here. For example, replacing literacy by "total gross enrollment ratio" would not require any basic change in the methodological approach developed here. We have reasons to question the quality of these data and their perspicuity in "telling" between poorer countries in terms of what has been called "first things first" (on which see Streeten et al. 1981), but the methodology has enough catholicity to deal with that option if it were chosen. The ball should now be at the UNDP's court.

APPENDICES

A.2.7.1 Properties of the gender-equity-sensitive indicator X_{ede}

In this section we derive some properties of the gender-equity-sensitive indicator, X_{ede}. In particular, we examine X_{ede} as a function of the female and male achievements, X_f and X_m, respectively. To our knowledge, these properties of X_{ede} have not previously been derived in the literature on the measurement of inequality.

We begin with the general definition of X_{ede} with respect to a *concave* increasing social valuation function $V(X)$. We leave the functional form of $V(X)$ unspecified and require only that $V'(X) > 0$ and $V''(X) \leq 0$. Then X_{ede} is defined through the equation

$$(n_f + n_m)V(X_{ede}) = n_f V(X_f) + n_m V(X_m).$$

Henceforth, we denote p_f and p_m as the *proportions* of females and males in the total population, which is of size $(n_f + n_m)$. By definition,

$$p_f = n_f/(n_f + n_m) \text{ and } p_m = n_m/(n_f + n_m).$$

It follows that $(p_f + p_m) = 1$, and

$$V(X_{ede}) = p_f V(X_f) + p_m V(X_m). \quad (1)$$

Hence

$$X_{ede} = V^{-1}(p_f V(X_f) + p_m V(X_m))$$

subgroups, p_f and p_m. A rise in the population proportion of the subgroup with a higher level of with $V^{-1}(.)$ a convex increasing function. As X_{ede} is a monotonic increasing function of a concave function, it will be at least quasi-concave in (X_f, X_m). But will it be *concave*? The answer to this question is of central interest in understanding the gender-equity-sensitive indicator (GESI).

The first property of X_{ede} that we wish to derive is simply that X_{ede} is monotonic increasing in both X_f and X_m. This follows directly from partial differentiation with respect to X_i of equation (1) above, for $i = f, m$:

$$V'(X_{ede}) \cdot \partial X_{ede}/\partial X_i = p_i V'(X_i).$$

Hence

$$\partial X_{ede}/\partial X_i = p_i V'(X_i)/V'(X_{ede}) \quad (2)$$
$$> 0 \text{ for } i = f,m$$

because $V'(X) > 0$. Thus X_{ede} is monotonic increasing in both female and male achievements.[18]

Furthermore, if female achievement X_f is less than male achievement X_m, and the female popula-

tion proportion p_f is greater than or equal to the male population proportion p_m, then a unit increase in female achievement will be *more* valuable socially than a unit increase in male achievement. This follows easily using equation (2). By assumption, $X_f < X_m$ and $V''(X) \leq 0$; hence $V'(X_f) \geq V'(X_m)$. Since also $p_f \geq p_m$, we have

$$\partial X_{ede}/\partial X_f = p_f V'(X_f)/V'(X_{ede})$$
$$\geq p_m V'(X_m)/V'(X_{ede})$$
$$\text{because } V'(X_f) \geq V'(X_m)$$
$$= \partial X_{ede}/\partial X_m.$$

Note finally the property of X_{ede} relating to changes in the population proportions of the two subgroups, p_f and p_m. A rise in the population proportion of the subgroup with a higher level of achievement will result in a higher value of X_{ede}. Thus if $X_m > X_f$, and since $p_f = 1 - p_m$, we have from equation (1) by partial differentiation with respect to p_m

$$\partial X_{ede}/\partial p_m = [V(X_m) - V(X_f)]/V'(X_{ede})$$
$$> 0 \text{ because } V'(X) > 0.$$

The results obtained hitherto are valid for *any* concave increasing social valuation function $V(X)$. But how precisely does X_{ede} depend on the "degree of concavity" of $V(X)$? We know that if $V(X)$ is linear then we have

$$X_{ede} = p_f X_f + p_m X_m = \overline{X}$$

where $\overline{X}$2 is the simple arithmetic average of the individual achievements X_f and X_m. If $V(X)$ is *strictly* concave, then we will have

$$X_{ede} < \overline{X}.$$

This is because, by definition of X_{ede},

$$V(X_{ede}) = p_f V(X_f) + p_m V(X_m)$$
$$< V(p_f X_f + p_m X_m) \text{ since } V(X) \text{ is strictly concave}$$
$$= V(\overline{X}).$$

Hence

$$X_{ede} < \overline{X}$$

because V(X) is monotonic increasing in X. The analysis suggests that a "more concave" valuation function than V(X) will imply a still lower value of X_{ede}. We define one monotonic increasing function to be *more concave* than another if the former can be expressed as a concave monotonic increasing transform of the latter.

It is indeed the case that a more concave valuation function will yield a *lower* value of X_{ede}. Thus, if an increasing concave transform φ(.) is applied to the concave function V(X), then the equally distributed equivalent achievement corresponding to φ(V(X)) will be *smaller* than that corresponding to V(X). This is demonstrated by applying the function φ(.) to $(p_f V(X_f) + p_m V(X_m))$, and using concavity of φ(.) to prove the result.

Let X_{ede}^v and X_{ede}^ϕ be the equally distributed equivalent achievements corresponding to the functions V(X) and φ(V(X)), respectively. Then

$$V(X_{ede}^v) = p_f V(X_f) + p_m V(X_m)$$
$$\textit{by definition of } X_{ede}^v$$

Applying φ(.) to both sides of this equation gives

$$\phi(V(X_{ede}^v)) = \phi(p_f V(X_f) + p_m V(X_m))$$
$$\geq p_f \phi(V(X_f)) + p_m \phi(V(X_m))$$
$$\text{because φ(.) is concave}$$
$$= \phi(V(X_{ede}^\phi)) \text{ by definition of } X_{ede}^\phi$$

Hence,

$$X_{ede}^\phi \leq X_{ede}^v$$

because φ(V(X)) is monotonic increasing in X.

This inference is analogous to the Arrow (1965)–Pratt (1964) result in the theory of uncertainty that a more risk-averse individual has a lower certainty equivalent income for any given risk.[19] It was also established as an inequality concerning convex functions in Hardy, Littlewood and Pólya (1952, pp. 75–6).

The general proposition proven above on "more concave" functions can be applied to demonstrate result (2) in the text. This relates to *iso-elastic* social valuation functions and states that the larger is the elasticity ε of the marginal valuation function V'(X), the smaller will be X_{ede}. We let

$$V(X) = \frac{1}{1-\varepsilon} X^{1-\varepsilon}$$

and prove the result for ε ≥ 0, ε ≠ 1. Thus consider the function

$$W(X) = \frac{1}{1-v} X^{1-v} \textit{ where } v > \varepsilon.$$

To apply the general proposition we must be able to write

$$W = \phi(V), \textit{ where } \phi'(V) > 0 \textit{ and } \phi''(V) < 0$$

so that φ(.) is an increasing concave function. We have

$$X = [(1 - \varepsilon)V]^{1(1-\varepsilon)}$$

and hence

$$W = \frac{1}{1-v} X^{1-v} = \frac{1}{1-v}[(1-\varepsilon)V]^{(1-v)/(1-\varepsilon)}$$
$$= \phi(V),$$

say, which provides a definition of the required function φ(V). It turns out that φ(V) is indeed an increasing concave function of V provided that v > ε. To show this, differentiate φ(V) with respect to V twice:

$$\phi'(V) = [(1-\varepsilon)V]^{(\varepsilon-v)/(1-\varepsilon)} > 0,$$

and

$$\phi''(V) = (\varepsilon-v)[(1-\varepsilon)V]^{(2\varepsilon-v-1)/(1-\varepsilon)}$$
$$< 0 \text{ since } v > \varepsilon.$$

Note that whether ε < 1 or ε > 1, the quantity $(1-\varepsilon)V$ is always *positive* (and equal to $X^{1-\varepsilon}$): when 0 ≤ ε < 1 both $(1-\varepsilon)$ and V are positive, and when $\varepsilon > 1$ both $(1-\varepsilon)$ and V are negative. Our definition of V(X) as $X^{1-\varepsilon}$ divided by $(1-\varepsilon)$ thus circumvents the need to prove separately results for positive and negative powers of X, i.e. separately for the cases $0 \le \varepsilon < 1$ and $\varepsilon > 1$.[20]

A.2.7.2 On the concavity of X_{ede} with respect to (X_f, X_m)

Earlier we showed that X_{ede} was a monotonic increasing function of its arguments (X_f, X_m), demonstrated in equation (2). This is clearly a desirable property for a measure of social achievement, even once it has been adjusted for equity. Moreover, we saw that if $X_f < X_m$ (and $p_f \ge p_m$), then a unit increase in X_f adds *more* to X_{ede} than a unit increase in X_m. But will there be "diminishing returns" to unit increases in X_f, and for that matter to unit increases in X_m? This might seem like an appealing property for the measure of social achievement X_{ede} to possess.

To address this question, we have to differentiate equation (2) partially with respect to X_i. This gives

$$V''(X_{ede}) \cdot (\partial X_{ede}/\partial X_i)^2$$
$$+ V'(X_{ede}) \cdot (\partial^2 X_{ede}/\partial X_i^2) = p_i V''(X_i).$$

Hence,

$$V'(X_{ede}) \cdot (\partial^2 X_{ede}/\partial X_i^2) = p_i V''(X_i)$$
$$- V''(X_{ede}) \cdot (\partial X_{ede}/\partial X_i)^2 = p_i V''(X_i)$$
$$- V''(X_{ede}) \cdot [p_i V'(X_i)/V'(X_{ede})]^2 \quad (3)$$

In general, therefore, the behaviour of $(\partial^2 X_{ede}/\partial X_i^2)$ will depend on both the first and second derivatives of the function V(X) at X_i and at X_{ede}.

Let us now consider two special cases of the function V(X): the constant elasticity marginal valuation (or constant *relative* inequality aversion) form; and the constant *absolute* inequality aversion form.[21] For the case we have $V'(X) = X^{-\varepsilon}$ and $V''(X) = -\varepsilon X^{-\varepsilon-1}$. Substituting into equation (3) above, we get

$$V(X) = \frac{1}{1-\varepsilon} X^{1-\varepsilon}$$

we have $V'(X) = X^{-\varepsilon}$ and $V''(X) = -\varepsilon X^{-\varepsilon-1}$. Substituting into equation (3) above, we get

$$X_{ede}^{-\varepsilon} (\partial^2 X_{ede}/\partial X_i^2) = p_i(-\varepsilon X_i^{-\varepsilon-1}) - (-\varepsilon X_{ede}^{-\varepsilon-1}) \cdot$$
$$[p_i X_i^{-\varepsilon} / X_{ede}^{-\varepsilon}]^2$$
$$= p_i^2 \varepsilon X_{ede}^{\varepsilon-1} \cdot X_i^{-2\varepsilon} - p_i \varepsilon X_i^{-\varepsilon-1}$$
$$= p_i \varepsilon X_{ede}^{\varepsilon-1} \cdot X_i^{-\varepsilon-1} (p_i X_i^{1-\varepsilon} - X_{ede}^{1-\varepsilon}). \quad (4)$$

But we know that for this functional form for V(X), X_{ede} satisfies

$$X_{ede}^{1-\varepsilon} = p_f X_f^{1-\varepsilon} + p_m X_m^{1-\varepsilon}.$$

Hence the expression

$$(p_i X_i^{1-\varepsilon} - X_{ede}^{1-\varepsilon})$$

is equal either to

$$(-p_m X_m^{1-\varepsilon})$$

or to

$$(-p_f X_f^{1-\varepsilon})$$

depending on whether $i = f$ or $i = m$. In any event, the expression

$$(p_i X_i^{1-\varepsilon} - X_{ede}^{1-\varepsilon})$$

in equation (4) will be negative[22], and therefore

$$(\partial^2 X_{ede}/\partial X_i^2) < 0 \text{ for } i = f, m.$$

For the isoelastic form for V(X), we have shown that X_{ede} does indeed increase at a *diminishing rate* in each of its arguments X_f and X_m.

The second special case we consider for the function V(X) is the constant absolute inequality aversion form:

$$V(X) = -e^{-\gamma X}$$

up to a positive affine transformation. Here γ is the (positive) parameter of absolute inequality aversion, which is defined in general as $-V''(X)/V'(X)$. In this case,

$$V'(X) = \gamma e^{-\gamma X} > 0,$$

and

$$V''(X) = -\gamma^2 e^{-\gamma X} < 0.$$

Substituting into equation (3), we get

$$V'(X_{ede}) \cdot (\partial^2 X_{ede} / \partial X_i^2)$$

$$= p_i(-\gamma^2 e^{-\gamma X_i}) - (-\gamma^2 e^{-\gamma X_{ede}}) \cdot [p_i e^{-\gamma X_i} / e^{-\gamma X_{ede}}]^2$$

$$= p_i^2 \gamma^2 e^{\gamma X_{ede}} \cdot e^{-2\gamma X_i} - p_i \gamma^2 e^{-\gamma X_i}$$

$$= p_i \gamma^2 e^{\gamma(X_{ede} - X_i)} \cdot [p_i e^{-\gamma X_i} - e^{-\gamma X_{ede}}]. \quad (5)$$

But we know that for this functional form for $V(X)$, X_{ede} satisfies

$$e^{-\gamma X_{ede}} = p_f e^{-\gamma X_f} + p_m e^{-\gamma X_m}.$$

Hence the expression

$$[p_i e^{-\gamma X_i} - e^{-\gamma X_{ede}}]$$

is equal either to

$$(-p_m e^{-\gamma X_m})$$

or to

$$(-p_f e^{-\gamma X_f})$$

depending on whether i = f or i = m. In any event, the expression

$$[p_i e^{-\gamma X_i} - e^{-\gamma X_{ede}}]$$

in equation (5) will be negative[23], and therefore

$$(\partial^2 X_{ede} / \partial X_i^2) < 0 \text{ for } i = f, m.$$

Thus in both the main cases of constant relative and of constant absolute inequality aversion, we have the result that X_{ede} increases at a diminishing rate with respect to the individual achievement X_i, for all i. But will this result be true of *any* concave function $V(X)$? An examination of equation (3) shows that $(\partial^2 X_{ede} / \partial X_i^2)$ can fail to be negative if $V''(X_i)$ is close to zero and $V''(X_{ede})$ and $(\partial X_{ede} / \partial X_i)$ are large in absolute terms.[24]

To construct a counterexample, we choose $V''(X) = 0$ in the neighbourhood of variation of X_i, and $V''(X) < 0$ in the range around X_{ede}, while noting that X_{ede} depends both on X_f and on X_m. Let $X_f < X_m$, and let us here evaluate $(\partial^2 X_{ede} / \partial X_m^2)$. Take $X_f = 0$ and let X_m lie on a linear segment of the function $V(X)$. Thus consider the function

$$V(X) = \begin{cases} X^{1/2} & \text{for } 0 \leq X \leq 1. \\[2mm] \dfrac{X}{2} + \dfrac{1}{2} & \text{for } X \geq 1. \end{cases}$$

Then $V'(X) = 1/2$ for $X \geq 1$.

Now we choose $X_m \geq 1$, but not so large that X_{ede} will also lie on the linear segment containing X_m. For simplicity, assume that $p_f = p_m = \frac{1}{2}$. Then

$$2V(X_{ede}) = V(0) + V(X_m) \quad \text{by definition of } X_{ede}$$
$$= 0 + (X_m + 1)/2$$

so that

$$V(X_{ede}) = (X_m + 1)/4.$$

For $V(X_{ede}) < 1$, i.e. for $X_m < 3$, we have

$$V(X_{ede}) = X_{ede}^{1/2}.$$

Therefore,

$$X_{ede}^{1/2} = (X_m + 1)/4 \quad \text{for } 1 \leq X_m < 3$$

and

$$X_{ede} = (X_m + 1)^2 / 16$$

which is strictly *convex* in X_m. Hence

$$\partial^2 X_{ede} / \partial X_m^2 = 1/8 > 0$$

for the parameters and ranges of the variables we have chosen.

It is easy to see that the result will still hold if a small curvature were added to the function $V(X)$ along its linear segment, so that $V''(X) < 0$

throughout. If the function were made slightly strictly concave in this range, we would still get

$$(\partial^2 X_{ede}/\partial X_m^2) > 0.$$

Moreover, using smoother splines, we could make higher-order derivatives of the function continuous at $X = 1$. (In our example, the second derivative of the function $V(X)$ is not continuous at $X = 1$; it is equal to $(-1/4)$ just to the left of $X = 1$, and to 0 just to the right of $X = 1$.)

The basic intuition behind the counterexample is that if social value from increasing an individual achievement goes up (essentially) linearly, then to bring about equal unit increases in $V(X)$ we will have to raise X_{ede} at an *increasing* rate if X_{ede} lies on a diminishing marginal returns segment of the function.

A.2.7.3 Properties of the relative gender-equality index E

In this subsection we examine the properties of the relative gender-equality index E, defined as $X_{ede}/\overline{X}$, for the isoelastic social valuation function $V(X)$. We have

$$X_{ede} = [p_f X_f^{1-\varepsilon} + p_m X_m^{1-\varepsilon}]^{1/(1-\varepsilon)}$$

and

$$\overline{X} = [p_f X_f + p_m X_m].$$

Hence

$$E = X_{ede}/\overline{X}$$

$$= [p_f X_f^{1-\varepsilon} + p_m X_m^{1-\varepsilon}]^{1/(1-\varepsilon)}/[p_f X_f + p_m X_m]$$

$$= p_f^{\varepsilon/(1-\varepsilon)} [(p_m/p_f) + (X_f/X_m)^{1-\varepsilon}]^{1/(1-\varepsilon)}/$$

$$[(p_m/p_f) + (X_f/X_m)].$$

From now on we assume that $p_f = p_m = \frac{1}{2}$, and we define $z = (X_f/X_m)$ as the *ratio* of female to male achievement. Then

$$E(z) = (1/2)^{\varepsilon/(1-\varepsilon)} [1 + z^{1-\varepsilon}]^{1/(1-\varepsilon)}/[1 + z]. \quad (6)$$

It is not difficult to check that, for any $\varepsilon > 0$, the index of relative equality E is maximized at $z = 1$,

and its maximum value is $E = 1$. In general, we have $0 \le E(z) \le 1$ for $z \ge 0$.

By differentiating $E(z)$ with respect to z, and simplifying, we obtain

$$E'(z) = (1/2)^{\varepsilon/(1-\varepsilon)} + (1 + z^{1-\varepsilon})^{\varepsilon/(1-\varepsilon)}(z^{-\varepsilon} - 1)/$$

$$(1 + z)^2.$$

Given $\varepsilon > 0$, it follows that $E'(z) > 0$ for $z < 1$, $E'(z) = 0$ for $z = 1$, and $E'(z) < 0$ for $z > 1$. By further differentiating with respect to z we can show that $E''(1) < 0$, i.e. $z = 1$ maximizes $E(z)$.

Manipulating the second derivative of $E(z)$, it can be seen that $E''(z) = 0$ when

$$-\varepsilon(1+z)^2 = 2z(1-z^\varepsilon)(1+z^{1-\varepsilon}).$$

Inspecting the left- and right-hand sides of this equation, it is evident that its solution must occur at a value of $z > 1$.[25] To the left of this point of inflection in $E(z)$ the second derivative $E''(z)$ will be negative, and to the right of this point the second derivative $E''(z)$ will be positive. The shape of $E(z)$ for different values of ε is shown in the figure below.

For $\varepsilon = 0$, there is no concern for equality and $E = 1$ for all values of z.
For $0 < \varepsilon < 1$, we have $E \to (1/2)^{\varepsilon/(1-\varepsilon)}$ both as $z \to 0$ and as $z \to \infty$.
For $\varepsilon = 1$, we have X_{ede} as the geometric mean of X_f and X_m, and

$$E = 2z^{1/2}/[1 + z] = 2/[z^{-1/2} + z^{1/2}]$$

$$\to 0 \text{ as } z \to 0 \text{ and as } z \to \infty.$$

For $\varepsilon > 1$, we can again check from equation (6) that $E \to 0$ both as $z \to 0$ and as $z \to \infty$.
For $\varepsilon = 2$, in particular, we have X_{ede} as the harmonic mean of X_f and X_m, and

$$E = 4/[1 + z][1 + (1/z)]$$

$$\to 0 \text{ as } z \to 0 \text{ and as } z \to \infty.$$

Irrespective of ε, the value of $E(z)$ will obviously be the same as $z \to 0$ and as $z \to \infty$; the index of relative equality E is clearly *symmetric* (given $p_f = p_m = \frac{1}{2}$) in z and (1/z). From equation (6) it is easy to verify that E(z) = E(1/z) for all z ≥ 0. For any $\varepsilon \geq 0$, E as a function of z must therefore always satisfy the following properties:

(1)   E(z) = E(1/z) → 0 for all z → 0.
(2)   E(z) is maximized at z = 1, and E(1) = 1.

Thus within this framework we cannot impose arbitrary functional forms for E(z) for z → 0, such as E(z) = z or E(z) = 1– [1–z], which violate properties (1) and (2).

ENDNOTES

[handwritten margin notes: "not published then as a paper = new" and "we did not receive ... could have been ... collection"]

1. This paper was prepared for the *Human Development Report 1995*. For helpful discussions, we are grateful to Mahbub ul Haq and to the other members of the "human development" team.

2. The situation is slightly different in the case of adjusted income, which is based on a logarithmic transform of per capita GDP for the country as a whole (truncated at the official poverty line income for the richer, developed countries). See Anand and Sen 1993.

3. *Human Development Report 1994*, table 5, p. 139.

4. See also Kolm 1969; Sen 1973; Anand 1977, 1983; Blackorby and Donaldson 1978, 1984; Osmani 1982; and Foster 1984, 1985.

5. Considering X_{ede} as a function of ε, we can write

$$X_{ede}(\varepsilon) = [p_f X_f^{1-\varepsilon} + p_m X_m^{1-\varepsilon}]^{1/(1-\varepsilon)}.$$

For X_f, $X_m > 0$, $X_{ede}(\varepsilon)$ is well-defined for all ε (positive or negative) except $\varepsilon = 1$. As $\varepsilon \to 1$, we can show that $\log X_{ede}(\varepsilon) \to (p_f \log X_f + p_m \log X_m)$, i.e. the logarithm of the geometric mean of X_f and X_m; hence $X_{ede}(\varepsilon)$ tends to the geometric mean of (X_f, X_m). If one of the X_i, say X_f, is equal to 0, then $X_{ede}(\varepsilon)$ is well-defined for $\varepsilon < 1$. But for $\varepsilon > 1$, $X_f^{1-\varepsilon} = 1/X_f^{(\varepsilon-1)} \to \infty$ as $X_f \to 0$. In this case,

$$X_{ede}(\varepsilon) = 1/[p_f/X_f^{(\varepsilon-1)} + p_m / X_m^{(\varepsilon-1)}]^{1/(\varepsilon-1)},$$

so that

$$p_f/X_f^{(\varepsilon-1)}$$

and the entire denominator of $X_{ede}(\varepsilon)$ tends to infinity as $X_f \to 0$. Therefore for $\varepsilon > 1$, $X_{ede}(\varepsilon) \to 0$ as $X_f \to 0$. Putting together the cases $\varepsilon = 1$ and $\varepsilon > 1$, the limiting value of $X_{ede}(\varepsilon)$ for $\varepsilon \geq 1$ is zero as one of the X_i, e.g. X_f, tends to zero. Thus we may simply *define* $X_{ede}(\varepsilon) = 0$ for $\varepsilon \geq 1$ when X_f or X_m is equal to zero.

6. The appendices contain a more general discussion and proofs of the major results.

7. There is some ambiguity as to whether this "extreme inequality aversion" leads to simple maximin, or to the lexico-

graphic version of maximin (sometimes called "leximin"), on which see Hammond 1975.

8. By result (2) above, we have the following relationship between the three means when the two numbers X_f and X_m are positive and different: the harmonic mean is less than the geometric mean, and the geometric mean is less than the arithmetic mean.

9. The corresponding measure of relative *inequality* I is simply the Atkinson index

$$I = 1 - (X_{ede}/\overline{X}).$$

Under the assumptions made on V(X) in the text, both E and I are *mean-independent* measures. Indeed, the constant elasticity marginal valuation form is both sufficient *and* necessary for E and I to be homogeneous of degree zero in (X_f, X_m).

10. There is indeed strong evidence that the maximal potential life expectancy for women is greater than for men – given similar care, including health care and nutritional opportunities (see Holden 1987; Waldron 1983; and the references cited there). Indeed, in most of the "developed" countries, women tend to outlive men by typically six to eight years.

11. On this see Sen 1992a, ch. 6.

12. The translation is from Nussbaum 1988, who also discusses the precise role that this qualification plays in Aristotle's "distributive conception" (pp. 146–150; italics added).

13. On the other hand, for $\varepsilon = 1$, X_{ede} is given through the logarithmic functional form. These formulations are based on the presumption that there are the same number of women as of men – hence the half-and-half division. When this does not hold, the gross mean and the gender-equity-sensitive measure involve weighting the achievements of each group by their respective population shares p_f and p_m (see appendix A.2.7.1).

14. See, for example, Goldschmidt-Clermont 1982, 1993; Folbre 1991; Folbre and Wagman 1993; Urdaneta-Ferrán 1993; and the references cited there. Many of the diverse underlying issues are discussed in Chen 1983; Bergmann 1986; Jayawardena 1986; Brannen and Wilson 1987; Sen and Grown 1987; Okin 1989; Goldin 1990; England 1992; Ferber and Nelson 1993; Folbre 1994; Agarwal 1995; and Nussbaum and Glover 1995.

15. For references to the literature on this, and an analysis of why this relationship is observed in situations of "cooperative conflict" (as family-living typically is), see Sen 1990. See also Anand 1979; Manser and Brown 1980; McElroy and Horney 1981; Lundberg and Pollak 1994; and the references cited there.

16. By partial differentiation with respect to ε, it is straightforward to show that

$$\frac{\partial}{\partial \varepsilon}\left[\frac{\partial X_{ede}/\partial X_f}{\partial X_{ede}/\partial X_m}\right] > 0 \text{ for } (X_m/X_f) > 1, \text{ and}$$

$$\frac{\partial^2}{\partial \varepsilon^2}\left[\frac{\partial X_{ede}/\partial X_f}{\partial X_{ede}/\partial X_m}\right] > 0.$$

17. On this see Kynch 1985 and Sen 1988, and the references cited there.

18. Note that this property does not necessarily obtain with arbitrarily specified measures of gender equity, such as (X_f / X_m) $(p_f X_f + p_m X_m)$. The latter measure is equal to $[(p_f X_f^2 / X_m) + p_m X_f]$, which is a strictly decreasing function of X_m.

19. It is equivalent to saying that a more risk-averse individual is willing to pay more to eliminate any given risk – one of several characterizations of "greater risk aversion". See, *inter alia*, Arrow 1965; Pratt 1964; Rothschild and Stiglitz 1970; Diamond and Rothschild 1989.

20. For the case $V(X) = \log X$, which corresponds to an elasticity of marginal valuation $\varepsilon = 1$, we have $X = e^V$. Now consider a more concave function, i.e. one with elasticity of marginal valuation $v > 1$. Then

$$W(X) = \frac{1}{1-v} X^{1-v} \ with \ v > 1$$

$$= \frac{1}{1-v} (e^V)^{1-v}$$

$$= \frac{1}{1-v} e^{(1-v)V}$$

This is an increasing concave function for all values (positive and negative) of V, because $(1-v) < 0$. Hence we can apply the general proposition on "more concave" functions.

21. These two forms, named as such by Atkinson (1970) in the inequality literature, correspond in the risk literature to constant relative risk aversion and to constant absolute risk aversion, respectively (Arrow 1965, Pratt 1964).

22. When there are more than two arguments, we will have

$$(p_i X_i^{1-\varepsilon} - X_{ede}^{1-\varepsilon}) = -\sum_{j \neq 1} p_j X_j^{1-\varepsilon} < 0.$$

23. When there are more than two arguments X_f and X_m we will have

$$[p_i e^{-\gamma X_i} - e^{-\gamma X_{ede}}] = -\sum_{j \neq i} p_j e^{-\gamma X_j} < 0.$$

24. $(\partial X_{ede} / \partial X_i)$ is always less than unity for the case of constant absolute inequality aversion. Here

$$(\partial X_{ede} / \partial X_i) = p_i e^{-\gamma X_i} / e^{-\gamma X_{ede}}$$

$$= p_i e^{-\gamma X_i} / (\sum_j p_j e^{-\gamma X_j})$$

$$< 1.$$

But for the case of constant relative inequality aversion, we can make $(\partial X_{ede} / \partial X_i)$ as large as we like. For example, let $(X_m / X_f) = \lambda$, $p_m = p_f = 1/2$, and $\varepsilon = 1/2$. Then

$$\partial X_{ede} / \partial X_f = \frac{1}{2} [\frac{1}{2} (1 + \lambda^{1-\varepsilon})]^{\varepsilon/(1-\varepsilon)}$$

$$= \frac{1}{4} (1 + \lambda^{1/2}) \ for \ \varepsilon = 1/2$$

$$\rightarrow \infty \ as \ \lambda \rightarrow \infty.$$

25. For certain parameter values of ε, this equation can be solved immediately. Thus the solution is $z = 2$ for $\varepsilon = 2$, and $z = 2.1547$ for both $\varepsilon = 1/2$ and $\varepsilon = 1$. (For these parameter values, the equation is a quadratic.)

REFERENCES

Agarwal, Bina. 1995. *A Field of One's Own: Gender and Land Rights in South Asia*. Cambridge: Cambridge University Press.

Anand, Sudhir. 1977. "Aspects of Poverty in Malaysia." *Review of Income and Wealth*, series 23, no. 1, March, pp. 1–16.

——. 1979. "Models of the Farm Household in Less Developed Countries." St. Catherine's College, Oxford, July. Mimeographed.

——. 1983. *Inequality and Poverty in Malaysia: Measurement and Decomposition*. New York: Oxford University Press.

——. 1993. "Inequality Between and Within Nations." Center for Population and Development Studies, Harvard University, Cambridge, Mass. Mimeographed.

Anand, Sudhir and Amartya K. Sen. 1993. "Human Development Index: Methodology and Measurement." Human Development Report Office Occasional Papers No. 12. UNDP, New York.

Arrow, Kenneth J. 1965. *Aspects of the Theory of Risk-Bearing*. Yrjö Jahnsson Lectures. Helsinki: Yrjö Jahnssonin Säätiö.

Atkinson, Anthony B. 1970. "On the Measurement of Inequality." *Journal of Economic Theory* 2(3), September: 244–63.

——. 1973. "How Progressive Should Income-Tax Be?" In M. Parkin (ed.), *Essays on Modern Economics*, Longman. Reprinted in E. S. Phelps (ed.), *Economic Justice*, Penguin Education, Harmondsworth, Middlesex, pp. 386–408.

Bergmann, Barbara. 1986. *The Economic Emergence of Women*. New York: Basic Books.

Blackorby, C. and D. Donaldson. 1978. "Measures of Relative Equality and Their Meaning in Terms of Social Welfare." *Journal of Economic Theory* 18.

——. 1984. "Ethically Significant Ordinal Indexes of Relative Inequality." *Advances in Econometrics* 3.

Brannen, Julia and Gail Wilson. 1987. *Give and Take in Families: Studies in Resource Distribution*. London: Allen and Unwin.

Chen, Martha A. 1983. *A Quiet Revolution: Women in Transition in Rural Bangladesh*. Cambridge, Mass.: Schenkman Publishing Inc.

Desai, Meghnad J. 1991. "Human Development: Concepts and Measurement." *European Economic Review* 35: 350–57.

Diamond, Peter A. and Michael Rothschild (eds). 1989. *Uncertainty in Economics: Readings and Exercises*. Revised edition. New York: Academic Press.

Edgeworth, F. Y. 1922. "Equal Pay to Men and Women for Equal Work." *Economic Journal* 32: 431–57.

——. 1923. "Women's Wages in Relation to Economic Welfare." *Economic Journal* 33: 487–95.

Elson, Diane (ed.). 1991. *Male Bias in the Development Process*. Manchester, UK: Manchester University Press.

England, Paula. 1992. *Comparable Worth: Theories and Evidence*. New York: Aldine.

Ferber, Marianne A. and Julie A. Nelson (eds). 1993. *Beyond Economic Man: Feminist Theory and Economics*. Chicago: University of Chicago Press.

Folbre, Nancy. 1991. "The Unproductive Housewife: Her Evolution in Nineteenth Century Economic Thought." *Signs: Journal of Women in Culture and Society* 16(3): 463–84.

——. 1994. *Who Pays for the Kids? Gender and the Structures of Constraint*. London and New York: Routledge.

Folbre, Nancy and Barnet Wagman. 1993 "Counting Housework: Revised Estimates of Real Product in the United States, 1800–1860." *The Journal of Economic History* 53(2): 275–88.

Foster, James E. 1984. "On Economic Poverty: A Survey of Aggregate Measures." *Advances in Econometrics* 3.

——. 1985. "Inequality Measurement." In H. P. Young (ed.), *Fair Allocation*. Providence, RI: American Mathematical Society.

Glendon, Mary Ann. 1989. *The Transformation of Family Law: State, Law, and Family in the United States and Western Europe*. Chicago: University of Chicago Press.

Goldin, Claudia. 1990. *Understanding the Gender Gap*. Oxford: Oxford University Press.

Goldschmidt-Clermont, Luisella. 1982. *Unpaid Work in the Household*. Geneva: International Labour Office.

——. 1993. "Monetary Valuation of Unpaid Work." Paper presented at the International Conference on the Measurement and Valuation of Unpaid Work, Statistics Canada, Ottawa, April 28–30.

Hammond, Peter J. 1975. "A Note on Extreme Inequality Aversion." *Journal of Economic Theory* 11: 465–67.

Hardy, G. H., J. E. Littlewood and G. Pólya. 1952. *Inequalities*. Second edition. Cambridge: Cambridge University Press.

Hartmann, B. 1987. *Reproductive Rights and Wrongs: The Global Politics of Population Control and Reproductive Choice*. New York: Harper and Row.

Holden, Constance. 1987. "Why Do Women Live Longer Than Men?" *Science* 238: 158–60.

Jayawardena, Kumari. 1986. *Feminism and Nationalism in the Third World*. London: Zed Books.

Kolm, Serge Ch. 1969. "The Optimal Production of Social Justice." In J. Margolis and H. Guitton (eds.), *Public Economics*. London: Macmillan.

Kynch, Jocelyn. 1985. "How Many Women Are Enough? Sex Ratios and the Right to Life." *Third World Affairs 1985*. London: Third World Foundation.

Lundberg, Shelly and Robert A. Pollak. 1994. "Noncooperative Bargaining Models of Marriage." *American Economic Review*, Papers and Proceedings 84(2): 132–37.

McElroy, Marjorie and Mary Jean Horney. 1981. "Nash-Bargained Household Decisions: Toward a Generalization of the Theory of Demand." *International Economic Review* 22(2): 333–49.

Manser, Marilyn and Murray Brown. 1980. "Marriage and Household Decision Making: A Bargaining Analysis." *International Economic Review* 21(1): 31–44.

Moen, P. 1989. *Working Parents: Transformations in Gender Roles and Public Policies in Sweden*. Madison, Wisconsin: University of Wisconsin Press.

Nussbaum, Martha C. 1988. "Nature, Function, and Capability: Aristotle on Political Distribution." *Oxford Studies in Ancient Philosophy* (supplementary volume).

Nussbaum, Martha C. and Jonathan Glover (eds.). 1995. *Women, Culture, and Development*. Oxford: Clarendon Press.

Okin, S.M. 1989. *Justice, Gender and the Family*. New York: Basic Books.

Osmani, Siddiq R. 1982. *Economic Inequality and Group Welfare*. Oxford: Clarendon Press.

Pratt, John W. 1964. "Risk Aversion in the Small and in the Large." *Econometrica* 32: 122–36.

Rothschild, Michael and Joseph E. Stiglitz. 1970. "Increasing Risk: I. A Definition." *Journal of Economic Theory* 2(3), September: 225–43.

Sen, Amartya K. 1973. *On Economic Inequality*. Oxford: Clarendon Press.

——. 1988. "Africa and India: What Do We Have to Learn from Each Other?" C. N. Vakil Memorial Lecture, 8th World Congress of the International Economic Association; published in K. J. Arrow (ed.), *The Balance Between Industry and Agriculture in Economic Development*. London: Macmillan.

——. 1990. "Gender and Cooperative Conflicts." In Irene Tinker (ed.), *Persistent Inequalities: Women and World Development*. New York: Oxford University Press.

——. 1992a. *Inequality Reexamined*. Oxford: Clarendon Press; and Cambridge, Mass.: Harvard University Press.

——. 1992b. "Missing Women." *British Medical Journal* 304: 587–88.

——. 1993. "Life Expectancy and Inequality: Some Conceptual Issues." In P. K. Bardhan, M. Datta-Chaudhuri and T. N. Krishnan (eds.), *Development and Change*. Bombay: Oxford University Press.

Sen, Gita and Caren Grown. 1987. *Development, Crises, and Alternative Visions: Third World Women's Perspectives*. New York: Monthly Review Press.

Stern, Nicholas H. 1977. "Welfare Weights and the Elasticity of the Marginal Valuation of Income." In M. Artis and R. Nobay (eds.), *Current Economic Problems*. Oxford: Basil Blackwell.

Streeten, Paul, with Shahid J. Burki, Mahbub ul Haq, Norman Hicks, and Frances Stewart. 1981. *First Things First: Meeting Basic Human Needs in the Developing Countries*. New York: Oxford University Press.

UNDP (United Nations Development Programme). 1993. *Human Development Report 1993*. New York: Oxford University Press.

——. 1994. *Human Development Report 1994*. New York: Oxford University Press.

Urdaneta-Ferrán, Lourdes. 1993. "Measuring Women's and Men's Economic Contribution." In proceedings of the ISI 49th Session, Firenze.

Waldron, Ingrid. 1983. "The Role of Genetic and Biological Factors in Sex Differences in Mortality." In Alan D. Lopez and Lado T. Ruzicka (eds.), *Sex Differentials in Mortality: Trends, Determinants and Consequences*, 141–64. Canberra: Department of Demography, Australian National University.

2.8

CONCEPTS OF HUMAN DEVELOPMENT AND POVERTY: A MULTIDIMENSIONAL PERSPECTIVE*

Sudhir Anand and Amartya Sen

The contrast between a commodity-focus view and the approach of human development has been much discussed in the previous *Human Development Reports.* This paper is concerned with a different distinction: that between (1) concentrating specifically on the living conditions of the poor, and (2) the more traditional broader approach of looking at the conditions of all the people in the society. The human development index (HDI) belongs to the latter – more inclusive – approach. As *Human Development Report 1997* is aimed at the conditions specifically of the poor, there is a need for a more focused approach concentrating specifically on the lives of the poor.

HUMAN DEVELOPMENT AND HUMAN POVERTY

The process of development in the contemporary world can be seen in two rather different ways. It can be characterized in terms of the progress being made by different groups in each community, putting weight on the fortunes of the rich as well as the poor, the well-provided as well as the deprived. This "conglomerative perspective" can be contrasted with an alternative, more specialized, viewpoint in which development is judged by the way the poor and the deprived, in particular, fare in each community. This "deprivation perspective" is specifically concerned with those who are forced to live deprived lives. In this accounting of the process of development, lack of progress in reducing the disadvantages of the deprived cannot be "washed away" by large advances – no matter how large – made by the better-off people.

are reasons for taking an interest in the process of development from both the perspectives. At a very basic level, the lives and suc-

cesses of *everyone* should count, and it would be a mistake to make our understanding of the process of development completely insensitive to the gains and losses of those who happen to fare better than others. It would go against the right of each citizen to be counted, and also clash with the comprehensive concerns of a universalist ethic. Yet a part – a *big* part – of the general interest in the progress of a nation concentrates specifically on the state of the disadvantaged. The reasoning behind public concern with development relates particularly to the advancement of those who are less privileged than others and who are forced to live distinctly reduced lives.

This deprivational focus contrasts sharply with the conglomerative perspective, in which even a sharp regress in the conditions of the poor can be, quite possibly, outweighed by a suitably large surge in the fortunes of the affluent. To see a "great advance" – on aggregative grounds – even as the devil takes the hindmost cannot really be very convincing. The rationale of the present paper relates to this general recognition.

The conglomerative and the deprivational perspectives are not, in fact, substitutes of each other. We need *both,* for an adequate understanding of the process of development. The plurality of our concerns and commitments forces us to take an interest in each. The specialized focus of the deprivation perspective is needed to supplement – not to supplant – the universalist solicitude of the conglomerative approach.

The *Human Development Reports,* which have been published every year since 1990, have been generally concerned with the removal of disadvantages and the creation of opportunities to lead worthwhile lives. Right from the beginning, these Reports have taken a special interest in poverty and deprivation, and have tried to provide a wide range of information – in various tables and commentaries – on relevant features of the misery and restricted lives of the worst off. However, the specific index of progress in the form of the HDI has taken a conglomerative perspective. For example, a rise in the life expectancy of any group – no matter how affluent – is reflected in a corresponding increase in the average life expectancy of that nation, and this in turn enhances the HDI, since average life expectancy is one of the constitutive components of the HDI. The particular approach of "human development", with its focus on human lives and the quality of living, with which these Reports have been concerned, can of course be fruitfully combined with the deprivational perspective. While that connection has been explored in terms of particular investigations of the conditions of impoverished people, it has not, up to now, been reflected in any specific index of the burden of deprivation.

Focusing on the conglomerative HDI has not, of course, been pointless, even in understanding the nature of deprivation. The disadvantages of the worst off have *inter alia* figured in the index. Given its general concentration on the quality of life and substantive opportunities of all people, the HDI has played a role in broadening evaluative attention from such gross measures of economic progress as the gross national product (GNP) per head (or the average national income) to lines of analysis that are sensitive to the removal of deprivation of different kinds as well as expansion of opportunities in general. Indeed, the Reports have contributed to a substantial change in the nature of public discussion and debate on the successes and failures in the process of development. The focus has been on development in a very broad sense, not just on the expansion of real income per head, but on the enhancement of some of the central features of the quality of life of those who lead diminished – and often physically shorter – lives.

Nevertheless, the possibility of reflecting in a usable and uncomplicated index the bearing of "human development" on the "deprivational perspective" – concentrating specifically on people who are particularly deprived – has not been,

so far, pursued. To undertake that task would require the development of an index of "human poverty", which would focus exclusively on the specially deprived and impoverished. This is part of the exercise undertaken in the *Human Development Report 1997,* and calls for a human poverty index (HPI). In devising such an index, it is important that the purpose of its contribution and the motivation behind it are properly understood.

In particular, some possible pitfalls must be avoided. First, the human poverty index must not be seen as a *substitute* for the human development index. As has been already discussed, both perspectives – deprivational and conglomerative – have their own interests and complement each other. Perhaps the motivational distinction between the HDI and HPI can be explained with an analogy, drawn from the income-based evaluation of economic success. The growth rate of GNP per head gives an account of progress seen in the conglomerative perspective – everyone's income counts in the GNP total. In contrast, the reduction of an *income-based poverty index* (such as the deprivation of the proportion of the population below the poverty-line income), while also based on income information, uses the deprivational perspective, concentrating specifically on the incomes of the poor (in contrast with GNP's interest in the incomes of all). Within the income-based perspective, it would make little sense to argue that since GNP is already based on income information, any income-based poverty measure must be a substitute for the GNP. Nor would it be sensible to suggest that the availability of the GNP as an indicator makes it redundant to seek a measure of income poverty.

The GNP and the income poverty measures use the income information in *different perspectives,* with the GNP taking a conglomerative view, while the income-poverty measures focus specifically on the income-poor.

The relationship between the HDI and HPI has to be seen in a similar way. Both have to use the rich categories of information that are associated with "human development": characteristics of human lives and quality of living that go much beyond what income information can provide. But while these characteristics are used by the HDI in the conglomerative perspective, the HPI must use them in the deprivational perspective. The availability of GNP measures does not obviate the need for an income-based poverty indicator (using income information), and similarly, the presence of the HDI measure does not eliminate the need for a human poverty index (using information related to the deprivation in human lives).

The relationship between these different measures can perhaps be usefully seen in the form of a table (table 2.8.1) where the rows distinguish between the conglomerative and deprivational perspectives, while the columns discriminate between the use of income information and that of characteristics of living associated with human development.

A second misunderstanding to avoid relates not to the relationship between the HDI and the new HPI, but between income-based poverty measures and the new HPI (that is, the contrast between the *columns* rather than the *rows* in table 2.8.1). Both the HPI and the income-poverty indicators share the deprivational perspective, but while the latter sees nothing in poverty other than lowness of incomes, the HPI must take a much broader view, in line with the approach of human development. It would, in fact, be useful to see how the values and rankings of the HPI relate to the results of income-based poverty analysis.

MULTIDIMENSIONALITY OF POVERTY

Poverty is, in many ways, the worst form of human deprivation. It can involve not only the lack of necessities of material well-being, but also the denial of opportunities of living a tolerable life. The lives could be prematurely shortened, made hard, painful or hazardous, deprived of understanding and communication, and robbed of dignity, confidence and self-respect. It is ultimately in the poverty of the lives that people can lead that poverty manifests itself.

Income-based poverty measures concentrate exclusively on deprivation in one variable in particular, viz. income. It has the advantage of simplicity in refraining from taking an interest in different aspects of deprivation. A similarly rudimentary approach cannot be used in developing an index of "human poverty", since the lives of human beings can be blighted and impoverished in quite different ways. Someone can, for example, enjoy good health and live quite long, and yet suffer from being illiterate and remain cut off from learning as well as communication and interactions with others that rely on literacy. Another person may be literate and quite well educated, but in fact be particularly prone to premature mortality because of the epidemiological characteristics of the region or country. If illiteracy were our only criterion, the first person would be seen as deprived, but not the second, whereas with proneness towards premature mortality as the only criterion, the second would be seen as handicapped, but not the first. But both are, in important ways, quite deprived, and it would be a mistake to concentrate only on one of the two types of information and ignore the other. When we consider several other ways in which a person can be severely deprived, we find other dimensions of disadvantage.

This line of reasoning also throws light on the inadequacy of income-based poverty measures. A person with an above-poverty-line personal income may still be deprived in the sense of being illiterate, or being subject to epidemiological vulnerabilities that can lead to premature mortality, or being without crucial services (such as safe water or health care) which are often provided by public provisioning (going well beyond what is purchased by personal incomes). The need for a multidimensional view of poverty and deprivation

Table 2.8.1

	Income information	Information on human living
Conglomerative	GNP per head	Human development index
Deprivational	Income poverty measures	Human poverty index

not only guides the search for an adequate indicator of human poverty, it also clarifies why an income-based poverty measure cannot serve the same purpose.

The HPI must, therefore, use a multidimensional procedure in assessing poverty. This is entirely in line with the "human development" approach. The human development index examines different features of the quality of life and arrives at an aggregate judgement on the extent of overall human development. In the same way, the human poverty index must examine different features of deprivation in the quality of life, and then arrive at an aggregate judgement on the extent of overall deprivation of the impoverished. In getting an adequately broad view of deprivation (including its different aspects), this multidimensionality is important and inescapable, and despite the complications of dealing with several variables at the same time, taking a multidimensional approach must, ultimately, be seen as an asset rather than a liability.

This is not to deny that any reduction of a multidimensional indicator into a numerical index, such as the HPI, must involve an exercise in weighting. The exercise of specifying usable weights supplements the evaluative task already involved in making a selection of the particular dimensions of deprivation on which to concentrate. These evaluative decisions have to be guided not only by practical considerations of measurability and data availability, but also by the reading of the prevailing values as to what counts as deprivation and how this is to be recorded. Since any choice of weights should be open to questioning and debating in public discussions, it is crucial that the judgements that are implicit in such weighting be made as clear and comprehensible as possible, and thus be open to public scrutiny. After proposing a particular system of weighting, we must supplement it by a thorough and transparent investigation of its properties and implications.

CONTEXT DEPENDENCE
AND DEPRIVATION IN POOR COUNTRIES

The identification of principal deprivations tends to vary with social and economic conditions of the community in question. Premature mortality is an extensive problem in impoverished countries in a way it may not be in highly developed countries where most people live quite long. Also, illiteracy may be a frequent form of significant deprivation in many countries with educational backwardness, but not in others. The choice of the indicators to be used in the human poverty index cannot but be sensitive to the context of the evaluation, and in particular to the characteristics of the countries for which this index is primarily intended. For example, an index that concentrates on illiteracy and premature mortality may be able to discriminate between, say, Sri Lanka and Pakistan much more easily than it can between, say, Germany and France.

To some extent this problem is also present for the human development index itself, and the case for having more specialized indicators in the conglomerative perspective may well be worth considering. But the difficulty is particularly immediate and powerful in characterizing poverty and in examining the condition of the deprived. Issues of poverty in the developing countries crucially involve such matters as hunger, illiteracy, epidemics, lack of health service or of safe water, but these deprivations may not be at all common in the more developed countries, where hunger is rare, literacy is close to being universal, most epidemics are well controlled, health services are typically widespread, and safe water is easy to access. Not surprisingly, studies of poverty in the more affluent countries have tended to concentrate on other variables, such as social exclusion, or inability to take part in the life of the community. These too can be quite forceful sources of deprivation of human lives and very hard to eliminate, but they involve different types of deprivation. There is no real possibility of getting an index of human poverty that would be equally relevant in the different types of countries.

Given the peculiar importance of poverty in poor countries, the HPI to be presented here is aimed at that context. The variables chosen reflect that. The nature of poverty in rich countries deserves a separate study – and a more specialized index, focusing on those deprivations that are particularly relevant for these countries. This motivational point has to be borne in mind in interpreting and examining the HPI, in the light of its context.

DEPRIVATION IN SURVIVAL AND IN EDUCATION

Of the three basic components of the human development index, two deal respectively with survival and education. The aspect of survival in the quality of life is captured in the human development index through the use of life expectancy at birth. This draws on the age-specific mortality rates that currently obtain. A weighted average of survival years is calculated, using this information. Different people do, of course, die at different ages, but the pattern of ages at death can be calculated by using the prevailing age-specific mortality rates, and the life expectancy gives the statistical expectation of an average person's length of life at the prevailing mortality rates.

The average value of life expectancy uses a firmly conglomerative approach, and is an average over the entire community. The deprivational perspective applied to survival makes us concentrate on vulnerability to death at a remarkably early age. By using the same age-specific mortality rates, it is possible to calculate the proportion of people who can be expected to die before a specified age (such as 40 years), at the prevailing rates. That proportion is a measure of vulnerability to having a substantially shortened life and reflects the incidence of serious deprivation in terms of length of life.

Turning now to education, it is reasonable to argue that illiteracy is indeed a strikingly sharp educational deprivation. The proportion of illiteracy expresses the incidence of this kind of deprivation in the population. The illiteracy rate can, thus, be used for the educational component in deriving a human poverty measure, the HPI. The consequent narrowing from the broad coverage of the educational component in the human development index to the specific concentration on illiteracy in the human poverty index should be an appropriate move.

There is an issue of data availability and reliability which also deserves attention here. The narrowing of the education focus from a general ed-ucational index in the HDI to just illiteracy in the HPI will probably be an improvement in terms of data access and quality, since, comparatively speaking, the literacy data tend to be better than the data on enrolment at educational establishments at different levels.[1]

So far as survival is concerned, the calculation of life expectancy and that of non-survival to a specified age (such as 40 years) have to draw on the same informational base, viz. the prevailing age-specific mortality rates. The latter needs a little less, since it is independent of mortality rates beyond the specified age (40 years). However, doubts about the quality of mortality statistics that are available apply to both, and this should be taken into account in making use of the results of the HPI calculation (just as it is relevant for using the HDI results as well).

DEPRIVATION IN ECONOMIC PROVISIONS

The third component of the HDI is based on income, and concentrates on per capita national income of GNP. It is used at an aggregative level for each country, and reflects not only the average personal incomes of individuals but also the provision of public services (such as public health care) paid out of the aggregate national income. The income component of HDI is, thus, an amalgam of private and public facilities, attempting to reflect overall economic provisioning. In adapting this aspect of living standard in the measurement of poverty, the focus has to be disaggregative and oriented towards individual life experiences. In line with the general idea behind the use of the income variable in HDI (as an indicator of overall economic provisioning), the HPI must pay attention to personal affluence as well as public services.

One of the problems in assessing the prevalence of income poverty is that the use of the same cut-off poverty line in different countries can be very misleading. Adam Smith noted in the *Wealth of Nations*, as early as 1776, that, depending on the prevailing consumption patterns in the respective societies, the minimum income needed to achieve the same elementary freedom from deprivation would vary from one community to another. In Adam Smith's example, a person who cannot afford to buy a linen shirt or leather shoes in England may well be ashamed to appear in public, but the inability may not be seen as a crucial deprivation in a society where linen shirts or leather shoes are not widely worn.

This variation of "necessary" commodities between one society and another makes the use of the same poverty line in different countries (with diverse levels of general opulence and disparate consumption patterns) extremely deceptive. Depending on the prevailing patterns of observable consumption (of clothing, accommodation, means of communication and interaction such as radios, televisions, telephones, etc.), many provisions are taken to be essential for social participation in one community without being treated to be so in another. As a result, the minimum income needed to escape social estrangement can be quite different in different communities. Given the social pressure generated to fulfil these felt "needs", they may compete – for relatively poor people – even with the provision of resources for food, nutrition and health care, which can be significantly squeezed – often for the children – as a result of this socially induced influence (and a corresponding sense of cultural compulsion). This can, in fact, help to explain the observed presence of hunger and undernourishment even in societies such as the United States in which the general income levels are very high, but where inequalities generate a heavy burden of "necessity" in the direction of socially obligated consumption, often to the detriment of nutritional and health expenditure. Thus, the assessment of poverty on the basis only of the level of income, with the same cut-off point in different societies, can record little or no poverty in generally affluent societies, even when the relatively poor in these societies may lack social participation and – more starkly – may suffer even from hunger and undernourishment (because of the competing pressure of "social necessities").[2]

An alternative is to use different poverty lines in different countries. But it is not easy to decide what the appropriate variations would be and how the respective poverty lines could be estimated. The officially published national "poverty lines" cannot, obviously, serve this purpose, since those variations reflect other influences, particularly the impact of politics and pressures. The general need for a variable cut-off line of poverty is easy to appreciate, though it may be hard to find an adequate procedure for determining the appropriate values of a variable poverty line in different communities.

A more practical possibility in dealing with the component of economic deprivation in the HPI is to choose to be less ambitious and to concentrate on material deprivation in the form of hunger and undernourishment in particular, rather than on income in general. Since a very high proportion of personal income is expended on acquiring food and nourishment, this is not a tremendously severe departure for poor countries. We can either use information on the intake of food and nutrition, or go by estimates of prevailing undernourishment. The former relates more closely to personal incomes, but the latter incorporates also the influence of other variables that affect nourishment, such as metabolic rates, climatic conditions, activity patterns and epidemiological circumstances. Since our ultimate concern is with the nature of the lives that people can lead, there is a case for going straight to the prevalence of undernourishment, rather than to the intake of calories and other nutrients[3]. This is what has been done in the human poverty index, concentrating specifically on the undernutrition of children, which is easier to diagnose (by such criteria as weight for age) and on which useable data are easier to get.

So far as specifically public provisions are concerned, access to health service and to safe water have been chosen as the indicators to be used. The absence of access to health service or the unavailability of safe water can indeed be seen as a significant deprivation. Combining these two access variables with the prevalence of undernutrition, we get a fairly broad picture of the deprivation of economic provisioning – private and public – to supplement the information on survival and literacy.

These, then, are the basic informational ingredients of the HPI. It must be emphasized that there is some inescapable arbitrariness in any such choice. The choice was made on the basis of balancing considerations of relevance, on the one hand, and the availability and quality of data on the other. There are inevitable compromises here. Even though some variables could not be used because the quality of data seemed particularly bad (information on access to sanitation was a variable that was considered seriously, but could not ultimately be used given the limitations of the available data), it would be idle to pretend that even the variables that have been included have high-quality data for every country. There has been an attempt, in these selections, to strike a balance between the demands of relevance and the need for tolerably useable data, and these choices would certainly remain open to criticism and public scrutiny.

WEIGHTING AND AGGREGATION

There are two distinct problems of weighting in moving from this diverse and multidimensional informational base to a combined index of human deprivation in the form of the HPI. While two of the three components to be dealt with have clear numerical values (viz., proportion of population expected to die by the age of 40 and the proportion of illiteracy), the description of economic deprivation includes disparate elements in the form of undernourishment, lack of access to health care and lack of access to safe water.

These sub-components are, however, themselves numerically specific, and we can identify the percentage of population without access to health care (h), the percentage without safe water (w), and the percentage of children who are undernourished (n). In the absence of any clearly agreed way of discriminating between the respective importance of these three sub-components, the economic provisioning component has been chosen to be simply the mean of these three deprivations, that is the unweighted average of these three percentage deprivations: $e = (1/3) [h+w+n]$. It should be pointed out, to make the scrutiny of the implicit assumptions easier, that this procedure amounts to assuming that the three deprivations act additively and have the same relative values vis-à-vis each other throughout.

There is now the further problem of moving from this three-dimensional indication of human poverty to a numerical index of human poverty, the HPI. The three components are reflected respectively by:

(1) survival deprivation (s), given by the expected incidence of mortality by age 40 (that is, the proportion that would be expected to die before becoming 40 years old at the current age-specific mortality rates);
(2) deprivation of education and knowledge (k), given by the percentage of people who are illiterate;
(3) economic deprivation (e), given by the mean of the three sub-components already discussed.

While these three components of human poverty are all important, it is not unreasonable to assume, given their dissimilarity, that the relative impact of the deprivation of each would increase as the level of deprivation becomes sharper. For example, as we consider higher and higher percentages of people who may perish before the age of 40, this deprivation will become more and more intense per unit, compared with other deprivations. This is, of course, equivalent to assuming that as the incidence of early death diminishes (and, correspondingly, as there are more plentiful survival prospects), the relative value of this consideration will diminish.

A simple, symmetric and regular way of reflecting this requirement is through the formula:

$$H = [(1/3)s^{\alpha} + (1/3)k^{\alpha} + (1/3)e^{a}]^{1/\alpha},$$

if we choose a value of a more than 1.[4] This is in line with a general procedure we had recommended for constructing indices in earlier *Human Development Reports* (see, for example, Anand and Sen 1995 on the construction of the gender-related development index, GDI), and this general approach has indeed been used in *Human Development Reports* already (see, for example, UNDP 1995). The procedure is discussed in the accompanying technical note, which also examines the properties of this type of weighting and their implications.

TECHNICAL NOTE 1. PROPERTIES OF THE HUMAN POVERTY INDEX

This technical note states, establishes and discusses some important properties of the human poverty index. Intended as an aid to understanding the index, these properties are derived with respect to a more general definition of the human poverty index $P(\alpha)$ than that actually used in the Report. This allows the possibility that the weights on the three poverty subindices may differ, so that $P(\alpha)$ is a weighted mean of order α of P_1, P_2, and P_3.

Thus, letting $w_i > 0$ be the weight on $P_i (\geq 0)$, for $i = 1, 2, 3$, we define the generalized mean $P(\alpha)$ as

(1)
$$P(\alpha) = \left(\frac{w_1 P_1 + w_2 P_2^{\alpha} + w_3 P_3^{\alpha}}{w_1 + w_2 + w_3} \right)^{1/\alpha}$$

The weighted mean reduces to the ordinary mean of order α when $w_1 = 1$ for every i. With $w_1 = w_2 = w_3 = 1$, we have simply

(2)
$$P(\alpha) = \left[\left(\frac{1}{3} \right) P_1^{\alpha} + \left(\frac{1}{3} \right) P_2^{\alpha} + \left(\frac{1}{3} \right) P_3^{\alpha} \right]^{1/\alpha}$$

The mean order 1 ($\alpha = 1$) is the simple weighted or unweighted arithmetic mean of P_1, P_2 and P_3. Thus

$$P(1) = \frac{w_1 P_1 + w_2 P_2 + w_3 P_3}{w_1 + w_2 + w_3}$$

$$= \frac{1}{3}(P_1 + P_2 + P_3)$$

when $w_1 = 1$ for every i.

Can the human poverty index $P(\alpha)$ be interpreted as a headcount or incidence of poverty? While P_1, P_2 and P_3 are the headcount or incidence of poverty in each of three separate dimensions, $P(\alpha)$ cannot be generally thought of as the headcount ratio with respect to a poverty line (hyperplane) drawn in the product space of the tree variables. Instead, $P(\alpha)$ is an average, albeit of

order α, of the three subindices P_1, P_2 and P_3. If the incidence of poverty happened to be the *same* in every dimension, then $P(\alpha)$ would clearly be equal to this common number, since

$$\left[\frac{w_1 P(\alpha)^{\alpha} + w_2 P(\alpha)^{\alpha} + w_3 P(\alpha)^{\alpha}}{w_1 + w_2 + w_3} \right]^{1/\alpha}$$

$$= P(\alpha) = \left(\frac{w_1 P_1^{\alpha} + w_2 P_2^{\alpha} + w_3 P_3^{\alpha}}{w_1 + w_2 + w_3} \right)^{1/\alpha}$$

This observation allows us to interpret $P(\alpha)$ as the degree of overall poverty that is equivalent to having a headcount ratio of $P(\alpha)\%$ in every dimension. The first property of $P(\alpha)$ that we establish is central to understanding it as a mean of P_1, P_2, and P_3. This property is that $P(\alpha)$ always lies between the smallest and largest values of P_i for $i = 1,2,3$.

PROPOSITION 1.

$$\min\{P_1, P_2, P_3,\} \leq P(\alpha) \leq \max\{P_1, P_2, P_3,\}$$

PROOF. By definition of $P(\alpha)$, we have

(3)
$$P(\alpha)^{\alpha} = \frac{w_1}{w_1 + w_2 + w_3} P_1^{\alpha} + \frac{w_2}{w_1 + w_2 + w_3} P_2^{\alpha}$$
$$+ \frac{w_3}{w_1 + w_2 + w_3} P_3^{\alpha}$$

But for each $i = 1,2,3$,

$$\min\{P_1, P_2, P_3,\} \leq P_i \leq \max\{P_1, P_2, P_3,\}$$

Therefore, since $\alpha > 0$,

$$[\min\{P_1, P_2, P_3,\}]^{\alpha} \leq P_i^{\alpha} \leq [\max\{P_1, P_2, P_3,\}]^{\alpha}$$

Using the right-hand-side inequality for each P_i^{α} in equation 3 gives

$$P(\alpha)^{\alpha} \leq \frac{w_1 + w_2 + w_3}{w_1 + w_2 + w_3} [\max\{P_1, P_2, P_3\}]^{\alpha}$$

$$= [\max\{P_1, P_2, P_3\}]^{\alpha}$$

Similarly,

$$P(\alpha)^\alpha \geq [\min\{P_1,P_2,P_3,\}]^\alpha$$

Hence

$$[\min\{P_1,P_2,P_3,\}]^\alpha \leq P(\alpha)^\alpha \leq [\max\{P_1,P_2,P_3,\}]^\alpha$$

Since $\alpha > 0$, it follows that

$$\min\{P_1,P_2,P_3,\} \leq P(\alpha) \leq \max\{P_1,P_2,P_3\}. \quad \square$$

The generalized mean $P(\alpha)$ is constructed for values of $\alpha \geq 1$. As shown, its limiting value when $\alpha = 1$ is simply the arithmetic mean of P_1, P_2 and P_3. In proposition 7 we show that the larger α is, the larger $P(\alpha)$ will be. For expositional reasons, it is convenient to demonstrate at this stage that as α tends to infinity, the limiting value of $P(\alpha)$ is max $\{P_1, P_2, P_3\}$.

PROPOSITION 2. As $\alpha \to \infty$,

$$P(\alpha) \to \max\{P_1,P_2,P_3\}.$$

PROOF. Let P_α be the largest – or in the case of ties, one of the largest – P_α for $i = 1,2,3$. Thus

$$P_\alpha = \max\{P_1,P_2,P_3\}$$

Then from proposition 1, for any $\alpha > 0$ we have

$$(4) \qquad P(\alpha) \leq P_\alpha = \max\{P_1,P_2,P_3\}$$

Now

$$P(\alpha)^\alpha = \frac{w_1}{w_1+w_2+w_3}P_1^\alpha + \frac{w_2}{w_1+w_2+w_3}P_2^\alpha$$

$$+ \frac{w_3}{w_1+w_2+w_3}P_3^\alpha$$

$$\geq \frac{w_k}{w_1+w_2+w_3}P_k^\alpha$$

since P_k is one of P_1, P_2, P_3.

Therefore, since $\alpha > 0$.

$$P(\alpha) \geq \left(\frac{w_k}{w_1+w_2+w_3}\right)^{1/\alpha} P_k.$$

Letting $\alpha \to \infty$, $\left(\dfrac{w_k}{w_1+w_2+w_3}\right)^{1/\alpha} \to 1,$

so that $\lim\limits_{\alpha\to\infty} P(\alpha) \geq P_k.$

But from equation 4 we also have

$$\lim\limits_{\alpha\to\infty} P(\alpha) \leq P_k.$$

Hence

$$\lim\limits_{\alpha\to\infty} P(\alpha) = P_k = \max\{P_1,P_2,P_3\}. \quad \square$$

The next property of $P(\alpha)$ that we demonstrate is that the index is homogeneous of degree 1 in the subindices P_1, P_2 and P_3. In other words, if the incidence of poverty in each dimension is halved (multiplied by $\lambda > 0$), the value of the aggregate index $P(\alpha)$ will be halved (changed to λ multiplied by $P(\alpha)$).

PROPOSITION 3. $P(\alpha)$ is homogenous of degree 1 in (P_1, P_2, P_3).

PROOF. Let $\lambda > 0$ be a scalar number, and let $P(\alpha)$ be the value of the human poverty index corresponding to (P_1, P_2, P_3).

Then

$$P(\alpha) = \left(\frac{w_1 P_1^\alpha + w_2 P_2^\alpha + w_3 P_3^\alpha}{w_1+w_2+w_3}\right)^{1/\alpha}$$

The value of the human poverty index corresponding to $(\lambda P_1, \lambda P_2, \lambda P_3)$ is then given by

$$\left[\frac{w_1(\lambda P_1)^\alpha + w_2(\lambda P_2)^\alpha + w_3(\lambda P_3)^\alpha}{w_1+w_2+w_3}\right]^{1/\alpha}$$

$$= \left[\frac{\lambda^\alpha(w_1 P_1^\alpha + w_2 P_2^\alpha + w_3 P_3^\alpha)}{w_1+w_2+w_3}\right]^{1/\alpha}$$

$$= \lambda P(\alpha). \quad \square$$

The next property of $P(\alpha)$ that we derive is that $P(\alpha)$ is monotonic increasing in each P_y for $i = 1,2,3$.

PROPOSITION 4. For each $i = 1,2,3$,

$$\frac{\partial P(\alpha)}{\partial P_i} > 0.$$

PROOF. From the definition of the generalized mean $P(\alpha)$ we have

$$(w_1 + w_2 + w_3)P(\alpha)^\alpha = w_1 P_1^\alpha + w_2 P_2^\alpha + w_3 P_3^\alpha$$

Differentiating partially with respect to P_i

$$(w_1 + w_2 + w_3)\alpha P(\alpha)^{\alpha-1}\frac{\partial P(\alpha)}{\partial P_i} = w_1 \alpha_i^{\alpha-1}$$

Therefore

$$(5) \qquad \frac{\partial P(\alpha)}{\partial P_i} = \frac{w_i}{(w_1 + w_2 + w_3)}\left[\frac{P_i}{P(\alpha)}\right]^{\alpha-1}$$

$$> 0 \text{ because } w_1 > 0. \quad \square$$

In the unit weights case ($w_1 = 1$, for $i = 1,2,3$) this reduces to

$$\frac{\partial P(\alpha)}{\partial P_i} = \frac{1}{3}\left[\frac{P_i}{P(\alpha)}\right]^{\alpha-1}$$

Moreover, for $\alpha = 1$, so that $P(1)$ is simply the weighted or unweighted arithmetic mean of P_i, we have

$$\frac{\partial P(1)}{\partial P_i} = \frac{w_1}{w_1 + w_2 + w_3}$$

or

$$\frac{\partial P(1)}{\partial P_i} = \frac{1}{3}.$$

For an aggregate poverty index $P(\alpha)$ composed of distinct poverty subindices $P_1, P_2,$ and P_3, it seems clearly desirable that $P(\alpha)$ should be increasing in each P_i – in other words, that $P(\alpha)$ should be convex with respect to P_i. This is equivalent to saying that $P(\alpha)$ decreases with reductions in P_i, and at a diminishing rate. The next proposition establishes that our aggregator function $P(\alpha)$ for $\alpha > 1$ does satisfy this property.

PROPOSITION 5. For each $i = 1,2,3$,

$$\frac{\partial^2 P(\alpha)}{\partial P_i^2} > 0.$$

PROOF.

$$\frac{\partial^2 P(\alpha)}{\partial P_i^2} = \frac{\partial}{\partial P_i}\left[\frac{\partial P(\alpha)}{\partial P_i}\right]$$

$$= \frac{w_1}{w_1 + w_2 + w_3}\frac{\partial}{\partial P_i}\left\{\left[\frac{P_i}{P(\alpha)}\right]^{\alpha-1}\right\}$$

from equation 5.

Now

$$\frac{\partial}{\partial P_i}\left[\frac{P_i}{P(\alpha)}\right]^{\alpha-1}$$

$$= (\alpha-1)\left[\frac{P_i}{P(\alpha)}\right]^{\alpha-2}\frac{\partial}{\partial P_i}\left[\frac{P_i}{P(\alpha)}\right]$$

$$= (\alpha-1)\left[\frac{P_i}{P(\alpha)}\right]^{\alpha-2}\left[P(\alpha) - P_i\frac{\partial P(\alpha)}{\partial P_i}\right]/P(\alpha)^2$$

$$= (\alpha-1)\frac{P_i^{\alpha-2}}{P(\alpha)^\alpha}\left[P(\alpha) - \frac{P_i w_i P_i^{\alpha-1}}{(w_1 + w_2 + w_3)P(\alpha)^{\alpha-1}}\right]$$

substituting for $\dfrac{\partial P(\alpha)}{\partial P_i}$ from equation 5

$$= \frac{(\alpha-1)P_i^{\alpha-2}}{P(\alpha)^\alpha}\left[\frac{(w_1 + w_2 + w_3)P(\alpha)^\alpha - w_i P_i^\alpha}{(w_1 + w_2 + w_3)P(\alpha)^{\alpha-1}}\right]$$

Hence

$$\frac{\partial^2 P(\alpha)}{\partial P_i^2} = \frac{w_i P_i^{\alpha-2}(\alpha-1)}{(w_1 + w_2 + w_3)^2 P(\alpha)^{2\alpha-1}}$$

$$[(w_1 + w_2 + w_3)P(\alpha)^\alpha - w_i P_i^\alpha] > 0$$

because $\alpha > 1$ and

$$(w_1 + w_2 + w_3)P(\alpha)^\alpha - w_i P_i^\alpha = \sum_{j=i} w_j P_j^\alpha > 0. \ \square$$

The next property we consider is the effect on the aggregate index $P(\alpha)$ of increasing the weight w_i on a particular poverty subindex P_i. We expect that increasing the weight on the largest subindex, max $\{P_1, P_2, P_3\}$, will increase $P(\alpha)$, while increasing the weight on the smallest subindex, min $\{P_1, P_2, P_3\}$, will reduce $P(\alpha)$. But what would be the effect of increasing the weight on a middle P_i? The answer depends on the relationship between P_i and $P(\alpha)$.

PROPOSITION 6. For any i,

$$\frac{\partial P(\alpha)}{\partial w_i} \gtrless 0 \text{ as } P_i \gtrless P(\alpha).$$

PROOF. From the definition of $P(\alpha)$ we have

$$(w_1 + w_2 + w_3)P(\alpha)^\alpha = w_1 P_1^\alpha + w_2 P_2^\alpha + w_3 P_3^\alpha.$$

Differentiating both sides partially with respect to w_i,

$$(w_1 + w_2 + w_3)\alpha P(\alpha)^{\alpha-1}\frac{\partial P(\alpha)}{\partial w_i} + (P(\alpha)^\alpha = P_i^\alpha.$$

Therefore

$$(w_1 + w_2 + w_3)\alpha P(\alpha)^{\alpha-1}\frac{\partial P(\alpha)}{\partial w_i} = P_i^\alpha - P(\alpha)^\alpha.$$

Hence, since $\alpha > 0$,

$$\frac{\partial P(\alpha)}{\partial w_i} \gtrless 0 \text{ as } P_i^\alpha \gtrless P(\alpha)^\alpha$$

that is,

$$\text{as } P_i^\alpha \gtrless P(\alpha). \ \square$$

For $\alpha = 1$ we have

$$= \frac{\partial P(1)}{\partial w_i} = \frac{1}{(w_1 + w_2 + w_3)}[P_i - P(1)]$$

$$\gtrless 0 \text{ as } P_i \gtrless P(1).$$

The next property we consider is the effect on $P(\alpha)$ of raising the parameter value α for given values of the subindices P_i, for $i = 1,2,3$. It shows that the value of the aggregate index will be higher when a higher-order mean is formed of P_1, P_2 and P_3. In particular, a mean of order $\alpha > 1$ will result in a $P(\alpha)$ that is greater than $P(1)$, the simple arithmetic mean of P_1, P_2 and P_3.

PROPOSITION 7. For given P_1, P_2 and P_3 that are not equal, if $\alpha > \gamma > 0$, then $P(\alpha) > P(\gamma)$.

PROOF. Let $\alpha > \gamma > 0$. By definition of $P(\alpha)$ and $P(\gamma)$, we have

$$P(\alpha)^\alpha = \frac{w_1}{w_1 + w_2 + w_3}P_1^\alpha + \frac{w_2}{w_1 + w_2 + w_3}P_2^\alpha$$
$$+ \frac{w_3}{w_1 + w_2 + w_3}P_3^\alpha$$

and

$$P(\gamma)^\gamma = \frac{w_1}{w_1 + w_2 + w_3}P_1^\gamma + \frac{w_2}{w_1 + w_2 + w_3}P_2^\gamma$$
$$+ \frac{w_3}{w_1 + w_2 + w_3}P_3^\gamma.$$

Raising both sides of the second equation to the power (α/γ) (> 1 because $\alpha > \gamma > 0$.)

$$[P(\gamma)^\gamma]^{\alpha/\gamma} = \left(\frac{w_1}{w_1 + w_2 + w_3}P_1^\gamma + \frac{w_2}{w_1 + w_2 + w_3}P_2^\gamma \right.$$
$$\left. + \frac{w_3}{w_1 + w_2 + w_3}P_3^\gamma \right)^{\alpha/\gamma}$$

Now $f(x) = x^{\alpha/\gamma}$ is a strictly convex function, since

$$f'(x) = (\alpha/\gamma)x^{(\alpha/\gamma)-1}$$

and

$$f''(x) = (\alpha/\gamma)[(\alpha/\gamma) - 1]x^{(\alpha/\gamma)-2}$$
$$> 0 \text{ because } (\alpha/\gamma) > 1$$

Hence, by Jensen's inequality applied to strictly convex functions $f(\cdot)$, since P_1, P_2 and P_3, are not equal, we have the strict inequality

$$f\left(\frac{w_1}{w_1+w_2+w_3}P_1^\gamma + \frac{w_2}{w_1+w_2+w_3}P_2^\gamma + \frac{w_3}{w_1+w_2+w_3}P_3^\gamma \right)$$

$$< \frac{w_1}{w_1+w_2+w_3}f(P_1^\gamma) + \frac{w_2}{w_1+w_2+w_3}f(P_2^\gamma)$$

$$+ \frac{w_3}{w_1+w_2+w_3}f(P_3^\gamma)$$

Using the strictly convex function $f(x) = x^{\alpha/\gamma}$ gives

$$[P(\gamma)^\gamma]^{\alpha/\gamma} < \frac{w_1}{w_1+w_2+w_3}P_1^\alpha + \frac{w_2}{w_1+w_2+w_3}P_2^\alpha$$

$$+ \frac{w_3}{w_1+w_2+w_3}P_3^\alpha,$$

that is,

$$P(\gamma)^\alpha < P(\alpha)^\alpha.$$

Since $\alpha > 0$, it follows that

$$P(\gamma) < P(\alpha). \quad \square$$

Letting $\gamma = 1$, and $\alpha > 1$, we have the corollary that

$$P(\alpha) > P(1) = \frac{w_1P_1 + w_2P_2 + w_3P_3}{}\,,$$

The simple weighted arithmetic mean of P_1, P_2, and P_3.

We next investigate the "decomposability" of the human poverty index among groups within a country. Suppose the population of a country is divided into m mutually exclusive and exhaustive groups. The groups may be defined in terms of stratum (urban, rural), region (by state, province or district) or gender (male, female). Let n be the size of population group $j = 1, 2, \ldots, m$, and let n be the size of the total population of the country. Then

$$n = \sum_{j=1}^{m} n_j.$$

Let P_{1j}, P_{2j} and P_{3j} be the values of the three poverty subindices P_1, P_2 and P_3 for group j, where $j = 1, 2, \ldots, m$. Finally, let $P_j(\alpha)$ denote the mean of order α of P_{1j}, P_{2j} and P_{3j} for group j. By definition, we have

$$P_j(\alpha) = \left(\frac{w_1P_{1j}^\alpha + w_2P_{2j}^\alpha + w_3P_{3j}^\alpha}{w_1+w_2+w_3} \right)^{1/\alpha},$$

for $j = 1, 2, \ldots, m$.

What is the relationship between $P(\alpha)$ and the $P_j(\alpha)$ for $j = 1, 2, \ldots, m$? Strict decomposability of the index $P(\alpha)$ would require that $P(\alpha)$ be a population-weighted average of the $P_j(\alpha)$, the population weights being n_j/n. But strict decomposability does not generally obtain.

The relationship between the values of a given subindex for different groups (for example, P_{1j}, for $j + 1, 2, \ldots, m$) and the overall value of the subindex (for example, P_1) is straightforward enough. As the indices are simple headcounts of poverty, we have

$$\sum_{j=1}^{m} \frac{n_j}{n}P_{1j} = P_1,$$

$$\sum_{j=1}^{m} \frac{n_j}{n}P_{2j} = P_2, \text{ and}$$

$$\sum_{j=1}^{m} \frac{n_j}{n}P_{3j} = P_3$$

But when the α-averages of P_{1j}, P_{2j} and P_{3j} are formed for each j to give $P_j(\alpha)$ the population-weighted average of the $P_j(\alpha)$s exceeds $P(\alpha)$.

PROPOSITION 8. For $\alpha \geq 1$.

$$\sum_{j=1}^{m} \frac{n_j}{n} P_j(\alpha) \geq P(\alpha)$$

PROOF. For each $j = 1,2,...,m$, we have

$$\frac{n_j}{n} P_j(\alpha) = \left[\frac{\left[w_1 \left(\frac{n_j}{n} P_{1j} \right)^{\alpha} + w_2 \left(\frac{n_j}{n} P_{2j} \right)^{\alpha} + w_3 \left(\frac{n_j}{n} P_{3j} \right)^{\alpha} \right]}{w_1 + w_2 + w_3} \right]^{1/\alpha}$$

Applying Minkowski's inequality (Hardy, Littlewood and Pólya 1952, p. 30) to $(n_j/n)P_{1j}$, $(n_j/n)P_{2j}$, $(n_j/n)P_{3j}$, for $j = 1,2, \ldots, m$ yields

$$\sum_{j=1}^{m} \left[\frac{w_1 \left(\frac{n_j}{n} P_{1j} \right)^{\alpha} + w_2 \left(\frac{n_j}{n} P_{2j} \right)^{\alpha} + w_3 \left(\frac{n_j}{n} P_{3j} \right)^{\alpha}}{w_1 + w_2 + w_3} \right]^{1/\alpha}$$

$$\geq \left[\frac{w_1 \left(\sum_{j=1}^{m} \frac{n_j}{n} P_{1j} \right)^{\alpha} + w_2 \left(\sum_{j=1}^{m} \frac{n_j}{n} P_{2j} \right)^{\alpha} + w_3 \left(\sum_{j=1}^{m} \frac{n_j}{n} P_{3j} \right)^{\alpha}}{w_1 + w_2 + w_3} \right]^{1/\alpha}$$

Hence

$$\sum_{j=1}^{m} \frac{n_j}{n} P_{1j}(\alpha) \geq \left(\frac{w_1 P_1^{\alpha} + w_2 P_2^{\alpha} + w_3 P_3^{\alpha}}{w_1 + w_2 + w_3} \right)^{1/\alpha}$$

Therefore

$$\sum_{j=1}^{m} \frac{n_j}{n} P_{1j}(\alpha) \geq P(\alpha). \quad \square$$

The weak inequality in proposition 8 will be a strict inequality unless either $\alpha = 1$ or (P_{1j}, P_{2j}, P_{3j}) and (P_{1k}, P_{2k}, P_{3k}) are proportional for all j and k.

A simple example with non-proportionality of the group poverty subindices shows why decomposability (equality in proposition 8) does not obtain for $\alpha > 1$. Suppose the population is divided into two mutually exclusive and exhaustive groups $j = 1,2$ of equal size ($n_1/n = n_2/n = \frac{1}{2}$), with values of poverty subindices as follows:

$$(P_{11}, P_{21}, P_{31}) = (0.25, 0.5, 0.75)$$
and $$(P_{12}, P_{22}, P_{32}) = (0.75, 0.5, 0.25)$$

Hence

$$(P_1, P_2, P_3) = (0.5, 0.5, 0.5)$$

and obviously $P(\alpha) = 0.5$.

Now for group 1

$$P_1(\alpha) = \left[\left(\frac{1}{3} \right)(0.25)^{\alpha} + \left(\frac{1}{3} \right)(0.5)^{\alpha} + \left(\frac{1}{3} \right)(0.75)^{\alpha} \right]^{1/\alpha}$$

$$> 0.5, \text{ by proposition 7 since } \alpha > 1.$$

and for group 2

$$P_2(\alpha) = \left[\left(\frac{1}{3} \right)(0.75)^{\alpha} + \left(\frac{1}{3} \right)(0.5)^{\alpha} + \left(\frac{1}{3} \right)(0.25)^{\alpha} \right]^{1/\alpha}$$

$$> 0.5, \text{ by proposition 7 since } \alpha > 1.$$

Therefore

$$\left(\frac{1}{2} \right) P_1(\alpha) + \left(\frac{1}{2} \right) P_2(\alpha) > \left(\frac{1}{2} \right)(0.5) + \left(\frac{1}{2} \right)(0.5)$$

$$= 0.5$$
$$= P(\alpha).$$

Taking the group arithmetic means of each poverty subindex tends to reduce or leave unchanged the relative disparity among the three poverty subindices. As a result of this feature the α-average of the arithmetic means of group subindices is smaller than the arithmetic mean of α-averages of group subindices.

Finally, for a given value of α (≥ 1), we discuss the degree of substitutability between the poverty subindices P_1, P_2 and P_3 in the aggregate measure $P(\alpha)$. The elasticity of substitution between, say P_1 and P_2 along an iso-$P(\alpha)$ curve (holding P_3 constant) is defined as the percentage change in (P_1/P_2) for a unit percentage change in the slope of the tangent along this curve (projected onto P_1-P_2 space at the given value of P_3). For the index $P(\alpha)$ the elasticity of substitution is constant along each level set of $P(\alpha)$ and the same for different level sets. By proposition 3, $P(\alpha)$ is homogenous of degree 1 in (P_1, P_2, P_3), and therefore its level sets are homothetic.

PROPOSITION 9. The elasticity of substitution σ between any two subindices of $P(\alpha)$, that is, between any two of P_1, P_2 and P_3, is constant and equal to $1/(\alpha-1)$.

PROOF. Consider the elasticity of substitution between P_1 and P_2, holding P_3 constant. The slope of the tangent along an iso-$P(\alpha)$ curve in P_1-P_2 space is given by

$$x = \frac{\partial P(\alpha)}{\partial P_1} \Big/ \frac{\partial P(\alpha)}{\partial P_2}.$$

By definition, the elasticity of substitution σ between P_1 and P_2 is

$$\frac{\partial \log(P_1/P_2)}{\partial \log x}.$$

From equation 5 in proposition 4 we have

$$\frac{\partial P(\alpha)}{\partial P_1} \Big/ \frac{\partial P(\alpha)}{\partial P_2} = \frac{w_1}{w_2}\left(\frac{P_1}{P_2}\right)^{\alpha-1} = x$$

Therefore

$$\frac{P_1}{P_2}\left(\frac{w_2}{w_1}\right)^{1/(\alpha-1)} = x^{1/(\alpha-1)}$$

and

$$\log\left(\frac{P_1}{P_2}\right) = \frac{1}{\alpha-1}\log\left(\frac{w_2}{w_1}\right) + \frac{1}{\alpha-1}\log x.$$

Hence the elasticity of substitution

$$\sigma = \frac{\partial \log(P_1/P_2)}{\partial \log x} = \frac{1}{\alpha-1}. \qquad \square$$

Thus, if $\alpha = 1$, there is infinite, or perfect, substitutability between P_1 and P_2. And as $\alpha > \infty$, there is no substitutability between P_1 and P_2. As α increases from 1, the elasticity of substitution decreases monotonically from ∞ to 0. If we choose $\alpha = 1$ (the case of perfect substitutability), the aggregate index $P(\alpha)$ is the simple arithmetic mean of the three subindices P_1, P_2, P_3. As α tends to infinity, the substitutability becomes zero, and the aggregate index tends to the maximum of the three subindices, max $\{P_1, P_2, P_3\}$. In general, the elasticity of substitution between any two of the subindices, holding the other constant, is $\sigma = 1/(\alpha-1)$.

With $\alpha = 1$ and infinite substitutability, the impact on $P(\alpha)$ from a unit increase (or decrease) of any subindex is the same, irrespective of the level of deprivation in the different dimensions. This contradicts the usual assumption that as the extent of deprivation in any dimension increases (given the others) the weight on further additions to deprivation in that dimension should also increase. For this we need $\alpha > 1$. The value of α also influences, correspondingly, the relative weight to be placed on deprivation in the different dimensions. Consider, for example, $P_1 = 60\%$ and $P_2 = 30\%$ (with, say, $P_3 = 45\%$). In this case, for any α the relative impact of a unit increase in P_1 compared with a unit increase in P_2, which is given in general by $(P_1/P_2)^{\alpha-1}$, equals $2^{\alpha-1}$. With $\alpha = 1$, the relative impact is given by 1. As was remarked earlier, as α tends to infinity, P_1 becomes the only determinant of $P(\alpha)$, so that its impact is infinitely larger than that of a unit increase in P_2, which has, in this case, no impact at all.

The relative impact increases as α is raised from 1. With α = 3, the relative impact is 4, giving the dimension of doubly greater deprivation (P_1) much greater weight. The relative impact rises very fast with the raising of α, as is clear from the formula. For α = 5, the relative impact of a unit increase in P_1, is as much as 16 times that of a unit increase in P_2.

For calculating the human poverty index, α = 3 has been chosen. This gives an elasticity of substitution of 1/2 and places greater weight on those dimensions in which deprivation is larger. It does not, however, have the extremism of zero substitutability (given by α tending to infinity), nor the very high values of relative impact that are generated as α is raised (increasing the relative impact, in the case discussed above, from 4 to 16 as α grows from 3 to 5). There is an inescapable arbitrariness in the choice of α. The right way to deal with the issue is to explain clearly what is being assumed, as has been attempted here, so that public criticism of this assumption is possible.

As a matter of intellectual continuity, it should be mentioned that the value of α = 3 corresponds exactly to the weighting used to calculate the gender-related development index (GDI).

ENDNOTES

not on Econ & rather

* Editors' note: This article is reproduced from *Human Development Papers 1997*, UNDP, New York.

1. See Drèze and Sen 1995.

2. On this question of interdependence, see Sen 1992.

3. On these and related issues, see the important study of Peter Svedberg 1997. He also provides extensive comparison of the levels of nutritional deprivation respectively in Sub-Saharan Africa and in South Asia.

4. In the *Human Development Report 1997*, the HPI is constructed with an assumed value of α = 3.

REFERENCES

Anand, Sudhir. 1977. "Aspects of Poverty in Malaysia." *Review of Income and Wealth*, series 23, no. 1, March, pp. 1–16.

——. 1983. *Inequality and Poverty in Malaysia: Measurement and Decomposition.* New York: Oxford University Press.

——. 1993. "Inequality Between and Within Nations." Center for Population and Development Studies, Harvard University, Cambridge, Mass. Mimeographed.

Anand, Sudhir, and Ravallion, Martin. 1993. "Human Development in Poor Countries: On the Role of Private Incomes and Public Services." *Journal of Economic Perspectives* 7.

Anand, Sudhir and Amartya K. Sen. 1993. "Human Development Index: Methodology and Measurement." Human Development Report Office Occasional Paper 12. UNDP, New York.

——. 1995. "Gender Inequality in Human Development: Theories and Measurement." Human Development Report Office Occasional Paper 19. UNDP, New York.

Atkinson, Anthony B. 1970. "On the Measurement of Inequality." *Journal of Economic Theory* 2(3), September: 244–63.

——. 1973. "How Progressive Should Income-Tax Be?" In M. Parkin (ed.), *Essays on Modern Economics*, Longman. Reprinted in E. S. Phelps (ed.), *Economic Justice*, Penguin Education, Harmondsworth, Middlesex, pp. 386–408.

——. 1987. "On the Measurement of Poverty." *Econometrica* 55(4), July: 749–64.

Atkinson, Anthony B. and François Bourguignon. 1982. "The Comparison of Multi-Dimensional Distributions of Economic Status." *Review of Economic Studies* 49: 183–201.

Arrow, Kenneth J. 1965. *Aspects of the Theory of Risk-Bearing*. Yrjö Jahnsson Lectures. Helsinki: Yrjö Jahnsson in Säätiö.

Basu, Kaushik. 1987. "Achievements, Capabilities, and the Concept of Well-Being." *Social Choice and Welfare* 4: 69–76.

Blackorby, C. and D. Donaldson. 1978. "Measures of Relative Equality and Their Meaning in Terms of Social Welfare." *Journal of Economic Theory* 18.

——. 1984. "Ethically Significant Ordinal Indexes of Relative Inequality." *Advances in Econometrics* 3.

Desai, Meghnad J. 1991. "Human Development: Concepts and Measurement." *European Economic Review* 35: 350–57.

Diamond, Peter A. and Michael Rothschild (eds.). 1989. *Uncertainty in Economics: Readings and Exercises*. Revised edition. New York: Academic Press.

Drèze, Jean and Amartya K. Sen. 1995. *India: Economic Development and Social Opportunity*. Delhi, New York: Oxford University Press.

Foster, James E. 1984. "On Economic Poverty: A Survey of Aggregate Measures." *Advances in Econometrics* 3: 215–51.

——. 1985. "Inequality Measurement." In H. P. Young (ed.), *Fair Allocation*. Providence, RI: American Mathematical Society.

Foster, James E., Joel Greer and Erik Thorbecke. 1984. "A Class of Decomposable Poverty Measures." *Econometrica* 52(3), May: 761–65.

Graaff, J. de v. 1977. "Equity and Efficiency as Components of General Welfare." *South African Journal of Economics* 45.

Hammond, Peter J. 1975. "A Note on Extreme Inequality Aversion." *Journal of Economic Theory* 11: 465–67.

——. 1978. "Economic Welfare with Rank Order Price Weighting." *Review of Economic Studies* 45.

Hicks, J. R. 1940. "The Valuation of the Social Income." *Economica* 7.

Hardy, G. H., J. E. Littlewood and C. Pólva. 1952. *Inequalities*. Second edition. Cambridge: Cambridge University Press.

Kolm, Serge Ch. 1969. "The Optimal Production of Social Justice." In J. Margolis and H. Guitton (eds.), *Public Economics*. London: Macmillan.

Martinetti, Enrica Chiappero. 1994. "A New Approach to Evaluation of Well-Being and Poverty by Fuzzy Set Theory." *Giornale deggli Economisti e Annali di Economia,* Luglio – Settembre: 367–88.

Nussbaum, Martha C. 1988. "Nature, Function, and Capability: Aristotle on Political Distribution." *Oxford Studies in Ancient Philosophy* (supplementary volume).

Orshansky, Molly. 1965. "Counting the Poor: Another Look at the Poverty Profile." *Social Security Bulletin* 28: 3–29.

Osmani, Siddiq R. 1982. *Economic Inequality and Group Welfare*. Oxford: Clarendon Press.

Pratt, John W. 1964. "Risk Aversion in the Small and in the Large." *Econometrica* 32: 122–36.

Ravallion, Martin. 1994. *Poverty Comparisons*. Chur, Switzerland: Harwood Academic Publishers.

Roberts, K.W.S. 1980. "Price Independent Welfare Prescriptions." *Journal of Public Economics* 13.

Rothschild, Michael and Joseph E. Stiglitz. 1970. "Increasing Risk: I. A Definition." *Journal of Economic Theory* 2(3), September: 225–43.

Sen, Amartya K. 1973. *On Economic Inequality*. Oxford: Clarendon Press.

——. 1976a. "Poverty: An Ordinal Approach to Measurement." *Econometrica* 46: 219–31; reprinted in Sen 1982.

——. 1976b. "Real National Income." *Review of Economic Studies* 43; reprinted in Sen 1982.

——. 1979. "The Welfare Basis of Real Income Comparisons." *Journal of Economic Literature* 17.

——. 1982. *Choice, Welfare and Measurement*. Oxford: Blackwell; and Cambridge, Mass.: MIT Press.

——. 1983. "Poor, Relatively Speaking." *Oxford Economic Papers* 55.

——. 1985. *Commodities and Capabilities*. Amsterdam: North-Holland.

——. 1992. *Inequality Reexamined*. Oxford: Clarendon Press; and Cambridge, Mass.: Harvard University Press.

——. 1993. "Life Expectancy and Inequality: Some Conceptual Issues." In P. K. Bardhan, M. Datta-Chaudhuri and T. N. Krishnan (eds.), *Development and Change*. Bombay: Oxford University Press.

——. 1997. *On Economic Inequality,* with a new annex by James Foster and Amartya Sen. Oxford: Clarendon Press.

Stern, Nicholas H. 1977. "Welfare Weights and the Elasticity of the Marginal Valuation of Income." In M. Artis and R. Nobay (eds.), *Current Economic Problems*. Oxford: Basil Blackwell.

Svedberg. Peter. 1997. *Poverty and Undernutrition in Sub-Saharan Africa*. WIDER, Helsinki. Mimeographed.

Streeten, Paul, with Shahid J. Burki, Mahbub ul Haq, Norman Hicks, and Frances Stewart. 1981. *First Things First: Meeting Basic Human Needs in the*

Developing Countries. New York: Oxford University Press.

UNDP (United Nations Development Programme). 1990. *Human Development Report 1990.* New York: Oxford University Press.

——. 1995. *Human Development Report 1995.* New York: Oxford University Press.

——. 1996. *Human Development Report 1996.* New York: Oxford University Press.

2.9
A Technical Note: Calculating the Human Development Indices*

The diagrams here offer a clear overview of how the five human development indices used in the *Human Development Report* are constructed, highlighting both their similarities and their differences. The text on the following pages provides a detailed explanation.

HDI

	A long and healthy life	Knowledge		Decent standard of living
DIMENSION	**A long and healthy life**	**Knowledge**		**Decent standard of living**
INDICATOR	Life expectancy	Adult literacy rate	Gross enrolment ratio (GER)	GDP per capita (PPP US$)
		Adult literacy index	GER index	
DIMENSION INDICES	Life expectancy index	Education index		GDP index

Human development index (HDI)

HPI-1

	A long and healthy life	Knowledge	Decent standard of living	
DIMENSION	**A long and healthy life**	**Knowledge**	**Decent standard of living**	
INDICATOR	Probability at birth of not surviving to age 40	Adult illiteracy rate	Percentage of population not using improved water siurces	Percentage of children under five who are underweight
			Deprivation in standard of living	

Human poverty index for developing countries (HPI-1)

HPI-2

	A long and healthy life	Knowledge	Decent standard of living	Social exclusion
DIMENSION	**A long and healthy life**	**Knowledge**	**Decent standard of living**	**Social exclusion**
INDICATOR	Probability at birth of not surviving to age 60	Percentage of adults lacking functional literacy skills	Percentage of people living below the poverty line	Long-term unemployment rate

Human poverty index for selected OECD countries (HPI-2)

GDI

	A long and healthy life		Knowledge				Decent standard of living	
DIMENSION								
INDICATOR	Female life expectancy	Male life expectancy	Female adult literacy rate	Female GER	Male adult literacy rate	Male GER	Female estimated earned income	Male estimated earned income
DIMENSION INDICES	Female life expectancy index	Male life expectancy index	Female education index		Male education index		Female income index	Male income index
EQUALLY DISTRIBUTED INDICES	Equally distributed life expectancy index		Equally distributed education index				Equally distributed income index	

Gender-related development index (GDI)

GEM

	Political participation	Economic participation and decision-making		Power over economic resources
DIMENSION				
INDICATOR	Female and male shares of parliamentary seats	Female and male shares of positions as legislators, senior officials and managers	Female and male shares of professional and technical positions	Female and male estimated earned income
EQUALLY DISTRIBUTED EQUIVALENT PERCENTAGE	EDEP for parliamentary representation	EDEP for economic participation		EDEP for income

Gender empowerment measure (GEM)

The human development index (HDI)

The HDI is a summary measure of human development. It measures the average achievements in a country in three basic dimensions of human development:

• A long and healthy life, as measured by life expectancy at birth.
• Knowledge, as measured by the adult literacy rate (with two-thirds weight) and the combined primary, secondary and tertiary gross enrolment ratio (with one-third weight).
• A decent standard of living, as measured by GDP per capita (PPP US$).

Before the HDI itself is calculated, an index needs to be created for each of these dimensions. To calculate these dimension indices —the life expectancy, education and GDP indices—minimum and maximum values (goalposts) are chosen for each underlying indicator.

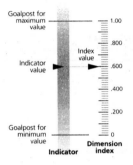

Performance in each dimension is expressed as a value between 0 and 1 by applying the following general formula:

$$\text{Dimension index} = \frac{\text{actual value} - \text{minimum value}}{\text{maximum value} - \text{minimum value}}$$

The HDI is then calculated as a simple average of the dimension indices. The box at right illustrates the calculation of the HDI for a sample country.

Goalposts for calculating the HDI

Indicator	Maximum value	Minimum value
Life expectancy at birth (years)	85	25
Adult literacy rate (%)	100	0
Combined gross enrolment ratio (%)	100	0
GDP per capita (PPP US$)	40,000	100

Calculating the HDI

This illustration of the calculation of the HDI uses data for Armenia.

1. Calculating the life expectancy index
The life expectancy index measures the relative achievement of a country in life expectancy at birth. For Armenia, with a life expectancy of 72.7 years in 1999, the life expectancy index is 0.795.

$$\text{Life expectancy index} = \frac{72.7 - 25}{85 - 25} = \textbf{0.795}$$

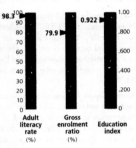

2. Calculating the education index
The education index measures a country's relative achievement in both adult literacy and combined primary, secondary and tertiary gross enrolment. First, an index for adult literacy and one for combined gross enrolment are calculated. Then these two indices are combined to create the education index, with two-thirds weight given to adult literacy and one-third weight to combined gross enrolment. For Armenia, with an adult literacy rate of 98.3% and a combined gross enrolment ratio of 79.9% in 1999, the education index is 0.922.

$$\text{Adult literacy index} = \frac{98.3 - 0}{100 - 0} = 0.983$$

$$\text{Gross enrolment index} = \frac{79.9 - 0}{100 - 0} = 0.799$$

$$\text{Education index} = 2/3 \text{ (adult literacy index)} + 1/3 \text{ (gross enrolment index)}$$
$$= 2/3 \text{ (0.983)} + 1/3 \text{ (0.799)} = \textbf{0.922}$$

3. Calculating the GDP index
The GDP index is calculated using adjusted GDP per capita (PPP US$). In the HDI income serves as a surrogate for all the dimensions of human development not reflected in a long and healthy life and in knowledge. Income is adjusted because achieving a respectable level of human development does not require unlimited income. Accordingly, the logarithm of income is used. For Armenia, with a GDP per capita of $2,215 (PPP US$) in 1998, the GDP index is 0.517.

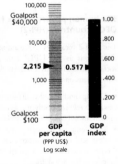

$$\text{GDP index} = \frac{\log (2,215) - \log (100)}{\log (40,000) - \log (100)} = \textbf{0.517}$$

4. Calculating the HDI
Once the dimension indices have been calculated, determining the HDI is straightforward. It is a simple average of the three dimension indices.

$$\text{HDI} = 1/3 \text{ (life expectancy index)} + 1/3 \text{ (education index)}$$
$$+ 1/3 \text{ (GDP index)}$$
$$= 1/3 \text{ (0.795)} + 1/3 \text{ (0.922)} + 1/3 \text{ (0.517)} = \textbf{0.745}$$

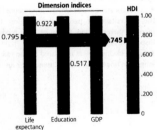

The human poverty index for developing countries (HPI-1)

While the HDI measures average achievement, the HPI-1 measures *deprivations* in the three basic dimensions of human development captured in the HDI:

• A long and healthy life—vulnerability to death at a relatively early age, as measured by the probability at birth of not surviving to age 40.
• Knowledge—exclusion from the world of reading and communications, as measured by the adult illiteracy rate.
• A decent standard of living—lack of access to overall economic provisioning, as measured by the percentage of the population not using improved water sources and the percentage of children under five who are underweight.

Calculating the HPI-1 is more straightforward than calculating the HDI. The indicators used to measure the deprivations are already normalized between 0 and 100 (because they are expressed as percentages), so there is no need to create dimension indices as for the HDI.

In this Report, because reliable data on access to health services are lacking for recent years, deprivation in a decent standard of living is measured by two rather than three indicators—the percentage of the population not using improved water sources and the percentage of children under five who are underweight. An unweighted average of the two is used as an input to the HPI-1.

The human poverty index for selected OECD countries (HPI-2)

The HPI-2 measures deprivations in the same dimensions as the HPI-1 and also captures social exclusion. Thus it reflects deprivations in four dimensions:

• A long and healthy life—vulnerability to death at a relatively early age, as measured by the probability at birth of not surviving to age 60.
• Knowledge—exclusion from the world of reading and communications, as measured by the percentage of adults (aged 16–65) lacking functional literacy skills.
• A decent standard of living—as measured by the percentage of people living below the income poverty line (50% of the median disposable household income).
• Social exclusion—as measured by the rate of long-term unemployment (12 months or more).

Calculating the HPI-1

1. Measuring deprivation in a decent standard of living
An unweighted average of two indicators is used to measure deprivation in a decent standard of living.

$$\text{Unweighted average} = 1/2 \text{ (population not using improved water sources)} + 1/2 \text{ (underweight children under five)}$$

A sample calculation: the Dominican Republic
Population not using improved water sources = 21%
Underweight children under five = 6%

$$\text{Unweighted average} = 1/2\,(21) + 1/2\,(6) = 13.5\%$$

2. Calculating the HPI-1
The formula for calculating the HPI-1 is as follows:

$$\text{HPI-1} = [1/3\,(P_1^{\alpha} + P_2^{\alpha} + P_3^{\alpha})]^{1/\alpha}$$

Where:
P_1 = Probability at birth of not surviving to age 40 (times 100)
P_2 = Adult illiteracy rate
P_3 = Unweighted average of population not using improved water sources and underweight children under age five
$\alpha = 3$

A sample calculation: the Dominican Republic
P_1 = 11.9%
P_2 = 16.8%
P_3 = 13.5%

$$\text{HPI-1} = [1/3\,(11.9^3 + 16.8^3 + 13.5^3)]^{1/3} = \textbf{14.4}$$

Calculating the HPI-2

The formula for calculating the HPI-2 is as follows:

$$\text{HPI-2} = [1/4\,(P_1^{\alpha} + P_2^{\alpha} + P_3^{\alpha} + P_4^{\alpha})]^{1/\alpha}$$

Where:
P_1 = Probability at birth of not surviving to age 60 (times 100)
P_2 = Adults lacking functional literacy skills
P_3 = Population below income poverty line (50% of median disposable household income)
P_4 = Long-term unemployment rate (lasting 12 months or more)
$\alpha = 3$

A sample calculation: Australia
P_1 = 9.1%
P_2 = 17.0%
P_3 = 2.1%
P_4 = 14.3%

$$\text{HPI-2} = [1/4\,(9.1^3 + 17.0^3 + 2.1^3 + 14.3^3)]^{1/3} = \textbf{12.9}$$

Why $\alpha = 3$ in calculating the HPI-1 and HPI-2

The value of α has an important impact on the value of the HPI. If $\alpha = 1$, the HPI is the average of its dimensions. As α rises, greater weight is given to the dimension in which there is the most deprivation. Thus as α increases towards infinity, the HPI will tend towards the value of the dimension in which deprivation is greatest (for the Dominican Republic, the example used for calculating the HPI-1, it would be 16.8%, equal to the adult illiteracy rate).

In this Report the value 3 is used to give additional but not overwhelming weight to areas of more acute deprivation. For a detailed analysis of the HPI's mathematical formulation see Sudhir Anand and Amartya Sen's "Concepts of Human Development and Poverty: A Multidimensional Perspective" and the technical note in *Human Development Report 1997* (see the list of selected readings at the end of this technical note).

The gender-related development index (GDI)

While the HDI measures average achievement, the GDI adjusts the average achievement to reflect the *inequalities* between men and women in the following dimensions:

- A long and healthy life, as measured by life expectancy at birth.
- Knowledge, as measured by the adult literacy rate and the combined primary, secondary and tertiary gross enrolment ratio.
- A decent standard of living, as measured by estimated earned income (PPP US$).

The calculation of the GDI involves three steps. First, female and male indices in each dimension are calculated according to this general formula:

$$\text{Dimension index} = \frac{\text{actual value} - \text{minimum value}}{\text{maximum value} - \text{minimum value}}$$

Second, the female and male indices in each dimension are combined in a way that penalizes differences in achievement between men and women. The resulting index, referred to as the equally distributed index, is calculated according to this general formula:

Equally distributed index
$= \{[\text{female population share (female index}^{1-\epsilon})]$
$+ [\text{male population share (male index}^{1-\epsilon})]\}^{1/1-\epsilon}$

ϵ measures the aversion to inequality. In the GDI $\epsilon = 2$. Thus the general equation becomes:

Equally distributed index
$= \{[\text{female population share (female index}^{-1})]$
$+ [\text{male population share (male index}^{-1})]\}^{-1}$

which gives the harmonic mean of the female and male indices.

Third, the GDI is calculated by combining the three equally distributed indices in an unweighted average.

Goalposts for calculating the GDI

Indicator	Maximum value	Minimum value
Female life expectancy at birth (years)	87.5	27.5
Male life expectancy at birth (years)	82.5	22.5
Adult literacy rate (%)	100	0
Combined gross enrolment ratio (%)	100	0
Estimated earned income (PPP US$)	40,000	100

Note: The maximum and minimum values (goalposts) for life expectancy are five years higher for women to take into account their longer life expectancy.

Calculating the GDI

This illustration of the calculation of the GDI uses data for Israel.

1. Calculating the equally distributed life expectancy index

The first step is to calculate separate indices for female and male achievements in life expectancy, using the general formula for dimension indices.

FEMALE
Life expectancy: 80.4 years

$$\text{Life expectancy index} = \frac{80.4 - 27.5}{87.5 - 27.5} = 0.882$$

MALE
Life expectancy: 76.6 years

$$\text{Life expectancy index} = \frac{76.6 - 22.5}{82.5 - 22.5} = 0.902$$

Next, the female and male indices are combined to create the equally distributed life expectancy index, using the general formula for equally distributed indices.

FEMALE
Population share: 0.507
Life expectancy index: 0.882

MALE
Population share: 0.493
Life expectancy index: 0.902

Equally distributed life expectancy index $= \{[0.507\ (0.882^{-1})] + [0.493\ (0.902^{-1})]\}^{-1} = \mathbf{0.891}$

2. Calculating the equally distributed education index

First, indices for the adult literacy rate and the combined primary, secondary and tertiary gross enrolment ratio are calculated separately for females and males. Calculating these indices is straightforward, since the indicators used are already normalized between 0 and 100.

FEMALE
Adult literacy rate: 93.9%
Adult literacy index: 0.939
Gross enrolment ratio: 83.5%
Gross enrolment index: 0.835

MALE
Adult literacy rate: 97.8%
Adult literacy index: 0.978
Gross enrolment ratio: 82.1%
Gross enrolment index: 0.821

Second, the education index, which gives two-thirds weight to the adult literacy index and one-third weight to the gross enrolment index, is computed separately for females and males.

Education index = 2/3 (adult literacy index) + 1/3 (gross enrolment index)

Female education index = 2/3 (0.939) + 1/3 (0.835) = 0.905

Male education index = 2/3 (0.978) + 1/3 (0.821) = 0.926

Finally, the female and male education indices are combined to create the equally distributed education index:

FEMALE
Population share: 0.507
Education index: 0.905

MALE
Population share: 0.493
Education index: 0.926

Equally distributed education index $= \{[0.507\ (0.905^{-1})] + [0.493\ (0.926^{-1})]\}^{-1} = \mathbf{0.915}$

3. Calculating the equally distributed income index

First, female and male earned income (PPP US$) are estimated (for details on this calculation see the addendum to this technical note). Then the income index is calculated for each gender. As for the HDI, income is adjusted by taking the logarithm of estimated earned income (PPP US$):

$$\text{Income index} = \frac{\log(\text{actual value}) - \log(\text{minimum value})}{\log(\text{maximum value}) - \log(\text{minimum value})}$$

FEMALE
Estimated earned income (PPP US$): 12,360

$$\text{Income index} = \frac{\log(12,360) - \log(100)}{\log(40,000) - \log(100)} = 0.804$$

MALE
Estimated earned income (PPP US$): 24,687

$$\text{Income index} = \frac{\log(24,687) - \log(100)}{\log(40,000) - \log(100)} = 0.919$$

Calculating the GDI continues on next page

Calculating the GDI (continued)

Second, the female and male income indices are combined to create the equally distributed income index:

FEMALE
Population share: 0.507
Income index: 0.804

MALE
Population share: 0.493
Income index: 0.919

$$\text{Equally distributed income index} = \{[0.507\,(0.804^{-1})] + [0.493\,(0.919^{-1})]\}^{-1} = \mathbf{0.857}$$

4. Calculating the GDI

Calculating the GDI is straightforward. It is simply the unweighted average of the three component indices—the equally distributed life expectancy index, the equally distributed education index and the equally distributed income index.

$$\text{GDI} = 1/3\ (\text{life expectancy index}) + 1/3\ (\text{education index}) + 1/3\ (\text{income index})$$
$$= 1/3\ (0.891) + 1/3\ (0.915) + 1/3\ (0.857) = \mathbf{0.888}$$

Why $\epsilon = 2$ in calculating the GDI

The value of ϵ is the size of the penalty for gender inequality. The larger the value, the more heavily a society is penalized for having inequalities.

If $\epsilon = 0$, gender inequality is not penalized (in this case the GDI would have the same value as the HDI). As ϵ increases towards infinity, more and more weight is given to the lesser achieving group.

The value 2 is used in calculating the GDI (as well as the GEM). This value places a moderate penalty on gender inequality in achievement.

For a detailed analysis of the GDI's mathematical formulation see Sudhir Anand and Amartya Sen's "Gender Inequality in Human Development: Theories and Measurement," Kalpana Bardhan and Stephan Klasen's "UNDP's Gender-Related Indices: A Critical Review" and the technical notes in *Human Development Report 1995* and *Human Development Report 1999* (see the list of selected readings at the end of this technical note).

The gender empowerment measure (GEM)

Focusing on women's opportunities rather than their capabilities, the GEM captures gender inequality in three key areas:

• Political participation and decision-making power, as measured by women's and men's percentage shares of parliamentary seats.
• Economic participation and decision-making power, as measured by two indicators—women's and men's percentage shares of positions as legislators, senior officials and managers and women's and men's percentage shares of professional and technical positions.
• Power over economic resources, as measured by women's and men's estimated earned income (PPP US$).

For each of these three dimensions, an equally distributed equivalent percentage (EDEP) is calculated, as a population-weighted average, according to the following general formula:

$$\text{EDEP} = \{[\text{female population share (female index}^{1-\epsilon})] + [\text{male population share (male index}^{1-\epsilon})]\}^{1/1-\epsilon}$$

ϵ measures the aversion to inequality. In the GEM (as in the GDI) $\epsilon = 2$, which places a moderate penalty on inequality. The formula is thus:

$$\text{EDEP} = \{[\text{female population share (female index}^{-1})] + [\text{male population share (male index}^{-1})]\}^{-1}$$

For political and economic participation and decision-making, the EDEP is then indexed by dividing it by 50. The rationale for this indexation: in an ideal society, with equal empowerment of the sexes, the GEM variables would equal 50%—that is, women's share would equal men's share for each variable.

Finally, the GEM is calculated as a simple average of the three indexed EDEPs.

Calculating the GEM

This illustration of the calculation of the GEM uses data for Singapore.

1. Calculating the EDEP for parliamentary representation

The EDEP for parliamentary representation measures the relative empowerment of women in terms of their political participation. The EDEP is calculated using the female and male shares of the population and female and male percentage shares of parliamentary seats according to the general formula.

FEMALE
Population share: 0.496
Parliamentary share: 6.5%

MALE
Population share: 0.504
Parliamentary share: 93.5%

$$\text{EDEP for parliamentary representation} = \{[0.496\,(6.5^{-1})] + [0.504\,(93.5^{-1})]\}^{-1} = 12.24$$

Then this initial EDEP is indexed to an ideal value of 50%.

$$\text{Indexed EDEP for parliamentary representation} = \frac{12.24}{50} = \mathbf{0.245}$$

2. Calculating the EDEP for economic participation

Using the general formula, an EDEP is calculated for women's and men's percentage shares of positions as legislators, senior officials and managers, and another for women's and men's percentage shares of professional and technical positions. The simple average of the two measures gives the EDEP for economic participation.

FEMALE
Population share: 0.496
Percentage share of positions as legislators, senior officials and managers: 21.5%
Percentage share of professional and technical positions: 41.7%

MALE
Population share: 0.504
Percentage share of positions as legislators, senior officials and managers: 78.5%
Percentage share of professional and technical positions: 58.3%

$$\text{EDEP for positions as legislators, senior officials and managers} = \{[0.496\,(21.5^{-1})] + [0.504\,(78.5^{-1})]\}^{-1} = 33.91$$

$$\text{Indexed EDEP for positions as legislators, senior officials and managers} = \frac{33.91}{50} = 0.678$$

$$\text{EDEP for professional and technical positions} = \{[0.496\,(41.7^{-1})] + [0.504\,(58.3^{-1})]\}^{-1} = 48.69$$

$$\text{Indexed EDEP for professional and technical positions} = \frac{48.69}{50} = 0.974$$

The two indexed EDEPs are averaged to create the EDEP for economic participation:

$$\text{EDEP for economic participation} = \frac{0.678 + 0.974}{2} = \mathbf{0.826}$$

3. Calculating the EDEP for income

Earned income (PPP US$) is estimated for women and men separately and then indexed to goalposts as for the HDI and the GDI. For the GEM, however, the income index is based on unadjusted values, not the logarithm of estimated earned income. (For details on the estimation of earned income for men and women see the addendum to this technical note.)

FEMALE
Population share: 0.496
Estimated earned income (PPP US$): 13,693

MALE
Population share: 0.504
Estimated earned income (PPP US$): 27,739

$$\text{Income index} = \frac{13,693 - 100}{40,000 - 100} = 0.341$$

$$\text{Income index} = \frac{27,739 - 100}{40,000 - 100} = 0.693$$

The female and male indices are then combined to create the equally distributed index:

$$\text{EDEP for income} = \{[0.496\,(0.341^{-1})] + [0.504\,(0.693^{-1})]\}^{-1} = \mathbf{0.458}$$

4. Calculating the GEM

Once the EDEP has been calculated for the three dimensions of the GEM, determining the GEM is straightforward. It is a simple average of the three EDEP indices.

$$\text{GEM} = \frac{0.245 + 0.826 + 0.458}{3} = \mathbf{0.509}$$

Female and male earned income

Despite the importance of having gender-disaggregated data on income, direct measures are unavailable. For this Report crude estimates of female and male earned income have therefore been derived.

Income can be seen in two ways: as a resource for consumption and as earnings by individuals. The use measure is difficult to disaggregate between men and women because they share resources within a family unit. By contrast, earnings are separable because different members of a family tend to have separate earned incomes.

The income measure used in the GDI and the GEM indicates a person's capacity to earn income. It is used in the GDI to capture the disparities between men and women in command over resources and in the GEM to capture women's economic independence. (For conceptual and methodological issues relating to this approach see Sudhir Anand and Amartya Sen's "Gender Inequality in Human Development" and, in *Human Development Report 1995*, chapter 3 and technical notes 1 and 2; see the list of selected readings at the end of this technical note.)

Female and male earned income (PPP US$) are estimated using the following data:

• Ratio of the female non-agricultural wage to the male non-agricultural wage.
• Male and female shares of the economically active population.
• Total female and male population.
• GDP per capita (PPP US$).

Key
W_f / W_m = ratio of female non-agricultural wage to male non-agricultural wage
EA_f = female share of economically active population
EA_m = male share of economically active population
S_f = female share of wage bill
Y = total GDP (PPP US$)
N_f = total female population
N_m = total male population
Y_f = estimated female earned income (PPP US$)
Y_m = estimated male earned income (PPP US$)

Note

Calculations based on data in the technical note may yield results that differ from those in the indicator tables because of rounding.

Estimating female and male earned income

This illustration of the estimation of female and male earned income uses 1999 data for Israel.

1. Calculating total GDP (PPP US$)
Total GDP (PPP US$) is calculated by multiplying the total population by GDP per capita (PPP US$).

Total population: 5,910 (thousand)
GDP per capita (PPP US$): 18,440
Total GDP (PPP US$) = 5,910 (18,440) = 108,980,400 (thousand)

2. Calculating the female share of the wage bill
Because data on wages in rural areas and in the informal sector are rare, the Report has used non-agricultural wages and assumed that the ratio of female wages to male wages in the non-agricultural sector applies to the rest of the economy. The female share of the wage bill is calculated using the ratio of the female non-agricultural wage to the male non-agricultural wage and the female and male percentage shares of the economically active population. Where data on the wage ratio are not available, a value of 75%, the unweighted average (rounded value) for countries with available data, is used.

Ratio of female to male non-agricultural wage (W_f/W_m) = 0.75
Female percentage share of economically active population (EA_f) = 40.7%
Male percentage share of economically active population (EA_m) = 59.3%

$$\text{Female share of wage bill } (S_f) = \frac{W_f/W_m (EA_f)}{[W_f/W_m (EA_f)] + EA_m} = \frac{0.75 (40.7)}{[0.75 (40.7)] + 59.3} = 0.340$$

3. Calculating female and male earned income (PPP US$)
An assumption has to be made that the female share of the wage bill is equal to the female share of GDP.

Female share of wage bill (S_f) = 0.340
Total GDP (PPP US$) ($Y$) = 108,980,400 (thousand)
Female population (N_f) = 2,995 (thousand)

$$\text{Estimated female earned income (PPP US\$) } (Y_f) = \frac{S_f(Y)}{N_f} = \frac{0.340 (108,980,400)}{2,995} = 12,372$$

Male population (N_m) = 2,915 (thousand)

$$\text{Estimated male earned income (PPP US\$) } (Y_m) = \frac{Y - S_f(Y)}{N_m} = \frac{108,980,400 - [0.340 (108,980,400)]}{2,915} = 24,675$$

Selected readings

Anand, Sudhir, and Amartya Sen. 1994. "Human Development Index: Methodology and Measurement." Occasional Paper 12. United Nations Development Programme, Human Development Report Office, New York. (HDI)

———. 1995. "Gender Inequality in Human Development: Theories and Measurement." Occasional Paper 19. United Nations Development Programme, Human Development Report Office, New York. (GDI, GEM)

———. 1997. "Concepts of Human Development and Poverty: A Multidimensional Perspective." In United Nations Development Programme, *Human Development Report 1997 Papers: Poverty and Human Development.* New York. (HPI-1, HPI-2)

Bardhan, Kalpana, and Stephan Klasen. 1999. "UNDP's Gender-Related Indices: A Critical Review." *World Development* 27(6): 985–1010. (GDI, GEM)

United Nations Development Programme. 1995. *Human Development Report 1995.* New York: Oxford University Press. Technical notes 1 and 2 and chapter 3. (GDI, GEM)

———. 1997. *Human Development Report 1997.* New York: Oxford University Press. Technical note 1 and chapter 1. (HPI-1, HPI-2)

———. 1999. *Human Development Report 1999.* New York: Oxford University Press. Technical note. (HDI)

CALCULATING THE TECHNOLOGY ACHIEVEMENT INDEX

The technology achievement index (TAI) is a composite index designed to capture the performance of countries in creating and diffusing technology and in building a human skills base. The index measures achievements in four dimensions:

- Technology creation, as measured by the number of patents granted to residents per capita and by receipts of royalties and license fees from abroad per capita.
- Diffusion of recent innovations, as measured by the number of Internet hosts per capita and the share of high- and medium-technology exports in total goods exports.
- Diffusion of old innovations, as measured by telephones (mainline and cellular) per capita and electricity consumption per capita.
- Human skills, as measured by mean years of schooling in the population aged 15 and above and the gross tertiary science enrolment ratio.

For each of the indicators in these dimensions the observed minimum and maximum values (among all countries with data) are chosen as "goalposts". Performance in each indicator is expressed as a value between 0 and 1 by applying the following general formula:

$$\text{Indicator index} = \frac{\text{actual value} - \text{observed minimum value}}{\text{observed maximum value} - \text{observed minimum value}}$$

The index for each dimension is then calculated as the simple average of the indicator indices in that dimension. The TAI, in turn, is the simple average of these four dimension indices.

Goalposts for calculating the TAI

Indicator	Observed maximum value	Observed minimum value
Patents granted to residents (per million people)	994	0
Royalties and license fees received (US$ per 1,000 people)	272.6	0
Internet hosts (per 1,000 people)	232.4	0
High- and medium-technology exports (as % of total goods exports)	80.8	0
Telephones (mainline and cellular, per 1,000 people)	901[a]	1
Electricity consumption (kilowatt-hours per capita)	6,969[a]	22
Mean years of schooling (age 15 and above)	12.0	0.8
Gross tertiary science enrolment ratio (%)	27.4	0.1

a. OECD average.

Note

Calculations based on data in the technical note may yield results that differ from those in annex table A2.1 in chapter 2 (*Human Development Report 2002*) because of rounding.

Editor's note: This chapter is taken from *Human Development Report 2002*. For the latest versions of the methodologies for constructing these indices, see the technical appendix in the most recent *Human Development Report*.

Calculating the TAI

This illustration of the calculation of the TAI uses data for New Zealand for various years in 1997–2000.

1. Calculating the technology creation index

Patents and receipts of royalties and license fees are used to approximate the level of technology creation. Indices for the two indicators are calculated according to the general formula.

$$\text{Patent index} = \frac{103 - 0}{994 - 0} = 0.104$$

$$\text{Royalty and license fee index} = \frac{13.0 - 0.0}{272.6 - 0.0} = 0.048$$

The technology creation index is the simple average of these two indices:

$$\text{Technology creation index} = \frac{0.104 + 0.048}{2} = \textbf{0.076}$$

2. Calculating the diffusion of recent innovations index

Using Internet hosts and the share of high- and medium-technology exports in total goods exports, the same formula is applied to calculate the diffusion of recent innovations index.

$$\text{Internet host index} = \frac{146.7 - 0.0}{232.4 - 0.0} = 0.631$$

$$\text{High- and medium-technology export index} = \frac{15.4 - 0.0}{80.8 - 0.0} = 0.191$$

$$\text{Diffusion of recent innovations index} = \frac{0.631 + 0.191}{2} = \textbf{0.411}$$

3. Calculating the diffusion of old innovations index

The two indicators used to represent the diffusion of old innovations are telephones (mainline and cellular) and electricity consumption per capita. For these, the indices are calculated using the logarithm of the value, and the upper goalpost is the OECD average. For a detailed discussion see annex 2.1 in *Human Development Report 2002*.

$$\text{Telephony index} = \frac{\log(720) - \log(1)}{\log(901) - \log(1)} = 0.967$$

For electricity consumption New Zealand's value is capped at 6,969, since it exceeds the goalpost.

$$\text{Electricity index} = \frac{\log(6,969) - \log(22)}{\log(6,969) - \log(22)} = 1.000$$

$$\text{Diffusion of old innovations index} = \frac{0.967 + 1.000}{2} = \textbf{0.984}$$

4. Calculating the human skills index

The human skills index is calculated according to the general formula, using mean years of schooling and the gross tertiary science enrolment ratio.

$$\text{Mean years of schooling index} = \frac{11.7 - 0.8}{12.0 - 0.8} = 0.973$$

$$\text{Gross tertiary science enrolment index} = \frac{13.1 - 0.1}{27.4 - 0.1} = 0.476$$

$$\text{Human skills index} = \frac{0.973 + 0.476}{2} = \textbf{0.725}$$

5. Calculating the technology achievement index

A simple average of the four dimension indices gives us the technology achievement index.

$$\text{TAI} = \frac{0.076 + 0.411 + 0.984 + 0.725}{4} = \textbf{0.549}$$

SECTION 3:
SOME POLICY EXPLORATIONS

N A rest of book

3.1

FINANCING
HUMAN DEVELOPMENT

Chapter 3, *Human Development Report 1991*
Based on a background paper by Gustav Ranis and Frances Stewart

The human development challenge for the 1990s is formidable. Millions in developing and industrial countries lack the most basic requirements of a decent and satisfying life – food, safe water, education, health care, adequate shelter and a clean environment.

THE COMPLEMENTARITY BETWEEN PRIVATE AND PUBLIC SPENDING

Above all, a low income frustrates people's development, for they simply do not have the means to acquire the basic goods they need. Nor in many cases do their governments offer as much support through health, education or other services as they should.

Most of what people need comes from individual or family efforts – from what they earn or from what they grow or make for themselves. This is their primary income (as distinct from secondary income received in kind from government). The size of the primary income determines what food or other essential items any household can afford. The best strategy for human development is to increase the primary incomes in a society by unleashing the creative energies of its people, its resources and its capacities, and by ensuring that these incomes benefit the majority of the population.

Strong policy action is needed for the generation and better distribution of primary incomes. Sustained and more equitable economic growth puts households in a much better position to meet their needs – as the experience of the newly industrializing East Asian economies shows. But if those in power maintain unjust patterns of land distribution, or neglect to promote employment opportunities, they will keep people poor and impede the country's entire development effort.

Governments do, of course, withdraw some of this primary income in taxes. In return, they are expected to ensure personal and national security, and provide physical infrastructure (like roads and electricity) as well as social infrastructure and services (like health clinics, schools and food subsidies). For the poorer people, government services can help make up for the inadequacy of their primary incomes. But there can be striking differences between one country and another in the amounts of money raised in taxation – and in the ways it is spent. This chapter explores the opportunities for public financing of human development. It looks closely at the proportion of each country's income spent through the government budget on social priority areas.

Before analysing the patterns and efficiency of public social spending in developing countries, however, the role of the state should be placed in a broader perspective.

First among the state's several functions that bear on human development is the responsibility for encouraging the creation of productive, remunerative, satisfying employment – including self-employment. Jobs do more than provide income and produce goods and services. They also engage people in the activities of the community, making them agents of change.

Sensible macroeconomic policies can help achieve this. The exchange rate, for example, should not be overvalued, and there should be no trade restrictions that handicap labour-intensive exports. Inflation should be controlled, and interest rates should not lead to credit rationing that excludes small borrowers. Nor should the country's distribution of assets discriminate against small entrepreneurs and their workers, stifling initiative and worsening poverty.

But even the best macroeconomic policies may fail unless they are complemented by effective *meso* policies – policies that link the macro and the micro level and that bear directly on people's lives. Chief among these are the level and structure of government social expenditures and the design of the policy measures and programmes they support (see country studies at the end of this chapter).

To play as productive a part as possible the state should:

- *Allow markets to work properly* – The small enterprises should not be stifled with excessive regulations. But regulations must be in place to ensure competition.
- *Correct for failures of the market* – discouraging activities like pollution or traffic congestion, certain types of stock exchange speculation or the consumption of goods like cigarettes or drugs or petrol. Conversely, the state should subsidize activities, such as public transport, that it wishes to encourage.
- *Create physical infrastructure* – such as roads, railways, harbours, electric power stations and telecommunications. The state is often best suited to providing infrastructure itself, but where private enterprise can provide it efficiently, and does so, policies must promote private investment.
- *Support important public goods* – including a legal framework, public parks, and defence and national security.
- *Ensure that people are at the centre of development* – investing in the formation of human capabilities, mobilizing and using people's productive and creative potential and making social security arrangements available to those who may not be able to help themselves – especially for the unemployed, the elderly and disabled or otherwise incapacitated persons.

The following discussion focuses on this last point, particularly on how public spending responds to existing priority needs with investments in people -- investments to build capabilities.

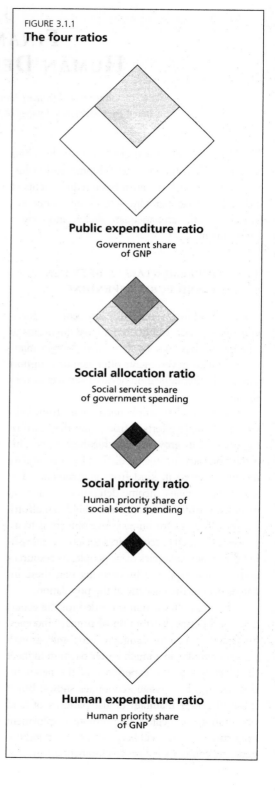

FIGURE 3.1.1
The four ratios

Public expenditure ratio
Government share
of GNP

Social allocation ratio
Social services share
of government spending

Social priority ratio
Human priority share of
social sector spending

Human expenditure ratio
Human priority share
of GNP

THE ANALYSIS OF PUBLIC SPENDING

To analyse how public spending on human development can be designed and monitored, the *Human Development Report 1991* suggests the use of four ratios (figures 3.1.1 and 3.1.2):

- *The public expenditure ratio* – the percentage of national income that goes into public expenditure.
- *The social allocation ratio* – the percentage of public expenditure earmarked for social services.
- *The social priority ratio* – the percentage of social expenditure devoted to human priority concerns.

- *The human expenditure ratio* – the percentage of national income devoted to human priority concerns.

The human expenditure ratio is the product of the first three ratios. It is a powerful operational tool that allows policy-makers who want to restructure their budgets to see existing imbalances and the available options.

If public expenditure is already high (as in many developing countries), but the social allocation ratio is low (as in Tanzania), the budget will need to be reassessed to see which areas of expenditure could be reduced (figure 3.1.2). Military spending, debt servicing and loss-making public enterprises would all be likely candidates.

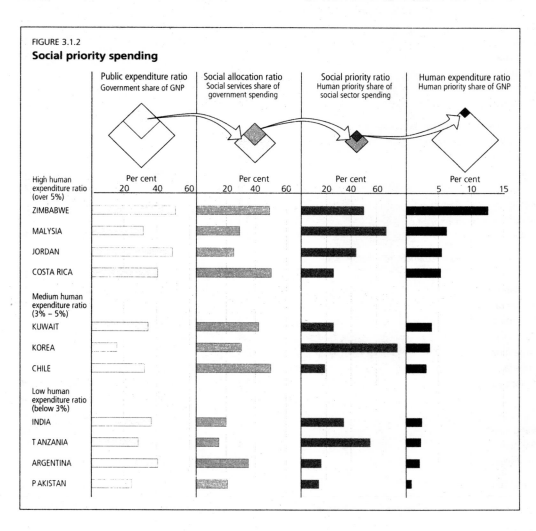

FIGURE 3.1.2
Social priority spending

If the first two ratios are high, but the ultimate human development impact, as reflected in human development indicators, is low (as in Pakistan), the social priority ratio must be increased. For the poorest countries, this is likely to involve seeking a better balance between expensive curative hospitals and preventive primary health care, between universities and primary schools, and between focusing greater attention on the cities and on the rural areas, where most poor people live.

The human expenditure ratios for 25 countries, covering 74% of the developing world, present some interesting patterns (table 3.1.1). They illustrate how it is possible to arrive at similar expenditures on social priority areas, but from very different directions.

TABLE 3.1.1
Analysis of public social spending, 1988

	Human expenditure ratio (columns 2x3x4) (%)(1)	Public expenditure ratio (%)(2)	Social allocation ratio (%)(3)	Social priority ratio (%)(4)
High levels of human expenditure – above 5%				
Zimbabwe	12.7	52	49	50
Botswana	7.7	51	37	41
Malaysia	6.3	32	29	68
Morocco	6.3	29	42	52
Jordan	5.5	50	25	44
Costa Rica	5.4	41	50	26
Medium levels of human expenditure –				
between 3% and 5%				
Singapore	4.3	35	35	35
Brazil	4.2	34	32	38
Kuwait	4.0	36	42	26
Korea	3.7	16	30	77
Mauritius	3.1	27	40	29
Chile	3.1	33	50	19
Low levels of human expenditure – below 3%				
India	2.5	37	20	34
Thailand	2.5	16	37	42
Sri Lanka	2.5	31	43	18
Philippines	2.4	21	22	53
Tanzania	2.4	29	15	55
Argentina	2.3	41	35	16
Nigeria	2.2	29	20	38
Colombia	2.1	15	40	36
China	2.1	19	24	46
Sierra Leone	1.6	13	39	31
Bangladesh	1.2	12	24	42
Pakistan	0.8	25	21	14
Indonesia	0.6	25	13	18
Weighted average	2.9	28	28	38

Note: The social priority ratio is the expenditure on primary health care and basic education as a percentage of total social sector expenditure.

Pakistan and Indonesia have a low human expenditure ratio, despite reasonable overall levels of public expenditure. The reason is that their social allocation and social priority ratios are low. The Republic of Korea, on the other hand, directs a large share of its relatively small public budget towards social priorities and has, as a result, a much better human expenditure ratio.

Even countries with a high human expenditure ratio (such as Jordan) rely on large public expenditure ratios, while others (including Malaysia and Morocco) have particularly high social priority ratios.

What probably matters more than the human expenditure ratio is human development spending per person in absolute terms (figure 3.1.3 and table 3.1.2). This helps place the ratio in its proper perspective. For instance, the Republic of Korea and Malaysia spend similar amounts on social priority concerns per person ($128), even though Malaysia's human expenditure ratio is twice that of the Republic of Korea, because the latter's GNP per capita is twice that of Malaysia. Similarly, Kuwait's human expenditure ratio is half that of Botswana, yet its absolute expenditure per person is nearly seven times that of Botswana.

Several important policy conclusions emerge from all of this:

- The human expenditure ratio may need to be around 5% if a country wishes to do well in human development.
- This can be achieved in different ways – both efficient and inefficient. A preferred option is to keep the public expenditure ratio moderate (around 25%), allocate much of this to the so-

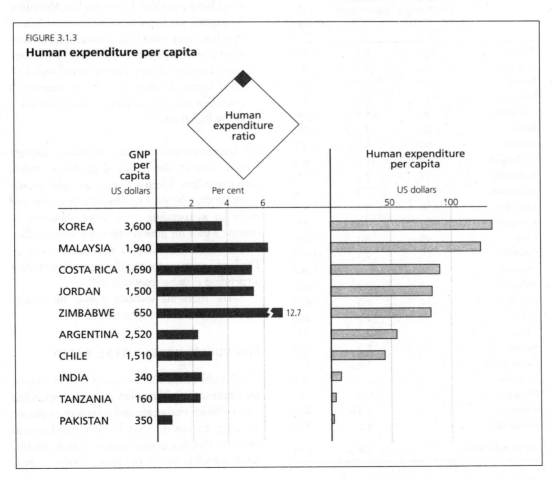

FIGURE 3.1.3

Human expenditure per capita

cial sectors (more than 40%) and focus on the social priority areas (giving them more than 50%). An inefficient option is to withdraw a large proportion of national income into the public sector, to depress private investment and initiative, and to restrict the economic growth and resource expansion that can ultimately finance human development. In several cases, total public expenditure can be cut back (that might encourage more private investment) and yet the government can spend more public money on human concerns.

- Budgetary interventions need not be extensive if GNP growth is rapid and equitable – or

if the private sector and non-governmental organizations are extremely active in social spending. Even when the funding is public, the implementation can still be private. Many governments find that the private sector and NGOs can provide social services more efficiently, and are increasingly channelling public funds through them.

- High government spending with low social priorities is the worst case. If 25% or more of national income is channelled through the government budget, and yet less than 1% of GNP goes into human priority concerns (as in Pakistan and Indonesia), this is the worst of all possible worlds. The public sector is huge, yet the majority of the population does not benefit from public social expenditure.
- Several developing countries have moved beyond basic priorities. Countries like Mauritius, Singapore, the Republic of Korea and Chile may have only a moderate human expenditure ratio when the priorities considered are basic ones. But they already have achieved high levels of human development and can therefore shift their focus to supporting social services at the higher levels.

The human expenditure ratio should increasingly become one of the principal guides to public spending policy. When resources are tight, greater attention must be paid to allocation priorities and efficiency in spending. It is wrong, however, to confuse a plea for greater efficiency with indifference to the mobilization of additional resources. The best argument for mobilizing more resources is spending existing resources well.

The following sections analyse the human expenditure ratio's components in detail.

THE PUBLIC EXPENDITURE RATIO

A high public expenditure ratio is neither a virtue nor a necessity. Public policy and public spending must facilitate, encourage and complement private spending to ensure that human development needs are met. If a government is to allow for sufficient spending on priority areas, a public expen-

TABLE 3.1.2
Human expenditure per capita, 1988

	Human expenditure per capita (US$)	Human expenditure ratio (%)	GNP per capita (US$)
Kuwait	536	4.0	13,400
Singapore	390	4.3	9,070
Korea	133	3.7	3,600
Malaysia	123	6.3	1,940
Costa Rica	92	5.4	1,690
Brazil	90	4.2	2,160
Jordan	83	5.5	1,500
Zimbabwe	83	12.7	650
Botswana	77	7.7	1,010
Argentina	57	2.3	2,520
Mauritius	56	3.1	1,800
Morocco	52	6.3	830
Chile	46	3.1	1,510
Colombia	25	2.1	1,180
Thailand	25	2.5	1,000
Philippines	15	2.4	630
Sri Lanka	10	2.5	420
India	9	2.5	340
China	7	2.1	330
Nigeria	6	2.2	290
Sierra Leone	5	1.6	300
Tanzania	4	2.4	160
Pakistan	3	0.8	350
Indonesia	3	0.6	440
Bangladesh	2	1.2	170
Weighted average	17	2.9	570

diture ratio of 20–25% is probably desirable. For a series of countries the public expenditure in 1988 varied from a high of 52% in Zimbabwe, to a low of 12% in Bangladesh.

For the few countries having reliable data – such as Argentina, India and the Philippines (table 3.1.3) – private spending often exceeds public spending. One study on the private financing of health care found that the relative significance of the private sector does not correlate with a country's GNP – richer and poorer countries alike can have heavy private involvement. In Africa, in 11 of the 15 countries covered, expenditures in the private sector exceeded those of all levels of government (table 3.1.4).

But there are questions to ask: What are the aims of public spending? Who benefits from it? Does it encourage or discourage private initiative? Does it crowd out private investment? Many developing countries spend one-quarter or more of the national income through the government budget, yet very little of this goes to human priority concerns – less than 3% of national income.

Taxation is the main source of finance for public expenditure. The possibilities for raising tax revenue will obviously vary among countries, depending, among other things, on the structure of the economy, on the stage of development and on the country's institutional capacity.

A government's expenditure can (and often does) exceed its revenues, but such "deficit financing" can lead to a very unstable economy. Bolivia in the 1980s is an extreme example: its deficit rose to 28% of GNP – leading to hyperinflation and a serious economic crisis. So, each country should aim at roughly balancing its budget and raising the taxes to do so.

TABLE 3.1.3
Private social sector expenditure as % of total, 1988

Philippines	69
India	64
Argentina	55
Mauritius	54
Ghana	53
Costa Rica	28
Jordan	26

TABLE 3.1.4
Total spending on health in Africa

Country	Year	Government share (%)			Private share (%)			
		Central and external aid	Local	Total	NGOs	Modern	Traditional	Total
Botswana	1979	62.8	10.5	73.3	7.6	11.8	7.3	26.7
Burkina Faso	1981	72.6	1.9	74.5				25.5
Burundi	1986			70.5	7.2	22.3		29.5
Cent. Afr. Rep.	1986			41.2				58.8
Ethiopia	1986			35.6	1.7	53.7	9.0	64.4
Kenya	1984	43.3	5.6	48.9	7.2		44.0	51.2
Lesotho	1986			40.6	7.5	51.9		59.4
Madagascar	1985	44.8	0.8	45.6	4.1	35.5	14.8	54.4
Mali	1985			42.4		18.8	38.8	57.6
Rwanda	1982			46.5	29.1		24.4	53.5
Somalia	1982			49.2				50.8
Swaziland	1984			32.4	12.0	17.6	38.0	67.6
Uganda	1982	15.2	4.5	19.7	4.4	22.9	53.0	80.3
Zambia	1981	43.0	0.8	43.8	7.1	33.1	16.0	56.2
Zimbabwe	1987	53.0	8.8	61.8	4.3	33.9		38.2

Source: Vogel 1990.

Taxes in developing countries typically come from three major sources: direct tax (on personal incomes or on corporations), indirect tax (usually on sales) and taxes on foreign trade.

- Personal income taxes are relatively insignificant in developing countries, generally averaging about 10% of total tax revenues (compared with around 30% in industrial countries). The main reason is the small number of people earning salaries in the formal sector. But there also are high rates of tax exemption, as well as widespread evasion. In Bangladesh, only 0.5% of the population is liable to pay personal income tax.
- Corporate tax is more important, typically contributing around 17% of total revenue. The share often exceeds 25% in countries that export oil or minerals, and in some cases 50% – as in Congo, Indonesia, Oman, Venezuela, and Trinidad and Tobago.
- Indirect taxes, predominantly on sales, are more heavily relied on in many developing countries – contributing about 28% of total tax revenue on average. And in some cases – like Cote d'Ivoire, Mauritius and Morocco – they contribute over 75%.
- Foreign trade taxes – import and export duties – typically amount to 25% of total revenue. Import duties are the single most important source of revenue in developing countries, particularly in Africa, South Asia and the Arab States.

Other, less widespread forms of taxation, such as social security contributions, are significant for some countries in Latin America (representing about 27% of revenue in Uruguay). But they are not collected at all in many other parts of the world. Wealth taxes are even less common, though they can be found in Nepal, Singapore, El Salvador and Jamaica.

The level of taxation largely determines the possibilities of government spending. But the design of the tax system is also important, since it has implications for both equity and efficiency in the economy.

Direct taxes tend to be progressive, since the rich pay a higher percentage of their income than the poor. But indirect taxes may have different distributional effects, depending on their design. If they apply to basic goods, they can be regressive, since every buyer of a loaf of bread pays the same, taking a higher proportion of a poorer person's income. In Tanzania, for example, indirect taxation is regressive since it applies to basic commodities like sugar. But in most developing countries, food and other basic items tend to be exempt, so the poor pay less sales tax than those who buy luxury goods.

The "revenue ratio" for any country is the government's total revenue from all sources expressed as a percentage of GNP (table 3.1.5). If a government wants to spend more money on human development (while still balancing its budget), it will have to raise its revenue ratio, or reallocate revenue from other parts of the budget to the social sector. The potential for doing either

TABLE 3.1.5
Total revenue as a % of GNP, 1988

High ratios	
Botswana	74.1
Gabon	47.1
Nicaragua	40.7
Oman	35.9
Brazil	34.4
Egypt	34.3
Tunisia	33.2
Zimbabwe	32.0
Panama	31.9
Chile	31.7
Low ratios	
Haiti	10.8
Paraguay	10.6
El Salvador	10.5
Guatemala	10.3
Nepal	10.3
Peru	9.0
Bangladesh	8.6
Uganda	8.2
Sierra Leone	7.3

Note: Central revenue only.

will vary greatly from one country to another, but some general observations can be made.

- *Administration* – The tax systems in most developing countries are complex and unstable. Much more revenue could be gained by simplifying the procedures, collecting all the information required and then enforcing collection. Reducing the number of exemptions, expanding the tax base and perhaps reducing tax rates would help rationalize existing systems and increase total revenues. Brazil has – in the wake of the 1988 reforms that reduced tax rebates and introduced a modest wealth tax – managed to increase its tax ratio by four percentage points. Likewise, Ghana succeeded, through a series of tax reforms aimed at both efficiency and equity, in increasing its tax ratio from 5% in 1983 to about 14% in 1989.
- *Tax handles* – These refer to administratively simple ways of collecting taxes. The opportunities for taxation are often quite limited in economies that are largely agricultural – or where production is for subsistence, or takes place in small enterprises. Taxes on mineral exports, as in diamond-producing Botswana, are usually more promising. Indeed, the countries with the highest tax ratios tend to be those with the highest share of mining in their GNP. A recent study showed that countries where tax ratios were falling tended to be those relying on indirect taxes.
- *Income* – A country's wealth and its efforts to raise taxes are not necessarily correlated. Colombia is much richer than India, for example, yet has much the same tax ratio. And while Bolivia and Zimbabwe have similar levels of GNP per head, their tax ratios are very different. This shows the untapped potential for raising public resources.
- *Economic growth* – What does matter, however, is whether the economy is expanding. Economic growth facilitates increasing revenue ratios – as happened in the 1980s in Botswana, Burkina Faso, Colombia, Indonesia, the Republic of Korea and Sierra Leone.

Burkina Faso, for example, is poor, with few minerals and little manufacturing. Yet it has managed to increase its tax ratio while reducing inflation to a very low level.

Colombia has achieved economic growth even while adjusting its economy. It has also raised its tax and public expenditure ratios. Colombia's tax system appears to be fairly progressive, based on income and property taxes and on value-added taxes that exclude basic goods.

The link between economic growth and taxes is complex, however. Both Malaysia and Morocco collected relatively less tax in the 1980s, even though their economies grew. This very fact may, however, have been critical in encouraging growth, increasing private spending and reducing (or at least holding constant) the need for public spending.

THE SOCIAL ALLOCATION RATIO

Governments also differ greatly in how much of their spending goes to social areas like nutrition, health and education. The social allocation ratio varies greatly – from 13% in Indonesia to 50% in both Costa Rica and Chile. Unfortunately, data on total government spending are not available for many countries, so that the ratios are unknown for them.

For some countries, the social allocation ratio refers only to central government spending. Regional or local authorities also contribute to social sector spending – and this can be a significant proportion for federally structured governments like India's, where 85% of expenditure on education and health comes from provincial or local governments. Similarly in Brazil, around 18% of health expenditure comes from state or local governments. Again, however, the data on local spending are not available for all countries, so the social spending figures here are incomplete in some cases. If social sector budgets were available in a consolidated form for all countries, this would permit more valid international comparisons.

"Social spending" includes that on education, health, welfare, social security, water, sanitation, housing and amenities. In many countries, particularly in Sub-Saharan Africa and South Asia, education and health make up the bulk of social expenditures. In Latin America (in Argentina, Brazil and Chile, for example) social security payments are much more significant. High social spenders devote over 40% of public expenditure to the social sector, and the low spenders, 20% or less (table 3.1.6).

A high social allocation ratio does not guarantee a good human development performance, but it does make an important contribution. Some developing countries have high social allocation ratios and social priority ratios – and have also attained high levels of human development. Almost all start from a large public expenditure ratio – one-third or more of GNP. But many of these countries could find ways to reduce the size of the public sectors and yet maintain, or even increase, their human development spending.

The trend in social spending in developing countries over recent years is disturbing. In many countries, the real expenditure per head has been declining (table 3.1.7). In five of the seven Latin American countries shown, spending was lower during 1985–87 than in 1979–81. Half the African countries saw similar falls, with Tanzania as the worst case, with its social spending falling by half during the 1980s.

Asian countries and the Arab States – probably due to economic growth – managed to raise social spending during the 1980s, though in most

cases the rate of increase was smaller than that during the 1970s.

Increasing the social allocation ratio

Financing human development usually involves switching resources from other areas of government expenditure.

But restructuring budgets can be difficult. Each government has existing commitments to fulfil and operates under political constraints. Still, it is easy to exaggerate these constraints and encourage passive attitudes towards highly undesirable spending patterns. The large changes by some countries show just what can be achieved.

The constraints tend to be less when government expenditure is rising and when aid flows can be committed in new directions. The time-scale is also important: there is much more flexibility in the medium and long term because of fewer contractual commitments.

Human development and economic growth need to be promoted together. Expenditure on economic items – including infrastructure such as roads and telecommunications – is very important for overall development. So, increasing social expenditure should not mean diverting resources from the economic sector. There may be some potential for savings in this sector, but widespread economic cut-backs could undermine the potential for growth.

But there are a number of other expenditure items where savings no doubt can be made. Defence is one of the largest components in this category – and a prime candidate for cut-backs. In many poor countries, military spending is now two to three times higher than spending on education and health.

Beyond defence spending, the other areas that have a great potential for releasing funds for more productive uses are:

- External debt
- Internal debt
- Internal policing
- Public enterprise losses

TABLE 3.1.6
Social allocation ratio, 1988

High social spending – above 40%	
Costa Rica	50
Chile	50
Zimbabwe	49
Sri Lanka	43
Kuwait	42
Morocco	42

Low social spending – 20% or less	
India	20
Nigeria	20
Tanzania	15
Indonesia	13

EXTERNAL DEBT REPAYMENTS. The burden of debt, and the reversal of net resource transfers to developing countries, constitute fundamental obstacles to human development. The latest figures for external debt repayments (1989) totalled $171 billion, a sum that claims an even larger share of the developing world's resources than the military. By the end of 1990, the highly indebted Latin

TABLE 3.1.7
Economic growth and social spending

	% change from 1973/75 to 1979/81		% change from 1979/81 to 1985/87	
	Expenditure on education and health	GNP per capita	Expenditure on education and health	GNP per capita
Latin America				
Barbados	24.6	23.3	5.2	1.4
Chile	22.8	32.8	−12.5	−7.5
Costa Rica	127.4	13.0	−32.5	−9.8
Mexico	53.8	21.9	−21.3	−6.6
Panama	5.1	14.8	19.5	4.2
Uruguay	−4.6	28.3	−24.2	−13.2
Venezuela	14.1	−0.8	−20.5	−16.8
Arab States				
Bahrain	20.7	17.8	36.5	−9.6
Egypt	7.4	41.8	5.9	−9.4
Kuwait	−17.4	−32.0	22.7	−42.9
Oman	67.7	75.9	235.8	53.2
Syria	4.8	29.8	7.0	−13.7
Tunisia	25.2	30.1	6.4	8.1
Yemen	712.4	30.8	36.0	15.9
Asia				
India	8.9	9.6	72.6	22.3
Indonesia	102.3	38.7	32.4	11.6
Iran	31.6	−23.2	−23.3	−0.3
Korea	95.2	45.1	47.7	43.7
Malaysia	28.1	31.1	26.7	12.7
Myanmar	−0.2	22.0	41.7	16.5
Nepal	45.8	4.4	58.9	5.3
Pakistan	119.9	16.2	22.2	24.2
Singapore	65.9	47.3	84.6	30.4
Sri Lanka	20.5	21.2	14.7	21.0
Thailand	68.8	30.6	38.1	21.0
Africa				
Burkina Faso	34.7	15.1	10.4	10.9
Ethiopia	−18.2	−20.5	..	..
Liberia	16.2	−17.1	−14.0	−22.3
Mauritius	87.6	23.6	−16.9	5.4
Tanzania	0.2	−2.9	−52.6	−12.1
Zimbabwe	..	..	53.4	3.4

American countries had over $423 billion in long-term loans outstanding, and they paid out almost 5% of GDP (or 24% of export receipts) in debt service (and even this did not cover all interest due). Although the total debt that African countries owed is much less (US$70 billion, or less than that of Mexico alone), the relative burden there is even more severe. The total debt of the low-income African countries is typically five times their annual export income. For ten of these countries, it is ten times that income, and scheduled debt service averages 80% of their exports.

Developing country debt doubled over the past decade, as economic growth was generally depressed and interest rates remained at historically high levels. The problem was particularly severe for commodity-dependent countries. Worsening terms of trade and the inability to increase export earnings made their debt burden worse. Attempts to obtain trade surpluses to cope with sudden increases in debt obligations failed, as the increasing supply of price-inelastic goods led to falling prices. Continued efforts to adjust failed to bring the promised results.

Most external debt in developing countries is owed by the government, because either the public sector undertook the initial loan or because it guaranteed private liabilities. The net negative resource transfers from high debt obligations and the collapse of voluntary lending have imposed a severe resource constraint on public expenditure – inhibiting policies for restructuring, investment and growth. The attempt to maintain debt service in the face of deteriorating terms of trade entailed fiscal deflation and devaluation. In the Philippines, debt service increased its share of government expenditure from around 2% in 1975 to 36% in 1988, when social services accounted for 22% of the total budget. In Kenya in 1984, debt service represented 20% of government expenditure, compared with the 23% spent on education. In Mexico, debt service is 20% of the government budget compared with 18% for the social sectors.

Clearly, there is a need for some medium-term resolution of the debt problem. The focus has recently shifted from rescheduling to debt and debt service reduction. There have been various schemes for debt conversions, debt buy-backs, special bonds, and so on. More formal schemes for debt relief, initiated by US Secretaries of State, have had disappointingly limited results. Although the Brady Plan has the laudable goal of restoring sustained growth, it is doubtful whether it will make much difference to the amount of service that debtors are paying. For example, the arrangement for Costa Rica merely cut contractual obligations to the levels of repayment that had previously been maintained.

In reality, debt relief has been considerable, as the majority of countries in Latin America and the Caribbean are in substantial arrears on their commercial debt. This situation is widely accepted as a fact of life by bankers and their shareholders as well as governments. But there still is a major haemorrhage of resources that stymies economic growth and social expenditures in developing countries.

Measures to improve the trade situation would also make an important contribution to financial viability. These measures include improving the access to industrial country markets in such areas as textiles and clothing, tropical goods and agriculture.

Further, large-scale debt relief or default – of much greater magnitude than the Brady Plan now envisages – will be essential to restore the conditions for growth and provide the resources for primary social and economic expenditures.

INTERNAL DEBT. Internal debt – money a government owes to its own citizens in its own currency – is a virtually unexplored aspect of the contemporary debt problem. Yet in some cases it exceeds the external debt – as in India, Malaysia and the Philippines (table 3.1.8).

Countries acquire this debt in several ways, including national saving schemes and selling government bonds. Internal debt may seem of less concern than external debt, since interest payments and amortization do not involve resources leaving the country – they are transfer payments from one group of citizens to another. But the problem of internal debt is still serious.

Servicing the debt takes up resources that could be used in the social or productive sectors.

In the Philippines, for example, internal debt service absorbs 23% of expenditure – while only 22% goes towards social sector spending.

Interest rates on internal debt are sometimes higher than those on external debt – as in Pakistan, Colombia and Mauritius. And it is politically very difficult (and perhaps unfair) for a government to obtain debt relief from its own citizens.

Policies to reduce the internal debt burden may therefore offer good potential for increasing social sector finance. The most direct way to reduce internal debt is through raising revenue and repaying the debt. Many countries made major improvements in their budgetary position in the 1980s – such as Botswana, Burkina Faso, Colombia and Indonesia. In each case, the improvements were made while raising government expenditure per head, by increasing taxation. Other countries have also improved their position but at the expense of government expenditure – Malaysia, Peru, Zambia and Uruguay.

Devices have been suggested for reducing the debt burden by converting it to equity or other forms of asset. Other options might be to reschedule debt or index it to reduce the current costs.

Each of these mechanisms can significantly reduce the short-term debt burden. Improving the budgetary position would do so permanently. Others, such as indexation, would offer short-term gains but only at the expense of increasing the long-term debt burden and perhaps passing the problem on to the next generation.

INTERNAL POLICING. A great deal of security expenditure in many developing countries is aimed at maintaining law and order, or policing the country's people. But quantifying this expenditure is not easy. Security spending takes diverse forms. And the budget for internal policing may be shown under various government departments – the President's Office (as in Pinochet's Chile), the Ministry of Defence (Zaire) or the Home Secretary (United Kingdom).

The sensitivity of the subject also restricts information on police numbers and expenditure. Governments often do not report the full expenditure, and estimates from other sources can vary widely. So, it is probably more useful to consider figures for overall security expenditure rather than those for civil police.

For some developing countries, there is also specific information on "public order and safety expenditures". The most striking case is that of Sri Lanka, where the proportion of government expenditure spent on police almost trebled between 1982 and 1987. In Ethiopia, the share of public resources devoted to internal policing remained at about 5% during the 1980s. In the latest Indian

TABLE 3.1.8
Domestic debt in selected countries, 1988

	Domestic debt service as a % of total government expenditure	Domestic debt service as a % of total debt service	Total debt as a % of GNP	Domestic debt as a % of total debt
Malaysia	33.7	69.9	49	70.2
Philippines	22.5	62.6	60	59.0
Chile	14.5	61.5	68	34.1
Nigeria	9.2	38.2	101	26.0
Zimbabwe	8.8	55.7	37	47.3
Côte d'Ivoire	8.2	20.7	93	12.8
Jordan	8.1	23.6	94	34.8
Pakistan	7.1	67.6	37	55.7
India	4.1	92.3	19	90.0

Source: UNDP 1990.

Plan, the budget for internal policing exceeds that for central expenditures on social services – partly a response to growing ethnic and religious strife.

Democratization at all levels could be the key to reducing expenditure on internal policing. If civil liberties are enhanced, the political functions of control and the financial demands imposed by the security forces are correspondingly reduced – and funds can be released for human development. This process could then become self-perpetuating. Progress in human development, with open and participatory systems responsive to the needs of all people (including minorities), reduces the need felt for enforced security.

PUBLIC ENTERPRISE LOSSES. Many developing countries have engaged in a range of economic activities through public enterprises. These include manufacturing, natural resource extraction, agricultural marketing and the provision of utility services.

Public enterprises consume a major part of the budgetary resources in many countries of Sub-Saharan Africa, but they are also significant elsewhere. In Uruguay, one in four workers is employed by the state – whose monopolies include insurance, ports, gambling and cement production. Sri Lanka has more than 270 public enterprises, which employ 40% of the formal sector workforce.

The record of most public enterprises is very poor, with few successful examples. Management has more often been incompetent, and the resulting losses constitute a massive drain on many national budgets. Net transfers from government to public enterprises are about 3% of GDP annually in Egypt and 2% in the Philippines. In Sri Lanka, public enterprises account for 20% of government expenditure and 62% of the budget deficit. In Cameroon, the losses have often exceeded oil revenue. In some cases, part of these losses might be justified in social terms – such as extending marketing or distribution services to poor and remote areas. But there is enormous room for improvement.

The obstacles to satisfactory performance are various. Politicians frequently interfere in the daily running of public enterprises, using them as important instruments of patronage and making many unmerited appointments to positions of power. Public enterprises have often become the employer of last resort – resulting in falling productivity and morale and a decline in real wages. Weak management and secrecy about their operations have compounded the problems. In the end, the state is usually willing to subsidize these loss-making enterprises.

An increasingly important way to deal with inefficient public enterprises has been privatization. Many developing countries find that efforts to privatize elicit protests from employees and other affected groups and look for alternative solutions. But half-hearted measures are unlikely to succeed, as shown by Argentina, Brazil, Pakistan, Poland and the USSR. Wherever bold privatization has been attempted, it has begun to yield satisfying results – after an admittedly painful transition. Wherever half-way measures have been tried, neither economic efficiency nor social justice has been achieved.

Even without privatization, certain significant reforms are possible. There is a need to match greater autonomy with improved financial reporting and greater accountability. The links with consumers could also be made more efficient – particularly through pricing policies. In many cases, the prices for telephones, energy and water are well below marginal cost. It might be thought that charging more realistic prices would hit the poor unduly, but this is not usually so. Around 90% of publicly provided electricity and water services are consumed by industry and by the better off. The poor often have to rely on more expensive alternatives, such as water delivered in trucks by private companies.

Recovering the real cost of services from those who can afford paying would generate more resources for the government (or at least reduce losses) and thus release funds for social expenditure. Prices could, in any case, be differentiated with poor groups in mind. For instance, charges should be lower for water from yard taps, which are used by the poor.

Freeing up the financial constraints would also allow for expansion of services – say, by making labour-intensive infrastructure improvements to extend services to poorer areas.

Resources are dissipated in many other ways: capital flight (box 3.1.1), corruption (box 3.1.2) and prestige projects (box 3.1.3). The examples show the wide scope for increasing social expenditures by squeezing expenditures in other sectors – or by eliminating government waste. But how much of the expenditure allocated to the social sector is actually earmarked for human priority concerns?

THE SOCIAL PRIORITY RATIO

The social priority ratio is the percentage of social expenditure directed at the priority areas. What is considered to be a priority will naturally change from one country to another, and change over time as human development proceeds. Countries

that have already achieved high standards of literacy may well regard higher education as their next priority area. Where basic standards of health have been achieved, health ministries will want to increase attention to more sophisticated kinds of curative care.

Many developing countries, however, have very low standards of public health, education and water. For them, the priority must be basic education, primary health care and the extension of basic water systems to poor areas of both cities and rural areas.

Of course, even the poorest country should have an efficient hospital system and good universities. All countries need skilled local people to teach children, to mend broken limbs, to design bridges, and to formulate economic and social policy. But countries where the illiteracy rate is be-

---

BOX 3.1.1

Capital flight

The export of capital by nationals and corporations represents a serious drain of resources from many developing countries. Estimates of the magnitude of the outflow differ enormously, in view of the inherent difficulties of measurement. But reliable sources suggest that for Mexico, Argentina and Venezuela (three of the largest Latin American debtors) an amount equivalent to at least half of the money borrowed in the last 15 years has flown out again. In the Philippines, it has been estimated that capital flight amounted to 80% of the outstanding debt between 1962 and 1986.

The wealthy benefit from such capital movements. They often incurred the original debt and then bought, at subsidized rates, dollars that they transferred abroad. Many Latin American governments later assumed these debts as a public responsibility – leaving the wealthy with tax-free dollar assets abroad, placing the burden of adjustment and fiscal austerity on the poor. If governments were pursuing sound macroeconomic policies, this would create scope for local investment and reduce the need for capital to flee.

More realistic exchange rates would also contribute – along with exchange controls, if appropri-

ate – as the Republic of Korea and Colombia reflect. But controls are no panacea, as evidenced by the failures in Mexico and France.

The problem of capital flight is exacerbated by the practices of the commercial banks in the haven countries – soliciting funds for tax-free interests and offering high interest rates.

Tax reform is also needed – in Latin America, all interest earned overseas is free of tax, while in the USA, only local residents are liable for tax – creating obvious incentives to keep tax-free accounts abroad. Ideally, the governments in haven countries should eliminate the tax exemptions enjoyed by foreign-held interest rates that intensified capital flight in the 1980s.

These proposals could help prevent future losses. But there are ways, too, of repatriating capital that has already fled. Governments can announce amnesties both on unpaid taxes and on violations of exchange controls. Above all, however, there must be stability and confidence in the economy.

Source: Lessard and Williamson 1987, Pastor 1990 and Rodriguez 1987.

yond 40% probably should not be spending the largest share of their education budgets on financing free universities.

Likewise, social security systems may not be a good use of available funds for developing countries. Social security payments tend to go to those in formal employment – not the poorest people. In Chile in 1985, for example, it was estimated that only 13% of social security payments benefited the poorest 40% of the population. Of health spending, by contrast, 64% did reach the poor.

The *Human Development Report 1991* makes the assumption that, for most developing countries, the basic services should be given priority. And calculating the social priority ratio on this basis highlights the cases where the social sector spending is badly skewed (table 3.1.9). Pakistan is one clear case. It has the lowest priority ratio in the sample. In a country where literacy rates are only 31%, the government is directing less than a third of social expenditure towards basic education.

Priorities change with the level of development. Argentina is a country that spends a significant amount on the social sector. Yet it, too, has a low social priority ratio – the share of overall social spending flowing to health and education has been falling at the expense of social security payments. In Argentina's case, however, this could be seen as a case of shifting priorities after some of the basic goals have been achieved. Human development levels are now high – the literacy rate equals 95%.

Health priorities

Primary health care for many countries would be the cheapest and quickest way to improve health standards. It costs between $100 and $600 to save each additional life through preventive health care, while the corresponding figure for curative care is between $500 and $5,000. Part of the reason: a primary health worker costs about $500 to train, a fully qualified doctor around $60,000.

BOX 3.1.2

Corruption

Corruption, the use of one's position for illegitimate private gain, is a serious problem in many countries – and a waste of time and money that could be better used elsewhere.

The Recruit scandal in Japan and the savings and loan debacle in the USA are two of the most infamous recent examples in the North. And developing countries – from Indonesia to Zaire to the Dominican Republic – have often suffered from chief executives who amass huge fortunes for themselves and their families.

But corruption generally takes place on a much smaller scale. There are often vast bureaucracies in developing countries operating extensive administrative controls. The rules and the lines of authority are frequently unclear. And they are often less constrained by legal principles than their counterparts in the North. Given the low pay of officials and the striking inequalities in income, status and wealth all around them, the temptation to supplement their incomes can be great.

Corruption is not easy to combat. Major anti-corruption drives tend to have only a limited impact – as in the USSR in the late 1980s and Nigeria in the mid-1970s.

Openness in the conduct of public business can help minimize corruption. This requires, among other things, open tendering for contracts and keeping registers of the business interests of officials. Together with an educated electorate and a free press, this approach can remove the easier opportunities and raise the deterrent of detection. But openness does not guarantee probity, as the frequency of scandals in the industrial countries attests.

This is an area in which some new thinking would be welcome. Since corruption often operates at the highest levels, involving rich and powerful elites, it can be difficult for local people to expose. There might thus be a role for an international organization that could operate along lines similar to those of Amnesty International.

Sources: Theobald 1990 and UN 1990.

Most countries spend a high proportion of their health budgets on hospitals – over 90% in Malawi and Sierra Leone and over 80% in Argentina, Bolivia, the Republic of Korea, Liberia, Panama, Tanzania, Togo and Uruguay. Many countries that spend a high proportion of their budgets on hospitals also have very high infant mortality rates (as in Liberia and Tanzania).

Things often get worse when a country is undergoing a severe economic adjustment programme. If health budgets come under pressure, primary health care is often hit hardest. It is a case of choosing priorities. One kind of health priority need not displace the other completely. The two need to be kept in balance.

Despite a low ranking in the social priority tables, Bangladesh provides an illustration of restructuring health expenditures. It inherited an urban-biased, curative health care system. Now the system, based on the primary health care concept, has an institutional network for providing health care facilities from the grassroots level upwards. This shift is reflected in the increasing share of rural health clinics in the health budget – rising from less than 10% in 1978 to 60% in 1988, implying greater access for the poor, especially in rural areas. In Malaysia, successive national governments have had the political impetus to redistribute income towards the Malays (*bumiputras*), who are generally poorer and live in rural areas. As a result, expenditures per head on education, health and pensions in Malaysia are higher in the rural areas than in the towns and cities.

Other governments have promoted low-cost, high-impact interventions. Indonesia introduced a nationwide programme of this type in the 1980s, and an estimated 85% of mothers and children now have access to preventive health facilities. This *posyandu* programme, based on meetings in private homes and village halls, concentrates on basic priorities like nutrition, immunization, diarrhoeal disease control and health education.

Chile's dramatic reduction in child mortality rates over the 1970s and 1980s was achieved

---

BOX 3.1.3

Prestige projects

There are many projects whose principal aim seems to be to enhance the prestige of national leaderships. One example is the recently constructed $250 million basilica to rival St. Peter's, in a country where only 10% of the population is even nominally of that denomination – and where 82% of people lack access to safe water. Quite apart from squandering scarce resources, such projects destroy the credibility of the government at home and abroad.

The construction of new capital cities can also be a questionable use of public resources. These capitals have sprung up from Canberra to Islamabad. There are some arguments in their favour. They help promote national unity and identity, and for newly independent nations a fresh seat of government can symbolize a break from the colonial past. But this cannot justify extravagance, which will ultimately undermine, rather than further, national solidarity.

Some prestige projects, designed in conjunction with foreign donors, can result in undertaking that are totally inappropriate and an excessive drain on local expenditure. The institute for malaria research in the Solomon Islands is one of several such projects funded by Japan in the South Pacific. The air-conditioning costs alone exceed what the government could afford.

The World Bank, too, has funded large and expensive ventures that proved technically poor and ill-designed for their intended purpose. One infamous example is the Morogoro shoe factory in Tanzania, built to produce high-quality exports. Expensive (and totally inappropriate) Italian technology was installed in what is one of the largest shoe factories in the world. At the peak of production, it operated at only 7% capacity, and the quality was so poor that the shoes were difficult to sell locally, let alone overseas.

Such projects would not get off the ground if development planning and aid programming were more participatory and if social priority needs were clearly identified.

through a series of targeted programmes, including subsidies to poor pregnant women, primary school feeding schemes and nutritional rehabilitation for severely malnourished children. This success is controversial, however. Some argue that the narrow focus on child health and nutrition was at the expense of other social measures. And while more children survived, the overall living standards of the poor fell during the same period, due to declining primary incomes.

Education priorities

Although the first priority in education should be a well-organized system of basic schooling, the primary level accounts for less than half the total education expenditure in every region. Over 100 million children worldwide receive no primary education. A further 200 million receive no education beyond the age of 12.

This is a wasted opportunity. Not only is primary education of fundamental importance in itself, it is also a good way to direct resources more specifically towards the poor, since a far greater share of the benefits of primary education accrues to those who are less well off. In Costa Rica, for example, 57% of the benefits of primary education go to the poorest 40% of the people, while only 8% go to the wealthiest 20%.

TABLE 3.1.9
Social priority ratio, 1988

High ratios	
Korea, Republic of	77
Malaysia	68
Tanzania	55
Philippines	53
Morocco	52
Zimbabwe	50
Low ratios	
Chile	19
Sri Lanka	18
Indonesia	18
Argentina	16
Pakistan	14

Source: UNDP 1990.

Basic education also brings high economic returns. In many countries, the economic returns to primary education are almost twice as high as those to higher education. Yet, throughout the developing world, a disproportionate share of spending goes to the higher levels. In francophone Africa, East Asia, Latin America and the Pacific, tertiary education receives a greater proportion of government funds than primary.

Restructuring is taking place in some countries – indeed, it is more common in education than in health. In 22 countries in Sub-Saharan Africa, the share of education budgets for primary schooling rose during the 1980s in 15 countries, fell in five and remained constant in one. In Latin America, there seem to have been clear improvements in Brazil, Chile and the Dominican Republic. In Argentina and Jamaica, the share of primary education fell as that of tertiary education rose. In Jamaica, this shift may reflect a move in the right direction – the adult literacy rate is 98%, and the combined primary and secondary school enrolment ratio is 82%. Higher education is thus the next challenge to address.

The training of scientists and engineers is important – particularly in East Asia and Latin America, where literacy rates are high. But a good deal could be gained from even limited restructuring. Reducing government expenditure on tertiary education by just 12% in the Arab States would permit a doubling of expenditure on primary schools – a critical need in a region where literacy rates are low.

Water and sanitation priorities

The inequalities evident for health and education services are matched by those for water supply. Clean water and safe sanitation, along with adequate food, are the foundations of human development. Yet the poor are badly served: around 50% of rural households, and 20% of urban ones, have no safe water supply. In some countries the disparities are much greater. In Ethiopia, people in urban areas have 14 times greater access to sanitary facilities than those in the countryside.

Around $10 billion is spent each year on water supplies in developing countries, and an estimated 80% of this goes to services for the better off. To provide safe water through stand pipes would cost only $5 per person per year. It is ironic that in many countries the wealthy receive a good service very cheaply while the poor get inadequate services at a high price.

Private sector response to social priority needs

National human development strategies work best when they seek to achieve complementarity and interaction between the public and private sectors. That has often been confirmed. But what is the response of the private sector to social priority needs?

The data on this point are patchy, but some assessments are possible.

In education, it appears that in all regions, except the Arab States, the private sector contribution is weighted towards higher education (table 3.1.10).

There are, however, wide variations among countries in the same region. Asia as a whole has relatively little private primary education, but it is significant in Bangladesh (11%) and Thailand (9%). Private secondary education in Asia shows even greater variation – from 93% in Bangladesh to 2% in Sri Lanka and zero in China and Laos. Tertiary education also varies, from 83% in the Philippines to zero in China.

Sub-Saharan Africa shows a different pattern. The private sector is much more significant in anglophone countries, where it accounts for a third of primary enrolment and almost a half of secondary enrolment. In the francophone and other countries, the figures for both levels are 8% or less.

For health, there are many well-known examples of well-equipped, private hospitals in developing countries. In Morocco, for example, 90% of the hospital beds are in private institutions.

But one also finds that large segments of the population – between 60% and 80% in some parts of Peru – are treated privately, by local, traditional healers.

The most interesting cases are probably those between these two alternatives. For example, both the Gandhigram Institute of Rural Health and Family Welfare in India and the Association of Rwandan Tradipractitioners of Bare encourage cooperation between traditional and modern health practitioners.

Other "mixed" strategies in health – of special interest in meeting basic health needs and those of the poor – encourage interaction between the public and the private sectors. Many examples could be cited of private hospitals working under contract to a ministry of health.

Another significant aspect is that private health care – particularly that of NGOs – has in some cases moved in to make up for failures of public provision. In other cases, traditional care has retained a significant role in health – notably in Uganda, Kenya and Swaziland. Elsewhere, private medicine may have been introduced to offer a higher standard of care to those who can afford it.

TABLE 3.1.10
Enrolment in private schools*, 1985
As % of total enrolment at that level

Region	Primary		Secondary		Higher	
	%	Number of countries	%	Number of countries	%	Number of countries
Asia	3.9	10	26.0	9	28.6	13
Sub-Saharan Africa	15.4	32	26.4	31	..	..
Latin America	17.7	19	29.1	19	33.6	7
Middle East and North Africa	8.8	15	8.1	17	3.3	15

* Includes schools that rely solely on private contributions and those that receive some government aid.
Source: Tan and Mingat 1989.

INTERNATIONAL AID

Aid programmes also offer great potential for restructuring – and an enormous pay-off. If only one-third of existing aid were committed to human priority areas, the aid allocation to these sectors would increase fourfold.

Aid budgets, like government expenditures, can be examined through four ratios:

- *The aid expenditure ratio* – the percentage of a donor's GNP that it gives in aid.
- *The aid social-sector ratio* – the percentage of each donor's aid that goes to the social sector.
- *The aid priority ratio* – the percentage of social sector aid committed to human priority areas.
- *The aid human expenditure ratio* – the product of the three foregoing ratios, and thus the percentage of a donor's GNP going to human priority areas in recipient countries.

The aid expenditure ratio

Most donor countries have failed to reach the internationally agreed target of 0.7% of GNP for official development assistance (ODA). While there is considerable variation among countries – Norway allocated over 1% of its GNP to aid, and the USA only 0.15% – the general trend in the 1980s has been downwards (table 3.1.11).

TABLE 3.1.11
ODA as a percentage of GNP

	1970	1980	1989
Norway	.33	.90	1.04
Sweden	.41	.85	.97
Netherlands	.60	.90	.94
Denmark	.40	.72	.94
Canada	.41	.47	.44
Australia	.59	.52	.38
Japan	.23	.27	.32
United Kingdom	.42	.43	.31
USA	.31	.24	.15
Average for industrial countries	.33	.35	.32

Source: Vogel 1990.

Despite these declining ratios, the share of ODA in net financial flows to developing countries has risen dramatically over the past decade – from about one-third to over two-thirds – largely because of the unavailability of private loans. This is particularly true for the poorest countries. Indeed, in some 40 countries, the ODA they receive exceeds 10% of their GDP.

The aid social-sector ratio

It is not possible, however, to be precise about how aid was used – particularly to estimate how much of it went to the social and productive sectors. Some aid is given to support a government's general expenditure programme. This programme aid may not be tied to any one sector, so that it can be used for defence or infrastructure or for social sectors. On the other hand, aid given specifically for the social sectors may – in theory, though rarely in practise – only substitute for funds the government would have provided anyway, and which it can now spend elsewhere.

Untied programme aid formed a rising proportion of aid flows in the 1980s, partly because of the increasing importance of structural adjustment loans. From the World Bank, adjustment lending in 1989 accounted for 18% of its IBRD commitments and 8% of its IDA funding, compared with 8% and 4% for 1980–82. Within adjustment lending, an increasing proportion – two-thirds in 1989 – has been directed towards specific sectors. But until 1989, only two such sectoral adjustment loans were for the social sectors, so the effect has been to reduce the proportion of funds specifically available for human development.

Aid social-sector ratios have also been falling in bilateral lending, as seen in the sectoral allocation of aid from western donors (accounting for over 85% of bilateral, or government-to-government aid) (table 3.1.12). For bilateral aid, the proportion for health and education together dropped from 24.5% to 17.4% between 1979 and 1989. For multilateral aid, the proportions are even lower. There are, however, considerable variations among donors: ranging from the relatively low allocations of Japan (8.4%) and Sweden (13.8%) to the higher proportions of Belgium (38%) and New Zealand (54%).

Even if the social allocation ratio is falling generally for certain recipient countries, the aid allocated to education and health can form a substantial proportion of their total social expenditure. In some cases, it exceeds the amount spent by national governments.

Much of the aid not allocated to the social sector is still important for human development – which involves both the economic and social aspects of people's lives. Support for some forms of infrastructure, say, will be of great value. Indeed, for countries already at a high level of human development, certain types of social spending may have a lower priority. Countries like Chile, Cuba and the Philippines, which already have high literacy rates, need to be spending more on higher education.

One part of non-social-sector aid that is very questionable is assistance to the military. Military assistance is an important instrument of US foreign policy. The real level of military assistance from the USA peaked during the Korean war. There has since been a major regional shift away from Asia and towards Israel, Egypt and the Gulf area. The next largest share goes to a group of countries where the USA has rights to military bases – Turkey, Greece, Portugal, Spain and the Philippines, though Pakistan was also an important recipient during the 1980s at the time of the Afghanistan war. Elsewhere, the assistance to Africa (excluding Ethiopia in the early 1970s) and Latin America (apart from El Salvador) has been relatively low. Most US military aid since 1974 has been in the form of credit sales rather than grants. But the loans have largely been forgiven (as at various times for Israel, Egypt, Turkey and Pakistan).

The aid priority ratio

The proportion of social sector aid allocated to priority areas (such as primary health care, basic education, family planning and rural water supply) has been small. The aid priority ratio is only about 36.6% (figures 3.1.4 and 3.1.5 and table 3.1.13) – despite repeated pronouncements from the international community about the importance of basic education and health care and rural services. Italy has a particularly low ratio, and those for France, Australia and Canada are not much higher. The Nordic countries and Switzerland have the highest aid priority ratios.

The aid priority ratio in table 3.1.13 is based on the Credit Reporting System (CRS) database of the OECD. But its coverage – approximately 70% of total bilateral ODA – is notably incomplete in the cases of some large donors, like France, Germany and the United Kingdom. Rough assumptions have been made about the sectoral distribution of bilateral grants. It must be noted, however, that actual figures are only approximations and need to be carefully checked: what matters is the method of this analysis.

Education received only 11% of all bilateral aid during the 1980s. Flows to primary education were limited, and declined in real terms for middle- and low-income countries.

TABLE 3.1.12
Allocation of aid by sector

	Bilateral*		Multilateral
	1979	1989	1988
Health and population	8.0	6.7	7.8
Education	16.5	10.7	4.3
Total social and administrative infrastructure including planning and public administration	30.8	25.7	19.9
Agriculture	17.9	11.3	23.2
Other	51.3	63.0	56.9
Total	100.0	100.0	100.0

* OECD/DAC, accounting for 85% of total bilateral aid.

Educational assistance to Sub-Saharan Africa in the early 1980s, for example, was heavily skewed towards higher education. This bias is reflected in the allocations per student – $1.10 per primary pupil, $11 per secondary pupil and $575 per university student – though the discrepancy arises, to some extent, because higher education is more expensive.

Social sector aid is skewed in this way when donors prefer their contributions to be more visible – the city hospital rather than the rural clinic. But even when there is a real desire to promote primary programmes, it can be very difficult to channel funds to small-scale, highly dispersed local initiatives

and to ensure that they are replicable. It certainly is possible, however – as with the success in promoting primary health care in Senegal (box 3.1.4).

Social sector aid that has a high priority ratio will tend to direct resources more towards the poor. But it is also possible to have much the same effect in economic sectors by supporting poverty-oriented projects.

Aid directed towards small-scale agriculture and industry, for example, can improve the incomes of the poor. Indeed, the evidence shows that poverty-oriented projects have a high rate of return and that attempts to reach the poor do not undermine economic efficiency.

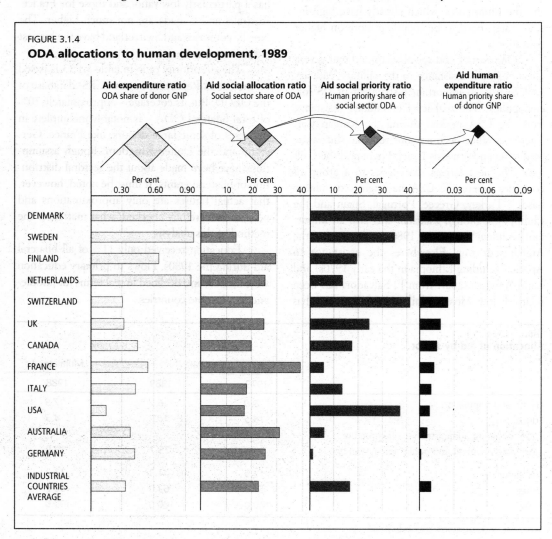

FIGURE 3.1.4

ODA allocations to human development, 1989

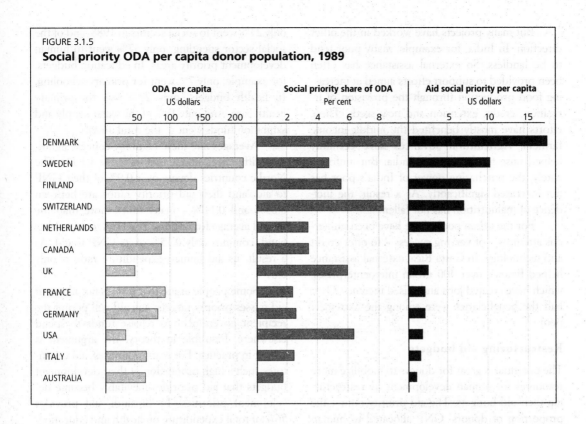

FIGURE 3.1.5
Social priority ODA per capita donor population, 1989

	ODA per capita US dollars	Social priority share of ODA Per cent	Aid social priority per capita US dollars
DENMARK			
SWEDEN			
FINLAND			
SWITZERLAND			
NETHERLANDS			
CANADA			
UK			
FRANCE			
GERMANY			
USA			
ITALY			
AUSTRALIA			

TABLE 3.1.13
Analysis of ODA social spending, 1989

	Aid human expenditure ratio (%)	Aid expenditure ratio (%)	Aid social allocation ratio (%)	Aid social priority ratio (%)
Average	0.026	0.32	22.6	36.6
Netherlands	0.128	0.94	25.2	53.8
Denmark	0.110	0.94	22.4	52.2
Sweden	0.070	0.97	13.8	51.9
France	0.053	0.54	39.1	25.1
Finland	0.051	0.63	29.3	27.4
Switzerland	0.047	0.30	20.1	78.7
Germany*	0.047	0.41	25.6	44.4
Australia	0.029	0.38	30.7	25.2
United Kingdom	0.028	0.31	24.8	36.6
Canada	0.023	0.44	19.9	25.9
Italy	0.017	0.42	18.0	22.4
USA	0.012	0.15	17.1	46.1

Note: Column 1 is the percentage of a donor's GNP allocated to priority sectors (primary health care and basic education) in recipient countries through ODA. It is calculated as columns 2 x 3 x 4.
* Excluding the former German Democratic Republic.

But many projects have worked in the other direction. In India, for example, many poor tend to be landless. So external assistance has often been provided to support efforts aimed at increasing food production through the provision of irrigation, credit, extension and new seeds. These efforts have mostly benefited the middle-income farmers. Agricultural advances have certainly helped raise food output in India. But, unfortunately, the purchasing power of India's poor has not increased significantly. As a result, the incidence of malnutrition has not fallen.

For the urban poor, there have been numerous attempts – of varying success – to offer credit and technology. In Costa Rica, external assistance helped finance over 400 urban microenterprises, which have created jobs and raised incomes. Over half the beneficiaries were among the extremely poor.

Restructuring aid budgets

The potential is great for donors to mobilize more resources for human development by restructuring their aid budgets. The aid priority ratio – the proportion of donors' GNP allocated to human priority concerns – is extremely low. For OECD donors as a whole, it is only 0.026% of their combined GNP.

The arithmetic is simple. Official development assistance (ODA) for all countries currently represents 0.32% of their combined GNP. Of this,

only 23% went to social sectors in 1988, and of the social sector spending, only 37% went to human development priority areas. In education budgets, for example, only 7% went for primary schooling. In health budgets, only 27% was for primary health care. And only 19% of the water supply and sanitation funds went to the rural areas.

Averages like these naturally conceal significant differences among donors (table 3.1.11). The Nordic countries devote over 0.9% of their GNP to aid, and their aid priority ratios are between 0.05% and 0.11% – many times more than the overall average for donors. The USA, on the other hand, commits only 0.15% of its GNP to aid. As a result, its aid human expenditure ratio is only 0.01%.

Some people argue that it does not matter if aid misses priority targets: any aid will permit the recipient government to release funds to spend elsewhere. Plausible in theory, the argument is wrong in practice. For many countries, aid constitutes such a high proportion of their development budgets that aid priorities inevitably become development priorities. In Burundi, aid provides 56% of total expenditure on health and education. The proportion of total expenditure is also high in Chad (53%), Uganda (48%), Somalia (38%) and Ethiopia (35%).

Finance ministers of developing countries are, in any case, unlikely to respond well to such arguments. They are reluctant in the best of times

---

BOX 3.1.4

Assistance for community health care in Senegal

The Pekine project, a successful primary health programme in Senegal, was initiated with external assistance in 1975 to provide health care to a poor part of Dakar, the capital.

By 1985, the project had 24 health posts, with two higher level health centres, seven maternity units and two dental units. The emphasis in the 800,000 medical visits during that period was on preventive medicine; the local rate of immunization rose from 5% to 60%. But cures were also offered for fairly straightforward conditions.

Participation was important. The beneficiaries were consulted on the programme from the beginning, and local health committees were established to control and administer the health posts. Training local staff was a high priority.

Central funding, including external assistance, was reduced over time and locally raised funds covered an increasing portion of costs – part of which came from small user charges. By 1983, local funds financed 70% of the recurrent costs.

Source: Bobiash 1988.

to undertake social expenditures – which offer little immediate financial return and demand recurring expenditure long into the future. Ministers will hardly be encouraged to increase social spending if donors, too, are reluctant to finance recurring expenditure – and prefer instead to give money for capital-intensive schemes that happen to require machinery and technical assistance from the same donor countries.

Of all the categories of development aid, technical assistance must be the ripest for reassessment. Africa receives $6 billion in technical assistance each year, and this figure keeps rising. Yet Africa still has some of the lowest levels of human development in the world.

The problem is that too much is being spent on the salaries of expensive foreign experts and too little on building up local institutions and expertise. Shifting the main focus of technical assistance to building up national capacity would not only reduce the cost of assistance. It would also release millions of dollars that could be put to more productive purposes.

Donor countries must thus reassess their aid priorities and commit themselves to the support of human development. If recipient countries adopt the same priorities, the way will be open to a new and productive era for official development assistance – one based on a mutual commitment to human development.

A restructuring of aid budgets will require much better disclosure and publication of information. The OECD Development Assistance Committee (DAC) could make a valuable contribution here. It could analyse the effects of existing aid priorities on the human development levels of recipient countries. It could also help by regularly publishing aid social allocation ratios and aid priority ratios for each donor.

ANNEX

Summary of county studies

Republic of Korea
Primary income distribution: Good
Human expenditure ratio: Medium
Public expenditure ratio: Low

Social allocation ratio: Medium
Social priority ratio: High

The main force behind human development in the Republic of Korea has been the rapid, widespread expansion of primary incomes, through economic growth. Land reform in 1949 laid the foundation for broad access to the country's most productive asset. There also was an emphasis on education, especially primary education, to develop the human resources needed for growth with equity. And macroeconomic policy encouraged the shift from import substitution to employment-intensive production for export.

But the experience has shown that high growth rates alone are not enough to ensure human development. Since 1976, the government has extended medical insurance to cover more than half the population and developed high-quality public health and education systems. It also provides free, or heavily subsidized, medical care to poor families – especially to mothers and children.

Human development thus started with the government's promotion of primary incomes. But now the government also directs a significant proportion of public resources towards the social sector, especially to social priority areas.

Zimbabwe
Primary income distribution: Poor/Moderate
Human expenditure ratio: High
Public expenditure ratio: High
Social allocation ratio: High
Social priority ratio: High

Zimbabwe illustrates the power of a high human expenditure ratio. The government's commitment to priority areas has resulted in human expenditures per person greater than those of wealthier countries – and accounts for the country's impressive achievements in literacy, child mortality and life expectancy.

After independence, the social allocation ratio rose from under 20% in 1978 to nearly 30% in 1981 and 49% today; the public expenditure ratio remained high but constant. Defence and administration spending dropped correspondingly, from 44% to 28%.

The social priority ratio rose as health expenditure shifted from urban hospitals to preventive rural services. Enormous progress was also made in education, where the share of the budget allocated to primary schooling rose from 38% to 56%, doubling the real expenditure per head. All primary school age children are now attending school, and for the secondary schooling, the gross enrolment ratio has risen to 51%.

Even in the 1980s, during periods of economic adjustment and severe drought, the falling infant mortality rates and rising school enrolment ratios showed how human development continued to progress.

Zimbabwe also shows what properly structured foreign aid can do. Aid financed almost a fifth of the budget for immunization in 1983. Aid also played a major role in financing the Child Supplementary Feeding Programme, from its inception in 1981. The contribution of aid to rural water supply rose from 32% in 1983 to 58% in 1985.

Tanzania

Primary income distribution: Moderate
Human expenditure ratio: Low
Public expenditure ratio: Medium
Social allocation ratio: Low
Social priority ratio: High

Tanzania's impressive progress in human development over the past three decades is reflected in increasing literacy (from less than 30% to an estimated 52%) and life expectancy (from 41 to 54 years). Although income per head, at $160, is less than half the regional average, Tanzania's performance in human development – as reflected in child mortality and nutritional status – compares favourably with its neighbours in Africa.

These achievements are the outcome of a philosophy to provide basic social services to the entire population. Tanzania has one of the oldest national health care systems in Sub-Saharan Africa. Since the late 1960s the rural population

has been organized in registered village settlements, facilitating the extension of basic social services. Over 80% of the population has access to health care, and almost 90% of the one-year-olds are immunized.

Even so, significant deprivation persists. Half the population lacks access to safe water, and nearly half the children do not attend primary school. Primary school enrolment dropped in the second half of the 1980s. Secondary enrolment rates are less than 5%.

Despite a high priority for primary education and health care, the country's human expenditure per person was only $3.80 in 1988. Reasons for this paltry spending are low income per head and the inadequate attention to social sector expenditures.

Budget strains since the mid-1970s have resulted in severe cut-backs, including basic social services. Health expenditures per person have declined by one-quarter over the period. These cutbacks have led to decreasing quality, and reduced access for the poor, who cannot afford to purchase those services.

The need to restructure public expenditures is urgent. Tanzania's social allocation ratio is only 15%, while debt servicing, public enterprises and military expenditures drain the government budget.

Human development is hampered by high rates of population growth (averaging 3.4% annually between 1960 and 1990) and poor economic performance. The restoration of growth and expanding income-earning opportunities, together with restructuring public expenditures towards the social sectors, are crucial factors in improving human development in Tanzania.

Costa Rica

Primary income distribution: Moderate
Human expenditure ratio: Medium
Public expenditure ratio: High
Social allocation ratio: High
Social priority ratio: Medium

Costa Rica has an outstanding record of human development. With high public expenditure and social allocation ratios, it has attained human development indicators close to those of Europe.

The basis for the social reforms was laid in the 1940s, when the Army was abolished and "autonomous institutions" were created for health, education and social insurance. A long history of democracy reinforced the pressure for welfare policies, underpinned by a rapid expansion in the export of cash crops, like coffee, which helped generate income-earning opportunities.

Primary health care was emphasized from the early-1970s, through programmes of rural health and community health. Both stressed preventive action (especially against infectious and parasitic diseases) as well as community participation.

In education, the proportion of girls completing primary school rose from 17% in 1960 to 65% in 1980. The high percentage of educated mothers helped bring down infant mortality – which in turn contributed to a decline in the desired family size and the fertility rate.

The social security system in Costa Rica is universal, whereas elsewhere in Latin America it tends to be regressive, benefiting only those in formal employment. By 1980, almost all Costa Ricans were covered be a combination of pensions, health insurance, social welfare and public health. The moderate social priority ratio does not include the contribution of social security payments (in this case positive).

Eventually, however, the country's income started to lag behind its social spending. The growing deficits were financed by both domestic and foreign debt, and when foreign assistance dried up in the 1980s, Costa Rica suffered a serious recession.

But Costa Rica's human development achievements have proved resilient even in these adverse conditions. Once women know about family planning and have been educated in hygiene and nutrition, such gains are not quickly lost. Infant mortality rates and malnutrition have continued to fall (although at a declining rate) as economic conditions have worsened.

There have been some warning signs, such as a disturbing drop in primary school enrolment in the 1980s. But Costa Rica remains an outstanding example of human development in Latin America – and the world.

Jordan
Primary income distribution: Moderate
Human expenditure ratio: High
Public expenditure ratio: High
Social allocation ratio: Low
Social priority ratio: Medium

Jordan has a level of human development that is high by the standards of the Arab region. High levels of public expenditure and a moderate social priority ratio have resulted in a high human expenditure ratio.

With the majority of the population under 15 years of age, there has been a strong emphasis on education. Jordan raised literacy rates from 47% in 1970 to 74% in 1985. And though still low (62%), female literacy rates are significantly above the average for the region.

The high educational levels of Jordanians has paid off in economic and financial terms. Skilled labour is the country's most valuable resource. Remittances from skilled Jordanian labour in the Gulf area has constituted a major source of hard currency.

Jordanians have also made considerable progress in health. Since 1960, life expectancy increased from 47 years to 67, and child mortality rates fell from 217 per 1,000 births to 55. Health services have been focused on Amman, the capital, where over a third of the population lives. But the government is now improving the quality of rural primary health care by establishing rural health centres capable of offering a wide range of basic services.

Jordan's experience is of special relevance to higher income countries in the region and elsewhere, who failed to reach human development levels compatible with their incomes. Astute allocation of scarce resources, together with a fairly equitable distribution of income, have contributed to human development levels that are better than in other countries with per capita incomes several times Jordan's.

Indonesia

Primary income distribution: Good
Human expenditure ratio: Low
Public expenditure ratio: Medium
Social allocation ratio: Low
Social priority ratio: Low

Indonesia has enjoyed broad-based economic growth since the 1970s. It reaped large windfall profits from its oil production – and used them to provide for the time when the oil revenues dwindled. The government has advanced human development, both by generating widespread primary incomes, particularly in agriculture, and by supplementing these through social services. The proportion of people below the poverty line fell considerably in the 1980s – though the incidence of poverty is much higher in the eastern parts of the archipelago.

The government launched a massive primary education programme and eliminated school fees in 1978 – achieving high basic enrolment rates.

Significant problems remain, however. A high proportion of the population is part of the "marginal poor", with incomes only slightly above the poverty line. Indonesia still lags behind many of its neighbours in nutrition, life expectancy and infant mortality.

The social allocation and social priority ratios are far below average, and the human expenditure ratio is very poor. Health expenditure is relatively low, biased heavily towards urban curative care. Higher priority needs to be given to preventive health facilities in the villages – through programmes, such as "posyanda".

Safe water and sanitation are also only available to a minority of Indonesians, usually the better-off urban residents. Much more attention needs to go to the public provision of priority social services.

Argentina

Primary income distribution: Poor
Human expenditure ratio: Medium
Public expenditure ratio: High
Social allocation ratio: Medium
Social priority ratio: Low

Argentina has achieved high rates of literacy and school enrolment (both stood at over 95% by the mid-1980s), and child mortality rates are less than one-third of the developing country average.

Nonetheless, Argentina's human development performance is disappointing, considering its level of GNP per head ($2,520). Substantial proportions of the population, especially in the north and the slum areas around Buenos Aires, have only limited access to education, health care or safe water and sanitation. Social conditions have worsened with the prolonged economic crises. The share of the population with access to safe water declined by nine percentage points over the 1980s, to 51%. Since the mid-1970s, average household income declined by more than one-fifth, in real terms, and income distribution became more skewed.

The public expenditure ratio is high. Although the social allocation ratio is moderate (35% in 1998), 70% of this is directed to social security payments, which benefit only those working in the formal sector, rather than the poor. Since Argentina has, over an extended period of time, achieved high rates of access to health care and basic education it can, to a certain extent, be seen as a case of shifting priorities in the light of past achievements in providing pensions, higher education and more sophisticated health care.

At the same time, it is vital that these achievements – largely attained before 1970 – be preserved. This has not always been the case, as the experience of the 1980s reflects. In this sense Argentina's low priority ratio is a cause for concern: social services that mainly benefit the poor – primary education, public hospitals, primary health care and slum improvement programmes – have suffered more severe deterioration over the past decade than social expenditures directed towards the better-off Argentines.

REFERENCES

Anderson, Dennis. 1989. "Infrastructure Pricing Policies and the Public Revenue in African Countries." *World Development* 174: 525–42

Ball, Nicole. 1985. "The Security Sector, the Budget and Development." *IDS Bulletin* 16 (4).

Bayley, D. 1985. *Patterns of Policing.* New Brunswick: Rutgers.

Bobiash, Donald J. 1988. "South-South Trade: West African Case Studies." Oxford University. Unpublished thesis.

Cassen, Robert and others. 1987. *Does Aid Work?* New York: Oxford University Press.

Cornia, G. Andrea, Richard Jolly and Frances Stewart (eds.). 1987. *Adjustment with a Human Face.* Volume I. New York: Oxford University Press for UNICEF.

Cornia, G. Andrea and Frances Stewart. 1990. *The Fiscal System, Adjustment and the Poor.* Queen Elizabeth House Development Studies Working Paper 29. Oxford.

Faber, Mike and Stephanie Griffith-Jones (eds.). 1990. "Approaches to the Third World Debt Reduction." *IDS Bulletin* 21 (2).

Grimmit, Richard F. 1988. "An Overview of US Military Assistance." CRS Report for the U.S. Congress. Washington, D.C.: Congressional Research Service.

Gulhati, Ravi. 1990. *The Making of Economic Policy in Africa.* EDI Seminar Series. Washington, D.C.: World Bank.

Humphreys, Charles and John Underwood. 1989. "The External Debt Difficulties of Low Income Africa." In I. Husain and I. Diwan (eds.), *Dealing With the Debt Crisis.* Washington, D.C.: World Bank.

Knight, John. 1991. "Parastatals in Africa." In Stewart, Lall and Wangwe (1991) *Alternative Development Strategies in Sub-Saharan Africa.* London: MacMillan.

Lessard, Donald and John Williamson (eds.). 1987. *Capital Flight and Third World Debt.* Washington, D.C.: Institute of International Economics.

Lewis, John P. and others. 1988. *Strengthening the Poor: What Have We Learned.* U.S. Third World Policy Perspectives 10. Overseas Development Council. New Brunswick: Transaction Books.

Lipton, Michael and John Toye. 1990. *Does Aid Work in India?* London: Routledge.

MacAndrews, Collin (ed.). 1986. *Central Government and Local Development in Indonesia.* Oxford: Oxford University Press.

Mesa-Lago, Carmelo. 1983. "Social Security and Extreme Poverty in Latin America." *Journal of Development Studies* 12: 83–110.

Newbery, David and Nicholas Stern (eds.). 1987. *The Theory of Taxation for Developing Countries.* New York: Oxford University Press.

OECD (Organisation for Economic Co-operation and Development). 1990. "Development Co-operation; Efforts and Policies of the Members of the Development Assistance Committee DAC." Report by Joseph C. Wheeler, Chairman of the DAC. Paris.

Pastor, Manuel. 1990 "Capital Flight from Latin America." *World Development* 18 (1): 1–18.

Rodriguez, Miguel A. 1987. "Consequences of Capital Flight for Latin American Debtor Countries." In Lessard, Donald and John Williamson (eds.) (1987), *Capital Flight and Third World Debt.* Washington, D.C.: Institute of International Economics.

Sivard, Ruth L. 1989. *World Military and Social Expenditures.* Washington, D.C.: World Priorities.

Tan, Jee-Peng and Alain Mingat. 1989. "Educational Development in Asia: A Comparative Study Focusing on Cost and Financing Issues." Asia Regional Series Internal Discussion Paper. Washington, D.C.: World Bank.

Theobald, Robin. 1990. *Corruption, Development and Underdevelopment.* London: MacMillan.

UN (United Nations). 1990. "Justice in the Context of Development: Realities and Perspectives of International Co-operation. Practical Measures Against Corruption." Report prepared by the Secretariat. Eighth United Nations Congress on the Prevention of Crime and the Treatment of Offenders. New York. A/CONF.144/8.

UNDP (United Nations Development Programme). 1990. "Human Development Country Studies in Selected Countries." New York. Mimeographed.

UNICEF (United Nations Children's Fund). 1990. *Children and Development in the 1990s - a UNICEF Sourcebook.* On the occasion of the World Summit for Children. New York.

Urrutia, Miguel, Shinichi Ichimura, and Setsuko Yukawa (eds.). 1989. *The Political Economy of Fiscal Policy*. Tokyo: United Nations University.

Vogel, Ronald J. 1990. "Trends in Health Expenditures and Revenue Sources in Sub-Saharan Africa." Paper prepared in conjunction with the World Bank Sub-Saharan Health Policy Study. Washington, D.C.: World Bank.

Williamson, J. 1990 "The Debt Crisis at the Turn of the Decade." *IDS Bulletin* 21 (2): 4–6.

World Bank. 1988. *Argentina: Social Sectors in Crisis*. A World Bank Country Study. Washington, D.C.

——. 1990a. *World Development Report 1990*. New York: Oxford University Press.

——. 1990b. "Indonesia Poverty Assessment and Strategy Report." Asia Regional Office, Country Department V. Washington, D.C.

——. 1990c. *Primary Education*. A World Bank Policy Paper. Washington, D.C.

3.2
VALUING WOMEN'S WORK

Chapter 4, *Human Development Report 1995*
Drafted principally by Terry McKinley based on background papers
by Githinji, Goldschmidt-Clermont, Harvey and Urdaneta-Ferrán

Much of women's work remains unrecognized and unvalued. This has an impact on the status of women in society, their opportunities in public life and the gender-blindness of development policy. In an attempt to understand the critical dimensions of women's work, this chapter sets out to measure the scale and nature of their economic contribution. A survey of time-use data from a range of countries highlights the contribution by women to household and community work. The chapter concludes that if the unpaid contributions by both women and men were recognized, there would be far-reaching consequences for social and economic policy and for social norms and institutions.

Women's work is greatly undervalued in economic terms. This is due in part to the restricted definition of economic activity. But part of the problem is the notion of value itself.

For the purposes of economic valuation, value is synonymous with market value. National income statistics were originally derived by adding the market value of all the goods produced and sold and all the services provided for hire. But many goods and services with economic value are not marketed. In theory, this problem is resolvable if these items could be sold, for a market value could then be imputed to them on this basis – as is done for subsistence crops consumed by the producers themselves. A rental value can be imputed to owner-occupied housing. And the 1993 revision of the System of National Accounts (SNA) imputes market value to some goods produced and consumed within the household. Yet much household and community work remains unvalued. The total product of society is thus underestimated – and the economic contributions of many people, especially women, are unrecognized and unrewarded.

The general problem of unpaid or non-market work has long been noted. At the start of this century, Arthur Cecil Pigou, the pioneer of welfare economics, wrote that if a woman employed as a housekeeper by a bachelor were to marry him, national income would fall, since her previously paid work would now be performed unpaid. But unpaid work goes far beyond housekeeping, and its omission leaves a major gap in national income accounting.

An additional consideration is that the value of much household and community work transcends market value. This activity has an intrinsic use value or human value that is not captured by its value for exchange. At the heart of human development is the expansion of human choices by developing human capabilities. Income becomes one of the means to ensure the development of capabilities, but it is not an end in itself. The pursuit of good health, the acquisition of knowledge, the time devoted to fostering social relationships, the hours spent in the company of relatives and friends – all are worthwhile activities, yet they carry no price tag.

Human value is not an attribute solely of activity pursued for its own sake – for the benefit of the individual. Much of such activity is imbued with value precisely because it is interactive – relational. Some of it may even have by-products that are useful and for which a market value can be imputed. But that is not its driving purpose. Take preparing meals as an example. This naturally involves work, but sharing a meal with other members of the household is also a way of enjoying and reproducing a relationship. A by-product, of course, is nourishment and building the capacity for work.

These comments are not made as a criticism of national income accounting but as a recognition of its limitations. The System of National Accounts was never designed to measure human well-being – only output, income and expenditures. But to accomplish this limited goal, the SNA should become more comprehensive, more encompassing in how it defines economic activity. The reason: much of the work of society remains "invisible", and the people performing it do not get their proper economic reward or recognition.

The question of value is simplified by assuming that an hour of market work and an hour of non-market work have the same value. This implies that productivity differences between market and non-market work are not an issue. While this may be a simplifying assumption for measuring economic output, it is not for measuring human well-being. When the real concern is with human development, it is difficult to argue that time spent producing goods and services for the market has greater value than time spent creating, nurturing and sustaining human life.

For the 1995 *Human Development Report*, extensive research was undertaken on the amount of time women and men spend on market and non-market activities. Spanning industrial and developing countries, the data generated by this research are used here to provide estimates of the value of household and other unpaid work.

A review of the 31 countries in the sample tells a fairly dramatic story:

• Women work longer hours than men in nearly every country (figure 3.2.1). Of the total burden of work, women carry on average 53% in developing countries and 51% in industrial countries.
• Of men's total work time in industrial countries, roughly two-thirds is spent in paid SNA activities and one-third in unpaid non-SNA activities. For women, these shares are reversed. In developing countries, more than three-fourths of men's work is in SNA activities. So, men receive the lion's share of income and recognition for their economic

contribution – while most of women's work remains unpaid, unrecognized and under-valued (figure 3.2.2).

THE EVIDENCE OF TIME USE

Time-use studies have been collected for 14 industrial countries, 9 developing countries and 8 countries in Eastern Europe and the Commonwealth of Independent States (CIS). For four industrial countries – Canada, Norway, Sweden and the United Kingdom – data are available to trace historical trends as well. Two developing countries, Kenya and Venezuela, are studied in detail. The data also allow an interesting comparison of

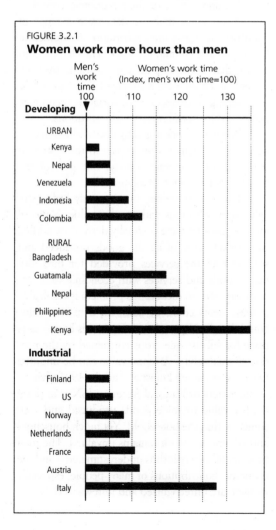

FIGURE 3.2.1
Women work more hours than men

an Eastern European country, Bulgaria, with a Nordic one, Finland.

All countries in the sample have been selected on the basis of the availability and reliability of time-use data. Originally, data were collected for a much larger set of developing countries, but the quality of the data did not permit a sizable selection to be included in the final analysis. The conclusions rely on the sample of countries studied.

The studies vary in data collection methods (diaries, yesterday recall or other), in representativeness of samples and the handling of non-response, in age groups covered, in time units defined and in treatments of seasonal variations. These small methodological differences should be kept in mind in interpreting the data. Variations based on urban and rural data, available for a few countries, can be highlighted. Trends can be discussed for the four countries for which there is

historical information. But beyond that, only the broadest conclusions are valid across countries.

Time is measured in hours and minutes per day, after averaging it over the week or month, and then divided in two ways. The first division is between the category of personal (non-economic) activities and that of productive (economic) activities. The criterion here is that personal activities cannot be delegated to third parties. No one else can eat your breakfast on your behalf or catch up on your sleep. You must do it yourself. Others could, however, cook a meal for you if you were to hire them. This third-person rule is standard in time-use studies for allocating time between economic and non-economic activities.

The second division is between productive activities that are market-oriented – and therefore qualify for entry in national income accounts – and those that are not. Market-oriented activities in-

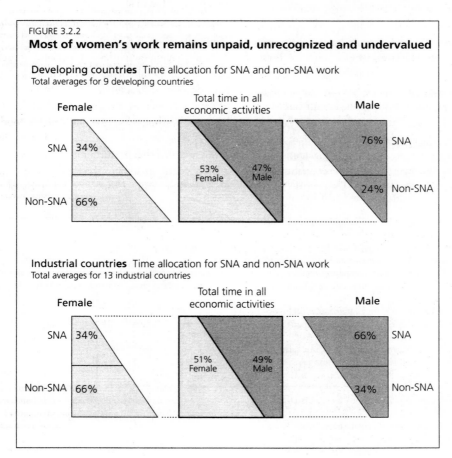

FIGURE 3.2.2

Most of women's work remains unpaid, unrecognized and undervalued

Developing countries Time allocation for SNA and non-SNA work
Total averages for 9 developing countries

Female

SNA 34%

Non-SNA 66%

Total time in all economic activities

53% Female   47% Male

Male

76% SNA

24% Non-SNA

Industrial countries Time allocation for SNA and non-SNA work
Total averages for 13 industrial countries

Female

SNA 34%

Non-SNA 66%

Total time in all economic activities

51% Female   49% Male

Male

66% SNA

34% Non-SNA

clude production of the self-consumed products of subsistence agriculture, since they could be marketed. The boundary between these two categories corresponds roughly to the production boundary defined by the UN System of National Accounts (1968 SNA). The 1993 revision of the SNA will lead to the addition of a few items to the national accounts, such as producing household goods for own-consumption and carrying water. But the bulk of household work and voluntary community work will remain excluded. Also excluded will be education, which should be considered an economic activity and a critical investment.

The question in valuing women's work is the amount and value of non-SNA time spent by women as well as men relative to the amount and value of time spent in SNA activities.

Hours in SNA activities

A large study was undertaken of the share of total market hours worked by women and men in developing countries and in some Eastern European and CIS countries. Using the number of hours women and men spend in market work is preferable to the standard method of merely counting the number of participants in the labour force (figure 3.2.3). In many sectors, women work fewer hours on average than men, but this underemployment usually is not captured by official statistics.

In Africa, women's economic contribution is higher than in other regions. They work almost 44% of all market hours, mainly because of their work in agriculture and services. They contribute only 17% of the hours in industry.

In Latin America, women's relative contribution is much smaller, at only 28% of all market hours, with the highest share in services.

In Asia, women contribute 36% of all market hours, with fairly even shares in industry services and agriculture. What is noteworthy is that women participate in industry much more in Asia than in Africa or Latin America.

In Eastern Europe and the CIS countries, women may well contribute more hours than men to market work, based on a very limited sample. They are active in agriculture and participate much more in industry than do women in the developing regions. They are most active, however, in services.

Intensity of work

Most time-use research regards people's activities as individual tasks that occur one after the other. In reality, many activities – especially household tasks – are simultaneous. Women in particular have developed a facility for juggling many activities at once, such as carrying a child while sweeping up or washing clothes while cooking food.

A time-use study in the United States in the 1980s revealed that performing simultaneous tasks is more common among women than men, particularly in household chores. And a study of rural

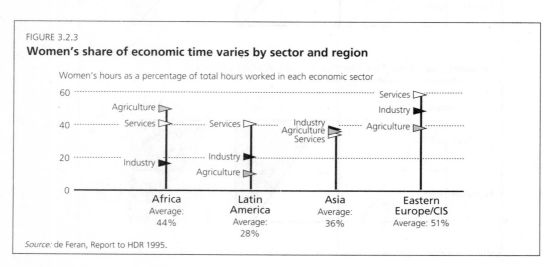

FIGURE 3.2.3
Women's share of economic time varies by sector and region

Women's hours as a percentage of total hours worked in each economic sector

Source: de Feran, Report to HDR 1995.

women in Saint Lucia showed that more than three-quarters of household activities involved multiple tasks.

In many developing countries, production activities outside the household are difficult to separate from household work, and women's multiple tasks often combine the two. In other words, the distinction between SNA and non-SNA work is often blurred. Non-marketed output and the corresponding labour input are thus both underestimated.

Many household tasks are unrelenting. Meals must be prepared three times a day. Child care cannot be delayed until there is free time. This becomes clear on weekends. During weekdays, men and women may have relatively equal total workloads, but data from 18 industrial countries show that on Saturday women work almost two more hours than men and on Sunday an hour and three-quarters more – a difference that widens if the family has young children.

The nature of work, especially household work, is very different in developing countries and industrial countries. Women in industrial countries have appliances to ease heavy work. And they can buy consumer goods and services that already incorporate many of the earlier stages of preparation that women in developing countries must perform themselves. Women in developing countries must carry water from a distance, collect firewood and clean and grind food grains. So, it is not only the quantity of time but the intensity of effort (and its drudgery) that are also important – though missing – dimensions.

There are only 24 hours in a day. With time a scarce resource relative to the tasks that need to be done, the frequent alternative is to heighten the intensity of work. This is a particular problem among poor women. They cannot rely on modern appliances. As their economic conditions deteriorate, they cope by increasing the output of their one productive resource – their labour. They produce more goods at home rather than purchase them. They take on contract work at home that they can do at the same time as household work. Or they choose informal employment, such as street vending, because it allows them to take their children along. Hours for leisure activities or even

sleep are reduced. Conventional measures of well-being, which focus on the production of goods and services, neglect this debilitating aspect of intense work. A human development perspective cannot afford to overlook it.

TIME USE IN DEVELOPING COUNTRIES

Time-use data are available from 13 surveys in nine developing countries. Four surveys are available from Nepal, one urban and three from different rural areas. General urban and rural surveys are available from Kenya. And the survey of the Republic of Korea is nationwide.

There are general problems in comparing the results of time-use studies because of a lack of uniformity in the design of surveys, the sample taken, the method of collection or the year of the survey. Surveys that examine only the allocation of time by women and men during workdays tend to underestimate the contribution of women to economic activity because their work continues unabated during "days off". The same is true with surveys of economic activities during the day, since a significant portion of women's work occurs at night.

Despite these problems – and in the absence of better data – the studies assembled here give a valuable glimpse of the general pattern of time use by women and men in developing countries (tables 3.2.1 and 3.2.2). Because of the limited selection of countries, simple arithmetic averages, unweighted by population, are used to present summary results.

Several features of the total time women and men spend in market and non-market activities are worth noting from the 13 surveys:

- The overall burden of work varies greatly from one country to another. It ranges from about 6.25 hours a day in Colombia to 10.5 hours in Guatemala. But such cross-country comparisons must be handled cautiously because of the different coverage of surveys.
- More important, women work longer hours than men in all countries. The difference ranges from as little as eight minutes a day in the Republic of Korea to almost two hours in

the mountainous regions of Nepal to almost three hours in rural Kenya (box 3.2.1 and figure 3.2.4). On average, women put in 13% more time than men do in market activities and unpaid work taken together.

- Of the total burden of work, women carry 53%, men 47%. In rural areas, this widens to 55% and 45%. In urban areas, it is 51% and 49% (figure 3.2.5).
- The disparity between rural and urban areas is startling. Normally, the total work time for both women and men is much longer (about 20% longer) in rural areas than in urban areas. Women spend an average of 20% more time than men working in rural areas, 6% more in urban areas.

- In Nepal, as life moves from the placid urban areas to the more rugged mountains and hills, men do not increase their hours of work appreciably – in fact, they work fewer hours. It is women who take on the extra burden of work, including working for a worthwhile livelihood in inhospitable conditions.

How much of this total work is in market-related economic activities and how much in unpaid activities? From the 13 surveys, the main conclusions are these:

- The proportion of daily time spent by women in paid economic activities varies enormously – from about a quarter in Colombia and urban Nepal to more than 40% in

TABLE 3.2.1
Burden of work by gender, selected developing countries

Country	Year	Work time (minutes a day)			Women's work burden compared with men's (% difference)
		Average	Women	Men	
Urban					
Colombia	1983	378	399	356	12
Indonesia	1992	382	398	366	9
Kenya	1986	581	590	572	3
Nepal	1978	567	579	554	5
Venezuela	1983	428	440	416	6
Average		471	481	453	6
Percentage share			51	49	
Rural					
Bangladesh	1990	521	545	496	10
Guatemala	1977	629	678	579	17
Kenya	1988	588	676	500	35
Nepal	1978	594	641	547	17
Highlands	1978	639	692	586	18
Mountains	1978	592	649	534	22
Rural hills	1978	552	583	520	12
Philippines	1975–77	499	546	452	21
Average		566	617	515	20
Percentage share			55	45	
National					
Korea, Rep. of	1990	479	488	480	2
Average for sample countries		514	544	483	13
Percentage share			33	47	

Source: Harvey 1995.

rural Kenya to more than half in the highlands of Nepal. Obviously, women adjust their work patterns to different economic environments and different family needs.

- The allocation of time by women and men to market-oriented and household activities differs greatly between urban and rural areas. In urban areas, women spend an average of 31% of their total work time in paid economic activities – in rural areas, 38%. The difference often arises because women carry a large burden of work in agriculture, generally in family-owned farms, and there are greater barriers to their entry in the more organized urban labour market. On average, women in all areas spend 34% of their work time in paid economic activities.
- Men normally spend no more than a quarter of their work time in unpaid activities –

though there are large variations, from 13% in Venezuela to 44% in the Republic of Korea. In Korea, those surveyed spend a significant share of their economic time in educational activities.

- In the ratio of market work to non-market work, the Republic of Korea shows the least inequality. For men it is 1.3:1, and for women 0.5:1. For Venezuelan men the ratio is 6.7:1 (box 3.2.2).

Women's work affected by the environment

Many time-use studies show that women's work is affected much more than men's by environmental degradation. Men receive most of the benefit from the timber and livestock industries because they get the jobs or own the productive assets. But the deforestation and overgrazing of pasture land that

TABLE 3.2.2

Time allocation by women and men, selected developing countries
(as a percentage of total work time)

Country	Year	Total work time		Female		Male	
		SNA	Non-SNA	SNA	Non-SNA	SNA	Non-SNA
Urban							
Colombia	1983	49	51	24	76	77	23
Indonesia	1992	60	40	35	65	86	14
Kenya	1986	46	54	41	59	79	21
Nepal	1978	58	42	25	75	67	33
Venezuela	1983	59	41	30	70	87	13
Average		54	46	31	69	79	21
Rural							
Bangladesh	1990	52	48	35	65	70	30
Guatemala	1977	59	41	37	63	84	16
Kenya	1988	56	44	42	58	76	24
Nepal	1978	56	44	46	54	67	33
Highlands	1978	59	41	52	48	66	34
Mountains	1978	56	44	48	52	65	35
Rural hills	1978	52	48	37	63	70	30
Philippines	1975-77	73	27	29	71	84	16
Average		59	41	38	62	76	24
National							
Korea, Rep. of	1990	45	55	34	66	56	44
Average for sample countries		54	46	34	66	76	24

Source: Harvey 1995.

BOX 3.2.1

Women and girls are Kenya's breadwinners

Women in rural Kenya work on average about 56 hours a week, men only about 42 (figure 3.2.4). Children between the ages of 8 and 16 also work many hours. If time for education is counted, girls spend about 41 hours a week in economic activity, boys 35 hours.

Women shoulder the heaviest burden in household work, including firewood and water collection: 10 times the hours of men! This carries over to girls, whose household work takes about 3.7 times the hours of boys.

Women in households that farm such cash crops as tea and coffee work the most hours of any rural women – 62 total hours a week. As Kenya's farming becomes more cash-oriented, women tend to shoulder more work, not less.

The average workload for urban men and women is more equal: 49.2 hours a week for women, and 47.7 for men.

Almost 80% of men's work, but only 41% of women's, is income-earning. But girls, not boys, are the "breadwinners" for the family – spending 10 times the hours of boys in work outside the household.

Self-employed women and men work a lot, but their workload is unequal – more than 75 hours for women and more than 61 hours for men. Urban self-employed women are clearly worse off than other urban women and even worse off than rural women. Among urban men and women who are not self-employed, the hours per week are nearly the same – about 46.

Source: Githinji 1995.

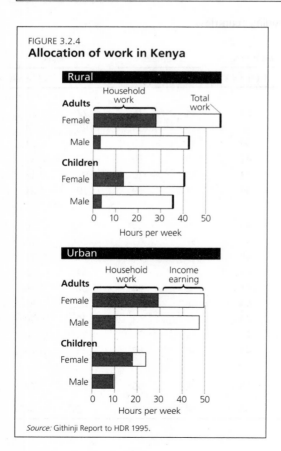

FIGURE 3.2.4
Allocation of work in Kenya

Source: Githinji Report to HDR 1995.

often ensue cause soil erosion, loss of fuel wood and depletion of water resources. And that increases the time and energy that women must devote to collecting water and wood.

When land and water are depleted, much more labour – usually women's labour – is required to maintain the same output. The workload of children also rises, for girls more than boys.

A study of Kenya shows that women are much more involved than men in such activities as farming, collecting fuel wood and water, cooking and cleaning – spending almost 45 hours a week on them, men only 20 hours. And girls spend more hours in these activities than boys.

Most immediately and directly affected by deforestation and overgrazing are fuel wood and water collection, activities to which women devote more than 10 times as many hours as men – 9.7 hours compared with 0.9 hours. Girls spend more than 7 times as many hours as adult males in these activities and 3.5 times as many hours as boys.

The story is much the same elsewhere:

- In Peru, women must spend about 2.5 hours a day solely in gathering and cutting wood, and in Gujarat, India, 3 hours a day.

- In the Himalayas, gathering firewood took no more than 2 hours a day in the foothills a generation ago. Now, with deforestation, it takes a full day of trudging further up the mountains.
- In the Sudan, the time spent gathering fuel wood has increased fourfold in a decade.

FIGURE 3.2.5
Burden of work in developing countries

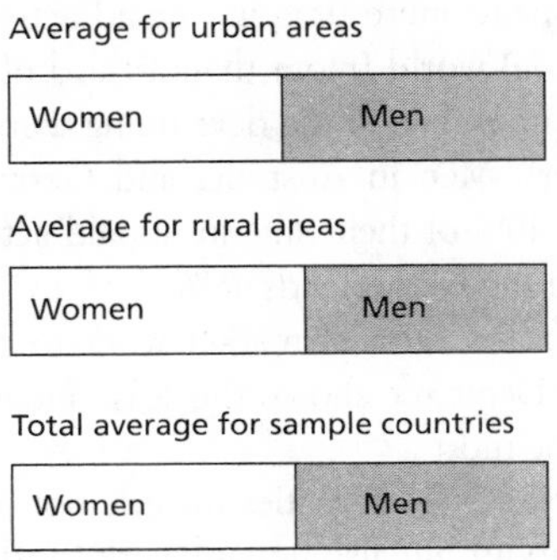

Average for urban areas

Average for rural areas

Total average for sample countries

- In Mozambique, women spend more than 15 hours a week collecting water, and in Senegal, about 17.5 hours. Where desertification is a problem, women may spend up to 4 hours a day retrieving water.

TIME USE IN INDUSTRIAL COUNTRIES

Unrecorded economic activity is as large as recorded economic activity. Comparisons across 13 industrial countries suggest important differences – but again, definitive cross-national conclusions should be avoided. An effort was made to minimize differences in time units, age groups under observation and categorizations of activities. Hours and minutes per day are used as time units. In most cases, data are provided for the population aged 15 and above. Major differences in categorization are eliminated. Yet important differences remain in data collection methods, the handling of seasonal variations and the representativeness of the survey sample.

BOX 3.2.2

Women do 56% of the work in Venezuela

In Venezuela, women are a minority in the labour force, but they work more total hours than men, according to a study of urban time-use by the central bank. Time is divided into five categories: income-earning activities, household activities, personal care, studying, and social activities and leisure.

As expected, men have a distinct advantage over women in income-earning activities: 6 hours a day, compared with only 2.25. But women's time in household work is a striking 11.5 multiple of men's time. Men's overall advantage shows up in about 10% more time enjoyed in social activities and leisure.

In the economically active population, men's time in household work stays at half an hour, but women's contracts from 4.5 to about 3 hours, still six times the amount of time devoted by men. So, economically active women have considerably less time for social activities and leisure. In this sense, they are worse off, relative to men, than women not involved in market work.

Economically active men spend only about 30 minutes a day in household work, whether married or not. But when single economically active women get married, their daily household work increases by about 30% – from 162 minutes to 211 minutes. With children under 13, women's daily household work increases further – to 246 minutes, or well over four hours.

What are the overall contributions of women and men to the Venezuelan economy? In 1988, women and men spent 12.3 billion hours in SNA-defined activity – men 8.9 billion hours, women 3.4 billion. But if all working hours are included, market and non-market, the total rises to 22.1 billion.

Of this, women contribute 12.4 billion hours, men 9.7 billion. So, 56% of all work in Venezuela is done by women, only 44% by men.

Source: Urdaneta-Ferrán 1994c.

- Total work time in industrial countries is about 7 hours a day (averaged over the week), about 20% less than in developing countries. The range is from about 6 hours in the Netherlands to about 7.5 hours in Denmark (table 3.2.3).
- Women carry 51% of the total work burden, men 49% (table 3.2.4).
- The longest workday is put in by women in Italy (over 7.75 hours) and men in Denmark (over 7.5 hours), and the shortest by men and women in the Netherlands.
- In Australia, Canada and Germany, there is near-parity in the work burdens of women and men. But women work many more hours than men in Italy (28% more), Austria (12%) and France (11%). In Denmark, men put in more hours than women, but this difference is within the margin of error of the study.
- Slightly less than half the total work time is spent in paid SNA activities, and slightly more than half in unpaid non-SNA activities.
- Of men's total work time, about two-thirds is spent in paid SNA activities and one-third in unpaid non-SNA activities. For women, these shares are reversed. As a result, men receive the lion's share of income and recognition in society for their economic contribution.
- There are significant variations in these shares. The male share in SNA activities ranges from 58% in Denmark to 73% in Italy. Women's share in non-SNA activities ranges from 64% in Canada, Finland and Germany to 81% in Italy.

Men spend more time in unpaid activities in the industrial world (more than a third of their total work time) than in the developing world (nearly a quarter). Men in Australia and Germany spend nearly 40% of their time in unpaid activities, and men in the Netherlands 48%.

In the ratio of market work to non-market work, Denmark shows the least inequality, and Italy the most.

Non-SNA activities include not only household labour but also unpaid work for the community. Among the 13 industrial countries, people in the Netherlands devote the highest proportion of their total non-market work to the community – 11%. The next highest share is 8% in both Canada

TABLE 3.2.3
Burden of work by gender, selected industrial countries

Country	Year	Work time (minutes a day)			Women's work burden compared with men's (% difference)
		Average	Women	Men	
Australia	1992	443	443	443	0.0
Austria	1992	416	438	393	11.5
Canada	1992	430	429	430	−0.2
Denmark	1987	454	449	458	−2.0
Finland	1987/88	420	430	410	4.9
France	1985/86	409	429	388	10.6
Germany	1991/92	441	440	441	−0.2
Israel	1991/92	376	375	377	−0.5
Italy	1988/89	419	470	367	28.1
Netherlands	1987	361	377	345	9.3
Norway	1990/91	429	445	412	8.0
United Kingdom	1985	412	413	411	0.5
USA	1985	441	453	428	5.8
Average for sample countries		419	430	408	5.8
Percentage share			51	49	

Source: Goldschmidt-Clermont and Aligisakis 1995.

and the United States. The lowest shares are 2% in the United Kingdom and 1% in France. There are no clear gender trends in the amount of time people spend in community work. In about half the countries, men spend more time than women in this work – in the other half, women do. In the Netherlands, for example, men's average time per day is twice that of women's – 34 minutes compared with 17 minutes. In the United States, it is the opposite – 20 minutes for women compared with 15 minutes for men.

Just as total work time varies across industrial countries, so does total personal or non-economic time. The average daily amount of personal time in a country could be considered an important aspect of human development. Averaging 17 hours or more for the population aged 15 and above are Finland, France, Italy and the United Kingdom. In contrast, Australia, Canada and the United States have averages below 17 hours – showing that these societies have less time available for leisure than other industrial nations. These results should be interpreted with caution, however, because of important differences in the surveys.

Historical trends

Three major historical trends in time use emerge clearly from data for Norway and the United Kingdom:

- There has been a decrease in total work for the population as a whole as well as for both women and men.
- Men's and women's contributions to total work are becoming more equal. In the United Kingdom, both women and men now spend about 29% of their day in work.
- There is also a tendency towards equalization of men's and women's contributions to both SNA and non-SNA work, more so for SNA work.

Time-series data from Canada, Norway and the United Kingdom show that women have decreased their work in traditional women's activities, such as cooking and washing. In general, non-SNA time devoted to preparing food, caring for clothes and maintaining the home has dropped, while that devoted to household management and shopping has risen. Men have increased their

TABLE 3.2.4
Time allocation by women and men, selected industrial countries
(as a percentage of total work time)

Country	Year	Total work time		Female		Male	
		SNA	Non-SNA	SNA	Non-SNA	SNA	Non-SNA
Australia	1992	44	56	28	72	61	39
Austria	1992	49	51	31	69	71	29
Canada	1992	52	48	39	61	65	35
Denmark	1987	68	32	58	42	79	21
Finland	1987/88	51	49	39	61	64	36
France	1985/86	45	55	30	70	62	38
Germany	1991/92	44	56	30	70	61	39
Israel	1991/92	51	49	29	71	74	26
Italy	1988/89	45	55	22	78	77	23
Netherlands	1987	35	65	19	81	52	48
Norway	1990/91	50	50	38	62	64	36
United Kingdom	1985	51	49	37	63	68	32
USA	1985	50	50	37	63	63	37
Average		49	51	34	66	66	34

Source: Goldschmidt-Clermont and Aligisakis 1995.

share of child care and shopping, but taken over little cooking, cleaning or general housework.

A separate study in Sweden found that leisure is on the rise, but how it is being used poses interesting questions (box 3.2.3).

TIME USE IN EASTERN EUROPE AND THE CIS

The trend in industrial countries towards equalization of work between men and women for both SNA and non-SNA activities is reversed for several countries undergoing economic restructuring in Eastern Europe and the Commonwealth of Independent States.

In Bulgaria, men's total work burden was 15% less than that of women in 1977, but 17% less in 1988. Women increased their participation in SNA activities – and their share of household work. In 1977, men did 52% as much household work as women, but in 1988, only 48% as much. So women's workload relative to men's increased on all counts – total time, SNA time and non-SNA time.

Women and men work much more in Bulgaria than in Finland – for the market as well as in the household, according to a comparative study for 1987–88. Finland, of course, is a richer country.

Women's work burden is 21% greater than men's in Bulgaria – and about 8% greater in Finland. Even Bulgarian men work more than Finnish women – 29% of their day, compared with 28% (figure 3.2.6).

Appliances such as dishwashers and washing machines are less common in Bulgaria. So, women there spend more time than Finnish women washing up, doing laundry and preserving food. They are also more likely to grow their own food and make their own clothes. And they do many typically male tasks, such as household maintenance and repairs. This means more equality, but also more total work.

Other Eastern European countries and countries that are now in the CIS show similar results for the 1980s. Both women and men in Hungary, Latvia, Lithuania, Poland and the CIS countries work long hours, but women work on average about 5.5 more hours a week. The average differ-

---

BOX 3.2.3

Leisure time rises in Sweden

A recent study shows that total work is becoming more equal between women and men in Sweden: in 1984, women worked 4 more hours a week than men, and in 1993, 1.75 more hours. Women now work more than 46.5 hours a week, men less than 45. The main reason for the greater equality is a decrease in women's household work.

Men have taken up about an hour's more household work but still spend 10.5 fewer hours on it than women do. Women spend 3.5 fewer hours than before – mainly because of less cooking and dishwashing – but their total household work is still about 21.5 hours a week.

Men still avoid doing laundry, spending about 20 minutes a week at this task. Women spend 2 hours a week taking care of laundry – others' as well as their own. Women also devote about twice as much time as men to childcare. While women in their twenties devote almost 2 more hours to child

care than before, men of the same age have reduced their time at this task by more than half an hour.

Leisure has increased for both women and men by about 2%, but the biggest increase, 10%, is among men in their twenties. Among women, it is mainly those in older age groups who enjoy increased leisure. In general, women are taking on more market work. Men's hours in market work have stayed about the same, with younger men affected more by unemployment.

More leisure means mainly more time watching TV and videos. Women spend 14.5 hours a week, and men 17.5 watching the screen. Reading time is down – by 26% for men, 12% for women. With people increasingly flicking on the TV rather than reading a newspaper or book, Sweden may have to find a more valuable use for its increased leisure time.

Source: Goldschmidt-Clermont and Aligisakis 1995.

---

ence in work burden between women and men is 9%, higher than in Western Europe, with the biggest difference, 15%, in Poland.

In many of the CIS countries, women appear worse off than those in Eastern Europe. There are sharp differences in time use, for example, between Bulgaria and the Republic of Moldova, which is poorer and more agricultural.

In Bulgaria, women work on average about 59 hours a week, and in Moldova, 73.5 hours a week. One reason: the majority of Moldovan workers are women, so they carry a heavy double burden of paid work and household work. Moldovan men work 51 hours a week, with only 11 hours of household work.

In Kyrgyzstan, the work burden is even heavier with women working 76.3 hours a week, and men 59.4 hours. And the total work of employed women increased 1.5% from 1980 to 1990, because of the increase in household work as economic conditions worsened. Because of the problems in buying food products and the short supply of semi-prepared products, time for food preparation increased by 12% from 1980 to 1990.

EXPLAINING VARIATIONS IN TIME USE

Time-use varies by region and historical period. And within a country, the time use of particular groups can be affected by the kind of household (number of adults and children) and the employment status of its members.

Survey data for 18 industrial countries from the early 1960s to the early 1990s show that the

unpaid work burden of women is highest in Eastern Europe – Bulgaria, the former Czechoslovakia, the former East Germany, Hungary, Poland and the former Yugoslavia. It is also higher in Western Europe than in Nordic countries, North America, Australia and Israel. Compared with the average for all 18 countries, women spend 25 more minutes a day on household work in Eastern Europe and 18 more minutes in Western Europe.

Once a woman has a child, she can expect to devote 3.3 more hours a day to unpaid household work – while her paid work declines by only about one hour. And a woman with a child under five can expect to put in 9.6 hours of total work every day. Many women would probably consider this an underestimate.

Women who work full-time still do a lot of unpaid work. So, the mere fact of getting a job increases a woman's total work burden, both paid and unpaid, by almost an hour a day on average.

Married women who are employed and have children under 15 carry the heaviest work burden of any group – almost 11 hours a day. A man in the same situation works about 10.5 hours a day.

Men contribute most to household work in North America and Eastern Europe – about 12 more minutes a day than the average. Men's total work burden is lowest in Nordic countries and Western Europe – highest in Eastern Europe.

Since the early 1980s, there has been a clear increase in the time men spend in household work – and a clear decrease in their market-oriented work. The total work burden of men decreased noticeably in the 1970s and early 1980s, but by the late 1980s the trend flattened.

Since the early 1960s, the total work burden of women has declined by a little more than one hour. Most of the decrease, however, took place before the early 1980s.

THE VALUATION OF NON-SNA OUTPUT IN INDUSTRIAL COUNTRIES

To aggregate the output of household goods and services and compare it with the aggregates of conventional national accounts, such as gross domestic product, it is necessary to express its value in

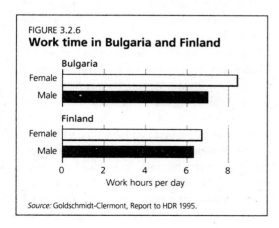

FIGURE 3.2.6
Work time in Bulgaria and Finland

Source: Goldschmidt-Clermont, Report to HDR 1995.

monetary units. The method chosen in the study of 13 industrial countries is to value household production at the cost of inputs – labour and capital. For unpaid labour, a market wage is imputed to the labour time needed to produce household goods and services.

The market wage selected is that of a substitute household worker – a worker who can perform, within the household, most of the economic activities carried out by unpaid household members. Because such workers tend in industrial countries to be women with low pay, using their wage as a yardstick gives a conservative estimate of the value of household labour. After selecting this wage, the choice is among using net wages (after taxes), gross wages (before taxes) or extra gross wages, which include employers' social security contributions. The choice here is extra gross wages, because it is most comprehensive.

With extra gross wages as the yardstick, a conservative estimate of the value of non-SNA production is about half the value of gross domestic product. A 1992 study of Australia estimates this production to be 86% of GDP, and a study of Germany in the same year gives an estimate of 55%. The lowest estimate of non-SNA output is 46% in Finland. Most of the value of non-SNA output is attributable to labour. Labour valued at extra gross wages accounts for 72% of GDP in Australia, 53% in Germany and 45% in Finland.

What is the contribution of unpaid household production to private consumption? To determine this requires accounting for the value of marketed goods and services privately consumed plus the value of the goods and services the household produces for its own consumption. The value of the household inputs used to produce these goods and services is then subtracted – to give the value of what can be called extended private consumption. For three industrial countries – Bulgaria, Finland and Germany – non-SNA production contributes some 60% of extended private consumption.

Clearly, the value of non-SNA production in industrial countries is considerable, whatever the standard. It is at least half of gross domestic product, and it accounts for more than half of private consumption.

THE INVISIBLE CONTRIBUTION

The undervaluation of women's work is reflected in the lack of recognition of their contribution. The debate therefore must cover equality of rewards as well as equality of opportunity.

Is there any reason that only work for the market-place should be valued and that work must have an exchange value, not just a human value, to be recognized in economic terms?

The idea should be resisted that, to be valued, human activity must always be assigned a market price. Many of the things that make life worth living carry no price. We do not advocate that all activities within a family or a community must be monetized to be given adequate recognition. Most of these activities have a value that extends far beyond any economic valuation.

Yet, we face the dilemma that not giving an economic valuation to these activities risks seriously underestimating the contribution of women. There is no adequate reward or recognition for the burden of work that women carry. In fact, the failure to value most of their work reduces women to virtual non-entities in most economic transactions – such as property ownership or offering collateral for bank loans. Because status in contemporary society is so often equated with income-earning power, women suffer a major undervaluation of their economic status. This is so despite their larger share of the total work burden and notwithstanding the reality that men's paid work in the market-place is often the result of "joint production", much of which might not be possible if women did not stay at home looking after the children and the household.

How can we recognize this reality without advocating an exchange value for all non-monetized activities and without arguing for a radical shift in the way families organize their work? Some countries are dealing with this issue by developing "satellite accounts" to register non-monetized work, particularly by women. On a global level, some rough estimates can also be made to highlight the problem. If these unpaid activities were treated as market transactions at the prevailing wages, they would yield huge monetary valuations – a staggering $16 trillion, or about 70% more than the officially estimated $23 trillion of global output. This estimate includes the value of the *unpaid* work performed by women and men as well as the value of the *underpayment* of women's work in the market at prevailing wages. Of this $16 trillion, $11 trillion is the non-monetized, "invisible" contribution of women.

This estimate is not meant to imply that this is the amount that would have to be paid for non-market work – since the entire wage structure would change if all activities entered the market. What it shows, however, is that the unpaid and unrecognized work is substantial.

The monetization of the non-market work of women is more than a question of justice. It concerns the economic status of women in society. If women's unpaid work were properly valued, it is quite possible that women would emerge in most societies as the main breadwinners – or at least equal breadwinners – since they put in more hours of work than men.

POLICY IMPLICATIONS

The research for this chapter confirms the findings of many other studies that document the heavier work burden of women. The division of labour in many societies, particularly in rural areas of developing countries, leads to long hours of drudgery for women in fetching water and firewood, tilling and weeding fields for food crops and processing food for consumption – often while simultaneously looking after young children. This Report goes a step further by systematically reviewing available data for a larger number of countries – and attempting to quantify non-market work and the disparities between men and women in the burden of work and in the income earned. The research for this chapter represents a modest contribution. Much more needs to be done.

If the results here are further substantiated at the country level and if full recognition is given to the need to reward non-market work, the implications for the way that society is structured are revolutionary.

In almost every country, women contribute as much total labour as men – and in many, they contribute more. But they receive a much smaller share of the goods and services produced by total labour.

The inescapable implication is that the fruits of society's total labour should be more equitably shared. Whether a family member works outside the household is a matter of choice. But each working member of a family is entitled to a share of the income generated by market work proportional to her or his total labour contribution – including unpaid labour. For husbands to share income with their wives will become an act of entitlement rather than benevolence.

On this basis, the entitlement to income and wealth would change radically, and the legal system would be overhauled accordingly. Rights to property and inheritance would change, as would access to credit based on collateral, direct entitlement to social security benefits, tax incentives for child care and terms of divorce settlements.

Women's vital social functions for maintaining families and communities – which become only too visible when juvenile delinquency rates rise, the elderly are left to die alone or cultural traditions wither – would gain full recognitior . Now considered largely women's responsibility in many societies, these functions would be recognized as the responsibility of both men and women as well as of society. For public policy, this implies incentives, investments and other measures to provide quality child care and care for the elderly, to do community work and so on. It means taking measures to ensure that men share more equally in the burden of family life and community service.

Such restructuring is unavoidable to liberate both women and men from artificial and restrictive social roles. But the needed changes in policy require relevant data and more refined analysis. As an essential first step, labour force surveys should incorporate all economic time use by household members. These surveys should include questions on the simultaneous performance of tasks and the intensity of labour.

It should always be clear, however, that a monetary value is imputed to unpaid work to make economic valuation more accurate and comprehensive, not because this is the only way to value these activities. In fact, in valuing much unpaid work, especially such household activities as the care of children or the sick, the human perspective of valuation should always supersede the economic perspective.

REFERENCES

Githinji, Mwangi wa. 1995. "Time Allocation and Gender in Kenya." Background paper for *Human Development Report 1995*. UNDP, New York.

Goldschmidt-Clermont, Luisella and Elisabetta Aligisakis. 1995. "Measures of Unrecorded Economic Activities in Fourteen Countries." Background paper for *Human Development Report 1995*. UNDP, New York.

Harvey, Andrew S. 1995. "Market and Non-Market Productive Activity in Less Developed and Developing Countries: Lessons from Time Use." Background paper for *Human Development Report 1995*. UNDP, New York.

Urdaneta-Ferrán, Lourdres. 1994a. "Measuring Women's Economic Contribution in the Subsistence Sector." Background paper for *Human Development Report 1995*. UNDP, New York.

Urdaneta-Ferrán, Lourdres. 1994b. "Methodology of Estimates of Women's Contribution to Human Development." Background paper for *Human Development Report 1995*. UNDP, New York.

Urdaneta-Ferrán, Lourdres. 1994c. "Venezuelan Women in Human Development." Background paper for *Human Development Report 1995*. UNDP, New York.

3.3

GROWTH FOR HUMAN DEVELOPMENT?

Overview, *Human Development Report 1996*
Drafted principally by Sakiko Fukuda-Parr and Richard Jolly

Human development is the end – economic growth a means. So, the purpose of growth should be to enrich people's lives. But far too often it does not. The recent decades show all too clearly that there is no automatic link between growth and human development. And even when links are established, they may gradually be eroded – unless regularly fortified by skilful and intelligent policy management.

The *Human Development Report 1996* explores the nature and strength of the links between economic growth and human development. Two disturbing findings. Growth has been failing over much of the past 15 years in about 100 countries, with almost a third of the world's people. And the links between growth and human development are failing for people in the many countries with lopsided development – with either good growth but little human development or good human development but little or no growth.

The *Human Development Report 1996* concludes that more economic growth, not less, will generally be needed as the world enters the 21st century. But more attention must go to the structure and quality of that growth – to ensure that it is directed to supporting human development, reducing poverty, protecting the environment and ensuring sustainability.

OVER THE PAST 15 YEARS THE WORLD HAS SEEN SPECTACULAR ECONOMIC ADVANCE FOR SOME COUNTRIES – AND UNPRECEDENTED DECLINE FOR OTHERS.

Since 1980 there has been a dramatic surge in economic growth in some 15 countries, bringing rap-idly rising incomes to many of their 1.5 billion people, more than a quarter of the world's population.

Over much of this period, however, economic decline or stagnation has affected 100 countries, reducing the incomes of 1.6 billion people – again, more than a quarter of the world's population. In 70 of these countries average incomes are less than they were in 1980 – and in 43 countries less than they were in 1970. Over 1990–93 alone, average incomes fell by a fifth or more in 21 countries, mostly in Eastern Europe and among the CIS countries.

Although many are aware of this economic stagnation and decline, the full extent and gravity are too often obscured – because of the stunning success of the fast-growing countries, because most of the richer countries have maintained their growth and because of repeated hopes that many of the economies with falling incomes are poised to resume growth. After 15 years of such disappointing performance, international policy-makers need to question whether that optimism is warranted.

The advances have often been at rates exceeding anything seen since the start of the industrial revolution some two centuries ago. The declines have also been unprecedented, far exceeding in duration, and sometimes in depth, the declines of the Great Depression of the 1930s in the industrial countries.

In much of this success and disaster, many of the poor have missed out, and even the better off have often been left vulnerable to unemployment and downsizing – to cutbacks in health and welfare services. Although per capita incomes in the OECD countries now average $20,000, surveys reveal growing insecurity and considerable dissatisfaction.

WIDENING DISPARITIES IN ECONOMIC PERFORMANCE ARE CREATING TWO WORLDS – EVER MORE POLARIZED.

The world has become more polarized, and the gulf between the poor and rich of the world has widened even further. Of the $23 trillion global GDP in 1993, $18 trillion is in the industrial countries – only $5 trillion in the developing countries, even though they have nearly 80% of the world's people.

- The poorest 20% of the world's people saw their share of global income decline from 2.3% to 1.4% in the past 30 years. Meanwhile, the share of the richest 20% rose from 70% to 85%. That doubled the ratio of the shares of the richest and the poorest – from 30:1 to 61:1.
- The assets of the world's 358 billionaires exceed the combined annual incomes of countries with 45% of the world's people.
- During the past three decades the proportion of people enjoying per capita income growth of at least 5% a year more than doubled, from 12% to 27%, while the proportion of those experiencing negative growth more than tripled, from 5% to 18%.
- The gap in per capita income between the industrial and developing worlds tripled, from $5,700 in 1960 to $15,400 in 1993.

Increasing polarization is reflected in the growing contrasts in regional performance. Most of Asia, with more than half the world's people, experienced accelerating and often spectacular per capita income growth over the 1980s. OECD countries generally maintained slow but steady growth in per capita income. But failed growth was the dominant experience in four groups of countries.

- In Sub-Saharan Africa declines mostly began in the late 1970s. Many reform efforts have been launched, often spurring recoveries, but 20 countries are still below their per capita incomes of 20 years ago.
- Among the Latin American and Caribbean countries, several began to recover slowly in the late 1980s, but 18 of them are still below their per capita incomes of 10 years ago.

- Eastern Europe and the CIS countries maintained at least slow growth over most of the 1980s, but then suffered steep declines in per capita income – which fell on average by a third from the peaks in the mid-1980s.
- Many Arab states also suffered sharp declines in income in the 1980s, with falling oil prices and other setbacks in the world economy.

Although very rapid population growth explains part of the negative per capita income growth, blaming population growth for all or even most of the decline is too simple. Even with lower fertility and slower population growth, per capita incomes would have fallen in many countries.

EVERYWHERE, THE STRUCTURE AND QUALITY OF GROWTH DEMAND MORE ATTENTION – TO CONTRIBUTE TO HUMAN DEVELOPMENT, POVERTY REDUCTION AND LONG-TERM SUSTAINABILITY.

Policy-makers are often mesmerized by the quantity of growth. They need to be more concerned with its structure and quality. Unless governments take timely corrective action, economic growth can become lopsided and flawed. Determined efforts are needed to avoid growth that is jobless, ruthless, voiceless, rootless and futureless.

- *Jobless growth* – where the overall economy grows but does not expand the opportunities for employment. In the OECD countries in 1993 the average unemployment rate was 8% – ranging from 2.5% in Japan to 10% in the United Kingdom, 18% in Finland and 23% in Spain. In the developing countries too, jobless growth has meant long hours and very low incomes for the hundreds of millions of people in low-productivity work in agriculture and the informal sector.
- *Ruthless growth* – where the fruits of economic growth mostly benefit the rich, leaving millions of people struggling in ever-deepening poverty. During 1970–85 global GNP increased by 40%, yet the number of poor increased by

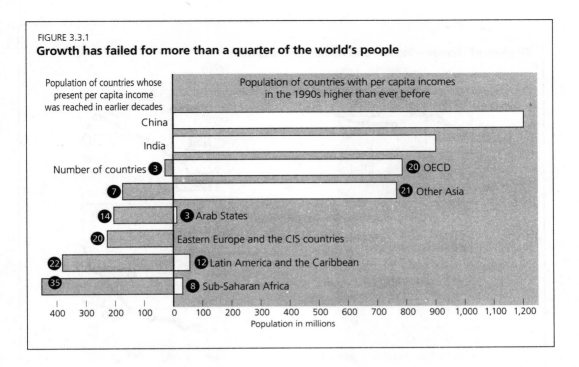

FIGURE 3.3.1

Growth has failed for more than a quarter of the world's people

Population of countries whose present per capita income was reached in earlier decades

Population of countries with per capita incomes in the 1990s higher than ever before

China

India

Number of countries ③ — ⑳ OECD

⑦ — ㉑ Other Asia

⑭ — ③ Arab States

⑳ — Eastern Europe and the CIS countries

㉒ — ⑫ Latin America and the Caribbean

㉟ — ⑧ Sub-Saharan Africa

400 300 200 100 0 100 200 300 400 500 600 700 800 900 1,000 1,100 1,200
Population in millions

When did countries with failed growth first reach their present per capita income?

1960 or before
Armenia
Central African Rep.
Chad
Georgia
Ghana
Haiti
Iraq
Kuwait
Liberia
Madagascar
Nicaragua
Niger
Rwanda
Senegal
Sudan
Tajikistan
Venezuela
Zaire
Zambia

In the 1960s
Bahamas
Bolivia
Côte d'Ivoire
Estonia
Guyana

Kiribati
Libyan Arab Jamahiriya
Lithuania
Mauritania
Peru
São Tomé and Principe
Saudi Arabia
Sierra Leone
Somalia
South Africa
Togo

In the 1970s
Albania
Algeria
Argentina
Bahrain
Brunei Darussalam
Cameroon
Comoros
Djibouti
El Salvador
Gabon
Gambia
Guatemala
Guinea-Bissau
Honduras

Iran, Islamic Rep. of
Jamaica
Kazakhstan
Kyrgyzstan
Latvia
Malawi
Mali
Mexico
Mozambique
Namibia
Nigeria
Poland
Romania
Tanzania
Trinidad and Tobago
Turkmenistan
Ukraine
United Arab Emirates
Uzbekistan
Vanuatu
Zimbabwe

In the 1980s
Azerbaijan
Barbados
Belarus
Benin

Brazil
Bulgaria
Burkina Faso
Burundi
Canada
Congo
Czech Rep.
Dominican Rep.
Ecuador
Egypt
Ethiopia
Finland
Hungary
Iceland
Jordan
Kenya
Mongolia
Morocco
Myanmar
Panama
Paraguay
Philippines
Slovakia
Suriname
Swaziland
Syrian Arab Rep.

Note: GDP per capita figures are in constant prices. Data are the latest available, 1995 for OECD countries, 1993 for most others.
Source: UN 1995, World Bank 1995.

FIGURE 3.3.2

30 years of change – income and human development

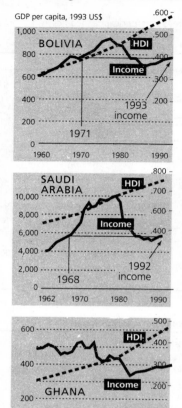

GDP per capita, 1993 US$

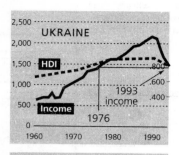

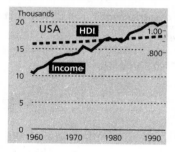

Countries with per capita incomes in the 1990s higher than ever before

Antigua and Barbuda	Equatorial Guinea	Lesotho	Seychelles
Australia	Fiji	Luxembourg	Singapore
Austria	France	Malaysia	Solomon Islands
Bangladesh	Germany	Maldives	Spain
Belgium	Greece	Malta	Sri Lanka
Belize	Grenada	Nepal	Sweden
Botswana	Guinea	Netherlands	Switzerland
Cambodia	Hong Kong	New Zealand	Thailand
Cape Verde	India	Norway	Tunisia
Chile	Indonesia	Oman	Turkey
China	Ireland	Pakistan	Uganda
Colombia	Israel	Papua New Guinea	United Kingdom
Costa Rica	Italy	Portugal	Uruguay
Cyprus	Japan	Saint Kitts and Nevis	USA
Denmark	Korea, Rep. of	Saint Lucia	Viet Nam
Dominica	Lao People's Dem. Rep.	Saint Vincent	

Note: GDP per capita figures are in constant prices. Data are the latest available, 1995 for OECD countries, 1993 for most others.
Source: UN 1995, World Bank 1995.

17%. While 200 million people saw their per capita incomes fall during 1965–80, more than one billion people did in 1980–93.

- *Voiceless growth* – where growth in the economy has not been accompanied by an extension of democracy or empowerment. Political repression and authoritarian controls have silenced alternative voices and stifled demands for greater social and economic participation.

  Policy-makers once debated whether they should choose economic growth or extensive participation, assuming that these were mutually exclusive. That debate is dead. People do not want one or the other – they want both. But too many people are still denied even the most basic forms of democracy, and many of the world's people are in the grip of repressive regimes.

  Voiceless growth can also be growth that gives women only a minor role in an economy's management and direction. As *Human Development Report 1995* showed, human development, if not engendered, is endangered.

- *Rootless growth* – which causes people's cultural identity to wither. There are thought to be about 10,000 distinct cultures, but many risk being marginalized or eliminated. In some cases minority cultures are being swamped by dominant cultures whose power has been amplified with growth. In other cases governments have deliberately imposed uniformity in the pursuit of nation-building – say, with a national language.

  This can be dangerous. The violence in the former Soviet Union and in the Balkan states of former Yugoslavia is a tragic legacy of culturally repressive governance. The nations that have held together best, from Switzerland to Malaysia, are often those that have recognized cultural diversity and decentralized economic and political governance to try to meet the aspirations of all their people.

- *Futureless growth* – where the present generation squanders resources needed by future generations. Rampant and uncontrolled economic growth in many countries is laying

waste to forests, polluting rivers, destroying biodiversity and depleting natural resources.

This damage and destruction is increasing, driven overwhelmingly by demand in the rich countries, inadequate conservation in the developing countries and the pressure of poor people pushed onto marginal lands in poor countries. On past trends, global production will triple by about 2030. Unless serious conservation and pollution controls are in place soon, production will be long past the point of sustainability.

In sum: development that perpetuates today's inequalities is neither sustainable nor worth sustaining.

PROGRESS IN HUMAN DEVELOPMENT HAS MOSTLY CONTINUED – BUT TOO UNEVENLY.

Despite the economic downturns and difficulties, key indicators of human development have advanced in almost all developing countries. Indeed, developing countries have made much more progress in human development than in income. Between 1960 and 1993 the North-South gap in life expectancy was more than halved, from 23 years to 11 years.

Human progress has nevertheless been very slow in some regions, and in some cases it even deteriorated. In the past 15 years the primary enrolment ratio stagnated in Sub-Saharan Africa as a whole, and in 17 countries it declined by 37–50%. And while the human development index (HDI) of most regions has improved, in Eastern Europe and the CIS countries it has declined sharply.

Overall, countries already in the high human development category (with an HDI of more than 0.800) have been able to reduce their HDI shortfall (the difference between the maximum possible HDI of 1 and the value achieved) by nearly 2.7% a year. For low human development countries (with an HDI of less than 0.500) the reduction was only 0.9% a year. So, there was a clear widening of the gap in human development as well.

Countries with similar levels of income and growth can have very different rates of advance in human development. During the past three decades both Tunisia and Congo enjoyed the same economic growth from similar starting points of income and human development. But Tunisia reduced its HDI shortfall by 60%, Congo by only 16%.

This record contains a warning. Unless economic growth is restored for countries in decline, their gains in human development may be ever more difficult to sustain – and present disparities will grow. At present rates of progress, it will take a century or more for the low human development countries to reach high human development.

THERE ARE STRIKING CONTRASTS IN TODAY'S RELATIONSHIP BETWEEN HUMAN DEVELOPMENT AND PER CAPITA INCOME.

- *Rankings by the human development index do not always match income rankings* – For 37 countries in 1993 their ranking by the HDI is more than 20 places higher or lower than their ranking by per capita income, highlighting the far from perfect correlation between income and human development in many countries.
- *Higher human development at lower income* – Some countries fall in the category of high human development despite modest per capita incomes. These include Colombia, with a per capita income of $1,400, and Thailand, with $2,100.
- *Lower human development at higher income* – Other countries have remained at medium levels of human development despite the advantage of greater incomes. These include South Africa, with a per capita income of nearly $3,000, and Gabon, with nearly $5,000.
- *Striking contrasts within countries* – In Mexico the HDI for indigenous people is only 0.700, compared with 0.890 for the rest of the population.
- *Human development weaknesses in OECD countries* – Despite high per capita incomes ($20,000), more than 100 million people in

OECD countries live below national poverty lines, and more than 5 million are homeless.

These and numerous other indicators in this Report spotlight the dangers of complacency. Many policy-makers assume that a rapidly expanding economy will sweep poverty and deprivation away. They are wrong. The challenge is broader and deeper – and demands close attention to a range of policy actions. This Report examines these actions in detail and reaches the following main conclusions.

SHORT-TERM ADVANCES IN HUMAN DEVELOPMENT ARE POSSIBLE – BUT THEY WILL NOT BE SUSTAINABLE WITHOUT FURTHER GROWTH. CONVERSELY, ECONOMIC GROWTH IS NOT SUSTAINABLE WITHOUT HUMAN DEVELOPMENT.

Improvements in human development have clearly been possible even in times of economic setback. But such advances can be sustained over a long time only if supported by economic growth. At the same time, for economic growth to be sustained, it must be constantly nourished by human development. Human development and economic growth should move together, strongly linked.

The record of economic growth and human development over the past 30 years shows that no country can follow a course of lopsided development for such a long time – where economic growth is not matched by advances in human development, or vice versa. Lopsided development can last for a decade or so, but it then shifts to rapid rises in both incomes and human development, or falls into slow improvements in both human development and incomes. Countries follow one of four patterns:

- *Slow economic growth and fast human development.* Countries achieving human development with only slow economic growth in one decade either increased economic growth in the next (the Republic of Korea in the 1960s and China and Indonesia in the 1970s) or slipped back into poor economic growth and slow human development (Cameroon, Sierra Leone and others in the 1980s).

- *Fast economic growth and slow human development.* Lopsided development tilted against human development is a dead end, with economic growth petering out after a decade or so of fast growth (such as Brazil and Egypt in the 1980s). No country with fast growth and slow human development maintained fast growth and accelerated human development.
- *Mutually reinforcing growth and human development.* Some countries enjoyed rapid improvements in both human development and incomes, sustained over three decades, in a mutually reinforcing virtuous circle.
- *Mutually stifling growth and human development.* Other countries suffered slow advances in human development and slow economic growth.

THERE NEED BE NO CONFLICT BETWEEN GROWTH AND EQUITY.

The traditional view that economic growth in the early stages is inevitably associated with deteriorating income distribution has been proved false. The new insight is that an equitable distribution of public and private resources can enhance the prospects for further growth.

The assertion that the benefits of growth in the early stages would inevitably be skewed towards the rich rested on two principal arguments. The first came from Nobel laureate Simon Kuznets, who said that inequality would first rise, as workers left agriculture for industry, and then fall as industrial production became more widespread. The second was advanced by Nicholas Kaldor, who emphasized the importance of savings. He argued that the only way to finance growth would be by channelling the initial benefits into the pockets of rich capitalists. Since they have a higher propensity to save, only they could provide the funds for investment.

These hypotheses have been disproved by recent evidence of a positive correlation between economic growth and income equality (as represented by the share of the poorest 60% of the population). Japan and East Asia pioneered this form of equitable development, and China, Malaysia and Mauritius have been following a similar route more recently.

The discovery of this reinforcing relationship between equity and growth has far-reaching implications for policy-makers. Well-developed human capabilities and well-distributed opportunities can ensure that growth is not lopsided and that its benefits are equitably shared. They can also help in getting the most growth.

FOR POLICY-MAKERS EVERYWHERE, THE FOCUS MUST BE ON STRENGTHENING THE LINKS BETWEEN ECONOMIC GROWTH AND HUMAN DEVELOPMENT.

To ensure that these links work efficiently and effectively in both directions, policy-makers need to understand how the links connect. Some of the most important issues determining how growth contributes to human development:

- *Equity* – The more equally GNP and economic opportunities are distributed, the more likely that they will be translated into improved human well-being.
- *Job opportunities* – Economic growth is translated into people's lives when they are offered productive and well-paid work. An important way to achieve this is to aim for patterns of growth that are heavily labour-intensive.
- *Access to productive assets* – Many people find their economic opportunities stifled by a lack of access to productive assets – particularly land, physical infrastructure and financial credit. The state can do much in all these areas by stepping in and levelling the playing fields.
- *Social spending* – Governments and communities can greatly influence human development by channelling a major part of public revenue into high-priority social expenditure – particularly by providing basic social services for all.

- *Gender equality* – Fairer opportunities for women and better access to education, child care, credit and employment contribute to their human development. They also contribute to the human development of other family members and to economic growth. Investing in women's capabilities and empowering them to exercise their choices is the surest way to contribute to economic growth and overall development.
- *Population policy* – Education, reproductive health and child survival all help lower fertility, thus creating the conditions for slower population growth and lower education and health costs in the longer run.
- *Good governance* – When those in power give high priority to the needs of the whole population, and when people participate in decision-making at many levels, the links between economic growth and human well-being are likely to be stronger and more durable.
- *An active civil society* – Non-governmental organizations and community groups also play a vital part in enhancing human development. They not only supplement government services, extending them to people and groups who would otherwise remain unserved. They also play a vital advocacy role, mobilizing public opinion and community action and helping shape human development priorities.

A determined effort to expand human capabilities – through improved education, health and nutrition – can help transform the prospects for economic growth, especially in the low-human-development, low-income countries. A World Bank study of 192 countries concluded that only 16% of growth is explained by physical capital (machinery, buildings and physical infrastructure), while 20% comes from natural capital. But no less than 64% can be attributed to human and social capital. An extensive analysis of earlier experience in the Asian industrializing tigers, including Japan, comes to similar conclusions.

NEW APPROACHES ARE NEEDED TO EXPAND AND IMPROVE EMPLOYMENT OPPORTUNITIES, SO THAT PEOPLE CAN PARTICIPATE IN GROWTH – AND BENEFIT FROM IT.

Without growth, it is difficult to create jobs and increase wages. With growth, job opportunities normally expand. But again, the process is not automatic. Witness several recent periods of "jobless growth". And even when jobs have been created, they have not met the aspirations of people in search of job security, remunerative work or creative work. They have also bypassed whole groups of society – including women, young adults, the uneducated, the unskilled and people with disabilities.

To forge a strong link between economic growth and employment requires employment-generating growth strategies. The experience of the fast-growing Asian economies – Hong Kong, the Republic of Korea, Singapore and Taiwan (province of China) – shows how sustained long-term growth can expand employment (by 2–6% a year), reduce unemployment (down to less than 2.5%) and raise productivity and wages. This in turn reduced inequality and poverty. Such growth was led by small-scale agriculture in Taiwan (province of China) and by labour-intensive export-oriented manufacturing in Hong Kong, the Republic of Korea and Singapore.

The Latin American experience stands in stark contrast. During the 1960s and 1970s the average annual growth in per capita income was more than 4% in Brazil, 3.5% in Mexico and 2.5% in Costa Rica. But this growth was not accompanied by the creation of enough jobs to absorb the growing labour force or by increases in productivity. The region's productivity growth during the past three decades was only 0.5% a year, an eighth that of the Asian tigers' 4%. Growth was concentrated in capital-intensive activities – mining and import-substitution industries. Employment expanded, but mostly in the service sectors and without a sustained increase in productivity.

A strategy for economic growth that emphasizes people and their productive potential is the only way to open opportunities. Although most of the action must be taken at the country level, it is increasingly clear that new international measures are also needed to encourage and support national strategies for employment creation and human development.

Some of the specifics:

- *A political commitment to full employment* – The countries achieving the greatest success in employment have generally been those that deliberately set out do so. Rather than assuming that employment would materialize automatically, they have publicly identified it as a central policy objective.
- *Enhancing human capabilities* – High-employment economies have generally invested heavily in the development of human capabilities – particularly education, health and skills. They also have constantly upgraded technical skills to enable workers to adapt to rapidly changing international conditions. The Republic of Korea invests $160 per person a year in health and education, Malaysia $150. India, by contrast, invests only $14, Pakistan $10 and Bangladesh $5.
- *Strengthening small-scale and informal sector production* – In many countries such production has demonstrated the potential for generating employment and incomes for millions of people while providing a wide range of the basic goods and services needed in daily life. It needs to be encouraged and supported, not restricted. Some countries have increased opportunities for employment – particularly self-employment – by extending access to credit. There are many encouraging examples among small farmers, microenterprises, and poor and marginal communities. And extension services and other mechanisms to enable small-scale producers to get better and quicker access to technology and information can often make a big difference in their productivity.
- *Broader and more egalitarian access to land* – Numerous studies show that small farmers achieve higher output per hectare than large farmers. So, providing greater access to land can increase productivity, employment and growth while reducing poverty and easing the pressure on scarce resources.
- *Research and development* – Another part of successful employment strategies is intensive investment in research and development for labour-intensive technology, including the adaptation of imported capital-intensive technologies to fit local needs.

NEW PATTERNS OF GROWTH WILL NEED TO BE DEVELOPED AND SUSTAINED WELL INTO THE 21ST CENTURY – TO PREVENT EVER MORE EXTREME IMBALANCES AND INEQUALITIES IN THE WORLD ECONOMY.

The imbalances in economic growth over the past 15 years are clear enough. But if allowed to continue well into the next century, they will produce a world gargantuan in its excesses and grotesque in its human and economic inequalities.

- Poverty in Sub-Saharan African and other least developed countries would deepen, with per capita income falling to $325 by 2030.
- Meanwhile, per capita income in the OECD countries would rise to nearly $40,000.
- Although East Asia would catch up to the incomes of the OECD countries in 15–25 years, it would take China about 50 years, and India a century or more.

Such scenarios do not pretend to be a forecast. They simply suggest what could happen if current trends continued, to emphasize the need for purposeful action – both national and international. Much attention is now given to the rapid rates of population growth. Equal attention needs to be given to the much larger and more rapidly growing imbalances in the growth of consumption and resource use.

NEW MECHANISMS MUST BE DEVELOPED TO HELP THE WEAK AND THE VULNERABLE SEIZE THE OPPORTUNITIES OF THE NEW GLOBAL ECONOMY, WHILE PROTECTING THEM FROM MARGINALIZATION.

Globalization is one of the most dramatic developments of recent years. During 1965–90 world merchandise trade tripled, and global trade in services increased more than fourteenfold. Meanwhile, financial flows have reached unimaginable dimensions. More than a trillion dollars roam the world every 24 hours, restlessly seeking the highest return. This flow of capital is not just offering unprecedented opportunities for profit (and loss). It has opened the world to the operation of a global financial market that leaves even the strongest countries with limited autonomy over interest rates, exchange rates or other financial policies.

Many developing countries have seized globalization as an opportunity. Countries that combine low wages with high technology skills have out-competed more established countries. In just ten years India has expanded its software development industry, centred on "Silicon Bangalore", to become the world's second largest software exporter. Other developing countries need to escape their debilitating dependence on exports of low-value primary products by combining their natural resources with their human capital. In the 21st century rapid strides in technology and communications will open the prospect of "leapfrogging" several decades of development – but only for the poor countries that can master the new skills and compete.

While globalization has often helped growth in the strong countries, it has bypassed the weak. The poorest countries, with 20% of the world's people, have seen their share of world trade fall between 1960 and 1990 – from 4% to less than 1%. And they receive a meagre 0.2% of the world's commercial lending. Although private investment flows to developing countries increased between 1970 and 1994 from $5 billion to $173 billion, three-quarters of this went to just ten countries, mostly in East and South-East Asia and Latin America. Countries elsewhere, particularly in Sub-Saharan Africa, have been left behind.

The agenda to achieve the new patterns of growth for human development would have four priorities:

First, three groups of countries need faster economic growth, especially after the declines of the 1980s.

- *The low human development countries* – With nearly two billion people, these countries must accelerate their human development, backed by rapid economic growth. A massive expansion of education and health must be at the core, especially when half the population often lacks these most basic requirements. Each of these countries has to revamp its domestic social and economic policies, with stronger priorities for human development, economic growth and poverty reduction. And most will also need a new level of long-term international commitment for debt relief, more and better-focused financial assistance, and actions to open export markets and move to sustained economic growth. All the least developed countries need to reach a minimum annual economic growth rate of 3% per capita, with a higher rate in countries still below their per capita incomes of a decade or more ago.

- *The formerly socialist countries, now in transition* – With their per capita incomes having fallen by about a third since 1990, these countries must restart growth and sustain it for several decades. Domestic reforms backed by loans and other international economic and social support can help achieve this and end the free fall of many of these economies.

- *The middle range of developing countries* – Most countries in Latin America, the Middle East, North Africa and South and South-East Asia need an acceleration in growth to support human development.

Second, in two groups of countries the priority is to improve the quality of growth and to sustain – rather than increase – the rate of growth.

- *The fast-growing developing countries* – For China and the countries of East and South-East Asia the challenge is not so much to accelerate growth further. It is to ensure the long-term sustainability of this growth and to give more attention to poverty reduction and human development.
- *The OECD countries* – With very high incomes and growth averaging about 2% per capita during the 1980s, the human development challenge for the OECD countries is to move to new approaches to employment, equity and satisfying life styles in ways consistent with steady growth. Another part of that challenge is to provide support for health care, pensions and other social services – for children, the working poor and the growing numbers in their postretirement years.

The limits to growth and material consumption will become more obvious as countries reach higher levels of income – but there are no limits to human creativity, human compassion and the human spirit.

Third, global action is needed to support national efforts to expand employment opportunities.

Both developing and industrial countries need international support if their national efforts towards full employment are to succeed. New forms of international action are required, and the United Nations and the Bretton Woods organizations should work together to devise them. This Report recommends:

- New measures to support countries in reversing downward employment trends, including more effective multilateral and bilateral debt relief, reformed development assistance backed by concessional resources, and access

to export markets, often through trade preferences.
- A global commission to study and propose international measures for national policy and action for full employment.

Fourth, a global safety net should be created to move all countries with low levels of human development to medium levels in the next ten years.

National and international efforts for human development may have continued over time – but those supporting it with economic growth and resources have too often failed. A major international priority must be to move all countries to at least medium levels of human development in the next ten years – laying a human foundation for accelerating growth, reducing poverty and achieving more equitable development in the 21st century.

- High-profile monitoring and reporting on the situation of the poorest and least developed countries, at least until rapid growth in human development and income is achieved.
- Serious and sustained support for any least developed country that has a plan for widespread and solid human development.

Often this assistance needs to be accompanied by a radical overhaul of the domestic management of their economies. But not always. A good number of the poorer and weaker economies have already taken far-reaching measures to reform and restructure their economies, but with little growth to show for their efforts.

Richer countries need to provide greater support – with an international safety net, fashioned perhaps through compacts between poor and rich nations. The poor nations can demonstrate their willingness to invest in their people and in their economies. The rich nations can offer a package of resources (through aid, debt relief and trade concessions) sufficient to generate a respectable rate of growth and to provide universal coverage of basic social services. This will strengthen the link between economic growth and human development, both nationally and internationally.

• • •

In a fast-changing global economy there are no simple answers, no easy rides. And as this Report so graphically demonstrates, inertia is not an option. Economic growth should lead to fuller choices for all people – rather than few choices for most people or many choices for a few. But it is never enough to wait for economic growth automatically to trickle down to the poor. Instead, human development and poverty reduction must be moved to the top of the agenda for political and economic policy-making. And even when links between economic growth and human development have been painstakingly established, they must be protected against being blown apart by sudden shifts in political power or market force.

REFERENCES

UN (United Nations). 1995. *Statistical Yearbook 1993*. 40th issue. New York.

World Bank. 1995. "World Data 1995." World Bank indicators on CD-ROM. Washington, D.C.

3.4

THE POLITICS OF POVERTY ERADICATION

Chapter 5, *Human Development Report 1997*
Drafted principally by Håkan Björkman based on background papers by Gita Sen and Paul Streeten

Politics, not just economics, determines what we do – or don't do – to address human poverty. And what is lacking is not the resources or the economic solutions – but the political momentum to tackle poverty head on.

Much is known about what is needed to eradicate poverty – job-led growth, access to credit, redistribution of land, investment in basic social services, promotion of the informal sector and sound macroeconomic policies. But too little attention has gone to finding ways to ensure that such actions are taken. How can an environment be created that ensures that state policies, market forces, civil activism and community mobilization contribute to the eradication of poverty? What political reform is needed to ensure pro-poor policies and pro-poor markets?

A political strategy for poverty eradication has three essential elements:

POLITICAL EMPOWERMENT OF POOR PEOPLE. People must organize for collective action to influence the circumstances and decisions affecting their lives. To advance their interests, their voices must be heard in the corridors of power.

PARTNERSHIPS FOR CHANGE. All agents in society – trade unions, the media, community groups, private companies, political parties, academic institutions, professional associations – need to come together in a partnership to address human poverty in all its dimensions. And that partnership must be based on common interests and brokered compromises. Society must be open enough to tolerate a complex web of interests and coalitions and to ensure stability and progress towards human development.

AN ENABLING AND RESPONSIBLE STATE. The state needs to foster peaceful expression of people's priorities and to ensure democratic space for brokering the interests of society's many groups. Thus it needs to promote participation and encourage private-public partnerships. It also needs to be transparent and accountable – and to resist pressure from the economically powerful.

A FORMIDABLE CHALLENGE

Building peaceful political momentum for poverty eradication is a formidable challenge. Poverty often serves the vested interests of the economically powerful, who may benefit from exploiting the pool of low-paid labour (box 3.4.1).

The realities of economic, social and political disparities and injustices are so overwhelming that few believe that things can change. And some think that only violence and confrontation can produce real change in favour of the poor. Poverty is brutal. It can provoke violent reactions. Those who profit from the status quo have often defended their position with violence. And when disappointment and frustration have risen to a crisis point, the poor have sometimes turned to armed struggle.

Progress in human development and in eradicating human poverty has often been won through uprisings and rebellions against states that have advanced the interests of the economically powerful while tolerating rigid class divisions, unbearable economic conditions and human suffering and poverty.

History is marked by uprisings and rebellions sparked by poverty. English peasants revolted against an impoverishing poll tax in 1381.

German peasants rose up against their feudal overlords in opposition to serfdom in 1524.

Among developing countries, India has a long tradition of peasants' movements. As far back as the 17th and 18th centuries, when India was ruled by the British East India Company, peasants rose up against their British landlords.

In Bangladesh as recently as the 1950s, there was another large-scale peasants' movement, a response to unjust sharecropping practices. Although sharecroppers were responsible for providing all the inputs, including labour, they received only a third of the yield, with two-thirds going to the landlords. The Three-Division Movement that arose in opposition to this exploitation demanded a 50:50 split. Violence erupted, and the authorities responded with force. But ultimately the peasants' demands prevailed, and the principle of equal distribution of sharecroppers' production was enacted into law.

Full-scale revolutions have their roots in people's reactions to poverty and economic injustice. Spontaneous uprisings instigated the French Revolution in 1789, the revolutionary movements throughout Europe in 1848 and the Bolshevik Revolution in 1917. The wars of independence in Africa and Asia in the 19th and 20th centuries were not only an expression of nationalism – they were also a struggle against economic and social injustice. The civil rights movement in the United States in the 1960s too was a struggle for economic and social emancipation – at times resulting in violence despite the pacifist philosophy of its leader, Martin Luther King Jr.

Sometimes it was the violence itself that sabotaged the achievements of these struggles. Many revolutions replaced one evil with another through harsh recriminations, self-serving leadership, misguided utopianism or betrayals.

Naturally, not all progress in eradicating poverty was achieved through confrontation. Some strides in reducing poverty, especially since 1960, have been gradual and peaceful, as with the formation of welfare states in industrial countries and the reduction of infant mortality, the increase in life expectancy and other achievements in developing countries.

This chapter looks at the need for peaceful – but fundamental – reform through collective action and democracy. The challenge facing today's leaders, activists and citizens is to learn from history and work towards non-violent change, understanding the risks of confrontation and the backlashes it can produce. Avoiding violence and chaos is in all people's interest, and the imperative of avoiding disorder must be the motivation to share power more equitably.

BOX 3.4.1

Vested interests in perpetuating poverty

Poor people are often seen as an economic burden on society. Yet poverty often serves the vested interests of the economically powerful, who may depend on the poverty-stricken to ensure that their societies run smoothly. A mobile pool of low-paid and unorganized workers is useful for doing the "dirty, dangerous and difficult" work that others refuse to do. In industrial countries many jobs considered menial are taken by immigrants, legal and illegal. With no legal protection or opportunity for collective action, workers are often exploited, receiving wages far below the minimum.

The poor can also be politically convenient. In some countries they serve as scapegoats for the ills of society as immigrant workers do in Europe and North America. But they can also serve as a useful pool of voters for politicians who claim to serve their interests – even if they never consult them.

In the end, poverty reduction must involve some redistribution of resources – economic, social or political – and that will sometimes be vigorously opposed. Any strategy to eradicate poverty must therefore take into account the fact that many people have a vested interest in the perpetuation of poverty.

Source: Øyen 1997.

THE NEED FOR COLLECTIVE ACTION

Achievements in eradicating human poverty depend first and foremost on people's ability to articulate their demands and mobilize for collective action. Isolated and dispersed, poor people have no power and no influence over political decisions that affect their lives. But organized, they have the power to ensure that their interests are advanced. As a group they can influence state policies and push for the allocation of adequate resources to human development priorities, for markets that are more people-friendly and for economic growth that is pro-poor. It is the pressure from people to defend their rights and to remove obstacles and enhance their life opportunities that will eradicate human poverty.

Putting local initiatives and community action at the centre of poverty eradication strategies is the only way, though a difficult one, to ensure that those strategies are truly people-centred. This has profound implications. Poor people must no longer be seen as beneficiaries of government largesse, but instead as legitimate claimants of entitlements. That is why years of action by community groups and others have focused increasingly on rights – to employment, to health, to reproductive freedom, to participation. This approach recognizes the inherent dignity of all members of the human family – a dignity that states have a duty to protect.

People's mobilization for collective action to eradicate poverty may take many forms.

Community mobilization

Poor people must mobilize themselves and build solidarity to improve their life opportunities. Individual empowerment is the starting point of community action. As the women's movement has so successfully demonstrated, the personal is political (box 3.4.2).

At the core of collective action against poverty is self-help. Under normal circumstances most communities already have systems of mutual support. One of the main assets people have to defend themselves against poverty is the network of family and community to which they can turn to cope with sudden crises.

BOX 3.4.2

Alagamma gains control of her life

Empowerment is about change in favour of those who previously exercised little control over their lives. This has two sides. The first is control over resources (financial, physical and human). The second is control over ideology (beliefs, values and attitudes).

Alagamma is an illiterate Indian woman of scheduled caste. She used to earn a pittance from Ganesan, a quarrying contractor, by breaking granite blocks into smaller stones. Her entire family was bonded to Ganesan because her father once borrowed money from him secured on their quarter acre of land.

Then the government gave quarrying rights to groups of women workers like Alagamma, breaking the hold of contractors and the Indian mafia.

Alagamma and her father took Rs 1,000 ($40) to the shop where Ganesan was sitting. They told him that they had come to repay the money they had borrowed eight years ago and reclaim their quarter acre. Ganesan was not inclined to take the money and told them to come back in two or three years. But Alagamma and her father were adamant: they told Ganesan they would plough their land the next day. And they did.

Empowerment starts with changes in consciousness and in self-perception. This can be the most explosively creative, energy-releasing transformation, one from which there is no looking back. Empowerment taps powerful reservoirs of hope and enthusiasm among people used to viewing themselves negatively.

Governments, NGOs and other institutions do not empower people; people empower themselves. But through policies and actions governments can either create a supportive environment or put up barriers to empowerment.

Source: G. Sen 1997.

At times, however, these networks are stretched beyond breaking point. Historical processes such as wars or colonization have sometimes weakened the social capital of communities. This has happened, for example, in large areas of Indochina – Cambodia, the Lao People's Democratic Republic and Viet Nam – as a result of the Viet Nam War and its aftermath.

Much the same could be said of the impact of colonialism in Africa. The belittling of African culture and identity and imposition of Western values sabotaged social cohesion and solidarity in many communities. Strengthening cultural traditions can be an important part of building the capacity for taking collective action.

There are striking examples of communities coming together to fight poverty. In Senegal villagers have set up development associations for village improvement, water management, road construction, cooperative marketing, mosque building and a range of other activities. The emergence of "local corporatism" in recent years in China is another example of small-scale economic solidarity. Township and village enterprises are spreading fast in rural areas of Guangdong, Hebei and Jiangsu Provinces. Part of the profits are put into community funds to help support adult education and finance informal insurance schemes for protection in case of illness.

In many other countries cooperative associations based on traditional forms of solidarity manage small irrigation systems, ensuring that the poorest households get the water they need. In the Philippines these self-managed schemes are called *zanjeros,* in Thailand *muang-fai* and in Bali *subaks.*

Community organizations, whatever the terms used to describe them, are multiplying the world over. Kenya has 23,000 registered women's groups, and the Philippines about 12,000 people's organizations. In India the state of Tamil Nadu alone has more than 25,000 community organizations. Counting non-registered groups would push the figures even higher.

Non-governmental organizations

A vibrant civil society working towards the eradication of poverty also depends on the mobilization of people in more formal organizations. Strong communities of NGOs are particularly active in some countries – such as Bangladesh, Brazil, India, Indonesia, Kenya, the Philippines, Thailand and Zimbabwe – playing a vital role in poverty eradication and in advocating people-friendly development strategies. In Thailand, for example, government-NGO consultations and partnerships are frequent and dynamic in many important policy areas – from environmental protection to housing rights for slum dwellers to HIV/AIDS prevention. NGOs must have the space and freedom to play this essential role.

NGOs can be an important force for poverty eradication – pressing for land reform, for example, or protecting slum dwellers from property developers (box 3.4.3). They can also represent people's views and priorities in contacts with governments.

In addition, NGOs can reinforce and complement government activities – tending to be more flexible, more responsive and more effective than official agencies in reaching some communities. This role should not be seen as "filling gaps" because it does not relieve governments of their responsibilities, a result that might be repugnant to some proponents of NGOs. But there are many productive partnerships achieving things that governments alone could not. In India, for example, government resources combined with NGO energy and creativity reaped spectacular results in the Total Literacy Campaign.

Trade unions

Throughout the 20th century and before, trade unions have played a vital part in promoting better living and working conditions. In the industrial countries years of trade union activism were part of the struggle for higher wages, better benefits, shorter working hours and stronger safety precautions in the workplace. But trade unions have also had a much broader social and political impact. In many countries trade unions were influential in the development of welfare states and people-friendly markets (box 3.4.4).

But their power has been waning, and membership is down almost everywhere. In the United

States union membership declined from 23% of the labor force in 1970 to 16% in 1990. In France it has fallen from 22% to 10%, and in Spain from 26% to 10%. Only in the Nordic countries has union membership increased since 1970.

In developing countries the shares tend to be smaller, because there are fewer workers in the formal sector. In Sub-Saharan Africa only 1–2% of workers are unionized – and they tend to be the ones with better-paying, stable jobs. In Latin America and the Caribbean the share is about 20%.

As developing countries industrialize, unions become more important. In the Republic of Korea they have been the impetus for democratization. But in Asia generally, they are under pressure from governments and from multinational corporations, which often make their absence a condition of investment.

Trade unions have had trouble adapting to the changing times. They have lost influence as the workforce has shifted away from the ranks of production-line workers and towards the more dispersed workers in the services sector. The rapid increase in unemployment has further weakened the economic clout of trade unions. Many critics of trade unions now accuse them of contributing to unemployment and poverty by pushing the price of labour too high. If trade unions are to remain relevant, they clearly need to reinvent themselves – to represent a new generation of workers in a context of reduced demand for labour and to build broader alliances.

BOX 3.4.3

Empowering the urban poor in Mumbai, India

In developing countries NGOs play an indispensable role in helping to reduce and eliminate poverty. Their activities vary widely, but their aims are the same.

Yuva – Youth for Unity and Voluntary Action – is one of many NGOs working in Mumbai (Bombay) for the rights of the urban poor. It organizes youth and women for social action in housing, health, education and the judicial system and offers counseling. Yuva is also active in policy advocacy – and made its voice heard at the Habitat II conference in Istanbul in 1996.

One of its main activities is providing support to pavement dwellers, who are under constant threat of being evicted and of having their makeshift homes bulldozed by the municipal authorities. Often when people are evicted, the authorities offer to relocate them to the outskirts of the city far from their work and from their children's schools. Most soon trickle back to their old locations, and the cycle starts again.

These people can find themselves powerless in the vice between politicians and large urban developers – a situation that also offers considerable scope for petty corruption by local officials. Yuva educates people about their rights – with respect to housing, employment and schooling for their children Recognizing that, as elsewhere most responsibility for household survival falls on women, Yuva also supports such activities as women's savings funds.

One of the pavement dwellers, Lalitabai, explains their concerns: "We have lived here for many years, most of us for more than 15 years. We have ration cards, and our names are on the voting lists. We have a right to this ground. We are saying that we will not move from here until we have been given land and a house. And not housing miles away in the jungle outside Mumbai. No, what use would that be to us? We need housing here so we can continue to work in our jobs."

The success of organizations such as Yuva will always depend on the determination and courage of the poor people with whom they work. These qualities are clearly demonstrated by another pavement dweller, Shantabai, who says: "If we were not alert, they would simply come and take away our belongings. But we will fight them. We know this is a just fight. They claim they are enforcing the law, but we have been told and we know that these laws are wrong. It is right to resist them."

Source: G. Sen 1997.

People's movements

Another essential form of collective action is the self-mobilization of people into large movements. Although these movements are often equated with unrest and violence, it is often the resistance to them by repressive regimes and corporate interests that causes the violence – not the movements themselves. To be effective, people's movements must emerge spontaneously from grass-roots initiatives, not be controlled or manipulated from above. This is not to downplay the importance of leadership in harnessing the energies of people towards common goals.

The most spectacular example of a people's movement: the enormously strong women's movement. Global in reach, empowering half the world's people, the women's movement has driven the progress towards gender equality. The recognition of equality as a human right, the near-universal right to vote and the increasing equality in educational enrolment in most countries – these are just some of the revolutionary achievements of this century-old movement.

Another notable example: the struggle against British rule in India, led by Mahatma Gandhi. His policies of *ahimsa* (non-violence) and *satyagraha* (passive resistance) have been the inspiration for many popular movements since – notably the civil rights movement in the United States. Gandhi's legacy includes the aspiration to eradicate the unjust social and economic aspects of the caste system.

Some movements – such as the anti-apartheid movement in South Africa and the movement for democracy in the Philippines that brought Corazon

---

BOX 3.4.4

Trade unions led poverty reduction in Germany

Trade unions work solely for the benefit of their members. True? Not always. Many have had a much broader social and political impact – such as those in Germany.

Since the late 19th century the work week in German industry has been virtually halved. The union movement has also succeeded in ensuring the steady extension of financial safeguards against the kind of economic downturns that led to rampant poverty and misery in the 1870s and 1930s.

Many things now taken for granted are social rights that were fought for and won with much struggle by the trade unions: freedom of association, the right to strike and to bargain collectively, industrial health and safety standards, industrial law, universal suffrage, co-determination, and worker participation in the workplace and the company and representation on public bodies responsible for everything from social insurance to radio.

Trade unions proved to be the biggest organized force working not only for social reform but also for democracy. Alongside other associations and political parties and often against strong opposition, they struggled for a more people-friendly market and a "social state", basic political rights and democratization. Trade unions became "schools" and guarantors of democracy. With the creation of the Federal Republic, they strongly supported the strengthening of democratic traditions and the creation of a "social market economy".

In the postwar era the German economy has been a powerful exporter. Social progress did not inhibit international competitiveness – contrary to what some critics of the social welfare state and strong unions still contend.

Although in Germany labour does not have the same influence over national politics as it does in Austria or Sweden, workers' councils and co-determination at local levels have been decisive in guaranteeing social progress, even in times of slow growth. Both unions and management are prohibited from taking actions that could endanger the welfare of the company. The outcome is referred to as "socially oriented business policy".

The German labour union movement stands in stark contrast to the antagonistic labour relations in the United Kingdom and the United States. The underlying difference is that the German model is based on negotiation and compromise, the Anglo-American model on exclusion and polarization.

Source: Schneider 1991 and Block 1995.

Aquino to power – have profoundly affected national human development.

Smaller movements focused on specific issues or reacting to a specific threat are also important collective action. Many local groups have mobilized against development projects or private company activities that threaten the natural environment and the livelihoods that depend on it. Others have focused on more general environmental concerns – for example, the Green Belt movement in Kenya (box 3.4.5). And still other have focused on health and nutrition issues – such as the Hunger Campaign in Brazil (box 3.4.6).

THE NEED FOR PARTNERSHIPS

The success of political mobilization against poverty hinges on winning broad and diverse support. Poor people alone, however well organized, cannot force the policy shifts for poverty eradication. All groups in society must be involved – not just those representing the poor. Alliances, partnerships and compromises are the only viable vehicles for peaceful, sustained reform.

What does it take to mobilize those alliances and partnerships? A clear, shared vision of the future that provides an unshakable focus for action. And not just for the poor. Visionary ideals can rally groups normally seen as elite – politicians, academics and other leading members of society – to form alliances with the poor.

When enough people rally to a cause, many ideals can become realistic. Consider the abolition of slavery in the 19th century. And consider many of the welfare reforms of the 20th century, which would have seemed unthinkable a few decades before. Idealists should thus continue to think the unthinkable, but with clear commitment, presenting their proposal with the same detail and elaboration typically devoted to a meticulous defence of the status quo.

Reformers need to work out the best strategy for negotiating their way through the power structure. Each strategy must of course take local circumstances into account, but experience shows the value of some general approaches, such as finding common interests and exploiting differences among elite groups.

BOX 3.4.5

Environmental protection brings status to Kenyan women

People's movements have been hugely successful in protecting the environment and blocking the most destructive activities of multinational corporations.

In Kenya some 100,000 women have planted more than 20 million trees as part of the Green Belt movement. Begun 20 years ago, the movement arose in response to the alarming rate of soil erosion, which was threatening rural livelihoods.

Its success has been not only in planting trees and combating soil erosion, but also in empowering women – giving them self-esteem and status in their communities and enabling them to earn extra income by selling seedlings. The movement has also made people more aware of the importance of the environment to their survival.

Although the central government has in the past been suspicious of such powerful grass-roots move-

ments, local forestry officials are now closely involved in the Green Belt movement, providing extension services to the women.

The movement is a good example of how a narrowly focused initiative gradually expands into a broad-based politicized movement. The members are benefiting from civic education, debating a wide range of political issues – corruption, human rights and security of tenure for slum dwellers.

The movement now has an advocacy role beyond protecting the environment. With wide popular support it has an impact on policies and is helping to build a solid base for more equitable development and democratic governance.

Source: Maathai 1997.

Finding and creating areas of common interest

No child should die of hunger. On this the whole community can probably agree. The community may also agree that all citizens, regardless of their ability to pay, should have basic health and education services. Common interests may also reinforce these common concerns. Reducing levels of infectious disease by spraying or immunization makes everyone safer. Similarly, a more literate population benefits all of society through the associated productivity gains.

Common interests also abound between employers and employees. Enlightened employers want their workers to be well fed and energetic, and so are likely to support low food prices. But they also want workers to be literate and skilled, and so will support investment in education and training.

Alliances may also be possible between groups that seem to have little in common. In Norway urban and rural poor found a common interest in promoting rural development that discour-

aged migration to the towns and kept industrial labour in short supply (box 3.4.7).

Common interests can also emerge between beneficiaries and providers of social services. Nurses, social workers, extension workers, para-medical personnel, primary school teachers – all stand to benefit from an expansion of services. And since they are often better organized and more vocal than the poor, they can be powerful allies.

In Kenya and Sri Lanka in the 1980s, for example, resources devoted to primary education increased partly as a result of pressure from powerful teachers unions. And in Peru in the 1980s, primary education expanded largely because of efforts by political parties to win the votes of teachers.

Just last year in Zimbabwe, nurses went on strike to demand not only higher wages but also more public investment in health care. The government assumed that this was mere pleading on behalf of a certain group of employees. In fact, despite the disruption to health services, the strike enjoyed widespread popular support.

BOX 3.4.6

How one campaign helped shape public policy in Brazil

Brazilians' struggle against dictatorship taught them the value of solidarity and collective action. Organized through informal committees, church initiatives and trade unions, women and men have challenged prevailing social inequities and human poverty. Under the umbrella of the Citizen Action Group against Hunger and Misery (the Hunger Campaign, for short), an innovative form of collective action emerged, mobilizing both non-poor and poor people in a popular alliance to fight poverty.

The Hunger Campaign is a network of committees supporting food campaigns, income-generating projects, maternal and child health initiatives, support services for the elderly and care for people living with AIDS. The campaign has advocated greater political commitment to eradicating poverty, a sense of public responsibility and people-centred solutions.

The campaign has had a marked impact on attitudes and behaviour, particularly of government officials. And it has made people less fatalistic

about the scourge of poverty and more hopeful about the future.

The campaign has also helped shape government policy, persuading national and local governments to adopt social equality as a priority. It successfully pushed for a social agenda as part of Rio de Janeiro's bid for the Summer Olympics in 2004.

The campaign's main aim is to eradicate absolute poverty by meeting five targets: quality education for all children and teenagers, homes for the homeless, adequate nutrition for all children, upgrading of slum areas and investment in sports activities for youth.

The success of the campaign in mobilizing private and public support, forming partnerships and influencing public policy is proof that solidarity and collective action can achieve much in fighting human poverty and social inequality.

Source: Correa 1997.

Exploiting differences among elites

Most ruling elites are coalitions of different groups, and the poor can sometimes take advantage of this.

In 19th-century Britain factory workers allied themselves first with the industrialists – to support the repeal of the Corn Laws, which kept the price of food high. But they also allied themselves with the landowners against the industrialists when it came to supporting laws that protected the workforce. Both landowners and industrialists protested that they would be ruined – but both agriculture and industry flourished for a quarter of a century. As has been shown many times, promoting the interests of the poor does not run counter to the long-term interests of the rich.

Another example is the expansion of food stamps in the United States in the 1960s. In this case the interests of poor people coincided with those of people in the food-producing rural districts, whose representatives in Congress allied themselves with welfare-minded liberals.

THE NEED FOR AN ACTIVIST STATE

Individuals and groups can do a great deal on their own to combat poverty. But much will depend on the environment created by government action. The state has a central role – not just through its activities but through its influence on many other elements of society. And the call for people's mobilization must not be a justification for the state to abdicate its responsibilities.

In the era of structural adjustment many states have slashed expenditures on social services,

---

BOX 3.4.7

A rural-urban alliance for poverty reduction in Norway

Almost everybody in society benefits from the reduction and eradication of poverty, and disparate groups can be brought together to work towards that goal once a common interest has been identified. Let's take a simple example.

In Norway poverty was virtually eliminated in the first half of the 20th century – largely thanks to an alliance between rural smallholders and urban industrial workers.

In 1900 Norway was a poor country. Although natural resources, especially fish, were plentiful and the country was sparsely populated, rural people (70% of the population) lived in hunger and poverty.

Like many developing countries today, Norway could have remained a rich country with poor people. Why didn't it? Three reasons:

- Education. Early investment in education ensured that by 1900 illiteracy was virtually zero.
- Secure land tenure. Land was of little commercial value, so even poor people had secure tenure and thus access to natural resources.
- Democratic institutions. By 1913 universal adult suffrage meant that the rural poor were strongly represented in parliament.

This last point is particularly important. Unlike in many other European countries, in Norway democracy came first and industrialization second. A modern economy developed under a government representing the people, resulting in more equitable and people-centered policies to alleviate poverty.

Also distinguishing the Norwegian experience is the solid alliance that emerged between rural smallholders and urban workers. Both groups had a strong interest in accelerating rural development. For the rural poor this was a matter of direct self-interest. For urban workers it meant preventing large-scale migration to the cities, which would lead to a labour surplus and weaken the trade unions.

The strength of the rural poor lay in their voting numbers, while that of urban workers lay in their ability to disrupt production. Their coalition was so successful in ensuring heavy investment in rural areas that as late as 1960 half the population still lived there.

Only recently has this equilibrium been disturbed, with unemployment rising in both rural and urban areas.

Source: Brox 1996.

---

often with the argument that the gap can be filled by community self-help. At times the pressure on spending has motivated the introduction of user fees for health services – in countries where there is no capacity for effective means-testing and where people cannot afford even the lowest fees. This is a perversion of the ideals of self-help.

A poverty eradication strategy requires not a retreating, weak state but an active, strong one, and that strength should be used to enable the poor rather than disable them.

The disabling state

Some states use much of their power for actions that run counter to the interests of poor people. Politicians use government resources to strengthen their hold on power. Public officials demand bribes before they allow access to government benefits (box 3.4.8). And well-connected citizens use political influence to gain preferential access to public resources. The result: not just inefficient and inequitable allocation of resources, but also less freedom and more human deprivation.

In the worst cases politicians have used their offices ruthlessly to amass personal wealth and power and benefit those on whose support they depend – with no regard for efficiency or the public interest. The most extreme examples include Trujillo in the Dominican Republic, Somoza in Nicaragua, Amin in Uganda, Marcos in the Philippines and the Duvaliers in Haiti.

But it is not necessary to point to a handful of dictatorships to find ways in which governments are dominated by vested interests. Health and education services are frequently biased towards the wealthy in urban areas. Food policy too is often skewed towards the well off: prices are kept low so that urban officials and the military get subsidized supplies – at the expense of poor farmers and landless labourers.

The structure and operations of the economy may be pro-rich and antipoor, biased towards serving vested interests. Government policy can lead to underpriced capital, overpriced labour and an overvalued exchange rate – encouraging techniques that are capital and import intensive. And governments may support monopolies and cartels rather than labour-intensive microenterprises in the informal sector or small-scale agriculture. In Malawi until recently, smallholder farmers were forbidden to grow some of the more profitable cash crops, protecting the interests of a powerful consortium of estate owners.

Market competition offers an important way in which people, especially poor people, can escape economic domination by exploitative government, big landlords and big retailers. But for markets to help in this way there must be real competition, not monopolies. Worst of all are markets corrupted by biased government influence – when the market enters the government and the government sells off monopoly power to the highest bidder.

Various forces can encourage real competition, even where governments are weak or self-seeking. First, there are the profit-seeking ambitions of producers and retailers, who can be relied on to argue their own case. Second, there are influences and interests from abroad – foreign competitors eager to enter the market and donor governments and others wanting opportunities for their own exporters and investors. Third, there are the international agencies, supporting the doctrine of free trade and free competition. The result is rarely a textbook example of perfect competition, but poor people can often benefit from this diffusion of market power – and can certainly fare better than they would under a monopoly or under total government domination of the economy.

Probably the most shocking example of states' use of power contrary to the interests of poor people is the squandering of limited budgetary resources in the continued obsession with military might. Global defence spending amounted to roughly $800 billion in 1995 (in 1995 prices). South Asia spent $15 billion in 1995, more than what it would cost annually to achieve basic health and nutrition for all worldwide. Sub-Saharan Africa spent $8 billion, about the same as the estimated annual cost of achieving universal access to safe water and sanitation in all developing countries. And East Asia spent $51 billion, nine times the annual amount needed to ensure basic education for all worldwide.

If a government is more concerned about its military establishment than its people, the imbalance shows up in the ratio of military to social spending. Some countries have corrected this imbalance; others have not (table 3.4.1).

States can also add to impoverishment by squandering resources on prestige projects. Abortive projects have become a graveyard of white elephants in many poor countries. Factories have been built that have failed to reach full production capacity and need big state subsidies to keep going. Railways have been built that are now impassable because of lack of maintenance. Large sums have been spent on presidential palaces and other showpieces. And other infrastructure projects that are built might have some benefit, but not for poor people. A political decision to build a new international airport – one that will replace an

---

BOX 3.4.8

Poverty and corruption

Like blackmail, corruption makes you pay to end the nuisance it creates: it puts sand in the gears of the administrative machinery and charges you for its removal.

Corruption in government increases poverty in many ways. Most directly, it diverts resources to the rich people, who can afford to pay bribes, and away from the poor people, who cannot. But it also skews decisions in favour of capital-intensive enterprise (where the pickings are greater) and away from labour-intensive activities more likely to benefit the poor.

Corruption also weakens governments and lessens their ability to fight poverty. It reduces tax revenues and thus the resources available for public services. And if administrations are assumed to be corrupt, honest people tend to avoid public service, so the quality of personnel suffers. More generally, corruption eats away at the fabric of public life – leading to increased lawlessness and undermining social and political stability.

To focus attention on this issue, a recently established NGO, Transparency International, publishes an annual Corruption Perception Index based on a survey of international businesspeople's perception of corruption in the countries in which they operate. In 1996, according to this index, the most corrupt country was judged to be Nigeria, followed by Pakistan, Kenya, Bangladesh and China; the least corrupt was New Zealand.

Many countries are now making greater efforts to root out corruption. They are introducing systems to improve transparency and accountability in public administration, including regular independent auditing and incentives and protection for whistle-blowers.

In Botswana the parliament passed the Corruption and Economic Crime Act in August 1994. This act establishes a directorate, reporting to the president, with a mandate to prevent, investigate and report on corruption. The act also provides a comprehensive legal framework for the government's anticorruption drive, which is already showing results.

Other countries are addressing what is often considered the root cause of corruption – inadequate government salaries. Uganda has tripled the salaries of teachers in the hope that this will reduce the widespread practice of selling grades and test results. And Philippine tax authorities have reduced corruption through employee bonuses and merit-based promotions.

Corruption also requires an international response, and corporations from industrial countries must bear some of the responsibility. They often consider paying bribes a reasonable way to do business – and it is frequently tax-deductible. The US government has made corruption by US citizens of officials in other countries a criminal offence, something that other countries are now also considering.

Discussions about corruption have intensified at the United Nations, and in 1996 the Economic and Social Council adopted the United Nations Declaration against Corruption and Bribery in International Commercial Transactions. In addition, the Crime Prevention and Criminal Justice Branch of the UN Secretariat continues to provide guidelines and recommendations to governments on rooting out corruption.

Source: Transparency International 1996 and Frisch 1996.

old but fully functional airport – might run into strong opposition from local organizations demanding that the millions of dollars be invested instead in human development.

The enabling state

Fortunately, this bleak view of the state is only a partial one. The interaction among people, markets and states is generally more subtle. Many states can and do act in the common interest or in the interest of poor people – taking measures to, say, protect children, redistribute wealth or reduce poverty.

South Africa stands out as an example of a country with a political commitment to poverty eradication and a strategy based on public-private partnerships and a people-driven process of development. The political momentum of the struggle against apartheid is now driving the struggle against human poverty (box 3.4.9).

Government that acts in the interest of poor people is easier to achieve in democratic systems where the poor represent a significant electoral bloc. In Malaysia the government has promoted the interests of the Malays, who, although the majority of the population, are generally poorer than other groups. In Zimbabwe after independence, the government took many measures to benefit the poor majority, including a big shift in education priorities – between 1980 and 1984 it doubled the expenditure per primary student. And in Malawi after the 1994 shift to democracy, the government introduced free primary education, which increased net enrolment from 53% to 76%.

But free elections are not sufficient to motivate states to become more enabling and responsible. Studies on the link between development and type of government have established no clear correlation between electoral democracy and successful eradication of poverty. One important reason is low voter turnout. It is especially low in some industrial countries, implying that many poor people do not use their vote to influence policies (table 3.4.2).

During the cold war era the threat of communism was an important force in motivating non-communist regimes – whether or not they were democratic – to improve the conditions of poor people. Just as Bismarck introduced social policies to stem the tide of socialism in Germany, the governments of such countries as Indonesia, the Republic of Korea, Malaysia and Thailand advanced the interests of the poor to avoid social unrest and political upheaval. With this motivating force removed, it has now become even more critical to find ways to build political commitment to poverty eradication. The fall of communism has left only one prevailing economic ideology in the political marketplace. Does the lack of competition mean that the concerns of poor people are forgotten?

Most states are neither wholly harmful nor wholly beneficial. They are not monoliths, but collections of institutions and structures. This complexity offers the potential for checks and balances that can restrain corrupt officials and predatory government. It also offers openings for reform and alliances within state structures.

States committed to building the political momentum and policy environment for the eradication of poverty can take steps in several important areas. More important, even states that are

TABLE 3.4.1
Big military spenders

Country	Military expenditure as % of GDP 1995	Military expenditure as % of combined education and health expenditure 1991
Korea, Dem. People's Rep. of	25.5	..
Oman	15.1	283
Iraq	14.8	271
Croatia	12.6	..
Kuwait	11.8	88
Saudi Arabia	10.6	151
Israel	9.2	106
Russian Federation	7.4	132
Tajikistan	6.9	..
Pakistan	6.5	125
Myanmar	6.2	222
Brunei Darussalam	6.0	125
China	5.7	114

Source: IISS 1993 and 1996.

not fully committed can be encouraged to take such steps, through lobbying, democratic pressure and international influence. These actions put poor people on the political map and support a society-wide mobilization and partnership for pro-poor action.

BOX 3.4.9

South Africa – the struggle continues

"My government's commitment to creating a people-centred society of liberty binds us to the pursuit of the goals of freedom from want, freedom from hunger, freedom from deprivation, freedom from ignorance, freedom from suppression and freedom from fear. These freedoms are fundamental to the guarantee of human dignity." In these words at the opening of the first democratically elected parliament in South Africa, President Nelson Mandela captured the hopes, aspirations and needs of the population, particularly of the black majority.

For many the situation has not yet changed much – the landless; the homeless; the black African majority, more than 40% of whom live in absolute poverty; women and children, who are the majority of those living in deprivation, especially in rural areas; and the growing numbers of those who are unemployed, underemployed or living on less than $1 a day.

South Africa must operate in an increasingly competitive global environment with a limited pool of skills and an economic system that needs major restructuring to promote growth. The level of inequality is among the highest in the world, and crime and violence of all sorts, particularly against women and children, are on the rise. Government spending must be redirected towards those in greatest need. But cuts in social expenditures make sustainable development based on progressive redistribution difficult to achieve.

South Africa is in search of ways to eradicate poverty through a people-driven process – one that has people and government working in a new partnership to identify common priorities. This partnership would work towards processes for restoring and redistributing land; a legal framework to ensure more equitable access to loans, housing, education, health care and paid work; and the effective promotion of racial and gender equity.

A participatory study, conducted in more than 150 communities nationwide, surveyed people's perceptions of the problems affecting them and of the most effective ways to transform their situation. People expressed a desire to be informed and to participate in new ways of governance. An essential need voiced by the people is for channels of communication that are accessible, appropriate and timely. "We cannot draw up collective plans and strategies with government if the bureaucracy is antipeople and the language inaccessible," said one person.

Another need is for solutions to the violence—institutional, political, criminal and domestic—that people face in their daily lives. As another person said: "We are at war in our townships, we live in fear for our lives every day, and nothing is being done to safeguard us or our children. How much more must we take before something is done? We will no longer wait for others to do anything for us, because whether we live or die does not matter to those who have the resources. We will empower ourselves through mass action and education to solve our problems ourselves."

The new constitution has created an environment in which partnerships, coalitions and alliances can be forged, based on past common struggles against apartheid. This will unleash a process driven by people at the grass-roots that could mobilize both human and material resources to address widening and deepening poverty.

The political success that has been achieved provides the space for critical action, based on a shared history of struggle. A range of people's organizations are emerging, born out of political resistance and unique strategies of local mobilization. These organizations can work with the new government to plan joint strategies to energize reconstruction and development. And they can push for government support of a people-driven, sustainable process of development – a process that generates work, ensures sustainable livelihoods, builds a sense of pride and reclaims the community as a dynamic force for social transformation.

Source: Taylor 1996 and 1997.

- *Promote political participation by all.* The government must enable people's active participation at many levels of debate, dialogue and decision-making. This requires tolerant government institutions and free discussions of policy, development and change. Such an open atmosphere is greatly assisted by freedom of speech, democratic institutions, free elections and respect for human rights. And ensuring the full participation of women and minorities is likely to require affirmative action.

- *Encourage public-private partnerships.* Ideally, the relationship between governments and NGOs should be one of partnership, resulting, as in many countries, in a constructive division of labour in which the standard service delivery by provincial and district authorities is complemented by the more flexible, responsive activities of NGOs. To support such partnership, governments should create an adequate space for NGOs and engage them in policy dialogue. Partnerships with private sector firms also hold promise.

- *Facilitate bottom-up planning.* Governments have to offer adequate means for communities to feed in views, information and policy recommendations through every tier of administration. A useful tool for participatory planning and one that is proving highly appropriate is participatory rural appraisal (box 3.4.10).

- *Ensure accountability and transparency.* All organizations, public and private, should be accountable not just to their shareholders or members but to society as a whole. This also means that NGOs should be held accountable not just to their donors but also to the communities they serve.

- *Prevent the criminalization of politics.* State action for human development and poverty eradication requires a clear separation of economic and political power. In the complex web of power relations and self-serving economic interests, weak governments cannot find a counterweight to economically powerful groups and individuals, leaving corruption a major obstacle to poverty eradication. Legal mechanisms, institutional arrangements and political commitments are needed to fight corruption at every level.

- *Protect the freedom of the press.* A free press is essential for providing people with the information they need to make rational choices about political action. It helps establish the right political incentives for policy-makers.

- *Promote judicial activism.* NGOs, community groups and people's movements are using legal action to achieve their goals. Many countries already have a legal framework recognizing economic, social and political rights, with constitutions that commit the government to human development – laws often underused. In other countries activism is needed to amend laws, do away with biases and anachronisms and contribute to a pro-poor legal framework for just settlements.

- *Promote civic education,* People need to understand how their own political system works – or could work. Governments should

TABLE 3.4.2
Political participation in industrial countries

Country	Eligible voters voting (%) 1991–94
Lowest turnout	
USA	39
Switzerland	46
Russian Federation	50
Poland	53
Finland	68
France	69
Highest turnout	
Malta	96
Belgium	93
Latvia	90
Iceland	88
Slovenia	86
Denmark	84

Source: UNECE 1995.

make greater efforts to ensure that people are aware of their history, their constitution and their rights. If they lack the resources for this work, they should encourage NGOs to do it.

THE NEED FOR DEMOCRATIC SPACE

Ending human poverty requires an activist state to create the political conditions for fundamental reform. Above all, this requires a democratic space in which people can articulate demands, act collectively and fight for a more equitable distribution of power. Only then will adequate resources be invested in human development priorities, and access to productive assets become more equitable. Only then will macroeconomic management be more pro-poor, and markets provide ample opportunities for the poor to improve their standard of living.

Since 1986 the proportion of governments that are democratically elected has risen from 40% to 60%. Although an important start, a democratically elected government is not enough, however. The challenge now is to ensure that democratic practices and principles permeate every level and dimension of society. When it comes to eradicating poverty, political reform is not an option – it is an imperative.

BOX 3.4.10

The power of participation

The great value of participatory rural appraisals (which are not exclusively rural) is in the way they empower communities and build their capacity for self-help, solidarity and collective action. Such appraisals can be best described as a family of approaches, methods and behaviours that enable people to express and analyse the realities of their lives and conditions, plan what action to take and monitor and evaluate results. They provide ways to give poor people a voice, enabling them to express and analyse their problems and priorities. Used well, they can generate important (and often surprising) insights that can contribute to policies better fitted to serving the needs of poor people. More fundamentally, they can challenge the perceptions of those in authority and begin to change attitudes and agendas.

The methods used enable people to share information, and stimulate discussion and analysis. Many appraisals use visual tools. Maps show where people live and where water, forests, farmland, schools and health facilities are located. Flow diagrams help to analyse problems and find solutions. Seasonal calendars aid in planning agricultural activities, and matrices in comparing the merits of different crop varieties.

Participatory rural appraisals have also proved to be of direct value to policy-makers. By obtaining information from communities, the appraisals can build a detailed picture of the complexity and diversity of local people's realities – and do it far better than such conventional survey techniques as questionnaires. They provide an opportunity to meet people face to face and a means of gaining quick and accurate assessments of the implications and impact of policies.

In Jamaica an appraisal showed that the stigma of living in an area with a reputation for violence makes it difficult to find a job. In Zambia an appraisal identified the wide gap between policy and practice on exemptions from health care charges for the destitute, showing that the poorest often lose out. In Honduras and Panama appraisals showed that the areas where indigenous people's land rights were threatened also had the greatest biological diversity in the country, strengthening the people's claim to the land and the right to manage and conserve its resources. In Scotland an appraisal identified villagers' interest in purchasing and managing forests to generate jobs.

Participatory rural appraisals have evolved and spread with astonishing speed since the early 1990s. Originating mainly among NGOs in East Africa and South Asia, they have since been adopted by government departments, training institutes, aid agencies and universities around the globe. They are now used in at least 100 countries.

Source: IDS 1996 and Attwood 1996.

REFERENCES

Athreya, V.B. and S. R. Chunkath. 1996. *Literacy and Empowerment*. New Delhi: Sage Publications.

Attwood, Heidi. 1996. "PRA: What Is It and Why Should We Use It? and Illustrations of Poor People's Perceptions of Poverty and Well-Being as Disclosed through PRA Expenditures." Special contribution to the *Human Development Report 1997*. UNDP, New York.

Ba, Hassan. 1990. "Village Associations on the Riverbanks of Senegal: The New Development Actors." *Voices from Africa* 2, January: 83–104. UNCTAD/NGLS, Geneva.

Berger, Peter L. 1976. *Pyramids of Sacrifice: Political Ethics and Social Change*. New York: Anchor Books.

Block, Thorsten. 1995. "Human Development and Economic Growth in Germany." Background paper for *Human Development Report 1996*. UNDP, New York.

Brox, Ottar. 1996. "Out of Poverty: The Case of Norway." Special contribution to the *Human Development Report 1997*. UNDP, New York.

Correa, Sonia. 1997. "Brazil: The Citizen Action against Hunger and Misery." Brazilian Institute for Economic and Social Analysis. Special contribution to the *Human Development Report 1997*. UNDP, New York.

Freedom House. 1995. "Freedom in the World." New York.

Frisch, Dieter. 1996. "The Effects of Corruption on Development." *Courier* 158 (July–August): 68–70.

Ghai, Dharam and Jessica M. Vivian, eds. 1992. *Grassroots Environmental Action: People's Participation in Sustainable Development*. London: Routledge.

Government of Malawi and UNICEF (United Nations Children's Fund). 1996. "Malawi: Programme Plan of Operation for Youth and Education, 1997–2001." Lilongwe.

Haq, Mahbub ul. 1995. *Reflections on Human Development*. Oxford: Oxford University Press.

Human Development Center. 1997. *Human Development in South Asia 1997*. Karachi: Oxford University Press.

IDS (Institute for Development Studies). 1996. "The Power of Participation: PRA and Policy." *Policy Briefing Issue* 7 (August). Sussex.

IISS (International Institute for Strategic Studies). 1993. *The Military Balance 1993–94*. London: Brasseys.

———. 1996. *The Military Balance 1996–97*. Oxford: Oxford University Press.

Kapadia, K. 1996. "Housing Rights for the Urban Poor: Battle for Mumbai's Streets." *Economic and Political Weekly* 31 (24).

Kohli, Atul. 1994. "Democracy in the Developing World: Trends and Prospects." Background paper for the *Human Development Report 1994*. UNDP, New York.

Kothari, Smitu. 1993. "Social Movements and the Redefinition of Democracy." Background paper for the *Human Development Report 1994*. UNDP, New York.

Lal, Deepak and H. Myint. 1996. *The Political Economy of Poverty, Equity and Growth*. Oxford: Clarendon Press.

Lewis, Paul. 1996. "A World Fed up with Bribes." *New York Times*, 28 November.

Maathai, Wangari. 1997. "The Green Belt Movement." Special contribution to the *Human Development Report 1997*. UNDP, New York.

Øyen, Else. 1997. "The Utility of Poverty." Special contribution to the *Human Development Report 1997*. UNDP, New York.

Riddel, Roger. 1992. "Grassroots Participation and the Role of NGOs." Background paper for the *Human Development Report 1993*. UNDP, New York.

Rodrik, Dani. 1996. "Understanding Economic Policy Reform." *Journal of Economic Literature* 34 (March): 9–41.

Saggar, I. and I. Pan. 1994. "SCs and STs in Eastern India: Inequality and Poverty Estimates." *Economic and Political Weekly*, 5 March.

Schneider, Michael. 1991. *A Brief History of the German Trade Unions*. Bonn: Verlag J.H.W. Dietz Nachf.

Sen, Gita. 1997. "Empowerment as an Approach to Poverty." Background paper for the *Human Development Report 1997*. UNDP, New York.

Streeten, Paul. 1993. "Markets and States: Against Minimalism." *World Development* 21 (8): 1281–98.

Taylor, Vivienne. 1996. "Social Mobilization, Reconstruction and Development: Lessons from the Mass Democratic Movement." Cape Town: UWC Press for the Southern African Development Education and Policy Research Unit.

——. 1997. "South Africa: Transcending the Legacy of Apartheid and Poverty." Special contribution to the *Human Development Report 1997*. UNDP, New York.

Transparency International. 1996. *Sharpening the Response against Global Corruption: Transparency International Global Report 1996*. Berlin.

UNDP (United Nations Development Programme). 1996a. *Development and the HIV Epidemic: A Forward-Looking Evaluation of the Approach of the UNDP HIV and Development Programme*. New York.

——. 1996b. "Governance for Sustainable Development." UNDP Policy Document. New York.

UNECE (United Nations Economic Commission for Europe). 1995. *Trends in Europe and North America: The Statistical Yearbook of the Economic Commission for Europe*. New York and Geneva: United Nations.

——. 1996. Database. Geneva.

3.5
UNEQUAL HUMAN IMPACTS
OF ENVIRONMENTAL DAMAGE

Chapter 4, *Human Development Report 1998*
Drafted principally by Selim Jahan

Environmental damage almost always hits those living in poverty the hardest.

The overwhelming majority of those who die each year from air and water pollution are poor people in developing countries. So are those most affected by desertification – and so will be those worst affected by the floods, storms and harvest failures caused by global warming. All over the world poor people generally live nearest to dirty factories, busy roads and waste dumps.

There is an irony here. Even though poor people bear the brunt of environmental damage, they are seldom the principal creators of the damage. It is the rich who pollute more and contribute more to global warming. It is the rich who generate more waste and put more stress on nature's sink.

Yet there are also environmental challenges that stem not from growing affluence but from growing poverty. As a result of increasing impoverishment and the absence of alternatives, a swelling number of poor and landless people are putting unprecedented pressure on the natural resource base as they struggle to survive.

Poor people and environmental damage are often caught in a downward spiral. Past resource degradation deepens today's poverty, while today's poverty makes it very hard to care for or restore the agricultural resource base, to find alternatives to deforestation to prevent desertification, to control erosion and to replenish soil nutrients. People in poverty are forced to deplete resources to survive, and this degradation of the environment further impoverishes people.

When this self-reinforcing downward spiral becomes extreme, poor people are forced to move in increasing numbers to ecologically fragile lands. Almost half the world's poorest people – more than 500 million – live on marginal lands.

The poverty-environmental damage nexus in developing countries must be seen in the context of population growth as well. In the developing world pressures on the environment intensify every day as the population grows. United Nations projections indicate that the global population in 2050 will be 9.5 billion, with 8 billion in developing countries. By 2050 the population of Africa will be three times that of Europe, and China's will be four times North America's.

To feed this projected 9.5 billion human beings adequately will require three times the basic calories consumed today, the equivalent of about 10 billion tons of grain a year. To produce that much, all the world's current cropland would have to be farmed at three times the current global average productivity.

Yet each year almost 15 million acres of drylands are added to the 3.2 billion acres that have already been moderately or severely desertified. And population growth will contribute further to land degradation – the rough overgrazing, overcutting and overfarming. The situation can be expected to get worse.

The issue of the poverty-environmental damage nexus is complex, and explaining it in terms of income levels only is too simple. Questions of the ownership of natural resources, of access to common resources, of the strength or weakness of communities and local institutions, of the way information about poor people's entitlements and rights to resources is shared with them, of the way people cope with risk and uncertainty, of the way people use scarce time – all these are important in explaining people's environmental behaviour (box 3.5.1).

Some kinds of environmental degradation are truly global concerns, such as global warming and the depletion of the ozone layer. Others are

Poverty-environmental damage nexus – going beyond income

Often in discussions of the relationship between poverty and environmental damage, impoverishment is identified as the sole reason for the environmental behaviour of poor people. But many factors shape such behaviour, some related to poverty or affluence, others independent of either income or poverty.

- *Ownership.* Many of the natural resources being degraded – pastureland, rivers, lakes and forests – are not private but communal property. But rights are ill defined, often because they were originally defined in a local social and political system that is no longer viable.

- *Institutions.* Institutions for managing common property that reflect the consensus of the owners and can control use are lacking. Indige-

nous institutions that were once effective have eroded.

- *Risk and uncertainty.* People's decisions are influenced by the way they deal with risk and uncertainty. In ecologically fragile ecosystems people tend to minimize risks, not maximize output, whether they are poor or not.

- *Time.* Collecting firewood and water are tasks carried out by women who are already overworked, and the time available for these activities is limited. Thus overexploitation of sources of fuelwood is linked more to the time available to women than to their poverty status. There is a gender dimension, but not necessarily an income dimension.

Source: Human Development Report Office.

international – acid rain, the state of the oceans, the condition of rivers that run through several countries. Others still are more localized, though they may occur worldwide – air pollution, water pollution, soil degradation.

And regardless of the categorization, the costs of environmental degradation for human well-

being are enormous (table 3.5.1). Fewer than a fifth of poor households in developing countries have water connections to their houses, so poor people bear the brunt of water pollution. The rural poor suffer too because they are at the bottom of the energy ladder: of the 2.7 million deaths related to air pollution each year, 1.8 million are

TABLE 3.5.1

Estimated costs of environmental degradation in selected Asian countries

Country	Year of period	Environmental damage	Annual cost (US$ billions)	Cost as a percentage
China	1990	Productivity losses caused by soil erosion, deforestation and land degradation, water shortage and destruction of wetlands	13.9 – 26.6	3.8 – 7.3
		Health and productivity loses caused by environmental pollution in cities	6.3 – 9.3	1.7 – 2.5
Indonesia	1989	Health effects of particulate and lead levels above WHO standards in Jakarta	2.2	2.0
Pakistan	Early 1990s	Health impacts of air and water pollution and productivity losses from deforestation and soil erosion	1.7	3.3
Philippines	Early 1990s	Health and productivity loses from air and water pollution in the vicinity of Manila	0.3 – 0.4	0.8 – 1.0
Thailand	1989	Health effects of particulate and lead levels above WHO standards	1.6	2.0

Source: ADB 1997.

caused by indoor pollution in rural areas, most among poor households relying on traditional fuels. And the degradation of 1.5 billion hectares of land in developing countries ruins the lives and livelihoods of poor people. In all these cases the damage falls disproportionately on those least able to bear it.

This chapter analyses the disproportionate consequences of local and global environmental damage for poor people, presenting the geography of environmental impacts. It also presents a scenario for future environmental degradation, recognizing positive developments, concluding with some relevant policy issues.

LOCAL ENVIRONMENTAL DAMAGE HURTS POOR PEOPLE MOST

Local environmental concerns – water pollution and contamination, air pollution, waste disposal – have immediate and directly attributable effects on people. Dirty water causes disease; air pollution and inadequate waste disposal make people sick. They affect not only human health, but people's livelihoods and survival.

Water pollution and contamination

Water pollution and contamination affect people the world over, but by far the greatest impact on human well-being is in developing countries, especially in the poorest. Concerns about the effects of toxic chemicals and minerals, such as pesticides and lead, in drinking water in industrial countries are serious and well founded, but the effects seem small beside the widespread illness from simple contamination by sewage in developing countries.

Recent years have seen big improvements in access to safe water and adequate sanitation (figure 3.5.1). In developing countries nearly 2 billion people have gained access to safe water and 400 million people to basic sanitation during the past one and a half decades. But these gains in many cases have passed by the poor.

As a result nearly 30% of the population of developing countries, more than 1.3 billion people, lack access to safe water – and nearly 60%, or over 2.5 billion, to basic sanitation (table 3.5.2).

Excrement ends up in ponds, streams and ditches and on open ground. More than 90% of the waste water of the developing world is discharged directly into streams, open drains, rivers, lakes and coastal waters without treatment. On average, Asian rivers carry 50 times as much bacteria from human excrement as do those in industrial countries (box 3.5.2). Water pollution as measured by

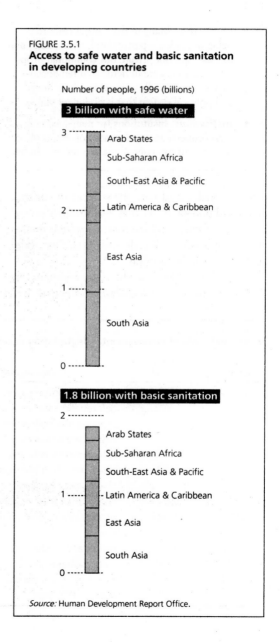

FIGURE 3.5.1
Access to safe water and basic sanitation in developing countries

Number of people, 1996 (billions)

3 billion with safe water

3 — Arab States
Sub-Saharan Africa
South-East Asia & Pacific
2 — Latin America & Caribbean

East Asia

1 —

South Asia

0 —

1.8 billion with basic sanitation

2 —
Arab States
Sub-Saharan Africa
South-East Asia & Pacific
1 — Latin America & Caribbean
East Asia
South Asia
0 —

Source: Human Development Report Office.

TABLE 3.5.2
Lack of access to safe water and basic sanitation – a regional profile, 1990–96
(percent)

Region	People without access to safe water	People without access to basic sanitation
Arab States	21	30
Sub-Saharan Africa	48	55
South-East Asia and the Pacific	35	45
Latin America and the Caribbean	23	29
East Asia	32	73
East Asia (excluding China)	13	..
South Asia	18	64
Developing countries	29	58
Least developed countries	43	64

Source: Human Development Report Office.

organic pollutants and suspended solids is most serious in Asia and Africa (figure 3.5.2).

As a result of this pollution, water-borne diseases – diarrhoea, dysentery, intestinal worms and hepatitis – are rife in developing countries, particularly among poor people. Diarrhoea and dysentery account for an estimated 20% of the total burden of disease in developing countries. Every year polluted water produces nearly 2 billion cases of diarrhoea in the developing world, and diarrhoeal diseases cause the deaths of some 5 million people (including 3 million children). Con-

---

BOX 3.5.2

The Ganges – pure or polluted?

Myth has it that the goddess Ganga descended to earth in the form of a river, the Ganges, to purify the souls of the 60,000 sons of the ancient ruler King Sagara who had been burned to ashes by an enraged ascetic. Today the river symbolizes purification to millions of Hindus the world over, who believe that drinking or bathing in its waters will lead to *moksha,* or salvation.

If Ganga originally came to bring salvation to Sagara's 60,000 sons, the poor goddess has ended up with a burden 10,000 times greater than she bargained for. Supporting a staggering 400 million people along its 1,560 mile course, the Ganges forms the most populous river basin in the world, with about 1,000 people per square mile.

Today there are more than 29 cities, 70 towns and thousands of villages along the Ganges's banks, depositing nearly all their sewage – more than 1.3 billion litres a day – directly into the river. Another 260 million litres of industrial waste are added to this by the hundreds of factories along the river's banks. All this waste enters the river largely untreated. To the raw sewage and factory effluents are added the runoff from more than 6 million tons of chemical fertilizer and some 9,000 tons of pesticides. And the Ganges serves as the final resting place for thousands of Hindus, whose cremated ashes or half-burned corpses are put into the river for spiritual rebirth.

The result is deeply ironic: the ancient symbol of purity and cleansing has become a great open sewer along much of its length. When the 15th century poet Kabir wrote of the Ganges, "hell flows along that river, with rotten men and beasts", few would have believed that this impious lament would one day prove so prophetic. But under the 20th century's pressures of burgeoning population and industrial growth, the Ganges's cleansing capacity cannot keep up. Today, in the basin of a half-billion souls, purification and pollution swim together in unholy wedlock.

Source: Sampat 1996.

taminated water also leads to 900 million cases of intestinal worms and 200 million cases of schistosomiasis. If everyone had access to safe water and basis sanitation, 2 million young lives would be saved every year.

Fisheries, one of the main sources of livelihood for poor people – and of protein for many more – are being damaged by sewage. Major declines in fish catches have been documented in rivers near cities in China, India, Senegal and Venezuela. And in Manila Bay, heavily polluted by vast quantities of sewage carried by two major rivers, fish yields have declined by nearly 40% during the past decade. About 100 million of the world's poorest people depend on fishing for all or part of their livelihoods.

In industrial countries the overuse of fertilizers causes great water pollution problems. Over the years nitrates from overloaded fields work their way through the groundwater supplies. Nearly a quarter of the groundwater in Europe – west and east – has contamination levels above the European Union's maximum permissible concentration. Meanwhile, nutrients from fertilizers wash off the land into inland waters and the sea, causing blooms of toxic algae. Fertilizers are less of a problem in developing countries, though nitrates have been found in the water supply of both São Paulo and Buenos Aires. High levels of arsenic, linked to heavy use of phosphatic fertilizers, have appeared in groundwater in six districts in West Bengal, India, and one in Bangladesh – killing some of those who drink the water.

In industrial countries a third of waste water is discharged untreated. Rivers generally are becoming cleaner in OECD countries, but there still are major problems in Eastern Europe and the former Soviet Union. Four-fifths of water samples from 200 rivers in the former Soviet Union were found to be dangerously contaminated, and the water of the river Vistula is too dirty over much of its length even for industrial use.

In developing countries public water utilities have often failed to serve people because of inefficiency and leakages. As a result in many parts of the developing world the private sector and communities are launching initiatives to provide safe water to people (box 3.5.3).

Air pollution

Air pollution from industrial emissions, car exhaust and the burning of fuels at home kills more than 2.7 million people every year – mainly from respiratory damage, heart and lung disease and cancer (table 3.5.3). The toll is heaviest where it is most overlooked.

Although air pollution is normally seen as predominantly a problem of industrial countries, more than 90% of the deaths occur in the developing world. Although it is normally seen as affecting the air outdoors, more than 80% of the casualties are from indoor pollution. And although it is normally seen as affecting towns and cities, more than two-thirds of the mortalities are in rural areas.

Poor people in developing countries, at the bottom of the energy ladder, must burn dung,

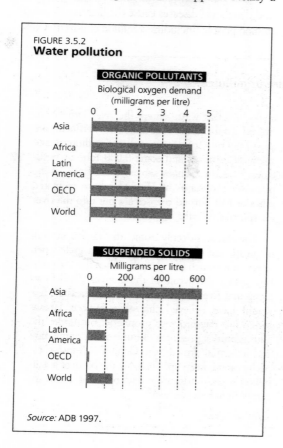

FIGURE 3.5.2
Water pollution

ORGANIC POLLUTANTS
Biological oxygen demand (milligrams per litre)

SUSPENDED SOLIDS
Milligrams per litre

Source: ADB 1997.

Improving access to safe water – public-private alliance in Guinea

In the 1980s less than 15% of the population in Guinea had access to safe water. By 1996 that share had increased almost fourfold to 55%. In a decade Guinea had brought one of the least developed water supply services in Sub-Saharan Africa to the point at which it could provide safe water to more than half the population. Guinea still has a long way to go, but its progress is impressive.

These significant achievements in the provision of safe water are the result of a public-private alliance. After 1989 Guinea restructured the water sector, transferring the water supply authority and responsibility for planning and investment to a new autonomous authority, SONEG. A new company, SEEG, was created to operate and maintain the facilities. SEEG is a joint venture, 49% owned by the government and 51% by a foreign private consortium.

The strength of the Guinean arrangement lies in the clarity of responsibilities and incentives. Under a ten-year lease contract SEEG operates and maintains the system at its own risk, with remuneration based on the user charges it collects as well as new connections. SEEG can increase its profits by improving the collection rate and reducing operating costs and unaccounted-for water.

The collection rate has increased dramatically, from 20% to 70%, and technical efficiency and coverage have improved. Tariff collection has increased from 60 Guinean francs per cubic metre before the lease contract to 680 Guinean francs in 1993 and is expected to reach full cost recovery this year.

SONEG has steadily increased the number of customers in Conakry and other cities. Between 1989 and 1993 it added 8,000, raising the total from 13,000 to 21,000. Since SONEG has ultimate responsibility for capital financing, it also has incentives to seek adequate tariffs and invest prudently.

Source: World Bank 1995.

wood and crop residues indoors for their cooking and heating, especially in Sub-Saharan Africa, the region with the majority of the least developed countries. In most other regions traditional fuel use has declined substantially during the past two decades (figure 3.5.3). Traditional fuels are much more polluting than modern alternatives such as kerosene, propane, biogas and electricity. Burning such fuel fills houses with smoke swirling with hundreds of toxic substances, killing 2.2 million people a year, mostly in rural areas, where most of the poor live. Both indoor air pollution and poor nutrition increase susceptibility to respiratory infections in the developing world.

TABLE 3.5.3
Air pollution takes its toll – a regional picture, 1996
(thousands)

Region or country	Deaths from indoor pollution		Deaths from outdoor pollution in urban areas	Total
	Rural	Urban		
India	496	93	84	673
Sub-Saharan Africa	490	32	..	522
China	320	53	70	443
Other Asian countries	363	40	40	443
Latin America and the Caribbean	180	113	113	406
Industrial countries	..	32	147	179
Arab States	..	..	57	57
Total	1,849	363	511	2,723

Source: WHO 1997.

Nearly two-thirds of the deaths from indoor air pollution are in Asia. In Latin America, where a large proportion of the poorest people live in city slums, nearly two-fifths of the deaths from causes related to indoor pollution are in urban areas. Women and children, particularly girls, spend the most time indoors and are disproportionately affected.

Outdoor air pollution – once almost entirely concentrated in the industrial countries – is now growing rapidly in the developing world. Rapid industrialization in many countries has greatly increased pollution, and the spread of motorized vehicle ownership is raising emissions all over the world. Vehicle exhaust, coal burning and smoke from factories form small particles in the air that cause serious health damage.

High vehicle densities also lead to congestion, noise, rising traffic accident rates and lost time – all at significant cost (table 3.5.4).

Lead, often added to petrol and so emitted by car exhaust, has been eliminated from petrol in some OECD countries and is being phased out in others, but it is still used heavily in developing and transition economies (figure 3.5.4). In these countries it continues to harm human health, permanently impairing children's development. In 1990 in Bangkok 30,000–70,000 children were reported to be at risk of losing four or more IQ points because of high lead emissions. In Latin America and the Caribbean, where almost three-fourths of the people live in urban areas, nearly 15 million children below two years of age are particularly at risk. The children of the poorest urban dwellers often are worst affected, because they tend to live near busy roads.

TABLE 3.5.4
Estimated losses due to traffic jams in selected cities, 1994

City	Annual cost of time delay (US$ millions)	Cost as a percentage of local GNP*
Bangkok	272	2.1
Kuala Lumpur	68	1.8
Singapore	305	1.6
Jakarta	68	0.9
Manila	51	0.7
Hong Kong	293	0.6
Seoul	154	0.4

* GNP in the region in which the city is located.
Source: WRI 1996.

FIGURE 3.5.3
Changing reliance on traditional fuel sources

Traditional fuel as a percentage of total fuel use

- Sub-Saharan Africa
- South-East Asia & Pacific
- South Asia
- Latin America & Caribbean
- East Asia
- Arab States

1980   1995

Source: Human Development Report Office.

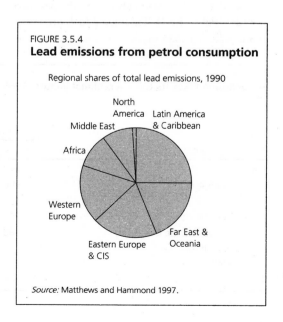

FIGURE 3.5.4
Lead emissions from petrol consumption

Regional shares of total lead emissions, 1990

North America, Latin America & Caribbean, Middle East, Africa, Western Europe, Eastern Europe & CIS, Far East & Oceania

Source: Matthews and Hammond 1997.

Studies suggest that outdoor air pollution causes 2–3% of all urban deaths in the Czech Republic, Poland and the United States. Particulates alone – tiny particles in black smoke – are estimated to kill 24,000 Britons each year, and several times as many Americans. Some parts of Eastern Europe and the CIS are affected even more. Nearly 5% of deaths and 4% of disabilities in Hungary are attributed to air pollution. More than 70% of the deaths from outdoor air pollution are in developing countries.

Although few studies have been done on the effects of air pollution in developing country cities, estimates in Mexico City suggest that particulates kill 6,400 residents a year. Air pollution caused more than 175,000 premature deaths in China in 1995 and nearly 2 million cases of chronic bronchitis. Damage to health and buildings from air pollution may cost Bangkok $1 billion a year. The total health costs of particulate air pollution in developing country cities were esti-mated to be nearly $100 billion in 1995, with chronic bronchitis accounting for $40 billion. Many municipalities, from Los Angeles to cities in Eastern Europe and the CIS – such as Katowice, Poland – are implementing broad-based strategies to curb pollution. Some cities in developing countries are successfully managing their air quality (box 3.5.4).

Besides harming human health, air pollution causes direct economic losses. Germany loses an estimated $4.7 billion in agricultural production every year as a result of air pollution, Poland $2.7 billion, Italy $1.8 billion and Sweden $1.5 billion. The adverse effects from crop damage hit the poor particularly hard.

Domestic solid waste

Domestic solid waste continues to increase worldwide in both absolute and per capita terms (table 3.5.5). With affluence, the composition of waste changes from primarily biodegradable organic ma-

---

BOX 3.5.4

Successful air quality management – the Chilean story

Air pollution in Santiago, the capital of Chile, is the most obvious environmental problem in the country. About 5.5 million people, 40% of the country's population, live in the metropolitan area. The urban transport system must handle 8.5 million trips a day within greater Santiago. The nation's fleet of motor vehicles doubled between 1985 and 1996, from 284,000 to 561,000. Now Santiago is one of the most polluted population centres in the world.

But recently the government has been quite successful in combating the problem through legislation and enforcement of laws. New legislation is based on the Framework Environmental Law, which provides the basis for a gradual improvement in environmental quality, while avoiding conflict between industry, government and pressure groups.

Earlier, Santiago had been characterized by unregulated public transport services and unlimited air pollution. In response, a bidding system for route concessions was introduced in the early 1990s. The system established a scheme allowing only modes of transport that meet certain requirements to use the busiest streets.

To encourage more environmentally sound use of automobiles, the Pollution Prevention and Clean-Up Plan for the Metropolitan Region proposes such measures as toll roads, the elimination of parking lots and changes in their rate structures. The ultimate goal of the plan, which was drafted by the National Environment Commission, is to reduce the levels of certain pollutants to acceptable standards by 2011. The steps include revamping private and public transport fleets, using improved fuels, curbing urban sprawl and establishing sustainable mechanisms for controlling airborne emissions from industry.

As a result of these efforts, Chile today has good and improving air quality management capabilities with an excellent monitoring network, an emissions inventory, and strengthening regulatory and administrative structures.

Source: Larenas 1997.

terials to plastic and other synthetic materials, which take much longer to decompose, if they do at all.

In developing country cities an estimated 20–50% of the domestic solid waste generated remains uncollected, even with up to half of local government recurrent spending going for waste collection. In most industrial countries the entire urban population is served by municipal waste collection, but with rising consumption, cities confront ever-growing mounds of garbage.

TABLE 3.5.5

Domestic solid waste generation: a regional picture, early 1990s

Region or country group	Per capita waste generated annually (kg)	Population served by municipal waste services (%)
Developing countries	100–330	50–70
OECD	510	96
European Union	414	99
North America	720	100

Source: UNCHS 1997.

Poorly managed domestic solid waste seriously threatens health. In areas lacking sanitation, waste heaps become mixed with excreta, contributing to the spread of infectious diseases. Again, the poor suffer most. They live near waste disposal sites, and their children are the waste-pickers.

Uncollected domestic waste is the most common cause of blocked urban drainage channels in Asian cities, increasing the risk of flooding and water-borne diseases. But in the developing world there is increasing concern about dealing with domestic solid waste. Innovative attempts have even been made to transform waste into fertilizer (box 3.5.5).

Industrial hazardous waste

Toxic effluents from mines, chemical producers, pulp and paper plants, and leather-tanning factories are playing an increasing role in environmental pollution. The typical contaminants are organo-chlorines, dioxins, pesticides, grease and oil, acid, and caustic and heavy metals such as cadmium and lead. Most are generated in industrial countries (table 3.5.6).

BOX 3.5.5

Managing solid waste – the experience in Alexandria, Egypt

Alexandria, the second largest city in Egypt, generates around 1,700 tons a day of domestic solid waste. And with nearly 40% of Egypt's industry, Alexandria also generates nearly 800 tons of industrial waste a day.

The high percentage of domestic waste in total solid waste creates problems because of its high moisture content. It contaminates water and pollutes the environment, spreading disease and posing health risks. In the short run industrial wastes produce toxicity by ingestion, inhalation and skin absorption or corrosivity. And in the long run they pose a potential carcinogenic hazard through polluted underground and surface water.

But Alexandria found an innovative way to deal with its solid waste – turning it into organic fertilizer, or compost. That takes care of the waste itself and in the process produces something useful for agriculture. The idea has received strong support from the national government.

In the mid-1980s a composting plant was established in the city's central district, Abbis. The processing technology is window-type fermentation. At first the plant was running a deficit, but within two years it started generating profits as prices for compost increased.

The Abbis compost plant produces 160 tons of fertilizer every day, at a price per ton of about $8. There is a heavy demand for compost among farmers, who have found that it boosts agricultural productivity.

The Abbis plant has shown that waste can have productive uses. With the demand for compost in Egypt estimated to be as high as 8 million tons a year, many observers have recommended replicating the experiment on a larger scale.

Source: Serageldin, Cohen and Sivaramakrishnan 1995.

Workers in facilities that produce toxic materials and people living close to waste disposal sites are the main victims of the effects of these contaminants. Illegal dumping and improper disposal are common in many developing countries, allowing wastes to leach into and contaminate water supplies. Asia's rivers contain 20 times as much lead on average as those in industrial countries. Jakarta Bay, where some 30,000 small industries discharge untreated waste, has a high accumulation of toxic heavy metals. In Peru 20,000 tons of mining waste laden with cyanide washed into the Pacoy River last year.

In addition to causing health-related risks, contamination of water threatens shipping and fishing industries. In China most toxic solid wastes are disposed of in the municipal waste streams without treatment – contaminating soils and waterways with such heavy metals as lead, arsenic

TABLE 3.5.6
Hazardous waste in industrial regions, early 1990s
(thousands of metric tons)

Region or country group	Hazardous waste produced
OECD	258,000
North America	220,000
European Union	27,000
Nordic countries	1,300

Source: Human Development Report Office.

and mercury, and threatening or destroying marine life. Recently, however, there have been initiatives to control industrial effluents in the developing world through the use of fees, as has been done in Malaysia.

Pesticides are used most widely in industrial countries. Indeed, the effects in industrial countries may be more widespread than in developing countries, if more subtle. As many as 50 million Americans may be drinking water polluted by pesticides, and the US National Research Council has estimated that up to 20,000 may die each year from the effects of the relatively low levels in food.

But again it is the world's poor who suffer the most acute effects from pesticides. They pose a major occupational health hazard for poor farmers and farm workers, who are easily exposed to dangerous levels. These workers use pesticides without training or protective clothing and are often unable to read even simple instructions. As many as 25 million agricultural workers in the developing world – 11 million of them in Africa – may be poisoned each year, and hundreds of thousands die. In recent years, however, alternatives to pesticides have sometimes been used to reduce the adverse effects of pesticide use in Africa and Asia (box 3.5.6).

The poor are most at risk, too, from accidents and discharges involving factories – for they tend to live nearest to them. Population growth,

---

BOX 3.5.6

Alternatives to pesticide use

Integrated pest management and biological control have proved to be successful alternatives to pesticides. The first method relies on such techniques as crop rotation and intercropping to inhibit the proliferation of weeds, pests and pathogens. Biological control relies on nature's own checks and balances. Natural predators are introduced to keep pest populations to a minimum, or pest breeding is disrupted by the release of sterilized males.

Integrated pest management has produced good results in Brazil, China and India. In Brazil its introduction in soyabean production has reduced pesticide use by more than 80% over seven years.

In cotton production in Jiangsu Province in China, pesticide use decreased by 90%, pest control costs were reduced by nearly 85% and increases in yields were reported. The introduction of integrated pest management in Orissa, India, has cut insecticide use by 30–50%.

Biological control has worked well in Sub-Saharan Africa and Costa Rica. In Africa it has brought mealy bug pests under control in some 65 million hectares of land planted with cassava. And in Costa Rica it has reduced banana pest populations.

Source: Lean 1992.

increasing urbanization and rural-urban migration have given rise to large squatter settlements in developing countries – *favelas* in Brazil, *juggias* in India and *barrios* in Venezuela. Squatter housing accounts for more than 50% of the total housing stock in Caracas and Dar-es-Salaam, more than 40% in Karachi and between 25% and 30% in Tunis. In Asia a quarter of the urban population lives in slums. These slums are made of cardboard and scrap materials, poorly served with water and sewerage and built on hazardous landfills.

The Bhopal disaster in India in 1984 – when a cloud of lethal gases swept out of the Union Carbide factory – was particularly severe because a squatter settlement was pressed up against the factory grounds. It killed nearly 8,000 people and injured more than 50,000. In the aftermath the lawsuit was moved to India from the United States so that a smaller compensation could be negotiated. After a long drawn-out legal process the victims were reportedly paid a meagre amount. Thus the Bhopal disaster was not just a severe industrial accident – it was also a case of environmental injustice.

The rising costs of responsible toxic waste management (now up to $3,000 a ton) have encouraged the export of toxic waste from industrial to developing countries, where it can be buried untreated for as little as $5 a ton. In the late 1980s it was reported that several African countries – in urgent need of foreign currency as commodity prices plunged and their debt soared – became dumping grounds for industrial country waste.

Between 1984 and 1986 the former Soviet Union dumped tons of hazardous waste in Benin. Between the late 1980s and early 1990s Paraguay and Uruguay were reported to be destinations for waste shipments from Europe and the United States. But in early 1998, in a meeting in Malaysia of the Parties to the Basel Convention on the Ban on Hazardous Waste, more than 100 countries agreed to ban such exports.

Soil degradation and desertification

Water contamination, air pollution and indiscriminate waste disposal have the most immediate

human impact – and their effects are relatively easy to quantify. But in the longer term the effects of the degradation of the world's natural systems are just as serious, for they both further impoverish hundreds of millions of poor people and undermine the very basis of development. They also are much harder to reverse. It is generally easier to provide safe drinking water or to clean up dangerous waste dumps than it is to restore badly degraded land – and given the political will, it can be done much faster.

Nearly a third of the world's people – almost all of them poor – depend directly on what they can grow, gather or catch. And while everyone on earth ultimately depends on its natural systems, the poor are particularly vulnerable to degradation of those systems.

The geography of soil degradation shows that the problem is severest in Asia and Africa, where two-thirds of the world's poor people live (figure 3.5.5). Population growth has often been identified as the driving force behind soil degradation. But increasing population density need not undermine environmental sustainability (box 3.5.7).

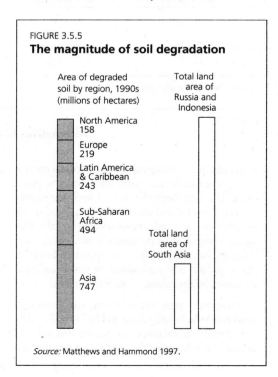

FIGURE 3.5.5
The magnitude of soil degradation

Area of degraded soil by region, 1990s (millions of hectares)

North America 158
Europe 219
Latin America & Caribbean 243
Sub-Saharan Africa 494
Asia 747

Total land area of Russia and Indonesia

Total land area of South Asia

Source: Matthews and Hammond 1997.

Soil degradation affects human life in three main ways:

- It reduces the availability of agricultural land per capita and agricultural productivity. Pressure on arable land stemming in part from soil degradation has reduced per capita farmland in developing countries to a tenth of a hectare, compared with half a hectare in industrial countries.
- It reduces the fodder available for cattle.
- It turns people into environmental refugees searching for more fertile land.

The crisis is worst in the drylands, which stretch across a third of the world's land surface. Here the soils are particularly fragile, vegetation is sparse, the climate is especially harsh – and land degradation is defined as desertification. Patches of degraded land erupt and spread like a skin disease, joining up to produce desertlike conditions over vast areas.

Desertification already costs the world $42 billion a year in lost income – Africa alone, $9 billion a year. But the human cost is even higher. Some 250 million people, and the livelihoods of a billion, are at risk from slashed crop yields. The poor people on the drylands of developing countries are among the most marginalized on earth – economically, politically and geographically. Extraordinarily vulnerable, they rarely have rights to their land. Traditional methods of managing the

---

BOX 3.5.7

Population growth and environmental sustainability – the Machakos miracle

Many people believe that rapid population growth is incompatible with sustainable management of the environment. But the experience of Machakos District in Kenya clearly demonstrates that this need not be so. In some cases increasing population density is required for environmental sustainability.

Between 1932 and 1990 the population of Machakos increased from 240,000 to 1.4 million. Until the late 1930s significant soil degradation and erosion had been observed in the district, most of which is semi-arid and often subject to moisture stress. This suggests the likelihood of population-induced degradation on a large scale, and that was the assessment in the 1930s. But the population-environment nexus affected the situation positively – in two ways.

First, the concern about soil degradation and erosion led to such measures as bench terracing to conserve soils. The activity was rooted in the community through a variant of the traditional work party, *mwethya*. In the 1950s more than 40,000 hectares of land were terraced, a success described as the Machakos miracle. In the 1980s more than 8,500 kilometres of terraces were constructed annually, compared with a peak of about 5,000 kilometres earlier.

Second, increasing population density has had positive effects in Machakos. The increasing scarcity (and rising value) of land promoted investment, both in conservation and in high-yielding improvements. Integrating crop and livestock production improved the sustainability of the farming system.

Many social and institutional factors – a good policy framework, better physical infrastructure, a secure land tenure system, indigenous technology, an improved health and education system – facilitated the agricultural changes in the Machakos District. More and more women took on leadership roles. In this setting farmers were receptive to suggestions regarding soil conservation, moisture retention and tree planting.

The results have been impressive. Between 1930 and 1987 the productivity of food and cash crops increased more than sixfold. Horticulture productivity grew fourteenfold.

The Machakos experience offers an alternative to the Malthusian models. It clearly demonstrates that even in an area vulnerable to land degradation, a large population can be sustained through a combination of endogenous and exogenous technological change supported by a conducive policy framework and much local initiative.

Source: Montimore and Tiffen 1994.

ecologically sensitive soils are being edged out as more and more good land is used for monoculture, often for export, pushing poor farmers onto ever more marginal territory.

This is not just a developing country phenomenon. The continent with the greatest share of dryland suffering moderate to severe desertification is North America, with 74%, just beating Africa, with 73%. In all, more than 110 countries are at risk.

Drought can cause disaster. One person in six in Burkina Faso and Mali has had to leave land as it turns to dust. About 135 million are in danger of becoming environmental refugees.

Deforestation

About a third of the earth's original forests have disappeared, and about two-thirds of what is left has been fundamentally changed (figure 3.5.6).

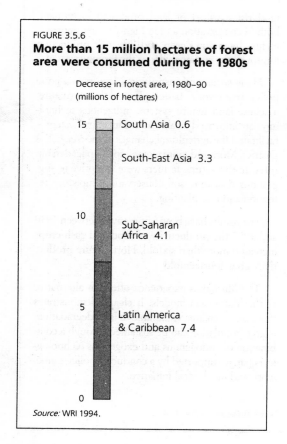

FIGURE 3.5.6

More than 15 million hectares of forest area were consumed during the 1980s

Decrease in forest area, 1980–90 (millions of hectares)

South Asia	0.6
South-East Asia	3.3
Sub-Saharan Africa	4.1
Latin America & Caribbean	7.4

Source: WRI 1994.

Deforestation has significant human costs. Forests have been a major source of food, fodder, fuel, fibre, timber, dyes and oils for medicine. Cutting them can rob poor people of their livelihood as well as their medicines. In many parts of the developing world poor communities able to draw at least half their food from forest products have never had famine. That ability is now diminishing. In the Philippines, for example, 50% of the forest was lost to commercial logging during the Marcos regime; a few hundred families shared the $42 billion in revenue, leaving 18 million forest dwellers impoverished.

Forests do wonderful things. They bind soil to the ground, regulate water supplies and help govern the climate. Cutting them seriously impairs these attributes. Two-fifths of the world's people depend on water absorbed by the forests of mountain ranges. But when the trees have been felled, rainwater sheets off the land, causing first floods, then drought. Tens of millions of hectares in India have become more vulnerable to flooding as a result of deforestation.

Perverse economic incentives, political motives and insecurity of land tenure often cause deforestation. Poor people are encouraged to clear forests and build settlements, only to find later that the soil quality is not good for agriculture. That leads to further deforestation. People are also encouraged to build new settlements as a wall of defense against rebels or invaders. Insecurity of land tenure also leads to deforestation, by promoting uncontrolled cattle ranching.

Forests are now generally replanted in industrial countries, with tree cover increasing slightly in Europe, Australia and New Zealand. But many of the original ecologically rich forests have been felled, and the new plantations are usually far poorer mixes of at best a few species. Only 1% of Europe's original forest remains, and such "old-growth" forests are still being cut. Temperate rain forests are thus far more endangered than their more celebrated tropical counterparts.

But in recent times increasing awareness about deforestation has led to serious reforestation efforts in some countries. China increased its forest area by more than 7 million hectares in the

1980s – and India, by more than 6 million hectares. Other countries – for example, Brazil – have formulated laws and regulations to reverse deforestation. Communities also have been playing an increasing role in conserving forests for economic and environmental benefits (box 3.5.8). Such measures may slow deforestation so that forests may thrive again in the lives and livelihoods of poor people.

Loss of biodiversity

Biodiversity refers to diversity of species of life forms. Biodiversity is important for everybody. It is an important factor in safeguarding the world's food supplies. Medicines developed from wild species have saved countless lives, and every year drugs worth more than $100 billion are derived largely from forest plants and animals. Exports of palm nuts, kernels and rattan are worth $2 billion a year.

But more important, biodiversity is the means of livelihood and the means of production for poor people who have no access to other assets and productive resources. For food and medicine, for energy and fibre, for ceremony and craft, poor people depend on the wealth of biological resources and their knowledge of a diverse biosphere. Biodiversity helps poor people survive in times of scarcity.

The erosion of biodiversity thus has more than ecological consequences. It also translates into destroyed livelihoods and unfulfilled basic needs for the poorer two-thirds of humanity living in a biodiversity-based economy. An estimated 3 billion people depend on traditional medicine as the principal source of cures for illness.

In today's world biodiversity is lost through various processes. Biopiracy is on the rise (box 3.5.9). In developing countries it can cause poor

---

BOX 3.5.8

Forest conservation in Zanzibar – community action

Jozani Forest is the largest remaining natural forest on the main island of Zanzibar in the United Republic of Tanzania. In the surrounding community livelihoods depend on supplying firewood and charcoal to the town and timber for building. As a result of rapid growth in local communities, in the town and in tourism, demand for wood products – poles, firewood and charcoal – is rising on all sides. This threatens the sustainability of the forest as a renewable resource as well as its potential to raise revenue from visiting tourists.

Past conflict between the government and communities, poorly defined property rights and weak community organizations have led to a situation of rapid degradation of the forest's resources. The Jozani Chwaka Bay Conservation Project was set up in 1995 to reduce community dependence on forest products, improve community livelihoods, encourage common resource management and develop a protected forest area.

The villages set up committees to produce plans for managing their surrounding forest resources. Local forest guards were recruited to curb wood cutting without licences. Workshops have helped to educate villagers about the wider issues involved, and visits to other villages with very degraded resources have alerted the communities to the need to preserve their own.

Jozani is probably the most visited forest in East Africa. In 1997 it attracted 18,000 tourists, generating $40,000 in entrance fees. The government, lobbied to share these revenues with local communities, has allowed the retention of 30% of revenues for a community development fund. The communities have chosen to use this money to improve schools and health centres, repair wells and upgrade roads. Alternative microenterprise is promoted both to diversify income generation away from dependence on timber and to increase the value added of those resources used.

The Jozani experience is also an example of an effective alliance between local communities, the government and international organizations. The Commission for Natural Resources in Zanzibar and CARE Tanzania are partners in the project and are actively working with village communities around Jozani.

Source: Wild 1998.

people to lose access to their livelihoods, means of production and sources of energy and medicine. Their survival and sustenance may be endangered as a result. In addition, global consumption patterns encourage developing countries to export commodities, the production of which results in environmental damage and loss of biodiversity. And globally mobile investments may bring resource – and pollution-intensive industries to developing countries, activities that may adversely affect biodiversity.

Consider the explosion in shrimp and prawn production in developing countries and in their export to the industrial world. In the past decade annual production of giant tiger prawns in Thailand has gone from 900 tons to 277,000. In 1996 alone Thailand exported 235,000 tons of shrimp and prawns, mostly to Europe and North America. This production has serious environmental, economic, social and political consequences.

The most serious environmental impact is the large-scale pumping of sea water into the shrimp farms, which causes salinization of ponds. The extraction of large volumes of fresh water from underground aquifers to control salinity is another problem. Still another is the seeping or overflow of saline water onto neighbouring agricultural farms – and into the water table. The degraded ponds can rarely be used for agriculture. That is why shrimp farming is termed a rape-and-run industry.

But more important, shrimp farming is directly linked to the loss of mangroves – the nurseries of marine life (table 3.5.7). In Thailand 200,000 hectares of mangroves have been lost to shrimp farming, in Ecuador 120,000 and in Viet Nam almost 70,000. The result is eroding coastal land and dwindling shelter and habitat for fish and other marine life.

Shrimp farming has two distinct economic effects on poor people. First, in most cases shrimp farms have been developed on productive agricultural lands, and the activities monopolized by rich local farmers, big exporters and multinationals. So poor people find themselves facing constraints in

---

BOX 3.5.9

Biopiracy

Biopiracy refers to the appropriation and pirating, through the enforcement of the intellectual property rights of scientists and corporations, of the intrinsic worth of diversified species and the community rights and innovations of indigenous people.

The intellectual property right implies four things: private rights as opposed to common rights; recognition of knowledge and innovation only when they generate profits, not when they meet social needs; innovation in a formal institutional setting rather than embodiment of indigenous knowledge; and international perspective rather than domestic and local use. Immediately it becomes apparent that the intellectual property right excludes all kinds of knowledge, ideas and innovations that arise in intellectual commons – in villages among farmers, in forests in tribes. It excludes all sectors that produce and innovate outside the industrial mode of organization of production.

Today a process is under way to strengthen enforcement of intellectual property rights. As a result, in many cases the collective and cumulative innovation of millions of people over thousands of years can be pirated and claimed as an innovation of professional scientists or corporations. This is happening for two reasons. The first is the idea that science is unique to formal institutions and indigenous knowledge systems cannot be treated as scientific. The second is that many countries do not recognize existing knowledge of other countries as intellectual property.

Such biopiracy inevitably leads to intellectual and cultural impoverishment, since it displaces other ways of knowing, other objectives for knowledge creation and other modes of knowledge sharing. It denies creativity, collective well-being and informal ways of knowledge creation and dissemination. But more important, it makes poor people poorer as their resources and knowledge are appropriated and privatized.

Source: Shiva 1997b.

producing staples for their families. Second, to produce each ton of industrial shrimp requires 10 tons of marine fish, limiting the access of poor people to a low-priced but nutritious source of animal protein.

Shrimp farming also leads to social and political problems. Land takeovers for shrimp production and actions to safeguard against shrimp theft have resulted in local conflicts and deaths.

TABLE 3.5.7
Relationship between mangrove loss and shrimp production

Country	Mangrove area loss by 1989 (thousands of hectares)	Shrimp production in 1995 (thousands of tons)
Thailand	200	280
Ecuador	120	90
Viet Nam	67	37
India	35	96
Bangladesh	9	34

Source: Shiva 1997a.

The act of robbing poor people of their resources and livelihoods at the global level is repeated at the national level, particularly against indigenous people (box 3.5.10). It makes people extremely vulnerable.

INTERNATIONAL ENVIRONMENTAL PROBLEMS ARE ALSO A BURDEN FOR THE POOR

The international and truly global environmental issues, such as the changes in the earth's atmosphere, are the hardest to quantify. The effects, usually occurring long after the pollution that causes them, cannot be observed, only estimated. Yet they may be the most devastating of all to human well-being – and some cannot be reversed within human time-scales.

Acid rain and forest fires may originate in one country but have an effect on others. Ozone depletion and global warming pertain to the whole globe. All these phenomena have impacts, direct and indirect, on human well-being. And even

---

BOX 3.5.10
Invading the environmental resources of indigenous people – the Brazilian case

Today in Brazil indigenous people account for only 0.2% of the total population, and their lands for about 12% of national territory. During the past few years their existence has become ever more precarious as a result of increasing invasion of their territory through land confiscation and exploitation of natural resources. The invaders are mostly dispossessed marginal workers who engage in illicit activities on indigenous land, illegally mining gold or extracting luxury woods such as mahogany, cherry and cedar. Their numbers are estimated at 45,000. Another type of invasion is by the public sector, to build highways, hydroelectric power plants and other infrastructure projects.

The number of invasions nearly doubled in 1996, affecting around 43% of the indigenous population. More than two-fifths of the invasions were motivated by illegal exploration for and theft of timber, mostly in the states of Amazon and Pará. But illegal logging activity on indigenous land was also carried out in more than half the Brazilian states. In Rondônia 40% of indigenous lands were subject to illegal activities. In Maranhão about 37% of the territories were invaded by loggers, and in the states of Pará and Mato Grosso there was exploration for luxury species of hardwoods on 33% of indigenous lands.

Cases of environmental damage on indigenous land increased eightfold in 1996, including illegal exploitation and degradation of natural resources and usurpation of indigenous land. The outcome: devastation of vegetation, contamination of products from mining and agriculture and endangered fish species. Also during 1996 nearly 33% of all illnesses were linked to environmental degradation. Invasion of indigenous territory in Brazil has aggravated the survival conditions of nearly a third of the country's indigenous population.

Source: Sodré 1997.

though their ultimate consequences for human lives and livelihoods cannot be well quantified, they are believed to impose a greater burden on poor people than on rich.

Acid rain

Polluted air drifts inexorably across national frontiers, with emissions of sulphur dioxide and other gases in one country raining acid on another. Only 7% of the polluting sulphur in Norway originates in that country. In Sweden it is 10%. The environmental damage from acid rain – to forests and agriculture, critical for the livelihoods of poor people – is more fundamental and longer-lasting than first believed.

Acid rain is causing heavy damage in industrial countries, particularly in Canada, Poland and the Nordic countries. About 60% of Europe's commercial forests suffer damaging levels of sulphur deposition. In Sweden about 20,000 of the 90,000 lakes are acidified to some degree – in Canada 48,000 lakes are acidified.

Acid rain also is becoming a major problem in the developing world. Acid depositions are particularly high in such industrial areas as South-East China, North-East India, the Republic of Korea and Thailand. The effects are already being felt in agriculture. In India wheat yields have been cut in half in areas close to large sources of sulphur dioxide emissions.

Over the years most industrial countries have reduced their sulphur dioxide emissions drastically. Japan reduced its emissions from nearly 5 million tons in 1970 to 900,000 in 1993. Canada, Norway, Sweden and the United Kingdom have been quite successful too, though the last two started from a lower base. Yet sulphur dioxide emissions are still serious in some industrial countries. The United States alone emitted 20 million metric tons in 1993 – compared with 38 million metric tons for 20 Asian countries.

There have also been attempts in some developing countries to reduce emissions of sulphur dioxide. In Chile a decree adopted in 1992 is aimed at reducing industrial emissions of air pollutants – and cutting sulphur dioxide emissions drastically. Early estimates show a reduction of 20–30% in sulphur dioxide emissions.

Forest fires

Forest fires are also a transnational environmental problem. They originate in one country, but the smoke and air pollution they create travel to others, affecting human health and economic well-being. The Indonesian forest fire in 1997 exported smoke haze to Malaysia, the Philippines and Singapore. By mid-October nearly 1.7 million hectares had burned, though this was only the fifth largest fire in the past two decades. Poor visibility due to smoke caused major accidents and left drought victims without aid. And thousands of tourists cancelled trips to the region. Economic losses to some of the countries in the region have been estimated at 2% of GDP.

It was the fire in Indonesia that captured international headlines, but every continent experienced large blazes. Annual forest fires in the Amazon increased by nearly 30% in 1997. Unusually dry conditions in Africa and pressure for land led to vast fires in Kenya, Senegal and the United Republic of Tanzania. And fires burned out of control in Australia, Colombia and Papua New Guinea. Worldwide in 1997, fires destroyed at least 5 million hectares of forest and other land.

In health and in livelihoods these fires affected poor people most. In the Indonesian fire more than 1,000 people died and more than 20 million suffered smoke-related respiratory problems; most of these victims were poor. Yet poor people often have little to do with causing the fires. Logging by multinational corporations and clearing to speed development are the primary culprits, causing negative economic effects that will be felt for years. Sometimes forest fires are an outcome of tension between poor settlers in forest areas who are not given proper territorial rights and multinationals that are provided logging concessions. Small farmers burn trees planted by the multinationals, which in turn burn land to drive out the smallholders.

Depletion of the ozone layer

Ozone – a molecule of oxygen with three atoms instead of the normal two – is a troublesome pollutant near the earth's surface, but a lifesaver far overhead. Scattered so finely through the stratosphere, 15–50 kilometres up, that if collected it would form a shell around the earth no thicker than the sole of a shoe, it filters out the harmful ultraviolet rays of the sun. Without it, no terrestrial life would be possible.

The small amount of ultraviolet light that does get through damages health. It is the main cause of skin cancers, which have been fast increasing. The incidence of melanoma, the most dangerous, increased 80% in the United States during the 1980s alone. The ultraviolet light is also a major cause of cataracts, which cause more than half the blindness in the world and claim the sight of 17 million people a year. And it may suppress the immune system, helping cancers to become established and grow and increasing people's susceptibility to such diseases as malaria.

Even the slightest damage to the ozone layer would increase this toll on human health. It would also affect food supplies. More than two-thirds of crop species are damaged by ultraviolet light, which also penetrates the surface of the sea, killing the plankton so vital in the marine food chain.

Today the ozone layer has thinned by about 10% over temperate regions. Ozone depletion may provide one exception – at least among global issues – to the general rule that the poor suffer most from environmental degradation. It mainly affects temperate and polar regions, and ultraviolet light has its most severe effects on people with light skin. Yet in industrial countries the poor – who are less able to afford protection and more likely to work outdoors – may be more vulnerable.

Global warming

Global warming may be considered one of the most serious of all the environmental challenges. It threatens to disrupt the remarkably stable climate the world has enjoyed since the beginning of settled agriculture some 10,000 years ago – a climate that has made possible the growth of all civilizations and the expansion of human numbers from a few million to nearly 6 billion. Global warming is likely to aggravate most other environmental problems, and could exceed both what the planet can take and what human societies can stand.

Although the industrial world accounts for most of the emissions that lead to global warming, the effects will be felt all over the globe. A rate of climate change faster than at any time in the past 10,000 years is expected, and it is likely to cause widespread economic, social and environmental destruction over the next century. Developing countries, particularly their poorest people, are expected to be hit hardest by the failing harvests, growing water shortages and rising seas that will accompany global warming.

By the best estimates the world's harvests will be slightly reduced in the next century. This in itself is likely to increase food prices and hunger. More important, the effects will be distributed in a way that will generally worsen existing inequalities and patterns of poverty and hunger. Some areas, such as Europe and Canada, are expected to benefit from better harvests. But yields are expected to fall in Africa, South Asia and Latin America, where most of the world's poor and hungry live. A recent study predicts that harvests will decline by more than 30% in India and Pakistan by 2050.

It is the same story for rainfall. By and large the haves, who get enough now, are expected to get more, while the have nots will get less. Water shortages are expected to increase, with Sub-Saharan Africa, the Arab States, South Asia and Europe particularly affected. Deserts are expected to spread in all these regions except Europe.

Rising seas may threaten the lives of millions in developing countries. With a one-metre rise in sea level, due in part to global warming, Bangladesh could see its land area shrink by 17%, though it produces only 0.3% of global emissions. Egypt could see 12% of its territory, home to 7 million people, disappear under the waves. Rising seas threaten to make several small island nations – such as the Maldives and Tuvalu – uninhabitable and to swamp vast areas of other countries.

HUMAN IMPACTS OF ENVIRONMENTAL DAMAGE – A SUMMARY

This discussion of the human impact of environmental damage establishes three appalling facts:

- Whether it is pollution, degradation or waste, environmental damage has serious consequences for human heath, livelihoods and human security. An attempt has been made to estimate such costs in India (box 3.5.11).
- The geography of environmental damage indicates that the rich contribute more, with larger shares in outdoor pollution, global warming, acid rain, solid waste and toxics. But the poor bear the brunt in loss of lives and risks to health from pollution and toxics – and in loss of livelihoods from soil degradation, desertification, deforestation and biodiversity loss. And among the poor, women face greater risks, largely because of their social and economic roles (box 3.5.12).
- Environmental damage threatens both the earth's carrying capacity and people's coping capacity. And it may have serious consequences for future generations.

THE FUTURE NEED NOT BE GLOOMY

During the next 20 years the worldwide demand for energy, under various scenarios, is projected to increase by 30–55%, with developing countries accounting for four-fifths of the growth. But with energy-saving measures, this demand growth could be limited to 30%.

Air pollution, on past trends, will rise with energy use – and so will its toll. Sulphur dioxide emissions in Asia will overtake those in industrial countries in 2010, causing extensive damage through acid rain, particularly in South China. In another 25 years the number of cars in the world, now more than 500 million, may well double to top a billion. With much of this increase in countries that still use lead in petrol – most of them developing – emissions of lead could increase five-fold between 1990 and 2030.

Adding to global warming, energy-related carbon dioxide emissions are projected to rise between 30% and 40% by 2010 under moderate growth conditions. Much of the growth in these emissions will occur in the developing world. During the early 1990s carbon dioxide emissions in OECD countries were projected to increase some 24% by 2010 from their levels in 1990. Annual emissions in developing countries are projected to more than double, though from a much smaller base. If current trends continue, developing countries, with four-fifths of the world's population, will account for nearly half the annual global carbon dioxide emissions, up from a third today. China and India will account for more than half the developing world total. The issue of carbon dioxide emissions must be seen in a historical context, however, and from the perspective of cumulative accumulation over many years.

BOX 3.5.11

Costs of environmental degradation – estimates for India

Economic development has been the watchword in India's march into the 21st century. But the country may be paying an enormous price for this march, which has brought in its wake ecological devastation and numerous health problems. A conservative estimate of environmental damage in India puts the figure at more than $10 billion a year, or 4.5% of GDP in 1992. If higher estimates are used, the total environmental costs would be $13.8 billion, or 6% of GDP.

A breakdown of the conservative cost estimate of about $10 billion shows that urban air pollution costs India $1.3 billion a year. Water degradation

leads to health costs amounting to $5.7 billion every year, nearly three-fifths of the total environmental costs. Soil erosion affects 83–163 million hectares of land every year. Land degradation causes productivity loss equal to 4–6.3% of total agricultural output every year – a loss amounting to $2.4 billion. And deforestation, which proceeded at the rate of 0.6% a year between 1981 and 1990, leads to annual costs of $214 million.

These estimates, however, do not include the major environmental costs that arise out of biodiversity loss or pollution due to hazardous wastes.
Source: Agarwal 1996.

The renewable natural resources on which we all depend – the poor disproportionately more – will become scarcer. Today nearly a third of the world's people depend directly on renewable resources for much of their livelihoods. And in 2025 much of the population of Sub-Saharan Africa and South Asia might still be highly dependent on such resources – as might many people in rural Latin America and the Caribbean, given the extreme disparities in income and land ownership.

The use of firewood and other traditional fuels – indeed, the use of most renewable resources – is driven by expanding populations. Within 40 years the amount of cropland available per person is projected to fall by half from today's already meagre 0.27 hectare. By 2050 more than 2 billion people will live in regions facing land scarcity, with extensive and increasing desertification and land degradation, particularly in parts of South Asia and Sub-Saharan Africa.

Worldwide, water use is expanding rapidly, and by 2025 it will have risen by 40%. By then, three-quarters of the world's available freshwater run-off could be pressed into service, up from half today. By 2050 the number of people short of water may rise from 132 million to 1–2.5 billion. Regions home to nearly two-thirds of the world's people will face moderate to high water scarcity. Many authorities predict that water will become an important cause of war and human conflict in the 21st century.

If trends continue, the world may see a five-fold increase in waste generation by 2025, adding to pollution and the related health risks in developing countries.

The possible result of all this: poor people will be pushed more and more onto ecologically fragile lands, increasing their vulnerability. By the end of the next decade a billion poor people may

---

BOX 3.5.12

Environmental deterioration and women – a disproportionate burden

In developing countries women are doubly affected by environmental deterioration, first because of poverty and second because they are women. Environmental degradation places a disproportionate burden on women largely because of their social and economic roles, which expose them to greater numbers of environmental hazards.

Women have primary responsibility for household chores, activities that keep them inside the house most of the time. As the household food preparers, women are often exposed to high levels of smoke for long periods. Thus it is no wonder that the majority of the 2.2 million deaths every year from indoor air pollution occur among women. They also take primary responsibility for obtaining water and washing the family's clothes – activities that can be hazardous where sanitation is poor, washing facilities are inadequate and water supplies are contaminated. And women are usually responsible for caring for sick children, increasing their exposure to disease-causing organisms.

Moreover, the kind of employment that women have access to often puts them at risk as well. In rural areas many women work in agricultural fields, where they are exposed to toxics from fertilizers and pesticides. Many urban women work in small-scale industries, where toxic chemicals are often used without adequate safeguards. Another common source of income for women is piece work done at home, such as fabricating sandals or articles of clothing, which can involve the use of dangerous adhesives and other flammable or toxic materials.

In poor households women have the responsibility of collecting fuelwood and cow dung to meet the family's energy requirements. In an environmentally degraded setting that may mean long hours of walking to collect fuel. These activities significantly reduce women's time for other activities, as well as exposing them to health risks. Moreover, girls often help their mothers fetch water and fuelwood, depriving them of education.

Physiological factors also play a part in making women's health more vulnerable. Women are particularly at risk during pregnancy and after childbirth, when they are more vulnerable to such diseases as malaria.

Source: WRI 1996.

be living on such lands, twice the number today. Scarce resources and unequal access to natural resources and sinks will make it difficult for them to escape impoverishment. This continuing disproportionate impact of environmental degradation will hamper their health, lives and livelihoods.

Is humankind heading for doomsday? Yes and no. The future is bleak if we continue with business as usual. But there are alternatives and we can shape the future accordingly – with big commitments, big changes in policies, institutions and values, and a big sense of collective responsibility. New patterns of consumption, new technologies and greater efficiency in resource use can make resources available to poor people and minimize damage to the environment.

Progress has already been made in the dematerialization of production and consumption – in reducing the natural resource content per unit of production, and thus consumption. Suggestions have also been put forward for knowledge-based societies to ensure sustainable development (box 3.5.13). This will ease pressure on resources and reduce environmental damage. Both would be good for poor people.

Dematerializing production and consumption

Economic growth has been directly linked to increasing use of resources. If this link could be weakened by reducing the materials required for production and using resources more efficiently, there would be many advantages for both industrial and developing countries.

Could this delinking of growth and natural resource use be applied throughout economies? To some extent it already is. Energy use no longer necessarily parallels economic growth. Japan reduced the energy used to produce each (constant) dollar of GNP by nearly a third between 1973 and 1985. But in most countries energy use continues to rise because consumption has increased faster than efficiency. The amount of steel, timber and copper used per person in industrial countries has generally stabilized or declined, showing some delinking (figure 3.5.7). But in most cases the absolute amounts have increased.

BOX 3.5.13

Potential of the knowledge-based society

The advent of the knowledge-based society opens up a promising path to dematerialization, making intensive use of information and skills, rather than natural resources.

A knowledge-based society, emphasizing creativity and diversity, can enlarge human choices. Although knowledge is created by private individuals, knowledge is a public good because we can share it without diminishing it.

Three important issues:

• First, a knowledge-based society is more than a service economy. In a knowledge-based society typical workers are highly skilled, and their knowledge resides in their brains and life experience rather than in the machines that they operate.

• Second, any restriction on the sharing of knowledge is inefficient, because knowledge can be shared at no cost and can make others better off. But without some restrictions, there may be no incentive to create new knowledge. Solving this paradox of knowledge may require new institutions.

• Third, a knowledge-based society is also an information society. An information society requires *information infrastructure,* encompassing such modes of telecommunications as cable and satellite coverage and telephone lines; *computer infrastructure,* such as personal computers and the Internet; and *social infrastructure,* such as educated people and an open society that allows information to flow freely within a society and to and from the rest of the world.

Source: Chichilnisky 1997.

Much more will have to be done if the environmental crises of our time are to be avoided – and it can be done. Energy consumption can be cut by up to half in present industrial installations and by up to 90% in new ones – using technologies already available. *Factor Four,* the 1997 report to the Club of Rome, shows how output can be doubled while halving resource use, and describes concrete techniques to achieve this. Beyond cuts in energy consumption, there are possibilities for heavily reducing the use of wood, water and minerals while increasing living standards.

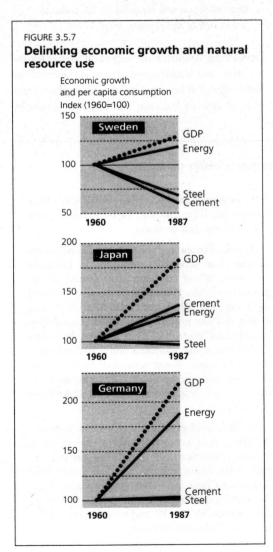

FIGURE 3.5.7

Delinking economic growth and natural resource use

Economic growth
and per capita consumption
Index (1960=100)

A broad consensus is growing, however, that industrial countries must go far beyond such delinking, to embrace the dematerialization of their economies. Both sustainability and equity demand that they reduce their use of resources – such as fisheries and natural forests – and their emissions by more than tenfold in the coming decades. This target for sustainability, "Factor Ten," has been broadly endorsed by a group of ministers from both industrial and developing countries.

Recycling can help, by reducing the use of new materials. If France doubled its reuse and recycling of non-renewable materials, it would reduce natural resource use by three-fifths. Every ton of recycled steel saves more than a ton of iron ore, half a ton of coal and 9 kilograms of limestone – as well as several tons of hidden material flows associated with mining and processing. Recycling can also save energy – recycling aluminium requires only 5% of the energy needed to refine and smelt new aluminium from bauxite. In industrial countries today, the recycling rate for paper is about 45%, and that for glass 50%. In the mid-1980s the rates were 33% and 26%. Recycling on a large-scale commercial basis is not yet significant in developing countries.

But recycling is only one option for dematerialization. Reusing products, repairing them and increasing their durability are also part of the package. So is cleaner production – designing the production process to minimize raw material use and waste and thus reducing pollution at the source (box 3.5.14). There is also increasing evidence that transforming effluents into commercial products, such as fertilizer, can be profitable for private firms.

Just as environmental damage seriously limits the well-being of poor people, these solutions can enhance it. Technologies that use fewer resources and create less pollution generally employ more people. Recycling waste, for example, creates jobs, particularly for women (box 3.5.15). Many studies show that ecological tax reform – which substitutes taxes on resource use and pollution for taxes on jobs and income – could help.

One study by the European Union suggests that such tax reform could produce 4 million new jobs in the EU countries.

TECHNOLOGY IS CRUCIAL

But dematerialization should not undermine the technologies needed to meet the requirements of poor people. Renewable sources of energy offer particular promise both for reducing poverty and for reducing indoor pollution for poor people – and for cutting the use of polluting forms of energy by the rich.

Technology is one of the make-or-break factors in the delinking of economic growth and natural resource use:

- Clean production processes must be broadly introduced so that industry becomes less

polluting. And clean and efficient technologies must be developed for waste management.

- Efficient "next-generation" technologies must be made available to developing countries so that their pollution levels do not rise as they industrialize and develop. These countries should advance to better technology by leap-frogging phases of technological development rather than progressing gradually.

- Low-cost, simple but efficient technology should be developed to meet the requirements of poor people. Without access to such technology, it will be difficult for them to break out of the poverty trap.

Developing countries are important arenas for innovation and leapfrogging. There is potential for leapfrogging in both processes and products, and often a synergy between the two. For example,

---

BOX 3.5.14

Cleaner production – prevention is better than cure

Cleaner production marks a new approach to enlisting technology to protect the environment. It reflects the old adage: "prevention is better than cure."

This approach aims to eliminate pollution at the source and to conserve raw materials such as energy and water through efficient production processes. It also aims to reduce the environmental impact of products throughout their life cycle, from the first extraction of raw materials to their ultimate disposal. This proactive, preventive approach contrasts sharply with traditional pollution control or waste management, which aims to mitigate damage after it occurs. It is more effective and much cheaper.

There are many examples of successful implementation of cleaner production in both industrial and developing countries. In the industrial world Dow Chemical's WRAP (Waste Reduction Always Pays) programme has cut emissions of 58 pollutants by more than half since 1985, and is continuing to bring about further reductions. Pollution by 3M has been cut 90% worldwide. In New Zealand companies that have reduced waste have saved 50–

100% of annual costs and where reuse is involved, have produced extra income. Payback times in many cases are only days or weeks.

Eastern Europe and the CIS are also beginning to take clean production seriously. In Lithuania only about 4% of companies had started cleaner production in the 1960s; that proportion increased to 35% in the 1990s. In the Czech Republic 24 case studies of clean production found that generation of industrial waste had been reduced by nearly 22,000 tons a year, including nearly 10,000 tons of hazardous waste. Waste water had been reduced to 12,000 cubic metres a year. The economic benefits have been estimated at more than $2.4 million every year.

In the developing world a cement company in Indonesia is saving $350,000 a year by using cleaner production techniques. The payback period of the investment was less than a year. Pilot projects in China, in 51 companies spanning 11 industries, found that cleaner production techniques cut pollution by 15–31% and were five times as effective as traditional methods.

Source: Hillary 1997.

---

lighting in isolated villages is predominately kerosene lanterns and candles. Switching to a compact fluorescent lightbulb (CFL), which is four times as efficient as a conventional incandescent bulb, would make it economical to supply power from a solar photovoltaic (PV) panel. Connecting to an electric grid – probably required if inefficient bulbs are used – would be unnecessary, allowing vast savings in capital equipment. These savings could be reflected in improved education, health and livelihoods. The PV-CFL solution leapfrogs over its alternative: a large, expensive electricity generating system.

A second dividend from leapfrog technologies derives from the avoided costs of long-term environmental clean-up, such as mopping up old toxic sites and scrubbing coal power plants. Using leapfrog technologies minimizes clean-up costs, as well as health care costs linked to environmental pollution and degradation.

Leapfrog technologies are not only ideas – they are a reality (box 3.5.16). And they are being used in many developing as well as industrial countries.

But technology alone is not the solution. It must be supplemented with policy reforms, institutional arrangements and changes in collective responsibility.

POLICY ISSUES

Reversing and minimizing the human impacts of environmental damage, particularly the unequal impacts on poor people, and ensuring environmental sustainability raise a number of important policy questions. These cover efficiency in resource use, clean production, reduction of waste generation, poor people's access to natural resources, their rights and entitlements to common property, low-cost next-generation technologies

---

BOX 3.5.15

Waste recycling – women in Ho Chi Minh City

Over the past six years the amount of garbage generated annually in Ho Chi Minh City has quadrupled, from 198,000 tons to 839,000. Each person produces three-fourths of a kilogram of waste per day. Non-decomposable garbage makes up about a third of the total. Of this, about 62 tons a day enter the recycling chain, mainly through women.

The urban waste recycling chain of Ho Chi Minh City involves several links for the collection of waste products, their transformation into low-priced consumer items and their sale, predominantly to poor people. Women are involved in all these links as buyers, shopkeepers and recyclers.

Women waste buyers ply their trade by walking door to door in self-designated areas where they know the clientele. Walking approximately 15 kilometres daily, they collect an average of 41 kilograms of waste, such as newspapers, old books, shoes, bottles, tin and aluminium. On average, buyers earn a daily income of VN$14,000 (US$1.30); in most cases this represents the largest share in their household income.

Women make up a little more than half of all shopkeepers dealing in waste. On average, a medium-size shop buys about 523 kilograms of waste and 115 bottles daily, while the big shops can buy up to 30 tons a day. Shopkeepers enjoy a fairly high living standard. The average monthly income per shop is VN$3–4 million (US$280–370) and can go as high as VN$ 10 million (US$930).

The waste recycling activities by women in Ho Chi Minh City have brought three distinct benefits. First, they relieve some of the pressure posed by the large amount of solid waste that must be collected by the city's public works department. Second, they transform waste into consumer goods purchased by poor people. Third, they create employment and income. About 10,000 people are employed in these activities, most of them women. More than 5,000 women are engaged in buying waste from households, more than 500 work as shopkeepers and more than 40% of the workers in recycling factories are women. Even though their earnings are not high, they contribute an important share of household incomes.

Source: Ngoc and others 1994.

---

for poor people and changes in production and consumption patterns. And in several areas public provisioning of goods and services for poor people is critical.

Another important issue is environmental management. Strengthening it will require a role for communities as well as the state and a stronger alliance between local communities, institutions of civil society and governments. Inspiration can be drawn from grass-roots environmental movements in alliance with antipoverty and women's movements.

Addressing all these issues effectively requires first exposing five myths that often surround policy discussion on the poverty environment nexus.

FIRST MYTH: SUBSIDIES ON RESOURCES ARE ALWAYS FOR THE BENEFIT OF POOR PEOPLE. This myth becomes exposed when one looks at water and energy. In most cases, throughout the world, the cost of providing water to consumers exceeds what they pay. The average price paid covers only a third of the cost, and government subsidies make up the difference. Since water prices are too low to recover investment costs, new connections are not seen as profitable and poor people remain unserved as a result.

Energy also receives significant subsidies in developing countries. Even in the early 1990s the average price paid per unit of electricity was only 40% of its production cost. But such subsidies are not passed on to poor people, because they are not connected to the grid. In developing countries it is the urban middle class that enjoys access to such facilities.

Not only have subsidies failed to benefit poor people. They have often provided incentives to the rich for wasting resources rather than conserving them.

SECOND MYTH: POOR PEOPLE ARE UNABLE OR UNWILLING TO CONTRIBUTE TO COSTS. This myth too is false. Most poor people already pay for the basics. Many poor families lacking a connection to piped water must purchase water

---

BOX 3.5.16

Leapfrog technologies

In developing countries there have been many attempts to develop technologies that can help leapfrog over steps in the traditional development path followed by industrial countries. These technologies include engine fuel from ethanol, electricity from biomass and zero-emission cars.

Ethanol produced from fermented sugar cane juice is used as a substitute for petrol to fuel cars in Brazil. Around 200,000 barrels a day of ethanol are used, reducing the petrol needed for the 10 million Brazilian automobiles by 50%. Although ethanol has lower caloric content than petrol, it is an excellent motor fuel; it has a motor octane of 90, exceeding that of petrol; and it is suitable for use in high-compression engines. The development of high-compression motors in Brazil is itself an example of technological leapfrogging. Nearly 400 processing plants have been established for ethanol production, creating more than 700,000 jobs. The substitution of ethanol for petrol avoids emissions of nearly 10 million tons of carbon dioxide a year.

Burning fuelwood, bagasse and other agricultural residues to generate electricity is a proven technology used in many countries. In the United States some 8,000 megawatts of electricity is generated from biomass. But generation efficiency is less than 10%. Using an integrated gasifier-gas turbine system would increase efficiency to more than 45%. This emerging technology is two and a half times as efficient as the conventional way of producing electricity (steam cycle), and the cost of the electricity from this system would be 5 cents per kilowatt-hour, compared with more than 8 cents per kilowatt-hour in the traditional system.

The zero-emission cars will operate on electricity. Two options exist – using energy stored in batteries and generating electricity on-board, for example, in fuel cells using hydrogen as fuel and yielding only water as a by-product. Buses are probably the ideal first candidate for zero-emission vehicles.

Source: Goldemberg 1997.

from private vendors – at a cost that is sometimes 10–12 times what a middle-class family with a connection pays. More positively, poor people are willing to contribute their time and effort to improving community water supply and sanitation systems. In low-income parts of Haiti and Nigeria more than a fifth of household expenditure goes to the purchase of water.

THIRD MYTH: DEVELOPING COUNTRIES SHOULD SIMPLY IMITATE WHAT INDUSTRIAL COUNTRIES HAVE DONE IN DEALING WITH THE ENVIRONMENT. Developing countries can certainly learn from the experiences of industrial countries. But that does not mean that they should adopt their practices wholesale. During the past decade and a half most OECD countries have been quite successful in reducing lead, carbon monoxide and sulphur dioxide emissions and in cleaning up their lakes and rivers. They have also increased forest cover. But their approach may not be the least-cost one. In seeking to reduce emissions, for example, governments have often imposed technologies on firms and industries, rather than looking for the cheapest solutions. And they have introduced emissions standards late in industrialization, after significant investments had already been made in polluting processes. Developing countries should avoid these mistakes.

FOURTH MYTH: DEVELOPING COUNTRIES SHOULD RESTRAIN THEIR CONSUMPTION, INDUSTRIALIZATION AND DEVELOPMENT, BECAUSE THESE WILL CONTRIBUTE TO FURTHER ENVIRONMENTAL DAMAGE. Developing countries face a fundamental choice. They can mimic the industrial countries, and go through a development phase that is dirty and wasteful and creates an enormous legacy of pollution. Or they can leapfrog over some of the steps followed by industrial countries and incorporate modern, efficient technologies into their development process. Leapfrogging would allow them to increase their consumption, industrialization and development without contributing to environmental damage. Their consumption is still so low that the issue should not be restraining it, but seeing how they can advance technologically to increase consumption without the adverse environmental impacts.

FIFTH MYTH: THE SCOPE FOR CHEAP, EFFECTIVE AND POLITICALLY ACCEPTABLE ANTI-POLLUTION POLICIES IS VERY LIMITED IN DEVELOPING COUNTRIES. This contention also is incorrect. There are many such policy options for developing countries. For example, to ensure clean air, governments can introduce measures to phase lead out of petrol. Or they can tax unleaded fuel less heavily, to give drivers more incentive to use it. The cost of taking lead out of petrol is minimal, and the belief that using unleaded petrol harms engines has been found to be false. With a large share of the emissions in many developing countries caused by motorcycles and three-wheelers, another important option would be to encourage the use of four-stroke engines through differential taxation, as has been done in Thailand. In the extreme, the use of such engines could be made mandatory.

• • •

All environmental issues, particularly the unequal impacts of environmental damage on poor people, demand urgent attention, for the time lags built into the world political system ensure that medium- and long-term threats require action just as immediate as that demanded by short-term threats. The millions of deaths each year from dirty water and indoor air pollution cry out for action without delay. But desertification and deforestation also have to be tackled now to avert disasters that would affect many millions of lives. And the inertia built into the world's climate system is so great that immediate steps to reduce greenhouse gas emissions are essential if runaway global warming is to be avoided.

All this would mean big changes and a big shift from business as usual. The changes would encompass structural shifts in natural resource use, in the production and consumption patterns of societies and in values and the sense of collective responsibility.

REFERENCES

ADB (Asian Development Bank). 1997. *Emerging Asia – Changes and Challenges*. Manila.

Agarwal, Anil. 1996. "Pay-offs to Progress." *Down to Earth*. Centre for Science and Environment, New Delhi. 5(10): 31–39.

Bernardini, Oliviero and Ricardo Galli. 1993. "Dematerialization: Long-term Trends in the Intensity of Use of Materials and Energy." *Futures* 25(4): 431–48.

Chichilnisky, Graciela. 1997. "The Knowledge Revolution: Its Impact on Consumption Patterns and Resource Use." Background paper for *Human Development Report 1998*. UNDP, New York.

Crocker, David, Luis Camacho and Ramón Romero. 1997. "Globalization, Consumption Patterns and Human Development: The Cases of Costa Rica and Honduras." County study for *Human Development Report 1998*. UNDP, New York.

Goldemberg, José. 1997. *Leapfrog Energy Technologies*. San Francisco: Energy Foundation.

Hillary, Ruth (ed). 1997. *Environmental Management Systems and Cleaner Production*. New York: John Wiley and Sons.

Janicke, Martin, Harald Monch, Thomas Ranneberg and Udo E. Simonis. 1989. "Economic Structure and Environmental Impacts: East-West Comparisons." *The Environmentalist* 9(3): 171–83.

Larenas, Stefan. 1997. "Globalization and Changes in the Patterns of Consumption in Chile." County study for *Human Development Report 1998*. UNDP, New York.

Lean, Geoffrey. 1992. *WWF Atlas of the Environment*. Oxford: Helican.

Matthews, Emily and Allen Hammond. 1997. "Natural Resource Consumption." Background paper for *Human Development Report 1998*. UNDP, New York.

Montimore, Michael and Mary Tiffen. 1994. "Population Growth and Sustainable Development: The Machakos Story." *Environment* 36(8): 10–31.

Myers, Norman. 1997a. "Consumption and Sustainable Development: The Role of Perverse Subsidies." Background paper for *Human Development Report 1998*. UNDP, New York.

—— 1997b. "Consumption in Relation to Population, Environment and Development." *The Environmentalist* 17: 33–44.

Ngoc, Du and others. 1994. "Women and Waste Recycling in Ho Chi Minh City." ICRW Report in Brief. International Centre for Research on Women. Washington, D.C.

OECD (Organisation for Economic Co-operation and Development). 1997a. *Economic Globalisation and Environment*. Paris.

——. 1997b. *Environmental Data: Compendium 1997*. Paris.

Panayotou, Theodore. 1997. "Market Instruments and Consumption and Production Patterns." Background paper for *Human Development Report 1998*. UNDP, New York.

Prescott-Allen, Robert. 1997. "Consumption Patterns, Ecosystem Stress and Human Development." Background paper for *Human Development Report 1998*. UNDP, New York.

Raskin, Paul and others. 1996. *The Sustainability Transition – Beyond Conventional Development*. POLESTAR Series Report No. 1. Stockholm: Stockholm Environment Institute.

Reddy, Amulya, Robert H. Williams and Thomas B. Johansson. 1997. *Energy after Rio: Prospects and Challenges*. New York: UNDP in collaboration with International Energy Initiative, Energy 21 and Stockholm Environment Institute.

Sampat, Payal. 1996. "The River Ganges' Long Decline." *Worldwatch* 9(4): 24-32.

Seragledin, Ismail, Michael A. Cohen and K. C. Sivaramakrishnan. 1995. *The Human Face of the Urban Environment*. Environmentally Sustainable Development Proceedings. Washington, D.C.: World Bank.

Shiva, Vandana. 1997a. Biodiversity, Consumption Patterns and Globalization." Background paper for *Human Development Report 1998*. UNDP, New York.

——. 1997b. *Biopiracy – The Plunder of Nature and Knowledge*. Boston, Mass.: South End Press.

Sodré, Marcelo Gomes. 1997. "Globalization and Changes in Consumer Patterns: The Case of Brazil." Country study for *Human Development Report 1998*. UNDP, New York.

UN (United Nations). 1997. *Critical Trends: Global Change and Sustainable Development*. Department for Policy Coordination and Sustainable Development. New York.

UNCHS (United Nations Centre for Human Settlements). 1997. "Changing Consumption Pattern in Human Settlements: Waste Management." Settlement Infrastructure and Environment Programme, Nairobi.

UNEP (United Nations Environment Programme). 1996. *Our Planet* (Nairobi) 7(6).

——. 1997a. *Global Environment Outlook*. Nairobi.

——. 1997b. *Our Planet* (Nairobi) 8(6).

Von Weizsäcker, Ernst, Amory B. Lovins and L. Hunter Lovins. 1997. *Factor Four: Doubling Wealth, Halving Resource Use*. London: Earthscan.

Welch, Wilford. 1997. "A World Standard for Measuring Information Societies." *On the Internet* (March/April): 41–45.

WHO (World Health Organisation). 1997. *Health and Environment in Sustainable Development: Five Years after the Earth Summit*. Geneva.

Wild, Robert. 1998. "The Jozani-Chwaka Bay Conservation Project, Zanzibar." Background notes for *Human Development Report 1998*. UNDP, New York.

World Bank. 1995. *A Continent in Transition: Sub-Saharan Africa in the Mid-1990s*. Wahington, D.C.

WRI (World Resources Institute). 1994. *World Resources 1994–95*. New York: Oxford University Press.

——. 1996. *World Resources 1996–97*. New York: Oxford University Press.

Zhang, Amei. 1997. "Globalization, Consumption and Human Development in China." Country study for *Human Development Report 1998*. UNDP, New York.

3.6

THE INVISIBLE HEART – CARE AND THE GLOBAL ECONOMY

Chapter 3, *Human Development Report 1999*

Drafted principally by Sakiko Fukuda-Parr based on a background paper prepared by Nancy Folbre

Studies of globalization and its impact on people focus on incomes, employment, education and other opportunities. Less visible, and often neglected, is the impact on care and caring labour – the task of providing for dependents, for children, the sick, the elderly and (do not forget) all the rest of us, exhausted from the demands of daily life. Human development is nourished not only by expanding incomes, schooling, health, empowerment and a clean environment but also by care. And the essence of care is in the human bonds that it creates and supplies. Care, sometimes referred to as social reproduction, is also essential for economic sustainability.

Globalization is putting a squeeze on care and caring labour. Changes in the way that men and women use their time put a squeeze on the time available for care. The fiscal pressures on the state put a resource squeeze on public spending on care services. And the wage gap between the tradable and non-tradable sectors puts an incentive squeeze on the supply of care services in the market. Gender is a major factor in all these impacts, because women the world over carry the main responsibility for these activities, and most of the burden.

In a globally competitive labour market, how can we preserve time to care for ourselves and our families, neighbours and friends? In a globally competitive economy, how do we find the resources to provide for those unable to provide for themselves? And how can societies distribute the costs and burdens of this work equitably – between men and women, and between the state and the family or community, including the private sector (box 3.6.1)?

To answer these questions requires an understanding of what care is, how it is provided, who bears the costs and the burdens and what the critical paths are to negotiating an equitable solution. These are little-explored issues, but an exciting new body of work is probing them.

HUMAN DEVELOPMENT, CAPABILITIES AND CARE

The role of care in the formation of human capabilities and in human development is fundamental. Without genuine care and nurturing, children cannot develop capabilities, and adults have a hard time maintaining or expanding theirs. But the supply of care is not merely an input into human development. It is also an output, an intangible yet essential capability – a factor of human well-being.

Most adults need care in the emotional sense, even if not in the economic sense of relying on one another. A clear manifestation of this is the positive effect of social support and social relationships on life expectancy – at least as significant as the negative effects of cigarette smoking, hypertension and lack of physical exercise. Married adults enjoy lower risks of mortality than those who are unmarried.

The difference that care makes for child health and survival is also well documented. A UNICEF analysis identifies caring as the third underlying factor in preventing child malnutrition, after household food security and access to water, health care and sanitation facilities. It is what translates available food and health resources into healthy growth and development. For example, risks of malnutrition and illness depend significantly on whether a child is breastfed and how long, at what age it is given complementary foods and whether it receives immunizations on schedule. Many studies show that malnourished children grow faster when they receive verbal and cognitive stimulation – special attention can encourage a child in pain to eat.

Another link between human development and care relates to equity for the providers of caring labour. These activities are often identified with women's unpaid work in the domestic sector. This is an important source, but there are others. Not just the family but the community plays an important role. So do men, though their contribution is smaller than women's in most countries. The private sector provides domestic service, teaching, nursing and similar services. The public sector also provides many services in these areas (figure 3.6.1).

But in almost all societies the gender division of labour hands the responsibility for caring labour to women, much of it without remuneration – in the family or as voluntary activity in the commu-

---

BOX 3.6.1

If we are going to compete, let it be in a game of our choosing

Once upon a time the goddesses decided to hold a competition, a kind of Olympics, among the nations of the world. This was not an ordinary race in which the distance was determined and the winner would be the runner who took the shortest time, but a contest to see which society, acting as a team, could move all its members forward.

When the gun went off, one nation assumed that the race would not last long. It urged all its citizens to start running as quickly as possible. It was every person for himself. Very soon the young children and the elderly were left behind, but none of the fast runners bothered to help them out because it would have slowed them down.

At first those who were in front were exhilarated by their success. But as the race continued some became tired or hurt and fell by the wayside. Gradually all the runners grew exhausted and sick, and there was no one to replace them. It became clear that this nation would not win the race.

Everyone's attention turned to a second nation, which adopted a slightly different strategy. It sent all its young men out ahead to compete, but required all the women to come along behind, carrying the children, the sick and the elderly and caring for the runners who needed help. The nation's leaders explained to the women that this was a natural and efficient arrangement from which everyone could benefit. They provided great incentives for the men to run fast, and gave them authority over the women.

At first this seemed to work, but the women found that they could run just as fast as the men if they were not burdened with caring for the weak. They began to argue that the work they were doing – caring for the runners – was just as important as the running and deserved equal reward. The men refused to make any changes. The nation began to waste a great deal of energy in bargaining and negotiation. Gradually it became clear that this nation, too, was losing the race.

So attention turned to a third nation, which had started out moving quite slowly, though making steady progress. In this nation everyone was required both to run and to take care of those who could not run. Both men and women were given incentives to compete, to run as fast as possible, but the rules required them all to share in carrying the burden of care.

Having agreed to rules that rewarded both kinds of contribution to the collective effort, people were free to choose their own speed, to find a balance between individual effort and collective responsibility. This freedom and equality contributed to their solidarity. Of course, it was this nation that won the race.

Perhaps this is a utopian fairy tale. But the global economic system tells us that we are all in a race. It tells us to hurry up. It tells us all to worry about our speed. But it does not tell us how long the race will last – or what the best long-term strategy is. And it does not tell us how victory will be defined. If we are going to compete, let it be a game of our own choosing. That is, in a nutshell, the challenge of the new global order: how to define a world economy that preserves the advantages of market competition, but establishes strict limits and rules that prevent competition from taking a destructive turn.

Source: Folbre 1999.

nity. *Human Development Report 1995* estimated that women spend two-thirds of their working hours on unpaid work (men spend just a fourth), and most of those hours are for caring work. The hours are long and the work physically hard – fetching water and fuel, for example – especially in rural areas of developing countries. In Nepal women work 21 more hours each week than men, and in India, 12 more hours.

In Kenya 8- to 14-year-old girls spend 5 hours more on household chores than boys. These inequalities in burden are an important part of the obstacles women face in their life choices and opportunities.

Women also make up a disproportionate share of workers in domestic service and in professions such as child care, teaching, therapy and nursing. These occupations offer low pay relative to their requirements for education, skills and other qualifications – another source of gender biases in opportunities.

CARE – OR "TENDER LOVING CARE"

Care can mean a feeling of care, an emotional involvement or a state of mind. Personal identity and personal contact – especially face-to-face contact – are key elements of care services, involving a sense of connection between the givers and receivers. The care-giver may be motivated by affection, altruism or social norms of obligation. The care-receiver has a sense of being cared for. These elements are frequently there even when the care-giver is a paid employee. Individuals often choose caring jobs because they are a way to express caring motives and earn a living at the same time.

The commitment to care for others is usually thought to be altruistic – involving love and emotional reciprocity. But it is also a social obligation, socially constructed and enforced by social norms and rewards. A compelling example: when a mother gets up for the fifth time in the night to soothe her crying child, it is not necessarily because she gets pleasure from doing so. She may feel quite irritated. But she accepts a social obligation to care for her child, even at some cost to her health or happiness.

The word *care* often refers to looking after people who cannot take care of themselves: children, the sick, the needy, the elderly. But this misses the fact that even the healthiest and happiest of adults require a certain amount of care. Their need for that care may ebb and flow, but it sometimes comes in tidal waves.

GLOBALIZATION AND CARE

Economic analysis of care offers three insights into the impact of globalization on human development:

- Women's increased participation in the labour force and shifts in economic structures are transforming the ways care services are provided. Needs once provided almost exclusively by unpaid family labour are now being purchased from the market or provided by the state.
- Increases in the scope and speed of transactions are increasing the size of markets, which are becoming disconnected from local communities. As market relationships become less personal, reliance on families as a source of emotional support tends to increase – just as they are becoming less stable economically and demographically.

FIGURE 3.6.1
Four sources of caring labour

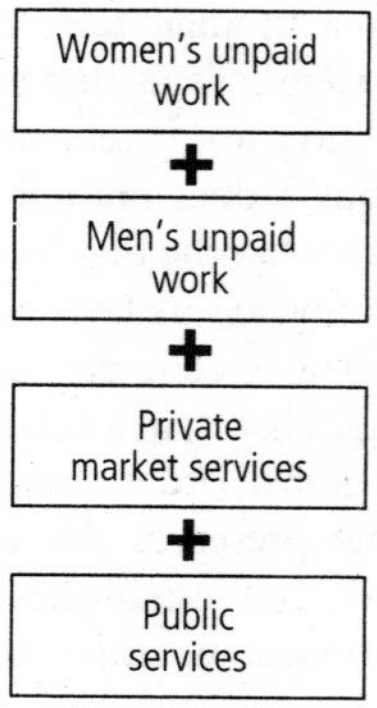

Women's unpaid work
+
Men's unpaid work
+
Private market services
+
Public services

Source: Human Development Report Office.

- Perhaps most important, the expansion of markets tends to penalize altruism and care. Both individuals and institutions have been free-riding on the caring labour that mainly women provide. Whether women will continue to provide such labour without fair remuneration is another matter.

Globalization is dominated by the expansion of markets and rewards profitability and efficiency. While economic growth reflects increasing private and public incomes, human development needs people to provide goods and services that fall outside the market – such as care and other unpaid services. A country can speed the growth of GDP by encouraging a shift in production from unpaid services such as care to market commodities. Care thus has clear analogies to environmental resources, with the characteristics of a resource outside the market. But a deficit of care services not only destroys human development – it also undermines economic growth.

This may be just what is happening in many OECD countries today, where there is a shortage of reliable, skilled labour in the midst of widespread unemployment. And despite universal schooling, there are widespread gaps in skills. Data from the International Adult Literacy Survey in OECD countries show that nearly half the population in almost all these countries score below the level needed to be trained for a skilled occupation.

The traditional restrictions on women's activities once guaranteed that women would specialize in providing care. Globalization's shifts in employment patterns have promoted and to some extent enforced the participation of women in wage employment. The supply of unpaid care services may be reduced, and daughters, cousins or nieces may have to take on more of the work. Nonetheless, women in most countries continue to carry the "double burden" of care services – ending up exhausted.

A challenge for human development is to find the incentives and rewards that ensure the supply of services – from the family, the community, the state and the market – all recognizing the need for gender equality and distributing the burdens and costs of care fairly (boxes 3.6.2 and 3.6.3).

Noble. But trends are moving in the opposite direction. In OECD countries the problem is that globalization has pulled back on state services and pushed more to private services. Many social commentators protest the ensuing deterioration in quality.

BOX 3.6.2

Globalization leads to the feminization of labour – but the outcome is mixed

Many empirical studies now allow analysis of how shifts in trade patterns affect employment. A study covering 165 countries from 1985 to 1990 concludes that greater trade openness increases women's share of paid employment. Further analysis of plant-level data from Colombia and from Turkey – both with rapid export growth – shows that firms producing for export employ more female workers, often in skilled functions.

But increasing participation has not always meant less discrimination. Women constitute a large share of workers in informal subcontracting, often in the garment industry – at low wages and under poor conditions. Highly competitive international markets in garments also mean that the work is volatile – with contracts moving with small changes in costs or trade regulations.

Globalization has also been associated with home work, tele-work and part-time work. In the United Kingdom the share of workers with unconventional work arrangements rose from 17% in 1965 to 40% in 1991. In 1985 the shares of such work arrangements were up to 15% in Japan, 33% in the Republic of Korea and 50% in Mexico, Peru and Sri Lanka. And in Greece and Portugal women constitute 90% of the home workers. This is a mixed blessing. Informal work arrangements can accommodate women's care obligations in the family. But such jobs are often precarious and poorly paid.

Source: Özler 1999.

In the transition economies of Eastern Europe and the CIS these trends have been dramatic, contributing to the huge human costs of the transition. The dismantling and weakening of the welfare state have meant cuts and deterioration in services in health and education – across the board – contributing to the deteriorating human outcomes. Life expectancy was lower in 1995 than in 1989 in 7 of 18 countries – falling as much as five years since 1987. Enrolment in kindergarten declined dramatically – falling from 64% to 36% of 3- to 6-year-olds in Lithuania between 1989 and 1995, and from 69% to 54% in Russia. Responsibility for pre-primary education was transferred from the state to parents, with enormous consequences for mothers of children this age.

CARE AND MARKET REWARDS

The market gives almost no rewards for care. Much of it is unpaid – most of it provided by women, some by men. The market also penalizes individuals who spend time in these activities, which take time away from investing in skills for paid work or from doing paid work.

BOX 3.6.3

More paid work doesn't reduce unpaid work

Women are responsible for most unpaid care work – a social norm slow to change. A review of time-use surveys in *Human Development Report 1995* showed a general trend to greater gender equality in unpaid work in the OECD countries, but no equalization in developing countries and a deterioration in the transition economies of Eastern Europe and the CIS.

Bangladesh had one of the largest increases in the share of women participating in the labour force – from 5% in 1965 to 42% in 1995. This has been important for export growth, with women as the main workers in the garment industry. But women still spend many hours in unpaid work. A survey of men and women working in formal urban manufacturing activities shows that women put in on average 31 hours a week in unpaid work – cooking, looking after children, collecting fuel, food and water (box table 3.6.3). Men put in 14 hours in activities such as house repair. Workers in the informal sector show similar patterns.

Women in Eastern Europe and the CIS spend more hours in paid employment than those in most other countries. But the gender disparity in sharing the burden of unpaid work remains stark, and it is worsening under the economic dislocations of the transition. In Bulgaria men's total work burden was 15% less than women's in 1977 but 17% less in 1988. Women increased their share of both paid and unpaid work – in 1977 men did 52% as much household work as women, but in 1988 only 48% as much. In Moldova women work 73.5 hours each week.

In OECD countries men's contribution to unpaid work has been increasing. But a woman who works full time still does a lot of unpaid work. Once she has a child, she can expect to devote 3.3 more hours a day to unpaid household work. Married women who are employed and have children under 15 carry the heaviest work burden – almost 11 hours a day.

BOX TABLE 3.6.3
Time spent in paid and unpaid work in Bangladesh, 1995 (hours per week)

	Formal sector workers		Informal sector workers	
	Men	Women	Men	Women
Unpaid work	14	31	14	24
Paid employment	53	56	23	21
Total	67	87	37	45

Source: Zohir 1998 and UNDP 1995.

Care services are also provided in the market, usually underremunerated. What explains the financial penalty for doing caring work? Gender bias is one factor. A second is the intrinsic reward people get from helping others, allowing employers to fill jobs at lower pay. A third is that people feel queasy about putting a price on something as sacred as care.

And global economic competition has tended to reinforce these trends, as the wage gap increases between the tradable and non-tradable sectors. Wages for teaching, domestic service and other caring work have stagnated – or even fallen – in the industrial countries.

Care produces goods with social externalities – widespread benefits for those who do not pay for them. It creates human and social capital – the next generation, workers with human and social skills who can be relied on, who are good citizens. But mothers cannot demand a fee from employers who hire their children. This care will be underproduced and overexploited unless non-market institutions ensure that everyone shares the burden of providing it. The traditional patriarchal family, and gender biases in society that limit opportunities for women outside the role of wife and mother, have been the traditional way to solve this problem. But this is obviously inequitable, and no solution at all.

REDISTRIBUTING THE COSTS AND RESPONSIBILITIES OF CARE – TO FAMILY, STATE AND CORPORATION

Where do the effects of globalization fit in the larger conflicts over the distribution of the costs of care? Consider a mother who devotes much time and energy to enhancing her children's capabilities and a country that devotes much of its national budget to family welfare. In the short run both are at a competitive disadvantage: they devote fewer resources to directly productive activities. But in the long run their position depends on their ability to claim some share of the economic benefits produced by the next generation.

The family today is a small welfare state. Women invest time and energy in children –

essentially a "family public good". They pay most of the costs – while other family members claim a greater share of the benefits. What they do is far less transferable outside the family than investments in a career. The resulting loss of bargaining power can mean less consumption or leisure time for women, even if they remain married and enjoy some of their husband's market income.

Public spending on children is modest compared with that by parents. Take public spending in the United States, about 38 percent of all spending. Over the past 30 years the elderly in the United States have received far more than the young for a simple reason – the elderly have more votes than parents with children. Studies in Western and Eastern European countries show similar biases against children. Parents who invest in the next generation of workers are not explicitly rewarded for their efforts. Their efforts are socially important but economically unproductive.

For much of the past 200 years nations have exercised a lot of control over the production of care services such as education, health and provision for dependents. The analogy of the family to the state is clear. Both institutions demand commitment to the welfare of the collective rather than the individual. But on the negative side, both institutions can generate oppressive hierarchies that interfere with the development of human capabilities.

Take a multinational corporation, tired of the frustrations of negotiating taxation and regulation with host governments, that buys a small island, writes a constitution and announces a new country – Corporation Nation. A citizen automatically receives a highly paid job. Sounds good, but some restrictions apply. Individuals must have advanced educational credentials, be physically and emotionally healthy, have no children and be under the age of 60. They do not have to emigrate but can work from their country over the Internet. And they immediately lose their new citizenship if they require retraining, become seriously ill, acquire children or reach the age of 60.

Corporation Nation can free-ride on the human capabilities of its citizen workers without paying for their production or their maintenance when ill or old. It can offer high wages to attract the best workers from around the world without threatening its profitability. Footloose capital of the globalized economy weakens the connections between corporations and communities, and the obligations to citizens. Why then would multinational firms remain in countries that tax them to support the production of human capabilities when they can go elsewhere and free-ride? They will remain for a while, out of habit and loyalty. But the ones that jump first to take advantage of new opportunities will win the race if the finish line is defined by maximizing the short-term value of market output.

THE CHALLENGE OF CARE IN THE GLOBAL ECONOMY

How can societies design new arrangements for care in the global economy – to make sure that it is not squeezed out?

Many fear that there is no alternative to the traditional model of the patriarchal household in which women shoulder much of the responsibility through unpaid work. The resurgence of religious fundamentalism around the world testifies to the anxieties about changing traditional patriarchal relationships that have ensured a supply of caring labour. Many social conservatives fear that globalization fuels market-based individualism at the expense of social commitments to family and community. A consistent theme of religious fundamentalism worldwide: reestablish rules that restrict women's rights for fear that women will abandon caring responsibilities.

At the other end of the spectrum is market provision of care – but often the people who need care cannot afford to pay for it. And finally there is state provision. But the search for efficiency in today's global economy imposes a "market discipline" that is at variance with quality. Cost-minimizing standards drive down quality in schools, hospitals and child-care centres. So public services alone are not a total answer, though state support must be a big part of it.

In all this, the challenge is to strike a balance between individual rights and social obligations of care. Competitive market societies emphasize values that encourage individualism – and say little about obligations and commitment to the family and community. The extreme responses of the patriarchal backlash and the marketization of care require far less effort and negotiation than the democratic response, which requires serious thinking about how to enforce responsibilities for care in the community.

So the first step must be to challenge social norms – to build commitment of both men and women to their responsibilities for caring labour. Societies – through public and corporate policy – then need to acknowledge care as a priority human need that they have a social obligation to foster.

A clear policy path is to support incentives and rewards for caring work, both paid and unpaid, to increase its supply and quality. This does not mean sending women back to the traditional role of housewife and mother, closing off other opportunities. It means sharing unpaid care services between men and women, reducing men's paid work time and increasing their time on family care. And it means increasing the supply of state-supported care services. Nordic countries have a long tradition of such approaches, which give public recognition and payment for care, rewarding family commitment but without reinforcing traditional gender roles (box 3.6.4).

Citizens could be given tax credits for contributing care services that develop long-term relationships between individuals. And this model could be extended further. For example, many young adults benefit from public support for higher education. They could repay the costs through mandatory national service that takes some responsibility for children and other dependents in their community. The care services they could provide would be at least as valuable as military service, and they could develop important skills as well as reinforce the value of care.

Policies to foster more caring labour appear unproductive or costly only to those who define them as narrowly contributing to GDP or short-

BOX 3.6.4

Support for men's child-care responsibilities in Western Europe

Although several countries in Western Europe have encouraged gender-neutral family-oriented work policies, in 1995 only 5% of the male workforce in the European Union (EU) worked part time, and only 5% of fathers took paternity leave. Men often cite their work environment as a constraint when explaining their reluctance to make full use of parental and paternal leave rights or to work part-time to care for a child. Private sector employers in particular are seen as unsupportive of such arrangements. Traditionally it has been women who have had to move into part-time labour or take a career break after the birth of a child. EU Commissioner for Employment and Social Affairs Padraig Flynn has stated that "even where there are policy instruments aimed at breaking down the gender imbalance in caring . . . the assumption that caring is the responsibility of women persists."

TIME USE

Austria. Men spend an average of 70% of their time in paid labour, 30% in unpaid; women spend an average of 30% of their time in paid labour, 70% in unpaid. Women make up 98% of part-time employees.

Denmark. About 65% of men in the labour force work 30–39 hours a week, 30% work more and 5% less; 69% of women work 30–39 hours, 11% work more and 20% work less. In 1987 men spent 10 hours a week in unpaid work, women 21 hours; in 1997 men spent 13 hours in unpaid work, and women 18.

Germany. A third of women work less than 35 hours a week; only 2–3% of men do so.

Italy. Married women with children spend 7.5 hours each day in care work, men 1.5 hours.

Netherlands. Women spend twice as much time in unpaid work at home as men (women 32 hours,

men 16). But women who work more than 30 hours a week spend only 18 hours in unpaid housework, compared with 19 hours for their husbands.

Spain. Women spend seven times as many hours doing domestic work as men.

PATERNAL AND PARENTAL LEAVE

Denmark. Fathers are allowed a 2-week paternal leave for the birth or adoption of a child. They can also use the last 10 weeks of maternity leave (10% of fathers do this). And there is a 4-week extension for fathers only.

Finland. Fathers may take 6–18 days of paternal leave, and 158 days of parental leave can be shared after maternity leave ends (parental leave is used by only 3% of fathers). One parent can take unpaid leave until the child is three. And parents are allowed 2–4 days a year to care for a sick child.

Italy. During the child's first year a 6-month parental leave can be taken after maternity leave ends (at 30% pay).

Norway. Employees may take parental leave for 42 weeks (at 100% pay) or 52 weeks (at 80% pay). Fathers must use at least 4 weeks of the parental leave; otherwise that period is lost. Parents may also combine their leave with part time work. Employees are allowed 10–15 days each year to care for a sick child, single parents 20–30 days.

Sweden. Employees are allowed 10 days paternal leave for the birth or adoption of a child, 450 days parental leave (at 80% pay). One parent, usually the father, has an absolute right to one month (at 85% pay). Parents have the right to a 25% reduction in their work hours until a child is eight; child care is a legal right.

Source: Flynn 1998 and EU Network 1998.

---

term profit. The erosion of family and community solidarity imposes enormous costs reflected in inefficient and unsuccessful education efforts, high crime rates and a social atmosphere of anxiety and resentment. The nurturing of human capabilities has always been difficult and expensive. In the

past it was assured by a gender division of labour based on the subordination of women. Today, however, the cost of providing caring labour should be confronted explicitly and distributed fairly – between men and women, and among the state, the family or community and the employer.

REFERENCES

Elson, Diane. 1998. "The Economic, the Political and the Domestic: Business, States and Households in the Organisation of Production." *New Political Economy* 3(2): 189–208.

England, Paula and Nancy Fobre. 1998. "The Cost of Caring." In Ronnie J. Steinberg and Deborah Figart (eds.), *The Annals of the American Academy of Political and Social Science on Emotional Labour.* London: Sage.

Folbre, Nancy. 1999. "Care and the Global Economy." Background paper for *Human Development Report 1999.* UNDP, New York.

Özler, Süle. 1999. "Globalisation, Employment, and Gender." Background paper for *Human Development Report 1999.* UNDP, New York.

Ruminska-Zimmy, Ewa. 1997. "Human Poverty in Transition Economies: Regional Overview for the *Human Development Report 1997.*" Occasional Paper Series. UNDP, Human Development Report Office, New York.

UNDP (United Nations Development Programme). 1995. *Human Development Report 1995.* New York: Oxford University Press.

UNICEF (United Nations Children's Fund). 1998. *The State of the World's Children 1998.* New York: Oxford University Press.

Zohir, Salma Chaudhuri. 1998. "Gender Implications of Industrial Reforms and Adjustment in the Manufacturing Sector of Bangladesh." Ph.D. dissertation. University of Manchester.

3.7

INCLUSIVE
DEMOCRACY SECURES RIGHTS

Chapter 3, *Human Development Report 2000*
Drafted principally by Omar Noman

*The primary meaning of democracy is that
all who are affected by a decision should
have the right to participate in making that
decision, either directly or through chosen
representatives ... to exclude the losing
groups from participation in decision-
making clearly violates the primary meaning
of democracy.*

*–Arthur Lewis, first Nobel Prize winner
in the economics of development*

The democratic liberalization sweeping the world
is making transitions more civil. One of the more
remarkable transitions: in Senegal President Ab-
dou Diouf's loss in an open election in February
2000 ended four decades of one-party rule. Senegal became part of the refreshing trend in Africa of leaders leaving office through the ballot,
a rare occurrence until recently. Yet despite un-
doubted benefits, the transition to democracy in
many countries remains imperilled, insecure, fragile. The spread of democracy is important, but we
must not overlook the challenges and dangers.

THE LINK BETWEEN HUMAN RIGHTS
AND DEMOCRACY

Democracy is the only form of political regime
compatible with respecting all five categories of
rights – economic, social, political, civil and cultural. But it is not enough to establish electoral
democracy. Several policy interventions are required to realize a range of rights under democratic government.

Democracy is defined by human rights

Some rights require mechanisms that ensure protection from the state. Others need active promotion by the state.

Four defining features of a democracy are
based on human rights:

- Holding free and fair elections contributes
  to fulfillment of the right to political
  participation.
- Allowing free and independent media
  contributes to fulfillment of the right to
  freedom of expression, thought and
  conscience.
- Separating powers among branches of government helps protect citizens from abuses of
  their civil and political rights.
- Encouraging an open civil society contributes
  to fulfillment of the right to peaceful assembly
  and association. An open civil society adds an
  important participatory dimension, along with
  the separation of powers, for the promotion of
  rights.

These rights are mutually reinforcing, with progress in one typically linked with advances in others. Openness of the media, for example, is usually
correlated with the development of civil society
institutions.

But democracy is not homogenous. From the
several forms of democracy, countries choose different institutional mixes depending on their circumstances and needs. For simplicity, it helps to
distinguish two broad categories of democracy –
majoritarian and inclusive. In a majoritarian democracy government is by the majority, and the role of
minorities is to oppose. The danger is that many minorities in plural societies may be permanently excluded, discriminated against and marginalized –
since this would not affect the electoral prospects of
majority-based political parties. That can lead to violence, the case under several democracies.

In the liberal democratic model all individuals are autonomous in displaying public loyalty to the state, while their various private loyalties – religious, ethnic or regional – are ignored. This puts the emphasis on a majority's right to decide. And when collectives of unequal size live together in a democracy and do not have identical or cross-cutting interests, conflicts become likely.

These dangers are evident in Nigeria, which has experienced much violence since its return to democratic rule. These concerns are emphasized in the special contribution by President Olusegun Obasanjo.

Majoritarian democracies have frequently been undermined by a minority's fear of repression. In 1947 the South Asian subcontinent split into two nations in part because the Muslims of India felt that Westminster-style majoritarian democracy would mean rule by the overwhelming Hindu majority. These fears echoed those of Catholics in Northern Ireland, who lived under a Protestant-elected government from 1921 to 1972. Both situations led to widespread violence.

Now consider an inclusive democracy built on the principle that political power is dispersed and shared in a variety of ways – to protect minorities and to ensure participation and free speech for all citizens. Inclusive democracy emphasizes the quality of representation by striving for consensus and inclusion, not the brute electoral force of the majority. An inclusive democracy also appreciates the need to promote civil society organizations, open media, rights-oriented economic policy and separation of powers. It thus creates mechanisms for the accountability of the majority to the minorities.

After the first elections in a free South Africa, President Nelson Mandela asked a prominent leader of the opposition to join his cabinet, even though the African National Congress has a comfortable majority. Mandela's accommodation of a threatened – and potentially violent – minority is an important lesson for other democracies. Having an opposition is important, and coalitions can make government unwieldy. But the price of ex-

clusion is often higher, especially when it leads to civil war.

Holding free elections to ensure participation and non-discrimination

When individuals are acknowledged as an important part of a system, they tend to take responsibility for it and make efforts to maintain and improve it. Voting is the opportunity to choose the government, and faith in the process of electing representatives confers legitimacy on the institutions of government. This basic right of participation, along with related rights, has been extended recently in the once colonized or satellite regimes of Africa, Europe and Asia. The initial progress in democratization has been impressive in parts of Central Asia, such as Kyrgyzstan and Mongolia. In sharp contrast are neighbouring Turkmenistan, which has a president for life, and Uzbekistan, where Inter-Parliamentary Union and other observers raised concerns about the electoral process.

There are other stirring developments. In the Islamic Republic of Iran the February 2000 parliamentary election – a democratic path to revolutionary change – is an example of people's power contributing to systemic structural changes.

Independent media – for freedom of expression

The freedom of individuals to openly debate and criticize policies and institutions guards against abuses of human rights. Openness of the media not only advances civil and political liberties – it often contributes to economic and social rights. Pricking the public conscience and pressuring for action have worked in several cases (box 3.7.1).

In many cases the media have raised awareness of rights violations. Child labour in making carpets and soccer balls and poor working conditions in the factories of multinational firms received extensive coverage. In most of these cases NGOs formed an alliance with the media – to mobilize the power of shame to protect the rights of the vulnerable.

The separation of powers – for the rule of law

The state is omnipresent in any discussion of human rights, as culprit and protector, as judge, jury and defendant. It often has to be ready to act against itself – if, say, extrajudicial killing or torture is carried out by its police. A democratic state can fulfill its human rights obligations only if it ensures the rule of law. The institutions that curb the arbitrary exercise of power are a democratically elected legislature, an independent judiciary and an executive that can retain a reasonable professional independence in implementing laws and policies. These key elements of democratic governance are embodied in the separation of powers. And their existence enhances the accountability of the state.

Little noticed by the world, reforms are taking place in this direction in a number of countries, with profound implications for the civil and political rights of people. Not least of these developments has been in China, where a series of fundamental reforms have been introduced into the

---

"SPECIAL CONTRIBUTION"
Transition to democracy and human rights

A main feature of Nigerian sociopolitical life of the recent dark years is the extent to which it spawned human rights activism. The more tyrannical the regime got, the more people became aware of what they were losing by way of freedom of expression and the right to determine how they were to be governed. In fact, human rights activism became the only form of political expression. It's thus hardly surprising that the protests all became generically known as pro-democracy movements.

The human rights groups aligned themselves into forces that were determined to force General Sani Abacha out of power. And, looking back, they had a strong chance of scoring a unique victory for the nation, had there not been the divine intervention that offered an opportunity for transition without the disadvantages of violent confrontation.

In the immediate years before the transition Nigerian society experienced evil governance. Nigerians were so traumatized by the experience that transition alone was not an adequate palliative. In recognition of this, our administration immediately set up a commission to look into all complaints of human rights abuses in the past. The commission has yet to conclude its findings, but already we seem to be achieving some of the desired effect: namely, that many people have felt a sense of relief simply because they have had the chance to air their grievances and put their cases before someone who is willing and prepared to listen.

By all standards, the transition in Nigeria has been most rapid, and we thank God that it has so far been without any major crises. However, the speed of liberalization is analogous to the sudden release of the lid from a boiling kettle. After years of oppression and suppression, many conflicts have suddenly found voices for public expression. Besides this, there are those forces of activism that are yet to lose their confrontational habits from the days of less sympathetic and undemocratic regimes. Some of these forces have even been hijacked by people with criminal intentions.

We fully accept the challenge of persuading all Nigerians to accept that transition is process and not a one-off event that was concluded on 29 May 1999. In that process all Nigerians should feel free to bring their legitimate grievances to the dialogue table, where they will be heard rationally, justly and constitutionally. That is the beauty of the unique advantage of democracy over other forms of government.

Our administration is not only fully committed to democratic rule, but our battle cry in the transition process is "Never again will this country sink into the abyss of recent past when human rights abuse was the order of the day!"

PRESIDENT OLUSEGUN OBASANJO
President of Nigeria

constitution. A major revision of the penal code introduces the principle of habeas corpus, and a new civil code incorporates the principle of rights and dignity of the individual. Reforms have moved towards greater independence of the judiciary from the executive, and within the judiciary, the functions of judge, prosecutor and legal counsel have been separated, and each of these professional groups has a code of conduct.

An open civil society – for deepening participation, expression and accountability

The state is accountable to its citizens – but a neutral public space is needed as an intermediary for the citizens to make the state fulfill its obligations. There may be independent auditing by citizens groups, such as the People's Union for Civil Liberties in India – or by international NGOs, such as Amnesty International or Human Rights Watch. Such pressure is aimed at advancing freedoms of press, of speech, of associations. A state may have signed all human rights treaties – but without an open civil society it may be under little pressure to honour its commitments.

In sum, democratic governance provides the ideal political framework for the realization of human rights – because it is based on the extension of civil and political rights, notably the right to participate in political life. And by allowing a voice in political decisions, it can be instrumental in realizing other rights. Democracy builds the institutions needed for the fulfillment of human rights.

HOW AND WHY SOME "DEMOCRACIES" HARM HUMAN RIGHTS

Many democracies nevertheless fail to protect or promote human rights. Although the global transition to democratic regimes is undoubtedly progress, problems of human rights are not resolved simply because an electoral system has replaced an authoritarian regime. The transition to a new order

---

BOX 3.7.1

The power of shame – a weapon for human rights NGOs

For many civil society agencies, shame is their only weapon. And it can be quite powerful.

BRAZIL

In February 1989, 50 prisoners were locked in an unventilated maximum security cell at the 42nd police station in São Paolo. Eighteen died of asphyxiation. To protest, NGOs filed a petition with the Inter-American Commission on Human Rights. This pressure prompted the federal government and São Paolo state government to pay compensation to the prisoners' families in 1997, and to close down the maximum security cells in São Paolo police stations. And partly as a result of this incident, Brazil has produced guidelines for the treatment of prisoners closely based on the UN framework.

HUNGARY

In 1997 municipal authorities in the town of Szekesfehervar began to relocate predominantly Roma families from a rundown building on "Radio Street" to a row of containers used to house soldiers stationed in Hungary during the Bosnian war. The containers were placed outside city limits. A number of NGOs banded together to form an ad hoc Anti-Ghetto Committee, which held public demonstrations and lobbied the national government. Municipal authorities finally agreed to purchase flats in the city.

NIGERIA

To resist human rights violations by Shell Oil in 1990, the Ogoni people formed the Movement for Survival of Ogoni People, a peaceful movement led by Ken Saro-Wiwa. Although Shell Oil suspended its activities in Ogoniland in 1993, it continued to pump more than 250,000 barrels of oil a day in Nigeria, nearly 12 percent of its international output. In the wake of Saro-Wiwa's execution in 1994, many NGOs and fair trade organizations started campaigning against Shell. The damage to the company's public image and profits compelled it to publicly admit its errors and adopt a human rights code.

Source: Neve and Affonso 1995; Cahn 1999; Shell Report 1999.

involves complex issues of human rights. In extreme cases of illiberal majoritarian democracy, the human rights of several groups have worsened. In other cases the world community has been too tolerant of human rights abuses under democracies.

Countries in the transition to democracy generally face four challenges in promoting human rights.

- A critical challenge is to integrate minorities and address horizontal inequality between ethnic groups or geographical regions. Perhaps the most persistent weakness of majoritarian democracies is discrimination against minorities and worsening of horizontal inequalities.
- A second key weakness is the arbitrary exercise of power. Elected governments frequently lose legitimacy and popular support when they behave in an authoritarian manner. When elite groups act as if they are above the law or when elected representatives arbitrarily remove judges, civil servants and others, faith in democratic institutions weakens.
- A third weakness is neglecting the economic dimension of human rights. Many democracies fail to address the economic and social rights of significant groups, typically because this neglect does not hurt the electoral outcomes of those in power.
- Finally, failing to deal adequately with the legacy of an authoritarian past can lead to the recurrence of violence and the reversal of democratic rule.

In each case, human rights are seriously affected. Minorities are punished. Children remain uneducated and hungry. Journalists are intimidated, judges threatened, political opponents tortured and human rights activists eliminated. These violations continue under many elected governments.

Exclusion and marginalization of minorities

The Achilles' heel of majoritarian democracies: the exclusion and marginalization of minorities. The scale and extent of discrimination differ, but the histories of India, Israel, Nigeria, Russia, Spain, Sri Lanka, Turkey, Uganda, the United Kingdom, the United States, to name a few, show that minorities suffer serious discrimination.

Rights are protections against the harms that people are likely to suffer. Minority rights protect groups against threats from majoritarian decision-making procedures. The threats typically include:

- *Exclusion from participation* – manipulating political rights and the media to increase the power of the majority in politics, such as through gerrymandering of constituencies.
- *Bypassing of the rule of law* – setting aside the rule of law in times of great social stress, often targeting minorities whose loyalty the majority questions. In assessing the rights of minorities in a democratic society, two questions are relevant. What rights for the protection of minorities are in the constitution? How well does the political system protect these rights in practice?
- *Oppression* – imposing social practices on minorities, a recurrent theme in many societies. The languages and cultures of minorities have often been banned or marginalized. Today the rise of religious intolerance in several countries is imposing alien cultural practices on minorities. And in some societies intolerance towards those wishing to practice their religion is a denial of the right to freedom of expression.
- *Impoverishment* – actions of the majority to further its economic interests at the expense of minorities, through, say, forced relocations from resource-rich areas.

Violence against minorities is a burning political issue the world over. Even with constitutional protection, minorities can face large threats. In Western Europe immigrant minorities are constantly exposed to violence and racism (box 3.7.2).

The failure to integrate minorities – the extreme of civil wars

An estimated 5 million people perished in civil wars in the past decade. The breakdown of trust and failure of internal political accommodation often occur because of horizontal inequalities and the absence of democratic processes for settling disputes. The paradox of the former Yugoslavia and Sri Lanka – two countries with reasonable progress in incomes alongside human rights violations, though there are many other examples – is at one level due to civil war. But why are these societies in civil war? The answer relates to the quality of democracy, particularly the way minorities have been excluded.

Yugoslavia in the 1980s was a multi-ethnic, multi-faith federation with much local autonomy for minority ethnic groups, as in Kosovo. But the country – once considered a model for dynamic workers' cooperatives, ethnic integration and non-Soviet socialism – imploded into vicious ethnic cleansing of minorities, which resulted in the first genocide in Europe since Nazi Germany.

In Sri Lanka two large communities – the Sinhalese and Tamil – started out as citizens in a liberal democratic framework with guaranteed rights. In this multi-ethnic society the Sinhalese speakers far outnumbered the Tamil speakers. But in 1956 the Sinhalese majority started imposing a single-language national identity, and had the numbers to force it through parliament.

After decades of troubles the majority has recognized that some form of recognition of the parity of the two communities is a prerequisite for reconstructing the Sri Lankan nation. But the assassination of a well-known human rights activist and lawyer in July 1999, a few months before attempts on the life of the president of Sri Lanka, is a gruesome reminder of the continuing obstacles (box 3.7.3).

So, despite reasonable progress in income, the failure to integrate minorities can lead to violations of human rights and to war. The spirit of democracy has to be inclusive, embracing the principle that power must be dispersed and shared. The multiple layers of people's identity and loyalty – to their ethnic group, their religion, their region and their state – have to be recognized and given fair play in democratic institutions – or explode into conflict (box 3.7.4).

Arbitrary exercise of power

Democracy suffered reversals in Ecuador, Pakistan and Sierra Leone, where elected regimes changed through unconstitutional mechanisms. In other, less extreme cases elected leaders have become more authoritarian.

An economic crisis might contribute to an elected regime's unpopularity, but a deeper disillusionment comes from the arbitrary exercise of power. In many countries suffering reversals, civilian governments behaved like their military pred-

---

BOX 3.7.2

Racism against immigrants and other minorities in Western Europe

The European Monitoring Centre on Racism and Xenophobia, in a comprehensive survey in 1998, confirmed that racism and xenophobia exist in all 15 member countries of the European Union, though the situation varies across countries.

The centre documented vicious attacks, intimidation and discrimination against foreigners, immigrants and racial groups in several countries in 1998 – while recognizing just how few cases are ever reported. In Germany there were 430 officially reported cases of xenophobic violence; in Spain 143 cases, mostly against "gypsies"; in France 191 cases, most of them anti-Semitic; in Sweden 591 "acts against ethnic groups"; and in Finland 194 reported racial crimes, most against immigrants and Roma. The study observed that racism is not always linked to social marginalization. Hate crimes are perpetrated in many cases by members of far-right organizations and parties, but also by other citizens and by police officers.

Such uncivil society poses threats to the human rights of minorities in many parts of the world. Refusing to keep silent, by documenting cases and reporting on them in the media, is the first step towards combating racism – bringing it to collective awareness and mobilizing a response.

Source: European Monitoring Centre on Racism and Xenophobia 1998.

ecessors. Elected to power in an institutional collapse, they did not institute any separation of powers. Instead, the judiciary, legislature and civil service were effectively merged into an instrument of arbitrary power, concentrated in the office of the chief executive. There was no effective check on the exercise of power, a legacy of long periods of military and colonial rule. Rather than undertaking major institutional reforms – which would introduce checks and balances and thereby protect rights – successive civilian governments continued to exercise arbitrary power. Rights to participate, as well as many other rights, have suffered in fragile democracies.

Persistent poverty and growing inequality

Despite half a century of elected governments, India has failed to provide universal primary education. There is no provision in the constitution for mandatory primary education as a right of all citizens. Resources are not the critical constraint. Countries with similar resources, such as China, have legal guarantees for this economic right, and have delivered it.

Mass poverty, particularly when combined with growing vertical or horizontal inequality, often leads to social instability. The resulting law and order problems have an economic base but undermine civil and political rights. Persistent poverty and growing inequality lead to social strife, which has often undermined civil liberties.

The troubled legacy of an authoritarian regime

Cambodia, Chile, Guatemala, Indonesia, Nigeria, Russia, South Africa – to name a few – have to

---

BOX 3.7.3

A murder that didn't silence a message

Dr. Neelan Tiruchelvam, human rights activist, member of the Sri Lankan parliament, scholar and constitutional lawyer, was brutally assassinated on 29 July 1999. He was a critical link in the discourse on ethnic politics and human rights in Sri Lanka, bringing his intellectual strength, activist inspiration and mediation skills to the peace effort. His contributions, both locally and internationally, to democratization and conflict resolution are most clearly visible in his efforts to mediate a negotiated settlement and his work in drafting constitutional amendments and legislation on equal opportunity and non-discrimination and establishing civil society institutions for human rights.

The politics of ethnicity and the politics of war require people with the commitment and capacity to confront the perpetrators of all forms of discrimination, extreme nationalism, human rights violations and injustices – and to do so at all levels, legal, constitutional, political, intellectual and moral.

Neelan, who belonged to one of the minority communities of Sri Lanka, advocated tolerance and celebration of diversity and pluralism in an environment where both the state and the people could be held accountable for their actions. His life's work was committed to these ideals and practice. The void he leaves behind is great in a world where the voices of moderation, negotiation, self-determination and liberalism are frequently threatened by violence.

On what would have been his 56th birthday, 31 January 2000, human rights activists, academicians, lawyers, political leaders and friends gathered from around the world to pay tribute to his memory and his work. Kofi Annan and Mary Robinson added their messages to this gathering. To quote from Neelan's last address to parliament on 15 June 1999:

We cannot glorify death, whether in the battlefield or otherwise. We, on the other hand, must celebrate life, and are fiercely committed to protecting and securing the sanctity of life, which is the most fundamental value without which all other rights and freedoms become meaningless.

We can only hope that all those individuals and institutions he engaged and inspired, both in Sri Lanka and around the world, will advance his work and his vision.

Source: Wignaraja 2000.

build democracies on the ashes of a brutal past. Healing deep wounds, taming repressive institutions, changing violent attitudes born of conflict and creating a culture of consensus are vital to the process of democratization.

How best to convert militaristic or fascist states into democracies? There have been three types of responses:

- A country accepts externally imposed democratic institutions because of military defeat and the promise of major financial assistance. This was the case in Germany and Japan after the Second World War – ironically, outsiders "imposed" democratic institutions, which have nonetheless taken root and grown for the past five decades.

- A country has an internal consensus on democracy as the system for the future, often supported by incentives from regional institutions – and by features of the past that provide a symbol of unity during radical institutional change. Spain chose not to rake up a difficult past in human rights, in part because of the consensus across the political spectrum on democracy and the lack of any serious threat of reversion to a militaristic, authoritarian government. As part of this

---

BOX 3.7.4

Horizontal inequality and conflict

AFRICA

Politics in several African countries are dominated by conflict among groups (horizontal conflict) rather than classes. The usual form is majority exclusion of minorities from political and economic resources. This has lead to conflict in Nigeria, Rwanda, Uganda and others. South Africa and Zimbabwe face the opposite challenge: protecting minorities previously associated with repressive rule over the majority. Such complexities need to be addressed within the framework of inclusive democracy being pursued by some African countries.

EASTERN EUROPE AND THE CIS

Threats to the Albanian minority in Serbia evoked memories of the massacre of Muslims in Bosnia and Herzegovina and led to international intervention in Kosovo. The form of the intervention, through the North Atlantic Treaty Organization (NATO), raised complex new issues of international law and sovereignty related to the rights of minorities and the obligations of the international community.

Other minorities face discrimination in the new democracies. The Roma, of Asian descent, have encountered violence, legal discrimination and prejudice in such countries as Bulgaria, the Czech Republic, Hungary and Romania. Estonia and Slovakia face the challenge of integrating Hungarian and Russian minorities. Armenia, Azerbaijan and Georgia face intense ethnic conflict, frequently involving other countries.

LATIN AMERICA

Constitutions recently adopted in Latin America include provisions on the protection and promotion of the rights of indigenous communities. They are an attempt to clear away the legacy left by the indigenism that was formally instituted following the Inter-American Indigenous Congress in Patzcuaro, Mexico, in 1940.

Indigenism has two main objectives: to speed up and consolidate the national integration of Latin American states, and to promote economic and social development in order to overcome the "centuries-long backwardness" of indigenous communities and assimilate them into the nation-state model. These nationalistic societies, dominated by the white and mestizo urban middle class, rejected cultural diversity and did not recognize the indigenous elements of their culture. Indigenism, which in practice assigned indigenous people the same legal status as minors, exacerbated rather than solved the problems of extreme poverty, marginalization and recognition of ancestral lands.

Political liberalization has begun to reverse legal discrimination against indigenous peoples. But in some Latin American countries such progress has been accompanied by growing economic inequality and social marginalization.

Source: Mendez 2000; Olokoa-Onyango 2000; Silovic 2000; Stewart 2000.

consensus, the major political parties agreed to a symbolic role for the monarchy in consolidating the transition to democratic governance.

- A country uses a truth and reconciliation commission to heal deep wounds. Many countries have felt the need to openly discuss human rights abuses – to recognize suffering and to put the perpetrators of such abuses on the defensive.

Formal truth and reconciliation commissions were first established in Latin America in the 1980s (table 3.7.1). They have since proved, in some countries, to be an ingenious device for balancing the divergent needs of healing and justice. Elsewhere, they have been superficial exercises in futility.

In 1983 the newly elected president of Argentina, Raúl Alfonsín, appointed a National Commission on the Disappearance of Persons, chaired by the writer Ernesto Sabato. In 1984 the commission produced *Nunca Más* (*Never Again*), a chilling account of the machinery of death created by the military dictatorship. Immediately thereafter, the Argentine courts heard the historic case against the members of the three successive military juntas that governed between 1976 and 1982. The process resulted in the sentencing of powerful figures, omnipotent only a few years before. Restlessness in the armed forces over continued prosecutions later led to presidential pardons for the convicted officers.

Following this experience, the democratic government in Chile also created a truth and reconciliation commission, with members representing a wide political spectrum. Rather than describe the patterns and structure of repression, as the Argentine commission had done, the Chilean commission gave each victim's family an account of what had happened – to the extent that it could reconstruct the facts.

Truth and reconciliation commissions gained global visibility with their adoption in Africa. The deep psychological wounds of apartheid in South Africa were bared in an intensely emotional, participatory process. Victims confronted perpetrators, recalling inhumane acts, but generously expressing forgiveness for unforgivable crimes.

Suddenly Africa, so defamed by its dictators, was leading the world through the wisdom of Nobel Prize winners such as President Mandela and Archbishop Desmond Tutu. The South African Truth and Reconciliation Commission was preceded by one President Yoweri Museveni established in Uganda to come to terms with the terrors of Idi Amin and Milton Obote. Rwanda created an NGO-led commission. The most recent significant example is that of Nigeria, whose return to democratic rule in 1999 was accompanied by President Obasanjo's announcement of a truth and reconciliation commission.

Advancing the human rights agenda during the transition to democracy does not always require a truth and reconciliation commission, particularly when there is a consensus in society about the direction of transition, and no perceived threat of a reversal. This was evident in many transitions from one-party to multi-party states (box 3.7.5).

Truth and reconciliation commissions have not only exposed sordid details of the past, however – they have also put the perpetrators to shame in the public eye. But some have been meek, tokenistic failures. Sceptics note that in proportion to the enormity of the crimes, truth commissions have often achieved very little justice and disclosed too little truth.

Countries that have already suffered a return to military government or fear the resurgence of authoritarian forces may well consider the utility of a truth and reconciliation commission to put such forces on the defensive. An open discussion of their role in brutalizing society and destroying institutions is preferable to appeasing unrepentant authoritarian forces by hiding ugly truths under the carpet. Some countries that protected their armies, by avoiding an open discussion of their human rights abuses, have paid a heavy price in the return to military rule.

Experience with truth and reconciliation commissions suggests, ironically, that the key to their success is to be forward-looking. Commissions should not be seen as an alternative to creating judicial institutions for the future – but as part of a policy of accountability for the past that helps the process of creating independent and just insti-

TABLE 3.7.1

Truth and reconciliation commissions – a selected list

Country	Year commission was established	Main features
Bolivia	1982	This commission focused on unearthing and documenting disappearances under military rule, a major issue in the Latin American transitions to democracy.
Argentina	1983	Established by President Raúl Alfonsín, this commission consisted of writers, judges, journalists and legislators. Its report focused on 9,000 disappearances under military rule.
Philippines	1986	Established by President Corazon Aquino with a broad mandate and powers to probe the Marcos era, this commission did not produce a final report.
Chile	1990	Led by Senator Raul Retting, this commission documented two decades of human rights abuses during the Pinochet era.
Chad	1992	Headed by Chad's chief prosecutor, this commission examined human rights violations and corruption.
El Salvador	1992	A distinctive feature of this commission was its international membership, including a former president of Colombia, a former foreign minister of Venezuela and a law professor from George Washington University. Its report, "From Madness to Hope", was released at the United Nations in 1993.
Germany	1992	This commission, headed by an eastern German member of parliament, covered 40 years of human rights violations under communist rule in East Germany.
Rwanda	1993	A unique model for truth commissions, this commission was created, funded and fully sponsored by international NGOs in response to a request by a coalition of Rwandan human rights organizations. The commission covered the civil war period, from 1990 to 1993. Its report was widely circulated in Rwanda.
Guatemala	1994	This famous commission was established in the wake of a peace accord, after 36 years of civil war. Its report, "Memory of Silence", was given to the government and international agencies at a public ceremony in Guatemala City. The commission has a mix of foreign and national lawyers.
Haiti	1994	Established by President Jean-Bertrand Aristide, this commission also contained a mix of international and national members, headed by a sociologist. The commission took 14 months to complete its findings.
Uganda	1994	President Yoweri Museveni's six-member commission, established a year before South Africa's, had an explicit forward-looking mandate. Its clearly stated objective is to prevent a recurrence of the events that traumatized Uganda under Milton Obote and Idi Amin.
South Africa	1995	This most well-known truth and reconciliation commission was established by parliament and chaired by Archbishop Desmond Tutu. The 17-member commission covered 25 years of human rights violations. One of its most significant features was its extensive series of public hearings. The commission submitted its report to President Nelson Mandela in 1998.
Nigeria	1999	This commission, established in June 1999 by President Olusegun Obasanjo, is headed by a senior judge and covers nearly two decades. Soon after its formation, the commission was inundated with submissions.
Sierra Leone	1999	Established a month after the Nigerian commission, this commission has strong amnesty provisions, allowing it to grant pardons and immunity from prosecution to perpetrators. The commission provides a public forum for victims and perpetrators to discuss a brutal past.

Source: Hayner 1994; United States Institute of Peace 2000; Garton Ash 1998.

tutions. Truth commissions succeed if society sees them as an effort not only to respect and acknowledge the plight of victims but also to ensure that state-sponsored abuses of human rights are not repeated.

POLICY RESPONSES – ADVANCING HUMAN RIGHTS THROUGH AN INCLUSIVE DEMOCRACY

The solution to the many dilemmas of democracy is not to return to authoritarian government. Nor are civil society organizations by themselves the answer. Reasonable progress requires a political framework conducive to human rights. And there is far more to that framework than elections, which can still produce governments that tolerate or are directly responsible for serious human rights violations.

Protecting rights of minorities and addressing horizontal inequalities

International comparative analysis studies have emphasized that acute horizontal inequalities in access to political and economic resources lead to conflict. They have also identified 267 minorities particularly at risk across the world.

Horizontal inequalities typically translate into discrimination and marginalization for minority groups. The lack of belonging spurs alienation from the political and economic system controlled by the majority. Incorporating minority groups requires a more enlightened view of sharing economic and political resources than simple majoritarian democracy. The institutional framework and values of inclusive democracy need to be promoted to prevent violence and civil war.

This does not mean that minorities are better off under authoritarian governments. The recent

---

BOX 3.7.5

The importance of laughter and forgetting

In *The Book of Laughter and Forgetting*, Milan Kundera noted that "the past is full of life, eager to irritate us, provoke us and insult us, tempt us to destroy or repaint it. The only reason people want to be masters of the future is to change the past." The link between past and future had a twisted logic in the totalitarianism that suffocated Czechoslovakia. Many communist regimes used the past as an ever-changing tool to justify the present – most crudely by obliterating figures in disrepute from historical photographs. That was the fate of Leon Trotsky in the USSR. And in Czechoslovakia, Foreign Minister Vladimir Clementis was airbrushed out of a famous photograph of communist leader Klement Gottwald making a historic speech in Prague in February 1948.

There was a particular irony to the airbrushing of Comrade Clementis. It was freezing, and the foreign minister had had the generosity to lend his hat to his bareheaded leader. So Clementis's hat remained in the photograph and became a symbol – for men such as Vaclav Havel – of the distortion of the past that was so much a part of totalitarian

societies. The democratic Czech Republic of the 1990s, under Havel's leadership, has come to terms with its past in a remarkably open way. This attitude contributed to perhaps the most amicable divorce in history, Czechoslovakia's voluntary split into two countries.

Countries such as the Czech Republic and Slovakia illustrate how much wider human development and human rights are than some of the indicators used to measure them. Even a composite indicator such as the human development index, while a broader measure of progress than gross national product, does not pretend to measure civil and political rights. Czechoslovakia has ranked higher in the human development index than in gross national product, indicating a fairer distribution of economic resources than that in many other countries at the same income level. But the index does not measure the political dimension of rights – an area in which many one-party states were seriously deficient.

Source: Kundera 1978, Human Development Report Office.

ethnic cleansings have not occurred under de-mocracies. Some of the worst abuses of minorities have been by dictatorships. But the transition to democracy will improve matters only if there is public policy intervention in favour of minority protection – and that goes far beyond the assumption that the ballot box is an automatic protector.

Several countries have recognized the need for additional measures to incorporate groups that may be left out from a narrowly defined majoritarian democracy. Belgium and Switzerland have taken policy and institutional measures to incorporate groups within representative institutions (box 3.7.6).

Similar efforts have been undertaken by other countries. Germany has cross-party representation in parliament, with many parliamentary committees chaired by the opposition. And when the second chamber of parliament blocks legislation, conciliation committees work out an acceptable compromise.

Two large new democracies facing major challenges with minorities and horizontal inequalities are Indonesia and Nigeria. They may have something to learn from Malaysia's experience in addressing horizontal inequalities, while Malaysia has much to learn about expanding other human rights from such neighbouring countries as Thailand, where the new constitution and supporting measures represent impressive gains for human rights (box 3.7.7). Much of East Asia is not only recovering from the economic crisis but doing so under greater political freedom than before.

Malaysia's policies on horizontal inequalities in the 1970s, inevitably contentious, have been admired by many. Race riots shook the nation in 1969. In response, Malaysia embarked on an ambitious programme to address the severe horizontal inequalities underlying the racial violence. The key elements of Malaysia's response are captured in box 3.7.8.

Other countries' experiences of promoting majorities have been less benevolent. But instituting affirmative action is unavoidable in any country where inherited horizontal inequalities favour a minority, and the majority acquires power – the dilemma in South Africa and Zimbabwe. In such situations public policy has to tackle inequities

---

BOX 3.7.6

Minority rights and horizontal inequality – the parliamentary responses in Belgium and Switzerland

Switzerland's political system has tried to incorporate the country's three major ethnic groups – German, French and Italian. The national executive – the Federal Council – has had representation of all three groups since 1959. While the Swiss have an informal criterion of ethnic representation, the 1970 Belgian constitution has a formal requirement of equal representation for the two ethnic groups – Dutch and French. This regulation must be honoured whether the government is formed by one or several parties.

Inclusiveness is also ensured by giving minorities special representation in the second chamber. In Switzerland the national council is the lower chamber, with freely elected members. The upper house, the Council of States, has a representational formula that favours smaller cantons and has real decision-making power. The cantons have extensive self-governing powers.

While Swiss federalism is territorial, Belgium introduced "non-territorial" federalism to protect some cultural rights. The Dutch and the French each have a cultural council, with members from both houses of the legislature, that acts as a legislature for cultural and educational issues affecting its ethnic group.

Political parties in these countries have naturally tended to reflect a multitude of ethnic, religious and socioeconomic cleavages. Such a complex weave of horizontal and vertical divisions could easily lead to neglect and alienation of minorities. The political systems created have tried to address this challenge. Other countries, such as Germany, have also established institutional mechanisms that encourage consensus rather than two-party, adversarial politics.

Source: Donnelly 1989; Lijphart 1999.

while maintaining the dynamism of markets historically dominated by the minority.

Much has been learned about the need to address horizontal economic inequalities to prevent political conflict. Governments should avoid nationalizing the economic assets of relatively prosperous minorities. And they should stimulate growth in the assets and incomes of impoverished

---

BOX 3.7.7

The values of Asia

The signs of economic revival in Asia – so soon after the 1997–98 East Asian financial crisis – appear to provide further evidence of the deep structural foundations for economic development laid by the region. But perhaps the most positive outcome has been the remarkable change in civil and political rights, whose neglect the crisis exposed.

There has been a major change in Thailand, where the main safeguard of human rights and human development is the 1997 constitution, the country's first democratic one. The constitution stipulates that "human dignity" is the basis of human rights, which include equality between people and genders, the presumption of innocence, freedom of religion, association and expression, the rights to life, to privacy, to 12 years' education, to property and to health care, the right of children against violence and injustice, the right to access public information and the rights to take action against public authorities and to use peaceful means against those who subvert the constitution.

Violations of the constitution can be contested in the courts. Unlike rights in past constitutions, many of which had no force unless enacted into law, many of the new provisions are immediately applicable. And while earlier constitutions subordinated rights to interests such as national security, the new constitution does not allow such interests to undermine the substance of rights.

Other Asian societies have made similar gains. Indonesia, the Republic of Korea and Taiwan (province of China) have become more open, with greater recognition of the need to advance civil and political rights. Indonesia, a complex case, has moved to civilian rule, although the new regime is having to grapple with the troubled legacy of East Timor.

The new talk of Asia advancing the cause of human rights and democracy is a far cry from earlier false claims that "Asian values" justified neglect of civil and political rights.

Source: De Barry 1998; Saravanamuttu 2000; Muntarbhorn 2000.

BOX 3.7.8

Malaysia's response to race riots – addressing horizontal inequality

Unlike many other countries, Malaysia refrained from nationalizing the assets of the richer minority community. This restraint ensured adherence to an efficient, market-led economic framework and reassured the Chinese minority. Political power rested in the hands of the Malay majority, the bumiputras. Their legitimate grievances were addressed largely through extensive intervention in the public sector, including programmes for affirmative action in education, technology and employment.

In 1969, around the time of the race riots, the per capita income of the Chinese was twice that of the Malays. Two decades later both communities were substantially richer. But while the average incomes of both communities rose, the gap between them narrowed – the Malay income was half of Chinese income in 1970, but nearly two-thirds by 1990. This outcome was made possible by an enabling economic environment that generated rapid growth – and more equal sharing of the pie.

Critics of the Malaysian system point to its extensive network of controls on the press, political parties and the judiciary. Others point to Malaysia's practical good sense in many areas – including the unfashionable imposition of temporary capital controls in the midst of the East Asian financial crisis. This pragmatic ethos, it is claimed, will lead to a deepening of democracy, as evidenced by the recent open presidential elections.

Source: Yoke and Leng 1992.

minorities through such targeted measures as small business promotion and measures to end discrimination in the labour market. Job quotas in the public sector are likely to work only in a rapidly growing economy. Economic stagnation and an overstaffed public sector are a poor environment for affirmative action in the labour market.

Widening participation and expression

A precondition for building an inclusive democracy is ensuring the right to elect representatives. Tampering with the ballot has often undermined the legitimacy of elected governments. In Bangladesh doubts about the independence of the election commission led to an agreement among political parties that elections would always be held under a temporary interim regime. This prevents the military's control over electoral politics, while ensuring that the results of elections are considered legitimate, an important advance in a new democracy. An independent election commission and international election monitors provide other tools for protecting the sanctity of the ballot where trust and autonomous institutions are lacking.

A key element in deepening inclusive democracy is a legal framework that protects the right to participation and free expression. Civil society organizations and open media are vital for monitoring violations of rights. People's participation in local institutions, including school boards, is as important a feature of democracy as participation in elections or in formal political parties.

Jordan shows how civil society organizations can lead in advancing rights in a country undergoing a gradual transition to democracy. Several members of the royal family have not only helped establish human rights NGOs directly but also supported an environment that promotes grass-roots civil society organizations struggling for human rights, including those fighting for women's rights.

An important element of the participatory principle is internal democracy in political parties. Too often, the organizational structure of parties engaged in democratic politics is anything but participatory. Parties that are not open and transparent are unlikely to be democratic in their policy commitments. Without internal democracy, parties become individual or family fiefdoms. Creating a

culture of democracy in political parties is thus vital. At the very least, this should involve open, competitive elections for the party leadership.

In Panama the military was abolished as part of wide-ranging structural political reform. The democratic features of the reform included an electoral code, adopted in 1995, that requires political parties to democratically elect their presidential candidates.

In addition to internal democracy, political parties in new democracies need to exemplify tolerant behaviour. The Institute for Democracy and Electoral Assistance, a policy institute based in Stockholm, has proposed a code of conduct for political parties to promote a public atmosphere of tolerance.

The code sets out principles of behaviour for political parties and their supporters relating to their participation in a democratic election campaign. Ideally, parties would agree voluntarily to this code and negotiate towards consensus on the text, which might later be incorporated in law.

The core prescriptions of such a code generally include:

- *Campaign management* – the right of all parties to campaign and to disseminate political ideas, and respect for the freedom of the press.
- *Election process* – peaceful polling, cooperation with election observers and acceptance of the outcome of the election.
- *Fair conduct* – avoiding defamatory language, destruction of the symbols of other parties or intimidation of voters and election officials.
- *Legal penalties* – for example, disqualification for corrupt practices, such as offering money to induce people to vote, or to stand or not stand.

Efforts to extend participation should also involve special measures to incorporate groups that are underrepresented because of a history of prejudice and discrimination. All over the world, social and structural barriers impede women from participating in politics. In many countries women have enhanced their participation by increasing gender sensitivity and awareness, by lobbying for party and parliamentary electoral quotas for women and by providing support services to women legislators. Gender-balanced local elections often represent the first step, enabling greater political participation at all levels.

In Trinidad and Tobago a network of NGOs conducted workshops to train 300 women to run as candidates in the 1999 local government elections. Of the 91 women contesting the elections, 28 won, virtually doubling the number of seats held by women since the 1996 election.

Sweden has the largest proportion of women in parliament. Although this cannot be attributed to any single factor, the quota system used by the majority party – the Green Party in 1983–90, the Left Party in 1990–93 and the Social Democratic Party since 1993 – has undoubtedly contributed.

In South Africa after the end of apartheid, the African National Congress expanded women's political participation in parliament by adopting a quota. According to the Inter-Parliamentary Union, the country now ranks ninth in the world in the proportion of women in parliament, with 119 women in its 399-member National Assembly (in 1994 it was 141st).

India reserves seats for women in local government institutions known as *panchayats,* challenging the traditional structures of policy-making. In 1993 the federal government passed the Panchayat Raj Act, reserving 33% of the three-tiered *panchayats* for women. The *panchayat* elections of 1998 showed that the reservation policy worked in most states: women won 33–40% of the seats.

In the Philippines improving the quality of women legislators' participation in policy-making is as important as increasing the number of elected women. The Centre for Legislative Development provides elected women, particularly at the local level, with the technical skills they need for their job – through training on legislative agenda setting and on the development of legislative proposals and deliberations. To sustain advocacy initiatives, the centre also helps build links between elected women and women's groups.

Widening the participation of those discriminated against – whether minorities, women or others – is linked to the process of changing norms and values. Instilling a democratic culture at all levels of society is a radical process – threatening existing values, inequities and injustices. The task is complicated further by a recent history of violence. Two societies struggling to create a culture of democracy on the ashes of violence are Cambodia and South Africa (box 3.7.9).

An independent press has been a vital ally in the recent advances in Eastern Europe. The Network of Independent Journalists, run by the Croatian-based Stina press agency, has campaigned vigorously for extension of freedoms long denied in the region.

Widening participation has several other dimensions. Even well-established democracies face the need for continual reform to adapt to changing circumstances and to correct deficiencies. Recent reforms in the United Kingdom are aimed at addressing the shortcomings of the Westminster model, the subject of debate in the country for decades.

While Thailand was forming its first democratic constitution, the United Kingdom's Labour government began to enact a series of wide-ranging reforms to the country's customary unwritten constitution. These include devolving power to regional assemblies, enhancing the powers of the Scottish parliament in particular. Apart from excessive centralization, another deficiency was the hereditary principle governing membership in the House of Lords, the upper chamber – a symbol of privilege rather than inclusion. The reforms changed its composition and the criteria for selection to reduce the power of inherited privilege. Other changes include a move towards a freedom of information act.

These reforms, linked to the expanded framework of the European Union's human rights legislation, have modernized British democracy. Many of the changes are in line with the EU principle of subsidiarity and decentralization – that power is more accountable when it is close to the beneficiaries. Some decision-making is retained at regional or central levels of authority, where justified for consistency and enforcement of common standards across national boundaries.

Implementing the separation of powers

When elected leaders behave like military rulers, arbitrary power undermines a basic principle of democracy, violating the checks and balances at the heart of democratic government. Human rights are most vulnerable when the exercise of power is not rule based. An elected leader must face institutional curbs to restrict arbitrary action. Most countries making the transition from authoritarian to democratic government still face this challenge.

There is tension in restricting arbitrary power. A newly elected leader typically inherits an environment in which arbitrary power has been part of authoritarian rule. The elected leader and party are entrusted with building institutions that place checks on their power. Visionary leadership is rare in such situations. Civilians carry on behaving in much the same way as their military and colonial predecessors. That is why a coalition of forces is required to create a culture of accountability for civilian rule – a coalition of an independent press, opposition parties, national civil society institutions and international human rights organizations.

Such a coalition needs to build opposition to arbitrary power. It has to exert pressure for the institutionalized separation of powers. If disputes cannot be settled in court, if corruption undermines the legal process and if the elite is above the law, a country is in no position to fulfil the rights of its citizens. Establishing a sound and supportive institutional framework is thus essential for any serious implementation of rights.

An important aspect of the separation of powers is the role of the judiciary. Argentina and El Salvador provide important examples of promising judicial reform (box 3.7.10).

BOX 3.7.9

Transition from a brutal past to an open society in South Africa and Cambodia

"This Constitution provides a historic bridge between the past of a deeply divided society characterized by strife, conflict, untold suffering and injustice, and a future founded on the recognition of human rights, democracy and peaceful co-existence and opportunities for all South Africans, irrespective of colour, race, class, belief or sex."

This quotation from the 1993 interim South African constitution provides a framework of values and institutions for advancing human rights and development. The constitution includes civil, political, economic, social and cultural rights.

But the wide gap between the constitutional promises and the lived realities of millions of poor South Africans remains a challenge. The constitution and new laws are means to overcome that challenge, and South Africa's national action plan for human rights provides a framework for doing so. The plan enables the government to evaluate its human rights performance, set goals and priorities within achievable time frames, devise strategies and allocate resources for promoting human rights. It can also be used as a tool by NGOs and the media to hold the government accountable for its human rights commitments – by monitoring the human rights impact of government policies, legislation and programmes.

Cambodia's recent past was even more violent than South Africa's. And it too has adopted a constitution respectful of human rights, after the Paris peace accords of 1991. But the gap between the constitution's ideals and reality led to heated exchanges in 1997 between the United Nations Human Rights Envoy Thomas Hammerberg and Cambodian leaders.

Over the past three years, however, there have been signs of progress. A coalition of 17 NGOs formed the Human Rights Action Committee, and another group of NGOs won prominence as the Coalition for Free and Fair Elections. The establishment of the Khmer Institute for Democracy, the widespread revival of Buddhism and the appearance of reasonably independent newspapers are all advances, although inevitably many acute problems remain as Cambodia continues its slow climb back from the heart of darkness.

Source: Neou 2000; Liebenberg 2000.

Besides independent judiciaries, democracies need a civil service protected from arbitrary instructions from the political leadership. But the actions of civil servants also have to be under public scrutiny. Several institutional mechanisms can curb bureaucratic arrogance. An increasingly popular one is the office of the ombudsman, typically created to examine abuses of authority by public officials. The protection of civil servants against arbitrary political intervention lies in genuinely independent civil service commissions responsible for recruitment, promotion and discipline. These need to be supplemented by open procedures for bureaucrats to take elected representatives to court if asked to do anything illegal.

These open procedures in turn require an independent judiciary, reinforcing the point that an effective separation of powers requires rule-based interaction between institutions. The US constitution and subsequent civil rights reforms provide a classic model for effective separation of powers.

Within the civil service, the police are particularly important for human rights. Recent shootings by the police in New York City, for example, have raised apprehensions among the African American minority, some of whom have called for federal monitoring of the city's police.

Investigative reporters across the world have exposed rape in prisons, extrajudicial killings, torture and many other human rights violations by the police and security forces. Such journalists have played a vital role in raising awareness and contributing to a culture of public outrage at abuses.

BOX 3.7.10

Strengthening the rule of law in Argentina and El Salvador

Access to justice is an important part of the rule of law. Partnerships of governments, civil society and international development organizations are implementing judicial reform programmes bringing timely and tangible results. Two promising examples, symbolic of similar initiatives being undertaken across the world: Buenos Aires and El Salvador.

Under the 1996 constitution of Buenos Aires, politicians and the people are collaborating on new institutions that will improve access to justice. All laws used by the courts are to be compiled and analysed. Experts, judges and citizens are to confer about the institutional barriers to justice and propose solutions. New laws are to be drafted, new institutions designed and judges retrained. In the words of the president of Argentina, Fernando De la Rua, who started the process when he was mayor of Buenos Aires, "the key objective of the new justice system is to promote and facilitate access to justice, mainly for poor people and women".

In El Salvador judicial reform, a product of the 1992 peace agreement, is a joint effort by government, civil society and international development agencies. Since its inception during the war years, judicial reform has been led and "owned" by Salvadorans working in partnership with international experts sponsored by bilateral and multilateral donors and the development banks. They have rewritten laws, reorganized the judiciary, retrained police and prosecutors and carried out public awareness campaigns.

These examples suggest some lessons:

- An efficient, high-quality justice system entails a social, economic and political commitment. Setting up institutions that protect rights, particularly where public opinion of political parties and the justice system is poor, involves serious resource commitments and substantial political risks

- Countries need international advisory services as well as national political will and social participation to succeed.

- The reform should be holistic to avoid setbacks and obstacles. Legal institutions must be made credible. Laws must fit with the constitution and international human rights conventions. To ensure access to justice, institutional barriers must come down, information about rights and how to exercise them must be freely available and the quality of the public service of justice must be increased.

Source: Yujnovsky 2000.

Recognizing the importance of police reform for advancing human rights, several countries have taken important steps. Luxembourg is training police to combat racism and xenophobia. In Honduras the police reform has been inspired by an integrated set of principles on demilitarization, subordination to civil authority, respect for human rights, citizen control and accountability. The government created a new Ministry of Security to inculcate a new ethos in what was considered a volatile and dangerous police force.

As with other separations of powers, there is a dual nature to police reform. The police have to be protected from arbitrary orders from the political system. At the same time, the people have to be protected from rights abuses by the police. An ombudsman can monitor police abuses and hear complaints. In addition, human rights NGOs should have the political space to monitor prisons and any abuses by the police system.

Such measures as public interest litigation, often involving an appeal to the supreme court, have advanced people's involvement in mechanisms of accountability. People's organizations have used similar instruments to appeal to other branches of government. In Hungary citizens groups representing the Roma have regularly filed discrimination complaints against employers with the Office of the Parliamentary Ombudsman for Minority Rights, including for refusal to hire them because of their ethnicity. After an investigation, the ombudsman recommended that the Ministry of Social and Family Protection compile a brochure informing prospective employees of their rights and that employment centres report all cases of discrimination. It also requested that the Ministry of Justice simplify the procedures for discrimination cases and recommended that the Ministry of Internal Affairs require officials to report such cases.

In Italy in 1993, the Federation of the Association of Haemophiliacs filed a case against the Ministry of Health on behalf of 385 haemophiliac patients infected with HIV by contaminated blood transfusions. No action was taken on the case, and in May 1998 some of the patients filed an appeal with the European human rights commission against the Italian government for violating Article 6 of the European human rights convention. The article asserts entitlement to a fair and public hearing "within a reasonable time". In November 1998 the case filed in 1993 was concluded in favour of the plaintiffs. And in July 1999 the European Commission ordered the Italian government to compensate the victims for its negligent behaviour.

Incorporating human rights into economic policy

The process of economic policy-making for human development should honour the rights of participation and freedom of expression. These rights imply that economic policy formulation must be open and transparent, allowing debate on the options and conferring the authority for the final decision on elected representatives.

Economic policies have large effects on the rights of people. Those hurt by decisions have the right to know – and to participate in debate and discussion. That does not mean that they have veto power, since many economic policies can hurt a few people justifiably, on grounds of efficiency in resource allocation, reduction of horizontal inequality or, indeed, improvements in human development. But those adversely affected must be heard and, if appropriate, compensated.

The importance of process for sustaining ownership of structural economic policy change is shown by India. Open debate helped embed the decision-making in the national discourse (box 3.7.11). Opposition remains and is desirable, but India debated the options far more openly than have most countries undergoing similar reforms.

The typical process for international policy-based lending often suffers from a democratic deficit of broad participatory debate, for example, lacking parliamentary debate. It is therefore ironic, but not surprising, that a constant refrain in the international community is "lack of ownership" of the agreed policy programme (box 3.7.12). And it was one of the weaknesses of adjustment policies in the 1980s, when international financial agencies and national finance ministries often agreed to policies behind closed doors.

Participatory processes can increase efficiency and economic sustainability, particularly for projects requiring community involvement. Many evaluations confirm that community participation in project design increases the efficiency and viability of projects in water and sanitation and in education and health. So, due process can do more than fulfil important participatory rights.

The other side of incorporating rights in economic policy-making relates to the outcome. Indi-

---

BOX 3.7.11

Ownership of structural adjustment – the rights approach in India

By the late 1980s there was wide consensus that India's economy had performed below potential since independence and recognition of the need for major policy change. Most, if not all, international agencies agreed.

Rather than signing a secretive agreement on a structural adjustment programme with international financial institutions, India engaged in an open policy discussion. There were, and remain, vociferous critics of the reform path being suggested. But the process of open participation and expression of opinion has led to two important results.

First, despite persistent political instability and fragile coalition governments, the broad consensus on economic policy reform has survived. All the major political parties have adhered to the programme. National ownership has not been at issue.

Second, India's economic reforms have produced the most rapid growth in its history – twice the average annual rate before the reforms. That has underscored the importance of the reforms – and led to public debate on how the benefits of the growth should be shared among regions, groups and classes.

Source: Human Development Report Office.

BOX 3.7.12

The John Le Carré approach to economic policy – structural adjustment by stealth

Structural adjustment has aroused strong passions. Its proponents have argued that poor performance was due to poor policy, pointing to the futility of huge project investments in a perverse policy environment. Its critics point to adverse social consequences and the lack of fine-tuning of a blunt "cookie cutter" approach.

This debate has often ignored a vital shortcoming in the process for negotiating and implementing these programmes – a level of secrecy of which the finest spy novelists, including John Le Carré himself, would be proud. Economic policies that will profoundly affect the lives of many citizens were often agreed in closed-door meetings between finance ministers and international financial institutions. Such secrecy would be considered scandalous in the countries of many of the representatives of these international institutions.

This process is fundamentally contrary to a rights-based approach to economic policy. Regardless of the merits of the programme, the process undermined accountability. This was a particularly serious neglect, since the citizens barred from debating the options are often those who must bear the burden of paying back the debts incurred.

But representatives of international financial institutions are increasingly recognizing this need for greater transparency. Joseph Stiglitz, chief economist of the World Bank from 1996 to 2000, has expressed concerns over a process that has left "a legacy of suspicion and doubt. Opponents see in development conditionality an echo of colonial bonds ... the process of negotiating policy conditionality is widely perceived to have undermined transparency and participation."

Getting the policy environment right, and honouring conditions linked to project loans consistent with this objective, are important aspects of economic management. But the process has to respect important rights if governments and nations are to be held accountable through national ownership of programmes.

Source: Stiglitz 1999a; Human Development Report Office.

viduals have economic and social rights, not all of which can be immediately realized because of resource and institutional constraints. The first step in a rights-oriented approach to economic policy is to recognize these rights. This implies that citizens have a claim to have these rights realized – and may have certain duties to perform to have them fulfilled.

Many human rights are subject to progressive realization. Rights-oriented economic policy-making would force a national debate on choices and on the priority given to fulfilling some rights before others. For example, the citizens of a poor country may find that the government can meet its obligations to fulfil the right to basic education more easily than the right of each individual to housing.

Difficult choices are inherent in economic decision-making, involving complex trade-offs due to scarce resources. Incorporating human rights into economic policy-making does not make these constraints vanish. But it honours certain rights in due process. It also recognizes that choices must produce outcomes that reflect the claims that individuals have to levels of human development – and honour the economic dimension of their human rights.

• • •

Implementing these four interconnected institutional reforms will go a long way towards creating a rights-based, inclusive democracy. But it will not be a technocratic, depoliticized exercise. The agenda will face strong internal opposition, for there are groups whose power, values and interests are threatened by such change. Implementation will require a committed coalition of the media, people's movements and civil society organizations, including professional bodies of lawyers and human rights advocates. Such reforms are possible only with the active involvement of democratic political parties.

Other reforms accompanying these four, such as decentralization, would deepen democracy by extending participation. Decentralization on its own may not further rights – but when allied to these four pillars of reform, it can strengthen democratic governance.

All this can be summarized in a 10-point policy agenda for inclusive democracy:

- An independent judiciary is the pillar in a system of checks and balances against arbitrary power. Judicial appointments, training and the court system have to curb executive authority – not succumb to it. Direct recourse of people's organizations to the judicial system, through public interest litigation, also helps protect rights.
- There are two dimensions to police reform. The police have to be protected from arbitrary orders from the political system. And the people have to be protected from rights abuses inflicted by the police. This requires monitoring of police actions and other measures to promote human rights norms in the police force.
- Ensuring non-discrimination against women in politics requires various interventions, including quotas – for the national parliament and at other levels of representation, particularly local.
- Minority participation in decision-making structures should be promoted by giving minorities special weight in legislative procedures and by having opposition and minority representatives chair parliamentary committees.
- Reducing horizontal inequalities requires economic measures. Countries need to consider what to do and what not to do. They should avoid nationalizing the private economic assets of privileged minorities, instead using targeted economic measures to promote asset accumulation and income opportunities for poor minorities.
- The sanctity of the vote must be guarded by autonomous election commissions, international monitors and, if necessary, interim regimes for the sole purpose of transferring power from one elected regime to another.
- Political parties must be internally democratic. Party leaders should be elected and replaced through open, competitive processes. Political parties should adopt codes of conduct for

internal democracy and for tolerant behaviour during the electoral process.

- Countries that have already suffered a return to military government – or fear the resurgence of authoritarian forces – might well consider the utility of a truth and reconciliation commission to create an environment conducive to democracy and respect for human rights.
- Governments should create the political space, and encourage partnerships, for monitoring and promoting human rights. Ultimately, governments and the people benefit when the media are open and civil society institutions free – conditions conducive to partnerships for creating norms and accountability for human rights.
- Pro-poor human development policies – and a reasonable distribution of the resources from economic growth – are vital companions to legal and institutional advances in human rights. The process of economic policy-making has to respect rights of participation and expression. And the content of pro-poor economic policies has to be aimed at increasing resources and targeting programmes to the vulnerable.

Democracy, as noted earlier, is not homogeneous. Developing a framework of institutions that fit a country's structure and circumstances requires measures that celebrate diversity. Happily, nations no longer face the choice between authoritarianism and democracy. Their challenge for the 21st century is to deepen and enrich fragile democracies.

REFERENCES

An-Na'im, Abdullahi A. 2000. "Human Rights in the Arab World – A Regional Perspective." Regional study for *Human Development Report 2000*. UNDP, New York.

CAD (Coalition against Dictatorship). 1995. "Nigerian Casefile: The Ken Saro-Wiwa-Ogoni Handbook." Committee Report, Paris. [http://www.hartford-hwp.com/archives/34a/023.html]. 12 April 2000

Cahn, Claude. 1999. Correspondence on examples of struggles that have achieved goals for Roma rights and the use of shame by a national NGO. European Roma Rights Center. 12 December. Budapest.

De Barry, Theodore. 1998. *Asian Values and Human Rights*. Cambridge, Mass.: Harvard University Press.

Desai, Meghnad. 2000. "Rights and Obligations: A Framework for Accountability." Background paper for *Human Development Report 2000*. UNDP, New York.

Diamond, Larry. 1999. *Developing Democracy: Toward Consolidation*. Baltimore, Md.: John Hopkins University Press.

Donelly, Jack. 1989. *Universal Human Rights in Theory and Practice*. Ithaca, N.Y.: Cornell University Press.

ECRI (European Commission Against Racism and Intolerance). 2000. "Combating Racism and Intolerance: A Basket of Good Practices." [http://www.ecri.coe.int/en/04/01/e04010001.htm]. 14 April 2000

European Monitoring Centre on Racism and Xenophobia. 1998. *Annual Report 1998: Part 2 – Looking Reality in the Face*. Vienna. [http://www.eumc.at/publications/anualreport/report1998.htm.]. 14 April 2000.

Federazione Italiana delle Associazioni Emofilici. 2000. "Cosa dicono i Giornali." [http://www.espero.it/emofilia/attualita'/news.htm]. 15 April 2000.

Garton Ash, Timothy. 1998. "The Truth about Dictatorship." *New York Review of Books* 45 (3). [http://www.nybooks.com/nyrev/WWWarchdisplay.cgi?19980219035F]. 12 April 2000.

Gurr, Ted Robert, Betty Brown, Pamela L. Burke, Michael Dravis, Jonathan Fox, Michael L. Haxton, Mizan Khan, Deepa Khosla, Monty G. Marshall, Beáta Kovás Nás, Anne Pitsch and Marion Recktenwald. 1999. *Peoples versus States: Minorities at Risk in the New Century*. College Park, Md.: University of Maryland. [http://www.bsos.umd.edu/cidcm/mar/trgpvs.html]. 10 March 2000

Hassan, Bahey El-Din. 2000. "Egypt Human Rights Report." Country study for *Human Development Report 2000*. UNDP, New York.

Hayner, Priscilla. 1994. "Fifteen Truth Commissions – 1974 to 1994: A Comparative Study." *Human Rights Quarterly* 16 (4): 597–655.

International IDEA (Institute for Democracy and Electoral Assistance). 1999. *Code of Conduct: Political Parties Campaigning in Democratic Elections.* Stockholm.

Khader, Asma. 2000. "Human Development and Human Rights – A Country Study of Jordan." Country study for *Human Development Report 2000.* UNDP, New York.

Kundera, Milan. 1980 [1978]. *The Book of Laughter and Forgetting.* New York: Penguin Books.

Liebenberg, Sandra. 2000. "A Country Study of South Africa – Human Development and Human Rights." Regional study for *Human Development Report 2000.* UNDP, New York.

Lijphart, Arend. 1999. *Patterns of Democracy: Government Forms and Performance in Thirty-Six Countries.* New Haven, Conn.: Yale University Press.

Mendez, Juan E. 2000. "Human Rights in Latin America and the Caribbean – A Regional Perspective." Regional study for *Human Development Report 2000.* UNDP, New York.

Muntarbhorn, Vitit. 2000. "Human Rights and Human Development: Thailand – A Country Study." Country study for *Human Development Report 2000.* UNDP, New York.

Muntarbhorn, Vitit and Charles Taylor. 1994. *Roads to Democracy: Human Rights and Democratic Development in Thailand.* Montreal: International Centre for Human Rights and Democratic Development.

Mutua, Makau. 2000. "The African Human Rights System: A Critical Evaluation." Regional study for *Human Development Report 2000.* UNDP, New York.

Neou, Kassie. 2000. "Country Study – Cambodia." Country study for *Human Development Report 2000.* UNDP, New York.

Neve, Christina and Beatriz Affonso. 1995. "Report on a Mass Murder: Death of 18 Prisoners at the 42nd Police Station, Parada de Lucas, São Paolo" (Relato de uma chacina. Morte de 18 detentos na 42a DP, Parada de Lucas, São Paolo). In Centre for the Study of Violence and Univerity of São Paolo and Teotônio Vilela Commission, *Human Rights in Brazil* (Os Direitos Humanos no Brasil), São Paolo.

Olcott, Martha Brill. 2000. "Regional Study on Human Development and Human Rights – Central Asia." Regional study for *Human Development Report 2000.* UNDP, New York.

Olokoa-Onyango, Joseph. 2000. "Human Rights and Human Development in Ecuador." Country study for *Human Development Report 2000.* UNDP, New York.

Pérez, Andres E. 2000. "Honduras: The Birth of Citizenship and State Conscience." Country study for *Human Development Report 2000.* UNDP, New York.

Reyes, Socorro. 2000. "Seeking Gender Balance: Women Strategize for Change." Women's Environment and Development Organization, New York.

Roma Rights. 1999a. "Bulgarian Roma Rights Organisation Scores Political Victory." *Roma Rights Quarterly.* [http://www.errc.org/rr_nr1_1999/snap02.shtml]. 12 March 2000.

——. 1999b. "Local Government in Hungary Taken to Court by Roma." [http://www.errc.org/rr_nr1_1999/snap11.shtml]. 12 March 2000.

——. 1999c. "Ombudsman Investigates Discrimination in Employment in Hungary." [http://www.errc.org/rr_nr1_1999/snap23.shtml]. 12 March 2000.

Saravanamuttu, Johan. 2000. "Country Study – Report of Human Rights in Malaysia." Country study for *Human Development Report 2000.* UNDP, New York.

Sarker, Lotika. 2000. "Country Study – India." Country study for *Human Development Report 2000.* UNDP, New York.

Shell Report. 1999. "People, Planet and Profits – An Act of Commitment." Houston, Tex. [http://www.shell.com/royal-en/]. 14 April 2000.

Silovic, Darko. 2000. "Regional Study of Human Development and Human Rights in Central and Eastern Europe." Regional study for *Human Development Report 2000.* UNDP, New York.

Stewart, Frances. 2000. "The Root Causes of Humanitarian Emergencies." In E. Wayne Nafziger, Frances Stewart and Raimo Vayrynen, eds., *War, Hunger, and Displacement: The Origins of Humanitarian Emergencies, Volume 1.* New York: Oxford University Press.

Stiglitz, Joseph. 1999. "Democratic Development as the Fruits of Labor." [http://www.worldbank.org/knowledge/chiefecon/stiglitz.htm]. 2 December 1999.

United States Institute of Peace. 2000. *Truth Commissions*. [http://www.usip.org/library/truth.html]. 10 March 2000.

Wignaraja, Kanni. 2000. Email correspondence on Sri Lanka. 18 February 2000. New York.

Yoke, The Hoe and Goh Kim Leng (eds). 1992. *Malaysia's Economic Vision. Issues and Challenges*. Malaysia: Pelanduk Publications.

Yujnovsky, Oscar. 2000. Email correspondence on judicial reforms in Latin America. 15 February 2000. New York.

ABOUT THE CONTRIBUTORS

Sudhir Anand is Professor of Economics at the University of Oxford, and Fellow at St Catherine's College, Oxford. He has also been Adjunct Professor at Harvard University, Cambridge, Massachussetts, where he served as Acting Director of the Center for Population and Development Studies. He has advised the Human Development Report Office since 1992.

Håkan Björkman is Deputy Resident Representative and Programme Director of the United Nations Development Programme in Thailand. From 2000 to 2002 he was Senior Adviser on HIV/AIDS, Bureau for Development Policy at the United Nations Development Programme. He was a member of the core team of the 1996, 1997 and 1998 *Human Development Reports*. From 1998 to 2000 he launched and managed the National Human Development Report Network and assisted different countries in the preparation of their National Human Development Reports.

Lord Meghnad Desai is Professor of Economics at the London School of Economics and Political Science, Head of the Development Studies Institute, and Director of the Centre for the Study of Global Governance at the LSE. He was made Lord Desai of St. Clements Danes in 1991. From 1984 to 1991, he was co-editor of the *Journal of Applied Econometrics*.

Nancy Folbre is Professor of Economics at the University of Massachusetts at Amherst. In 1995–96, she held the Visiting Chair in American Studies at Ecole des Hautes en Sciences Sociales in Paris. She is also co-founder and Chief Executive Officer of The Dancing Monkey Project.

Sakiko Fukuda-Parr is a development economist, and Director of the Human Development Report Office since 1995. She is the lead author of the *Human Development Reports* of 2001 and 2002, and the chief author with Richard Jolly of the 1996–2000 *Human Development Reports*. She also worked on the 1995 *Human Development Report* on gender with Mahbub ul Haq.

The late **Mahbub ul Haq** trained as an economist at Government College, Lahore (1948–53); King's College, Cambridge (1953–55); and Yale University (1955–57). He had a long and distinguished career as a policy-maker in his capacity as Chief Economist of the Pakistan Planning Commission (1957–70), Director of the World Bank's Policy Planning Department (1970–82), and Planning and Finance Minister in Pakistan's Federal Cabinet (1982–88). Between 1989 and 1995, he was Special Adviser to the Administrator of the United Nations Development Programme and chief architect of the *Human Development Report*. In 1995, he set up the Human Development Centre in Islamabad, Pakistan. Dr. Haq died in 1998.

Selim Jahan is Senior Adviser, Employment for Poverty Reduction, Bureau for Development Policy at the United Nations Development Programme in New York. Between 1996 and 2001, he was Deputy Director of the Human Development Report Office. He is one of the core authors of the 1992–2000 *Human Development Reports*.

Sir Richard Jolly is Professor Emeritus at the Institute of Development Studies at the University of Sussex. He succeeded Mahbub ul Haq as Special Adviser to the Administrator of the United Nations Development Programme, and was the principal coordinator of the 1996–2000 *Human Development Reports*. Before joining UNDP, he was Deputy Executive Director of the United Nations Children's Fund for 14 years. Prior to UNICEF, Dr. Jolly served for nine years as Director of the Institute of Development Studies at the University of Sussex. He was knighted in 2001.

Inge Kaul is Director of UNDP's Office of Development Studies. From 1989 to 1994, she was Director of the Human Development Report Office (UNDP) **and a member of the team of authors that produced Human Development Reports 1990-1995. She has a Ph.D. in sociology/economics from Konstanz University** in Germany. She is Editor of the books "Global Public Goods, International Cooperation in the 21st Century" (New York: Oxford University Press 1999) and "Providing Global Public Goods; Managing Globalization (New York, Oxford University Press 2003).

Terry McKinley is a Senior Policy Adviser on Poverty and Economic Policy in the Bureau for Development Policy, United Nations Development Programme, New York. He was contributor to the 1995 and 1996 Human Development Reports and principal author of the 1998 and 2000 UNDP Global Poverty Reports. He is currently Global Coordinator of case studies on the Macroeconomics of Poverty Reduction and specializes in Human Development and Poverty, Inequality and Pro-Poor Macroeconomic and Adjustment Policies.

Omar Noman is Senior Adviser to Regional Bureau Director for Asia and the Pacific at the United Nations Development Programme in New York. Between 2002 and 2004, he was Deputy Director of the Human Development Report Office. Before joining the United Nations Development Programme in 1996, he was a Senior Research Economist at Oxford University, where he taught political economy.

Alejandro Ramírez is Mexico's Deputy Permanent Representative to the Organisation for Economic Co-operation and Development (OECD), Paris. He specializes in the study of poverty and discrimination in Mexico. Prior to this job he was the chief of staff of Mexico's Social Cabinet and has worked for the World Bank and the Human Development Report Office of the United Nations Development Programme. He received a BA in economics and an MBA from Harvard, an M.Sc. in Development Economics from Oxford and is currently an economics PhD candidate at Cambridge.

Gustav Ranis is the Director of the Center for International and Area Studies and the Frank Altschul Professor of International Economics at Yale University. He has been an adviser to the Human Development Report Office from its early years.

Kate Raworth is a development economist and was a co-author of the *Human Development Reports* from 1998 to 2001. She is now a policy analyst with Oxfam. She holds a B.A. in politics, philosophy and economics, and an M.Sc. in development economics from the University of Oxford.

Amartya Sen won the 1998 Nobel Prize in Economic Science in recognition of his work on welfare economics. He is Master of Trinity College, Cambridge, and was the Lamont University Professor and Professor of Economics and Philosophy at Harvard University. Previously, he was Drummond Professor of Political Economy at Oxford University and fellow of All Souls College. He has taught at the London School of Economics, Delhi University and Cambridge University. He is a past President of the American Economic Association, Indian Economic Association, Development Studies Association, and Social Choice and Welfare Society. Amartya Sen has been a principal contributor to the *Human Development Reports* from the very beginning.

Gita Sen is a Sri Ratan Tata Chair Professor at the Indian Institute of Management, Bangalore, India, and Adjunct Professor at the Harvard School of Public Health. She is also a Research Co-ordinator on Alternative Development Frameworks for

DAWN (Development Alternatives with Women for a New Era). She has an MA in Economics from the University of Delhi and received her Ph.D. at Stanford University. She is a leading international researcher on the links between gender, inequity and health. Lately appointed as Honorary Doctor of Medicine by the Karolinska Institutet of Sweden (2003), she is a contributor of the 1997 *Human Development Report*.

A. K. Shiva Kumar is an economist and Special Adviser to the United Nations Children's Fund in India. Prior to that, he was a Research Fellow at the Harvard Institute for International Development, Harvard Center for Population and Development Studies, and Adjunct Lecturer in Economics and Public Policy at the John F. Kennedy School of Government. He has been a regular contributor to the *Human Development Report* from its early years, and was a member of the global team of the 1996, 1997 and 1998 *Human Development Reports*.

David Stewart is an economist at the Human Development Report Office. His recent work has been on measuring income inequality and progress towards the Millennium Developmen... He is also very involved in the production of the statistical tables of the report. He holds an economics degree from the University of Sussex and a masters in development economics from the University of Oxford.

Frances Stewart is Director of the International Development Centre at Queen Elizabeth House, University of Oxford, and Fellow of Somerville College. She is a board member of the United Nations Research Institute for Social Development, and has been a senior consultant in the preparation of the *Human Development Reports* from their beginning.

Paul Streeten is Professor Emeritus of Economics at Boston University. He is the founder and chair of World Development. He was Warden of Queen Elizabeth House; Director of the Institute of Commonwealth Studies; a Fellow of Balliol College, Oxford; Director of the Institute of Development Studies at the University of Sussex; Deputy Director-General at the Ministry of Overseas Development and Special Adviser to the World Bank.